Sikh Soldier

FORGOTTEN REGIMENTS

Maharajah Ranjit Singh
(1780-1839)
The Sikh Emperor

Dedication

To Laurie Michael Singh Dhesi

This is an account of the Sikh soldiers and fighters; the ways of the Sikh warrior. It is a story about the regiments lost to the Sikh Soldier. Their martial traditions run deep in your blood.

Sat Siri Akal; from Baba Ji

This is an extract from Ella Wheeler Wilcox's "After the battles are over", written in 1872 after the American Civil War for a soldier's re-union, and not forgotten either are those who did not return:

> O boys who died for your country,
> O dear and sainted dead!
> What can we say about you
> That has not once been said?
> Whether you fell in the contest,
> Struck down by shot and shell,
> Or pined 'neath the hand of sickness
> Or starved in a prison cell.
>
> We know that you died for freedom,
> To save our land from shame,
> And we give you deathless fame,
> "Twas the cause of Truth and Justice
> That you fought and perished for,
> And we say it oh, so gently,
> "Our boys who died in the war."

Comments

Why the title 'Forgotten Regiments' has been given to this volume of the Sikh Soldier series is a question that has been asked by some, including such eminent participants in the military tradition as Lieutenant General BS Dhaliwal and Major General AJS Sandhu. Although the end of British colonial occupation and the partition of the Subcontinent did lead to the merging and renaming of many traditional units of the old Indian Army, many of the Regiments do still exist today, it is argued by the Generals. The answer is that in the very act of remembering that this book embodies, we fight against the forgetting that inevitably takes place, as the years pass, as memories fade, and as the last survivors of past conflict pass into the eternal peace that awaits us all. These proud regimental names are lost to the Sikh Soldier. The purpose of this book is to bring the feats of arms to life, to ensure that forgetting is resisted and to guarantee that these Regiments which are lost to the Sikh Soldier will be remembered for their martial glory.

This book will be a great boon to today's Regiments who were formed from them....a book which would be a must read by all military historians and by all officers whose parentage is linked with the 'Forgotten Regiments'.

Lieutenant General BS Dhaliwal, PVSM, AVSM, VSM (Retd) Indian Army.

'The Forgotten Regiments' is the sixth volume of the series on the Sikh Soldier by Narindar Singh Dhesi. The Sikhs are a warrior class who have borne arms since centuries. Initially they fought for the Khalsa armies before they were recruited in large numbers (due to their famed fighting qualities) for the British Indian Army regiments, where they distinguished themselves in the battles and campaigns of both the world wars and elsewhere. After Partition of the sub-continent in August 1947, most of these units went to Pakistan; some of them were merged to form new entities while many others were demobilised. The author has lucidly encapsulated the histories of these regiments and highlighted their contribution in warfare for future generations. Researching the histories of so many regiments is a very onerous task indeed, but he has traced the journey from their raising till their eventual transfer to Pakistan in detail. This treatise will surely be of immense interest to those interested in military history. In bringing out this volume, Narindar Singh Dhesi has ensured that these great Sikh regiments will never be 'forgotten'!

Major General AJS Sandhu, VSM (Retd) Indian Army.

Sincere thanks to Major General AJS Sandhu, for his valid criticism, corrections and additions to the final text of this book. He belongs to an illustrious military family. His father and uncle commanded the 7 Punjab. (See Page 127)

I must also thank Vice Admiral Harinder Singh (Retd.) Indian Navy, for his wise consul.

My sincere thanks, to Major General BS Dhillon, VSM (Retd) for writing the Foreword to this book.

Narindar Singh Dhesi

Published by

The Naval & Military Press Ltd
Unit 5 Riverside, Brambleside,
Bellbrook Industrial Estate,
Uckfield, East Sussex,
TN22 1QQ England

Tel: +44 (0) 1825 749494
Fax: +44 (0) 1825 765701

www.naval-military-press.com
www.nmarchive.com

Copyright: Narindar Singh Dhesi

Sardar Bahadur Captain Ishar Singh OBI
First Sikh Victoria Cross winner
(15th Punjab Regiment)

Contents

Comments	3
Contents	5
Foreword	7
Introduction	8
The Khalsa	9
Sikh States Forces	16
The Corps of Sikh Pioneers	35
The Corps of Bombay Pioneers	59
Punjab Regiments	72
1ST Punjab Regiment	73
2ND Punjab Regiment	99
8TH Punjab Regiment	128
12TH Frontier Force Regiment	157
13TH Frontier Force Rifles	199
14TH Punjab Regiment	231
15TH Punjab Regiment	251
16TH Punjab Regiment	277
Probyn's Horse (5TH KEVO Lancers)	301
6TH DCO Lancers (Watson's Horse)	312
Guides Cavalry (10TH QVO Frontier Force)	328
Pavo Cavalry (11TH Frontier Force)	343
19TH King George V's Own Lancers	349
Burma Military Police	357
Burma Mounted Rifles	360
85TH Burma Rifles	362
The Burma Regiment	363
Shanghai Municipal Police	364
Auxiliary Military Police Battalion	365

Contents

Hong Kong Police	365
Hong Kong & Singapore, Royal Garrison Artillery	366
Malay States Guides	368
North Borneo Defence Force	376
The Sarawak Rangers	378
Central African Rifles	379
Uganda Rifles	388
Kings African Rifles	390
Free Indian Legion	394
Indische Freiwillegen Legion Der Waffen SS	394
Azad Hind Fauj	395
Indian Long Range Squadron	401
Appendix	402
Bibliography	403
Index	405

Captain Gian Singh VC
(15TH Punjab Regiment)

Foreword

Narindar Singh Dhesi has done it again in his sincere research and admirable work to further add and compile the history of Sikh soldiering, which spans over a large canvas of time and space. It was a matter of proud privilege to read his earlier books Sikh Soldier Volume Four-Warriors and Generals and Sikh Soldier Volume Five-At War. Sikh Soldier-Forgotten Regiments is work that would have taken tremendous amount of patience, devotion and efforts to dig out the historical facts when no eye witnesses are alive to assist in such a difficult task. He has gone into the details making it an easy reading for even non military readers. It's like going through a war diary or Digest of service of Regiments by a military man. The stead fastness and bravery of highest order in the face of the enemy were at display by Infantry and Cavalry. Author has explained in layman's language as to how well were they organised at that point of time when mobility and communications were not advanced as compared to present day warfare. An action of Sikh forces had very far reaching results in ensuring the state of territorial jurisdiction during the successive regimes in the country and has bearing on the present state area under control. Sikh Soldier-Forgotten Regiments is also a saga of valour that has been enshrined in the Sikh history wherein they fought away from their homes for years and yet never displayed any weakness of any kind. Fighting and fighting well, playing havoc into the enemy was their sole aim all the time. This brought out the best traits of soldiering and leadership. Narindar Singh Dhesi's deep research into Sikh soldiering has brought clearly the lightening terror that Sikh soldier carried into the enemy heartland during the actions. Some of the Regiments may have been forgotten while penning the history but it is this work of author that brings in the tough and resolute Sikh's spirit to win always. Compliments to Narindar Singh Dhesi, for his outstanding contribution in recording the heroic deeds of unmatching soldiering of the Sikh soldier, in various theatres of battles and wars. His works a treasure for our institutions at all levels and would go a long way to motivate the future generations to read, imbibe and keep up the traditions of never say die by our ancestors on the battle fields all over the world. A great work under taken by Narindar Singh Dhesi and one and all of the community should go through it. It will be in fitness of things if selected actions are included in the School/Colleges text books as part of motivation. Author has amply proved that Warriors and Regiments cannot be forgotten. A job indeed very well done! Narindar Singh Dhesi. I salute you for your consistent devotion, diligence and stamina to the cause and proud you have done to the community by your untiring efforts.

Major General BS Dhillon, VSM **(Retd) Indian Army**

Introduction

The inspiring and elevating history of the Sikh Soldier's battles and campaigns pertain to the bloodstained Mughal period, the tyrannical Afghan period, the feat of arms and the glorious period of the Sikh Empire. The main geographical footprint of the Sikh Empire was the Punjab region to Khyber Pass in the west, to Kashmir in the north, to Sindh in the south, and Tibet in the east. The religious demography of the Sikh Empire was Muslim (70%), Sikh (17%), and Hindu (13%).

The greatest legacy of the Sikh Soldier is the conquest of Hazara and Pashawar and the consolidation of the North-West Frontier of India. If it were not for this achievement, the entire trans-Indus territories, would have been lost to India forever, and would have remained part of Afghanistan. These territories would not have been part of the British Empire and would not have formed part of the newly formed state of Pakistan. Today we have all but forgotten the regiments and the indomitable men who played a major role in rebelling against the Mughals, the Afghans and the British.

In the Cis Satluj region, the Phulkian Confederacy had carved out petty Kingdoms in Malwa and Sirhind. With the establishment of British power, Cis-Satluj States Forces continued to exist and fight side-by-side with new governors. Shortly after Independence came to India, it was decided to take over these State Forces and merge them in the existing Indian Army. The result of this was the destruction of the identity of these forces, quickly and irrevocably. Today there are no Indian State Forces.

The reputation of the Sikh soldier as the premier colonial soldier was so great that from the outset the colonial administrators insisted that Sikhs, and Sikhs alone, must be supplied to them for the Para-Military policing needs of the colonial forces. They were organized into regular military regiments and were extensively used as the 'Motor Muscle' of imperial authority. During the initial period of pacification, the Sikhs performed the role of shock troops, leading attacks against various hostile elements. Subsequently they trained the native soldiers to meet the requirements of their respective territories. Once their work was done, their services were terminated. The regiments that they had created became part of their respective countries.

At the fall of the Sikh Kingdom the Sikh Soldier became the Sword Arm of the British Empire and served to the far corners of the British Empire. He went on to fight from the trenches of France and Flanders to the sands of the African Sahara, from the deserts of the Middle East to the steaming jungles of Burma. Sadly most of these regiments were allotted to Pakistan and lost to the Sikh Soldier.

If there was a single inspiration behind this book, it was admiration and fascination for all of the men of these diverse formations. I have endeavoured to present the glorious deeds of the brave Sikh soldier, who wandered far away from his homeland to impose his martial authority. If enough has not been said about some regiments, it is not due to the lack of effort on my part but due to non-availability of the material to me.

Narindar Singh Dhesi

The Khalsa

Sikh homeland, the Punjab, is a very fertile region in the Northwest of India. In 1947 the state of the Punjab was partitioned between British India's successor states, India and Pakistan. Historically the Punjab embraced the entire plain between the Rivers Jamuna and the Indus. Punjab was the main gateway and the first home of all conquerors coming into India from the northwest of India. It was fated to be a 'perpetual field of battle'.

Towards the close of the eighteenth century, the Punjab was in chaotic condition. It had suffered from repeated Afghan Durrani invasions since 1747, when Ahmed Shah had driven the Mughal governor from the Punjab's capital, Lahore. The fertility of the northern Mughal province had so sharpened the Afghan lust for plunder and wealth that between the years 1747 and 1767, Ahmad Shah repeated his invasions seven times, and altered the whole political structure of the Indus-Jumna region. But since his death in 1773, the Afghans, who had detached from the Mughal Empire some of its richest provinces, found it extremely difficult to maintain their authority.

In the heart of the Punjab it gave impetus to the rise of Sikh Confederacies. Every Sikh Gorchurra (Lancer) soldier was free to join any Confederacy he chose and free to cancel his membership of the Confederacy to whom he belonged and join another. If ordered by the Confederate Supreme Commander, the Confederate Barons against a hostile force would allow their armies to combine, or coordinate their defences together.

In the centre and the north, the *Bhangi* Confederacy had become prominent. They held the two major cities of the Punjab, Lahore and Amritsar and extended their territories between Jhelum and the Indus. The *Ramgharia* Confederacy held Jullundur Doab and their possessions included Kalanaur, Qadian and Dinanagar. The *Kanhaya Confederacy* established their supremacy over the Raikri tract including Hajpur, Mukerian, Pathankot and Gurdaspur. The *Singhpuria* Confederacy held sway in the area in the east and the west of the River Satluj. The *Ahluwalia* Confederacy had seized Raikot and Kapurthala, and the *Sukkarchakkia* Confederacy had acquired Gujranwala, Wazirabad and some areas in Sialkot, Rohtas and Pind Dadan Khan.

In the Cis-Satluj region, the *Phulkians* had carved out petty kingdoms in Malwa and Sirhind. The Jullundur Doab was completely in the hands of Sikh Chiefs. In Haryana, the Sikhs had overthrown Muslim authority.

The futile attempts of Taimur Shah, Ahmad Shah's successor, to establish the Afghan authority in the Punjab, Sind, Multan and Kashmir, exhibited to the Sikh and Muslim usurpers, the weakness of the Afghan power. During his 20 year rule the Durrani possessions in northern India slipped out of Afghan control. The Sikh Confederacies consolidated their possessions and seized new territories. Common interests and need for a concerted action against the foreign invader bound them together as a Sikh Commonwealth, the Khalsa.

(*The Khalsa,* A collective term for all baptized Sikhs. The word means pure ones. It also denotes the Sikh Armies).

The Khalsa

An ambitious young Baron of the Horse, Ranjit Singh of the Sukkarchakkia Confederacy, had inherited a force of 15,000 Horse and 5,000 Foot, with 6 pieces of artillery. He could also call on five feudal chiefs to supply him fighting contingents. From these humble beginnings, and by welding together the rude Barons of the Sikh Confederacies, he forged a powerful military machine that would not only overpower the outmoded and feudal armies of the petty principalities, but also contain the British, who were relentlessly expanding their frontiers. Ranjit Singh single-mindedly modernized the Khalsa forces on the European lines. He created and consolidated the most awesome military muscle ever seen in India, and became King of an Empire extending from Tibet to the deserts of Sindh, and from the Khyber Pass to the Satluj. His army was one of the most powerful at the time in all Asia. It was the first Indian force in a thousand years to carry invasion into the homelands of the traditional conquerors of India - the Pathans and the Afghans.

At the death of Maharajah Ranjit Singh, in the ensuing bloodletting between various competing factions for power, many a valiant Sardar had lost his life, and the survivors had bribed and used the Sikh Army for their own needs. Having no confidence in the ruling family and the executive, the Sikh Army assumed control and became the Khalsa, the People's Army, and the republican army. They had created the Sikh State and Kingdom. They were the State's defenders and preservers, and became an executive sovereign of the State. They controlled the affairs of the State but had to co-operate with a corrupt Government, and Sardars and the Sovereign, who were seeking British interference to safeguard their estates and privileges.

The Khalsa vigorously resisted any foreign intervention in the State and proceeded to punish the traitors. The Sovereign and the leading Sardars frantically sought British military intervention in the affairs of the Kingdom.

The British had been farsighted in their expansion of India. They wanted to extend their power to the continent's natural border, the North West Frontier. After the fall of Delhi, the British had a standoff against Maharajah Ranjit Singh, who was seeking to expand the Sikh State. The British checked Maharajah Ranjit Singh's ambitions, by taking the Cis Satluj territories under their protection. They also checked the Sikh State's expansion towards Sindh and the sea by taking the Amirs of Sindh under their protection. Additionally, the Anglo-Sikh treaty blocked the State's expansion towards Afghanistan. The British had made no secret of their intention to destroy the Sikh Kingdom and annex the Punjab to the British Empire. With the turmoil in the Punjab, and their under-estimation of the fighting qualities of the Sikh soldier, the British started massing their armies, the largest force ever assembled in India, on the Kingdom's borders. The British also had an understanding of co-operation with Punjab Government Minister Gulab Singh Dogra, Chief Minister Lal Singh and the Commander-in-Chief Tej Singh, whose intention was to shatter the Khalsa on the British bayonets. As the British advanced on the Sikh Kingdom, the Khalsa prepared for war.

The Khalsa

The morale of the Khalsa was extremely high. The Sikh soldier was extremely brave and had always carried everything before him. The weakness lay in the officer corps, who merely became the figureheads, as the Panchas (five elected elders) made all the decisions. The Sikh regimental officers were mostly illiterate and, brave that they might be, were not worthy of the men they commanded. Neither of the two principal generals, Lal Singh and Tej Singh, were Sikhs, but Brahmins, and were not committed to the cause for which they were fighting.

"A powerful, well-trained and confident Sikh army prepared for war under the leadership of a Commander-in-Chief under orders from a Vizier, and watched from the sidelines by a powerful and clever chieftain. All three men dedicated to the defeat of the army they lead, and secretly informing their British opponents of that fact!" (Donald Featherstone)

Traitors on the field and traitors at court commanded the Khalsa armies; their main aim was the destruction of the Khalsa. Gulab Singh Dogra was a feudal chieftain of the Sikh government, and commanded two divisions of Dogras and hill-men. Twice he had refused to reinforce the Khalsa during battle, with the aim of complete subjugation of the Khalsa by the British, and to be recognized as an independent sovereign of Jammu. He had been in direct communications with the British and had reached a secret understanding that the Durbar (Royal Council) would openly disavow the acts of the army, and that Maharajah Dalip Singh would be allowed to retain his nominal sovereignty, provided the British forces were allowed to occupy the capital of the Sikhs unopposed.

Thus with ignominious treachery and deceit were sold the lives of the valiant soldiers of the Khalsa by their rulers, and thus was fought the First Anglo-Sikh War.

Individual bravery and superb fighting qualities of the Sikhs were in vain. The Sikh army put up a very gallant fight against the British, against very heavy odds. They were disowned by their government and leaders who contrived for their destruction, the general people were apathetic to their fate as they feared their power. But in spite of these handicaps, the Khalsa, rallied their forces and fought the superior led and equipped British army to a standstill. The Lahore Durbar sued for peace and the Treaty of Lahore was signed between the warring parties in March 1946.

Even after end of the war and the virtual disbandment of the Sikh army, the Lahore state still clamoured for British help and 20,000 British troops stayed in Lahore. The feudal chiefs were still apprehensive of the Sikh army, and agreed to the continued stay of the British army and their occupation of the Lahore state, though in a truncated state.

The British government became the guardian of the young Maharajah Dalip Singh and the Punjab became a British protectorate. The Khalsa was restricted to 20,000 infantry and 12,000 cavalry and was crushed as a military power.

The Khalsa

The district of Multan was a tributary of the Sikh Kingdom. At the death of his father, Mulraj had taken over the governorship of Multan. As he was unable to pay the accession fee and the increased tribute to the central government, he submitted his resignation. His resignation was accepted. Sardar Kahan Singh was appointed as the new Governor. Two British Officers, Vans Agnew and Anderson would accompany him to Multan. Kahan Singh was to be a nominal figurehead; the British Officers would conduct the administration of Multan. Sardar Kahan Singh, along with the British Officers and an escort of 1500 troops, reached Multan on 14TH April. As the Multan troops were going to be set free, losing their livelihood and replaced, they mutinied and killed the two British Officers. They took Mulraj prisoner and compelled him to be their leader. They appealed to the people to join the rebellion. The Lahore escort deserted and went over to join the Multani soldiers. The rebellion was allowed to spread for five months, despite the leading British Officers straining at the leash for instant action, which would have forestalled any Sikh insurrection. The British were warned about the despatch of Sikh troops to Multan, that they would prove mutinous. The British deliberately despatched all the available Sikh forces to Multan, including the main force led by Sher Singh. All forces converged on Multan and laid siege to the massive Multan fort in preparation for the final annexation of the Punjab to British India.

Sardar Chattar Singh Attariwala was the Governor of the Northwest Frontier districts. His daughter was engaged to Maharajah Dalip Singh. He ardently supported the British in all measures they wished to take, as did his son Sher Singh Attariwala, who was energetically co-operating with the British at the siege of Multan. Since the Multan outbreak, which was allowed to spread, the British started inciting the tribesmen on the Frontier against the Sikh garrison. Captain James Abbot sought the help of Hazara chiefs and their Levies and advanced to expel the Sikh Governor. The Governor, for his own safety moved into the fort of Hajipur. His guns were in the charge of an American, Colonel Canora, who was in the Durbar's service. Canora refused to hand over the guns without orders from Abbot; he was instantly killed for insubordination.

At the court of enquiry, it was established that as Governor of the province, he had acted to defend the besieged capital of Hazara from Abbot's Muslim mercenaries. Notwithstanding the findings, Chattar Singh's estates were confiscated and he was dismissed from his post. The actions of the British Officers, in raising Muslim Levies to attack the Sikh garrisons and humiliation and dismissal of the Durbar Governor of the North West Frontier and moving a force of 10,000 to Lahore, the occupation of the Lahore citadel, and putting leading Sikh Sardars under guard, convinced Chattar Singh that the British were preparing for the final annexation of the Punjab. The old Sardar decided to fight the British and wrote to his son Sher Singh to join him. Sher Singh realized that the die was cast, and reluctantly left the British camp to join his father.

The Khalsa

The Governor General declared, "The die is cast; this is a national rebellion to expel us. It is a religious war for the Khalsa. Consequently, after anxious and grave deliberation we have without hesitation resolved that the Punjab can no longer be allowed to exist as a power and must be destroyed."

The British were the rulers of the Punjab and the guardians of the young Maharajah. The rebellion of the Attariwala Sardars was against the authority of the Durbar. The Guardian was set to punish and destroy the Ward, which he was bound to protect by the Treaty of Bhayirowal! Even the Commander in Chief, General Gough appears to have been in some doubt whether he was carrying out operations to suppress a rebellion on behalf of the Durbar or whether the Durbar in Lahore was itself to be regarded as an enemy.

The British invading force deployed at various points in the Punjab was a staggering total of 104,666 men, 61,366 Regular British Army; 5,300 Lahore Army; 38,000 Irregular troops; 13,542 Cavalry; 123 Field guns and 22 Heavy guns.

At the conclusion of the hard fought, First Anglo-Sikh War, the British had methodically destroyed the military power of the Sikhs. The soldiers had been disarmed, disbanded and dispersed. The pride of the Khalsa, the guns, were dismantled and taken away. What remained was but a shadow of the colossal military machine of Maharajah Ranjit Singh. The remnants of the Khalsa permitted were 20,000 men and 12,000 Cavalry.

The total force the Attariwala Sardars could muster was 23,000; these were the various contingents from Hazara, Pashawar, Tank, Bannu, Kohat and Attock including 10,000 Irregulars.

The major battle of the Second Sikh War was fought near Chillianwala. When darkness fell the British left the battlefield and fell back on the village of Chillianwala. The British casualties amounted to 2,446 men, with 132 officers killed and 4 guns lost. Chillianwala was the worst defeat the British had suffered in their annals of Indian warfare. However, re-enforced with fresh forces, they turned defeat into victory at the battle of Gujarat.

The observers who watched the Sikh surrender greatly admired the bearing of the Sikh soldiers, who still carried themselves with pride. They were tired and hungry, but their spirit was by no means broken. It was noticed that many of the older men threw down their Tulwars (swords) with a gesture of disgust. On 29TH March 1849, Maharajah Dalip Singh took his seat on the throne for the last time. The Punjab was annexed to British India, the Sikh Kingdom ended, and Dalip Singh was pensioned off to England.

While some of the soldiers from the following regiments were absorbed into the British Indian Army (for example the Horse Artillery was bodily transferred), the Regiments themselves were sadly disbanded. Tragically the magnificent feats of arms of these Regiments have been lost to the annals of time. These are the forgotten Regiments.

The Khalsa

The Khalsa (The Sikh Army) in 1845 is listed below:

Fauj-e-Ain (Regular Army) 22 Brigades
62 infantry battalions, 49,000 soldiers
13 cavalry regiments, 7,800 troopers
33 artillery batteries

The Fauj-e-Khas
4 infantry battalions
2 cavalry regiments
1 Jagirdari cavalry squadron
Artillery; 12guns horse artillery and 22 field guns

Dewan Jodha Ram's Brigade
4 infantry battalions
1 cavalry regiment
10 guns horse artillery and 8 heavy field guns

General Kahn Singh's Brigade
4 infantry battalions
12 guns horse artillery

General Mehtab Singh Majithia's Brigade
4 infantry battalions
1 cavalry regiment
12 guns horse artillery

General Tej Singh' Brigade
4 infantry battalions
1 cavalry regiment
12 guns horse artillery

General Gulab Singh Paoindia's Brigade
3 infantry battalions
14 guns, horse artillery

Suchet Singh's Brigade
2 infantry battalions
1cavalry regiment
10 heavy garrison guns and 4 guns horse artillery

General Gulab Singh Calcuttawala's Brigade
4 infantry battalions
1 cavalry regiment
16 guns, horse artillery

General Jawala Singh's Brigade
2 infantry battalions
4 guns, horse artillery

The Khalsa

General Lehna Singh Majithia's Brigade
2 infantry battalions
2 heavy garrison guns, 3 field guns and 10 guns horse artillery

General Bishan Singh's Brigade
2 infantry battalions
3 guns, horse artillery

General Gurdit Singh Majithia's Brigade
3 infantry battalions
8 artillery guns

General Dhonkel's Brigade
3 infantry battalions (Dogra)

General Courtland's Brigade
2 infantry battalions
10 guns, horse artillery

Sardar Nihal Singh Ahluwalia's Brigade
1 infantry battalion
11 heavy guns and 4 guns horse artillery

Dewan Sawan Mul's Brigade
3 infantry battalions
40 heavy garrison guns and 6 guns horse artillery

Heera Singh's Brigade
2 infantry battalions
1 cavalry regiment
5 heavy garrison guns and 3 heavy field guns

Raja Partap Singh of Punch's Brigade
3 infantry battalions

Raja Gulab Singh's Brigade
3 infantry battalions
40 heavy garrison guns and 15 guns horse artillery

Sheik Iman-ud-din's Brigade
3 infantry battalions
4 guns, horse artillery

Sheikh Ghulam Mohi-ud-din's Brigade
2 infantry battalions
8 heavy field guns and 6 guns horse artillery

Source: Bajwa, Military System of the Sikhs

Sikh States Forces

In the 18TH century, the political vacuum created by the downfall of the Mughals was successfully filled up by the Sikhs in Punjab, by thwarting the designs of both the Marathas and the Afghans. The Cis Satluj Sikhs rose to power at the same time as the Majha Sikhs were establishing their confederacies, and did not serve under the banner of the Dal Khalsa (The Sikh Army). The Majha Sikhs had defied any authority on their rise to power, but the Cis Satluj Sikhs prudently accepted the Imperial Sovereignty. As Cis Satluj Sikhs came to maturity at the decline of the Mughal power, they faced the ambitions of the Lion of the Punjab, Maharajah Ranjit Singh. Ranjit Singh was subverting all the independent states and absorbing them to the expanding Sikh Kingdom. The Cis Satluj States were saved from annihilation by the arrival of the British.

Delhi had fallen to the British on 11TH September 1803, and they had pushed the borders of British India to the River Jumna and then to the River Satluj, where they had a standoff with Maharajah Ranjit Singh. Ranjit Singh realised the power of the British and, with the Anglo-Sikh treaty of 1809, signed away the Cis Satluj territories.

The Phulkian House in Cis Satluj was subdivided into three principalities of Patiala, Nabha and Jind. The Cis Satluj Sikhs were familiar with the concept of Imperial Authority and willingly accepted the British protection. The Cis Satluj Princely States maintained their own armed forces within their States and were obliged to make their forces available to the paramount power in time of war or emergency.

After the hard-fought battles of the Anglo -Sikh wars and the annexation of the Punjab to British India, the Sikh principalities of Kapurthala and Faridkot, also allied themselves to the British, with the understanding to make their forces available to the paramount power in time of war or emergency.

The Sikh Princely States Forces fought alongside the British forces during the Anglo-Gurkha war of 1814 and numerous campaigns during the Sepoy Mutiny of 1857. They thereafter played a prominent part in the continuums punitive expeditions on the North-West Frontier of India. During the First World War, they took part in operations against the Turkish Army in Egypt, Palestine, Jordan and Mesopotamia, and went on to fight the Germans in East Africa. During the Second World War, the Sikh State Forces fought against the Japanese in Burma, Malaya and Singapore. The Nabha Akals won a cluster of Military Medals fighting the Germans in Italy.

All the Sikh Cis Satluj States acceded to the union of India in 1948. At that time the bulk of the State Forces were absorbed into the Indian Army, thus losing their distinct regimental identity, thus becoming The Forgotten Regiments.

Sikh States Forces

1st Patiala Infantry (Rajindra Sikhs)

The origins of the Patiala Army can be traced as far back as 1705, when a fighting Jatha (a fighting band) led by Ala Singh carved out the State of Patiala, in the Cis-Satluj region of the Punjab. By 1723 infantry wing of Patiala Army contained 700 foot soldiers. From this time onwards, the Patiala forces began the period of regular conquests and territorial possessions. By the turn of the century Patiala emerged as the most powerful state in the Cis-Satluj territories. It could go to the field at any time against any army in a disciplined way. At this time Maharajah Ranjit Singh was subverting all the independent states of the Punjab and absorbing them to the expanding Sikh Kingdom. The Raja of Patiala entered into a treaty with the British in 1808, thus becoming a collaborator in the grand empire building process by the British.

On 1st November 1814, the Government of India were compelled to declare war against the Gurkhas, who had for years been encroaching on British territory. The Raja of Patiala had more than once, before the declaration of war, been engaged in repelling these encroachments. In October 1814, Colonel Ochterlony led a British force, with the Patiala Infantry forming part of his force, into the hills by Ropar. After the capture of Nalagarh and Taragarh, the British force, in a desperate action took possession of Rangarh and completely defeated the Gurkhas on 15th April 1814. The Gurkha garrison was allowed to retire, completely evacuating the whole of that territory.

Colonel Ochterlony had this to say about the Patiala Infantry: - "in physique, discipline and fighting qualities of Patiala soldiers who fought along with the British troops were commendable."

In 1819 the designation of 1st Infantry (Rajindra Sikhs) was given to the Patiala infantry, as the Maharajah had ordered the raising of five more infantry units. During the Kythal Rebellion of 1843, which the British troops were hard pressed to suppress, 2000 soldiers of Patiala Infantry went to their aid. After a short skirmish in which some men were killed, the rebel leader Teg Singh and several other leaders were intercepted and taken prisoner by the Patialas.

During the Anglo-Sikh wars, Patiala State gave active support to the British; however, the authorities at Patiala were not able to control some troops whose sympathies were with the Khalsa Army.

During the Sepoy Mutiny of 1857, the Maharajah of Patiala sent his best troops in aid of the British. The infantry wing of the Patiala contingent consisted of 2,846 soldiers. The Patiala contingent was led by a galaxy of most distinguished commanders. Sardar Partab Singh commanded the detachment at Delhi, Kanwar Dip Singh at Thanesar; Sardars Hira Singh and Hazara Singh at Ambala; Sardars Karam Singh and Kahan Singh at Hissar; Sardars Dal Singh and Fateh Singh at Hansi, and Sardar Jiwan Singh at Ferozepore. The splendid feat of arms of the Patiala contingent was suitably rewarded by the British. Narnaul, Knauj and Kamaron were awarded to the Patiala State in perpetual sovereignty.

Sikh States Forces

1st Patiala Infantry (Rajindra Sikhs)

The Mohmand are a Pakhtun tribe who inhabit the hilly country to the north-west of Pashawar, in the North-West Frontier Province of India. The year 1897 witnessed an almost general outbreak among the tribes on the North-West Frontier. The tribes involved were practically independent, but the new frontier arranged with the Amir of Afghanistan, brought them within the British sphere of influence. The fear of these tribes was annexation. On 10TH June 1897, a detachment of Indian troops escorting a British frontier officer was suddenly attacked during the mid-day halt in the Tochi Valley, where certain armed posts had been established by the government of India.

On 29TH July, with equal suddenness, the fortified posts at Chakdara and Malakand, in the Swat valley, were for several days fiercely assailed by the Swatis under the leadership of the 'Mad Mullah' in the Siege of Malakand. On the 8TH of August the village of Shabkadar within a few miles of Pashawar, and in British territory, was raided by the Mohmands, while the Afridis besieged the fortified posts on the Samana ridge and within a few days, captured all the British posts in the Khyber Pass.

The 1ST Patiala Infantry formed part of the Malakand Field Force commanded by Major-General Sir Bindon Blood. The force was assembled at Nowshera and reached the post at Malakand on 1ST August and on the following day Chakdara was relieved. The Patialas totally overwhelmed the tribesmen, who were compelled to sue for peace. The Patialas then moved for the relief of Malakand. The garrison of Malakand fort was manned by the regiment of 45TH Rattray's Sikhs, and held against repeated day and night attacks by swarms of tribesmen. The Sikhs were required to make a desperate bayonet charge during the storm-laden night of 30TH, which scattered the tribesmen.

The next day 1ST Patialas pursued the tribesmen as they fled back to the safety of the hills. Later 1ST Patiala took an active part in the Tirah expedition. They resumed punitive operations in the Mamund valley, destroying numerous villages. On 30TH they encountered strong opposition at Agrah, and suffered 61 casualties. On 5TH the Mamund tendered their submission. After marching into Buner, the Malakand field-force was broken up on 21ST of January. The objects of the expedition were completely attained, in spite of the great natural difficulties of the country.

Due to heavy demand, another battalion of the State Force, 2ND Patiala (2ND Yadavindra Infantry) also formed part of the Malakand Field Force and took part in the operations against the tribesmen. A memorable feature of this campaign was the presence in the fighting line of the Imperial Service native troops under their own officers, while several of the best known of the Indian princes, such as the Maharajah of Patiala, served on Sir W. Lockhart's staff in these operations.

Sikh States Forces

1st Patiala Infantry (Rajindra Sikhs)

When the First World War broke out in 1914, Indian troops were mobilised for the defence of Egypt and the protection of Suez Canal. 1ST Patiala Infantry was mobilised and sailed for Suez Canal area for operations against the Turkish Army, which had joined the Axis Powers by then. The regiment, under the command of Colonel Gurbux Singh, was brigaded with 32ND Imperial Service Brigade and arrived at Suez on November 16TH and at Ismailia five days later. It defended the portion of the canal from Tinch to Port Said, during the Turkish attacks on the canal between January and February 1915. The first large scale actions were fought on 22ND and 28TH January 1915, when Turkish advances were defeated near Qantara. On 3RD February, the Turks made serious attempt to cross the Canal near Tussum, where they were decisively defeated, and defeated yet again in another action fought at Qantara. In July and September 1915, a company each of the regiment and 1ST Patiala Lancers reinforced 14TH Sikhs at Dardanelles and Gallipoli respectively. The battalion spent much of 1916 in the static defence of the Suez Canal line, while sending two companies to Jordan Valley to reconnoitre the enemy on foot in the directions of Bir-Abu-Tif and Abu Garad. The entire regiment remained on front line duty on various posts in Jordan. On 21ST December the regiment saw action in the capture of El Arisha and the rout of the Turks at Maghdada. An equally successful action at Magruntein on 9TH January 1917 finally saw the Sinai Peninsula cleared of the enemy. During September 1917 Colonel Ishar Singh took over the command of 1ST Patiala. On 27TH October the defences of Gaza were bombarded. Beersheba was attacked and captured the next day. The attack on Gaza continued and some of its strongest defensive positions fell to the attackers. After the capture of Gaza, 1ST Patialas were employed on lines of communication duties. On 14TH April 1918, it was incorporated in the Desert Mounted Corps. The regiment took part in the second Es-Salt operations, storming the positions at Kabar, Masjid, Kajahir, and on the hills near El-Houd. On 9TH January the regiment embarked at Suez to return home. It reached Patiala on 27TH January 1919, after five years active service overseas. Apart from the major campaign waged against the Turks, Indian forces in Egypt also took part in a series of smaller operations against the Senussi, a militant Islamic sect, in the western desert of Egypt. The 15TH Sikhs and the Patiala Infantry especially distinguished themselves in these operations.

Clusters of honours and awards were awarded to 1ST Patiala during the War, to include three I.O.M.s to Captain Bhagwan Singh, Subedar Kala Singh and Subedar Dharm Singh, a Military Cross to Major Budh Singh and eight Indian Distinguished Service Medals to; Captain Gurdial Singh, Lieutenant Jasmer Singh, Jemadar Partap Singh, Jemadar Jokal Singh, Naik Rattan Singh, Sepoy Sewa Singh and Sepoy Jawala Singh. Four Order of British India, to Sirdar Gurbaksh Singh, Lieutenant Colonel Ishar Singh, Major Narain Singh, and Subedar -Major Bhagat Singh.

Sikh States Forces

1st Patiala Infantry (Rajindra Sikhs)

The Third Afghan War was launched by Amir Amanullah, who had been placed on the Afghan throne in February 1919 by the army and the Young Afghan radical party, after the murder of his father. He proclaimed a Jihad against Britain, and on 3rd May 1919 Afghan troops crossed the Indian border and occupied Bagh. As the war came soon after the bloodletting of World War I, when the decimated Indian regiments were being demobilised, Britain mobilised the leading Indian Princely States Forces in the month long war. The 1st Patiala Infantry was mobilised in May 1919 and joined the Kurram Force. The battalion performed in an exemplary manner as the British Indian troops recaptured Bagh on 11th May, and pushed on into Afghanistan, while British bombers attacked Jalalabad and Kabul. Amanullah sued for peace on 31st May, and peace was restored by the treaty of Rawalpindi.

In 1922, the regiment was formally designated as 1st Rajindra Sikh Infantry. The same year the command of the regiment devolved on Colonel, later Lieutenant General Gurdial Singh Harika, who commanded the regiment for eleven years. In 1932, Colonel, later Brigadier Balwant Singh Sidhu, assumed the command of the regiment and remained its Commanding Officer for a decade.

At the outbreak of the Second World War, 1st Rajindra Sikh Infantry was stationed at Razmak, in Waziristan. The Afghan tribes were asserting their authority in the area, often including sniping at the troops and raiding Piquets. With pressure on the Indian Army to send troops for the Allied Forces in Africa, Europe and against aggressive Japan, the British Empire did not want to face another war on the Afghan front. Thus, the regiment was tasked to fight off the raiding Afghans. The regiment distinguished itself particularly in the Shahwali and Tochi valley columns, on a punitive expedition against rebellious tribesmen, under very severe conditions, through an extremely hostile territory.

Meanwhile the Japanese had gained overwhelming successes, Singapore had fallen and they were in pursuit of the shattered ranks of Burma Army towards India. In early April 1942 the regiment was sent hurriedly to the Indo-Burmese frontier to stem the tide of Japanese advance into India. The regiment had received no training with modern weapons against a first class enemy. In fact their equipment was thirty-five years out of date. Notwithstanding the Sikh stalwarts covered the withdrawal of the Burma Army in May 1942. For about three months the regiment occupied the forward positions of their Brigade front. They moved to these positions at the height of the monsoon period, when the most unfavourable and difficult climate conditions prevailed. These conditions caused great personal hardship to the troops and made communications very uncertain. The delivery of supplies to the forward posts was always a serious problem and, at times, rations had to be considerably reduced. In addition to manning the forward posts, the battalion sent out constant patrols to forward areas. These involved long marches, the crossing of rivers in spate and sleeping in the mosquito and leech infested jungles in adverse weather.

Sikh States Forces

1st Patiala Infantry (Rajindra Sikhs)

One of the most striking achievements of these patrols was carried out by the Commanding Officer himself, involving a force of 118 officers and men. 331 miles were covered by this special patrol in 21 days, including 88 miles through almost virgin jungle, at a time when weather conditions were at their worst. Considerable hardships were met and overcome with determination. In the winter of 1942, the battalion established a bridgehead across the Chindwin River to facilitate the crossing of the First Wingate Expedient. On 24th March Wingate was ordered to withdraw. Non-essential equipment was dumped and mules no longer required were turned loose. By now the Chindits were tired and short of food, many were exhausted or sick, and faced a dangerous journey home pursued by the Japanese. The Patialas ensured Chindits withdrawal westwards. (The irony was that Wingate had refused to use Indian Army Formations in his force.) Patialas managed to better arm themselves with the excellent weapons and equipment jettisoned by the Chindits, and went on to perform prodigal feats against the Japanese and soon established ascendancy over them. In the spring of 1943, 1ST Patiala fulfilled with distinction a covering role on the right of 20TH Division's withdrawals at Chamol. A company found ample scope for Patiala skill in setting ambushes. Twice they allowed enemy parties, a platoon strong, to come within ten yards, where they delivered a knock-out blow which caused the Japanese to pause; and if it came to a close-quarter scrap, the Japanese found their masters. The skill and courage of this company played a material role in slowing up the advance for four days. In early 1944, when the Japanese cut Kohima- Imphal road, the Commanding Officer of 1ST Patiala, Colonel Balwant Singh Sidhu, volunteered to cut the Japanese route via Ukhrul to Kohima. He took the regiment through a jungle route and contacted the Japanese troops at Sakpao. Very careful Recce was made on the morning of 19TH for the main attack on Sakpao. The 'D' Company rose up at the start line and rushed forward, shouting the Patiala battle cry, "Sat Sri Akal." The Japanese taken by surprise were overwhelmed and in nine minutes the position had been captured. The fight had only begun. Six minutes later, when 'D' Company was still hastily reorganizing, the Japanese came from the east and hurled themselves on the rear of the Company. There was no time to take up fire positions; the Company Commander charged with his reserve at the oncoming Japanese; he fell in the hand-to-hand grapple, but his action checked the enemy for the moment. Five minutes later the Japanese came again a little further down the ridge and were held by 'B' Company, but he was not yet spent; a nine-minute interval and he came a third time between 'B' Company and battalion H.Q. Colonel Balwant Singh did not hesitate; as one of his officers had done a few minutes earlier, he charged magnificently into the fray at the head of his H.Q. The Japanese were halted at last. The Patiala account of the tremendous affair runs; "Balance of the battle from 1425 to 1455 hours simply hanged round the gutts, it was anybody's battle during this time."

Sikh States Forces

1st Patiala Infantry (Rajindra Sikhs)

The day cost the Patialas sixty-six casualties. Among the awards gained were Military Crosses for the resourceful and determined commander of 'A' Company Lieutenant Baldev Singh and Jemadar Rakha Singh in command of the leading assault platoon.

Field Marshal Slim had this to say about the Patialas: "I want it conveyed to 1ST Patiala that if I were to pick one unit for any special task, it would be 1ST Patiala. I am sanctioning a special one month's leave to the whole unit at Shillong." However their leave was cut short, when they received orders to concentrate at Nasik. It was here that Lieutenant General Balwant Singh Sidhu relinquished command of the regiment by the end of 1944 and Lieutenant Colonel Bikramdev Singh Gill, took over the command of the regiment.

On the 8TH August 1945, the world was shattered by the release of the most ghastly weapon yet devised; the dropping of atom bombs at Hiroshima and Nagasaki in Japan, which compelled the Japanese to surrender en masse. The Second World War was at an end.

At the Japanese surrender 1ST Patiala were ordered to Malaya. Their task in Malaya called for a speedy occupation of Northern Johor, Negri Sembilan and Pahang, so that the early appearance of the Army as they rounded up the Japanese should restore confidence, quell any uprising by dissentient elements and lead to the resumption of normal life. In early December 1945, 1ST Patiala moved to Indonesia, where it was deployed in Batavia (now Djakarta), and the capital city of Java. Trouble was brewing as a result of agitation by nationalists led by Dr. Sukarno, an Indonesian politician who had proclaimed himself President and had declared independence. Several other Indonesian politicians and a large number of armed extremists supported him. Until 1942 Java had been a Dutch colony, after the Japanese invasion in 1942, the Indonesians were not unhappy to see their former masters being imprisoned. When the Japanese surrendered in August 1945 they had handed over some of their weapons to the Indonesians and had withdrawn to camps inland to await the arrival of the Allied forces to which they would surrender. Thus by the time the Patialas arrived, Java was in the throes of popular uprising and the Indonesians had assumed control of the country. The Indonesian Republic existed and could not be disregarded. One problem facing the Patialas was the deployment of the Japanese battalion by Winston Churchill. While they had done much to re-establish order, and had since been deployed on guard duties throughout Semarang, their presence was not welcomed by the local people, many of whom had suffered during the Japanese occupation. The Patialas resented their proximity to the Japanese. The Patialas carried out a number of operations against local guerrillas, mostly freedom fighters who were fighting for independence for their country. Their objective was to re-establish the Dutch regime in Indonesia on behest of Winston Churchill. The Patialas had to resort to stiff fighting against well trained, highly motivated and well armed Indonesians.

Sikh States Forces

1st Patiala Infantry (Rajindra Sikhs)

Many a fine Sikh soldiers died in re-establishing Dutch rule in Indonesia, the soldiers who had fought valiantly on the North-West Frontier, the Arakan, Assam, Burma and Malaya. It was little wonder that the Commanding Officer of the Patialas bitterly lamented the loss of brave men killed in such affairs. For the 1st Patiala the war ended when they were relieved by Netherlands Marines early in 1946. The regiment left Batavia during the end of 1946, having been on active service for six years. The Patialas can be justly proud of their magnificent achievements in the cause of peace and freedom. During World War Two, the Patialas earned a total of 83 awards to include on the Commander a British Empire Medal, which had no parallel in the entire British Indian Army; two Distinguished Service Orders, awarded to both the Commanding officers; Lieutenant General Balwant Singh Sidhu, CBE and Brigadier Bikramdev Singh Gill, one Member British Empire; nine Military Crosses; one Indian Order of Merit; 12 Distinguished Service Medals; five Military Medals; one British Empire Medal and 51 Mentioned-in- Despatches.

When India gained freedom, all the Sikh Princely States opted for immediate integration with India. Pakistan sent in about 15,000 tribal Pathans to Kashmir under the clarion call of Jihad. Pakistan financed the expedition, armed the tribes with modern weapons, trained them and provided some leadership from the Pakistan Army. It was called 'Operation Gulmarg' and was led by a Major General Akbar Khan. These hordes poured into Kashmir by the third week of October. Muzaffarabad and Domel had been invaded and occupied on 22nd October. By 24th the invaders were at Baramula, 35 miles west of Srinagar. The Maharaja lost his illusions about independent Kashmir. His state forces were totally inadequate to check the invasion. Late at night on 24th October he asked the Indian Government for help and signed the Instrument of Accession on 26th October 1947.

1st Patiala was flown to Jammu on 3rd November 1947 under the command of Lieutenant Colonel Bikramdev Singh Gill. In 1948, the battalion fought at Chhamb, Naushera and Jhangar. In this operation, the battalion's finest moment was at Zojila Pass where despite being un-acclimatized and without adequate clothing and equipment for high altitude warfare in peak winter, the Patialas achieved resounding success under the command of Colonel (later Brigadier) Sukhdev Singh, earning eight Mahavir Chakra, 18 Vr Chakra, 34 Mention-in-Dispatches and 42 C-in-C Commendation Cards in the theatre, including the Battle Honour Zojila. 1st Patiala holds the record of having won eight Mahavir Chakras, the maximum in a single operation. No other battalion of the Indian Army has ever achieved such distinction in any battle before or since.

In 1951, the 1st Patiala Rajindra Sikh Infantry and the 2nd Patiala Yadavindra Infantry were integrated into the Indian Army and redesignated as 15th and 16th (Patiala) Battalion, The Punjab Regiment.

Sikh States Forces

1ST Patiala (Rajindra) Lancers *(B Squadron 2ND Patiala Lancers)*

This was fighting contingent (Jatha) founded by Maharajah Ala Singh in the Patiala State in 1722. The backbone of the State's armed contingent were 7000 horsemen, commanded by Bakshi Ganda Singh. 1722 onward began the period of regular battles for territorial possessions. In all the battles fought by the Patialas, victory was assured and certain, but the finest moment of glory attained at that time was during the Bhati war fought in 1738. The successor of Maharaja Ala Singh, Maharaja Amar Singh, fought and defeated the Nawab of Malerkotla in 1767, seizing important territory from him. Saifabad was captured the same year. He defeated the belligerent Bhatti Chiefs and extended his territories to Sirsa and Fatehbad. Thus, by the turn of the century, Patiala emerged as the most powerful state between the Satluj and the Jamuna.

In 1809 Patiala Sate accepted British protection and was obliged to make the State Forces available to the British in time of war. The Patialas participated in the Anglo-Gurkha war of 1814. At the request of the British, Patiala infantry formed part of the attacking force, with the Patiala cavalry guarding the foothills. The combined forces defeated the Gurkhas and were permitted to retire, after taking a firm commitment of abstaining from such misadventures in the future. In 1819 Maharajah Karam Singh had ordered the raising of five more infantry units, three additional cavalry regiments and a few more regular horsed artillery units. During the Kaithal Rebellion of 1843, the Patiala State sent some 2000 cavalry, and equal number of infantry and some artillery to help the British troops. The Patialas played a very important part in maintaining peace and security over a wide area during the Sepoy Mutiny of 1857. The Patialas thereafter played a prominent role in the Mohmand Expedition and also in Malakand in 1897. The Maharaja of Patiala offered the services of Patiala infantry and a battery each of artillery and cavalry to the Malakand Field Force. The battalion Group proved its mettle in the Swat Valley and areas adjacent to the Black Mountains. From 1902 onwards the Patiala units were trained on the Indian Pattern of War Establishment. Two full sized units, 1ST Rajindra Sikh Infantry and 1ST Patiala Lancers, as part of Imperial Service Troops, were kept in state of readiness to take to field at short notice, as and when required by the British government. The Great War began in August 1914 and an opportunity came for overseas service for the Patiala forces as well, and two of its units 1ST Rajindra Sikh Infantry and Patiala Lancers were mobilised.

The 15TH (Imperial Service) Cavalry Brigade was a brigade-sized formation that served alongside British Empire forces in the Sinai and Palestine Campaign, during the First World War. Originally called the Imperial Service Cavalry Brigade it was formed from Imperial Service Troops provided by the Indian Princely States of Hyderabad, Mysore, Patiala and Jodhpur, which each provided a regiment of lancers. The 1ST Patiala Lancers were commanded by Colonel Nand Singh Sardar Bahadur with twenty-six officers and 528 Sowars.

Sikh States Forces

1ST Patiala (Rajindra) Lancers *(B Squadron 2ND Patiala Lancers)*

In October 1914, the Imperial Service Cavalry Brigade was moved by sea to Egypt to become part of the Force in Egypt defending the Suez Canal. Patiala Lancers extensively patrolled the vicinity of the Suez Canal. Their first clash against the enemy came when they encountered a force of some 200 Bedouins and Turks near Bir-el-Nuss. The patrol lost one officer and twelve other ranks killed and three troopers wounded, but inflicted some sixty casualties on the enemy. In July and September 1915, a company each of 1ST Patiala Infantry and 1ST Patiala Lancers reinforced 14TH Sikhs at Dardanelles and Gallipoli respectively. In the first three years of the war, the soldiers were involved in several small-scale battles connected to the first Suez offensive, but spent most of their time patrolling in the Sinai Desert and along the west bank of the canal.

In 1916, 1ST Patiala Lancers were transferred to serve in the campaign in Mesopotamia with 53RD Brigade of 18TH Indian Division. They were involved in the actions at Fat-ha-Gorge and on the Little Zab between 23RD–26TH October 1918 and the Battle of Sherqat on 30TH October 1918. In 1919 the 1ST Patiala Lancers were rushed to Afghanistan. Sensing post-First World War fatigue and the frailty of British positions along the Afghan border, Amanullah, the new ruler of Afghanistan, suddenly attacked the British in two thrusts. The British were taken by surprise and the Afghan forces achieved some success in the early days of the war. The British mobilised eight divisions of the Indian Army and decidedly defeated the Afghans in some dogged battles, and the armistice was declared at the end of 1919. The 1ST Patiala lancers returned home in 1920 after 6 years service overseas. The Indian cavalry maintained its high standards between the two world wars. During World War Two the Indian armoured formations suffered from a lack of equipment and were supplied with equipment rendered surplus and under discard by the British, However they went on to fight on all theatres of war. Although 1ST Patiala Lancers were not mechanised or mobilised, they constantly supplied volunteers to most of the armoured regiments. At the time of Indian Independence in 1947, the only mounted cavalry remaining in service were the President's (formerly Viceroy's) Body Guard and several units that had formed part of the Imperial Service State Forces, provided by the Indian Princely States.

Upon the integration of the State Forces into the regular Indian Army, the remaining horsed cavalry units were reorganized and reconstituted into the new regiment as "61ST Cavalry" in January 1954. Today 61ST Cavalry is one of the limited numbers of un-mechanised mounted cavalry regiments in the world. However, the Patiala Lancers were integrated into the Indian Army in January 1950 and redesignated as '(2ND Patiala Lancers) 61 Cavalry' in 1954, thus losing their distinct identity.

Sikh States Forces

Patiala Mountain Battery

In the process of expelling the Afghans from the Punjab, the Sikhs had wrested most of their arms for the fledging Sikh Confederate Armies. By 1722 the Patiala Confederacy had a full-fledged fighting unit with an Artillery wing, which was involved in all the wars and conflicts in which the Patiala State Forces participated. In 1784 the Marathas, having dealt ruthlessly with the Mughal rulers, advanced towards Punjab. The Patiala forces intercepted the superior Maratha force at Mubarakpur, and during their subsequent attacks, compelled the Marathas to flee.

The Raja of Patiala had a dispute with the Raja of Nabha. The situation became critical leading to a bloody battle at Narwana, in which the Patiala Artillery decimated the Nabha Army; however, the Patiala forces lost 150 dead in the process. There seemed to be no end to the dispute. Then both parties invited Maharajah Ranjit Singh to mediate between them. This gave Ranjit Singh an opportunity to milk both sides!

During the Kaithal Rebellion of 1843, the Patiala State Forces, which included some artillery, were sent to help the British, in which they proved their uncanny fighting qualities. During the Sepoy Mutiny of 1857, Patiala forces swarmed in aid of the British. Besides the troops at Delhi, Karnal, Thanesar and Ambala, the Patiala forces aided in restoring order in Sirsa and Hissar; a contingent was employed at Sahaurnpur and Jagadari. The bulk of these actions were supported by the Patiala gunners. Patiala artillery also took active part in the Mohamed and Tirah expeditions on the North-West Frontier of India. When the First World War broke out in 1914, some of the Indian States and Patiala, provided a total of 7 Mountain and Field Batteries, which were added to various Indian army mountain and field regiments. They fought at Gallipoli, in East Africa, the Middle East, (Mesopotamia, Persia and Iraq), Palestine and on the North-West Frontier. During the Second World War, the Patiala gunners were once again absorbed in the Indian army, and fought in the Middle East, East Africa, Abyssinia, Malaya and Burma.

In September 1947, after Pakistan failed to persuade the ruler of Jammu and Kashmir to accede to it, she sent hordes of tribesmen supported and led by the Pakistani Army into Jammu and Kashmir, where they indulged in acts of loot, arson, rape and sabotage. The Maharaja of Kashmir frantically asked for, and received, an infantry battalion and a battery of Mountain artillery from the Sikh Maharaja of Patiala. The Patiala gunners were in the vanguard of defending Kashmir when 1948 closed with a cease-fire in Jammu and Kashmir. On integration of the Princely State Forces into the Indian Army, the Patiala Artillery was merged into the Indian Army in 1951 and redesignated as:

Patiala Mountain Battery	75TH (Patiala) Mountain Battery
Patiala Field Battery	85TH (Patiala) Field Battery

Regiment of Artillery Indian Army

Sikh States Forces

Jind Infantry

One Gajpat Singh with his Jatha (band) which contained both the mounted troopers and foot soldiers joined the Khalsa (Sikh Confederate Army) in 1763. He took part in the attack of the Sikhs on the province of Sirhind in 1763 in which Zain Khan, the Afghan governor of the province was killed. Gajpat Singh occupied a large tract of the country including Jind and Safidon as his share of the spoil. He made Jind his headquarters and built a large brick fort there. From this time onward, the Sikh chief ruled as an Independent Prince and coined money in his own name. Raja Gajpat Singh died in 1786 and was succeeded by his son Bhag Singh. He was the first of all the Cis-Satluj princes to seek an alliance with the British. He joined Lord Lake in his pursuit of Jaswant Rai Holkar in 1805, and was well rewarded for his services to the British. In 1809 the British declared suzerainty in Cis-Satluj territories. The Jind State accepted British protection and was obliged to make the State Forces available to the British in time of war. Like most of the Sikhs, Bhag Singh was a hard drinker, and the excess led to his death in 1819. After Bhag Singh's death, one of his successors Sarup Singh was very friendly and loyal to the British.

During the first Anglo-Sikh war the exertions of his people in providing supplies and carriage were great; his contingent served with the British troops, and a detachment of it, which accompanied the Patiala contingent to Ghumgrana, under Captain Hay, was highly praised by that officer for its steady conduct and discipline.

Still later, a detachment accompanied the expedition to Kashmir, where the Sikh governor was in revolt against Maharaja Gulab Singh. When the second Sikh war broke out, Raja Sarup Singh offered to lead his troops in person to Lahore, to join the British army. His services were declined as they were not needed. In 1857, immediately on learning of the outbreak of the Sepoy mutiny, he conducted his troops to Karnal by forced marches and undertook the defence of the city and cantonment. The Jind forces marched in advance of the British army recovering Samalkha and Rai, securing the road and collecting supplies for the army. The Jind force, under Commandant Khan Singh, took prominent part in the assault on Delhi, scaling the walls side by side with English troops, and of their number several were killed and wounded.

Raja Sarup Singh was the only Sikh Chieftain who was present with the army before Delhi. After the fall of Delhi, Sarup Singh returned to Sufidon. He left twenty-five men for service at the Larssowli Tehsil, and the same number at Delhi; sent a detachment of 200 men with General Van Cortland to Hansi, and 110 men under the command of Khan Singh to Jhajar with Colonel R. Lawrence. Besides these, 250 Jind troops remained stationed at Rohtak, and 50 at Gohana, about twenty miles to the north. Raja Sarup Singh died in 1864. He was succeeded by his son Raghbir Singh.

Sikh States Forces

Jind Infantry

When the second Afghan war broke out, Raja Raghbir Singh gave help to the British with men, money, and material. The British government conferred the title of Raja-i-Rajgan on him. Raghbir Singh died in 1887. His only son Balbir Singh had died during his own lifetime and therefore his grandson, Ranbir Singh, succeeded him. During the period of his minority, a council of regency administered the state; during this regime the state troops took part in the Tirah campaign of 1897. General Sir William Lockhart was in command of the Tirah Field Force, which numbered 35,000 men that included the Jind Infantry. The enemy, the Afridis, were masters of guerrilla tactics and knew the difficult terrain well and seized all the forts leading up to the Khyber Pass. The campaign was harsh, but the Jind Infantry gained an excellent reputation and valuable experience. The Force remained in occupation of Afridi` country until December 1897, but the campaign did not end until April 1898. The regiment's casualties were low, due to good discipline and outstanding musketry.

At the outbreak of the First World War, the Germans in East Africa not only cut the vital line of British communication from the Cape to Cairo but also provided Germany with a Naval base from where the German ships could operate in the Indian Ocean and destroy British ships en route to and from India. Consequently, the British Government decided to capture German East Africa. The Indian Government was given responsibility for this. The Indian Army maintained a force to at least Brigade strength throughout the fighting, and a total of 17,500 Indian soldiers served in East Africa. Jind maintained its loyal tradition by placing all the resources of his state at the disposal of the government. The Jind Infantry were in Africa from October 1914 to December 1917. They earned the highest opinions of all the Generals under whom they served, especially their fighting at Jassin. Major General Natha Singh, who commanded with great gallantry, was awarded the O.B.I., as well as C.I.E. Lieutenant Colonel Baldev Singh was awarded the O.B.I. and Captain Sundar Singh the French gallantry awards of Croix de Guerre and Naik Such Singh the Russian Cross of St. George.

Subedar Harnam Singh, Jind Infantry

Subedar Harnam Singh was awarded the I.O.M. for his gallant conduct at Jassin on 18TH January 1915. He rallied a small party to cover a retirement and held the enemy in check until his party were all killed and he himself severely wounded and taken prisoner.

Sepoy Sadda Singh, Jind Infantry

Sepoy Sadda Singh was awarded a posthumous I.O.M. for conspicuous gallantry in action on 9TH October 1916. He proceeded forward under a hot fire along a communication trench and removed a number of dead bodies which were impeding the advance. He was killed in the process.

Sikh States Forces

Jind Infantry

The Malaya Command was a formation of the British Army for the coordination of the defences of British Malaya. It consisted mainly of small garrison forces in Kuala Lumpur, Penang, Taiping, Seremban and Singapore. With the outbreak of the Second World War, the command reinforced its strength in anticipation. With the bulk of British forces being tied down in the war in Europe and the Near East, the command was mainly augmented by units from India. The Jind Infantry joined the command in 1941, and was responsible for the ground defence of two main aerodromes in Singapore. These areas were regularly and heavily bombed, and later dive-bombed and machine-gunned. In the later stages of the fighting when the forward troops withdrew in the Tengah area, leaving the flanks of the aerodrome unprotected, the battalion defended their position on 10TH and 11TH February with commendable tenacity, inflicting heavy casualties on the enemy. The regiment eventually withdrew in good order, having suffered considerable loss after the action of which and Indian State Force Unit should well be proud. Subsequently Jind Infantry took a prominent part in the defence of the outskirts of Singapore, where it again displayed a high degree of courage under continuous shelling and mortar machine gun fire. Lieutenant Colonel Gurbaksh Singh was most successful in avoiding heavy casualties in his unit by skill and resource in the dispositions of his command. He maintained a very high standard of morale and efficiency, for which his own gallant bearing under fire and his determined personality were responsible, for which Lieutenant Colonel Gurbaksh Singh was awarded the DSO. Singapore garrison surrendered to the Japanese on 15TH February 1942. From February 1942 to December 1942, he resisted all efforts to force him and his men, especially the Sikhs, to join the Indian National Army. (Indian National Army, also known as the Azad Hind Fauj, was formed for the liberation of India from the British rule). The majority of his Sikhs and many those of other units were dissuaded by him from wavering from their allegiance. To the end of his captivity Lieutenant Colonel Gurbaksh Singh concentrated his efforts on the welfare of his men. At the end he brought back to India his complete regiment, loyal almost to a man. By his wonderful example and leadership and the faith placed in him by all, he has earned and deserves the highest possible praise and distinction. Lieutenant Colonel Gurbaksh Singh was awarded: The Most Excellent Order of the British Empire.

He retired from the Indian Army with the rank of Lieutenant General.

In 1951, Jind Infantry Regiment was re-designated:-

'13TH (Jind) Punjab Regiment' the Indian Army

Sikh States Forces

Nabha Akal Infantry

Gurdit Singh laid the foundations of the House of Nabha. His grandson Raja Hamir Singh consolidated and extended the possessions and by the year 1760 had put the independent principality on a firm footing. His successor Raja Jaswant Singh sought British alliance in 1809. The Nabha State accepted British protection and was obliged to make the State Forces available to the British in time of war. Raja Jaswant Singh died in 1840 and was succeeded by his son Davindar Singh. The late Raja had been a faithful ally of the British Government. In 1814 he gave assistance in supplies and carriage during the Gurkha campaign, and in that of Bikaner in 1818; and during the northward march of the British army to Kabul in 1838, he advanced a loan of six lakhs or rupees to the Government. In 1845, during the Sikh war, Devinder Singh withheld supplies from the British, and as punishment was deposed in 1846 (He died at Lahore in 1865). Devinder's son, Bharpur Singh attained his majority a few months after the outbreak of the Sepoy Mutiny in 1857. At the time he was in possession of one Cavalry Regiment, two Infantry regiments and two batteries of Horse Artillery. He acted with exemplary loyalty to the British. He held charge of the station of Ludhiana and of the neighbouring Satluj ferries at the commencement of the outbreak. Nabha detachment of 300 men took the place of the Nasiri Battalion which had been detailed to escort a siege train from Phillaur to Delhi, but had refused to march. Another detachment of 150 Nabha troops assisted the British Deputy Commissioner in opposing the Jullundur mutineers at Phillaur and prevented their crossing the River. The Raja also despatched a contingent of 300 to Delhi, under Sardar Didar Singh throughout the siege. In addition to this, the Raja enlisted many hundred new troops, furnished supplies and carriage, arrested mutineers marching through his state, and performed every service required of him. He was amply rewarded by the British for his assistance. He died in 1863. One of his successors Raja Hira Singh also sent a force of two guns, 200 cavalry and 500 infantry for service on the frontier during the Afghan War of 1870-80, and these troops did excellent service in the Kurram Valley throughout the first phase of the campaign. In recognition of this the Grand Cross of the Star of India was conferred on the Raja in 1879. In 1893 he was given the title of Raja-i-Rajgan. The Nabha troops took part in the Tirah campaign of 1897. The enemy, the Afridis, were masters of guerrilla tactics and knew the difficult terrain well and seized all the forts leading up to the Khyber Pass. The forts were retaken and the force remained in occupation of Afridi` country until December 1897, but the campaign did not end until April 1898. They were back on the Frontier and advanced on Afghanistan and served there throughout Afghanistan in the war of 1919.

During World War Two, after serving in the Middle East, Nabha Akal Infantry joined 10TH Indian Infantry Division in March 1944, and was sent to Italy to join the Eighth Army on the Adriatic front. The Nabha Akals were involved in some hard fighting against the Germans northwards through Central Italy.

Sikh States Forces

Nabha Akal Infantry

Numerous mountain battles and River crossings followed with *Operation Olive* on the Gothic Line and then the spring 1945 offensive. The Nabha Akals suffered many casualties before final victory in Italy in May 1945.

Three Sikh officers of Nabha Akal Infantry were awarded the Military Cross in Italy including Jemadar Gurdial Singh and Major Inder Singh.

The citation of Jemadar Gurdial Singh's award reads: "On 5TH October 1944, 'C' Company of the Nabha Akal Infantry was ordered to take the high feature of Finnachio in Italy. Jemadar Gurdial Singh's platoon took part in the first wave of the assault. Jemadar Gurdial Singh led the charge up the steep side of the feature in a magnificent manner taking his place at the head of his assaulting party and shouting encouragement to his men under very heavy Spandau, grenade and mortar fire. On nearing the objective he came upon an enemy trench whose occupants had been giving the advancing troops a great deal of trouble. Unless this batch of the enemy was quickly neutralized, they would cause many more casualties among the assaulting section. Jemadar Gurdial Singh rushed up to them alone and firing his pistol into their midst and showing outstanding courage under heavy fire, succeeded in killing and wounding all the occupants. On the same day his Company was again employed in another attack in which Jemadar Gurdial Singh again led his men into assault with outstanding bravery, which encouraged his men to carry through the attack with success."

The citation of Major Inder Singh's award reads: "On 30TH November 1944, Major Inder Singh was in command of 'D' Company of the Nabha Akal Infantry during the attack on Alberto in Italy. Ten minutes before the starting time fresh information compelled him to make urgent alterations to his plan. At the outset of the advance the Company came under heavy enemy Artillery and small arms fire halting the Company. Casualties were heavy including all three Platoon Commanders. Without the slightest hesitation and with complete disregard for his own safety Major Inder Singh immediately ran forward to carry out a recce. He then moved from Platoon to Platoon still under very heavy fire encouraging his men and giving orders to continue the advance. The coolness, courage and leadership displayed by Major Inder Singh were outstanding and undoubtedly ensured the capture of his objective. He displayed a devotion to duty of a very high order and his personal example was an inspiration to the rest of his Company."

Havildars Nika Singh, Pritam Singh, Sobha Singh, Sher Singh, Naiks Bachan Singh, Gurbachan Singh, Joginder Singh, Sepoys Dalip Singh, Labh Singh and Ram Singh were awarded the Military Medal for their gallantry in battle in Italy.

In August 1947, at the independence and the partition of the Indian subcontinent in the sovereign states of India and Pakistan, Nabha State was merged into India. In 1954 the Nabha Akal Infantry Regiment was merged into the Indian Army and re-designated '14TH (Nabha) battalion, The Punjab Regiment'.

Sikh States Forces

Kapurthala Infantry

Founder of the Kapurthala state, Jassa Singh Ahluwalia, was one of the Chief architects of Sikh power in the Punjab. He took advantage of the troubled times in which he lived to annex territory on a large scale and make himself by his intelligence and bravery the leading Sikh of his day. In 1748 he attacked and killed Salabat Khan, Governor of Amritsar, seizing a large portion of the district; five years later he extended his conquests to the edge of Beas, defeating Adina Beg, Governor of Jullundur Doab, and taking possession of the Fatehbad Pargana. He next captured Sirhind and Dayapur south of the Satluj. Hoshiarpur, Bhairog and Narayagarh fell to his sword in the same year; and Rai Ibrahim Bhatti then the Muhammadan chief of Kapurthala, only saved himself from destruction, becoming feudatory of Jassa Singh Ahluwalia. Sardar Jassa Singh Ahluwalia was undoubtedly the foremost amongst the Sikhs north of the Satluj; he did more than any contemporary Sikh to consolidate the power of the Khalsa. One of his successors Fateh Singh was fast friend and ally of Maharaja Ranjit Singh. Fateh Singh and the Maharaja jointly signed the first treaty, dated 1ST January 1806, and entered into the British Government with the rulers of the Trans-Satluj. But they were never afterwards regarded as equals and in the end Fateh Singh found himself the feudatory of the Lahore Government. In the majority of Ranjit Singh's annual campaigns, Fateh Singh served with his contingent. He fought at the battle of Haidera, on 13TH July 1813, when Fateh Khan, the Kabul minister and General, was utterly defeated and driven from the Punjab; he held a command in Bhimber, Rajaori, and Bahawalpur campaigns. He was at the last famous siege of Multan in 1818, when the whole province fell into the hands of the Maharaja, and Nawab Muzafar Khan was slain; and established a military post of his own at Talambah, forty- five miles north-east of the city. During the Kashmir campaign of 1819 he remained in charge of the capital; and in 1821assisted at the reduction of the fort of Mankera in the desert of Sind Sagar Doab. The possessions of Sardar Fateh Singh being situated for the most part in the Jullundur Doab north of Satluj, his relations with the British Government were not very intimate, though his Cis–Satluj possessions were secured under the general agreement of 1809. Sardar Fateh Singh died in 1837, and was succeeded by his son Nihal Singh. During the Anglo-Sikh war in 1845, he withheld assistance from the British, for as a protected Cis-Satluj feudatory he was bound to place all his resources at the British disposal, and in this he failed. His estates south of the Satluj were declared an escheat to the British Government as he failed to act up to his obligations under the treaty of 1809.

The Kapurthala troops had broken away from Sardar Nihal Singh's control and fought against the British both at Aliwal and Budhowal. In the Second Anglo-Sikh War, he did all in his power to retrieve his affairs, by furnishing carriage and supplies to the British. At the close of the war he was created a Raja in acknowledgment of his valuable services. He died in 1852.

Sikh States Forces

Kapurthala Infantry

His successor Raja Randhir Singh, on the news of the outbreak of the Sepoy Mutiny, with his younger brother Kanwar Bikram Singh, marched into Jullundur at the head of his men and helped to hold the Doab, almost denuded of troops, until the fall of Delhi. The force the Raja employed during this time consisted of 1200 infantry, 200 cavalry and 5 guns. The Raja's able assistance was promptly acknowledged by the bestowal upon him of the title of Raja-i-Rajgan. In 1858, Raja Randhir Singh led his contingent of soldiers to Oudh and took part in the pacification of the disturbed districts. He, with his brother, remained in the field for ten months and was engaged with the enemy in six general actions, capturing nine guns. He is said to have avoided neither fatigue nor danger, remaining constantly at the head of his men, who fought at all times with conspicuous bravery, and earned for themselves the highest characters for discipline and soldiery behaviour. He died on the 2ND April 1870, and was succeeded by his son Prince Kharak Singh, who reigned for seven years and died in 1877, leaving a son, Jagatjit Singh, who was invested with the full powers of administration in 1890. During the Afghan war of 1879-80 the Kapurthala State furnished a contingent of seven hundred cavalry, artillery and infantry. The force was employed on the Bannu frontier and did good service. In 1889 the British Government accepted an offer from the state to maintain a select body of troops for Imperial Service, and this force was employed in the Tirah campaign of 1897-98, in which it gained great credit.

At the outbreak of the Great War in 1914, the Kapurthala Service Infantry regiment was dispatched for active service in East Africa, where it remained for nearly four years and did excellent work. On 2ND November 1915, the Kapurthala Infantry launched a frontal attack on the mountain positions at Longido. Subedar Gurdit Singh was awarded the I.D.S.M. for his conspicuous gallantry during this action.

On the successful termination of the Great War the regiment saw active service in Seistan during the Afghan War of 1919, and later spent six months performing imperial duties in Mesopotamia.

Kapurthala's two infantry regiments, 'The Kapurthala Jagjit Infantry' and 'The Kapurthala Parmjit Infantry' formed a composite battalion in 1939.

In the Second World the Kapurthala Regiment was the first among the Indian States to proceed on active service and took part in actual fighting at Singapore; where the Japanese unfortunately captured it.

In August 1947, at the independence and the partition of the Indian subcontinent in the sovereign states of India and Pakistan, Kapurthala State was merged into the republic of India.

The Kapurthala Infantry Regiment was mustered out by the Indian Army but its regimental band was retained by the Artillery Centre, at Nasik.

Sikh States Forces

Faridkot Sappers and Miners

At the expulsion of the Afghans from the Punjab, Sardar Hamir Singh added considerably to the family possessions. He built Faridkot and made it his capital, and kept up an armed force, and administered justice to the best of his ability. His son was deposed by Sardar Charat Singh and died in exile in 1798. Charat Singh was attacked and slain by his uncle Dal Singh, who in his turn, was assassinated by a cousin Fauja Singh. Then succeeded Gulab Singh, a minor, to whom the assassin acted as guardian. Maharaja Ranjit Singh took possession of the state in 1809, using all of his army. He assigned five villages for the maintenance of Gulab Singh and his brothers. The spoliation of the state was regarded with disfavour by the British Government, and the Maharaja was forced to relinquish this prey in the following year, with his other Cis-Satluj possessions. During the Anglo-Sikh war of 1846, then the reigning Sardar of Faridkot, Sardar Pahar Singh sided with the British, and helped them by collecting carriage and supplies for the army. In recognition of these services he received the title of Raja. Raja Pahar Singh was followed by his son Wazir Singh. He remained loyal to the British during the Second Anglo-Sikh war. During the Sepoy Mutiny of 1857, he guarded the ferries of the Satluj against the passage of the mutineers. His troops also served in Sirsa and elsewhere, and he, in person with a body of horse and two guns, attacked a notorious rebel and destroyed his village. Raja Bikram Singh succeeded his father in 1875. During the second Afghan war he furnished a contingent of two hundred and fifty horse and foot, which was employed on the Kohat Frontier. In 1888 the Faridkot forces, cavalry and infantry were formed into two battalions of 'Faridkot Sappers and Miners'. During World War One the Faridkot Sappers and Miners served on the Western Front in France and Flanders, and provided reinforcements to 39TH Garhwal Rifles, and fought as infantry in the trenches. A battalion of 130 strong were despatched to British East Africa in October 1914. They were in Africa from November 1914 to February 1918. Lieutenant Colonel Nand Singh was awarded the O.B.I. and the I.O.M. Lieutenant Colonel Bishan Singh was awarded the O.B.I. The following Sikh soldiers of Faridkot Sappers and Miners were awarded the I.D.S.M. for their conspicuous gallantry East Africa. Jemadar Mota Singh, Jemadar Chet Singh, Havildar Harnam Singh, Naik Sawan Singh, Naik Thana Singh, and Lance-Naik Kishen Singh.

During the Second World War, the Faridkot Sappers were incorporated in 4TH Corps in India, and were effectively engaged in operations against the Japanese in Burma. In August 1947, at the independence and the partition of the Indian subcontinent in the sovereign states of India and Pakistan, Faridkot State was merged into the republic of India.

Both Field companies of Faridkot Sappers and Miners were absorbed into the Indian Army in 1948 and their new designation was:

2ND Faridkot Field Co. became 94TH Field Co. (Faridkot) Bengal Group.

1ST Field Co. became 368TH Field Co. (Faridkot) Bengal Group.

The Corps of Sikh Pioneers

1ST Battalion

Punjab has always been a region of warriors though soldiering was only open to certain castes. The ascent of Sikhism and its bringing into being an order of saint-soldiers unfettered by caste restrictions gave a chance to everyone to take up the profession. The Mazhabi and Ramdasia communities imbued with the martial spirit of Sikhism stood out because of their hardy nature. The British started their recruitment in 1850 when a corps of Mazhbi Sikh Pioneers had been formed, largely from the men who had been in the Sikh Army. It had been sent to work on the Grand Trunk Road between Nowshera and Pashawar.

In 1857 they were known as 24TH Sikh Pioneers, later 32ND Sikh Pioneers Bengal Army. It was the first regiment recruited exclusively from the Mazhabi Sikh community of Punjab province. Despite being 'pioneers' by name, the regiment functioned as a Sikh infantry regiment specially trained as assault pioneers.

The Sepoys of Bengal Army mutinied at the Meerut cantonment near Delhi on 10TH May 1857. The Mutiny spread to Delhi, Agra, Cawnpore, and Lucknow, starting a year-long insurrection against the British. A rebellious and committed force of 30,000 mutineers defended Delhi, a well fortified walled city. The mutinous force was armed with a greater number of high calibre guns which was perhaps their strongest point. On 7TH June 1857, a hastily raised force succeeded in occupying a ridge overlooking Delhi. It was far too weak a force to retake the city. Reinforcements gradually arrived from the Punjab, including the newly raised unit of Sikh Pioneers of 960 ranks. Thus it was that the Mazhbis returned to Delhi where a few of their forbears had earned the outcaste race a title of distinction. They returned too, to be eagerly welcomed by an Army, in hard circumstances, and to gain military lore and credit that was to remain perhaps for all time. They had been constantly employed in the defence of ridge. Three or four times also the Sikh Pioneers sent detachments to some miles up the Ganges Canal destroying bridges over which the enemies' Horse used to scamper to attack the convoys coming from the north. In searing heat, the force held off repeated efforts by the mutineers to take the ridge. The assault on the city began on 14TH September, when the artillery breached the city walls, and the Sikh Pioneers accomplished the desperate task of blowing in the Kashmir Gate. The deeds of the gallant party have been commemorated for all time by a tablet on the shot-riddled Kashmir Gate in 1856 by General Lord Napier of Magdala, C-in-C. India. The assaulting troops had to make their way down long narrow lanes flanked by flat-topped buildings, from which the Sepoys and their allies maintained a heavy fire. It took a week of vicious street fighting before Delhi was finally taken. This ended the Delhi episode of the first Pioneers regiment. Yet there was little rest for 24TH Pioneers. The regiment was broken up into various detachments required to restore order, the most important being the detachment which was to march at once to the relief of beleaguered Agra.

The Corps of Sikh Pioneers

1ST Battalion

The Punjab had been stripped bare of most of its reliable troops other than the minimum frontier garrisons during the Sepoy Mutiny. The Mazhbi Pioneers at the siege of Delhi had shown unexpected staunchness under fire and loyalty to their leaders. The British wanted more troops for their safety and, therefore, decided to raise another Mazhbi Regiment in 1857, which consisted of 800 rank and file and 140 officers and N.C.O.s. The newly raised regiment, '15TH (Pioneer) Regiment of Punjab Infantry' was raised at Lahore on 15TH September 1857. Immediately it marched to Multan and picked up a good many of mutinous stragglers. Of the 1,300 mutineers involved very few made it to their homes. On 15TH September 1858, the regiment was ordered to march to Lucknow. The great battle and recapture of that city was over, but the huge province was full of rebel forces which needed to be chased and broken up. The second regiment, with its sister regiment, was split up by companies among the various armies, that were to trample out the mutineers, for several months and which brought the operations in Oudh down to a police basis.

The Chinese government was anxious about British opium trading activity in their country, forced the British to remain within Hong Kong. An incident in 1856, when the Chinese authorities seized 'Arrow', a ship flying the British flag, and arrested its Chinese crew for piracy, caused the British to mount an expedition to China, under Lord Elgin. In 1858, the British seized Canton and followed it up by an unsuccessful naval attack on Taku Forts, situated at the mouth of the Pei-Ho River. In 1860, the British attacking force consisted of 4 Infantry Brigades of British and Indian troops that included 15TH Ludhiana Sikhs, 15TH Pioneers, 20TH Punjab Regiment and 27TH Punjab Infantry. The Cavalry Brigade included Probyn's Horse and Fane's Horse. Both cavalry regiments were raised during the Sepoy Mutiny from the disbanded troopers of the Khalsa Armies of the Sikh Kingdom. They gathered in Hong Kong under Lieutenant General Sir Hope Grant. In all there were 11,000 British and Indian troops, plus 6,000 French troops. The expedition landed at Odin Bay on 1ST August and fought actions on 3RD, 12TH, and 14TH August around Sinho. Then a combined British and French force of infantry carried out the attack on Taku Forts. Inside the leading Fort, a bloody hand-to-hand encounter ensued and out of the Chinese garrison of 500 strong, only 100 succeeded in escaping, many indeed jumped from the walls, only to be impaled on the stakes outside. The fate of the fort had not been lost on the defenders of the succeeding fort and almost before the assaulting troops had reached the walls, flags of truce were put up. The allies took 2,000 prisoners, besides taking possession of several brass and iron guns. This completed the capture of the famous Taku Forts that had defied a strong Naval Contingent the year before, as the southern forts surrendered next day to a small force of 2ND Division that included 15TH Pioneers. The 15TH Pioneers, justly proud of their share in these successes, now looked forward to the march to and capture of Peking, which was resumed on 8TH September.

The Corps of Sikh Pioneers

1st Battalion

During the advance on Peking the allies fought several actions at Pa-li-Chio and Chan Chai Wan, compelling the Chinese to flee in utter consternation. On 21st September, at the battle of Palikao, 10,000 Chinese troops were completely annihilated after several doomed frontal charges against the concentrated firepower of the Anglo- French forces, which entered Peking on 6th October. The services of the Sikh Pioneers were brought to the notice of the Indian Government by Lieutenant General Sir Hope Grant, in his despatch dated 21st November 1860:

"The 15th Regiment of Punjab Infantry had accompanied the army in all the active operations in the field, and although owing to the nature of the operations, they have not come into collision with the enemy as frequently as they have perhaps wished, their services have not been of the less value to the expedition. The regiment was particularly forward during the action of the 18th September, and on the 21st September a detachment distinguished itself by crossing the River and capturing a gun which had opened on our lines."

The 15th Pioneers after their return from Tartary, became 23rd Regiment of Sikh Pioneers. In 1863, 23rd Pioneers formed part of the Umbeyla campaign directed against the 'Hindustani Fanatics' in Sittana and focused on the village of Malka. The 23rd Pioneers were constantly employed in their dual role of pioneering and infantry work, in the whole area ablaze with swarms of tribesmen with countless banners. General Sir Neville Chamberlain realized the seriousness of the occasion and collected troops of the most reliable kind and these included 23rd Pioneers. The force advanced up the Umbeyla Pass against strong opposition. Heavy casualties were sustained during attempts to hold the 'Eagle's Nest' and 'Crag Piquet'. Although the 'Hindustani Fanatics' had practically exterminated themselves on the bayonets of the Mazhbis. The pioneers then drove the rebels out of the valley, and then burnt Malka.

The 23rd Sikh Pioneers were to find themselves in a minor campaign left over from Umbeyla days. In 1865, it was necessary to chastise refractory villages in Yuzufzai country. The operations only lasted a few days, the punishment proceeded unhindered by neighbouring tribes, and towers and fortified hamlets were destroyed by the pioneers. The 23rd Pioneers then returned to Pashawar, where they remained till 1867, preparing for the Abyssinian campaign.

In 1868, a combined British and Indian force invaded Abyssinia to secure the release of captives held hostage by King Theodore. The decisive action was fought at Apogee, near the capital. A detachment of 23rd Sikh Pioneers charged forward and met the enemy in close combat. The Abyssinian courage could not stand up to the Sikh bayonets, and they were beaten off with very heavy losses. Subedar Major Natha Singh, Subedar Kharak Singh, Naiks Jowala Singh, Fateh Singh and Bugler Khushal Singh, of 23rd Sikh Pioneers were awarded the I.O.M. in consideration of their conspicuous gallantry in Abyssinia. They were the only gallantry awards made to Indian soldiers in during this expedition.

The Corps of Sikh Pioneers

1ST Battalion

The Battle of Peiwar Kotal was fought on 29TH November 1878 between British forces under Sir Frederick Roberts, which included 23RD Sikh Pioneers and Afghan forces under Karim Khan, during the opening stages of the Second Anglo-Afghan War. Indeed, Roberts was a great believer in the idea of martial races and valued the services of the Sikhs far above the other Indian troops. This was partly a natural reaction for anyone who had been involved in the Indian Mutiny as he had been. As Roberts' force moved up the Kurram valley, the Afghans, 1,800 in number with 12 guns, retreated before them until they reached Peiwar Kotal. They joined the existing garrison, so that 4,000 Afghans with 23 guns held the 4-mile long fortified position centred on Peiwar Kotal. Early on 28TH November, 1878, the attacking force advancing up a wide slope and halting beneath the Kotal by a steep ridge, up which wound the track to the Afghan position. An account of the fierce fighting relates how:-

"Time after time the enemy made determined charges from behind the barricades with which they had obstructed the narrow causeway in front of their position, only to be driven back. But when Roberts ordered a party of 23RD Sikh Pioneers to deliver a counter attack, they, in their turn, were repulsed, losing their leader, Major Anderson. With him fell Havildar Kharak Singh, Lance-Naik Jita Singh and Sepoy Ram Singh. A second party of the same regiment, after some hand-to-hand fighting, was likewise compelled to retire, with the loss of a Havildar and three men killed. It seemed as if the two forces might continue facing each other and firing into each other's ranks until the ammunition of one side, or both, ran short". The British and Indian troops then attacked along the ridge into the main Afghan positions. Heavy fighting developed as the troops continued to attack, making their way up the northern side of the valley until close to the Peiwar Kotal itself. The Afghan troops fled down the valley, pursued by the Cavalry, while the tribesmen ran for the hills. The British were victorious and seized the strategic Peiwar Kotal Pass leading into Afghanistan.

The death of the British resident Sir Cavignari, resolved the government in Calcutta for a full invasion of the country, the occupation of Kabul and punitive action against the killers of Cavignari's party. Roberts resolved on immediate attack on the Afghan army, blocking his road to Kabul. During the attack, it was a charge by 23RD Sikh Pioneers, which finally caused the Afghans to break. The brilliant victory of Charasia threw open the road to Kabul, gained over thirteen regular Afghan battalions and a host of tribesmen. The battle at Charasia was a critical one. As on several occasions in the Second Afghan War, the margin between success and disastrous failure was thin. The courage and resource of the Sikh soldiers won the battle against great odds. Eight Sikh soldiers of 23RD Sikh Pioneers were awarded the I.O.M. for gallantry in this action. Lord Roberts, on his march from Kabul to Kandahar in 1880, dispensed with his Sappers and Miners and relied on 23RD Sikh Pioneers as one of the four infantry regiments in the first of his three brigades, to act as engineers when necessary.

The Corps of Sikh Pioneers

1ST Battalion

Hundreds of Ghilzais surrounded a small garrison manned by 23RD Sikh Pioneers at Latabad on the North-West Frontier of India, and established a Piquet within close range. Subedar Mehtab Singh led forth forty Sikh Pioneers against this Piquet with great success. Subedar Mehtab Singh and Havildar Gulab Singh were awarded the I.O.M., for their gallantry in this action.

After the disastrous defeat at Maiwand in Afghanistan, the remnants of battle-wearied army were forced to fall back on Kandahar. The Amir, Ayub Khan then laid siege to Kandahar, defended by a well-supplied garrison of 5000 men and 13 guns under General Primrose. As soon as news of the defeat and siege reached Kabul, Lieutenant General Stewart ordered General Roberts to form a flying column of one cavalry brigade, three infantry brigades and four mountain batteries. The force comprised 2836 British troops and 7151 Sepoy and Gurkha troops which included 2ND Sikhs, 3RD Sikhs and 15TH Ludhiana Sikhs, 23RD, 24TH Sikh Pioneers and 25TH Punjabis, with its 7000 followers, left for Kandahar on 8TH August. The relief force finally entered Kandahar on 31ST August. After a brief rest, on 1ST September, Roberts sortied out of Kandahar and attacked the Afghan army. Battle commenced at 9.30 am and, after meeting considerable opposition amongst the village and surrounding orchards, 1ST and 2ND Brigades dislodged the enemy troops after fierce hand-to-hand fighting.

Both brigades then advanced to turn the Afghan position on Pir Paimal and take the rest of the Afghan army in the rear. The Afghans attempted to form a new line, but the British pressed home their advantage with 2ND Gurkha Rifles; 92ND Highlanders and 23RD Sikh Pioneers storming the Afghan defences in front of their camp. Ayub Khan fled, leaving his army to disperse, pursued by the British cavalry. The Battle of Kandahar ended the Second Anglo-Afghan War. Ayub Khan had been decisively beaten. He had lost the whole of his artillery, his camp, enormous quantities of ammunition and about 1,000 men killed. He became a fugitive along with the small remnants of his battered army. The British appointee Abdul Rahman was thus securely established, under British protection, as Emir of Afghanistan. Having achieved the aims of their invasion of Afghanistan, the British withdrew. Three Sikh soldiers of 23RD Sikh Pioneers were awarded the IOM for their conspicuous gallantry against the Afghans.

During the period under review 23RD Pioneers spent most of their time making barracks. During the autumn of 1897, owing to the outbreak of war along the Frontier of larger dimensions than had hitherto been known, 23RD Pioneers sent six of their British officers as reinforcements and various detachments to relieve regiments ordered on active service. The 23RD Pioneers remained at Mian Mir in peace, re-organising under the new double company system. Finally at the close of the year 23RD Pioneers proceeded on service to Waziristan to take part in the Blockade that it was proposed to enforce on that part of the North-West Frontier against the Mahsuds and Waziris.

The Corps of Sikh Pioneers

1ST Battalion

On the Frontier, the fines imposed on the Mahsuds for their raids into Tochi, the Tank Zam and the Gomal trade route amounted to large sums and were unpaid. It was decided to impose on them, the old-fashioned but formerly effective remedy of 'blockade' or ban. All entry into administered India, and the bazaars of the frontier towns was forbidden and no trade to them was allowed. The Blockade was proclaimed on 1ST December, and the Border Police were re-enforced by a strong force of troops. The Right Wing of 23RD Sikh Pioneers left Lahore on 3RD December, 1900, for Dera Ismail Khan on the Indus, whence they marched to Murtaza for various military works. They were joined a month later by the Left Wing and were entirely occupied by work on the Gomal. Apart from sniping the only soldier's affair was an attack on the Piquet at Khuzma Khula by Abdul Rehman Khels. On 23RD November, 1901, four punitive expeditions, one from Tochi, and three from the Gomal side, were mounted against the tribesmen. The 23RD Sikh Pioneers were attached to the force that raided Torwan from Wana. The column was lightly equipped and left Wana at midnight on 24TH, timed so as to reach Torwan at daybreak. This was entirely successful, and after destroying a recalcitrant village, and having marched forty-five miles in twenty hours, the force headed for the heights at Wachla Piazza, and for the next three days raided the whole of the Khaisora, returning to Wana on 28TH with 124 prisoners and much grain, fodder and cattle. There was a certain amount of skirmishing, the column suffering twenty casualties, out of which fourteen fell to 23RD Sikh Pioneers, two being killed and twelve wounded. The four raids, of which the above was one, were so successful that a series of further raids was decided on. A large column was assembling at Jandola and this was joined by 23RD Sikh Pioneers on 30TH November. Marching up the Shahur Nullah and destroying various towers.

The story of the Tibetan campaign in 1903 has been largely devoted to the daring of 32ND Sikh Pioneers, who took such a prominent part. However, 23RD Sikh Pioneers came up early in the day to share in the original advance to Gyantse and then proceeded to work on the rearward, but clearly difficult and supremely essential part of the road, a company working up as far as Kangma, the next post below Chumbi, which they garrisoned. After the severe fighting at Chumbi, it took part in the advance on Lhasa. General Macdonald in his despatches referred to their splendid work on the roads. Four soldiers of 23RD Sikh Pioneers were awarded the IOM for their conspicuous gallantry during this campaign.

At the beginning of World War One, the Sikh Pioneers mobilised two regiments forthwith, 34TH went to France and 23RD went to Aden and in due course to Egypt, then to Palestine. The 32ND garrisoned the North-West Frontier for three years, then proceeded to Mesopotamia in 1917, and remained there taking part in the suppression of the Arab Rebellion of 1920-1921. Later in the War, 2ND and 3RD battalions were raised for each of the three regiments, so that no less than nine battalions of Mazhbi Sikhs were serving the Empire at the Armistice.

The Corps of Sikh Pioneers

1ST Battalion

In 1914, 23RD Sikh Pioneers were posted to a force that was being rushed towards Egypt. However, on their way they were ordered to destroy the fort of Sheikh Saad. The fort lies at the end of a small peninsula of Arabia, whence the Red Sea traffic could be attacked. The Sikhs proceeded to attack the fort supported by the naval guns. They carried out demolitions at fort and guardhouses, which included the destruction of field guns. They then re-embarked and sailed for Aden. In January twelve pioneers left to join the Somaliland Contingent as an explosion party, who after some arduous and waterless marching attacked and destroyed five forts at Shimber Berries and then rejoined the battalion at Aden. The third of these put up a stout resistance, confident in its walls of eight foot thickness. The mountain guns with the contingent could not hope to batter these down, and the old last hope of an explosion party remained. Under hot fire from the walls the party laid their charge and the gateway was blown in. While placing the charge against the gateway, Naik Sher Singh was knocked over and rendered practically insensible by the discharge of the Dervish rifles through the door. After getting up, and joined by Havildar Teja Singh, they placed the charge in the correct place and thus blew the gate, enabling the rest of the party to attack and capture the fort. Havildar Teja Singh and Naik Sher Singh very properly received the IOM. By the end of February the demolition party rejoined the battalion at Aden.

In mid-1915 the Turks stirred up trouble amongst tribes in the Aden hinterland, threatening the friendly Sultan of Lahej. A British column was despatched to Lahej but numerous difficulties, not the least being the deadly summer heat, the breakdown of the water and ammunition transport arrangements, the desertion of local drivers, led to a disorganised British retreat. As soon as the news of the retirement from Lahej reached Aden, Majors Ottley and Hope with five Indian officers and 180 23RD Sikh Pioneers marched out to Sheikh Othman from Aden, they arrived to find stragglers of all kinds streaming in. Then they marched on another four miles to Bir Muhammad, where they took over rearguard to the returning remnants from Lahej and escorted them to Sheikh Othman. Such a situation as had occurred could not be left for long, quite apart from the threat to the defended port. Major-General Younghusband's 28TH brigade was at once embarked at Suez and sent to Aden. There was no opposition to so strong a force, both Turks and Arabs having disappeared, and Sheikh Othman was put into a proper state of defence. The detachment of 23RD Sikh Pioneers, 250 strong from Perim, had rejoined on 27TH of July and were at once, with the whole battalion, put on the defence works. On 25TH an attempt to deal with a body of Turks and Arabs, reported at Waht was undertaken. The Turks were hustled out of the various villages and then attacked at Waht. The 23RD were specially commended for their work. The period of service at Aden for 23RD Sikh Pioneers was over. On January 20TH, 1916, they proceeded to Egypt, Sinai and Palestine.

The Corps of Sikh Pioneers

1ST Battalion

In Egypt 23RD Sikh Pioneers became divisional troops of 10TH Division, consisting of 20TH, 29TH and 31ST Indian Infantry Brigades. By 1917 the demand for more Indian Corps was intense and 23RD was cut in two, half to become 2/23RD Sikh Pioneers. The actual formation to effect at Shallufah in Egypt from 3RD February and shortly after a draft of 669 men from India completed both battalions to a total of some 700 men. The new battalion was then posted as Divisional Pioneers to 75TH Division, and remained with it till the end of the campaign, though often detached for work on road or railway communication. The 2/23RD Sikh Pioneers was the first unit to enter Palestine, where they took over 850 German and Turkish prisoners including the commander of the Turkish 53RD Division. The two battalions of 23RD Sikh Pioneers were now kept at work principally on the outer flank of the force, as befitted their armed and disciplined state. However, 23RD Sikh Pioneers shot down a German plane at El Arish. "One of them left their formation and with a view to machine- gunning us. They picked up their rifles and with the Machine guns we opened fire. We could see the splinters flying out of the plane and down he came about a mile away. It gave the Germans a shock and we were not molested again." After the success of Bir Sheba and the capture of Gaza the pioneers entered Jerusalem on December 9TH. The history of the Sikh Pioneers henceforth in Egypt and Palestine is to a great extent, uneventful, save for the miracle of construction for which their name should long be famous in this phase of the World War. Seven Sikh soldiers were awarded the I.D.S.M. for their conspicuous gallantry in Egypt and Palestine.

The 1/23RD Sikh Pioneers leaving Alexandria on 25TH February arrived at Constantinople on 20TH of March, where they remained three days, and then made for Batoum across the Black Sea. They reached Batoum in ten days and were at once put to work on the Batoum-Tiflis-Baku railway. On April 7TH they reached Tiflis, and were at once ordered to Kars. Alexandropol and Kars had just been wrecked and burnt by Tartars out of vindictiveness. The Pioneers now proceeded to disarm the town, and re-establish order, remaining there till April 30TH, when more of the Armenians returned. By 15TH May they were required to prepare a camp for 27TH Division at Pendik. On June 29TH 1919 the Turkish peace was signed. The next duty for them was on the Hiader Pasha Ishmit portion of the Anatolian railway. This continued till the middle of November when the battalion arrived at Tuzla barracks en route for India. Subedar Sundar Singh, Havildar Phuman Singh, Havildar-Major Kaka Singh, Lance Naik Shamir Singh and Sepoy Lachman Singh, were awarded the I.D.S.M. for their conspicuous gallantry in Asia Minor.

In 1928 the Regiments of Pioneers became the Corps of Pioneers, in the Sikh case, the Corps of Sikh Pioneers. Sadly, the Corps of Sikh Pioneers was to be short-lived. Little more than three years later, on 10TH February 1933, the Corps was finally disbanded. The serving soldiers, however, were absorbed in the Bengal Sappers and Miners and Bombay Sappers and Miners.

The Corps of Sikh Pioneers

2ND Battalion

At the start of the Sepoy Mutiny, the rebels had seized Lucknow City, and besieged the British who were cooped up in the Residency. Havelock with a small force fought his way through to the beleaguered garrison, reaching them just in time, but both the beleaguered and the relievers then had to endure a second siege. In the autumn of 1857 Sir Colin Campbell, with a second relief column, managed to raise the siege, but had not sufficient strength to capture the city, and so retired with what remained of the garrison and its imprisoned Europeans. Now in February 1858 he was assembling a force of 20,000 men, which included 24TH Pioneers with the rank and file of 755, to march on Lucknow, which was held by 130,000 mutineers, many of who were regular sepoys, whilst others were followers of their hereditary chieftains. The city was assaulted and captured on 21ST March 1858. It had been gained at a loss of 127 officers and men killed and 595 wounded. Sikh Pioneers casualties being 8 other ranks killed and 25 other ranks wounded.

At the conclusion of the Sepoy Mutiny, 24TH Pioneers were ordered to the North West Frontier to chastise the Kabul Khel Wazirs. The Kabul Khel, a section of the larger group of the Utmanzai Wazirs, had a long history of crimes culminating in the murder of a British officer. The Maliks of this section refused to deliver up the murderers to the authorities. A punitive force was collected in December 1859, to which 100 men of 24TH Sikh Pioneers were added. The force assembled at Mandani, near Buland Khel, where the Kabul Khel had established an enceinte of strong Sangars to guard the valley. The attacking force drove the tribesmen from all their positions. Next day a foray captured all their winter stores, together with 5,000 sheep, 300 bullocks, and 60 camels, while the Sikh Pioneers accompanied a force in the destruction of fortified towers.

In April 1860, General Chamberlain took the field against the Mahsud Wazir clan. The climax of their iniquities had been their attempt to capture and sack the frontier town of Tank, which belonged to a protected Nawab of a settled Pawindah tribe. General Chamberlain had asked for 24TH Sikh Pioneers and 412 of them had joined him. As the Sikhs attacked, Mahsuds fled in confusion, the men in the front forcing back the men behind until all became a helpless rabble, straining to gain the safety of the mountains. The result was that about 300 Mahsuds were killed, including six leading Maliks, and many more wounded. By now the new Bengal line had been formed and 15TH and 24TH Sikh Pioneers became 23RD and 32ND Regiments of Sikh Pioneers, and by such they will now be known. Allusion have been made to the anomaly that the younger regiment should have senior number. No explanation has ever been given.

Towards the end of 1863, a force from Pashawar moved out under Brigadier-General Sir Neville Chamberlain, for punitive operations against the Hindustani Fanatics at Malka. This nest of fanatical exiles had been a thorn in the side of the Sikh authority before the British flag flew in the north. The Sikhs utterly defeated them in 1831.

The Corps of Sikh Pioneers

2ND Battalion

The night of 16TH December 1863 was a memorable one for both 23RD and 32ND Sikh Pioneers. Mr. J. Campbell of 93RD Highlanders has communicated this interesting account of the Ghazis charge to the Sikh Pioneer's history: - "I happened to be looking when the 200 Ghazis made their splendid charge on the two Mazhbi Regiments, and I shall never forget the scene. There were a great many of the enemy between the foot of the hills and the village of Umbeyla, but as the force advanced they all scuttled into the hills behind the village and charged 23RD and 32ND Sikh Pioneers. The Sikhs were taken aback, but recovered quickly and counter charged the Ghazis, of whom they killed over two hundred. The 23RD and 32ND Sikh Pioneers were the only regiments involved. These two regiments were within a few yards of the nullah before they could see that there was any nullah at all; it was very deep and narrow. The Ghazis left their matchlocks etc., in the nullah, and came in with Tulwars only. The Ghazis came down the front of the two regiments, cutting and slashing with their Tulwars, and every one of them was killed. They came out to die and they did die, but they did some mischief. Thus terminated the first important combined action of the sister regiments, in which they had but gloriously upheld the honour of the Muzbee, their regiments, and the Khalsa. As in the days of old in the Khalsa armies the Muzbee were in the front of the fight and bore the first onslaught of the enemy. Pushed back at first by weight of numbers and the suddenness of the attack, they soon rallied, and killed every Hindustani Fanatic of those two hundred, not allowing one to escape. The attack on the Sikh Pioneers was made almost entirely by the Hindustani Ghazis, the very object of the punitive efforts, who had practically exterminated themselves on the bayonets of the Mazbhis. During the night the bulk of the tribesmen whom the influence and misrepresentations of the Hindustanis had brought to the gathering fled towards their homes. The menace was over."

It was to the North-East Frontier that the scene was to change, almost before the troops in Umbeyla had marched back to their cantonment, the state of Bhutan was to be the theatre. The 32ND Sikh Pioneers arrived in Bhutan after two months of leaving the Punjab to join the punitive brigade. The raiders were met and overcame at Dhalimkote, Bhumsong and Charmoorchee. A detachment captured Dewanigiri on 2ND April 1865, after which the Bhutanese accepted defeat. The 32ND garrisoned Dewanigiri till the close of 1866, when the post was dismantled and abandoned as too unhealthy. The regiment then returned to Baksa and spent 1867 and 1869 in making roads to the interior. And after three years in the country, they marched down to Dinapore. Now we come to one of the main events of the last sixty years, the Second Afghan War. British Government in 1878 was anxious to counter Russian influence in Afghanistan and demanded the Afghans to receive a British military mission to Kabul. When the Afghan ruler Sher Ali refused, British Indian army invaded Afghanistan on 21ST November 1878.

The Corps of Sikh Pioneers

2ND Battalion

During the Second Afghan War 32ND Sikh Pioneers performed a record of two years hard work in constructing roads. However, an action fought against the local clans interrupted the work. The Afghans had gathered at a collection of walled villages known as Hisarak, with drums and flags flying. Before the British could close in on the enemy, estimated to be almost 1,500 strong, they moved out to the charge the British. Rushing forward in the centre with loud cries, and swarming on the flanks, they evidently hoped to overwhelm the small British force. A few well directed volleys from 32ND Sikh Pioneers, soon dispelled any such idea, and the tribesmen fell back. A further offensive was necessary and after certain points had been stormed with the bayonet, the enemy disappeared. The Sikh Pioneers now set out to work to blow up towers, in devastating heat before returning to Pesh Bolak on completion of this duty.

During 1889 the Black Mountain tribes were quiet enough. In 1890 the British announced their determination to make certain roads along the crest of the Black Mountain Ridge, which was the actual administrative border. The Hasanzais and Akazai objected. It was therefore decided to send a force against the sections who had given trouble. To this, the force marched with 32ND Sikh Pioneers. They were sent to work to make a road from Tilli to Kunhar. A force of Ghazis rushed a Piquet and occupied the Masjid, whence they made several sallies against the rest of the column. Two companies of the Sikh Pioneers hurried in support of the Piquet and cleared the village with a bayonet. By dawn the enemy had disappeared, leaving twenty five dead behind them, a company of Pioneers moving in their wake guided by the track of blood. Curiously enough at Umbeyla, at Kotkai and now at Ghazi-Kot, it was always the Sikh Pioneers who broke the attack, or any rate a very fair share of it! On the night of 19TH March, the camp Piquet at Kunhar was attacked during the night, the enemy actually entering part of the village, but being promptly expelled by the Sikh Pioneers, having three men wounded in the process.

In the first half of 19TH century, the British extended their influence to the Himalayas, and Sikkim signed an agreement with the British in 1861. We have seen the Sikh Pioneers in 1864 concerned in the adjustment of affairs in Bhutan, and now in 1886, they were bound for the same part of the world. The semi-independent state of Sikkim lies to the north-west of Bhutan and east of Darjeeling, with Tibet on the north and Nepal on the north-west. In 1886, 300 Tibetans crossed the frontier and occupied Lingtu in Sikkim, fortifying a position across the trade routes to Tibet. The British issued an ultimatum that unless the Tibetans withdrew, they would be expelled by force. On 25TH February Brigadier General Thomas Graham was ordered to march on Sikkim. His forces included 32ND Sikh Pioneers. His orders were to expel the Tibetans from Lingtu and re-establish Indian control of the road up to the Jelep La, while securing Gangtok and Tumlong from possible reprisals.

The Corps of Sikh Pioneers

2ND Battalion

The force was assembled at Padong and it was divided into two columns, the Lingtu column commanded by General Graham and the Intchi column by Lieutenant Colonel Mitchell. At Graham's advance the Tibetans had barricaded the road and erected a stockade on a hill that dominated the road. Graham advanced up the road with the pioneers in front clearing the path from bamboo and foliage. Once they reached the stockade the Tibetans retreated after a short struggle. In spite of the fortifications the defenders' bows and matchlocks were outgunned by the British modern rifles and artillery. After carrying the stockade, the British drove the defenders off a stone breastwork that covered the back of the stockade. Graham continued his advance down the road as far as Garnei, within a mile of the Lingtu fort, and camped there for the night. The next morning the column advanced slowly through the mist and snow to the Tibetan positions and around 11 o'clock, 32ND Sikh Pioneers occupied the gate of the fort which was guarded only by some 30 Tibetan soldiers. General Graham continued the attack on Tibetan positions and penetrated the defences and captured the Tuko La pass, after which the Tibetans retreated through the Nim La pass.

On 25TH September the force advanced beyond Jelap-La to Chumbi, the Sikkim capital, but the Tibetans had gone, and all the fighting was over. It was estimated that 11,000 Tibetans with miserable arms and no real aptitude or heart for the battle had come forward, advancing out of arrogance and bravado. They lost many hundreds killed and wounded and 200 prisoners out of the 8,000 who had come to Tuko La. Eventually an Anglo-Chinese convention was signed on 17TH March 1890 at Kolkata, which established the Tibetan renunciation of suzerainty over Sikkim, and delimited the border between Tibet and Sikkim. The campaign was now over and the Tibetans brought to some sort of terms. The troops were gradually withdrawn, but to protect the State of Sikkim from any more inroads a garrison has always remained. The 32ND Sikh Pioneers themselves stayed barracks and road building, till August 1889.

In 1893 began a period of three years in which 23RD and 32ND Sikh Pioneers were to add to their laurels, and 32ND Sikh Pioneers to undergo experience and perform service unique even in the annals of the British Army. In early 1895, following the death of a chieftain and conflict over the succession, a British force ended up besieged in Chitral fort, in the shadow of the Hindu Kush in what is now north-west Pakistan. The 32ND Sikh Pioneers set out from Gilgit to cover 220 miles of very poor road to Chitral. The importance of the Sikh Pioneer's epic march was never fully recognized, most of the publicity and fame for the relief being lavished on the well-known British regiments like 60TH Rifles and Gordon Highlanders. However, Subedar Bhaga Singh, Subedar Prem Singh, Havildar Wasawa Singh, Havildar Wadhawa Singh, Jemadar Sher Singh, Sepoy Gurdit Singh and Sepoy Ishar Singh, of 32ND Sikh Pioneers were awarded the I.O.M. for their conspicuous gallantry in the relief of the Chitral Fort.

The Corps of Sikh Pioneers

2ND Battalion

In early March 1895, 32ND Sikh Pioneers was ordered to Gilgit as the force at Chitral was facing hostile action by Umra Khan. The troops committed to the column were 400 soldiers from 32ND Sikh Pioneers and a 2 gun section of No1 Kashmir Mountain Battery. Before reaching Chitral, Kelly's force would have to cross the Shandur Pass. On 2ND April the guns were brought up to Teru and Borradaile's detachment began the struggle to cross the Shandur Pass leaving the gun section at Langar. The pass was filled with snow up to 5 feet deep causing the column to travel at less than a mile an hour. Borradaile's detachment reached the village of Laspur at the far end of the pass and fortified part of the village and sent porters back to assist in bringing Stewart's gun detachment from Langar. Stewart's detachment arrived in the evening after an exacting journey in which the heavy guns had to be carried through the snow by the soldiers. Reconnaissance along the road to Chitral showed that the Chitralis were in position in the Chakalwat Defile in strength and building Sangars. On 7TH April 1895 Colonel Kelly arrived at Laspur and decided to attack the Chakalwat Defile although many of the soldiers were suffering from snow blindness and the rest of the column was still on the track from Ghizr. The attack went in on 9TH April 1895 and the Chitralis were driven from the position to Nisa Gol. The British attack went in with ladders being used to cross the ravine and turn the Chitralis right flank causing the Chitralis to withdraw. On 18TH April 1895 the column reached Koghazi where Kelly received a letter from Robertson in Chitral saying that the besieging force of Sher Afzul and Umra Khan had withdrawn and the siege of Chitral Fort was over. On 20TH April 1895 Kelly's column marched into Chitral. The Relief of Chitral was the first expedition to take the Indian and British Armies over the Malakand Pass into Swat and Jandol. There were no roads, only tracks over the mountains. The first range of border hills was 3,000 to 6,000 feet in height. Beyond were further ranges of high mountains and 3 substantial Rivers without bridges, border hills, then the Swat River; Laram Range up to 6,000 feet, then the Panjkora River; Janbati Range and the Dir Valley; the Lowarai Pass into the valley of the Chitral. Until roads could be built the force would have to rely on pack animals to move supplies. Some 30,000 mules and camels were used in support of the force. No tents were taken and the baggage allowance was 40 lbs for officers and 10 lbs for soldiers, including greatcoat. The weather was snow, wind, rain and fierce sunshine. In order to reach Jandol and Dir and then to enter Chitral the Chitral Relief Force had to cross the territory of a number of other hostile tribes and rulers.

Thus ended the enduring Epic of 32ND Sikh Pioneers and Kelly's Relief Force, but it by no means comprised the whole story of the Sikh Pioneers in this campaign, which was to demand the energies of all the three Pioneer regiments in garrisoning Chitral, the infant son of the murdered Mehtar to be maintained on the throne, while various small states to be supported as friends and allies, and the Malakand to be held in perpetuity.

The Corps of Sikh Pioneers

2ND Battalion

To forestall the Russians, in 1904, a British expedition led by Colonel Francis Younghusband was sent to Lhasa to force a trading agreement and to prevent Tibetans from establishing a relationship with the Russians.

Younghusband's mission was expanded into a full scale military force consisting of 23RD and 32ND Sikh Pioneers and 8TH Gurkhas, with sixty-five Mounted Infantry, formed from the above regiments. Soon the Mounted infantry was to be raised to one hundred strong, with ten more men from 23RD Pioneers and sixteen from 32ND under the command of Jemadar Prem Singh. Three more Sikh officers were sent for from India. By early December, it was poised at the Jelap La Pass, the 14,000 foot entrance into Tibet the 'roof of the world'. To the hazards of travel over some of the roughest and highest terrain in the world, was added sub-zero winter cold. Conditions were frightful. Rifle-bolts froze into the breaches and subalterns kept the Maxims' bolts warm in their own beds. The troops' clothing, though lavish by the standards of those days, offered no real protection and was, in addition, too bulky to allow free movement for firing. Yet, although scouts kept reporting that they had sighted large Tibetan forces in the hills, Younghusband was not attacked. It was not until the two opposing forces reached the tiny village of Guru on March 31ST, 1904, that they came into direct conflict. Two thousand Tibetan troops were waiting there, blocking the caravan trail, which the British had to follow if they were to get to Gyantse. On March 31ST, 1904, the British reached the Tibetan fortifications. The Tibetan general galloped up and told them to withdraw. Younghusband replied giving them 15 minutes to clear the way. A quarter of an hour passed and nothing happened. Then, slowly the troops advanced until they were covering the Tibetans at point-blank range. Another company of Sikhs was brought up and formed into a line. Younghusband ordered the Sikhs to disarm the Tibetans. As the two forces wrestled with each other, the situation began to turn ugly. Then the Tibetan general, who in a sudden impulse of anger at seeing his orderly being disarmed, drew his pistol and blew off the jaw of the Sikh Sepoy who was taking the arms. Fighting broke out instantly. Volley after volley of British bullets crashed into the solid mass of Tibetans. There were certainly 1,500 Tibetans and had they not been fired on promptly, they would have rushed on and easily cut up the 150 Sikh Sepoys confronting them. On the outbreak of the firing, the Tibetans in the Sangars on the hill began throwing stones and firing on the Sikhs and 2ND Mounted Infantry, and then the fight became general. Suddenly Tibetans turned and fled for the village of Guru with the Sikhs, with the two companies of Mounted Infantry in hot pursuit. Guru village was rushed and cleared and as they retreated along the Gyantse road, they were pursued for twelve miles and thoroughly dispersed. After the fight, two companies of 32ND Sikh Pioneers and 2ND Mounted Infantry held Guru Village. The total Tibetan loss was 620 killed and wounded, besides the ones taken prisoners.

The Corps of Sikh Pioneers

2ND Battalion

The advance on Gyantse was resumed on 2ND April, but this was not affected without some opposition, for the Tibetans, about 2,000 strong, were found to be occupying a series of ridges above a deep gorge, the Zamdong (the Red Idol). They held a very strong position among some loose boulders on the right, two miles beyond the gully, which the Gurkhas had ascended to make their flank attack. The rocks extended from the bluff cliff to the path, which skirted the stream. No one could ask for better cover; it was most difficult to distinguish the drab-coated Tibetans who lay concealed there. To attack the strong position General Macdonald sent Captain Bethune with one company of 32ND Sikh Pioneers, placing Lieutenant Cook with his Maxim on a mound at 500 yards to cover Bethune's advance. Bethune led a frontal attack. The Tibetans fired wildly until the Sikhs with fixed bayonets were within fifty yards of them and then fled up the valley. Not a single man of 32ND Sikh Pioneers was hit during the attack, though one Sepoy was wounded in the pursuit by a bullet in the hand, from a man who lay concealed behind a rock within a few yards of him. While 32ND Sikh Pioneers were dislodging the Tibetans from the path and the rocks above it, the Mounted Infantry galloped through them to reconnoitre ahead and cut off the fugitives in the valley. They also came through the enemy's fire at very close quarters without a casualty. On emerging from the gorge, the Mounted Infantry discovered that the ridge the Tibetans had held was shaped like the letter S, so that by doubling back along an almost parallel valley they were able to intercept the enemy, whom the Gurkhas had driven down the cliffs. The unfortunate Tibetans were now hemmed in between two fires and hardly a man of them escaped. Finally, the Sikhs dashed through the gorge digging the enemy out of caves and from behind boulders. The honour of the day was an award of the I.O.M. to Sepoy Sahib Singh, who had entered a cave and bayoneted all the occupants in it. On May 3RD, Colonel Brander left Gyantse with his column of 400 rifles. The column comprised of three companies of 32ND Pioneers, under Captains Bethune and Cullen and Lieutenant Hodgson; one company of 8TH Gurkhas with two 7-pounder guns; the Maxim detachment of the Norfolks, and forty-five of 1ST Mounted Infantry, under Captain Ottley. The column marched up the pass and encamped about two miles from where the Tibetans had built their wall. A reconnaissance that afternoon estimated the enemy at 2,000, and they were holding the strongest position on the road to Lhasa. They had built a wall the whole length of a narrow spur and up the hill on the other side of the stream, and in addition held detached Sangars high up the steep hills. Their flanks rested on very high and nearly precipitous rocks. The fire from the wall was very heavy and the advance of Cullen's and Bethune's companies was checked. Then compelled by some fatal impulse, Bethune with half a company, left the cover of the Riverbed and rushed out into the open, within forty yards of the main wall, exposed to a withering fire from three sides. Bethune and seventeen men were killed.

The Corps of Sikh Pioneers

2ND Battalion

The guns had made no impression on their wall and a large reinforcement of at least 500 men coming up to join the enemy. The situation was critical. When the front attack had failed, fifteen men of 32ND Sikh Pioneers were sent up the hill. The party, led by Subedar Wasawa Singh, scaled the 'almost perpendicular face of the 1,500-foot southern scarp'. Subedar Wasant Singh's gallant section poured down deadly rifle fire on the Sangar. Twice the Tibetans rushed out, and, coming under a heavy Maxim fire, bolted back again. The third time they fled en masse, while the Maxims mowed down about thirty. From the position they had won the Sikhs could enfilade the main wall itself. The Tibetans on the wall turned and fled in three huge bodies down the valley. Thus, the fifteen Sikhs on the right saved the situation and Subedar Wasawa Singh and Sepoy Bhagwan Singh were awarded the I.O.M. for their conspicuous gallantry. Directly the flight began, 1ST Mounted Infantry poured into the valley and harassed the flying masses, riding on their flanks and pursuing them for ten miles to within sight of the Yamdok Tso. It showed extraordinary courage on the part of this little band of Sikhs and Gurkhas. They did not hesitate to hurl themselves on the flanks of the enormous body of men, like terriers on the heels of a flock of cattle, though they had had experience of their stubborn resistance the whole day long. They rode through the bodies of their fallen comrades. Not a man drew rein. The Tibetans were caught in a trap. The hills that sloped down to the valley afforded them little cover. Their fate was only a question of time and ammunition. The mounted infantry returned at night with only three casualties, having killed over 300 men. The sortie to the Karo la was one of the most brilliant episodes of the campaign. The expedition reached Gyantse on 11TH April. General Macdonald announced his intention of returning to Chumbi with the larger portion of the escort, leaving a sufficient guard with the mission. The guard left behind consisted of four companies of 32ND Sikh Pioneers under Colonel Brander; four companies of 8TH Gurkhas, under Major Row; 1ST Mounted Infantry, under Captain Ottley; and the machine-gun section of the Norfolk's, under Lieutenant Hadow. The next morning the post was attacked at dawn. It appears that the Shigatze forces, about 1,000 strong, on hearing that very few troops were guarding the mission, determined to make an attack on the post. The attack was sudden and simultaneous. A Gurkha sentry had just time to fire off his rifle before the Tibetans rushed to the walls and had their muskets through the loopholes. The enemy did not for the moment attempt to scale, but contented themselves with firing into the post through the loopholes they had taken. This delay proved fatal to their plans, for it gave the small garrison time to rise and arm. The brunt of the Tibetan fire was directed on the courtyard of the house, where the tents of the members of the mission were pitched. The Sikhs, emerging from their tents with bandolier and rifle, in extraordinary costumes, were directed towards the loopholes. Some were sent on the roof of the mission-house, whence they could enfilade the attackers.

The Corps of Sikh Pioneers

2ND Battalion

Lieutenant Franklin, the medical officer of 8TH Gurkhas, rallied Gurkhas and Pioneers to the loopholes on the east and north. Lieutenant Lynch, the treasure-chest officer, who had a guard of about twenty Gurkhas, took his men to the main gate to the south. There were at this time in hospital about a dozen Sikhs, who had been badly burnt in a lamentable gunpowder explosion a few days previously. These men bandaged and crippled as they were, rose from their couches, made their painful way to the tops of the houses and fired into the enemy below. A few of the enemy got inside the defences and were immediately shot down. The fire was so heavy and so well directed that it was not more than ten minutes from the time the first shot was fired to the time the enemy began to withdraw. They were pursued almost to the very walls of the fort. Indeed, but for the fringe of houses and narrow streets at the base of the jong, they would have gone on. The Tibetans, however, turned as soon as they reached the shelter of walls. It would have been madness to attack five or six hundred determined men in a maze of alleys and passages, with only a weak company. Major Murray accordingly made his way back to the post, picking up a dozen prisoners en route. The enemy in the jong began to fire into the camp and it was realized that the jong entirely dominated the post; that walls and stockades, protection enough against a direct assault from the plain, were no protection against bullets dropped from a height. On 18TH May, the enemy occupied a building 500 yards away from the post and as the fire from the Lhasa Martinis was disconcerting, it was decided to storm the building next morning. The two companies of 8TH Gurkhas under Major Murray, with an explosion party of Sikh Pioneers under Lieutenant Gurdon, were detailed to the storming, with two companies of 32ND Sikh Pioneers in reserve. Silently they slipped out of the Post at 3.30 a.m. and were not detected until close under the walls of the building. The defenders then woke up to hurl stones and fire heavily, while the jong also joined in. As an entrance could not be forced, the Gurkhas lay down to wait till the Sikhs had done their share; a roar and a column of smoke soon followed; after which a period of dead silence ensued and even the jong ceased firing. Then the Gurkhas, with kukri and bayonet, did their bit and those Tibetans who had not escaped met their fate. From the garrison of about sixty, forty were killed; twenty threw themselves from the walls, of whom the reserve Sikhs accounted for half. The Post was put into a state of defence and garrisoned by fifty Gurkhas. The Gurkhas were to spend an anxious time threatened by night attack and fired at from the jong. The inconvenience of the investment was instanced that very day, when a party of eight Mounted Infantry, bringing in the mails, were ambushed close to the River. Captain Ottley galloped out with his mounted infantry and was only just in time to save a party of his men, who were coming up from Kangma with the letter-bags. These Sikhs - eight in number - were riding along the edge of the River, when they were met by a fusillade from a number of the enemy, concealed amongst sedges on the opposite bank.

The Corps of Sikh Pioneers

2ND Battalion

Before the Sikhs could take cover, one man was killed, three wounded and seven out of the eight horses shot down. The remaining men showed rare courage. They carried their wounded comrades under cover of a ditch, untied and brought to the same place the letter-bags, and then lay down and returned the fire of the enemy. The Tibetans, however, were beginning to creep round, and the ammunition of the Sikhs was running low, when Captain Ottley dashed up to the rescue. Without waiting to consider how many of the enemy might be hiding in the sedge, Ottley took his twenty men splashing through the River. Nearly 300 Tibetans bolted out in all directions, like rabbits from a cover. The mounted infantry, shooting and smiting, chased them to the very edge of the plain. On reaching hilly ground the enemy, who must have lost about fifty of their number, began to turn, having doubtless realized that they were running before a handful of men. At the same time shots were fired from villages, previously thought unoccupied, on Ottley's left, and a body of matchlock men were seen running up to reinforce from a large village on the Lhasa road. Under these conditions, it would have been madness to continue the fight and Ottley cleverly and skilfully withdrew without having lost a single man. It now appeared that the Tibetans were drawing a cordon in the rear of the Post across the communications. 32ND accordingly moved out against the villages of Kaha, Chilra, and Tagu. The first two were empty and were set fire to, but the other two were obstinately held. Suddenly fire was opened from the upper windows of the two houses. All the doors were found blocked with bricks and stones. Two Sikhs were killed and, for the moment, it seemed as if they would lose heavily. But Lieutenant Gurdon, with half a dozen men, rushed up with a box of explosives. The first attempt to blow a breach failed, matches having got wet wading the River, but the next attempt in which Lieutenant Gurdon and Havildar Wasawa Singh laid the charge was successful, though Havildar Wasawa Singh was shot through the head. Many of the garrison jumped from the walls, only to fall into the hands of another company of Sikhs and the whole garrison was killed or captured. A posthumous I.O.M. was bestowed on Havildar Wasawa Singh, his widow receiving the special pension attached thereto, and the same to Sepoy Prem Singh. Preparations were now made for taking the remaining village. This was protected by a high loophole embankment, which sheltered about five or six hundred of the enemy. The Sikh Pioneers had just extended and were advancing, when someone who happened to be looking at the jong through his glasses suddenly uttered a loud exclamation. Turning round, they saw a dense stream of men, several thousands in number, forming up at the base of the rock, evidently with the intention of rushing the mission post whilst the majority of the garrison and the guns were engaged elsewhere. Colonel Brander immediately gave the order for the whole force to retire into the post at the double. The withdrawal was affected before the Tibetans made their contemplated rush, but all felt that it was rather a narrow shave.

The Corps of Sikh Pioneers

2ND Battalion

On the succeeding day, a large convoy and reinforcements under Major Peterson, 32ND Sikh Pioneers, came safely through. The additional troops included a section of 7TH (British) Mountain Battery, under Captain Easton; one and a half companies of Sappers and Miners, under Captain Shepherd and Lieutenant Garstin; and another company of 32ND Sikh Pioneers. Major Peterson reported that his convoy had come under heavy fire from the village and monastery of Naini. Accordingly, on 24TH, a column marched out to Naini. But the monastery and the group of buildings outside it were found deserted. The walls were far too heavy and strong to be destroyed by a small force, which had to return before nightfall, but Captain Shepherd blew up the four towers at the corners and a portion of the hall in which the Buddhas were enthroned. On 5TH June, Colonel Younghusband went through to Kangma and was to go on next morning to Kalatso. There was not sufficient room in the post to admit the extra Mounted Infantry being put inside and they were, therefore, picketed outside in the open, together with the Yak Corps and their escort of about twenty men of 1ST Battalion 2ND Gurkhas. About 4 a.m. next day, the Mounted Infantry saddled up and were waiting to start with Colonel Younghusband for Kalatso. Most of the men, at the invitation of their comrades, the two companies of 23RD Sikh Pioneers garrisoning Kangma, were inside the post having some warm tea. Subedar Sangat Singh and Jemadar Prem Singh and about six or eight men were with the ponies. Most of the yaks and over half the Gurkha escort were well on their way to Kalatso. The rest were just ready to go, when Jemadar Prem Singh, of the Mounted Infantry, walked about 200 yards up the hill. He espied about 1,000 Tibetans get up out of a Nullah, where they had concealed themselves, and make straight for the post. The Jemadar ran back and gave the alarm. Subedar Sangat Singh, thinking of his ponies, collected the five or six Sikh and Gurkha Mounted Infantry men, who were lying down practically in the open, prepared to defend their ponies, and well they did it, else the lot would have been killed, wounded or cut loose. The attack was so sudden that although the Subedar and his party shot down numbers of the enemy and checked them, some had got amongst the ponies and were killing them, cutting them loose, or trying to ride them away. Some Tibetans had even mounted, without losing the picketing rope, but were unused to the slippery English saddles, and the ponies, resenting this rude treatment, bucked them off again. Just then, the Mounted Infantry men inside the post, hearing the commotion outside, rushed out with fixed bayonets and drove the Tibetans out of the pony lines, untied the ponies and took them all inside the post, still covered by the Subedar and his party. The garrison of two companies of 23RD had commenced rifle fire on the Tibetans, who were compelled to retire, leaving numbers of dead behind. Immediately the Tibetans showed signs of going, Captain Pearson sallied out of the post with one company of 23RD Sikh Pioneers, led by their fine old Subedar Jiwan Singh, an old Afghan war veteran.

The Corps of Sikh Pioneers

2ND Battalion

They did not know that so large a body of Mounted Infantry was in the post and had tarried just too long; they were caught by the mounted men, who, led by their own native officers, rode through them, using their rifles from horseback, and chased them down the Gyantse road, and up the Ealung road. The attack had completely failed and the Tibetans had sense enough never to attempt another on posts in the lines of communication, which, though weakly held, were proved capable of withstanding their assaults. On their advance, the reduction of the village of Palla was decided on. In it was a strong, imposing building known as the Palace. The Tibetans had been seen fortifying it, but hitherto occupation of it had been out the question. At early dawn on 29TH, a force sallied forth, consisting of the four guns of the column, one maxim, two companies of Sikh Pioneers and one of Gurkhas, with two sapper storming parties. The first explosion gave access to the outer works, but the garrison was on the upper tier, with all the ladders removed. The firing of another charge frightened the garrison into one strong house, which the Sikhs now rushed, killing its defenders. Meantime the main body of the assaulting column, after extraordinary effort, took the Palace. Palla was now put into a state of defence and garrisoned with one company, 32ND Sikh Pioneers under Subedar Sher Singh. The fight at Palla was the last affair of any importance in which the garrison was engaged, pending the arrival of the relieving force. The Tibetans had received such a shock that in future they confined themselves practically to the defensive, with five half-hearted night attacks, which were never anywhere near being pushed home. On 26TH June, Lieutenant Colonel Brander led a small portion of his force with his guns to assist the attack on Naini monastery, where the Tibetans were reported to be barring the way. This force got into position close on the spurs above Naini and opened fire with its guns. The monastery was then captured with ease by the main column, which then marched into Gyantse without further incident. The force then proceeded to seize forts and high points in the vicinity, and generally engaging any Tibetans they encountered. On 6TH July, the force proceeded to attack Gyantse itself. The Pioneers furnished explosion parties, but a feeble attempt at resistance was experienced. The town and jong being carried easily once the breaches had been made. The force then started for Lhasa some 2,000 strong. By now the attitude of the Tibetans had changed. The British must be got rid of, and finally on 7TH September a treaty was signed, amid considerable ceremony. On 23RD, the force, which had been reduced to 180 Mounted Infantry and 1,450 rifles, marched out for India. It was a march almost as arduous as the advance and carried out for the most part in two columns. It is related that as the column marched away, several Tibetan magnates and Lamas rode after it to offer thanks for the orderly behaviour of troops and the magnanimous treatment of the city. The 32ND Sikh Pioneers had returned to Ambala by the autumn of 1904.

The Corps of Sikh Pioneers

2ND Battalion

September 1911, was to see it once more on active service, and this time again on the North East Frontier. They proceeded high up in the Himalayas, beyond Assam. One of the wilder aboriginal tribes, the Abors, had been raiding beyond all bearing, rejecting all civil and police warnings and it was decided to open their country and teach them a lesson. Proceeding to Calcutta by rail 32ND Sikh Pioneers moved by steamer up the Ganges and Brahmaputra on 18TH September, arriving at the Kobo base on 23RD. The actual campaign saw little fighting but the regiment was hard at work on roads behind the column in heavy jungle and malarias country. Subedar Sundar Singh and Havildar Budh Singh were mentioned in General Bower's despatches. The regiment then returned to Lahore to abide in peace till the opening of the World War.

Although 32ND Sikh Pioneers did not go overseas till 1917, it had sent re-enforcements to both 23RD and 34TH Sikh Pioneers during the First World War. It arrived at Basra on 8TH May, 1917, and followed the fortunes of 17TH Division until the war in Mesopotamia was over. The Great War had ended in Mesopotamia with the signing of an armistice on 31st October 1918, and the surrender of the remnants of the Turkish 6TH Army at Mosul. However, the country actually remained a theatre of warfare and in July the Arab rebellion broke out, in which 32ND lost thirty Pioneers killed and missing. Fierce fighting continued in Mesopotamia until the insurgency began to run out of steam towards the end of the year. The last action took place in February 1921. The 32ND returned to India in May 1921. The battalion now 2/3RD Sikh pioneers joined the Razmak Field Force in Waziristan. At the end of January 1924 the battalion was at work on roads and Piquet duty between Razani and Razmak under severe winter conditions. In November 1924, the battalion left Razmak for Manzai, a good deal of sniping occurred here while parties were on the road, the battalion having one killed and three wounded in a smart encounter, for which Subedar Sadda Singh, Lance-Naik Gujjar Singh and Sepoy Nand Singh received I.D.S.M. The battalion returned to Sialkot after one and half year's hard work in May, 1924.

We have seen 32ND Sikh Pioneers at Delhi, Lucknow, N.W. Frontier, Bhutan, Afghanistan, Sikkim, Tibet, Chitral, Afghanistan and Mesopotamia. We have seen them since the World War in the great Waziri Campaign of 1920-1921, and once more in the operations connected with the pacification and the making of the great motor roads of peace. Thus, be it on motor road, on camel track, or on mule path, the rifle and pick of the Mazhbi Pioneers had marched home to the setting sun. In 1922, 32ND became 2ND battalion, 3RD Sikh Pioneers. Sadly the Corps of Sikh Pioneers was to be short lived. Little more than three years later, on 10TH February 1933, the Corps was finally disbanded. The men were, however, absorbed in the Bengal Sappers and Miners and Bombay Sappers and Miners. The 32ND Sikh Pioneers had marched to the drums for nigh on 70 years.

The Corps of Sikh Pioneers

3RD Battalion

So famous and so greatly in request had been 23RD and 32ND Sikh Pioneer Regiments that it was decided to raise another of the same type and race. The organisation of the new regiment, raised in March, 1887, was like the others, eight companies each commanded by a Subedar, assisted by a Jemadar, with the usual wing commander and wing officers. The new regiment was set on a firm footing by the transfer of a nucleus mainly from 23RD and 32ND Pioneers. In 1888 the regiment proceeded on active service with Black Mountain Expedition where the newly-raised regiment of eighteen months' standing acquitted itself most honourably. The regiment found hard at work on barracks, roads and cantonments and took active part in the Miranzi and Samana expeditions of 1891. It continued with its pioneer work on the North-West Frontier when it was mobilised for service with the Tirah Expeditionary Force in 1897. During the Tirah campaign the regiment was involved in extensive destruction of enemy towers, working on the roads and performing Piquet duties. The regiment marched out of Landi Kotal on 1ST April, 1899, to return to India.

The 34TH Sikh Pioneers were now to be involved in the Boxer Rebellion in China. In 1900, in what became known as the Boxer Rebellion (or the Boxer Uprising), a Chinese secret organization called the Society of the Righteous and Harmonious Fists led an uprising in northern China against the spread of Western and Japanese influence there. The rebels, referred to by westerners as Boxers because they performed physical exercises they believed would make them able to withstand bullets, killed foreigners and Chinese Christians and destroyed foreign property. From June to August, the Boxers besieged the foreign district of Beijing (then called Peking), China's capital. On August 14TH, after fighting its way through northern China, an international force that included a force from India to strength of 10,000 troops, and included 34TH Sikh Pioneers, arrived to take Beijing and rescue the foreigners and Chinese Christians. An outline of events that had taken place from the time that Admiral Seymour had set off on his attempted relief of the Legations in Peking and Tientsin had been besieged and Taku Forts captured, has already been stated in the history of 23RD Sikh Pioneers. With the relief of Peking and the Legations, the main operations were brought to a close and it only remained for the troops scattered about China to conduct a series of minor operations against the roving bands of Boxers.

The Boxer Rebellion formally ended with the signing of the Boxer Protocol on September 7TH, 1901. By terms of the agreement, forts protecting Beijing were to be destroyed, Boxer and Chinese government officials involved in the uprising were to be punished, foreign legations were permitted to station troops in Beijing for their defence, China was prohibited from importing arms for two years and it agreed to pay more than $330 million in reparations to the foreign nations involved.

The Corps of Sikh Pioneers

3RD Battalion

Although the general story follows the important but less spectacular lines indicated, there are remarkable differences in opportunity which brought 34TH Sikh Pioneers the rare and supreme honour of being a Royal battalion. It is to be remembered in this connection that no unit of the Indian Army had ever been a Royal Corps before the World War. The 34TH Sikh Pioneers with 806 rank and file and 57 followers first landed in Marseilles on 26TH September 1914. On the 22ND October, a company took over an advanced post from the French at Festubert. It was attacked within the hour of relieving the French and all the British officers were wounded. Subedars Sher Singh and Natha Singh took over command and held the post very resolutely till the evening of 26TH October. For his gallantry Sher Singh received an immediate I.O.M. From 26TH to 29TH the whole battalion was in the first and second line trenches, under constant shelling and continuous sniping. The 28TH and 29TH were such days of mud and rain that the rifles could hardly be fired. On the night of 28TH a German attack was beaten off with twenty-five casualties to the Pioneers. The regiment which was holding a front of 600 yards lost fifteen other ranks killed and 189 wounded. During the night of 23RD November, the enemy pushed up his sap to within five yards of the trenches of 34TH Sikh Pioneers, and at dawn attacked with a shower of bombs and hand grenades, especially where a company of 34TH Sikh Pioneers joined the Connaught Rangers. The bombs fell fast and furious near 34TH Sikh Pioneers' machine gun, and many men fell. Subedar Natha Singh at once took charge and held his position against the enemy, who had broken in. He had previously distinguished himself on several occasions and received the I.O.M. When all the men of the machine gun team had been killed or wounded, Havildar Nika Singh carried the gun by himself under a withering fire back to the support trenches, for which act of bravery he also received the I.O.M. Captain McCain, who commanded the next Company, had already been wounded by a bomb, but as the Germans broke in got his men behind a traverse and fought through it, till he was mortally wounded in the head and carried to safety by Sepoys Ishar Singh, Bachittar Singh and Kanhaiya Singh. Sepoy Ishar Singh received the IOM for his devotion.

Lance-Naik Tota Singh was killed beside Captain McCain and was awarded the posthumous I.O.M. for his fidelity and valour. Colour-Havildar Chanda Singh, Havildar Naryan Singh and Sepoy Teja Singh held on to their position. When the enemy entered the trench, they blocked up the traverse and fired through loopholes in it, until after Naryan Singh had been wounded, they were ordered to retire. Naryan Singh was again wounded, this time mortally, while being carried to the aid post; his bravery was recognized by the posthumous award of Indian Distinguished Service Medal. Subedar Sant Singh rallied his half Company and held them in position when the enemy broke in. He received the Military Cross.

The Corps of Sikh Pioneers

3RD Battalion

During counter attack 34TH Sikh Pioneers were overpowered by numbers and bombs, and their left was pushed out into the Connaught Ranger's trench, while the Germans continued to clear each traverse with grenades as they advanced. Subedar Natha Singh distinguished himself by getting into the enemy's trench on the left with only twenty-six men. The Commanding Officer reported that his conduct during the whole of these operations was an exceptional example of the highest courage and coolness. He well merited the I.O.M. bestowed on him, to be followed later by the Order of British India.

The 34TH Sikh Pioneers had suffered heavy losses, among the killed were Subedars Natha Singh and Ram Singh, with Subedar Sant Singh and Jemadars Pala Singh and Mit Singh wounded. Of the Other Ranks, 161 were killed and 105 wounded. Captain Baldwin was killed in a counter attack and the command of the Company was then taken by Havildar Indar Singh, who held the position against heavy assaults until relieved the next morning, for which he was promoted to Jemadar and received the Military Cross. During the battle of Neuve Chapelle on the night of 14TH, a pioneer working party in the forward sap was suddenly rushed by the Germans, who in their turn were charged by the right half-company led by Subedar Natha Singh, three pioneers being killed and nine wounded. During the historic battle of Ypres the companies of 34TH Sikh Pioneers had been distributed one to each brigade, and the companies found themselves hard at work with their brigades, improving communications and making new defences.

On 17TH December, 1915, 34TH left Marseilles with the Lahore Division after 13 months arduous service in France. The Sikh soldiers of 34TH Sikh Pioneers had been awarded; eight I.O.M.s, and eleven I.D.S.M.s, for their conspicuous gallantry on the Western Front. They landed at Basra on 6TH January 1916, and joined 3RD Division, which was already marching up the Tigris. They proceeded to Sheikh Saad and then to Wadi. At the fighting front 34TH Sikh Pioneers were busily employed in every sort of work from the front line redoubts to the light railway that was being made from Sheikh Saad towards Hai. The Pioneers were actively in support of all the battles in Mesopotamia culminating in the capture of Baghdad. They had been awarded two Indian Order of Merits and four Indian Distinguished Service Medals for their conspicuous gallantry in Mesopotamia.

At the conclusion of the Great War 34TH Sikh Pioneers went on to distinguish themselves in Waziristan. Seven Sikh soldiers were awarded I.D.S.M. for their conspicuous gallantry in Waziristan.

In 1928, the Regiments of Pioneers became Corps of Pioneers, in the Sikh case, the Corps of Sikh Pioneers. Sadly the Corps of Sikh Pioneers was to be short lived. Little more than three years later on 10TH February 1933 the Corps of Sikh Pioneers was finally disbanded.

The Corps of Bombay Pioneers

1ST Battalion

The regiment was raised in 1780; however, on the conversion of the regiment into Pioneers in 1900, the class composition was altered to include 2 Companies of Lobana Sikhs. We take the military history of the regiment on the inclusion of the Lobana Sikhs into the ranks of the regiment.

The regiment, then as 7TH Bombay Pioneers, was selected for active service soon after its conversion into Pioneers and ordered to Somaliland for the subjugation of the 'Mad Mullah'. Previous to 1903, he had raided and harassed with impunity the tribes nominally under British protection. As his forays extended almost to the coast near Berbera, the authorities at last realized that something had to be done.

It was decided to send regular troops to Somaliland, to include 7TH Bombay Pioneers. They were detailed to the portion of the force operating from the North coast of Somaliland. In February, 1903, at the time the Southern force was advancing from Obbia, two double companies of the Pioneers were sent up to Bohotle, on the march clearing bad bits for throughway. The other two double-companies constructed a good road through the foothills of the Golis and improved the camel track up the Pass. At Bohotle a stone fort was started and over 100 wells cleaned out. A perimeter camp, large enough for all the troops and animals was constructed, with thorn abates 15 yards wide, and a field of fire of 400 yards was cleared. These companies were given the harassing duty of escorting the food convoys across the Haud to the Southern Force. In June, when a fall of rain had made movement easier, the Mullah with the whole of his following boldly crossed between the two British forces and reached unmolested the grazing grounds of the upper Nogal Valley. During the pause in active operations, all the detachments of 107TH Pioneers (The change of name took place while in Somaliland) were gradually concentrated to the Sheikh Pass. The work on the Sheikh Pass gave all the ranks an excellent opportunity of increasing their efficiency as Pioneers. On completion of this work, the Regiment was split up into detachments holding the advance posts, while operations were taking place in the upper Nogal Valley, which culminated in the battle of Jidballi on 10TH January, 1904. At this battle the 2 Maxim detachments of 107TH Pioneers, represented the Regiment. The Mullah, having been driven out of the upper Nogal Valley, moved with a dwindling following northwards to the country around Rat. Two companies of 107TH Pioneers formed part of a force sent in pursuit of Mullah. After hard marching, they fetched up at Las Khorai on the coast. There being no enemy left, the campaign closed down. The regiment remained behind as a garrison and held the advanced posts on the Southern frontier of the Protectorate. They left Somaliland on 29TH November, 1904 for India. During the years 1901-1904 small parties of men from the Bombay Pioneers served with the Uganda Rifles and in British Central Africa, and Jemadar Karam Singh received promotion for his services in Ashanti, in Ghana.

The Corps of Bombay Pioneers

1ST Battalion

During the First World War, the regiment reached Marseilles on 26TH September 1941, handed in their arms and were re-issued with machine-guns, rifles and bayonets of the latest pattern. They were initially dressed in their thin Indian Khaki uniforms. They worked on constructing traverses, and improving the trench, work for which their previous training in engineering and their equipment eminently fitted them. The shortage of troops made it necessary to use pioneers as infantry, although there was endless engineering work which required doing. Time and again they were ordered to relieve the infantry regiments in the trenches, suffering numerous casualties in the process. They were also employed by day in preparing material for wire entanglements and by night some parties put up the wire in 'no man's land' along the front of the position, and other parties repaired damaged parapets and dug up new trenches. The 107TH were also considered to be reserve for the line. They followed the fortunes of the Indian Corps in the battles of Festubert, 1914-15, Givenchy, 1914, Neuve Chapelle, Aubers, and Loos. During their service on the Western Front, six Sikh soldiers were awarded the I.D.S.M. for their conspicuous gallantry. The 107TH Pioneers left the Western Front and arrived at Port Said in Egypt on 16TH November. Meanwhile the critical state of affairs in Mesopotamia had caused the Indian Corps to be diverted to that country. On 20TH November, 1915, the Pioneers entrained for Suez and sailed for Basra in Mesopotamia. They reached Basra on 4TH December, and the rifles they had received on arrival in France were exchanged for the older pattern which they had left in India. One of the many difficulties was to get the constantly arriving troops up the river, owing to the shortage of suitable steamers, so it was decided to construct a track up the right bank of the river, to enable troops to march from Basra to Kut-al-Amara. The 107TH Pioneers were detailed to make this track and two companies started work on bridging the Euphrates at Gurmat Ali on the day after their disembarkation at Basra. The other two companies left Basra a few days later and proceeded higher up the Tigris, each company being given a long stretch of track to construct. Eleven channels and numerous smaller water-courses were bridged with the scanty material available and troops and transport began to march from Basra up this track on 14TH December. On 31ST December, the 107TH Pioneers arrived at Ali Gharbi, to join the rest of the force for the relief of Kut-al-Amara. After the relief of Kut-al-Amara and for the rest of the time until they left for India in 1916, 107TH Pioneers served with 7TH Division and participated in the battles at the Sheikh Saad, Wadi, Hanna, Dujailah, and the Sannaiyat. From Mesopotamia they were ordered to Southern Waziristan in April 1917. The 107TH proceeded to Murtaza and other posts on the Gomel, where the flooded River caused a deal of trouble. Then they marched with a Column, via Kajuri Kach, towards Sawakai, the battalion Piqueting the hills. Later the battalion marched across country from Murtaza to Khirgi, to assist in the advance up the Takki Zam.

The Corps of Bombay Pioneers

1ST Battalion

In November 1917, 107TH Pioneers returned to India. Early in the following year a tribe in Baluchistan, named the Marri, broke out in rebellion. The Marri Field Force had to be hastily organized, which included 107TH Pioneers, with the leading company arriving there on 23RD February. With the exception of one fight in which the Marri were quickly defeated, the rebels put up little resistance. The 107TH were at first split up into companies holding various posts and Piqueting the road by day between Harnai and Ashgara. The 107TH Pioneers had to do a good deal of punitive work, destroying villages, cutting crops and rounding up flocks of sheep. Amongst the other road making, 107TH Pioneers cut a camel track over a pass which crossed the Suleiman Range at a height of nearly ten thousand feet. In October, 107TH Pioneers were ordered to join the East Persian Cordon, where much road making was urgently required to enable motor convoys to supply the posts along the six hundred miles from rail-head at Duzdab, through Birjand, to Meshed, and then onwards to supply the small force under General Malleson operating against the Bolsheviks round about the Trans-Caspian railway from Krasnovokdsk, through Askhabad, to Merv. The 107TH Pioneers finally returned to Quettal from East Persia on 7TH November, 1920.

2ND Battalion 107TH Pioneers was raised at Bareilly on 26TH July, 1917, from a nucleus of volunteers from the fighting classes serving with 1ST Labour Corps in Mesopotamia. The battalion landed at Suez on 8TH July, 1918, and proceeded to Tel-el-Kebir, where they were allotted to be the Pioneers of 20TH Division of The Egyptian Expeditionary Force. By early August, General Allenby had the resources and the plan for a final offensive to rout the Turkish forces in what are now Palestine, Syria and Lebanon. The concentration of troops, which involved the move of the whole of the Desert Corps from the Jordan Valley to the sea-coast, without the enemy becoming aware of it, was a stupendous task which was successfully carried out. The corps had achieved what General Allenby called "a brilliant feat of arms." In his final despatch he said, "The Desert Mounted Corps took over 46,000 prisoners during the operations. The complete destruction of the V11 and V111 Turkish Armies depended mainly on the rapidity with which their communications were reached and in quick decisions in dealing with the enemy's columns as they attempted to escape." The performance and the endurance of the Pioneers throughout the campaign were absolutely outstanding.

In March, 1920, 2ND battalion, 107TH Pioneers entrained at Jenin for Suez, where they embarked for India and proceeded to Jhansi for disbandment. By August, 1920, 2ND battalion had ceased to exist.

In 1922 all battalions of the Indian Army were reorganized into groups and renamed. The pioneer battalions were grouped into a Regiment and named 2ND Bombay Pioneers and 107TH Pioneers became 1ST battalion. Sadly on 10TH February 1933, the Corps of Bombay Pioneers was struck off the strength of the Indian Army.

The Corps of Bombay Pioneers

2ND Battalion

The Regiment was raised in 1838. Until after the Sepoy Mutiny the Regiment appears to have been mainly composed of Brahmans, Rajputs, and Hindustani Mohammedans, all mixed up in the companies. On becoming a regular regiment of the line of the Bengal Army in 1861, its composition was changed to include Sikhs and this was again altered in 1883, when the Sikhs were mustered out. On becoming 12TH Bengal Pioneers in 1903, its composition was changed to include 2 Double Companies of Lobana Sikhs. On 21ST September, 1864, as 12TH (The Kelat-i-Ghilzie) Regiment proceeded with their fellow pioneers, 32ND Sikh Pioneers to the North-East Frontier, on account of trouble with Bhutan. The Bhutias had been raiding into Indian Territory to a considerable extent and carrying off the inhabitants of the Duars as slaves. This had culminated in an outrageous insult on the British official sent to remonstrate and to negotiate a treaty with Bhutan. Local forces had eventually entered Bhutan, had established certain protecting forts and had withdrawn. This was followed, almost before the troop's back were turned, by attacks on these forts. Two beat off their assailants, two were besieged, the fifth garrison, that of Dewanigiri, was forced to evacuate and in the retreat lost guns and baggage and sustained forty casualties. It was now necessary to mount punitive operations against the Bhutias. The raiders were met and overcame at Dhalimkote, Bhumsong and Charmoorchee. The final action of the campaign was fought at Dewanigiri, which was perched on a mountain ridge, protected by stockades and strongly held by the Bhutias. One party attempted to storm the stockade on the right and was driven back. Another party took the centre stockade, when indiscriminate slaughter of the defenders commenced, as nearly the whole of the garrison of this stockade were killed. After the fall of the centre stockade, the enemy evacuated the others and made their escape, and Dewanigiri was occupied by the Pioneers. The 12TH Pioneers had suffered twenty-one casualties during this action. Three Sepoys of 12TH (The Kelat-i-Ghilzie) Regiment, including Sepoy Kharak Singh received the I.O.M. for their conduct during the assault on Dewanigiri. The final action had terminated this campaign against the Bhutias. Early in 1866, 12TH Pioneers returned to India, when the post was dismantled and abandoned as too unhealthy.

During the Second Afghan War, 1878-80, 12TH Pioneers formed part of the Kabul Field Force. Major General Sir Frederick Roberts led the Kabul Field Force over the Shutargardan Pass into central Afghanistan, defeated the Afghan Army at Charasia on 6TH October 1879, and occupied Kabul two days later. Ghazi Mohammad Jan Khan Wardak, and a force of 10,000 Afghans, staged an uprising and attacked British forces near Kabul in the Siege of the Sherpur Cantonment in December 1879. Despite besieging the British garrison there, he failed to maintain the Siege of Sherpur, instead shifting focus to Roberts' force, and this resulted in the collapse of this rebellion.

The Corps of Bombay Pioneers

2ND Battalion

Amir of Afghanistan, Ayub Khan, rose in revolt, defeated a British detachment at the Battle of Maiwand in July 1880 and besieged Kandahar. General Roberts then led a force from Kabul and decisively defeated Ayub Khan on 1ST September at the Battle of Kandahar. Abdur Rahman then signed the Treaty of Gandamak, leaving the British in control of the territories ceded by his predecessor Yaqub Khan and ensuring British control of Afghanistan's foreign affairs. Having achieved all their other objectives, the British withdrew.

In December, 1883, a wing of 12TH (The Kelat-i-Ghilzie) Regiment, then stationed at Silchar in Assam, formed part of a small expedition against the primitive Aka tribe, inhabiting mountainous country on the eastern side of Bhutan. The expedition made determined attacks on the defences, which were held in strength by the tribesmen and compelled them to submit. The wing of 12TH had some tough marching and was present at the skirmishes. Sepoy Atar Singh was recommended for the I.O.M. for his gallantry in being the first to enter a stockade, after crossing the Tenga River and though twice wounded, having remained in front of the advance.

During 3RD Burmese War 12TH (The Kelat-i-Ghilzie) Regiment arrived at Mandalay on 30TH December, 1886. Battalion Headquarters were first at Katha and later moved to Bhamo, with numerous detachments at various posts and on mobile columns. Two companies were in the operations against the Sawbwa of Wuntho and 50 rifles took part in the Siu expedition. Later 100 rifles proceeded to the Silay Hills, where they lost 5 men killed and 5 wounded in an engagement on 3RD December, 1887. They also had a mounted infantry detachment. The 12TH (The Kelat-i-Ghilzie) Regiment, left Burma on 19TH December, 1888, and proceeded to India.

During 1895, 12TH (The Kelat-i-Ghilzie) Regiment was stationed at Nowshera and had a great deal of hard work in connection with the Chitral Relief Force, as Nowshera was the base of the expedition sent to the succour of the garrison besieged in Chitral.

In 1897 occurred the violent and widespread rising of the North-West Frontier tribes which led to the operations of the Mohmand, Tirah, and other Field Forces. On 23RD September, 1897, 12TH (The Kelat-i-Ghilzie) Regiment set out for Sadda, which lies in the Kurram Valley between Thal and Parachinar, to join the Kurram Movable Column, whose job was to maintain order in the valley and to co-operate with the main force in Tirah. Various reconnaissances were made from Sadda into the enemy's country in all of which a prominent part was taken by the regiment. The tribesmen having submitted, the force marched back to Sadda. The 12TH (The Kelat-i-Ghilzie) Regiment remained in the Kurram Valley till the middle of January, 1898, when they returned to Kohat. They eventually arrived back at Bareilly on 3RD June, 1898.

The Corps of Bombay Pioneers

2ND Battalion

It was the fate of 12TH (The Kelat-i-Ghilzie) Regiment to remain in India throughout the Great War, though this regiment sent many officers and large drafts of men as reinforcements to other regiments in France and Mesopotamia, notably one of its Sikh companies to 34TH Sikh Pioneers, which company later became the nucleus for re-formed 48TH Pioneers. 12TH (The Kelat-i-Ghilzie) Regiment also sent a machine gun section to East Persia to join General Dyer's force operating against the tribesmen.

In February, 1916, 12TH proceeded from Quetta to Pashawar, where it formed part of the Pashawar Flying Column which carried out punitive operations against a section of the Mohmunds beyond Shabkadar. The Mohmunds having been pacified, the regiment moved early in April, 1917, to Lahore. Measures had to be taken during this year to deal with the Mahsuds of Waziristan, who had been indulging in one of their recurring epidemics of raiding, and both 12TH and 107TH Pioneers took part in this little frontier campaign.

During 3RD Anglo-Afghan War, both battalions of 12TH served on the Northern Front. The Afghan force had crossed the frontier and taken up a position on the hills above Bagh, from which position they were driven with the loss of several guns. The force then proceeded to occupy Dakka on 13TH May, 1919. So demoralised were the Afghans that the Amir asked for armistice, which was granted on 3RD June, 1919. Peace was declared with Afghanistan on 9TH September, 1919, and the troops were speedily withdrawn from the country, 1/12TH going to Nowshera and 2/12TH to Landi Kotal. The 2/12TH remained in the Khyber Pass for next two years. In October, 1921 they proceeded to Ambala for disbandment

The 12TH (The Kelat-i-Ghilzie) Regiment served in Iraq (formerly Mesopotamia) during the Arab rebellion. After the insurrection had been suppressed, the regiment moved to Baghdad in February, 1921. In the meantime the regiment had become 2ND (The Kelat-i-Ghilzie) battalion, 2ND Bombay Pioneers. When the Arab insurrection was contained 2ND battalion sailed from Basra on 26TH May, 1923, and then proceeded to Meerut.

The 2ND battalion was ordered to the North-West Province in 1930, as the province was in a disturbed state owing to the revolutionary activities of Congress agitators, and of a political organization called 'Red Shirts.' After normal conditions had been restored in the Pashawar Valley 2ND battalion was then sent to Sarband, between Pashawar and Bara Fort, where the official intimation that the Government had decided to disband all Indian Pioneers was received on 22ND July, 1932.

Sadly on 10TH February 1933, the Corps of Bombay Pioneers was struck off the strength of the Indian Army. A final ceremony; that of laying up the Kelat-i-Ghilzie Colour in the Viceroy's House at Delhi, took place on 13TH March, 1933, after the disbandment had been completed.

The Corps of Bombay Pioneers

3RD Battalion

The Regiment was raised in 1846. In March 1897, it was converted into a Pioneer Corps, under the name of 28TH (Pioneer) Regiment of Bombay Native Infantry, with a class section that included 2 Companies of Lobana Sikhs. The name of the regiment was changed to 28TH Bombay Pioneers and then to 128TH Pioneers. We take the military history of the regiment on the inclusion of the Lobana Sikhs into the ranks of the regiment in 1897.

In 1897 occurred the violent and widespread rising of the North-West Frontier. To deal with the situation it was decided that one force should assemble at Kohat to operate against the Afridis and other tribes in the Tirah. Another force starting from Shabkadar should invade the Mohmad country; the Malakand Field Force should deal with the Swat tribes. On 19TH August 1897, 28TH Bombay Pioneers formed part of a force assembled at Jamrud because of the threatened attack on the Khyber posts by the Afridis. The 28TH took part in several demonstrations around the entrance of the Khyber Pass, which was held in strength by the Afridis. On 6TH September the regiment joined the Mohmand Field Force, when the advance in the Mohmund country began. On 23RD September the force advanced on the attack on the Bedmanai Pass, with 28TH Pioneers in close support. The enemy were driven back from ridge to ridge; the Pass was gained with only trifling loss to the attackers. Early on 25TH September the force started for Jarobi, the home of the Haddah Mullah, who had been chiefly responsible for stirring up the trouble amongst the Mohmunds. A company of 28TH was ordered to occupy a village, 'which was taken after some opposition. Another company was detailed to burn and destroy Jarobi, which was accomplished under long range fire from the tribesmen on the heights around the village. The next day the force moved down the valley in two columns, a wing of 28TH going with each, and forty-five towers, solidly built of stones, were blown up by the regiment and the Sapper Company on this one day, compelling the Mohmunds to accept the Government's terms and surrender the required number of rifles. 28TH Bombay Pioneers had scarcely arrived at Pashawar when they were ordered to join the Tirah Field Force. On 28TH October the two Divisions of the Tirah Field Force, attacked the Pass, 28TH Pioneers being with the reserve. The enemy was driven off in a spirited attack and the Pass was secured. The force next advanced and captured the Arhangi Pass and then entered the Maidan Valley in the heart of the Afridi country. The continues advance of the force, brought 28TH Pioneers to the Bara Valley, where it worked improving the road in case of further operations being necessary. They worked on making this road until 31ST March, when all the Afridi tribes having submitted, the campaign came to an end. The regiment then marched to Pashawar and entrained for Kirkee, where they arrived on 14TH April, 1898.During the years 1901-04 small parties of men from 28TH Bombay Pioneers served with the Uganda Rifles and in British Central Africa, and Jemadar Karam Singh received promotion for his service in Ashanti, in Ghana.

The Corps of Bombay Pioneers

3RD Battalion

During the Great War 128TH Pioneers (1903 became 128th Pioneers) received their orders to proceed to Suez in 1914. After a short wait at Suez the regiment proceeded up the Canal to Serapeum, where they disembarked and camped on the West Bank. The most practicable line of advance for an invading army from the Canal to Cairo is to follow the sweet-water canal from Ismailia to the Nile. Dragging their artillery, including two howitzers, and their pontoon train across the sandy desert, the Turks duly arrived within striking distance of the Canal by the end of January, 1915. Despite some feeble feint attacks towards each end of the Canal, it was evident that the enemy's main attack would fall on some part of the centre, and the portion of the Canal chosen by Djemal Pasha for this was the sector between Lake Timsah and the Great Bittier Lake. One platoon (Lobana Sikhs) of 128TH Pioneers was sent to this sector on 1ST February as an escort to 5TH Mountain Battery, Egyptian Artillery. They dug emplacements for the guns about a mile South of Tussum on the top of the high West bank, so as to give a good field of view. The 128TH Pioneers (less this platoon and 2 platoons at Ismailia ferry post) were in 31ST Brigade with the General Reserve at Moascar camp, Ismailia. The defence, which was so short of artillery, was supported by the guns of British and French ships stationed in each end of this section of the Canal, near the entrances to the lakes. Thus in this unique defensive position, infantry, artillery, and warships were strung out in one long firing line, the obstacle in front of the firer trench being the Empire's main communication ! Lack of organized transport and other circumstances of the time, however, had ruled out all other methods of countering the enemy's advance. The night of 2ND/3RD February, 1915, was pitch dark, with a sand-storm stinging the faces of the Sentries. All was quiet till the Turks began to approach the East bank in preparation for their crossing the Canal by means of pontoons, boats, rafts and swimming. A lack of discipline first gave their presence away, as shouting was heard along the East bank south of Tussum post, which quickly ceased on a machine-gun opening fire from the post. Nothing much more occurred for about an hour, when the moon emerging through the clouds just enabled the watchers on the West bank to make out parties of the enemy carrying pontoons down the East bank and launching them on the Canal; the three points where their most determined efforts were made being a little South of Tussum, opposite to the Egyptian Battery and the infantry near these points, including the platoon of 128^{TH,} opened fire and the Turks replied. Although much of it went high, the enemy's fire, especially from some sand-hills behind the East bank, soon began to cause casualties, amongst which were an Egyptian officer and two gunners killed, and two wounded, of the Battery, and the platoon of 128TH Pioneers lost Lieutenant FitzGibbon mortally wounded, three Sepoys killed and four wounded. After being grievously wounded, Lieutenant FitzGibbon ran a considerable way to the Egyptian Battery to point out some target.

The Corps of Bombay Pioneers

3RD Battalion

The action of this platoon of 128TH is best described in the words of Jemadar Inder Singh who took over command of the platoon when Lieutenant FitzGibbon became casualty.

Jemadar Inder Singh states:- "My platoon constructed emplacements for the Egyptian mountain guns and machine guns all day on 2ND February, and slept in a wood behind the Canal bank that night. At about 3 a.m. the sentry awoke me and reported that he had heard one rifle shot. I woke all the men. And then Lieutenant FitzGibbon arrived and ordered me to bring the platoon after him. He went off to the gun position on the top of the bank, and came down again, meeting me at the bottom of the bank. He then led the platoon past the South of the battery. He took half the men down to the water's edge, ordering me to take the remainder and search a belt of trees 50 yards farther south for some of the enemy who had landed from a boat and gone into it. I searched the trees and found nothing. Hearing firing, I came out of the trees on to the Canal bank, joining Lieutenant FitzGibbon and his men. I then saw three boats close to the East bank and we opened fire on them. Lieutenant FitzGibbon was standing and walking about behind the men, and he was wounded just as I joined him. Nanak Singh had already been killed. The platoon remained there firing and under fire for about half an hour, during which time one of the enemy's boats once came half way across the Canal and then went back again, and another boat returned after coming twenty yards towards us. Then a third boat started from the bank directly opposite us, went to our left front, and then made for a wooden hut on the West twenty yards to my right. I saw four men get out of the boat and run towards us, one of them was at once shot. Two other men started rowing the boat back again. I took Colour-Havildar Ganda Singh, Havildar Bhagat Singh and some of my men to attack the Turks on our bank. One of them fired killing Bugler Uttam Singh, and both Havildars immediately bayoneted this man. The remaining two then threw away their arms, held up their hands and were made prisoners. I then established the platoon on the top of the bank until we were relieved." Two other boatloads of Turks were either killed or escaped. The attempted crossing had thus definitely failed, and as it got lighter, many abandoned pontoons and rafts, as well numerous dead, were seen littered along the East bank. Finally all the surviving Turks in this area surrendered. When the Pioneers searched the East bank for wounded Turks, the body of a German staff officer was found amongst the dead. Over 700 Turks were captured during the fighting and some 300 of their dead were buried near the Canal. After the retirement of the Turks all was peaceful along the Canal for the remainder of the year, 128TH Pioneers being employed on various works and on garrison duty up and down the Canal, and they occasionally accompanied reconnoitring marches into the desert. Later it was decided to send eleven Indian battalions from the Canal garrison to Mesopotamia, and one of these, 128TH Pioneers, sailed from Suez for Mesopotamia on 11TH December.

The Corps of Bombay Pioneers

3RD Battalion

The 128TH Pioneers arrived at Ali Gharbi in Mesopotamia on 31ST December 1915, to join the rest of the force for the relief of Kut. By 3RD January 1916, sixteen battalions of infantry, five cavalry regiments and forty-two guns were concentrated at Ali Gharbi. The 128TH Pioneers were divided between 28TH and 35TH Brigades, both of which were in 7TH Division. The 7TH Division commenced the advance up both banks of the Tigres on 4TH January. Three companies of the 128TH Pioneers, marched on the right bank with the Cavalry Brigade and the remaining company of 128TH marched on the left bank with 35TH Brigade. They participated in the hard fought battle at the Sheikh Saad where in one action half a battalion had lost 26 men killed and 5 missing, believed killed. During the morning of 9TH the Turks were forced from their trenches, and 7TH Division advanced and occupied Sheikh Saad. Two companies of 128TH Pioneers were formed into half a battalion during the battle of Wadi, where the determination with which the Turks held off the advance saved their army from what promised to be a serious defeat. The Turks were decisively defeated at the battles of Hanna and Dujailah and the Sannaiyat. The 128TH Pioneers had pulled their full weight in Mesopotamia and Kurdistan and sailed for India on 17TH January 1920. The 128TH Pioneers was the only one of Bombay Pioneers who enjoyed a lengthy spell of peace after their return from overseas service in January 1920. Following a year at Meerut, they were transferred to Burma and were stationed at Mandalay, with a detachment at Maymo.

The 3RD battalion, 2ND Bombay Pioneers, as 128TH Pioneers were now named sailed from Rangoon on 30TH November, 1924 for Waziristan. The circular road through that country up the Takki Zam from Tank to Razmak and then down the Tochi Valley and so on to Bannu, had been roughly got through by the end of 1922, following which further operations again the Mahsuds had quickly brought the tribesmen to terms. This road now required to be more thoroughly constructed in order to be fit for motor traffic in all seasons of the year, and to get it done quickly, companies from all three corps of Sappers and Miners and several battalions from the Pioneers were employed. On the completion of the road in May, 1925, the garrison marched to Razmak. For the remainder of its time in Waziristan, 3RD Battalion did a good deal of infantry work, in addition to occasional technical tasks; it took its turn of duty on road protection.

In 1928 came disturbing rumours with regard to Pioneers that all the battalions of 2ND Bombay Pioneers were merged into a new organization to be called The Corps of Bombay Pioneers, which was implemented in 1929. Official intimation that the Government had decided to disband all Indian Pioneers was received on 22ND July 1932 and sadly on 10TH February 1933, the Corps of Bombay Pioneers was struck off the strength of the Indian Army.

The Corps of Bombay Pioneers

4TH Battalion

The battalion was raised in 1901 as 48TH Pioneers that included 2 Double-companies of Lobana Sikhs. This was the only one of the five battalions which was raised as Pioneers. The 48TH Pioneers received their mobilization orders on 13TH August, 1914, whilst stationed at Kirkee. They arrived at Sanniya in Mesopotamia on 14TH November, 1914. From Sanniya they marched with the main force to engage the Turkish force of 1,200 regular infantry, with 8 guns, and a larger force of Arabs at Sahil. The 48TH Pioneers had been detailed for the general reserve, but as soon as the action had started, they started to push on. Whilst still in close formation the battalion was caught by the artillery fire, but continued to advance. The enemy's rifle fire now began to tell. Casualties now became frequent and it was noticed that effective fire was coming from a concealed trench to the left, which enfiladed part of the firing line. Fire was concentrated on this trench and Subedar Ganga Singh and his platoon, who had worked up near to it, were just about to rush it with the bayonet, when the enemy bolted from the trench leaving behind a number of casualties. The Turks evacuated the fort at the same time they began a rapid retreat from all their trenches. The British force followed on as fast as the heavy going would let them and passed through the enemy position, 48TH being amongst the first to reach the edge of the Turkish camp, two miles north of the fort. Here the Pioneers were stopped by General Delamain, but the pursuit was carried on by part of the force until late afternoon. In this fight, this was their baptism of fire, 48TH suffered ninety casualties. From Sahil 48TH were ordered to Basra, as the town had been evacuated by the Turks and was being looted by the Arabs. Basra at this time was in a filthy condition. The lack of jetties, roads and bridges kept 48TH Pioneers hard at work for several weeks. As well as much road making and clearing sites, 48TH constructed six trestle bridges, many culverts and two reservoirs. Two infantry brigades had been concentrated at Shaiba because of the advance of a strong force of Turkish regular troops and Arabs down the Euphrates, with the intention of attacking Basra from the West and driving the British out of Mesopotamia. The 48TH Pioneers held the south salient of the British entrenched camp. The enemy's most determined attack was made against the south salient which was repulsed, 48TH Pioneers having lost one man killed and 7 wounded, while the Turks lost heavily, especially from the machine guns of 48TH Pioneers. The next morning some of the enemy were found to be entrenched within 150 yards of the south salient, having being pinned down to their trenches by heavy fire of 48TH, 7 Turkish officers and 112 ranks surrendered later in the morning. Half of 48TH moved out to reinforce the left of 16TH Brigade, which was engaged in clearing the front. After some fighting in which 48TH lost another 2 men killed and 7 wounded, this force returned to camp with 400 prisoners and 2 captured guns. Subedar Ganga Singh was mentioned for excellent leadership while Pipers Chander Singh and Narian Singh were commended for bringing in a dangerously wounded man under fire.

The Corps of Bombay Pioneers

4TH Battalion

Soon after the battle of Shaiba, operations were commenced to clear the eastern flank up the Karun River in Southern Arabistan of the enemy, who mainly consisted of Arabs, and a company of 48TH Pioneers was despatched for this campaign. The force marched 30 miles to the Karun River and then up its right bank to near Ahwaz. Thence the operations commenced against the enemy in the desert country between Ahwaz and Amara. The company of 48TH assisted the Sappers in making arrangements for 12TH Division to cross the swift and deep Kherke River, mostly on rafts made of brushwood and tarpaulins. In the fight at Kafiajiyeh they formed the vanguard of one column. They did a lot of ramping nullas, bridging and blew down some towers. On one occasion twenty men of the company swam across a river with some transport animals. The troops suffered much from the heat, lack of water and long desert marches. The operations lasted seven weeks and were completely successful. Then followed on 3RD June, the astonishing capture of Amara, with many prisoners of war, by a few officers and only 41 soldiers and sailors, who had pursued up the river in five small armed ships, although that town was held by a considerable body of Turks. The Division moved up the river from Amara, and by 16TH September had reached Sannaiyat, eight miles from the carefully prepared enemy position covering Kut-al-Amara, where after a hard fight it achieved a brilliant victory on 28TH September with the Turks retreating up the river. In this battle 48TH Pioneers were employed as escort to the guns. They dug up gun positions on the night prior to the attack and helped to bring up ammunition to the guns during the action. Their only causality was Jemadar Bhag Singh who was wounded. They had also assisted with the bridge of boats across the river, helped in disembarking the guns and other such work. Owing to the difficult navigation of the meandering Tigres, the pursuit lost touch with the Turks, who stopped their retreat at Ctesiphon and occupied an entrenched position which had been under construction for several months. The Turks had been reinforced at Ctesiphon; so 6TH Division was to attack an entrenched position in which the defenders numbered nearly double the attacking force. The force charged under a withering fire until checked by the wire entanglements. Unknown individuals, including a number of the Pioneers, then dashed forward and though many fell, managed to cut gaps in the wire, through which the assaulting troops passed and entered the redoubt, where a fierce bayonet fight took place till most of the garrison, who had fought with the stubbornness characteristic of the entrenched Turk, were either killed or captured. The survivors of 48TH penetrated through several lines of support trenches and then opened fire at the Turks retreating in disorder across the open, their fire causing the Turkish gunners to abandon a field battery. In the assault at Ctesiphon the casualties of 48TH Pioneers included, Jemadars Sundar Singh, Khushal Singh, Bhag Singh and 76 men were Killed and Subedar Major Dula Singh, Subedar Pala Singh, Jemadar Gardhara Singh, and 259 other ranks wounded.

The Corps of Bombay Pioneers

4TH Battalion

Many deeds of particular daring had been performed by individuals during the battle at Ctesiphon, most of those names are unknown, but for one such act Pipe-Major Dayal Singh, 48TH Pioneers, received I.O.M. Jemadar Gurdit Singh was the only Indian officer of 48TH who got through the assault at Ctesiphon unscathed, so of the 10 Indian Officers present at that action, not one marched into Kut-al-Amara with the battalion. On 2ND December 48TH marched into Kut-al-Amara. Soon after this the Turks moved some of their troops to the downstream side of the town. Kut-al-Amara was invested and the siege had begun.

The Tigres Corps had been struggling for nearly four months to relieve Kut-al-Amara, they had endured the greatest hardships and suffered over 23,000 battle casualties, and now they were to hear that they had failed. On 29TH April, 1916, Kut-al-Amara surrendered. Here is a description of 48TH Pioneers at the beginning of their captivity given by a British Officer eye-witness:-

"It was sad but inspiring sight to see 48TH Pioneers march off from Shumran in perfect order, as if on an inspection parade. A senior Turkish officer spoke most complimentarily of their soldiery bearing. Despite having no British or Indian officers, the Pioneers remained a battalion during the dreadful marches, whilst some other units deteriorated into mere mobs. They bivouacked properly, detailed orderly Havildars and rear parties to help stragglers, and issued battalion orders. Of some 300 Rank and File of 48TH Pioneers taken prisoner, only 90 returned from captivity. The rest had died, chiefly to the callous and inhuman treatment they received from the Turks, who were in charge of them".

For some weeks after the fall of Kut-al-Amara he independent company of 12TH Pioneers, after picking up some of the remnants of 48TH Pioneers, proceeded to join 15TH Division, here they were organized into a battalion known as 'The Re-formed 48TH Pioneers'. When the Kut-al-Amara prisoners were released at the conclusion of the war, the officers and the few men still fit for service of the original 48TH Pioneers joined this re-formed battalion. From Mesopotamia the battalion went on to serve in Afghanistan during the Third Afghan war. At the conclusion of the war in Afghanistan the battalion was posted to Iraq. In 1926 it was decided to reduce the garrison of Iraq by one battalion and the Pioneers were withdrawn to India for disbandment.

In 1922, 48TH became 4TH Battalion, 2ND Bombay Pioneers and was disbanded in 1926. The reasons for 4TH Battalion being chosen for disbandment were that it was the youngest of the Bombay Pioneer battalions and was returning from Iraq on reduction of the garrison there. The personnel of 4TH Battalion, instead of being discharged, were transferred to other battalions, which kept within establishment by mustering out some of their own personnel. In this way the disbandment of 4TH Battalion was shared by the whole Corps of Bombay Pioneers.

Sadly on 10TH February 1933, the Corps of Bombay Pioneers was struck off the strength of the Indian Army.

Punjab Regiments

The Punjab Regiments have their antecedents in the Old Coast Army of Madras Presidency. Its battalions were raised more than two hundred years ago during the upheaval of Mysore and Mahratta Wars, when the British were expanding their Indian forces. Over the next hundred years, as the British consolidated their hold over India, these battalions served in different parts of the sub-continent. But the years of inactivity had brought about visible deterioration in the standard of efficiency. Since 1857, the bulk of the Bengal Army had increasingly been made of Sikhs and Punjabi Mussalmans. The martial prowess of these people had never been in doubt. Between 1890 and 1898, the Madras Infantry regiments based in Burma were reconstituted with the Punjabis. This led to their coming together as 1ST, 2ND and 8TH Punjab Regiments in 1922.

Both 12TH Frontier Force Regiment and 13TH Frontier Force Rifles shared a common origin in recruiting the Khalsa veterans of the Anglo-Sikh Wars. They both sprang from the infantry elements of the Frontier Brigade authorised in 1846 after the First Sikh War. Authorisation was also given to the raising of a small irregular body of men, one troop mounted and two companies of infantry, to be called 'Guides'. Together with the Corps of Guides, the four regiments of infantry 1ST, 2ND, 3RD and 4TH Regiments of Sikh Local Infantry went to form the 12TH Frontier Force Regiment in 1923. The other five regiments, 1ST, 2ND, 3RD 4TH and 5TH Punjab Infantry Regiments of infantry of the Frontier Brigade, renamed in 1851 the Punjab Irregular Force, and went to form 13TH Frontier Force Rifles in 1923. When The Frontier Brigade was abolished all units were to be part of an all-India Army.

The 14TH, 15TH and 16TH Punjab Regiments were formed from the amalgamations of infantry regiments raised during the upheaval of the Indian Mutiny in 1857 from the disbanded veterans of the Sikh army, by John Lawrence in the Punjab. These men had been largely responsible for the British victory and the British were completely enamoured with these warlike people who had proven so reliable in their darkest hour.

The 14TH Punjab Regiment was formed in 1922 by the amalgamation of 19TH, 20TH, 21ST, 22ND, 24TH, and 40TH Pathans.

The 15TH Punjab Regiment was formed in 1922 by the amalgamation of 25TH, 26TH, 27TH, 28TH, and 29TH Punjabis.

The 16TH Punjab Regiment was formed in 1922 by amalgamation of 30TH, 31ST, 33RD, 46TH Punjabis and 9TH Bhopal Infantry.

An important change was that these previously individual regiments became Battalions of a large regiment.

1ST Punjab Regiment

62ND Punjabis (1/1ST)

The 62ND Punjabis was an infantry regiment was raised in 1759 as 3RD Battalion of Coast Sepoys and formed part of the Madras Army. The regiment had its antecedents in the old Madras Army of the British East India Company, which was largely responsible for the British conquest of south and central India. The men were mostly enlisted from South India and consisted of Muslims and Hindus. In 1840, the regiment took part in the First Anglo-Chinese War. In 1902, the regiment was reconstituted with Sikhs, Punjabi Mussalmans, and Rajputs. In 1903, as a result of the reforms brought about in the Indian Army, the regiment's designation was changed to 62ND Punjabis.

During the First World War, 62ND Punjabis were sent to Egypt to protect the Suez Canal. On January 23^{RD,} the regiment took a section of the Suez Canal defences. The Turks had dragged their pontoons and guns across the sands and hills of Sinai and were in force east of Ismailia and Serapeum. At the Turkish attack on the morning of February 3RD, the men rushed out of their trenches in the face of hot fire and charged down the steep, sandy bank to the water's edge. Soon they charged killing or wounding all the occupants of the boat. The Turks having failed at this point, pushed in an attack at a different point, where twenty-six Turks emerged from this point and succeeded in getting a foothold on the bank. These Turks were attacked, four were killed and six captured; the remainder surrendered. The battle was not over yet. The Turks reinforced, mounted another attack. A company of the regiment withstood their continuous assaults, till three companies arrived to reinforce these posts. The Turks had paid heavily for their persistence. This was the first battle 62ND Punjabis fought in the Great War. On February 3RD, the Turks attacked two of the regiments advanced posts on the eastern bank. In a counter- attack launched from Serapeum East, the trenches east of Tussum post were cleared of the Turks. However, on 4TH, they were still in strength, entrenched on the east bank of the Canal. Two companies of 92ND Punjabis were ordered to attack and round up the Turks in this position. After some initial success these companies found further advance difficult and one company each of 62ND Punjabis and 27TH Punjabis were ordered to reinforce the attack. The enemy was attacked and compelled to surrender. Six officers and two hundred men surrendered in the trenches facing the companies; the remainder on the ground to the east surrendered to 92ND Punjabis,

On July 12TH, 62ND Punjabis joined 28TH Brigade and embarked for Aden. The situation in the Aden Protectorate at the time was critical. Sheikh Othman, eight miles north of Aden and essential to the Aden water supply, was in Turkish hands and had to be recaptured. Operations had also to be undertaken to disperse the hostile Arabs from the waterless and sandy wastes on the mainland north of Aden isthmus. Sheikh Othman was recaptured on July 21$^{ST.}$ Operations to clear the mainland were undertaken in the following six months by sending out columns to Fiyush and Waht.

1ST Punjab Regiment

62ND Punjabis (1/1ST)

Operations against Waht were undertaken on September 25TH. The regiment formed a part of the advanced guard and encountered stiff opposition south east of Waht. The enemy was attacked and chased out of the area at the cost of seven casualties to the regiment. Havildar Bishen Singh won the I.D.S.M., for his exemplary courage in the operations of this day.

After operating in Aden, 62ND Punjabis arrived in Mesopotamia on 31ST December 1915. Here they were engaged in fierce fighting on the Tigris Front, as the British made desperate efforts to raise the Siege of Kut-al-Amara. The regiment took part in the failed battle of Hanna, where General Aylmer was compelled to arrange a truce with the enemy to enable him to collect his wounded. In this grim battle 62ND Punjabis had 372 casualties. Amongst the killed were Subedar Narain Singh, I.O.M. and Subedar Attar Singh, both of the Sikh Double Company. Within a month of its arrival in Mesopotamia the regiment suffered 443 casualties.

The 82ND Punjabis, who were destined to share with 62ND Punjabis the trials and fortunes of the Kut-al-Amara relief operation, and the subsequent advance on Baghdad, joined the brigade on February 8TH. The first battle which the regiments fought together took place on March 8TH and 9TH, 1916, on the Dujaila Redoubt. Both regiments commenced short advances over the flat plain almost completely devoid of cover in the face of Turkish gun fire as well as heavy machine-gun and rifle fire. So intense was the hostile fire that the assault died away within 200 yards of the enemy trenches. At midnight a withdrawal was ordered to Ora. The wounded comprised Subedar Sundar Singh and 36 other ranks. Havildar Mahil Singh won the I.D.S.M., for his exemplary courage in the operations of this day. On April 30TH, 1916, news was received the garrison of Kut-al-Amara, had surrendered. With the surrender of Kut-al-Amara, the fighting on the Tigres died down, both sides being exhausted. By the end of the year 62ND was again up to strength and had been re-organized on the new four-company system.

When the battle for the Hai Salient had started, the Turkish garrison had been estimated at about 3,700 men. The first attack on 25TH of January had gone well at first, and 1,800 yards of the Turkish front line had been captured. However, the Turks had eventually counter-attacked by heavy shell fire and had driven back 39TH brigade, having suffered over a thousand casualties. The following day the assault had been renewed by the Indian 14TH Division. After twelve hours of bitter fighting 82ND and 26TH with 62ND Punjabis in support had succeeded in retaking the line, which had been lost the previous day, the price had nonetheless been expensive. By the end of January the whole Turkish front line system to a depth of 1,000 yards had been in British hands.

On the morning of January 25TH, 36TH Brigade resumed the advance. In this advance 62ND Punjabis took a prominent part. By 5TH February the Turks had completely abandoned the Hai Salient to take up a new line at the Dahra Bend to the west of Kut.

1ST Punjab Regiment

62ND Punjabis (1/1ST)

On the morning of 9TH, 13TH Division launched an attack against the Turkish positions which had been sited near to an abandoned liquorice factory. After some vicious fighting and beating off several counter attacks, the Brigade had breached the Turkish defences. During the following day the 'liquorice factory' had been captured. Six days later the Turkish resistance had totally collapsed. For the first time since the early days of the campaign, over two thousand Turks had surrendered en masse.

In December, 1917, 36TH Brigade, with 62ND Punjabis moved to Khaniqin near the Persian border. In January, 1918, a force, known as 'Dunster Force', passed through Khaniqin into Persia to co-operate with the Russians against the Bolsheviks. For the remaining period of the war, 62ND Punjabis occupied posts along the Persian road which was the line of communication for this force. The posts stretched over eighty miles of road on the Khaniqin-Hamadan route at an average distance of seventeen miles and each were generally manned by two platoons. The regiment was mainly occupied in protecting the posts and stores from marauding Kurds, in road mending and in escorting motor ration convoys. The year 1919 opened with 62ND Punjabis still holding posts on the Persian Line of Communications. It was relieved in April and concentrated at Baghdad and provided guards for the huge dumps of rations, stores and equipment. The regiment also provided guards and escorts for Turkish prisoners of war.

Eventually in May, 1920, 62ND returned home. The 62ND was one of the Indian Army units which went on service in 1914 and were among the last to return to India. The casualties sustained by it amounted to 840, the strength of a regiment.

Havildar Sundar Singh and Sepoy Chanan Singh were awarded the I.D.S.M. while serving in Mesopotamia. The 62ND Punjabis did not serve in France as a unit, though Baldev Singh of the regiment earned the I.D.S.M. in that theatre. Sepoy Nihal Singh, 62ND Punjabis, was awarded the I.O.M. for the first day of the Battle of Loos, 25TH September 1915. Nihal Singh was attached to 35TH Divisional Signal Company. Nihal Singh was also awarded the French Croix de Guerre. Ultimately he became a Subedar and received the O.B.I. He was one of a very few veterans of the regiment to be recalled for service in 1939 and served with the newly raised 16TH Battalion of 1ST Punjabis.

In 1922 the Battalion was redesignated as 1ST Battalion, 1ST Punjab Regiment. During the Second World War, 1/1ST Punjab initially served in Iraq and then moved to North Africa in November 1941 to join 5TH Indian Division. Only to take part in the British withdrawal following Rommel's offensive in January 1942. Rommel's mobile forces swept eastwards along the El-Abiar-Mekili track as well as along the coast roads, and threatened to cut off the retreating Eighth Army. The 5TH Indian Division was ordered to hold a position covering the junction of the Cirene and Elfaidia roads.

1ST Punjab Regiment

62ND Punjabis (1/1ST)

The 1/1ST Punjab acted as rear guard in 5TH Brigade's retreat, which was accomplished without much interference, although the Germans were close on its heels. The 5TH Brigade was then ordered to Derna, where the Battalion, acting for the better part of the way as rear-guard, arrived on February 1ST. Dumps in Derna had to be destroyed and demolitions completed, before the brigade could move on to its next destination, Tmimi. The task was completed on February 2ND, and 1ST Battalion arrived on 3RD at Tmimi and took up defensive position on the northern flank in the dark. At dawn the positions were adjusted and the men, in spite of the past week's strain, worked hard to strengthen the defences. This stood them in good stead, for at noon the Germans opened a heavy artillery bombardment on the position and shortly afterwards launched a strong infantry attack supported by tanks. Neither the numerical superiority of the Germans nor their violent attacks could shake the determination of the men, who repulsed them with heavy losses. This was the first engagement of 1ST Battalion during the Second World War, and the Punjabis lived up to their traditions.

The Battalion was converted into motorized infantry and deployed at Ruweisat Ridge. Having completed its conversion, the battalion left with 161ST Brigade for El Alamein, where it joined the already famous 5TH Indian Division. For two weeks after its arrival the battalion helped to dig rearward defences in the El Alamein area, but on 19TH it went into battle on the vital Ruweisat Ridge.

Rommel had launched an attack on the Gazala line on May 27TH, and had not only overrun its defences but had captured Tobruk with its large garrison. He pressed hard on the heels of the retreating Eighth Army, which, after a fighting retreat, arrived back at El Alamein.

The battalion participated in the battle of Ruweisat Ridge; it advanced and captured a position against intensive artillery and medium-machine-gun fire. During the German counter attack, in spite of the heavy casualties they sustained, continued to fight back tenaciously, when it was finally decided to withdraw from the captured position. During this action the Battalion suffered some 140 casualties. For their courage during this fierce battle, Naik Hazara Singh and Lance-Naik Indar Singh were awarded the I.D.S.M. During the battle of El Alamein the battalion was given the task to raid enemy positions in order to kill as many of the garrison as possible and obtain identifications. On its advance heavy shell fire caused twenty-five casualties. The advance was halted. Havildar, later Subedar, Joginder Singh took command of the company and led it forward in an endeavour to get to the objective and out of the shelled area. But the hostile shelling increased in intensity and it was decided to withdraw. Havildar Joginder Singh received the award of the I.D.S.M. and the whole company was commended by the Corps Commander for its gallant effort. Although the company did not reach its objective, it succeeded in pinning down a German regiment on that critical night. It then participated in the British counter-attack in October, which turned the tide of war in North Africa.

1ST Punjab Regiment

62ND Punjabis (1/1ST)

On November 7TH, 1942, by which date Rommel had lost the El Alamein battle, the battalion was withdrawn and moved to Iraq, where it was split up in detachments to guard the oil pipe-line. The Arab Legion took over these duties in the middle of February, 1943, and the battalion concentrated at Baghdad and then moved on to Latafiya. Eventually the battalion sailed from Iraq for India. As 5TH Division, of which the Battalion was still part, was ordered for the Burma theatre, the battalion cut short its stay at Jhelum and on July 29^{TH,} 1943, left for Ranchi where it re-joined 161ST Brigade. In October 1943, 1/1ST Punjab arrived in Burma, where it fought in the Second Arakan Campaign.

Throughout the first week of January, 1944, the battalion probed its way forward on the east of the Bawli-Razabil road until it arrived north of Rehkat Chaung, where it came against the strongly fortified defences running along the Chaung, known as the Razabil Fortress. The battalion launched an attack on two features, to the south of Rehkat Chaung, having gained a footing on these features. The Japanese counter-attack was successful. After a long day of grim fighting, the companies were ordered to extricate themselves from their difficult situation. It was soon apparent that the capture of these hills was not a battalion task. A brigade attack was planned for January 25TH, and the battalion was to seize Squiggle and Bunker Hill. A company assaulted Squiggle and got to the top practically unopposed. In an attack to capture Bunker Hill, a company came under heavy fire from the front and flanks. Subedar Arjan Singh, who was with the leading section, personally led an assault on the enemy posts in the first line of trenches in the face of intense machine-gun and grenade fire, fell seriously wounded, at the second post and was taken down the hill, where he organized the evacuation of the wounded. The gallantry of Subedar Arjan Singh won him an I.O.M., and Sepoy Man Singh an I.D.S.M.

The battalion then fought in the Battles of Kohima on March, 30TH. The battle was fought in three stages from 4TH April to 22ND June 1944 around the town of Kohima in Nagaland in northeast India. From 3RD to 16TH April, the Japanese attempted to capture Kohima ridge, a feature which dominated the road by which the besieged British and Indian troops of IV Corps at Imphal were supplied. By mid-April, the small British force at Kohima was relieved. From 18TH April to 13TH May, British and Indian reinforcements counter-attacked to drive the Japanese from the positions they had captured. The Japanese abandoned the ridge at this point but continued to block the Kohima–Imphal road.

From 16TH May to 22ND June, the British and Indian troops pursued the retreating Japanese and reopened the road. The battle ended on 22ND June when British and Indian troops from Kohima and Imphal met at Milestone 109, ending the Siege of Imphal.

"The battles on the Tiddim Road were some of the fiercest of the whole Burma war". Once the Japanese invasion began, it was the route through which the Tiddim-based 17TH Indian Division made a fighting withdrawal.

1ST Punjab Regiment

62ND Punjabis (1/1ST)

For the majority of this period, the British forces consisted of 17TH Indian Division with 32 Brigade of 20TH Indian Division. It was on the Tiddim Road and on the Silchar-Bishenpur Track that some of the heaviest fighting in the entire Battle of Imphal-Kohima took place. As in the other sectors, the fighting on the Tiddim Road involved repeated and determined attempts by the Japanese to break through to Imphal, this time from the south.

On May 16TH, Subedar Chaiju Singh's fighting patrol contacted a party of thirty Japanese dug in on a small feature. Despite his numerical inferiority, the Subedar led a direct attack against the Japanese machine-gun post and personally killed a Japanese officer in close combat, while his patrol accounted for ten others; the remaining Japanese took to their heels. On another occasion on the same day, Subedar Sewa Singh took a reconnaissance patrol forward through dense jungle, directed artillery fire on the Japanese bunker holding up the advance and personally leading a small party, and drove the Japanese from their positions, killing three of them. Subedars Chaiju Singh and Sewa Singh were awarded the Military Cross, for their gallant leadership and personal bravery.

The British were equally determined to prevent the Japanese from recapturing the positions and the result again was ferocious to-and-fro fighting between the two sides, until the British finally prevailed. The battalion continued aggressive patrolling and harassing raids around and along Kennedy Peak-Dallung track. The trials and tribulations of the journey down the Tiddim Road had been most severe. For the greater part of the operations, the battalion had to fight in thickly wooded and precipitous hills, east of the main road. Enduring dismal discomfort in the pouring rain, the men were continuously on the move, digging, patrolling and raiding in this unhealthy country. The total casualties the Battalion had suffered in the operations were forty-four. Havildar Santa Singh and Havildar Badan Singh won the I.D.S.M., for organizing two ambushes and for gallantry during the advance down the Tiddim Road.

On March 6TH, 1945, the battalion commenced its long and strenuous march to take part in the operations for the final reconquest of Burma. The Battalion fought numerous actions in the Irrawaddy Basin until the final Allied victory in August 1945.

It then served in the Dutch East Indies as part of the Allied occupation forces. The patrolling in Batavia had to be constant and vigorous to prevent the looting of villages and towns. Villages were searched and a number of small-scale operations launched to capture the extremist leaders and stores of arms available to them. These trying and distasteful duties, to re-impose the Dutch rule on Indonesians lasted till May 23RD, when the Battalion embarked at Batavia for Ranchi in India.

In 1947, 1ST Battalion, 1ST Punjab Regiment was allocated to Pakistan Army. The Sikh soldiers from the battalion were routed to join the Indian Army.

1ST Punjab Regiment

66TH Punjabis (2/1ST)

The 66TH Punjabis was raised in 1761 as 7TH Battalion of Coast Sepoys. The regiment had its antecedents in the old Madras Army of the British East India Company, which was largely responsible for the British conquest of south and central India. The men were mostly enlisted from South India and consisted of Muslims and Hindus. For the next forty years, the regiment was engaged in constant warfare against the Sultans of Mysore. In 1902, the regiment was designated as 6TH Madras Infantry, and was reconstituted with Sikhs, Punjabi Mussalmans and Rajputs. In 1903 the regiment's designation was changed to 66TH Punjabis.

Between the years 1902 and 1914, these reconstituted regiments were employed on operational and garrison duties beyond and along the frontiers of India. The 66TH Punjabis served on the North-West Frontier from 1905 to 1908, and in Burma from February, 1913, to December, 1914.

On the outbreak of the Great War, 66TH Punjabis, then stationed in Burma, mobilized and returned to Jhelum. The situation in Mesopotamia took an unfavourable turn and 66TH Punjabis were ordered to join 33RD Brigade, which embarked on March 13TH, 1915, for Basra, where it arrived a week later. A Turkish offensive appeared to be imminent, as a Turco-Arab force concentrated between Nasiriyah and Nakhela with a view to advancing on Shaiba, which had been occupied by the British to protect the western approaches to Basra.

The British outposts at Ahwaz on the Karun River had been pressed back, and the Turks were gradually increasing their strength in Mesopotamia as a whole. The Headquarters and half 66TH were sent to Kurmat Ali and two other companies were sent to Fao and Abadan. Another detachment joined a combined naval and military force operating as a flotilla from Kurmat Ali against the Turkish supply sailing barges on their line of communication.

The long–awaited Turkish attack on Shaiba came on April 12TH. During the battle, which lasted three days, a double company of 66TH Punjabis protected the south-western approaches to Basra against a force of Turkish cavalry, while the regiment's machine-guns, operating from the rafts, guarded the approaches across the flooded area. Having repulsed the Turkish attack on Shaiba, the decision was taken to concentrate a force at Ahwaz to operate against the Turks and Arabs in Arabistan on order to secure the eastern flank of the British Army. The 66TH, embarked in two River steamers as divisional troops, a force which was to advance up the Karun River and drive the Turks across the Karkha River. The regiment disembarked at Salmaneh on April 24TH, and marched up the Karun with the advanced troops to Braika, where it arrived on 29TH.

On November 20TH General Townshend made his final preparations for the attack on the Turkish position at Ctesiphon. The attack started on 22ND. The advance was continuous and rapid in spite of the hostile artillery fire. When the troops came under enemy machine-gun and rifle fire, they carried on the advance in rushes of a hundred yards, halting only to take breath.

1ST Punjab Regiment

66TH Punjabis (2/1ST)

Covered by supporting fire, the first line reached the wire entanglements about forty yards in front of the hostile trench, but were brought to a standstill owing to the want of wire-cutters. The 66TH Punjabis pushed on, and with dahs (choppers) which they had brought from Burma, hacked down the wooden posts and forced their way into trenches, killing many of the enemy with their bayonets. As they forced their way forward, they came under heavy fire from a redoubt on their left. They swung around and attacked southwards against this redoubt. Having cleared the redoubt, 66TH Punjabis pushed on and drove the enemy from his intermediate position, capturing eight guns and penetrating towards the Turkish second line. Various units of this attacking force, though much intermingled, still occupied a position in front of the Turkish second line.

A fresh enemy division put in a counter attack and forced the brigade to fall back to the Turkish first line. The British advance all along the front had now to come to a halt, and 66TH Punjabis withdrew into the original first-line Turkish trenches. During the day many deeds of gallantry were performed. Jemadar Bishan Singh and Sepoy Mugh Singh were awarded the I.O.M. Other gallantry awards included the I.D.S.M. to Sepoy Dhir Singh.

The 16TH Brigade, to which 66TH Punjabis had reverted, was withdrawn on the morning of 23RD to the Water Redoubt to re-organize. That evening the Turks, coming to the conclusion that the British were shaken and disorganized by the fighting on the previous day, launched a counter-attack with the object of retaking their original first line of defence. Six furious attacks were made against the centre of the line occupied by 16TH Brigade, but all were repulsed. The Turks despaired of success and withdrew. The condition of the British force was equally critical. The wearied troops had hung on with the utmost tenacity to their trenches, but the strain on the infantry, already exhausted by the previous day's battle, had been great. The strength of the brigade was considerably reduced and it was decided to retire to Lajj. On 24TH, 66TH Punjabis, with the remainder of 16TH Brigade, commenced the long and arduous retreat to Kut-al-Amara. The first serious encounter with the pursuing Turkish army took place at Umm at Tubul, where the force bivouacked on November 30TH. The camp was shelled and the Turks attempted to rush an important Piquet manned by a detachment of 66TH Punjabis. The Piquet held its ground, and after two hours of futile attacks the enemy withdrew, leaving fifteen dead. On the morning of the 3RD, the 66TH marched into to Kut-al-Amara. Meanwhile, the Turks were closing round Kut-al-Amara. The historic siege, which was to last until 29TH had begun. Shortly after the garrison was besieged, the Turks began their attack on the Kut-al-Amara defences. Between December 8TH and 12TH, the enemy launched two attacks against the north-west sector. The 66TH Punjabis were in the front line and checked the enemy attacks with cool determination, bringing them to a halt.

1ST Punjab Regiment

66TH Punjabis (2/1ST)

On December 24TH, the Turks made their most serious and sustained effort to take the place by assault, their main attack being directed against the fort. The 66TH Punjabis were then in the rear and did not take part in the battle, but its two men, Havildar Chaman Singh and Sepoy Dhir Singh, with the machine-gun battery in the fort won the I.O.M., for conspicuous enterprise and courageous behaviour. Havildar Chaman Singh, later Honorary Lieutenant and Subedar–Major of the regiment, in command of the regimental machine-gun section, behaved with great coolness throughout and helped greatly in beating off attacks of the enemy. During hand-to-hand fighting which took place later, he displayed great bravery. Sepoy Dhir Singh was on this day in charge of a machine-gun detailed to man a flank post in the fort. All the other gun teams having been put out of action, this gallant soldier continued firing his gun until jammed. He then encouraged his companions to join him in opening rifle fire, and thus succeeded in beating off the enemy attack on this flank. Several casualties occurred from stray bullets, and one of the most regrettable being Havildar Chaman Singh, who was hit through the head while standing in a trench. He had distinguished himself greatly at Ctesiphon and had been a leader in many enterprises. They resisted all Turkish attempts to overwhelm the defences of Kut-al-Amara for 150 days, but after the failure of the British to relieve them, the starving garrison of Kut-al-Amara was forced to surrender on 29TH April 1916. The 66TH Punjabis became prisoners of war and suffered terrible privations during their long captivity. Out of the 538 officers and men present in the regiment on 14TH March, only about a quarter returned home after the war. The 66TH Punjabis were re-formed at Jhelum on 31ST December, 1916 and served on the North West Frontier of India.

During the Third Afghan War of 1919, fort was entirely cut off, and exposed the posts at Girni and Jata to enemy attacks. A force assembled at Khirgi for the relief of Jandola included 66TH Punjabis, who came from Manzai. Girni post, being seriously threatened, demanded urgent attention. Four thousand Mahsuds had surrounded it. A flying column that included a company of 66TH Punjabis moved from Khirgi camp on June 3RD, and met stiff opposition from the Mahsuds holding positions north and north-west of Girni post. An attack was launched by the infantry, which included two platoons of 66TH Punjabis. The Mahsuds were driven off at the cost of three casualties to the column.

Meanwhile, Jandola fort was surrounded on May 28TH by more than 6,000 Mahsuds and Bhitannis. On 29TH, the tribesmen attacked the Jandola fort and a detached tower on a hill about a mile away. Both attacks failed. The siege of Jandola fort continued until the Waziristan Field Force including 66TH Punjabis undertook the relief of it.

After the First World War, 66TH Punjabis were grouped with 62ND, 76TH, 82ND and 84TH Punjabis, to form 1ST Punjab Regiment. In 1922 the regiment was redesignated as 2ND Battalion, 1ST Punjab Regiment.

1ST Punjab Regiment

66TH Punjabis (2/1ST)

The 2/1ST Punjabis spent practically the whole period between the two World Wars on the North-West Frontier.

In February, 1923, eight units were selected to be officered by Indians. Among these were 2/1ST Punjabis. Indian officers holding commissions in the Indian Army were to be gradually transferred to these units, and the process of Indianisation was to continue as these officers gained seniority and fitness in other respects to hold senior posts. 2ND Lieutenant Kalwant Singh, who eventually attained the rank of Lieutenant-General in the Indian Army, was one of the officers to join 2/1ST Punjabis in April, 1926.

During the Second World War, 2/1ST Punjabis served in Burma, as a part of the 47TH Brigade, 14TH Indian Division. With surprising rapidity the Japanese had pushed back the Allied Forces in Burma to the Indian border. It was not only essential to stop the Japanese from invading India, but also imperative to regain Burma. On 21ST December 1942, British and Commonwealth forces launched a small assault against the Arakan region in western Burma, aiming to capture the Mayu Peninsula and Akyab Island's airfield. In spite of persistent efforts, 47TH Brigade could make little progress on the Donbaik front. In an action fought on February 2ND, 1943, Naik Shamsher Singh was awarded the I.D.S.M. for bravery.

In another action fought on 18TH, "D" Company of the Battalion had advanced with great gallantry, under the command of Captain Budh Singh, over the open and bullet swept country and captured its objective. Terrific fire from the front and flanks took a heavy toll. Captain Budh Singh realized that all he could do now was to withdraw across the open to his original position. This he did with cool courage, collecting as many of the wounded men as he could on his way back. The company strength was reduced to forty-four through casualties. Amongst them were, Jemadar Surjan Singh and Havildar-Major Indar Singh, both platoon commanders, wounded. For his gallantry during this engagement Captain Budh Singh was awarded the Military Cross and Jemadar Surjan Singh, the leading platoon commander, and Lance-Naik Karan Singh each got I.D.S.M. This attack had cost 2/1ST Punjabis 131 casualties. On March 8TH, 2ND Battalion moved up to the front line at Hitzwe. By then the British troops in the Kaladan valley had been forced to withdraw and the Japanese had quickly followed up, launching a vigorous offensive westwards towards Hitzwe. Captain Budh Singh's Company was the first to experience the momentum of this offensive. On the night of March 12TH / 13TH, six successive waves of Japanese assaulted in vain against this company, which repulsed the enemy with heavy losses, estimated at about 100 killed and many wounded. At dawn the Company withdrew, with its wounded, as the enemy had infiltrated during the night and dug in on the lower slopes of the hill, making further maintenance difficult. Soon after, the Battalion was told to take up another rearward position, where 'D' Company was again the first to be attacked. Just before dawn on 14TH, about 300 Japanese attacked Jemadar Kalyan Singh's platoon guarding the left flank of the Battalion Headquarters.

1ST Punjab Regiment

66TH Punjabis (2/1ST)

'D' Company commander, Budh Singh, hastened with reinforcements to his platoon, took charge of the situation and repulsed the assailants, who left seventy-three dead around the position. Captain Budh Singh was awarded a bar to his Military Cross for his valiant leadership of 'D' Company during this action. Jemadar Kalyan Singh won the I.D.S.M.

The Japanese managed to infiltrate and directed their medium-machine-gun fire on Battalion headquarters. The Battalion mortars brought down accurate fire on the enemy position till a successful counter-attack was put in by a platoon of "D" Company. The Japanese were badly shaken and started running away across open paddy-fields, where they were caught by guns, mortars and light automatics. Altogether, 103 dead Japanese were counted. Once again 'D' Company had taken a leading part in the day's fighting. Two of its viceroy's commissioned officers, Subedar Bhanwar Singh and Jemadar Kalyan Singh, were wounded. On 3RD April, 1943, Japanese reinforcements struck the Indian 14TH Division, forcing them to abandon their heavy equipment and retreat back across the Indian border. The 2ND retreated to Buthidaung, where Colonel Lowther left to take over the command of 4TH Indian Infantry Brigade. Major Sarbjit Singh Kalha took over command. He was the first Indian to command a Battalion of the Regiment.

On April, 21ST, the Battalion was once again on the march to the north. From now on, until the beginning of May, the Battalion was continually fighting rear-guard actions. In an action fought during this retreat Jemadar Mod Singh, was awarded the I.D.S.M.

The XV Corps launched a renewed offensive at the Mayu Peninsula in which the small port city of Maungdaw was captured on 9TH January 1944. The Japanese 55TH Division, under Lieutenant General Hanaya Tadashi, dispatched units of the Sakurai Force in small groups on 5TH February, penetrating positions held by Indian 7TH Division without being detected. On the following day, the Japanese crossed the Kalapanzin River and attacked the forward headquarters of the Indian 7TH Division in surprise, forcing the divisional staff to destroy all the orders and signal equipment before fleeing. The Japanese then advanced toward the Indian 7TH Division's administrative area at Sinzweya. In the subsequent Battle of the Admin Box, the Japanese failed to dislodge the Indian defensive point, and eventually the offensive was beaten off as the Japanese supplies dwindled; 3,106 Japanese were killed and 2,229 were wounded in this failed offensive. During this battle, Lieutenant-Colonel Sarbjit Singh Kalha's careful planning and bold executions was rewarded with a D.S.O. and Subedar Sukhmandar Singh was awarded the Military Cross.

In the second week of March, 1944, 5TH Division completed its task of capturing the Tunnels Area and thus securing the vital Buthidaung- Maungdaw road. Two days later the Battalion moved to Dohazari, thus ending its memorable part in the two campaigns in Arakan. Soon after its arrival at Dohazari, the Battalion was airlifted to join in the battle of Imphal.

1ST Punjab Regiment

66TH Punjabis (2/1ST)

The Battle of Imphal took place in the region around the city of Imphal, the capital of the state of Manipur in northeast India from March until July 1944. Japanese armies attempted to destroy the Allied forces at Imphal and invade India, but were driven back into Burma with heavy losses. Together with the simultaneous Battle of Kohima on the road by which the encircled Allied forces at Imphal were relieved, the battle was the turning point of the Burma Campaign, part of the South-East Asian Theatre of the Second World War. The defeat at Kohima and Imphal was the largest defeat to that date in Japanese history. During the Battle, Subedar Bhanwar Singh, who was in command of the two platoons, received three bullets in his leg during the attack on the second platoon, but refused to be evacuated till the situation stabilized. He was awarded the Military Cross. On Septembers 4TH, 2ND Battalion concentrated to take part in the advance down the Tiddim Road.

During the battles on the Tiddim Road, Lance-Naik Bhur Singh's platoon encountered forty Japanese with three light machine-guns. The platoon killed five Japanese and recovered two Gurkha prisoners of war. Lance-Naik Bhur Singh was awarded an I.D.S.M. for outstanding initiative and courage during this action.

On 25TH October 1944 at Kennedy Peak in the Tiddim area two platoons were ordered to attack a strong Japanese position. The platoon commanded by Subedar Ram Sarup Singh attained its objective and although Singh was wounded in both legs he insisted on carrying on. Later, the enemy's counter-attack was halted by Subedar Singh's dashing counter-charge in which he killed four of the enemy himself. He was again wounded, but continued to lead his men, killing two more of the enemy, before he was mortally wounded. He was 25 years old, and a Jemadar (acting Subedar) in 2/1ST Punjabis, when the deed took place for which he was awarded the Victoria Cross. It would be difficult to find a finer example of cool bravery, cheerfulness, leadership and determination. His action had a profound effect on the rest of the Company, and when volunteers were called for to bring in his body, under the heaviest fire, the entire Company volunteered.

On March, 17TH, 1945, the Battalion took part in the drive to reach Rangoon before the monsoon. The 2/1ST Punjabis were left to establish a firm base at Mahlaing, a small town half-way between Taungtha and Meiktilla. At the end of March the troops of the Division entered Meiktilla. They settled in quickly in the southern part of Meiktilla. Preparations for the pursuit of the Japanese to Rangoon were pressed forward. The distance between Meiktilla and Rangoon is 384 miles. During the race for Rangoon, a strong Japanese resistance was met at Yamethin. The road and rail crossing in the centre of Yamethin was secured and 2/1st Punjabis, with a squadron of tanks, were ordered to advance down either side of the road. Though the two leading companies had cleared the southern outskirts of Yamethin within two hours, considerable firing was still coming from the Japanese soldiers who had dug themselves in on the eastern edge of the town. Accordingly, two companies were diverted towards this quarter, but came under intense fire.

1ST Punjab Regiment

66TH Punjabis (2/1ST)

The leading platoon ran on to a minefield and suffered a dozen casualties within a minute. Then the companies were ordered back, to allow a Divisional artillery concentration to be brought down on the area. When the Battalion went forward with three companies, they were again held up and forced to retire under cover of a screen of mortar fire and snipers.

The 2/1ST Punjabis consolidated along the line of the main road. All through the night the Gunners harassed the enemy in the eastern streets and buildings, and Yamethin was captured. The advance had been held up for two days, the enemy had been difficult to dislodge and the fighting to secure Yamethin had been severe and costly. Between Yamethin and Pyinmana the main road runs alongside hilly country and thick jungle and at the Schwemyo Bluff, eight miles south of Tatkon, it was known that the Japanese would attempt to make a strong stand. The 2/1ST Punjabis and 1/17TH Dogras took the hills. And so a strong position, which the enemy would in earlier days have held with great tenacity, was wrested from his grasp.

The whole of 5TH Division then advanced to capture Taungoo airfield. From Taungoo onwards, 17TH Indian Division took over the lead, and 2/1ST Punjabis, besides guarding the Taungoo airfield, carried out extensive mopping-up operations along the banks of the Sittang River, to which a large body of the retreating Japanese had withdrawn. On May 27TH, 2/1ST Punjabis moved southwards to mop up Japanese pockets of resistance in the rear of 17TH Division. Meanwhile, Rangoon had been captured from the sea by a force of which 5TH Battalion of the Regiment formed part. The Japanese were now in a critical position. Hemmed in between the two corps, their only course was to withdraw over the eastern frontier of Burma across the Sittang River or through Moulmein. The task of preventing and intercepting the enemy forces seeking to escape across the main road south of Pegu was given to 5TH Division.

The 2/1ST Punjabis were given the task of operating in the Pegu Yomas against 5,000 Japanese, retreating in disorganization from Prome. This entailed strenuous patrolling and difficult marches in an area of small hillocks crossed with thick clumps of bamboos. No effort was spared to hunt down the disordered, leaderless, out of touch, dejected enemy. Liable to be trapped and faced with a country flooded by the violent monsoon rains, with rushing streams and rivers, paddy fields deep in mud, the Battalion was ready to destroy or capture the straggling Japanese as opportunity offered.

On May 31ST, 1945, 2/1ST Punjabis were relieved and then employed on road-protection duties till the middle of June, when it left with the remainder of 5TH Indian Division to Mingladon and began training in combined operations for an invasion of Malaya. The invasion never came, for the Japanese surrendered in August, 1945.

The 5TH Indian Division, detailed to reoccupy Singapore Island, landed on the Island on September. The 2/1ST Punjabis had the honour of being the first to land.

1ˢᵀ Punjab Regiment

66ᵀᴴ Punjabis (2/1ˢᵀ)

Seven days later, the official surrender of the Japanese in South Asia was received by Lord Louis Mountbatten from General Itagaki. Colonel Sarbjit Singh Kalha, D.S.O., was one of the officers escorting the six Japanese generals at the historic ceremony.

The 2/1ˢᵀ Punjabis were then moved to Soerabaja in Java. Soerabaja was the centre of the Indonesian Nationalist Movement and the strength of the Indonesian army was twelve thousand. In addition, the armed mobs were armed with Japanese weapons seized at the time of capitulation. The 5ᵀᴴ Indian Division's task was to restore order, and hand the country back to the Dutch!!

The 2/1ˢᵀ Punjabis landed on November, 2ᴺᴰ, and went into action on the 7ᵀᴴ, by which time the situation had become even tenser and the Indonesians increasingly aggressive. Considerable care and caution was shown in dealing with the Indonesians, who were in strength in the town and had numerous weapons, including tanks and artillery. They were given ample warning to surrender their arms; artillery fire was withheld until it was clear that any further advance without artillery support would incur heavy casualties, and leaflets were dropped urging the Indonesians to hand in their arms by 10ᵀᴴ.

On the expiry of the ultimatum, operations commenced against them. The 2/1ˢᵀ Punjabis captured the railway station and participated in the subsequent operations, which ended on November, 28ᵀᴴ, after the Indonesian army had been driven out of the city and its suburbs. The Indonesians then resorted to full-fledged guerrilla warfare and numerous patrol clashes took place in the following weeks. On December, 13ᵀᴴ, 2/1ˢᵀ Punjabis advanced against an Indonesian strong-hold covering the entrance to Soerabaja harbour and cleared it after two days' fighting.

On January, 11ᵀᴴ, 1946, 2/1ˢᵀ Punjabis and the Indian Army suffered a grievous loss. In an ambush the Battalion Commander, Lieutenant–Colonel Sarbjit Singh Kalha, in the foremost jeep was killed outright. It was tragic that the last actions of any importance in which 2/1ˢᵀ Punjabis were engaged should have been the most disastrous, in that Colonel Kalha lost his life. He had been at the Staff College and had served with the Battalion off and on from the first day it went into action. Calm and unruffled in battle, fearless with delightful manners, he had won the D.S.O. and bar. His remarkable ability included that of commanding both British and Indian officers. He was one of those senior Indian Army officers whom India could least afford to lose.

In March, 1945, 2/1ˢᵀ Punjabis handed over its commitments to the Dutch and left on April, 2ᴺᴰ, for India. After three months at Ranchi, it moved to Pashawar on July 27ᵀᴴ 1946, and on May 2ᴺᴰ 1947, it left for Bannu in North Waziristan, where it was stationed at the time of Independence and Partition of the sub-continent.

In 1947, 2/1ˢᵀ Punjabis were allocated to Pakistan Army. The Sikh soldiers from the battalion were routed to join the Indian Army.

1ˢᵀ Punjab Regiment

76ᵀᴴ Punjabis (3/1ˢᵀ)

The 76ᵀᴴ Punjabis were raised at Trichonopoly on 16ᵀᴴ December 1776, as 16ᵀᴴ Carnatic Battalion. The men were mostly enlisted from South India and consisted of Muslims and Hindus. The Rifle Company operated in Bihar and Oudh during the Sepoy Mutiny and rejoined the regiment in April, 1860. The detachment sent to the Madras Field Force, after ten months operating against the rebels, rejoined the Regiment in December, 1858.

It served with the Upper Burma Field Force in 1886. Soon after its arrival in Burma, the Battalion was split up into eleven detachments to man various posts. It provided many detachments and escorts and took part in numerous small actions until February, 1888, when it moved to garrison Mandalay, whence it left for India in March, 1889.

In 1902, the regiment was reconstituted with Sikhs, Punjabi Mussalmans and Hindu Jats. As a result of the reforms brought about in the Indian Army the regiment's designation was changed to 76ᵀᴴ Punjabis. Between the years 1902 and 1914, this reconstituted Battalion was employed on operational and garrison duties beyond and along the frontiers of India. 76ᵀᴴ Punjabis carried out garrison duties in China from April, 1908, to June, 1911.

On the outbreak of the First World War in 1914, 76ᵀᴴ Punjabis were dispatched to Egypt to protect the Suez Canal. The 76ᵀᴴ Punjabis were allotted the second of the defences south of the Little Bitter Lake. The general scheme for the defence of the Canal was a series of posts or bridgeheads on the east bank and the battalion manned these posts throughout its stay in the canal area. The main Turkish attack on the Suez Canal came further north, in the sector occupied by 62ᴺᴰ Punjabis, and 76ᵀᴴ Punjabis had practically no fighting. After the failure of their main attack, the Turks made no more attempts on the Suez Canal and the threat to its security diminished by the end of March, 1915, when the Regiment, accompanied the remainder of 30ᵀᴴ Brigade proceeded to Basra, in Mesopotamia, to join the newly formed 12ᵀᴴ Indian Division.

On the April 12ᵀᴴ, 1915, the Turks struck with a force of about 22,000 regulars and Arabs, at a vital position at Shaiba. The garrison, numbering 5,000 British and Indian troops, cut off from Basra by the floods, was hard pressed. Its commander asked for help and 30ᵀᴴ Brigade moved from Basra, with 76ᵀᴴ Punjabis leading the advance. Throughout April 13ᵀᴴ and 14ᵀᴴ the battle for Shaiba continued. On 14ᵀᴴ, a convoy of Arab boats, with the Regiments machine-gun section was sent across to Shaiba. The convoy, by its apparently unguarded appearance, succeeded in deceiving the Turks, who sailed forth in their boats to capture it, but were subjected to devastating fire from the machine-guns. The Turks fled from the watery battlefield, having paid dearly for their harshness. After taking part in the Battle of Shaiba, where the Turkish counter-attack was repulsed, 76ᵀᴴ Punjabis participated in the operations to punish Beni Turuf tribe, whose principal village was Khafajiya, with a mud fort. On May, 14ᵀᴴ, orders were sent out to Major Perrin to capture the fort.

1ST Punjab Regiment

76TH Punjabis (3/1ST)

Major Perrin sent a party round the far side of the fort under Subedar Indar Singh and launched the assault. The gateway of the fort was a narrow entrance some eight to ten feet broad, and this was charged by a party of six. This small band was opposed by some fifty Arabs armed with swords and spears and covered by rifle fire. The Arabs fled when charged by this party and attempted to escape over the walls of the fort. The majority were, however, killed by Subedar Indar Singh's party, who were skilfully placed. The fort was captured after some two hours' resistance, with a loss to the enemy of 31 killed, several wounded and 11 Arab prisoners. For the operations against Khafajiya, Havildar Kesar Singh was among the five officers and men who were awarded the I.O.M., while twenty I.D.S.M.s were awarded to other Indian officers and men who took part.

The 76TH Punjabis continued their advance along the River Euphrates, which led to the capture of the Akaika Channel on 5TH July. In the action at Akaika Channel, the enemy's strength that day was estimated at three hundred Turkish troops, two thousand Arabs, two guns and two launches, each armed with a 'pom-pom'. During the action they had been reinforced by two guns and seven hundred troops. Their casualties could not be estimated, but ninety-one prisoners, two guns and large quantities of ammunition and stores were captured. The 76TH Punjabis incurred 16 killed and 33 wounded. Five I.O.M.s, were won by the gallantry of Naik Sundar Singh, Naik Ram Singh, Lance-Naik Hukam Singh, Sepoy Jamal and Sepoy Bagga Khan,

Meanwhile, further reinforcements had arrived; an attack, which included half of 76TH Punjabis, was launched along the Euphrates on 24TH, July. Among the first to reach the enemy trenches were Jemadar Gulzara Singh and Sepoy Ishar Singh. The latter had hitherto been employed in the Mess soda-water 'factory' and had been chaffed about this by his companions, who said "We go and fight while you make soda-pani." This was too much for Ishar Singh, who went and made a petition to be allowed to join his company in action. He displayed marked gallantry, was one of the very first into the enemy trenches, and in this first battle, earned the I.D.S.M. Later he was to earn three more "mentions", stop a bullet, win the I.O.M. on the North-West Frontier and get promoted in the field for still further gallantry. Two field guns were captured by the regiment after hand-to-hand fighting and the crew of the third was put to flight. Nasiriyah was captured on 25^{TH,} July. The Turkish defeat had been complete. Their losses amounted to 700 killed, 740 wounded and 200 prisoners, and 17 guns of varying calibres, with large stores of rifles and ammunition. The gallantry awards included I.O.M. to Havildar Ganda Singh. In August, the regiment joined 6TH Indian Division in its advance towards Baghdad. It fought in the epic Battle of Ctesiphon. During the three days of battle ground Ctesiphon, the regiment suffered 289 casualties, comprising 50 killed, and 232 wounded. Awards for gallantry at Ctesiphon included an I.O.M. to Lance-Naik Battan Singh.

1ST Punjab Regiment

76TH Punjabis (3/1ST)

The 76TH Punjabis retired towards Kut-al-Amara, where they were besieged by the Turks with the rest of 6TH Division. The regiment resolutely resisted all Turkish attempts to overwhelm the defences of Kut-al-Amara, suffering 171 casualties during the 150 days long siege. For services during the siege Subedars Indar Singh and Sundar Singh were awarded the O.B.I. The starving garrison of Kut-al-Amara was forced to surrender on 29TH April 1916. The 76TH Punjabis became prisoners of war and suffered terrible privations during their long captivity. Out of the 341 officers and men present with the regiment at the commencement of the siege in December 1915, 72 died during the siege, while another 101 died during the captivity. The regiment was re-formed in January, 1917, and served on the North-West Frontier until 1919, when it was ordered to serve in Palestine. It served in Palestine until 1922, when it embarked for India.

The 76TH alongside 66TH and 82ND Punjabis served during the Third Afghan War of 1919. The Afghan war ended, but this did not improve the situation in Waziristan. The Government decided to offer terms of peace and prepared to take punitive action against those refusing to accept the terms. The Waziris accepted the terms, but the Mahsuds flatly refused them. Consequently, a force named the Derajat Column was assembled at Tank to deal with them. The 76TH Punjabis formed part of this column. This was the beginning of some of the most difficult and costly operations ever undertaken on the Frontier. During the epic battle of Flathead, 76TH Punjabis were in action continuously for nearly twelve hours and sustained 138 casualties and earned three awards of Military Cross and one I.O.M. An eyewitness account of the battle, written by Major Compertz states:

"It is a little epic, that day of 76TH Punjabis on Flathead. They were a very, very young second-line Battalion, and they bumped into a fight such as the oldest of veteran Frontier Force Battalions had never even dreamt of. Nevertheless, they attacked with go, when bidden, and when told to hang on, hung on to what they had got, exposed hour after hour to incessant torment of sniper's bullets; while from time to time the prone line of men huddled behind rocks and stones would swirl into sudden movement, as a rush of Mahsuds came up one or other of the nullas and folds leading unseen to the very crest-line.

But they stuck grimly to their ground the whole of that weary hard-fought day, doing all that men could do-just sticking to it, and dying in the process. Five separate times did the Mahsud counter-attack, and five separate times with bullet and butt, bayonet and bomb, did 76TH Punjabis, and later the Gurkha reinforcements for the picket, hurl him back down the slopes." As the column commander wired that day, "the safety of the column depends on the staunchness of the troops." Staunch indeed they proved, but none more so than those children of 76TH. Evidently they have a tradition of 'sticking it' in 76TH Punjabis, for their Battalion was part of the immortal garrison of Kut-al-Amara.

1ST Punjab Regiment

76TH Punjabis (3/1ST)

The column commander's hope of inflicting severe punishment had been fulfilled, for the tribesmen owned to 400 dead at the end of this fight. After the heaviest fight in all the annals of the Frontier, the road to Mahsud lay open. By the beginning of April, 1920, all the major resistance by the Mahsuds ceased, and the Derajat column dispersed.

In 1922, 76TH Punjabis were grouped with 62ND, 66TH, 82ND and 84TH Punjabis, to form 1ST Punjab Regiment, and were redesignated as 3RD Battalion, 1ST Punjab Regiment. The 3RD Battalion's life between the two world wars was spent on the North-West Frontier.

On the outbreak of the Second World War, 3/1ST Punjab was dispatched to North Africa in September 1939. Throughout the winter of 1939-40, the Battalion trained intensively for desert warfare. By May, 1940, when the call came to go to the Western Desert to meet the Italian threat in Libya, it was an efficient fighting machine with every man trained for his part in the battles to come. Meanwhile, Mussolini had poured a large number of troops into Abyssinia, Eritrea and Libya with the intention of overrunning the whole of North Africa. The Italian forces in Libya crossed the frontier on September, 11TH, 1940, and captured Sidi Barani, and established fortified positions on an arc of forty miles.

The Battle of Sidi Barani was the opening battle of 'Operation Compass', the first big British attack of the Western Desert Campaign. The battle of Sidi Barani opened on the morning of December, 9TH, with the capture of Nibeiwa Camp and the advance on Tummar West. Much greater resistance was met at Tummar West and the situation was further complicated by the fact that 3/1ST Punjab had taken over 2,000 prisoners and the men had to be detached to guard them. Soon all resistance ceased. Over 3,000 prisoners, including many senior officers were captured by 3/1ST Punjabis. During this battle, its first action, 3/1ST Punjabis suffered 32 casualties. Many deeds of gallantry were performed during this action. Havildar Kalyan Singh won a well-merited I.O.M. for rescuing the machine gun from his blazing carrier and showing great daring in helping his platoon commander by leading his crew and gun in action against an enemy strong-point. Havildar Natha Singh was awarded the I.D.S.M. for his gallantry in this action. The battle of Sidi Barani was not over yet. Although the Italian counter-attack had been defeated, the attack on Tummar East which was to follow was postponed and the Italians made good use of this postponement by retiring to Point 90. An attempt to obtain an unconditional surrender of the garrison having failed, the Battalion, supported by five infantry tanks, advanced in skirmishing order and arrived at Point 90 to find 2,000 Italians lined up with kit-bags and suitcases packed for travel. The task completed 3/1ST Punjab returned to Tummar West.

Having smashed the Italians in the desert, General Wavell sent forward an Australian Division to continue the pursuit and pulled back his highly trained mobile 4TH Indian Division to meet another threat.

1ˢᵀ Punjab Regiment

76ᵀᴴ Punjabis (3/1ˢᵀ)

The Italians had advanced from Eritrea into Sudan. The Indian 4ᵀᴴ Division poured down to the Sudan. The leading troops advanced across the frontier and began to chase after the retreating Italians. On January, 25ᵀᴴ, 3/1ˢᵀ Punjabis crossed the border of Eritrea to join in 4ᵀᴴ Division's pursuit to Agordat, which offered the first major obstacle to the pursuers. The Italian garrison of the town consisted of some Battalions of Blackshirts and three brigades, including 2ᴺᴰ Brigade of five Battalions which had fought well in British Somaliland and was considered the best brigade in Italian East Africa. The 5ᵀᴴ Brigade was given the task of cutting the Keren road running east from Agordat. The final attack on four fortified hills astride this road was launched by the companies of 3/1ˢᵀ Punjabis on January, 31ˢᵀ. By dusk the Italians had been driven off the four hills at the cost of three casualties. The loss of four hills cut the enemy's line of communication and he made haste to get away as many men as possible to the Keren positions, which were considered by him to be impregnable. The Italians had good reason to believe Keren to be impregnable, as it might well have been to troops not inured to warfare on the North-West Frontier of India. The road runs up a narrow, rocky valley, overlooked by towering mountains. To the east is Fort Dologorodoc, 1,475 metres high, a pinnacle with almost perpendicular sides, while to the west the great massif of Sanchil to a height of 1,786 metres. Behind them again were the towering heights of Zeban and Falestoh. Beside these were a group of peaks. The forces holding them were the flower of the Italian army, the Savoy Grenadiers, the Bersagliery and the Alpini, besides fully trained native levies, well supplied with artillery and mortars. The fate of Keren had been decided on March 16ᵀᴴ, when the important fort of Dologorodoc fell to 5ᵀᴴ Indian Division. This success changed the course of the battle. The attack was pressed home, and by March 26ᵀᴴ the road through the Gorge was opened. A mobile force organized for the pursuit included 3/1ˢᵀ Punjabis' carriers. On 27ᵀᴴ this force entered Keren and pushed forward on the road to Asmara. Thus ended the epic battle of Kere, which completed the conquest of Eritrea and in which 3/1ˢᵀ Punjabis sustained 450 casualties. Although the Battalion did not take part in the final assault on March, 15ᵀᴴ, it had borne the brunt of the fighting in 5ᵀᴴ Brigade's attacks on the Cameron ridge and Brig's Peak and had on one occasion, by sweeping the hills as far as the slopes of Mount Sanchil, brought success within the reach of 4ᵀᴴ Division. Its subsequent tenacious stand on Brig's Peak is an inspiring record of gallantry.

From Eritrea, 3/1ˢᵀ Punjabis were ordered to Syria. Syria was under the French mandate. After the fall of France, Syria had remained in the administration of men of anti-British Vichy French Government and Syria began to fill with Germans and Italians. The British Cabinet, well aware of the German eagerness to follow up the conquest of Crete by an entry into the Middle East, urged General Wavell to secure Syria. On 6ᵀᴴ June, 5ᵀᴴ Brigade crossed the frontier by the road to Deraa and Damascus.

1ˢᵀ Punjab Regiment

76ᵀᴴ Punjabis (3/1ˢᵀ)

Deraa was the first objective of 5ᵀᴴ Brigade. On 7ᵀᴴ June, 3/1ˢᵀ Punjabis took up a position south of the town, ready to attack on the following morning. Next morning a flag of truce with a summons to surrender approached Deraa. This was rejected and the attack commenced. At this 3/1ˢᵀ Punjabis, supported by artillery fire, entered the village. Stiff resistance was soon overcome. A 75 mm gun firing at point-blank range was silenced. While the greater part of the enemy garrison escaped to the east, 3/1ˢᵀ Punjabis managed to collect 250 prisoners. On June 12ᵀᴴ, 3/1ˢᵀ Punjabis supported the Free French troops when they met strong opposition along the line of Nahr-el-Ouaj.

On June 13ᵀᴴ, 3/1ˢᵀ Punjabis found itself facing the strongly held village of Kissoue, against which a four-company assault was launched on 15ᵀᴴ. After fighting a successful action at Kissoue, in which 3/1ˢᵀ Punjabis had sustained 33 casualties.

On the evening of June 18ᵀᴴ, 3/1ˢᵀ Punjabis set forth on what turned out to be one of its most heroic and desperate actions in the war. The Brigade plan was to capture the village of Mezze, a detached suburb, which dominated the road and railway through the mountains to Beirut. The first objective was the fortified village of Mouddamiya, five miles from Mezze. The 3/1ˢᵀ Punjabis led a determined attack against the machine-gun posts, armoured cars and strong points in Mouddamiya. In pitch darkness, lit by intense shelling, the men pushed on to the far edge of the wood. Yard by yard the gardens were cleared. One tank after another was found and destroyed. In this attack Jemadar Bhagat Singh set an example of gallant effort and confident leadership by destroying four strongly held machine-gun pill-boxes, in spite of his platoon having suffered heavy casualties. In the assault on a fourth pill-box he was killed. By midnight Mouddamiya was captured, but twenty-seven men only of the company remained on their feet. The advance continued and after an hour of hard and desperate fighting Mezze was secured.

The seven glorious days commencing with the battle of Kissoue and terminating in the valiant fight for Mezze must always be remembered with pride in the history of 3/1ˢᵀ Punjabis. For in these days the men of 3/1ˢᵀ Punjabis gave supreme expression to the great fighting qualities which had distinguished them during the past year on the stony plains of the Western Desert, in the scrub covered country of Eastern Eritrea and in the precipitous mountains of Keren. Not one, not a few, but scores of deeds of gallantry shine in the Battalion's heroic story of Kissoue, Madani and Mezze. Such was the sacrifice 3/1ˢᵀ Punjabis made towards securing Syria for allies. For the Sikhs, Subedar Dogar Singh and Jemadar Bhagat Singh were awarded the I.O.M., and Havildars Sapuran Singh, Harnath Singh, Naiks Bachan Singh, Sardara Singh, Lance-Naik Sultan Singh, and Sepoys Bakhtwar Singh, Karam Singh and Sardar Singh, were awarded the I.D.S.M., for conspicuous gallantry in the fighting in Syria. On September, 17ᵀᴴ, 3/1ˢᵀ Punjabis, still in 5ᵀᴴ Indian Infantry Brigade, left for North Africa.

1ST Punjab Regiment

76TH Punjabis (3/1ST)

On the night of November 21ST, 3/1ST Punjabis, moved forward to the battle area. Much had happened since the earlier victories of December 1940. Rommel with his Panzer units had appeared on the scene and the Afrika Korps, organized and equipped by him, was certainly a force to be reckoned with. In July, General Auchinleck took over the command in the Middle East.

On November 18TH, General Auchinleck launched his offensive in Cyrenaica. The 4TH Indian Division was given the task of capturing Libyan Omar, Omar Nuova and Cova. The defences of these encampments had been well prepared; belts of wire and minefields encircled the perimeters. In the defended area were many shell-proof strong-points with excellent fields of fire.

Omar Nuova was the first to fall, after fierce fighting. The capture of Libyan Omar cost 3/1ST Punjabis, 102 casualties. Subedar Fateh Singh, Jemadar Bhag Singh, 28 other ranks and 1 follower were killed. In this action Subedar Fateh Singh, won posthumous award of I,O,M., and Lance-Naik Ujagar Singh and Sepoy Chhotu Singh were awarded the I.D.S.M. Lance-Naik Ujagar Singh had penetrated deep into the enemy position, and although wounded in arm and face, had led attack after attack with grenades taken from wounded and dead comrades.

On December, 20TH, 3/1ST Punjabis came up against a strong enemy position in the hills south of Giovanni Berta. Against the well-defended position it made no progress throughout the day. At dusk another company of the Battalion went in with the bayonet and overran the stubborn garrison, 111 prisoners being taken, including 11 officers, while 40 of the enemy lay dead on the field.

Orders now reached 4TH Indian Division to withdraw to the Gazala line and on 4TH, 3/1ST Punjabis, tired and worn, arrived at Acroma, and took up a defensive position some nine miles west of Acroma. After a stint of defensive duties at Tobruk, the Battalion left for Cyprus. April, 1943, saw 3/1ST Punjabis back in Palestine, where it was allotted the role of protecting the oil installations. On March 19TH, 3/1ST Punjabis embarked for Italy, where on 23RD, it took over the position on the Adriatic Sea. While advancing along the Tiber, 3/1ST Punjabis captured Montone from a Battalion of 14TH Jaeger Division, after a stiff fight during which Jemadar Bachan Singh was killed. The same day 3/1ST Punjabis advanced to attack the Colle Di Pozzo Ridge, two miles west of Montone. During the forty-eight hours of fighting near Colle Di Pozzo, 3/1ST Punjabis suffered 29 casualties, amongst who was Naik Gurnam Singh, who was awarded a posthumous I.O.M. for his daring leadership and initiative on 11TH July. In the pitch-black night his platoon had come up against a difficult cliff. While the platoon waited, he forced his way up the cliff, hauled up his section one by one and personally silenced a number of machine-guns located in a well-defended house. On the following day, while the company lay dangerously held up at the start-line under intense shell fire, he was the first to rise and lead the company in the attack until killed by an enemy shell.

1ST Punjab Regiment

76TH Punjabis (3/1ST)

The pursuit to Bibbiena continued against minor opposition in the beginning of September. Early in October 10TH Indian Division moved through torrential rain over roads in mud to the relief of 4TH Indian Division on the Adriatic front. The Division lost no time in coming into action, and on the very day of its arrival 3/1ST Punjabis were told to capture Ronconfreddo. During its capture of Ronconfreddo, Subedar Bhanwar Singh, with great initiative, led his company to capture half of the village. Ronconfreddo, which had been a thorn in the flesh to the whole Army's advance, had fallen. The pursuit continued. Cesana was the next objective, to which 3/1ST Punjabis advanced soon after the fall of Ronconfreddo. Despite continuous and heavy shelling and the stubborn resistance of the Germans, 3/1ST Punjabis secured Acquarola by the first light on October 17TH, and gradually battled its way through to occupy the strongly held German positions on the north and north-west. It repelled a strong German counter attack supported by armour. Despite heavy casualties the company held on to the position. The Germans had had enough and withdrew on 19TH. On the same day, 3/1ST Punjabis were relieved in the Acquarola position and swung west across the Savio River. Having chased the Germans as far as Forli, the Battalion advanced to a position one mile east of Pideura. On the very day of its arrival, 3/1ST Punjabis were given the task of capturing Qarrada and the Colombara Ridge. So fierce had been the battles that both sides mutually agreed to a truce so that the casualties could be evacuated. The 3/1ST Punjabis had suffered 165 casualties during the eight days on the Ridge. The task was decidedly the toughest assigned to it since its arrival in Italy.

The big offensive by the Eighth Army began in the middle of April, 1945. The 3/1ST Punjabis reached Malalbego on the Reno River. This was virtually the end of the pursuit and of the Battalion's operations in Italy and the Second World War. The 3/1ST Punjabis were the first Battalion of the Regiment to go into action in the Second World War and it fought in some of the fiercest battles of the campaigns in the Middle East and Italy. During its four years of war it sustained 1,651 casualties in battle.

After celebrating VE Day in northern Italy, 3/1ST Punjabis were ordered for peacekeeping duties on the Yugoslav Frontier. The people on the frontier were mainly Slaves who hated anything Fascist and were well in favour of joining Yugoslavia. However, the terms of the timely Alexander-Tito agreement, were vigorously enforced by 3/1ST Punjabis. The battalion arrived in India in December to contend with communal frenzy which had swept certain areas of the Punjab. The 3/1ST Punjabis spent most of the time patrolling these areas and kept the peace.

In 1947, 3/1ST Punjab Regiment was allocated to the new Pakistan Army. The Sikh soldiers from the battalion were transferred to the 2 Sikh, Indian Army.

1ST Punjab Regiment

82ND Punjabis (5/1ST)

The 82ND Punjabis were raised in 1788, as 29TH Madras Battalion. It was designated as 82ND Punjabis in 1903. The regiment started life in the old Madras Army of the British East India Company, which was largely responsible for the British conquest of south and central India. The men were mostly enlisted from South India and consisted of Muslims and Hindus. In 1903, the regiment was reconstituted with Sikhs, Punjabi Mussalmans, and Jats.

Ever since the annexation of the Punjab in 1849, the rugged mountains on the North-West Frontier had been the scene of continual hostile tribal activities and uprisings. This frontier therefore became an important security problem necessitating again and again the concentration of troops to deal with tribesmen who refused to acknowledge the authority of the Government of India. Towards the end of 1907, many tribes were seething with unrest and troops were moved up to the border as a precautionary measure. Among these were 82ND Punjabis. During the next five years 82ND Punjabis remained on the Frontier. The Regiment was still on the Frontier when the Bunerwals raided British territory early in 1914. The 1ST and 2ND Brigades from Pashawar and Nowshera were sent to deal with the situation and exact compensation. The 82ND Punjabis formed a part of 2ND Brigade and marched forty-two miles in thirty-six hours without sleep, along the slippery track, including ten miles of rough path in the dark, to the summit of the Malandarai Pass, which led into the Buner country. Immediately on arrival 82ND Punjabis were sent to burn the village of Zangi Khan. In the face of harassing fire, the village was surrounded and set on fire. The task accomplished, 82ND Punjabis withdrew to the camp at Rustam. At Rustam the regiment remained part of a small force to Piquet the passes into Buner until April 2ND, 1914, when it returned to Nowshera.

At the start of the World War One, although the regiment did not get the opportunity of fighting during 1914 and 1915, many of its officers and men went as reinforcements to other units and fought in decisive battles in the various theatres of war. The draft totalled 5 British officers and 577 other ranks, the better part of the strength of a Battalion.

In January 1916, 82ND Punjabis were dispatched to Mesopotamia, where they were engaged in the desperate British efforts to relieve the besieged garrison at Kut-al-Amara. The regiment suffered 223 casualties in the Battle of Dujaila Redoubt in March 1916. In this action Sepoy Kesar Singh of the Regiment was awarded the I.O.M., for his gallantry and initiative in leading his section under heavy fire after his commander was killed and for subsequently extricating the remaining men of the section from a difficult position though he himself was wounded.

The 82ND Punjabis, destined to share with 62ND Punjabis the trials and fortunes of the Kut-al-Amara relief operation and the subsequent advance on Baghdad. The first battle which the regiments fought together took place on March 8TH and 9TH, 1916, on the Dujaila Redoubt.

1ST Punjab Regiment

82ND Punjabis (5/1ST)

Both regiments commenced short advances over the flat plain, almost completely devoid of cover, in the face of Turkish gun fire as well as heavy machine-gun and rifle fire. So intense was the hostile fire that the assault died away within 200 yards of the enemy trenches. At midnight a withdrawal was ordered to Ora. During this bloody battle 82ND Punjabis lost heavily, suffering 223 casualties. In January 1917, it fought in the Battle of the Hai Salient and then took part in the British advance towards Baghdad. In the fierce fighting at Shumran, while crossing the River Tigris, the regiment again suffered heavy casualties. After capture of Baghdad on 15TH March, 82ND Punjabis remained employed on guard duties, first at Baghdad and then on the Persian frontier.

Subedar Hira Singh and Subedar Dalip Singh were awarded the I.D.S.M. for their conspicuous gallantry in Mesopotamia.

The 82ND Punjabis returned home in February 1919, and later that year participated in the Third Afghan War. The war was fought in the wake of the Great War, when Amanullah, Afghanistan's Amir (ruler), aided by Pakhtun (Pathan) tribal allies, and emboldened by an alliance with the new Bolshevik regime in Russia, took advantage of Britain's post-Great War weariness and nationalist unrest in India itself, to launch two surprise strikes into the North-West frontier region of British India in May 1919. The short-lived war that followed saw Britain check the thrusts and launch a counter strike in Baluchistan which took the town of Dakka. The war ended with Britain granted autonomy in foreign affairs to the Afghanis in the Treaty of Rawalpindi.

In 1922, 82nd Punjabis were grouped with 62ND, 66TH, 76TH and 84TH Punjabis, to form 1ST Punjab Regiment. The 82nd Punjabis was redesignated as 5TH Battalion, 1ST Punjab Regiment.

During the Second World War, at the Japanese invasion of Burma, 5/1ST Punjabis fought in a number of rear-guard actions, as the British retreated to India. During the battle of Shwegyin on March 11TH, 1942, the enemy fled across the Shwegyin Chaung at the south end of the town, many being killed in the stream by light machine-gun. An hour later, a company commanded by Dial Singh joined the battle after having done a long march from the Burma-Thailand border. Immediately on arrival he was detailed to capture the ferry at Maduak, which was effortlessly accomplished. A little later 5/1ST Punjabis took up position in and around Shwegyin and started to search the village, which yielded large quantities of rifles, shot-guns, ammunition and rations. In this fight 5/1ST Punjabis killed 50 Japanese and Burmans and captured 40 hostile Burmans and Thais at the cost of 21 casualties. Lance-Naik Surjan Singh was awarded the I.D.S.M. for his gallantry against the Japanese.

The battle of Yenangyaung, in April, had been a severe test of the Battalion's courage and fortitude. It had endured excessive physical hardships from the heat and the shortage of food and water and had sustained heavy casualties which included Subedar Bhagwan Singh and Jemadar Narain Singh.

1ST Punjab Regiment

82ND Punjabis (5/1ST)

On February 5TH, 5/1ST Punjabis were in defensive positions guarding the Mountbatten Bride, south-west of Bawli Bazaar. During the following week various tactical positions were occupied on the western slopes of the Mayu Range. 'B' Company was the first to contact the enemy on an independent mission and on February 10TH, while advancing to its objective, was held up by the Japanese in a strongly entrenched position. Major Weighill went forward to reconnoitre and was killed almost immediately. Subedar Gurbachan Singh carried on and silenced a post by courageously crawling forward and throwing a grenade. Further progress could not be made and the company, along with its dead and wounded, withdrew on the morning of 11TH. Major Weighill and five other ranks were killed and Jemadar Lall Singh and seven other ranks were wounded. For his gallant conduct in this action Subedar Gurbachan Singh was awarded the Military Cross.

On February 4TH, 1945, 5/1ST Punjabis joined 71ST Brigade, which encountered formidable opposition on its advance on Ramree Island. By February 9TH all organized resistance on the Island ceased.

On May 11TH, 5/1ST Punjabis left Syriam for Myaungtaung on the Prome road to link up with the troops of the Fourteenth Army driving south. A large number of Japanese parties were reported in this direction and it was planned by this move to cut off the enemy parties retreating east. On the very day of its arrival at Myaungtaung, a patrol commanded by Naik Mob Singh was sent to mop up an enemy party reported in the vicinity. While the patrol was crossing a paddy-field, it was fired upon from close range on three sides by machine-guns and almost all the men were wounded or pinned down. The patrol commander continued to offer resistance until the arrival of reinforcements under Subedar Bhikha Singh, the Second-in- Command of the company. The Subedar was the first to arrive at the spot, and throughout the rest of a hot and strenuous day, he and his men pursued and destroyed the enemy with the help of supporting arms. His gallantry won him the Military Cross and Naik Mob Singh was awarded the I.D.S.M. After a week of continuous hunting and extensive patrolling, 5/1ST Punjabis returned to India on June 17TH, 1945; this ended 5/1ST Punjabis' operations in Burma and in the Second World War. It had seen the trials and triumphs of the entire major campaigns in Burma; from the grim privations of the long retreat in 1942 to the victorious landings at Rangoon in May, 1945.

On August 17TH, the Japanese forces made an unconditional surrender to the allied forces. A few months after the end of the hostilities, 5/1ST Punjabis were selected to form part of 268TH Indian Infantry Brigade and arrived at Tattori in Japan for the occupational duties.

The 5/1ST Punjabis were still in Japan at the time of the Partition of the Indian sub-continent into India and Pakistan. On its return, the battalion was allotted to the Pakistan Army in 1947. The Sikh soldiers from the battalion were transferred to the 3 Sikh, Indian Army.

1ST Punjab Regiment

84TH Punjabis (10/1ST)

The 84TH Punjabis were raised at Vellore on 12TH August 1794, and became the 10TH (Training) Battalion, 1ST Punjab Regiment in 1922. The regiment had its antecedents in the old Madras Army of the British East India Company, which was largely responsible for the British conquest of south and central India. In 1810, it took part in the expeditions to Bourbon Island and Mauritius in the Indian Ocean. In the latter part of 19TH century, the regiment did not see much action, although it saw active service in Burma.

In 1902, the Battalion, now designated as 24TH Madras Infantry, was reconstituted with Sikhs, Punjabi Mussalmans and Rajputs. Next year, as a result of the reforms brought about in the Indian Army, the regiment's designation was changed to 84TH Punjabis.

During the first three years of the First World War, 84TH Punjabis remained deployed on the North West Frontier of India. Although 84TH Punjabis did not go overseas until late in the war, it sent reinforcements to many units already serving overseas, and these officers and men took part in many battles fought in the various theatres of war. From the outbreak of the war till March, 1917, 84TH furnished reinforcements of 10 British officers, 16 Indian officers, 1,187 rank and file and 25 followers.

In March 1917, 10/1ST Punjabis were dispatched to Mesopotamia. By March, 1917, the situation in Mesopotamia had completely changed in favour of the British, who after the occupation of Baghdad were pursuing the defeated Turks. Until February, 1918, 84TH Punjabis, with the rest of the Brigade, were employed on internal-security duties in Najaf and Hilla on the Euphrates. There were occasional columns sent out to troubled areas and once the whole Battalion was sent to Kura and then to Hilla to deal with disturbing elements.

In November 1918, it moved to Salonika in Greece to confront Bulgarian incursion into Greece. The campaign concluded with the surrender of Bulgaria on 30TH September 1918.

At the Bulgarian surrender 84TH Punjabis were ordered to the Russian Transcaucasia in support of the White Russian forces fighting the Bolsheviks. After the defeat of the White Russian forces by the Bolsheviks 84TH Punjabis were ordered to Turkey.

After spending 1919–20 in Turkey as part of the Allied occupation forces, it returned home in October 1920. In the reorganization of 1921, it was converted into a Training Battalion of 1ST Punjab Regiment. During the Second World War, 10/1ST Punjabis was converted into 1ST Punjab Regimental Centre.

In August 1947, at the independence and the partition of the Indian subcontinent in the sovereign states of India and Pakistan and the division of the army in 1947, The Regimental Centre, 1ST Punjab Regiment was allocated to Pakistan Army. The Sikh soldiers from the Regimental Centre were transferred to the Sikh Regiment, Indian Army

2ND Punjab Regiment

67TH Punjabis (1/2ND)

The 67TH Punjabis were raised at Trichonopoly by Captain Cooke in 1761 as 8TH Battalion Coast Sepoys. The men were mostly enlisted from South India. In 1902, the regiment was reconstituted with Sikhs, Punjabi Mussalmans and Rajputs In 1903, as a result of the reforms brought about in the Indian Army, the regiment's designation was changed to 67TH Punjabis. Henceforth, the regiment was constantly employed on the North-West Frontier of India.

On 7TH March 1915, while in Loralai, 67TH Punjabis received orders to proceed to Basra in Mesopotamia. While the regiment was at Basra it was decided to capture Nasiriyah, on the Euphrates, which during the prevailing flood season furnished the Turks with the only possible line of advance on Basra. Nasiriyah was important not only in size and situation but also because it was the capital of the warlike tribe of Muntifiq Arabs, whose depredations had become a serious source of annoyance. At Nasiriyah the enemy had made strong defensive preparations by building entrenchments and embankments on both sides of the River, and it was obvious that the place would fall only to a really determined attack. On 8TH July orders were received for 67TH Punjabis to embark for the Nasiriyah operations as a unit of 12TH Division. In the fighting which immediately ensued, 67TH Punjabis had one Indian officer and three men killed and 39 of all ranks wounded. This first attack was followed by a short period of consolidation in trenches.

On 24TH July the regiment was moved to the front-line trenches and attacked the Turkish positions. Seeing the attack was being held up by determined resistance, a company of the regiment was ordered to attack directly over a high embankment. The enemy brought heavy fire to bear against this attack. Captain Gribbon led the assault in a series of short rushes and then charged with the bayonet. This was too much for the Turks, who broke and fled across the crazy bridge, only to be shot down to a man as they set foot on it. The rest of the Turks at last realized that further resistance, even flight, was impossible and surrendered. In this action four guns were captured.

The Brigade then received orders to resume the attack and 67TH Punjabis were committed to an advance in the face of heavy oblique fire, at times almost enfilade, over more than 1,000 yards of dead flat ground, without support other than that afforded by a single machine-gun from the other side of the River and a naval 3-pounder gun from a River tug. But the attack was pressed home with such persistence that the morale of the Turks was shaken; and although the attacking force found their advance hampered by a bridge that had been destroyed, the Turks fortunately refrained from mounting a counter-attack. Their failure to counter-attack, allowed time for the rest of the Brigade to come up on the left of 67TH, which was able to bivouac for the night where it stood. On the 25TH a bridge was thrown over a creek and 12TH Brigade marched into Nasiriyah. During the fighting 67TH Punjabis proportion of killed and wounded was exceptionally high, there being 31 of all ranks killed and 36 wounded.

2ND Punjab Regiment

67TH Punjabis (1/2ND)

In October 1915, 67TH Punjabis moved to the Tigris River, where it left detachments at Qalat Saleh and Ali-eh-Gharbi. Towards the end of November, Headquarters and two companies of 67TH Punjabis were located at Kut-al-Amara and were besieged with other units of General Townshend's force, and finally taken prisoner by the Turks. Other two companies were on detached duty and thus avoided captivity and it formed a nucleus around which 67TH Punjabis were reconstituted with the aid of reinforcements. As soon the regiment had been built up to full strength it was made part of a movable column operating in the country surrounding Ali-el-Gharbi, which was its base.

On 18TH February 1917, 67TH Punjabis joined 37TH Brigade in the vicinity of Kut-al-Amara. The 37TH Brigade was ordered first to cross the River and then to cover the crossing of the rest of the Division. The crossing met with severe opposition and led to very heavy casualties, but it was successfully achieved. The following morning, after short bombardment, an attack was made by 36TH and 37TH Brigades, led by the Norfolks on the right 67TH Punjabis on the left. On the left there were many towers occupied by enemy snipers, with the lane between the buildings constantly swept by machine-gun fire. The 67TH Punjabis suffered such heavy casualties that the men were eventually ordered not to expose themselves, while maintaining effective fire upon the enemy's positions; meanwhile other troops were sent round in rear of the Turks, who were eventually dispersed and forced to retreat. The casualties sustained by 67TH Punjabis in this operation were 2 Indian officers, 38 Indian other ranks killed; and 5 British officers, 6 Indian officers and 154 Indian other ranks wounded.

As the Turks retreated from Shumran they blew up magazines and destroyed many stores and dumps. The retreat developed into a rout and the Turkish force degenerated into a mob which was harried all the way back to Ctesiphon. Their total losses, including prisoners, were estimated at 30,000. The repercussions of this defeat were felt by the Turkish forces in northern Persia, who were obliged to retire, with General Baratoff and his force in hot pursuit, until they reached a point about 167 miles from Baghdad. By that time British forces were 14 miles from the city. Then 67TH Punjabis moved to Ruz and thence in March 1918 to Tawilah. On 10TH October 1918 the Punjabis embarked at Basra for service in Salonika. Eventually they arrived back in India on 1ST October 1920, after five and half years of overseas service.

The following Sikh officers were awarded the I.D.S.M. for their conspicuous gallantry against the Turks in Mesopotamia. Subedar Lachman Singh, Havildar Indar Singh, Havildar Mahan Singh and Jemadar Khem Singh

In 1922, 67TH Punjabis were grouped with 69TH, 72ND, 74TH and 87TH Punjabis, to form 2ND Punjab Regiment. The regiment was redesignated as 1ST Battalion, 2ND Punjab Regiment.

2ND Punjab Regiment

67TH Punjabis ($1/2^{ND}$)

In February 1924, the newly designated $1/2^{ND}$ Punjab moved from Pashawar to Khirgi in South Waziristan. Shortly after arrival at Khirgi, a company went to the assistance of a company of $2/3^{RD}$ Sikh Pioneers, which had been pinned down by a large body of raiders, while trying to extricate their casualties. By nightfall the company had covered the Pioneers' withdrawal back to the camp successfully and extricated themselves without any casualties.

Lance-Naik Sadhu Singh and Naik Mangal Singh were awarded the I.D.S.M. for gallantry in this action.

In February 1936, $1/2^{ND}$ Punjab was ordered for service in Malaya. This involved a lengthy journey, by way of Calcutta and Rangoon, to Taiping in the State of Perak in Malaya. The main role of $1/2^{ND}$ Punjab was internal security, but in the event of hostilities its duties would include the defence of Blakang Mati Island at the entrance to Singapore Harbour and the civil aerodrome at Singapore. It returned to India 1939, the six months' leave on which the men then dispersed was interrupted by the outbreak of the Second World War. During the Second World War the Battalion served in Aden, Somaliland, Italian East Africa, Egypt and Italy.

In 1940 the Battalion was posted to Aden. On arrival the immediate task of $1/2^{ND}$ Punjab was to make numerous reconnaissances on the borders of the colony and to construct and wire defences against possible lines of landward attack. A month after the Battalion's arrival the whole balance of military power in the Middle East was radically upset by the collapse of France and Italy's intervention on the side of Germany.

The situation in British Somaliland was even more sinister. A major complication was the certain neutrality of French Somaliland. The plans for the defence of British Somaliland had been based on the assumption that the French troops, and in particular those garrisoning Djibouti, would operate against the left flank of any Italian advance from Eritrea. The Higher Command, located in Khartoum, had to plan for the defence of an immense area, against which the Italians could bring a numerical superiority in Italian and colonial troops. The chance of war was to make this corner of north-east Africa the first war theatre of $1/2^{ND}$ Punjab and on 29TH June 1940, it received orders to proceed to Berbera. During this initial phase of the operations in British Somaliland there could be no question of taking offensive against an enemy so superior in infantry and artillery. Active operations developed early in August 1940, and in view of the overwhelming strength of the enemy a temporary evacuation of British Somaliland had at that time been decided. The $1/2^{ND}$ Punjab was evacuated to Aden on 15TH August, 1940.

During this period, the British rounded up soldiers and governmental officials to evacuate them from the territory through Berbera. In total 7,000 people were evacuated and British Somaliland was briefly occupied by Italy.

2ND Punjab Regiment

67TH Punjabis (1/2ND)

In March 1941, the British forces from Aden, which included 1/2ND Punjab, recaptured the Somaliland Protectorate, after a six month's Italian occupation. The 1/2ND Punjabis had advanced on Berbera and captured it with little opposition. The Battalion had captured 8 Italian officers, between 40 and 50 Italian other ranks, a great many Italian Colonial troops and irregulars, and had hoisted the British flag over Government House. For their gallant services during the Somali campaign Havildar Agar Singh and Sepoy Attar Singh were mentioned in dispatches.

On 30TH June 1/2ND Punjab returned to Aden. The 1/2ND Punjab left Aden in July for Egypt. It was then sent to Alexandria, Egypt in July 1941. It spent the rest of the year on garrison duties and training in Egypt. In February 1942, it moved to Qatatba to become part of 161ST Indian Motor Brigade. In the summer of 1942, when Rommel was approaching Egypt, the brigade moved to the Tanta area of the Delta to dig defences. It returned to Qatatba after this but returned at once to the front to reinforce 5TH Indian Infantry Division. It arrived at 5TH Divisional HQ on Ruweisat Ridge on July 21ST and put in an attack on Ruweisat Ridge on July 21ST-22ND. The 1/2ND Punjab was detached to 9TH Indian Infantry Brigade on July 24TH for an attack at Dier-el-Shein. Then after a week to ten days, it returned to its original formation to rest and refit.

It left the brigade on August 23RD, 1942 in Egypt. 1943 the Battalion remained as a garrison unit in Egypt from August 23RD, 1942 until July 1943. One company was detached in Palestine on February 14TH, 1943. It then moved to Palestine in July 1943. Jemadar Amar Singh and Naik Jagat Singh were awarded the I.O.M. while Havildar Gurcharan Singh, and Lance-Naiks, Kishan Singh, Tulsa Singh and Harbans Singh, of the Battalion were awarded the I.D.S.M. for their gallantry in the Western Desert.

For the rest of the time the Battalion did garrison and security duties until in 1944 it was called upon to play its part in the northward advance through Italy. During its service in the Italian theatre 1/2ND Punjab formed part of 20TH Infantry Brigade of 10TH Indian Division, except for a short period when it left its Brigade for detached duty. It first went into action at Ortona in May 1944. Here it carried out intensive patrolling duties which resulted in heavy casualties. For his leadership and personal gallantry in this action Jemadar Pritam Singh was awarded the Military Cross.

On 5TH September 1944, an action was fought by 1/2ND Punjab around Modina and Pratella. Both these places were commanding heights, strongly held by the enemy. After preliminary manoeuvres, the main attack and the high ground of Pratella was captured. Twelve Germans were killed and two taken prisoner during the process of consolidation. A counter-attack on Pratella was checked. It was followed by an hour's fire from guns and mortars and this in turn was followed by another infantry attack. This also was repulsed.

2ND Punjab Regiment

67TH Punjabis (1/2ND)

Other attacks were launched by the enemy, by which time Modina had been assaulted and taken by a company of 1/2ND Punjab. During its service in the Italian theatre, the Battalion fought a series of further actions at, Donato, Vignola, and Sogliano. The decorations awarded for operations included: a posthumous Indian Order Merit to Subedar Kehar Singh, Military Cross to Subedar Sunda Singh, and Military Medal to Lance-Naik Rai Singh.

On 27TH Jemadar Gurdit Singh took out a fighting patrol of about platoon strength, his orders being 'to raid known enemy positions in the Casa Nuova, to kill as many Germans as possible, and to secure identifications.' Covered by the bank of the Sillaro River, his patrol worked its way to within 50 yards of the enemy position before fire was opened on it. At this point another enemy party, estimated at about twenty strong, was seen moving down the Sillaro Ridge to take the Patrol in the rear. The Jemadar successfully disengaged himself from the action to his front and engaged the new party threatening his rear, inflicting several casualties and causing it to withdraw in disorder. One of the most strenuous actions in the Battalion's long history was fought on 20TH and 21ST April 1945, on the banks of River Idice against crack German troops belonging to 4TH Para troop Division. After this battle there was no further organized resistance by the Germans in the Italian theatre. Havildar Baldev Singh and Havildar Gurbux Singh were awarded I.D.S.M. for their conspicuous gallantry in Italy

In August 1947, at the independence and the partition of the Indian subcontinent in the sovereign states of India and Pakistan and the division of the army 2ND Punjab remained part of India's Army. Half the strength of the Battalion being Punjabi Mussalman opted for Pakistan.

The 1ST Battalion, 2ND Punjab Regiment was transferred to the Parachute Regiment and designated as 1ST Battalion, the Parachute Regiment (Punjab).

69TH Punjabis (2/2ND)

The regiment was raised in 1759 as 10TH Battalion Coast Sepoys. The men were mostly enlisted from South India and consisted of Muslims and Hindus. In 1902, the Battalion was reconstituted with Sikhs, Punjabi Mussalmans, and Dogras Next year; the regiment's designation was changed to 69TH Punjabis. At the outbreak of the First World War in 1914, 69TH Punjabis, part of 29TH Indian Brigade, were on the way to Egypt. When the convoy was approaching Aden, the orders were received for 29TH Brigade, to attack the Turkish Fort of Turba, on the mainland opposite the island of Perim. On 10TH November the Brigade affected a landing at Sheikh Saad. The 69TH and 89TH Punjabis provided the forward element of the landing force. After a fight which lasted about 10 hours, the Turks abandoned the fort and retired inland, leaving behind only few wounded soldiers but a considerable quantity of stores and guns.

2ND Punjab Regiment

69TH Punjabis (2/2ND)

Only one double company and machine-guns of 69TH became actually engaged, the rest of the regiment landing later. The machine-gunners were particularly commended for the way in which they carried out their task of providing covering fire from exposed positions. Naik Labh Singh of the Machine Gun Section was awarded an I.D.S.M., and later in the war rose to the rank of Subedar. Next morning 23RD Sikh Pioneers blew up the Turkish fortifications and guns and in the afternoon the Brigade rejoined the convoy in the Gulf of Suez. The Brigade arrived in Port Said on 20TH November and for the next six months the regiment was engaged in the defence of the Suez Canal. Turkey had allied herself with Germany and it was almost certain that the Canal would be the objective of a Turkish attack. The 69TH Punjabis were at Qantara when the first attack developed. The Turkish attacking force was about the strength of a brigade and after crossing the Sinai desert made, on 3RD February 1915, a singularly unsuccessful onslaught on the outpost line.

On 25TH April, 29TH Brigade sailed for Gallipoli, landing on 1ST May at W Beach. The 69TH Punjabis remained in reserve during its fortnight's stay on the Peninsula and only the Machine Gun Section became actively engaged. On 6TH May this section supported an attack made by 14TH Sikhs and on the conclusion of the attack was subsequently attached to 89TH Punjabis in the trenches. During their short stay in Gallipoli, 69TH had 89TH Punjabis were withdrawn for being predominately Muslim, as there were fears that they might have qualms fighting the fellow Muslims of the Ottoman Empire.

On 15TH May, 69TH embarked for France and disembarked on 30TH May. After spending three months in the trenches the regiment participated in the battle of Loos. The British offensive was part of the attempt by the Allies to break through the German defences in Artois and Champagne and restore a war of movement. During this battle the regiment was in the front line and emerged with fewer than 250 effectives after going into action with 600 officers and men. Subedar Major Jogindar and Lance-Naik Nidham Singh were awarded the I.O.M. for their conspicuous gallantry at Neuve Chapelle while Havildar Gurdit Singh, Havildar Bhulla Singh, Naik Punna Singh were awarded the I.D.S.M.

On 3RD December, 69TH Punjabis embarked at Marseilles for Egypt. It remained in Egypt for only a few weeks, spent in digging trenches at Ayun Moussa for the Canal defence scheme, and sailed for Aden on 12TH January 1916. They served in the Aden Field Force for over 3 years. It took part in most of the operations against the Turks' forces under Said Pasha and in manning the outposts for the defence of Aden. It also took its turn at providing detachments, for periods of three months at a time, at Steamer Point and the Crater, both in Aden and in the islands of Perim and Kamaran. The operations consisted mainly of periodical attacks on Turkish outposts and strong points covering Lahej, which was Said Pasha's Headquarters.

2ND Punjab Regiment

69TH Punjabis (2/2ND)

On June 1917, as the enemy began to advance, Lance-Naik Prabhu Singh, under the covering fire of the cavalry and levies, led a spirited charge and although outnumbered three to one, drove off the Turks and recovered the bodies of his comrades. For this gallant act and for his fine leadership Lance-Naik Prabhu Singh was awarded the I.D.S.M.

After the Armistice the Turkish forces came into Aden to surrender, and 69TH Punjabis took part in disarming them. The regular Turkish troops exceeded the strength of a British division, and in addition there were renegade Arabs and Somalis, and the garrison of the Yemen with their wives and families. On 19TH April 1919, after 4 and half years of continuous service overseas, 69TH Punjabis left Aden for India.

In less than a month after arriving in India from wartime duties overseas, 69TH Punjabis received orders to re-mobilize. It left Agra on 20TH May 1919, for Hangu on the North-West Frontier, whence it moved out as part of Brigadier-General Dyer's column for the relief of Thal, which had been invested by the Afghans. On 1ST June Dyer decided to attack the enemy who were holding the heights south-east of Thal Fort; their strength as estimated at 3,000 with 3 guns. The 69TH Punjabis had provided the advanced guard and part of the Piqueting troops earlier in the day and was now deputed to lead the attack. The attack was pressed home with such determination that, in spite of heavy hostile sniping, the heights were cleared within half an hour; the enemy were in full retreat, providing excellent targets for the machine-guns in Thal Fort. The two remaining companies of 69TH quickly came up to consolidate, and the leading companies pushed on at once to a position from which patrols were sent out to harass the enemy's withdrawal; these patrols found a camp, large enough for a brigade, which the enemy had hastily evacuated.

From 16TH to 20TH July, 69TH Punjabis took part in successful punitive operations against the Kabul Khel Wazirs, and were again commended for good work. From November onwards 69TH Punjabis had to provide an escort for the train running between Thal and Kohat. On 1ST December, a force of local tribesmen, estimated at 200, attacked the train in a cutting about three miles from Thal. The train was first derailed by an obstruction placed on the line. From hills only 300 yards away the tribesmen then opened a murderous fire on the escort, who were travelling in the open at the front of the train. The escort immediately returned the fire, but when most of their ammunition had been expended, they were fired on suddenly from the top of the cutting, directly above the train. When every round of ammunition had been expended, the survivors of the escort fixed bayonets, and awaited the arrival of the enemy. Most of the escort was killed. Survivors of the tragedy spoke with enthusiastic praise for the gallant fight put up by the men of the escort against the overwhelming odds with which they were faced. For this action Havildar Dhana Singh was awarded the I.D.S.M.

2ND Punjab Regiment

69TH Punjabis (2/2ND)

After the First World War, 69TH Punjabis were redesignated as 2ND Battalion, 2ND Punjab Regiment. Under its new designation 2/2ND Punjab Regiment continued to serve on the North-West Frontier at Ladha, until the post was evacuated on 1ST February 1923. The battalion, as a part of 9TH Brigade, then proceeded to Tauda China, for operations against the Mahsuds. It continuously mounted punitive expeditions against the turbulent tribesmen on the North-West Frontier. During one operation, Naik Mangal Singh was awarded the I.D.S.M for his gallantry and endurance in continuing to command his machine-gun after being wounded in the head.

The 2/2ND Punjab Regiment was still serving on the Frontier, when the Second World War broke out on 3RD September 1939. When the war broke out, a portion of the Indian Army was already fully occupied with operations against some tribes on the North-West Frontier. At this period the main location of operations was South Waziristan, where the trouble was being fomented by a mullah known as the Din Faqir. The most important task at the time for 2/2ND Punjab Regiment was the rather arduous one of intercepting raiding gangs directed by the Din Faqir. Early in the spring of 1940, 2/2ND Punjab Regiment moved up to Wana and took part with the Wana Brigade in successful punitive operations against the tribesmen at Kotkai. In addition to its normal duties of patrolling and convoying, Piqueting hills and closing passes, all which frequently resulted in actual fighting. The 2/2ND Punjab also provided trained personnel for the considerable expansion of the Indian Army which followed the outbreak of war.

A new threat developed on the eastern frontiers of India, as a result of penetration by the Japanese. In June 1942, after having spent nearly 7 years continuously on the North-West Frontier, 2/2ND Punjab Regiment was ordered to join 53RD Brigade in the newly formed 25TH Division. After a short spell in Ceylon, 25TH Division was ordered to Burma. In March 1944, 25TH Division, moved to hold part of the front of 15TH Corps during the hot weather, so as to give the battle-weary troops some rest. As soon as this move started, the Japanese launched a second offensive, this time towards Assam. This new offensive compelled 53RD Brigade the task of taking over the Tunnels area, and on 11TH April 2/2ND Punjab Regiment took up position in the area of the East Tunnel. Here it became involved almost immediately in severe fighting, and for their first 10 days, the men were harassed ceaselessly by the enemy's fire and vigorous night patrolling.

In early February 1944, the Japanese found themselves encircled by the Indian 26TH and British 36TH Divisions. The Indians with the two frontline British divisions re-established contact with the Japanese and went on the immediate offensive in the Mayu area. In fierce fighting which ensued, the 2/2ND Punjab Regiment drove through the Japanese Maungdaw position.

2ND Punjab Regiment

69TH Punjabis (2/2ND)

Fighting continued in the Mayu area through May, but with the British about to continue on to Akyab, they were obliged to break off the attack to send reinforcements to the Imphal area. Nonetheless, for the first time in Burma, British forces had met and decisively defeated a major Japanese attack. With victory in the Arakan, the tide had decisively turned in Burma. By 26TH February all the companies of 2/2ND Punjab Regiment had returned to Akyab and a month later the Battalion sailed for India, arriving on 31ST March after a year in the Arakan. The 2/2ND Punjab Regiment had sustained 63 killed and 317 of all ranks wounded for their fighting during the Arakan campaign in Burma.

On arrival in India, the men were put through a strenuous course of training for operations in Malaya, where in spite of the Japanese surrender the local situation was still uncertain. In October 2/2ND Punjab Regiment was sent to Kuantan, with orders to maintain internal security in a large area on the east coast of Malaya. There still remained a small party of Japanese to be dealt with. The bulk of the Battalion's work involved clearing the country of an irregular anti-Japanese force, which was interfering with the re-establishment of ordinary civil administration in many of the less accessible areas. This was perhaps the most satisfying job 2/2ND Punjab Regiment ever did. It was responsible for the rehabilitation of 250 miles of the east coast to a depth of 100 miles inland. The condition of the inhabitants was appalling, but by the time the Battalion left they were once again a thriving and healthy community. The 2/2ND Punjab Regiment remained in Kuala Lumpur until September 1946, when it left Malaya and proceeded to Lahore, in the Punjab. Here, after a strenuous and prolonged campaign, all ranks were enabled to have a well-deserved rest and the arrival of a number of young recruits permitted the release of an equal number of older and war-weary men.

In August 1947, at the independence and the partition of the Indian subcontinent in the sovereign states of India and Pakistan and the division of the army 2ND Punjab remained part of India's Army. Battalion's Punjabi Mussalman personnel opted for Pakistan.

The 2/2ND Punjab Regiment was transferred the Brigade of Guards and designated, 1ST Battalion, Brigade of Guards (2 Punjab).

72ND Punjabis (3/2ND)

The regiment could trace their origins to 1759, when they were raised as 16TH Battalion Coast Sepoys. The regiment had its antecedents in the old Madras Army of the British East India Company, which was largely responsible for the British conquest of south and central India. The men were mostly enlisted from South India and consisted of Muslims and Hindus. In 1902, the Battalion was reconstituted with Sikhs, Punjabi Mussalmans, and Dogras. In 1903, the regiment's designation was changed to 72ND Punjabis. The regiment's first battle was the Battle of Sholinghur in 1781, during the Second Anglo-Mysore War.

2ND Punjab Regiment

72ND Punjabis (3/2ND)

During the Indian Mutiny of 1857 they were stationed in Hong Kong and Singapore. Their next action was during the Third Burmese War. With the defeat of King Thibaw Min, the regiment remained in Burma. In 1887 the gradual withdrawal from Burma of the regular military garrisons began, but the country was still very unsettled. So it was decided that a part of the Madras Army should be converted into local Burma Battalions. One of the Battalions selected for this purpose was 3RD Battalion of the regiment; its title was changed to 2ND Burma Battalion. The class composition was changed from Madrassis to Punjabis, the latter included Sikhs and Punjabi Mussalmans. Shortly after the regiment had been thus reconstituted, it was sent to man posts along the Chindwin River, south of Manipur and east of the Chin Hills. Since the annexation of Upper Burma there had been continuous strife between the Burmese and the Chins, the later regularly raiding the plains during the cold-weather months. The Burmese occasionally retaliated by expeditions into the Chin Hills. The Burmese having now become the Queen's subjects, it was obvious the activities of the Chins would have to be checked. For the operations near Manipur which followed, Lieutenant Grant was awarded the Victoria Cross and fifty of the Indian other ranks who had volunteered to accompany him on his particularly dangerous mission were awarded the I.O.M. In May 1890, Subedar Gopal Singh, (a Sikh), took over the duties of Subedar-Major of the regiment from Subedar–Major Veerswami (a Madrassi). During a long and distinguished career in the Army Subedar-Major Gopal Singh had earned the I.O.M. and also the Order of British India with the title of Bahadur.

During 1892 the regiment remained on garrison duty, with Headquarters at Haka and detachments at various other posts scattered around Burma. In 1893 it moved to Rawran and Gangaw, and during 1895 and 1896 was quartered at Mandalay. While the regiment was at Mandalay its composition was altered to two double companies of Sikhs, one of Punjabi Mussalmans and one of Pathans. The conversion of the regiment from Madrassis to Punjabis antedated that of the other regiments by thirteen years. While quartered at Tlhayetmyo in Burma in 1904, 2ND Burma Battalion had its designation changed to 72ND Punjabis. In 1908 the regiment moved to Rangoon, furnishing a detachment at Port Blair in the Andaman Islands. Its long service in Burma soon ended and it was posted back to India on 30TH December 1908. Here it remained until the end of 1910, when it was posted to Dera Ismail Khan on the North-West Frontier. Regimental Headquarters remained at Dera Ismail Khan until 1913, detachments being provided at various posts further west, notably at Jandola, Zam, Jatta, and Drazinda. Apart from the normal alarms and excursions of Frontier service, one rather noteworthy event occurred during the regiment's stay in this part of the Frontier. In the area in which 72ND Punjabis was then stationed there was at that time a famous Mahsud outlaw named Musa Khan.

2ND Punjab Regiment

72ND Punjabis (3/2ND)

On 2ND May the gang of Mahsuds under the leadership of Musa Khan made a surprise attack on a party of 72ND Punjabis, who were marching from Khajuri Kach to Nili Kach. The first volley fired by the Mahsuds killed 3 of the advanced guard and wounded many of the others. The butt of Lance-Naik Pakhar Singh's rifle had been smashed by a bullet, and he lay low and allowed Musa Khan to come close to him. He then shot him dead and took his rifle. The rest of the party then drove off the attackers, and the march continued. Lance-Naik Pakhar Singh received the I.O.M. for his services; Lance-Naik Bishan Singh, who also did valuable work, received the I.D.S.M.

On the outbreak of the First World War in August 1914, 72ND Punjabis was stationed in Pashawar, on the North West Frontier of India. While engaged in various Frontier operations, it was called upon to supply trained personnel for new units that were being formed. It also supplied drafts to regular units serving in overseas theatres. Eventually 72ND Punjabis were ordered for service in Egypt. They disembarked at Suez on 10TH March 1918 and went into camp at Tel-el-Kebir. Then they proceeded to Palestine and were sent into the line immediately. On 28TH July, they were called upon to carry out a night raid on a ridge held by about 100 Turks with 3 machine guns.

The raiding party consisted of 3 Indian officers and 140 Sikhs. When the raiding party was 150 yards from the enemy trenches it was caught in a barrage of artillery and machine gun fire. The soldiers gallantly pushed on with great determination; a few succeeded in getting through the enemy wire and right up to the enemy defences, but they were too few to be effective, and eventfully aborted the raid. During the final operations against the Turks, 72ND Punjabis helped to capture El Tireh, a stoutly fortified village, where the enemy offered a determined resistance. On the conclusion of the First World War the Battalion was employed on garrison duties until 1921, first in Palestine and afterwards in Egypt. The following Sikh soldiers were awarded the I.D.S.M. for their conspicuous gallantry in Palestine; Jemadar Phuman Singh, Lance-Naik Jagat Singh and Sepoy Kishen Singh of the regiment were awarded the I.O.M. in Egypt, while Havildar Bhagat Singh, Lance-Naik Sohan Singh, Sepoy Hari Singh and Sepoy Gurdas Singh were awarded the I.D.S.M. for their gallantry in Palestine.

In 1922, 72ND Punjabis became 3RD Battalion, 2ND Punjab Regiment. In 1936, a revolt broke out in Waziristan, 3/2ND Punjab was part of the force, which put down the revolt, in which Lance-Naik Sadhu Singh and Naik Mangal Singh were awarded the I.D.S.M. for their gallantry in action.

During the Second World War, the battalion served Italian East Africa, Egypt, Burma, Singapore and Dutch East Indies. In East Africa 3/2ND Punjab served in 5TH Indian Division. The Indian 5TH Infantry Division was sent from India in early August 1940 to the Sudan to reinforce the British forces which had been attacked by Italian forces in Eritrea.

2ND Punjab Regiment

72ND Punjabis (3/2ND)

In Italian East Africa the 3/2ND Punjab Regiment did not become actively engaged as a complete Battalion until the end of January 1941. For some months before that time the Battalion had been stationed at Gebeit on the plateau above Port Sudan, engaged principally in training. Latterly this training had become more intensive, as it was expected that the Italian Colonial Army in Eritrea and Abyssinia would attempt to advance northwards. On 17TH January 1941, the enemy slipped out of Kassala. The 29TH Brigade with 3/2ND Punjab Regiment immediately headed for Tesseni, which was occupied on the following day without any encounter with the enemy. The Brigade then fought its way towards Barentu, and 3/2ND Punjab Regiment went into action at Gogni on 26TH January. They continued in action throughout the day, until the enemy withdrew. By 1ST February the advance still continued, though more slowly, for the enemy put up a stubborn resistance. An attack made on that day by 3/2ND Punjab Regiment was checked by the enemy light tanks. Pressure, however, was still kept up on the enemy; the garrison of Barentu steadily lost ground and during the night of 1/2ND February evacuated the place altogether. This evacuation was very hurried; the enemy left behind a great deal of equipment as well as a number of wounded in the hospitals. The advancing British forces captured field kitchens containing food ready prepared. For his services in the rather stiff action preceding the evacuation, a young Sepoy of 3/2ND Punjab Regiment, Kishan Singh, was awarded the I.D.S.M.

The advance on Keren then began. The 3/2ND Punjab Regiment played an important part in the battle for Keren, which was a very hard-fought action. The key to the pass into the plain of Keren was Fort Dologorodoc, which commanded the road through the gorge; it was captured by 9TH Brigade of 5TH Division. The 3/2ND Punjab was ordered to capture two heights, Zeban Major and Zeban Minor. They met with stiff opposition from the fire of automatic weapons and from a battery of 75-mm field guns firing over open sights, and the assault was held up. Meanwhile the enemy put in a stiff counter-attack, which was beaten off with heavy casualties on both sides. By this time 3/2ND Punjab Regiment became pinned down by heavy and accurate fire from artillery and automatic weapons. For 4 days under continuous fire 3/2ND Punjab Regiment hung on to its precarious position. During this action, for supplying the isolated Battalion and for his coolness and courage, Havildar Gurcharan Singh was awarded the I.D.S.M. Eventually the situation became so desperate that the Battalion had to be supplied by air. After 4 days of this ordeal 3/2ND Punjab Regiment was relieved and withdrew to comparative safety near Fort Dologorodoc.

During this prolonged action casualties among officers had left Jemadar Dhera Singh in command of 'C' Company. His bearing throughout the whole trying period was subsequently recognized by the award of I.O.M.

2ND Punjab Regiment

72ND Punjabis (3/2ND)

On 25TH March, 3/2ND Punjab Regiment mounted an attack on Railway Ridge in full daylight. The capture of Railway Ridge undoubtedly contributed greatly towards the final capture of Keren. For this resolute and successful attack on the Railway Ridge, Jemadar Amar Singh was awarded the I.O.M. for his coolness and courage. The 3/2ND Punjab Regiment held the Ridge for 3 days under heavy shell-fire and repeated counter attacks, thus enabling the Sappers to come up and clear the road blocks, a task which they successfully accomplished, although it was performed under heavy artillery and mortar fire. Once the road blocks had been cleared the British tanks came trundling through and Keren fell shortly afterwards.

On 28TH March, 29TH Brigade was lorried forward to Ad Teclesan. After a short reconnaissance 3/2ND Punjab Regiment attacked, carrying objectives ahead of the road blocks, which the Sappers once again cleared. Next day the Battalion followed up the enemy rapidly and by outflanking movement seized and secured the heights of Ad Teclesan. Early the following morning an enemy party came out with a white flag and surrendered Asmara, the capital of Eritrea; the operations in Eritrea were thus concluded. The 3/2ND Punjab Regiment did not play any further active part in the operations which resulted in the capitulation by the Duke of Acosta and the surrender of his garrison of over 4,000, and so far as further fighting was concerned the East African campaign was over.

The 29TH Indian Infantry Brigade was detached from 5TH Indian Division, after spending some time in the vicinity of Suez and moved early in September to the Western Desert. At the end of September the Brigade left for Giarabub, a small oasis about 200 miles due south of Bardia and about 100 miles west of the Qattara Depression. In the middle of October, the Brigade formed part of the Oasis Group, its role being to guard the dumps and landing-grounds, to harass the enemy as much as possible and to hold its positions in the event of attack. As a preliminary measure, transport activity was increased between Siwa and Giarabub and dummy camps were erected so as to make it appear that far greater forces were in the locality than were actually present. In addition to these arrangements, an attack was to be made on Gialo, more than 200 miles west by south of Giarabub.

On 21ST November a detachment of 'E Force' moved swiftly forward to the outpost of Agheila, west-north-west of Gialo. The detachment consisted of armoured cars, a troop of artillery and a Company of the 3/2ND Punjab. The main body of the Force was to follow and be prepared to move straight through to Gialo by nightfall. Another Company of 3/2ND Punjab was to move on Jakheira, another outpost; after capturing it, the Company was to go on Gialo. Agheila was successfully captured. The advance on Jakheira and the march of the main body was delayed by very bad going through soft sand and scrub.

2ND Punjab Regiment

72ND Punjabis (3/2ND)

The troops for the capture of Gialo covered 10 to 12 miles to their assembly point about 3,000 yards from the edge of the Oasis. The attack began with the armoured cars and at the same time a Company of 3/2ND Punjab Regiment moved to create a diversion towards El Libba and the Gialo aerodrome. The armoured cars came under heavy fire from Breda guns, but destroyed one aeroplane on the ground. In the meantime the other leading companies of 3/2ND Punjab Regiment had moved up through the soft heavy ground to a line 150 yards beyond the edge of the Oasis. Here they came under heavy fire from a series of large mounds covered by bush and it was obvious that almost every mound held a machine gun or a Breda. Soon after sunset, two companies of 3/2ND Punjab Regiment crept forward silently and, covered by armoured cars, captured the mounds one by one with hand-grenades and the bayonet. Soon the fort was attacked and captured with hand-grenades, tommy-guns and the bayonet. Straightaway they captured about thirty depressed looking Italian prisoners. Inside the Presidio they found about fifteen officers and seventy Italian other ranks, which looked as if they were just about to sit down to a very good dinner and all surrendered without resistance. In the meantime another force, which included a company of 3/2ND Punjab Regiment, had captured Jakheira with fifty prisoners, two heavy Bredas and several light Bredas. During the Gialo operations about 700 Italians had been captured and these were evacuated with the British and Indian wounded. Among the captured Italians were six bakers and cooks, who were retained with the British forces.

On the conclusion of the Gialo operation, Lance-Naik of 3/2ND Punjab Regiment received the I.D.S.M. Jemadar Dhera Singh, already wearing the I.O.M. for his services in Eritrea, won the rare distinction of the First Class of the I.O.M.; his daring and utter contempt for danger had been an inspiration to all.

During the following months 3/2ND Punjab Regiment was involved in unceasing desert warfare, at 'The Kennels', El Adem, and Baguush. On 25TH June, 3/2ND Punjab Regiment were given the task of stopping the enemy on the Mersa Matruh-Sidi Hamza minefield. Towards evening the German tanks attacked. Without mines and with only a few anti-tank guns, 'E Force' was soon overrun. Lieutenant Bhag Singh also managed to extricate some men of the Headquarters Company and after marching along the coast throughout the night, made contact and joined up with patrols of 12TH Lancers.

In August the remnants of the Battalion were collected at Mena. For some time there seemed to be a danger of its being disbanded and amalgamated with another Punjabi Battalion, as it seemed to be impossible to draw on trained reinforcements in sufficient numbers to build 3/2ND Punjab Regiment up to strength. There was a timely arrival of a large batch of reinforcements and they responded to training sufficiently well to play their part later on in the jungles of Burma and Java.

2ND Punjab Regiment

72ND Punjabis (3/2ND)

The 5TH Indian Division was moved back to India in 1943; 3/2ND Punjab, which had recently been converted to a machine-gun Battalion, arrived at Meerut in May of that year. The 3/2ND Punjab Regiment then moved to Burma and was originally sent to the Arakan. In March 1944, the men, guns, mules and jeeps of 5TH Division were flown 400 miles over mountains and jungles from the Arakan to Imphal.

On 16TH May 1944, at Kangla Tonbi in Burma, the Punjabis clashed with the Japanese. Both Companies engaged suffered considerable losses. Among the killed was Subedar Dhera Singh, having twice been awarded the I.O.M. in the Western Desert. For his gallantry in these actions Subedar Ram Singh was awarded the Military Cross

Another contact with the Japanese on 14TH September resulted in a short but fierce action, which cost the Punjabis six killed and six wounded. The killed included the Company Commander, Ram Singh M.C. Also Subedar Pritam Singh, whose gallant conduct on that day was followed by a posthumous award of I.O.M.

On 16TH September 1944, at the commencement of the operation against the Japanese rear guard at Tongzang in Burma, Major Bhag Singh was sent with his Company to cut the Imphal-Tiddim road in the area of Tutee. By skilful navigation, mostly at night over 3 miles and a 4,000 feet descent and climb, Major Bhag Singh led his Company through thick jungle over an un-recced Nullah crossing to the appointed position. There he positioned his men on the escape route of approximately 100 of the enemy. The following night the enemy, forced to withdraw, ran into the Company position and finding their way blocked prepared to attack it. Their determined attack was repulsed and the enemy left behind twelve dead, including two officers. The aim of this skilful and difficult operation was to separate two portions of the enemy rear guard and finally to force the withdrawal of some 200 disorganised Japanese soldiers, which was successfully carried out. Throughout this operation Major Bhag Singh had displayed outstanding leadership and determination and he was awarded the Military Cross.

Opposition was next met on 22ND September at Tongzang, where about 100 Japanese were strongly entrenched. Constant harassing fire and aggressive patrolling compelled the Japanese to withdraw and they were pursued to Phaisi Lui. At this point the Dogras passed through along the main road and 3/2ND Punjab Regiment was ordered to carry out an encircling movement, with the object of seizing the road south of Tiddim. This movement was made with the support of a section of mountain guns.

On 28TH September a company cleared Bumzang and then advanced on Haupi. The small garrison of the village remained unaware of the company's presence until 30TH September, when a strong fighting patrol took them completely by surprise, killing some of them and putting others to flight.

2ND Punjab Regiment

72ND Punjabis (3/2ND)

The advance continued on Valum, which was cleared of the Japanese and then a small hillock known as Babu was fiercely attacked on two occasions. On both occasions the attacks were driven off and the attackers lost heavily. During November Lieutenant-Colonel Lakhinder Singh was appointed the commander of the Battalion, but was detached shortly on staff duties.

The 3/2ND Punjab Regiment continued the pursuit of the retreating Japanese, until their unconditional surrender on September 2ND 1945. The 5TH Division was immediately ordered to Singapore. The task allotted to it was to disarm the surrendered Japanese, to assist in the collection and repatriation of Allied prisoners-of-war and to maintain law and order. The 3/2ND Punjab Regiment did not stay long in Singapore. Owing to the deteriorating situation in Java, it embarked for that country in on 29TH October and disembarked at Surabaya on 2ND November. During the Indonesian campaign, all ranks played their part in suppressing the Indonesian aspirations of independence from Dutch colonists. They carried out this difficult and often thankless task, in which some brave men who had fought right thorough the Burma campaign lost their lives.

On 23RD November 1945, during an attack in Ngemplak area of Surabaya in Java, two sections of the leading platoon of Subedar Kartar Singh's company, of which he was second in command, were pinned down to the ground by enemy automatic fire from two strong concrete bunkers. Subedar Kartar Singh dashed forward from Company Headquarters, under very heavy fire, to take charge of the situation. He then, at very great risk to himself, carried out a personal reconnaissance before leading the third section of the platoon in an outflanking movement, which culminated in a magnificent charge onto the enemy position. While leading this extremely gallant charge Subedar Kartar Singh fell severely wounded in the stomach. From where he lay, he continued to shout words of encouragement to his men until they had over-run the position. He refused to be evacuated until he was certain the platoon could continue its advance without him. Subedar Kartar Singh's outstanding leadership, utter disregard for his own safety and devotion to duty earned Subedar Kartar Singh an immediate Military Cross on 23RD November 1945. Havildar Sardhara Singh was murdered by Indonesian insurgents in Java and was awarded the posthumous I.O.M. The 3/2ND Punjab Regiment's embarrassing and highly unprofitable duties in Java ended finally on 5TH May 1946, when it left Surabaya for India.

In August 1947, at the independence and partition of the Indian subcontinent in the sovereign states of India and Pakistan and the division of the army, 2ND Punjab remained part of India's Army. Half the strength of the Battalion being Punjabi Mussalman opted for Pakistan. The third Battalion still continues as part of the Punjab Regiment, with the class composition of Sikhs and Dogras.

2ND Punjab Regiment

74TH Punjabis (4/2ND)

The 74TH Punjabis was raised in 1776, as 14TH Carnatic Battalion. The regiment had its antecedents in the old Madras Army of the British East India Company, which was largely responsible for the British conquest of south and central India.

In 1902, the Battalion was reconstituted with Sikhs, Punjabi Mussalmans and Dogras. Next year, as a result of the reforms brought about in the Indian Army, the regiment's designation was changed to 74ND Punjabis.

On 5TH August 1914, 74TH Punjabis received orders for the defence of Hong Kong. Ten platoons proceeded immediately to the defence of the eastern sector and six to those of the western sector. The 74TH Punjabis were then ordered to send Headquarters and eight platoons to Peking and Tientsin. Orders were then received for the contingent at Tientsin to proceed and to relieve 36TH Sikhs at Tsingtao, one of the German concessions in China. From Tsingtao the platoons escorted back to Hong Kong a small party of German prisoners.

At the outbreak of war in August 1914, 74TH Punjabis were stationed in Hong Kong. During 1914 to 1916 they remained at Hong Kong, from time to time providing drafts to other regiments on active service. A complete company went to join 67TH Punjabis in Mesopotamia, where Subedar Wariam Singh was awarded the I.D.S.M. for his conspicuous gallantry against the Turks.

From Hong Kong 74TH Punjabis proceeded to India. After a brief spell on the North West Frontier the regiment proceeded to Palestine. In Palestine they participated in the final breakthrough towards Damascus. They hotly pursued the Turks in the direction of Haifa, Aleppo and Damascus. Until 1920 they were employed on guard duties at a prisoner of war camp at Tel-el-Kebir, returning to India in January 1921.

After World War One the Indian government reformed the army moving from single Battalion regiments to multi Battalion regiments. In 1922, 74TH Punjabis became 4TH Battalion, 2ND Punjab Regiment.

The Battalion continuously served on the North-West Frontier, until 24TH November 1903, when a Punjabi Mussalman Sepoy ran amok and after killing the Commanding Officer, killed 4 British and 3 Punjabi Mussalman officers, until he was shot dead. At the court of inquiry, no reason was elicited for the man's actions.

Consequently, during January 1939, the very month in which the disbandment of 4TH Battalion's Punjabi Mussalman had been ordered, the Battalion was disbanded entirely. Some of the Sikhs were transferred to other Battalions, but the majority were discharged. Most of them re-enlisted in the Crown Representative's Police.

Despite the outbreak of the Second World War a few months later, 4TH Battalion was never re-raised and the Indian Government which inherited 2ND Punjab Regiment in 1947 has also kept the number vacant.

2ND Punjab Regiment

87TH Punjabis (5/2ND)

The 87TH Punjabis was raised in 1784, as 1ST Battalion, 14TH Madras Native Infantry. The men enlisted were from South India and consisted of Muslims and Hindus.

In 1902, the regiment was reconstituted with Sikhs, Punjabi Mussalmans and Dogras. Next year, as a result of the reforms brought about in the Indian Army, the regiment's designation was changed to 87TH Punjabis.

The 87TH Punjabis were at Jhelum when the First World War broke out in 1914. Almost immediately the Battalion began to suffer the penalties that fell to the lot of most units which were not at once sent overseas; for it was obliged to provide drafts not only for the linked Battalion, 76TH Punjabis, which were sent to Mesopotamia, but also for 10TH Jats and 47TH Sikhs in France. During its stay on the North-West Frontier, the regiment continued to supplement the earlier drafts it had already sent overseas and it was also required to find new drafts from time to time. A draft of 100 men was sent to 14TH Sikhs in Gallipoli, while a company of 200 men to 26TH Punjabis in Mesopotamia. When 87TH Punjabis had sent away more than 1,400 men as drafts to other units, and lost more than half of its officers, it was itself called upon to proceed to Mesopotamia in 1917. It was not until the summer of 1918 that preparations were put in hand for further major advance and 87TH Punjabis were ordered to join 55TH Brigade of 18TH Indian Division at Samara.

In the autumn the British forces advanced virtually un-opposed as far as the foot of Jebel Hamrin. At this point the Turks occupied a very strong position, against which an attack was launched by two divisions. The 87TH Punjabis were given the task of covering the preliminary reconnaissance and concentrations, and in October the actual attack was made. By night 87TH Punjabis secured their objective at the first bound; at dawn other regiments of the Brigade passed through them and they were followed by the rest to the Division. The Turks were followed up rapidly and within a short time the Turkish Army, battered ceaselessly on its front, found itself cut off in the rear by the able handling of the British Cavalry Brigade. During the last days of October Turkey capitulated.

The breakdown of Turkish authority in this territory inspired many sections of the local population to question British authority, and of necessity the civil administration set up by the British had to rely on military aid for the establishment and maintenance of order. Sheikh Mahmud, the Kurdish chieftain at Sulaimaniyah in South Kurdistan, was one of the first to proclaim independence and to attempt to eject the British civil officers. The 55TH Brigade was ordered to Kirkuk and was designated South Kurdistan Force. From Kirkuk, operations were launched against Sheikh Mahmud and 87TH played its part by capturing the Bazyan Pass. A further operation towards Sulaimaniyah, and the pursuit and rounding up of many parties of rebels, became necessary before the area was finally pacified.

2ND Punjab Regiment

87TH Punjabis (5/2ND)

During the months in which the regiment was engaged in these particular operations, no less than 670 miles of ground were covered. No sooner was order restored in South Kurdistan than trouble threatened further north, and this new danger necessitated the presence of troops in Central Kurdistan. Before long 87TH had established it's Headquarters at Erbil, with detachments spread out to a distance of nearly 100 miles. In July 1920, 87TH Punjabis were ordered again at very short notice to join a force which was being assembled for the relief of Rumaitha on the middle Euphrates. At this place a detachment of Rajputs had become invested by a body of local Arabs. Although these Arabs failed to assault and capture the post, they succeeded in opposing all efforts by the garrison to break out and forage for supplies. The force assembled to relieve Rumaitha became known as Coningham's Column and it had a formidable task to perform. Its arrival became the signal for a widespread Arab rising; the railway was attacked in many places and the opposition to the column's advance continued to harden. When Coningham's Column made its last bound to gain a jumping-off place for the relief of Rumaitha, it fell to 87TH Punjabis to fight and secure a footing on the River. In the face of bitter opposition this task was carried out with such success that both banks of the River were secured. Water could then be obtained and transported with comparative safety and very shortly the column was able to relieve Rumaitha, extract its garrison, and withdraw through a defensive line held by 87TH Punjabis. During the Rumaitha operations 87TH suffered 69 casualties. The 87TH Punjabis took part in all the operations and received the submission of many tribes and sub-tribes of Arabs. As further units came to Mesopotamia, as part of the post-war garrison and the civil administration of the country became more firmly established, 87TH Punjabis' hope of returning to India rose once again. At last, in April 1921, the Battalion actually embarked on its return voyage after 4 years overseas.

Sepoy Sohan Singh and Sepoy Bhan Singh were awarded the I.D.S.M. for their gallantry in Mesopotamia. After World War One, the Indian government reformed the army moving from single Battalion regiments to multi Battalion regiments.

In 1922, 87TH Punjabis became 5TH Battalion, 2ND Punjab Regiment. Shortly before the outbreak of the Second World War, 5/2ND Punjab, was sent to Malaya. At the time of the Japanese invasion of Malaya, which began early on 8TH December 1941, 3RD Indian Corps controlled the whole of Malaya, except its most southerly portion. On 12TH December 1941, 5/2ND Punjab Regiment received orders to move north as part of 12TH Indian Infantry Brigade Group and reached the Merbau Pulas on 15TH December. On the same day they were ordered to hold the bridge over the Muda River at Batu Pekaka. On 16TH the Japanese, who had advanced from Gurrun by the inland road instead of direct on Sungei Patani, attempted to rush the Batu Pekaka Bridge which had been only partly demolished.

2ND Punjab Regiment

87TH Punjabis (5/2ND)

This attempt, made by infantry disguised in native dress and led by a European in plain clothes, who was believed to have been a German, was shot dead by Jemadar Pritam Singh. Almost immediately heavy and effective mortar and rifle fire were opened on the Company's positions and an attempt was made by the Japanese to take and cross the bridge. The Company's resistance was resolute and after about an hour the Japanese gave up the attempt. The same evening, in a sudden and surprise attack, with heavy fire which now included artillery fire, the Japanese drove the Company back from the bridge. The rest of the regiment led a counter-attack on the bridge, which was successful; about 100 enemy troops were dispersed and the possession of the bridge regained. For gallantry during these operations, Jemadar Pritam Singh was awarded the I.D.S.M.

On 30TH December, 5/2ND Punjab Regiment had to deal with the Japanese near Telok Anson. Jemadar Pritam Singh's platoon arrived as the Japanese forward troops were crossing the bridge, but his men promptly drove them back and burned the bridge. The Japanese kept up their pressure along the Telok Anson road, assisted by almost continuous aerial bombardment. On 7TH January, the Japanese tanks came pouring down the road towards the Battalion. The two leading Japanese tanks were blown up and put out of action. Others came on and encountered only the resistance of men who had few anti-tank guns and only small-arms and hand-grenades to use against them. The noise was indiscernible. The tank engines were roaring and their crews were yelling at the top of their voices and firing gun and mortar shells and tracer bullets in every direction. To this din was added the noise made by the Battalion's weapons and the few rounds of anti-tank gun ammunition they were able to fire off, which accounted for another Japanese tank.

No men could have fought with greater gallantry. The withdrawal to Singapore had been carried out with skill and courage, under most difficult conditions. The fighting in which 5/2ND Punjab Regiment had been involved had been extremely fierce, with considerable casualties. During the weeks of difficult fighting the line held by the Battalion had never been broken, although it had been forced to retire continually by superior forces. It had always performed the tasks allotted to it and had never been forced to retire before the time ordered by Command.

Between 11TH and 15TH February, 5/2ND Punjab Regiment had fought its last battle. The Battalion was captured by the Japanese on Singapore Island in February 1942. After the fall of Singapore the survivors had to face what was perhaps their worst ordeal. The story of the Indian prisoners was a long tale of intimidation and cruelty. The Sikhs and Dogras were sent to New Guinea, where most of them perished.

These events conclude the record of 5/2ND Punjab Regiment, after 150 years of service. At the Japanese defeat, and by the time prisoners had been released and repatriated, a re-organization of the Indian Army was under way, and 5/2ND Punjab Regiment was disbanded in 1945.

2ND Punjab Regiment

7TH Battalion (7/2ND)

The 7TH Battalion, 2ND Punjab Regiment was raised in May 1941, by Lt. Col. Shallow, with the class composition of Sikhs, Punjabi Mussalmans and Dogras. During the Second World War, 7/2ND Punjabis served in Burma, as a part of the 89TH Brigade, 7TH Indian Division. With surprising rapidity the Japanese had pushed back the Allied Forces in Burma to the Indian border. It was not only essential to stop the Japanese from invading India, but also imperative to regain Burma. In September, 1942, the new battalion was rushed to the Arakan region in western Burma aiming to capture the Mayu Peninsula and Akyab Island's airfield.

The early operations in the Arakan were restricted to small local advances to clear up the Japanese forward positions north of the Maungdaw-Buthidaung road; during the monsoon months these had been lightly held. But beyond these minor tactical objectives the immediate strategic objective was Akyab, where the Japanese held the only port of importance in the Arakan. If Akyab was seized, it could be used as a stepping-stone for seaborne operations down the Arakan coast, and would also furnish and advanced aerodrome from which air cover could be provided.

Local tactical information about the enemy was scanty and unreliable, and to supplement this information reconnoitring patrols on large scale were essential. The, 7/2ND Punjabis was ordered to patrol extensively down the Mayu Range. The monsoon rains were not over, and movement and observation were difficult. Nor it was always easy to make accurate deductions from what had been observed.

On 25TH September, the 7/2ND Punjab Regiment had joined the HQ, 89TH Brigade of 7TH Indian Division, and had taken over the west side of the Mayu ridge crest in Arakan. The next move was in increasing the pressure on the Japanese, was the occupation of some low wooded hills near Zeganbyin and the 7/2ND Punjab Regiment moved to Waybin. These moves forward resulted in several sharp engagements, in which 7/2ND Punjab patrol brought off a very successful ambush, killing several Japanese with no loss to themselves. For the next few weeks patrolling was still further intensified. The 89TH Brigade made preparations to move over the Ngakyedauk Pass, and the Engineers started intensive work on making a road over the pass. By the end of December, in a truly remarkable feat of engineering, the road had been driven through dense jungle over a precipitous pass with a 1,000-foot rise and fall in three miles, well within artillery range of the enemy. Within few more weeks this road was fit for medium tanks and was the focal point of the battle which broke the Japanese power in Arakan.

On 14TH November the 7/2ND Punjabis moved down the eastern side of the pass. Progress was slow as the jungle in the foothills of the east of the range is very dense, and the task of the battalion was to form a screen behind which the rest of the brigade could cross the pass, and to establish a secure base while they took up their allotted positions.

2ND Punjab Regiment

7TH Battalion (7/2ND)

Two nights later the rest of the 89TH Brigade followed. Brigade headquarters was established at Sinzweya in the area occupied by the 7/2ND Punjabis. The consolidation by the 89TH Brigade of their new positions was uninterrupted and work on the road over the pass was pushed on at top speed.

On the night of 30TH November/1ST December, on the 89TH Brigade front the 7/2ND Punjabis in a short fight captured two prominent features south of the Tatmin Chaung. Already this young battalion was showing a fine fighting spirit. In the course of the next few months it was to receive many hard knocks, but always fought back fiercely, never giving ground, and on more than one occasion inflicting very severe losses to the enemy.

By the end of January, the 89TH Brigade's front the enemy defences were in considerable depth. A system of small but strong posts dug into the knife-edged ridges in the foothills and the many low jungle-covered knolls in the valley south of Tatmin Chaung, covered main positions north of the Buthidaung road

During the early part of January the 4/8TH Gurkhas in the foothills and the 7/2ND Punjabis in the valley made some progress in their efforts to infiltrate through the positions on to feature overlooking the road. They encountered gradually stiffening resistance, and in a series of sharp engagements, particularly in the 7/2ND Punjabis area, several enemy patrol bases were occupied, including a hill overlooking Htindaw, which was held in spite of attacks and considerable harassing fire from medium artillery.

It was evident that infiltration tactics were not going to achieve the desired object. The 89TH Brigade commander's appreciation was that the broad, thickly forested feature north of the junction of the Letwedet track and the main road, known as Able, was key to the positions covering the road. It was known to be held in strength and to be covered by mutually supporting positions. It was also probable that it would be defended with fanatical courage, and that any attack on it would have to be supported by all available artillery.

A short distance in the north-east of Able was a small feature known as Pimples, consisting of three small jungle-covered knolls, connected by the usual knife-edged cols. Unless these were captured the continued occupation of Able would obviously be impossible and their capture was therefore to be the first phase of the attack. On 20TH January an unsuccessful effort was made to clear Pimples and on the evening of the 21ST the enemy still held Pimples, and it was becoming evident that unless the position could be cleared a withdrawal from Able would have to be made. A plan had already been made for the 7/2ND Punjabis to go to the assistance of the K.O.S.B. regiment in the event of the latter not being able to clear Pimples as well as establish themselves on Able, and orders were issued for this plan to be put into operation.

By dawn on 22ND January, a detachment of two companies of 7/2ND Punjabis carrying out this attack, was able to report that North and Middle Pimples had been captured.

2ND Punjab Regiment

7TH Battalion (7/2ND)

It had taken three attempts to dislodge the enemy on Middle Pimple, and nearly quarter of the force had been killed or wounded. The plight of the troops holding the position was not an enviable one. The Pimples was an unmissable target and one well known to the enemy. Their artillery made accurate shooting, while from the north of Able to which the Japanese had infiltrated, continued harassing by mortars and automatics was maintained. Sepoy Gosain Singh was awarded a posthumous Indian Order of Merit for his part in this action.

Just before dawn on the 23RD the enemy launched a fierce attack on Pimples, which was beaten off, but party of enemy succeeded in getting between North and Middle Pimple and digging in, thus isolating the troops on Middle Pimple, who began to run short of ammunition. The situation was now so confused that it became necessary to place the 7/2ND Punjabis companies on Pimple under the command of the K.O.S.B., whose commander as instructed to concentrate on getting touch with the isolated garrison. A company of the K.O.S.B. attempted to reach Middle Pimple by working around the south end of the feature, but came under heavy small-arms and artillery fire while crossing the open paddy and were pinned down, though the company commander, after a long and hazardous crawl, was able to make contact and satisfy himself that the isolated garrison was in good heart.

Under the cover of darkness, supplies, ammunition and reinforcements reached the 7/2ND Punjabis on North Pimple, while most of the K.O.S.B. Company which had been unable to get to Middle Pimple from the south was reassembled on North Pimple. On the morning of the 24TH a combined assault by the detachments of the two regiments was launched, and the enemy finding themselves being overwhelmed slipped away, leaving much equipment and many dead in the position. The next day the two battered companies of 7/2ND Punjabis on Pimples were relieved by the 89TH Brigade Headquarters Company of 1/11TH Sikhs.

The 89TH Brigade, who had been relieved in the Mayu range foothills by the 9TH Brigade of the 5TH Division, had moved to the rear of the 33RD Brigade and were, on the morning of 4TH February, was to enjoy their first day's rest for over three months. It was before the 89TH Brigade was called to act. They were to find, fix and destroy the Japanese column, estimated at one battalion, which had overrun Taung. The brigade moved north with two battalions up: the 7/2ND Punjabis right, directed on Badana East; the 4/8TH Gurkhas left, directed on Badana West. The K.O.S.B. and brigade headquarters followed the 7/2ND Punjabis. The idea was to secure the line of the Badana Chaung and then turn east of Taung. During the advance, battalions were to endeavour to cut off and destroy any enemy patrols encountered and to prevent any move south through the areas allotted to them.

First contact was made that evening by the 7/2ND Punjabis near Ingyaung. The Japanese appeared to be taken by surprise, and hesitated, giving the 89TH Brigade a little breathing space on this so far somewhat breathless day.

2ND Punjab Regiment

7TH Battalion (7/2ND)

The Punjabis established themselves for the night near the village. Meanwhile, information coming through from widely separated points made it quite evident that the estimate of one battalion was far below the truth. The true figure was nearer 7,000 than 1,000. On the night of the 5TH and throughout the day on the 6TH, the enemy attacked the Ingyaung and Linbabi positions fiercely, incurring casualties he could ill afford. Time and again the enemy hurled himself on both positions and at one time nearly succeeded in isolating brigade headquarters from the K.O.S.B. The commander of the company of the 1/11TH Sikhs defending brigade headquarters was wounded. He was evacuated and the party was ambushed, but he survived to command the battalion during the destruction of the Japanese army in Burma.

On the early morning of the 7TH, the enemy attacked the 7/2ND Punjabis in the Awlanbyin West area. The battalion had been on the move all night and had no time to organize its new position. Battalion headquarters was cut off from the rest of the battalion, while companies and even platoons found themselves isolated, and the real "soldier's battle" ensued. Two companies on the Awlanbyin West finger were isolated without food or ammunition for four days, during which they beat off repeated attacks and inflicted heavy casualties on enemy trying to use the east-to-west tracks along the Chaung. Another company, endeavouring to find battalion headquarters, reached headquarters of 33RD Brigade, where it received a most friendly welcome, but all attempts to "borrow" it were firmly resisted by the 89TH Brigade and the company returned to its rightful owners.

One company of the 7/2ND Punjabis was left at Awlanbyin West throughout the battle in the old Japanese position captured on 1ST December, which dominated the east and west tracks along the Ngakyedauk Chaung. Except for this company the 89TH Brigade was withdrawn by degrees between the 11TH and 15TH February into the administrative area, as the Japanese pressure there increased.

In February during the Battle of the Boxes, the casualties had seriously reduced the garrison at the Admin Box and it was essential to bring in more troops. The 7/2ND Punjabis were ordered to abandon their positions at Awlanbyin, leaving one company on the very strong west finger well supplied with food and ammunition, and move into the Box. As the battalion arrived in the Box, three of its officers, Major Burfield and Lieutenants Graham and Tareen, were killed in an air-raid. Coming on top of the casualties they had already suffered in the last few days' hard fighting, this was a terrible blow.

The company left on the Awlanbyin West finger during the next ten days inflicted very heavy loss on Japanese supply parties and reinforcements trying to reach Tanahashi and Kubo force. In a position of great natural strength, well equipped with ammunition, and equipped with stout hearts and self-confidence, they drove back all attempts to dislodge them.

2ND Punjab Regiment

7TH Battalion (7/2ND)

During March a very fierce battle had been fought by the 7/2ND Punjabis on a feature known as the Bulge, situated on the west bank of the Kalapanzin River opposite Kyaukit. This battalion, due to very heavy casualties during the February fighting, had been withdrawn from the 89TH Brigade and their place had been taken by the 1/11TH Sikhs. The badly battered 7/2ND Punjabis had been ordered to occupy the Bulge feature where trouble was not expected, and reported on 8TH March that they were in position. The feature consisted of numerous small hills covered with thick undergrowth, in which it would have been and easy matter to conceal a whole brigade. This group of hills ha\d formerly been held by the Japanese, and their empty positions remained, and on the night 10TH/11TH March they re-infiltrated and got, unobserved, on to a ridge immediately overlooking the battalion headquarters. The position was critical and the C.O. Lt. Col. Rouse, was killed while personally leading an immediate attack.

The ridge was eventually cleared with the aid of covering fire from tanks, and at the end of the fight the whole position was strewn with bodies and arms and equipment, including several medium machine-guns. One dazed Japanese soldier who was taken prisoner stated that he was the only survivor of a suicide force of a hundred and twenty-seven officers and men who had been sent to occupy the feature and remain there until annihilated. It was impossible to make an accurate account of the Japanese dead, for many were buried beneath the debris of broken bunkers and in bombed-out tunnels. The Punjabis had suffered heavily; their casualties amounted to nearly a hundred and fifty killed and wounded, and it was probably the toughest battalion actions fought during the Arakan campaign. For the first time complete victory was gained over the enemy, and brought the following message from Mr. Churchill: 'I congratulate the 14TH Army heartily upon the successful outcome of the series of fierce encounters with the Japanese in Arakan. It must be a great satisfaction to all ranks and races engaged in our common effort that the Japanese had been challenged and beaten in jungle warfare in Burma and that their boastfulness should have received a salutary exposure.' For his services during this Japanese offensive Colonel Rouse was awarded the posthumous D.S.O.

Typical of all the fighting about this time was the capture of a spur in the Bulge, for which there was a "grand-stand view" from a parallel ridge. A platoon of the Punjabis was working along the ridge, covered by a tank of the 25TH Dragoons. A section leader with a signal flag on a pole was "pointing" the next bunker, which the tank commander was very quick in picking up, and within seconds the 75.mm. gun was at it with high-explosive followed by armour piercing shot and machine-gun fire. As soon the fire lifted, the leading section rushed in- a yell, the thud of grenades, bayonet thrusts into invisible slits in the ground, and the attackers moved on a few yards before the pointer flag again came into use.

2ND Punjab Regiment

7TH Battalion (7/2ND)

After the crushing of the Japanese attempt to destroy the British forces in Arakan, the situation became more stable. Many enemy troops had been destroyed, but they still occupied a few isolated hills in front of Buthidaung. About five miles north of Buthidaung and about a mile to the west of Kalapanzin Range was the village of Sinohbyin. A few hundred yards to the north-east of Sinohbyin was a height which, from its shape, came to be called Boomerang. It was by far the most dangerous of the enemy forward positions; it was held in considerable strength, and the enemy must have been able to supply it under cover of darkness. The British supply columns were constantly being fired on and harassed from Boomerang, and it was necessary to clear the enemy form it and not merely to by-pass it. On 6TH March the 7/2ND Punjabis was given responsibility for this area, and was ordered to make a reconnaissance of the Japanese position on Boomerang Hill. The enemy had excellent facilities for concealment and camouflage, and it was difficult to estimate accurately their numbers and dispositions. It was not until the battle for the position was over the immensity of the task came to be realized.

The first attempt to capture Boomerang was made by 'D' Company of the 7/2ND Punjabis on 7TH March. No sooner had 'D' Company gained a footing on the lower slopes of the hill than a veritable curtain of small-arms fire was put down by the enemy, and grenades came tumbling down the hill-side. Any further advance would have been suicidal, and 'D' Company therefore withdrew. On 9TH March a second assault was attempted by 'A' and 'C' Companies under cover of mortar and machine-gun fire from an adjoining hill. It was again found that the enemy were so strongly entrenched in deep bunker positions, and were able to bring so much fire to bear, that the attack could not succeed. In the early stages of this attack 'A' and 'C' Companies suffered considerable casualties, and for the second time the attack was called off.

It was then realized that much heavier support would be necessary if the hill was to be captured. The 7/2ND Punjabis now came under the direct orders of the 114TH Infantry Brigade, and was ordered to attack at dawn on 12TH March. The attack was to be launched by three companies the 7/2ND Punjabis, supported by Sherman tanks of the 25TH Dragoons and 25-pounders of the 139TH Jungle Field Regiment, Royal Artillery. 'B' Company was to lead the assault and to move during the night of 11/12TH March to a position slightly east of Boomerang. At dawn the tanks and artillery were to concentrate to fire upon the enemy position, and when the range was lengthened 'B' Company was to secure a footing on Boomerang from the east. 'A' and 'C' Companies were to assist by infiltrating into the enemy's position from the south and west. The attack on Boomerang was one of the toughest assignments the 7/2ND Punjabis was ever given. On all sides the approach to the crest was extremely steep, and the enemy posted there were prepared to fight to the last.

2ND Punjab Regiment

7TH Battalion (7/2ND)

A British officer who survived this attack has written the following tribute to the men of the 7/2ND Punjabis:

'The bravery displayed by our men, individually and collectively, in the face of such odds was beyond all praise. 'B' Company, after a long and arduous march, often through waist-deep water, attacked at the precise moment when the tanks and guns lifted their heavy curtain of fire. As soon as they started to climb the steep slopes casualties began to occur. Among the first was Major Little, who was hit near the heart by a fragment of hand-grenade. In attempting to get him clear of the fighting, his orderly was shot dead. Immediately two Sepoys took the orderly's place, and carried their officer to safety and then rejoined the battle. Men dropped right and left, but the advance continued. 'A' and 'C' Companies were also suffering their share of casualties. The Japanese were using machine-guns and were raining down grenades. Our tanks came into action again, and to reduce the power and intensity of the Japanese fire started firing with Bren guns and 37 mm. Armour piercing shells. At the end of day's really bloody fighting more than 130 of our men were killed or wounded. But they destroyed as many Japanese of not more, and had won the hill by the evening.'

By that time Boomerang presented a scene of desolation, mainly caused by the British tank and artillery fire. Well over 100 enemy dead were lying in the bunkers or in the open. A single Japanese soldier, who alone remained alive in one of the bunkers refused to surrender. Impatient with this truculent attitude some men of the 7/2ND Punjabis shovelled earth into the bunker over his body, and then he came out and was captured. Owing to the heavy casualties sustained in this action the Battalion was relieved at Boomerang and took over duty as Divisional Defence Battalion.

By the end of 1944 the general situation in Burma had changed to the advantage of the Allies. The decisive defeat of the two main Japanese offensives in the Arakan and against Imphal had been followed by an Allied advance into Burma from Assam and Manipur State.

The assignment given to the 7TH Division was to concentrate in the Gangaw valley and to advance to Pakokku by way of Tilin and Pauk. The 7/2ND Punjabis was allotted the duty of operating as a fighting reconnaissance force on the extreme left flank of the 4TH Corps, and of advancing southwards towards Pakokku along the west bank of the Chindwin. To carry out this task the 7/2ND Punjabis had first to concentrate on the banks of the Manipur River in the Gangaw valley. By 2ND January 1945, the 7/2ND Punjabis was placed on a pack-transport basis and was accompanied by 270 mules. On 11TH January the column reached Sitlingyaung, having crossed no less than seventeen times the shallow sandy-bottomed Chaung which meandered through the valley. On 16TH January the 7/2ND Punjabis occupied Thalin without having been in contact with the enemy.

2ND Punjab Regiment

7TH Battalion (7/2ND)

On 4TH February the 7/2ND Punjabis embarked on the last stage of the march to Pakokku, 22 miles south of Myaing. At midday news arrived that 'A' Company at Wegan had had clash with a superior enemy force. On the evening of the 4TH the column closed on Wetkya to find that 'B' Company had already cleared the village, killing in the process three of the enemy who had tried to lay an ambush. Jemadar Shiv Singh was killed during a fighting reconnaissance by 'C' Company on the same date. The action planned for the following day was a cautious advance on Ynbin and thence to Magylkobin, 4 miles short of Pakokku. In accordance with this decision 'B' Company moved forward on 5TH February to clear Magylkobin, but on coming in to touch with the Japanese outpost positions became pinned down by the enemy's possession of a 75 mm., gun, and was forced to dig in astride the road on a gentle reverse slope. During the night a section of mortars was moved forward from Battalion Headquarters in support of 'B' Company. The mortars opened fire on the morning of 6TH February, as soon it was light enough, but succeeded only in developing a long-range duel with the enemy's 75 mm. gun. During the night of 10/11TH February 'B' Company disengaged itself from this encounter, and accompanied by Battalion Tactical Headquarters made a long night march right round the enemy's flank. This threat forced the Japanese to withdraw in the direction of Pakokku.

The surrender of the Empire of Japan was announced by Imperial Japan on August 15TH bringing the hostilities in Burma to a close.

The 7/2ND Punjabis spent remainder of its time in Burma transferring itself from war-time to a peace-time footing. After a short spell in Siam (Thailand) in the middle of January 1946 orders were received for the 7/2ND Punjabis to move to Malaya. For the best part of the year the battalion passed pleasant time in Johor and Taiping, and the final 6 months in Malaya were spent just outside Kuala Lumpur. The battalion returned to India in time for the Independence, and the creation of Pakistan.

The 2ND Punjab Regiment was the only Punjabi Regiment allotted to India. H hence it was decided to use only the first digit of their nomenclature i.e. 1 Punjab (and not 1/2 Punjab etc).

After Independence 7 Punjab, was involved in Operation Polo, the Police Action to annex Hyderabad State to the union of India.

7 Punjab less 'B' Company with 'B' Squadron 63 Cavalry was given the special mission of establishing a road block at Saji Ali with a view to facilitate the advance of 32 Infantry Brigade along Axis Chaucha Jessore on 6TH December 1971. The unit was opposed by approximately one Battalion (6 Punjab) and some reconnaissance and support elements of enemy in complex Afra and Saji Ali. The enemy was taken aback by surprise by the outflanking move along Ramnagar-Durga Barkti-Saji Ali and was forced to abandon Afra complex.

Punjab Regiment

The Battalion advanced regardless of heavy enemy shelling; however, the enemy retreated, abandoning large quantity of equipment, including arms and large amount of ammunition. A captured prisoner, Taj Alam of 6 Punjab Regiment, revealed that his regiment had withdrawn to Jessore, due to the Indian speedy and massive armour attack, which they could not check. On 7TH December 1971, the Battalion was given the task of capturing Jessore Airfield. 'C' Company with 'B' Squadron 63 Cavalry led the advance of the Battalion. 'C' Company had rushed forward and captured the given objective. The enemy ran in panic, abandoning a large number of vehicles, equipment and ammunition. Headquarters 107 Infantry Brigade of Pakistan Army was found intact where the enemy had left valuable documents and marked maps. The interrogation of prisoners revealed that the enemy had planned to give pitched battle in and around Jessore but the sudden appearance of mechanised Battalion and tanks in large numbers had upset their plans. Lt. Gen. Riana, officer commanding 11 Corps alongside Major General Dalbir Singh, officer commanding 9 Infantry Brigade, visited the Battalion at Jessore Airfield immediately after its capture. He congratulated Lt. Col. US Sandhu, officer commanding the Battalion, and commended the Battalion for a job well done. With the fall of Jessore, the backbone of the enemy force was broken, and it had a devastating effect on the enemies overall position.

On the evening of 7TH December 1971, the Battalion regained contact with the enemy at road junction 147544 at Ramnagar. The enemy opened up with small arms, tanks, anti-tank guns and artillery. It was estimated that the enemy was occupying the Area Road Junction by two companies of infantry supported by guns and mortars. The enemy had laid mines and constructed strong bunkers. The Battalion had advanced so fast that it went out of the range of its own medium guns. Fire-fight continued throughout the night. The enemy reaction was vicious and violent, however, it was forced to withdraw, and was trapped by the 8 Madras. The enemy force was forced to surrender a large quantity arms, ammunition, vehicles and military equipment. After this action the enemy had no time to consolidate its defences and Hyderabad State annexed to the republic of India.

Lt. Col. (later Lt. Gen.) Jaswant Singh was posted initially to 3 Punjab and later to 7 Punjab. As commanding officer of 7 Punjab during the 1965 Indo-Pakistan War, Lt. Col. (later Lt. Gen.) Jaswant Singh, led the battalion to decisive victory by capturing the formidable Icchogil Canal in the Lahore sector. This battalion won the highest number of gallantry awards in this war.

In the 1971 Indo-Pakistan war his younger brother, Lt Col (later Brig) US Sandhu commanded the same battalion in the East Pakistan theatre and was the first to enter Jessore and capture the airfield. This is the only example of two brothers having commanded the same battalion in two different wars.

In 1979 7 Punjab converted into a mechanized battalion and was re-designated as 8 Mechanized Battalion (as it is known even today).

8TH Punjab Regiment

89TH Punjabis (1/8TH)

The regiment was raised on 9TH November 1798 at Masulipatam as 3RD Extra Battalion of Madras Native. It was composed mostly of Muslims, Tamils and Telugus of South India. In 1893, it was reconstituted with Sikhs, Punjabi Mussalmans and Rajputs, and permanently based in Burma. Its new designation was 7TH Burma Battalion of Madras Infantry.

For the next decade or so after their reconstitution, the Burma Battalions remained employed in operations against the recalcitrant tribes in the border districts of Burma. The Battalions were employed in small detachments on remote border posts in a country without railways or proper roads. This often entailed long and arduous marches through hilly jungle terrain, which could last for weeks. Isolation was compounded by tropical diseases and the absence of proper medical care, which made life harsh and dangerous. However, the troops held out very well and their performance during these operations was highly commendable.

Subsequent to the reforms brought about in the Indian Army in 1903, the regiment's designation was changed to 89TH Punjabis. In 1910, the Burma Battalions were delocalized from Burma. In 1914, the regiment moved to Dinapore in India, just before the outbreak of the First World War. The 89TH Punjabis have a most distinguished record of service during the First World War. They have the unique distinction of serving in more theatres of war than any other unit of the British Empire. These include Aden, Egypt, Gallipoli, France, Mesopotamia, North West Frontier, Salonika and Russian Transcaucasia.

The Turkish fort of Turba was situated on the Sheikh Saad Peninsula on the Red Sea Coast of Arabia, overlooking the island of Perim. The guns of the fort posed a threat to British ships passing through the narrow straits on their way to the Suez Canal and it was decided to neutralize them. The 29TH Indian Brigade, with 89TH Punjabis on their way to Egypt, was detached from the convoy with the objective of capture and destruction of the fort and its heavy guns. On 10TH November 1914, following a heavy bombardment of Turkish positions, 89TH Punjabis and two double-companies of 69TH Punjabis landed on the west coast of the peninsula. The covering party landed and seized Hill 70. The Turks, from their position on Camp Hill, tried to disrupt the landing with long-range rifle and shrapnel fire but were ineffective. The regiment concentrated at Hill 70 and then advanced towards Camp Hill. The ground over the first 100 yards was sandy but became rocky as the advance continued. Due to heavy enemy fire, the system of alternate rushes under covering fire was adopted. The Turks abandoned their position and retreated along the east coast allowing a double-company of 69TH Punjabis to capture Fort Turba without any opposition. The Sikh Pioneers then demolished the fort and its guns. During the operation one Sepoy was killed, while eight were wounded. Sepoy Dasaunda Singh was awarded the I.D.S.M. during this operation. The regiment re-embarked the next morning and joined the convoy, arriving at Suez on 14TH November, 1914.

8TH Punjab Regiment

89TH Punjabis (1/8TH)

The entry of Turkey in the war made the British situation in Egypt critical. The Germans were keen for the Turks to attack the Suez Canal, as it would not only disrupt British supplies and communications with the rest of their Empire, but also tie up large numbers of British forcers desperately needed in France. On November 14TH, a large Turkish force of six divisions under Djemal Pasha crossed into Sinai. The Turks set out in three columns; along the coast from El Arish through El Abd and Qatiya in the north, towards Suez through Nekhl in the south and in the centre from Beersheba through Kassaima, El Hassana and Bir Jiffjaffa towards the centre part of the canal between Lake Timsah and Great Bittier Lake. This was the main objective of the Turkish attack, where they planned to cross the canal in rafts and pontoons under cover of heavy machine-gun and rifle fire from the east bank. The other columns were to launch diversionary attacks on Qantara, Ismailia, Ferdan, Shaluf and Suez. The attacking force totalled around 12,000 men with six batteries of 6-inch guns.

On their arrival at Suez, 89TH Punjabis initially took up defences at Port Said but later move to Qantara in January. On the night of 3ND February, the patrols of the Piquets reported the advance of large bodies of Turks. Half an hour later, Turkish advanced parties blundered into the barbed wire defences of a Piquet. Heavy fighting broke out as the Turks tried to extricate themselves and came into contact with the other Piquets. Reinforcements were rushed and the Turkish attack beaten back. Thirty-six prisoners were captured and another twenty were found dead in the barbed wire entanglements. The Turks launched another attack, this time on the post of Tel-el-Ahmar and a double company was despatched to assist the post. It was here that Sepoy Dasaunda Singh again distinguished himself. He made nine trips to the camp, 800 yards in the rear, bringing ammunition to the Piquets and each time carrying back a killed or wounded comrade, all the while exposed to heavy enemy fire. The Turks broke off the attack and during the night withdrew from the area. During the action, the regiment's casualties were four Other Ranks killed and 23 wounded. For his gallant conduct, Sepoy Dasaunda Singh received the I.O.M

The Straits of Dardanelles is a narrow forty miles long channel joining the Sea of Marmara with the Aegean Sea. It is bounded on one side by the Turkish mainland and on the other by the Gallipoli Peninsula, a rocky and hilly strip of land jutting out from the European part of Turkey. As Turkey joined the Axis powers during the war, the British decided to force the Dardanelles, thus opening the Black Sea with its Russian ports, and at the same time threatening Constantinople, the Turkish capital.

In April 1915, 89TH Punjabis were ordered to Gallipoli. The 89TH Punjabis left Qantara and arrived at Cape Helles on 29TH. During the next few days, it came under heavy fire as the Turks launched their counter-attack on 1ST May. On 9TH May, 29TH Indian Brigade relieved 87TH British Brigade, taking over the left of the British line from the sea to Gully Ravine.

8TH Punjab Regiment

89TH Punjabis (1/8TH)

The 89TH Punjabis took over the trenches astride the ravine under heavy enemy fire. During the next three days, neither side made any effort to attack but exchange of fire continued and the regiment suffered several casualties, including Subedar Major Sundar Singh, who was wounded. On 12TH May, under cover of artillery and covering fire from 89TH Punjabis, the Gurkhas achieved their objective and linked up with the line held by 89TH Punjabis. As the Turks tried to escape from their trenches, they suffered heavy casualties from fire by 89TH Punjabis. Havildar Harnam Singh greatly distinguished himself throughout the day by his gallantry and cool headedness under fire.

Concerns about the loyalty of Muslim soldiers fighting their fellow Muslims, led to the withdrawal of the two Punjabi regiments. During the evening of 13TH May, 89TH Punjabis were relieved by 14TH Sikhs. On 15TH May, the regiment embarked for Egypt. During its short stay in Gallipoli, the regiment had suffered casualties of two British officers, five Indian officers and more than a hundred Other Ranks killed, wounded or missing. The fruitless struggle on the Gallipoli peninsula continued for several more months, the British finally withdrew in January 1916, having suffered more than 200,000 casualties.

During the summer of 1915, several new regiments were despatched to France as replacement of some of the shattered units of the Indian Corps. Among these were 89TH Punjabis who arrived at Marseilles on 27TH May. By 12TH June, the regiment was in the trenches in front of Neuve Chapelle. Although the regiment was not involved in any major fighting, it did much useful work manning the defences, sending out fighting patrols and enduring the hardships of trench warfare, suffering more than 300 casualties in the process. Considerable patrol activity took place during this period.

On 1ST September, a patrol of three under Havildar Harnam Singh came across a listening post with fifteen Germans inside. The patrol attacked and bombed the post.

The Battle of Loos was the last major engagement of 89TH Punjabis in France, in which Sepoy Indar Singh was awarded the I.O.M. Havildar Harnam Singh, Havildar Naryan Singh and Jemadar Bhaga Singh were awarded the I.D.S.M. for conspicuous gallantry in the operations on the Western Front in France. By 10TH November, all units of the Indian Corps had been relieved on the frontline and in January 1916, the last Indian infantry left France for other battle fields.

The 89TH Punjabis arrived in Mesopotamia in the first week of January 1916, and immediately marched towards the front. On 5TH February, they arrived at Orah and were posted to 7TH Brigade. On 8TH March, they waited with the rest of 7TH Brigade to attack Sinn Abtar, but the attack never materialized due to the failure to take Dujaila. Their action of the day was to capture a Turkish patrol by Lance-Naik Santa Singh and three scouts in the morning. On 11TH March, 89TH Punjabis advanced towards Thorny Nullah and were to occupy the Maxim Mounds and 400 yards of the nullah on the right.

8TH Punjab Regiment

89TH Punjabis (1/8TH)

However, in the dark the Punjabis crossed the shallow nullah, without being aware of it, and found themselves in front of the Turkish position at Abu Roman. Both sides were surprised. The 89TH Punjabis immediately charged the Turkish positions despite heavy fire and occupied the first line trenches. The two leading double-companies gallantly continued the attack against the second line trenches. During the intense fire-fight, all the British officers of the two companies were wounded and command was taken over by the Indian officers, who continued the attack with cool determination and skill. Both the flanks of 89TH Punjabis had become exposed and their situation was precarious. With their ammunition running out and having lost 75 percent of the strength, the two companies were ordered to withdraw. After collecting the wounded, the companies withdrew in perfect order. Havildar Gurdit Singh, in command, covered the withdrawal of the two companies, thwarting several attempts by the Turks to follow up. Reinforcements were immediately sent forward to continue the attack, but as heavy rain started to fall, all movement became difficult and the attack was abandoned. The performance of the regiment during the action was magnificent. Numerous acts of gallantry were performed. The regiment's casualties during the action were 220 killed, wounded or missing.

On 11TH April two companies of 89TH Punjabis went forward and occupied a position in some low sand hills halfway between the British and Turkish lines at Beit Isa. During the advance they suffered heavy losses. Despite the intense fire and heavy casualties, the Punjabis maintained their position at this critical time until the support arrived. Several attempts by the Turks to dislodge them were foiled by their excellent fire control.

During the Battle of Beit Isa, for his gallantry Lance-Naik Shamed Khan was awarded the Victoria Cross. However, his two equally brave comrades received nothing despite all remmendations. The 89TH Punjabis suffered 121 casualties during the inconclusive battle for Beit Isa.

On 17TH April, two Brigades launched their attack against Beit Isa. The advance was carried out so rapidly that the Turkish trenches were still under bombardment when the attacking infantry reached their targets. In a ferocious charge through the fire of their own artillery, the assaulting troops took the enemy trenches on the point of the bayonet, killing 300 and capturing another 180. The 89TH Punjabis leap-frogged over the leading regiments of their brigade and occupied the mouths of the six canals on the right bank of the brigade. "This assault was carried out with such dash that 89TH passed clear through our own barrage."

As 3RD Division prepared for the next day's operations, the Turks launched a furious counter-attack. The British were totally surprised by the ferocity of the Turkish attack, which was carried out with great gallantry despite horrendous casualties.

8TH Punjab Regiment

89TH Punjabis (1/8TH)

Absolute chaos reigned in the dim moonlight, as friends and foes mixed up in a confused mass and all attempts at reforming the units failed. Several British and Indian officers made desperate efforts to rally their men. As reinforcements started arriving, the Turkish attack was finally repulsed. Although the Turks had suffered some 4,000 casualties, they had effectively broken the back of the British attack. The 89TH Punjabis had suffered 111 casualties and their total strength was reduced to 164. Naik Kishan Singh, Lance-Naik Hazura Singh, Sepoys Wariam Singh, Mit Singh, Gurdit Singh and Mehr Singh were awarded the I.D.S.M. for conspicuous gallantry in the operations in Mesopotamia.

In July 1916, 89TH Punjabis left Mesopotamia for India. They spent the next fourteenth months based at Nowshera in the North-West Frontier Province. The regiment was frequently engaged in operations against the frontier tribesmen, taking part in Mohmad Blockade and Chitral Relief Column. Jemadar Battan Singh, Jemadar Kartar Singh and Sepoy Tara Singh, were awarded the I.D.S.M., for gallantry on the North -West Frontier.

In 1922, 89TH Punjabis were grouped with four other Regiments, 90TH, 91ST, 92ND Punjabis and 93RD Burma Infantry, to form 8TH Punjab Regiment.

When the war broke out in 1939, 1/8TH Punjab Regiment was stationed at Lucknow, where it had arrived in 1937 after more than three years in Hong Kong. In August 1940, it joined 6TH Indian Brigade, which was mobilising for service overseas. On 20TH October, the Battalion embarked at Bombay for Penang in North Malaya. On the night of 8TH December, a mechanized consisting of two companies and a carrier platoon of 1/8TH Punjab Regiment, one section of anti-tank guns and two sections of engineers, was ordered across the Thailand frontier to harass and delay the advancing Japanese. The column moved on the Singora Road and crossing the frontier arrived at the village of Ban Sadao, ten miles inside Thailand. They spotted the advanced guard of 5TH Japanese Division and consisted of a mixed force of about 3,000 men with artillery and twelve tanks. When the column was forty yards away, the anti-tank guns opened fire and the lead tank was hit. Soon, two more tanks were hit and destroyed. At the same time, the carriers opened up an intense fire on the Lorries carrying the troops. The Japanese were completely surprised and suffered heavy casualties. The Japanese recovered quickly and supported by mortars, started working around the Punjabis' flank. Two carriers of 1/8TH Punjab Regiment was hit and destroyed by mortar fire. The little force had given a sharp welcome to the Japanese, but it was in no position to engage in a prolonged fire-fight with a much stronger force. The two companies were ordered to withdraw to the south of the village, where their Lorries were waiting. In the meantime, the anti-tank guns and the carriers continued to fire until they too withdrew. The withdrawal was carried out just in time. Havildar Lal Singh was awarded the I.O.M. for gallantry during these operations.

8^(TH) Punjab Regiment

89^(TH) Punjabis (1/8^(TH))

The Japanese tactics worked with devastating effect against poorly trained and equipped British forces. The British were further handicapped by their self-imposed compulsion to defend the airbases, which not only dispersed their forces, but also tied them down to tactically unsound defensive positions. This meant that the initiative remained with the Japanese throughout and they could concentrate their forces at the point of decision, while the British could not.

On 6^(TH) Brigade front, the outposts of 1/8^(TH) Punjab Regiment were ordered to withdraw towards the main Jitra position. As their column approached the causeway at Manggoi in late evening, the Royal Engineer officer in charge of the demolition panicked and blew up the causeway. This stranded the column, which consisted of a mountain battery and seven anti-tank guns and half the trucks of 1/8^(TH) Punjab. The troops were ordered to abandon the vehicles with their loads and move to the rear, as it was believed that the causeway would be repaired later. It never was. The loss of equipment was a serious blow, as none of it could be replaced.

The Japanese unrelenting attacks defeated the British at Jitra and forced 1/8^(TH) Punjab Regiment to withdraw towards Gurun. The defeat at Jitra was an absolute disaster. The 11^(TH) Division had been thoroughly beaten and driven out from its prepared defensive position in less than two days by a Japanese force no more than a brigade. It had suffered heavy casualties and its moral was shattered. The retreat from Jitra, though, was a disorganised shambles that cost the division more casualties than they had incurred during the Battle of Jitra itself. Many units were left behind at Jitra when the order to withdraw did not reach them, but many more men and whole platoons and companies were lost trying to cross the Bata River and in the broken terrain south of Jitra. Some of these men would eventually make it back to British lines; many more were captured or killed.

The 11^(TH) Division withdrew south to unprepared positions at Gurun. The terrain at Gurun offered a natural defensive obstacle for the British to use in the hope of stopping the Japanese advance. The Japanese had moved with astonishing speed and supported by air force and led by three tanks, eleven Lorries filled with infantry over ran Guru. On 15^(TH) December, the Japanese broke into the Brigade Headquarters, killing everyone. The situation of 11^(TH) Division was now hopeless. The Division Commander therefore decided to withdraw the remnants of his division south of Muda River and by the morning of 16^(TH) December, the division was across the River. In the meantime, 1/8^(TH) Punjab Regiment continued its withdrawal towards Sungei Patani to find that the Japanese had taken Sungei Patani. The Japanese advance continued to push back the British along both coasts. On 23^(RD) December, Taiping was taken and on 27^(TH) December, the British abandoned Ipoh. The British decided to make their next stand at Kampar in Central Malaya. On 1^(ST) January 1942, the Japanese launched a major attack on Kampar. The 1/8^(TH) Punjab Regiment charged the advancing Japanese and lost heavily.

8TH Punjab Regiment

89TH Punjabis (1/8TH)

With only thirty men were left in a company, which was now led by Jemadar Vir Singh. Jemadar Vir Singh led his men gallantly until he too fell badly wounded. The survivors hung on until ordered to withdraw at night. Jemadar Vir Singh was awarded the Military Cross for his heroic conduct. The company finally ran into a concealed Dannert wire, but the survivors hung on until ordered to withdraw at night. Numerous acts of bravery were carried out by the 1/8TH Punjab Regiment. One of them was by Sepoy Suba Singh, a runner, who was twice sent to the nearest British company under heavy enemy fire to telephone Battalion Headquarters. While returning from his second trip, he was seriously wounded in three places including the pelvis. The gallant Sepoy insisted on crawling back to the company with the reply. He was killed while attempting a third trip.

The British were again forced to fall back, this time to the Batu Pahat-Kluang-Mersing. The Battle of Muar was a decisive blow by the Japanese and the British had no option but to disengage and retreat towards Singapore. The 1/8TH Punjab Regiment, crossed into Singapore on 30TH January. The Battalion's total strength was 150. Next day, the causeway connecting the island to Malaya was blown up. The long retreat was over. The remnants of 1/8TH Punjab Regiment after their arrival in Singapore had been located at Bidadari Camp, and the Battalion was reformed with the draft from India.

The Japanese launched their invasion of Singapore on 8TH February. All the efforts by the British to stem the Japanese onslaught had been ineffectual. Despite the gallant conduct of their soldiers, the disjointed and confused British campaign never really had a chance. As the noose tightened around Singapore, the British surrendered unconditionally on 15TH February. Soon after the surrender, British officers were separated from their Indian troops and sent to Changi Prison. The Sikh soldiers that had not succumbed to join the Japanese sponsored Indian National Army had to face what was perhaps their worst ordeal. Story of the Sikh prisoners was a long tale of intimidation and cruelty, majority of them were sent to New Guinea, where most of them perished.

After the surrender of the Japanese in 1945, the liberated Prisoners of War started returning home. On 25TH March 1946, the 1/8TH Punjab Regiment started reforming around the nucleus of repatriated Prisoners of War at Lahore. By 28TH April, the Battalion had been brought up to strength by draft of officers and men from 9/8TH Punjab, which was being disbanded. On 25TH May, the 1/8TH Punjab Regiment proceeded to Bannu on the North-West Frontier, moving to Mir Ali in February 1947, where it was stationed at the time of independence.

At time of independence and the division of the Indian Army into newly formed Pakistan Army in 1947, the 1ST Battalion, 8TH Punjab Regiment was allocated to Pakistan Army. The new designation of the battalion became, 1ST Battalion, The Baluch Regiment. The Sikh soldiers from the battalion were transferred to the Indian Army.

8TH Punjab Regiment

90TH Punjabis (2/8TH)

The Battalion was raised in 1799 at Masulipatam as the Masulipatam Battalion. The Battalion was composed mostly of Muslims, Tamils and Telugus of South India. In 1892, it was reconstituted with Sikhs, Punjabi Mussalmans, and Rajputs, and permanently based in Burma. Its new designation was 5TH Burma Battalion of Madras Infantry.

For the next decade or so after their reconstitution, the Burma Battalions remained employed in operations against the recalcitrant tribes in the border districts of Burma. The 5TH Burma Battalion was also engaged in operations against the Chins in 1892-93. A detachment of three British and six Indian officers with 300 men left Mandalay on 13TH December 1892 and was mostly employed around Mautok.

Subsequent to the reforms brought about in the Indian Army in 1903, the regiment's designation was changed to 90TH Punjabis, the latter part reflecting the new class composition of the regiment, which it had acquired in 1892. In 1910, the Burma Battalions were delocalized from Burma and in 1911, the regiment moved to Nasirabad in India, where it was stationed on the outbreak of First World War.

Mesopotamian Campaign began as a small security measure to protect British oil interests in the Persian Gulf but soon developed into a major theatre of war. On 12TH January 1915, the 90TH Punjabis then stationed at Nasirabad, received their mobilization orders. The regiment sailed for Basra on 30TH January, as part of the 12TH Infantry Brigade and joined the newly formed 12TH Indian Division, and the regiment was stationed at Qurna. On 3RD March, the regiment was despatched to Persian Arabistan as a part of a column to secure the oil fields at Ahwaz. By the end of May, Persian Arabistan had been cleared of the Turks and the oil pipeline from Ahwaz to Abadan was secure. Although the operations in Persian Arabistan had not entailed any major fighting except skirmishes with hostile Arab tribesmen, the troops suffered greatly due to heat, exhaustion and disease.

With Ahwaz and Amara secure, the British now turned their attention towards Nasiriyah on the River Euphrates, whose capture they considered essential for securing Basra. Nasiriyah is situated about seventy miles west of Qurna at the southern end of Shatt al Hai. The area around the town is rich agricultural land surrounded by marshes.

On 8TH July, the 90TH Punjabis proceeded up the Euphrates, moving along the left bank of the River. On 12TH July, two companies of the regiment arrived at the frontline on the left bank. The regiment suffered its first casualties of the campaign when two men were wounded during reconnaissance of the Turkish positions. During the day, the Punjabis repulsed three attacks by the Turks on their position. On 13TH July, the British attack on the right bank failed its objective of occupying Sand Hills but extended the British line up to Sixteen Palms-Sukhair.

8TH Punjab Regiment

90TH Punjabis (2/8TH)

More reinforcements were sent for and the next several days were spent extending and improving the frontline trenches. By 20TH July, another brigade along with more artillery had arrived and General Gorringe decided to attack frontally on both banks of the River. On 24TH July, under cover of an artillery barrage, the 12TH Brigade launched its attack on the left bank frontage of 200 yards. The attack was led by the Royal West Kent Regiment, with two double companies of the 90TH Punjabis in close support. The rest of the regiment covered the attacking force with machine-gun and rifle fire from the right. The advance was carried out with great dash and gallantry, and the Turkish trenches were taken after some intense close quarter fighting. The Turks offered stiff resistance, but their positions on the left bank had been completely overrun.

Sepoy Partab Singh was awarded the I.O.M. for continuing the attack despite receiving two bullet wounds in his right arm. This young soldier was again wounded, losing two fingers and was unable to handle his rifle. He refused to go back and remained engaged in tending the wounded and Lance-Naik Kunda Singh received a posthumous I.O.M. for carrying a wounded NCO back to the lines over a distance of a hundred yards, while exposed to heavy enemy fire, which mortally wounded him.

Meanwhile on the right bank, the 30TH Brigade was successful in its attack and the Turks fled Nasiriyah. Next day they evacuated the town, which was then occupied by the British. During this operation, the British had suffered 533 casualties including nine killed and 36 wounded in the 90TH Punjabis. Following the capture of Nasiriyah, all objectives set by the British in Mesopotamia had been attained.

The 12TH Division, which had moved to Butaniyah in January to divert Turkish attention during the Battle of Shaikh Saad, was ordered to return to Nasiriyah in February. The 12TH Brigade with 90TH Punjabis withdrew on 5TH February, but due to the hostile attitude of Arabs, a column was despatched the next day to cover the withdrawal of 34TH Brigade. Two double companies of 90TH Punjabis accompanied the column, which took up position halfway between Butaniyah and Nasiriyah. On 7TH February, as 34TH Brigade reached the covering force, both were attacked by hostile Arabs from all sides. Heavy fighting ensued in which the 90TH Punjabis lost fourteen men killed including Jemadar Mewa Singh. The 90TH Punjabis were again in action during the summer, taking part in punitive operations against hostile Arabs near Nasiriyah. On 11TH September, the regiment attacked and captured the village of As Sahilan. As the regiment was retiring, it came under intense hostile fire and sustained 69 casualties including their Commanding Officer, Lieutenant Colonel Carleton, who was severely wounded, and Captain Morris, who was killed while trying to rescue a wounded Sepoy. Naik Jhanda Singh was awarded the I.O.M. for bringing back Captain Morris's body under heavy fire despite being wounded himself.

8TH Punjab Regiment

90TH Punjabis (2/8TH)

The 12TH Brigade with 90TH Punjabis had arrived at Fallujah from Baghdad after marching across the desert in extremely trying conditions. By 26TH September, the strike force had assembled at Madhij, with 90TH Punjabis forming part of an outpost line covering the concentration of the force.

On 27TH September, the force began its advance and soon captured the crossing over Habbaniya Canal at the dam. Early on the morning of 28TH September, Muslhaid Ridge was also seized. Screened by Muslhaid Ridge, the force then turned sharply to the southeast and crossed the dam. The 12TH Brigade was ordered to seize Aziziya Ridge. The 90TH Punjabis and the 39TH Garhwalis advanced against Aziziya Ridge and captured its southern portion. Meanwhile the cavalry, which had arrived in the rear of the Turks, was ordered to seize the bridge over Aziziya Canal, but for some unknown reason failed to do so. The task was now given to the 12TH Brigade, which was to continue the attack eastwards after capturing the bridge on Aziziya Canal in the morning. On 29TH September, the 90TH Punjabis captured Shaikh Faraja Ridge but suffered heavy casualties in the process. During the attack, two platoons of 'C' Company lost direction, and moving too far to the right, came up against the Turkish position on Unjana Hill. The Punjabis attacked and captured the position, but then were pushed back by heavy Turkish counter-attack.

In the meantime, the Garhwalis and the Queens along with the elements of the 90TH Punjabis had captured the Turkish trenches on the northern end of Aziziya Ridge. Captain Rodgerson, taking a mixed force of the three regiments charged and captured the bridge over Aziziya Canal along with a battery of guns. The Turks started surrendering all along the front. The Second Battle of Ramadi resulted in complete destruction of the Turkish 'Euphrates Group' and opened up the River to the British. The British killed or captured almost 3,600 Turks, besides seizing a large amount of war material. Their own losses amounted to about thousand men. The 90TH Punjabis suffered 182 casualties including three British and seven Indian officers wounded, 32 Other Ranks killed or missing and 140 Other Ranks wounded. The next objective along the Euphrates was the town of Khan al Baghdadi. A mobile force was then sent on a wide flanking march around Khan Baghdadi, and dug in behind the Turkish positions. The remainder of the division then assaulted frontally in the normal fashion, and the Turkish retreated from the town. They then ran unexpectedly into the blocking force, and their discipline quickly crumbled. The entire force of about 5000 men was taken prisoner. The mobile force was then dispatched further up the Euphrates in the direction the Turks had expected to retreat. 46 miles further upstream was the settlement of Ana. Here was the main Turkish supply base, which was now captured along with some high-ranking German officers attached to the Turkish Army. This was the last attack on the Euphrates Front. During Mesopotamian Campaign, the 90TH Punjabis suffered 452 casualties including 158 killed.

8TH Punjab Regiment

90TH Punjabis (2/8TH)

90TH Punjabis were awarded a number of gallantry awards: Subedar Mula Singh Jemadar Kishan Singh, Naik Jhanda Singh, Lance-Naik Kunda Singh, Sepoy Ghanda Singh Sepoy Balwant Singh and Sepoy Partab Singh were awarded the I.O.M.

Subedar Bir Singh, Subedar Pir Singh, was awarded the Military Cross, and Subedar Harnam Singh, Subedar Narian Singh, Jemadar Kishan Singh, Jemadar Sundar Singh, Havildar Sobha Singh, Havildar Bishan Singh, Naik Puran Singh, Sepoy Mangal Singh, Sepoy Gurdit Singh, and Sepoy Bhagat Singh were awarded the I.D.S.M. for their conspicuous gallantry in Mesopotamia.

The regiment returned from Mesopotamia to Kamptee in India in March 1919. It was re-mobilised on 8TH May for service on the North-West Frontier, and immediately mounted a punitive expedition against the Mahsuds. At no time in their history had the Mahsuds and Wazirs been so well armed at this juncture, since in addition to their normal armament considerable quantities of government rifles and ammunition had fallen recently into their hands, and they constituted a formidable enemy. The regiment subdued these clans with the action at Jandola, Palosina, Mandanna Hill, Kotkai and Ahnai Tangi. During the next fourteenth months, the regiment remained deployed at Thal, Parachinar, Alizai and Dharsamand.

In 1922, the 90TH Punjabis were grouped with the 91ST and 92ND Punjabis, 93RD Burma Infantry and 89TH Punjabis to form the 8TH Punjab Regiment. The 90TH Punjabis became the 2ND Battalion, 8TH Punjab Regiment.

In 1936, trouble again flared up in Waziristan in the form of a political and religious agitator known as the Fakir of Ipi. There had been for some time growing unrest in the region, fuelled by a perception of a weakening of British resolve to govern, following a number of constitutional changes in India. However, following a trial of a Muslim student on a charge of abducting a Hindu girl, the Fakir of Ipi began spreading anti-British sentiment in earnest, claiming that the government was interfering in a religious matter. While the British attempted to stamp out the insurrection by drawing the tribesmen into decisive engagement, the tribesmen managed to avoid being drawn into battle using guerrilla tactics of ambush in order to keep the initiative. In doing so, they inflicted considerable casualties upon the British and Indian troops. The North West Frontier and remained volatile with occasional raid on a village or attack on a garrison, things would remain this way until the end of British rule in 1947.

Sepoy Rattan Singh was awarded the I.O.M. for conspicuous gallantry during the operations on the North West Frontier in 1936.

In February 1943, the Battalion was mobilised for war. *Because of the demand for Sikhs from other regiments, all the Sikhs were withdrawn from the 2/8TH Punjab Regiment.*

In 1947, 2/8TH Punjab Regiment was allocated to the new Pakistan Army. The new designation of the battalion became, 2ST Battalion, The Baluch Regiment.

8TH Punjab Regiment

91ST Punjabis (3/8TH)

The regiment can be traced back to 1759 when it was first raised as Irregular Troops of East India Company. The regimen was composed mostly of Muslims, Tamils and Telugus of South India. In 1892, it was reconstituted with Sikhs, Punjabi Mussalmans, and Rajputs, and permanently based in Burma. Its new designation was 6TH Burma Battalion of Madras Infantry.

In 1887, the Battalion was formed into Shwebo Battalion of Upper Burma Police, and engaged in eliminating the rebels of Shwebo area in Central Burma. Jemadar Mangal Singh of the Shwebo Battalion was awarded the I.O.M. for gallantry during the Ymatha operation of 1889. Reverting back to Burma Battalion it went to China in 1900, to suppress the Boxer Rebellion. The Boxers, a xenophobic movement in China, carried out series of attacks on foreign missionaries, merchants and property. The foreign legations in the Imperial capital Peking (Beijing) were besieged by the Boxers, and held out for three months despite having a small garrison. An international relief force was organised by seven nations, and in June 1900 the Taku Forts were captured. The force then moved on Peking, which was captured in August. Eventually peace was concluded in January 1901.

On 3RD October 1903 the Battalion was renamed as 91ST Punjabis. After 31 years of service in Burma the 91ST Punjabis proceeded to Mesopotamia in August 1916, with class composition of Sikhs, Punjabi Mussalmans, and Dogras. On 16TH December, a reconnoitring party of the 91ST Punjabis and 7TH Gurkhas from the 7TH Brigade was sent to the left bank to ascertain Turkish disposition between Sannaiyat and Magasis. The seven men swam across the river on empty oil tins at night. Sepoy Naurang Singh and two Gurkhas drowned, while the rest returned after accomplishing their mission, utterly exhausted and numbed from cold. For their gallant exploit, Sepoys Narinjan Singh and Kishen Singh received the I.D.S.M.

On July 11TH, three companies of 91ST Punjabis along with four armoured cars moved out towards the enemy positions but were soon checked by the fire from the bank of the Habbaniya Canal. The 7TH Gurkhas were despatched to cover the left flank of 91ST Punjabis who continued to attack in the intense heat of the day. But the troops could not be pulled back because of enemy fire, and they were ordered to stay where they were. They stayed out in the open all day, suffering both from enemy fire as well as the terrible heat. The casualties of 91ST Punjabis during the day were 35 Other Ranks killed and 52 wounded including two Indian officers. They were in no condition to resume the attack and they were pulled back. Concluding that it was not possible to attain his objectives in the intense heat with the force at his disposal, the Brigade Commander withdrew his force to Fallujah.

The 91ST Punjabis then participated in operations on both the Tigris and the Euphrates Fronts, including the Battle of Ramadi.

8TH Punjab Regiment

91ST Punjabis (3/8TH)

In Battle of Ramadi 120 Turkish troops were killed and another 190 were wounded. 3,456 prisoners were captured, including 145 officers. A great deal of materiel was seized, including 13 artillery pieces, 12 machine guns and large quantities of ammunition and other supplies. On 30TH October, the Turkish commander in Mesopotamia surrendered.

In January 1918, the regiment moved to Palestine, to join in General Allenby's advance on Megiddo. The task given to the 3RD Division on 19TH September, to break through the Turkish defences in front of the village of Sabieh, and then turning eastwards, capture the Turkish positions between Jaljulye and Qalqilye. The attack of 7TH Brigade was carried out rapidly, with 91ST Punjabis advancing in the second wave. The Turkish trenches were quickly overrun, and the brigade captured Qalqilye. In the afternoon, the 91ST Punjabis moved to the front of the brigade and continued the advance over broken and difficult terrain well into the night. Early in the morning 20TH September, they captured Azzun, the headquarters of the German Asia Corps, after overcoming some stiff resistance. The Turks finally sued for peace. The armistice came into force on 31ST October. The 91ST Punjabis stayed in Palestine till May 1920, when they left for home. It had seen almost 4 years of active service and suffered 443 casualties including 185 killed.

Sepoy Nard Singh was awarded the I.O.M., while Subedar Sundar Singh and Sepoy Kishen Singh the I.D.S.M., for very conspicuous gallantry and coolness during the Palestine campaign.

The Third Afghan War was followed by a general uprising in Waziristan. In 1921, the 91ST Punjabis then stationed at Poona, were mobilized for operations in South Waziristan. On 18TH November, they arrived at Kotkai on the Taki Zam and were detailed on road protection duties. On 18TH December, two companies of the Battalion took part in a punitive expedition against Mahsuds near Kotkai. During the operation a company held an advance position for three hours under heavy fire and suffered several casualties, before the Mahsuds were subdued.

In 1922, the 91ST Punjabis were grouped with the 90TH Punjabis and 92ND Punjabis, 93RD Burma Infantry and 89TH Punjabis to form the 8TH Punjab Regiment. The 91ST Punjabis became the 3RD Battalion, 8TH Punjab Regiment.

Up to 1939, the 3/8TH Punjab Regiment, operated in South Waziristan, Chitral, Wucha Garhi and Khujuri Plains against the fiercely independent tribesmen that inhabited this region.

In October 1940, it joined the 19TH Infantry Brigade of the 8TH Indian Division. After intensive training at Dhond, the Battalion arrived at Basra in Iraq on 17TH August 1941. After tours of duty at Buqoq, Baghdad and Kifri, the Battalion left for Syria in April 1943, spending next five months training hard for mountain warfare. In September 1943, it embarked for Alexandria from Tripoli, en-route to Taranto in Italy.

8TH Punjab Regiment

91ST Punjabis (3/8TH)

The 3/8TH Punjab Regiment landed at Taranto on 24TH September 1943, as part of the 19TH Indian Infantry Brigade, 8TH Indian Division. The 8TH Indian Division concentrated east of Taranto and then moved up to join V Corps of the Eighth Army, which was then approaching Gustav Line, also called the Winter Line. Two Rivers blocked the Eighth Army's approach to the Gustav line. These were the Biferno and the Trigno. On 7TH October, Termoli on the coast was captured and the crossing over River Biferno was secured. The advance then was halted and the Eighth Army regrouped. It was at this time that the 8TH Indian Division was brought into line and took over the Larino Sector on 19/20TH October. The advance of V Corps was led by the 78TH British Division on the right and the 8TH Indian Division on the left, with the objective of seizing bridgeheads over the River Trigno. On 25TH October, about five miles short of Trigno, 19TH Brigade passed through 17TH Brigade, with 1/5TH Essex and 3/8TH Punjab Regiment in the lead. The main objective of the brigade was the villages of Monte Falcone and Monte Mitro on the southern bank of the River. From there, the brigade was to attack and seize the village of Tuffilo, on the opposite bank, and beyond it, the 2000 feet high feature of Monte Farano.

The 3/8TH Punjab Regiment's first brush with the enemy came on 25TH October, when 'A' and 'D' Companies went into action at San Felice and suffered their first causality of the war. Next day 'B' Company captured a ridge south of Monte Falcone. On 27TH October, the Battalion launched a dawn attack on Monte Falcone under a creeping barrage of artillery and captured the village without much opposition. With the southern bank firmly in their hands, next objective was the crossing of the Trigno River itself.

The retreating Germans had blown up the bridges, and all the approaches were mined, and under direct observation of the enemy, occupying the high ground on the opposite bank. Finally, early on 2ND November, the 19TH Brigade began crossing the river in heavy rain. The attacking Battalions came under heavy German fire and suffered serious casualties. Both Battalions were forced to withdraw. That night the 3/8TH Punjab Regiment crossed the river, and the attack was resumed, but was repulsed, forcing the troops back to their original positions. However, during the night, the Germans pulled out and the Punjabis took Monte Farano. The advance of the 8TH Indian Division was resumed.

On 16TH November, 3/8TH Punjab Regiment occupied the high ground two miles south of the river in order to deny the enemy observation of the area below. Supported by two squadrons of Sherman tanks, it was ordered to capture the hilltop village of Perano to secure the south bank of the Sangro and gain observation for its crossing. As the tanks approached the Battalion's position, they raised a big column of dust, alerting the enemy. The Germans responded by plastering the area with high explosives and air burst fire. Several men were killed, while more were wounded.

8TH Punjab Regiment

91ST Punjabis (3/8TH)

In the meantime, a section under Havildar Kuldip Singh had been sent forward to reconnoitre a knoll near Perano. The position was held by the enemy, who opened fire on the reconnaissance party. Havildar Kuldip Singh charged the German position, wounding several of them and forcing the rest to flee. He then occupied the knoll and despite heavy counter-shelling, retained the position until the capture of Perano. Havildar Kuldip Singh was awarded the I.D.S.M., for his gallantry and initiative.

On 17TH November, the attack on Perano went in at 1200 hours. The Germans had prepared a strong-point to block the approach from the right, which they considered the only feasible line of attack. But 'C' Company, supported by a squadron of tanks, climbed precipitous slopes and entered the village from a different direction, taking the Germans by complete surprise.

Although the other squadron of tanks and the Battalion carriers were halted at the heavily defended strong-point, the damage had been done. By dusk, the Germans had withdrawn and the village was occupied by 3/8TH Punjab Regiment. The 19TH Brigade was then ordered to capture the San Angelo-II Calvario feature to secure the left flank of the division. The attack was led by, 3/8TH Punjab Regiment. They left Perano on 22ND November and concentrated on the southern bank for the assault. A company crossed the River in heavy rain, and undetected by the enemy, secured the bridgehead on Woody Spur, a thickly wooded mound. They were followed by the rest of the Battalion, with men wet and cold from the freezing rain. 'C' Company under Captain Girdhari Singh advanced towards II Calvario, while 'D' Company under Subedar Amar Singh moved towards the ring contour.

Thanks to the tracers being used, the men were able to avoid the lines of fire and did not suffer any casualties. By dawn, the company had taken its objective after inflicting heavy casualties on the enemy, ten of whom were captured. The Germans counter- attacked with about fifty men supported by three tanks. Subedar Amar Singh requested artillery support, which initially landed on his own position, injuring him. But as the range was adjusted, a second counter-attack was repulsed without artillery support. Throughout the day the Germans tried to dislodge the company, but the men grimly held on to their position. As Subedar Amar Singh was being evacuated by a party of four, they were ambushed by a German patrol. All four were wounded. Subedar Amar Singh immediately counter-attacked and captured the three Germans, who were then drafted in assisting the wounded back to the Regimental Aid Post.

Meanwhile, as 'C' Company reached the lower slopes of II Calvario, it came under heavy fire from machine-guns and tanks positioned in the area of the saddle. Captain Girdhari Singh decided to seek protection of a ridge on his left. But first, a German machine-gun post covering its approach had to be eliminated. A party of five men under a Jemadar was ordered to neutralize the threat.

8TH Punjab Regiment

91ST Punjabis (3/8TH)

The party crawled up to within a few yards of the unsuspecting enemy, and while their Bren gunner covered one machine gun, the rest charged the other machine – gun. Crew of one machine-gun surrendered while the other abandoned its post and fled. By dawn B Company had captured II Calvario. However, Calvario was soon recaptured by the Germans.

On the morning of 24TH November, as the Germans had taken a severe beating and were in no shape to continue the fight, they abandoned the Calvario, which was re-occupied. The Battalion won a number of awards for its gallant conduct. These included Military Cross for Captain Girdhari Singh and I.D.S.M.s, for Havildars Baldev Singh and Gurbux Singh.

On the night of 18/19TH February, the Commando Platoon of 3/8TH Punjab Regiment was ordered to capture a German prisoner from Orsogna. The platoon moved silently into the pitch-dark night and entering the enemy post, surprised a section of the Germans; two of them were killed while another two were taken prisoner. But the commotion alerted the entire garrison and they came under heavy fire from several directions. The platoon withdrew in good order carrying back the wounded safely. The Germans, who considered Orsogna to be impregnable, were much perturbed by this incursion. Jemadar Kuldip Singh was awarded the I.O.M. for his gallantry during this operation.

In January 1944, Allied forces begin a major assault on the Gustav Line, a German defensive line drawn across central Italy just south of Rome. The Gustav Line represented a stubborn German defence, built by Field Marshal Albert Kesselring, which had to be broken before the Italian capital could be taken. Gustav Line followed the course of Rivers Gari and Garigliono. The River Gari itself was a formidable obstacle. As the 3/8TH Punjab Regiment advanced, it came against the strongest part of the escarpment, twenty feet high and held by a series of strong-points, each manned by a platoon, there was little or no cover, the Battalion was pinned down by murderous German fire and advance no further. Casualties began to mount and the wounded could not be evacuated. All communication had broken down. As the mist lifted around noon, a line of Canadian tanks were seen approaching. The arrival of armour had been most timely. Under the covering fire of tanks, German strong-points were rushed and overwhelmed. Major Girdhari Singh personally led the assault, attacking with grenades and Tommy–gun; he crossed the wire and threw grenades into the trench. Nine Germans surrendered to Major Girdhari Singh. His men followed up and the post was captured with twenty-two Germans inside. Major Girdhari was awarded bar to his Military Cross for yet another display of raw courage and inspiring leadership under fire. All the Battalion objectives had been secured, although at a terrible cost. Out of the 400 men who had set out, 256 had become casualties, including Major Sujan Singh, who was killed. The 8TH Indian Division had smashed the Gustav Line; and 3/8TH Punjab Regiment had played a central role in it.

8TH Punjab Regiment

91ST Punjabis (3/8TH)

On 15TH May, the 8TH Indian Division turned the Cassino position from the flank by capturing Pignataro. The German position was precarious. They rushed four divisions southwards and tried to regroup on the Hitler Line. But on 23RD May, the Eighth Army smashed the Hitler Line. The Germans were now in headlong retreat. The 8TH Indian Division with 3/8TH Punjab Regiment, was in the van of pursuit of the retreating Germans and fought numerous small actions with the enemy rearguard.

On 26TH May, a column of 3/8TH Punjab Regiment and a squadron of 6TH Lancers with some tanks caught up with a party of German paratroopers in the Melfa Gorge. Twenty-five Germans were killed and fourteen were taken prisoner. Four days later, passing through Arce, the battalion moved towards Cle Lucinetta. Here, it was involved in a fire-fight with the German rearguard on 31ST May and suffered 28 casualties.

German forces withdrew to the Gothic Line, a string of heavily fortified positions north of Florence, and last of German major defensive lines. By 16TH September, the 8TH Indian Division had broken through the Gothic Line. The 8TH Indian Division was given the task of clearing the Germans from the mountains in the central sector. On 30TH September, 3/8TH Punjab Regiment was ordered to capture the feature east of Maradi Road up to Monte Casalino. On 1ST October, the villages of Dogara and Monte L'Alto were captured against stiff opposition. As the 3/8TH Punjab advanced; hell was let loose from three sides as machine-guns coughed and sent bullets whipping towards the sturdy men of 3/8TH Punjab Regiment. Not a single man hesitated; before the Germans realized what was happening, the Punjabis were all over them, and six prisoners were taken. During the inevitable German counter-attack, this came after heavy artillery and mortar fire. The attack was beaten back after inflicting heavy casualties on the Germans. Lance Havildar Bhup Singh, using captured German weapons, repulsed two more German attacks. In the last attack, the Germans were able to penetrate and occupy part of the position. Bhup Singh and his men rushed the infiltrators, killing or capturing all of them. The platoon had been reduced to half its original number and was ordered to withdraw. Lance Havildar Bhup Singh was awarded the I.D.S.M., for his remarkable feats of heroism.

On 25TH April, the 8TH Indian Division started crossing the Po and advanced towards the next river, the Aldige. The Germans were surrendering everywhere. Two days later, the 19TH Brigade moved across the Aldige, while on 28TH April. 3/8TH Punjab crossed the River Ripo and moved to Fratta. It was the last river it would cross in Italy. By now all German resistance had ceased. On 29TH April, the Germans in Italy signed the instrument of surrender. Nine days later, the war in Europe ended with the surrender of Germany.

The performance of the battalion in Italy had been nothing short of spectacular. The battalion had taken part in most of the decisive battles of the campaign and carried out the missions assigned to it with remarkable professionalism and élan.

8^(TH) Punjab Regiment

91^(ST) Punjabis (3/8^(TH))

The officers and men of 3/8^(TH) Punjab Regiment in had fought with ferocious determination and courage, as attested by the numerous gallantry awards won by them. Five times the Battalion met the formidable German paratroopers in battle; and each time they were outfought by the indomitable Punjabis. But the campaign had also exacted a terrible price. The Battalion suffered 1288 casualties in Italy, including 304 killed in action; nine of them officers. In July 1945, the 3/8^(TH) Punjab returned home. It left for another stint in Iraq in August 1946, returning to India on 7^(TH) June 1947.

The 3/8^(TH) Punjab were awarded numerous gallantry awards in Italy, including the Victoria Cross. It was on 12^(TH) May 1944 that Sepoy Kamal Ram was awarded Victoria Cross at Gustav Lines. He was the youngest VC of his time at the age of 19 years. Later he retired as Subedar Major from the Indian Army.

Captain Shamsher Singh Gill of the Battalion was awarded the (MBE) Member of the Order of the British Empire.

Captain Girdhari Singh and Subedar Joginder Singh of the Battalion were awarded the Military Cross, while Havildar Kuldip Singh the I.O.M. and Lance-Naik Kartar Singh and Sepoys Jagdish Singh and Sepoy S. Singh were awarded the Military Medal.

In 1947, at the time of independence, and the creation of Pakistan, the Battalion was allocated to the newly formed Pakistan Army. The new designation of the battalion became, 3^(RD) Battalion, The Baluch Regiment. The Sikh soldiers from the battalion were transferred to the Indian Army.

92^(ND) Punjabis (4/8^(TH))

The regiment was raised on 1^(ST) January 1800 at Madura as the 2^(ND) Battalion 16^(TH) Regiment of Madras Native Infantry. It was composed mostly of Muslims, Tamils and Telugus. In 1890, it was reconstituted with Sikhs, Punjabi Mussalmans and permanently based in Burma. Its new designation was 4^(TH) Burma Battalion of Madras Infantry.

In January 1891, a British post at Yadwin in the southern Chin District of Yaw in Burma, was attacked by the Chins, who captured several military personnel. A punitive expedition was launched to punish the tribesmen and free the captives. The force, known as the Chinbok Column, and consisting of 96 rifles of the 4^(TH) Burma Battalion, and 112 mounted infantry composed of Sikhs, arrived at Yadwin on 4^(TH) February. The villages implicated in the attack were severely punished and the entire Yaw District was pacified.

Subsequent to the reforms brought about in the Indian Army all the 8^(TH) Punjabi Battalions except the 33^(RD) Burma Infantry elected to become Punjabis and the regiment's designation was changed to 92^(ND) Punjabis. In 1910, the Burma Battalions were delocalized from Burma and in 1913, the 92^(ND) Punjabis moved to Benares in India.

8TH Punjab Regiment

92ND Punjabis (4/8TH)

On the outbreak of the First World War, the 92ND Punjabis sailed for Egypt in November 1914. They entrained at Suez for Ismailia, where they stayed till 8TH January, when they moved to Serapeum, two miles north of the Great Bitter Lake. On 23RD January, two double companies were deployed at Tussum, a mile north of Lake Timash, while the other two remained at Serapeum. From the middle of January, British patrols started reporting contact with the advancing Turks in several sectors.

The main Turkish attack was launched at about 2,000 yards south of the post of Tussum. Early on the morning of 3RD February, the sentries of 92ND Punjabis at Tussum heard movement of troops southeast of the post. The Commander immediately directed machine-gun fire on the east bank of the canal. Then, as moon came out of the clouds, parties of Turkish soldiers were seen moving towards the canal carrying pontoons and rafts. They were fired upon and checked by the 92ND Punjabis supported by 62ND Punjabis and an Egyptian battery of artillery on the opposite bank. Soon however, parties of Turks carrying pontoons were seen on the east bank of the canal on a frontage of a mile and half. Rapid and effective fire by the defenders resulted in the Turks abandoning most of their craft. Several vessels were sunk, while the few who managed to cross were immediately charged by the 62ND Punjabis, who killed or captured all the occupants.

As daylight approached, the Turks launched an attack against the Tussum Post, while their artillery opened up on British positions on the west bank and on ships in the canal. A Turkish trench was seen about 200 yards south of the post and enfilade fire by the 92ND Punjabis destroyed its occupants. Another group of about 350 Turks, occupying the day trenches of 92ND Punjabis, southeast of the post, were attacked by a party, who captured portions of the trenches, along with some prisoners. Another counter-attack, in which 70 Turks surrendered, was followed by another attack to re-capture remaining portion of trenches, and the task was completed after intense fighting. A total of eight Turkish officers and 280 men were killed or captured in the entire operation. The 92ND Punjabis suffered losses of two men killed and seven wounded. Naik Mihan Singh was awarded the I.O.M., for conspicuous bravery shown during the day's action, when he worked up to a Turkish trench alone and opened fire on the enemy, forcing him to take shelter in the trench. On being joined by other men of his squad, he kept the enemy pinned down, enabling his company to get to a point where they could enfilade the trench, after which the Turks surrendered. In an action near Tussum, after an intense fight, the Turks surrendered. 92ND Punjabis took 299 prisoners, while 59 lay dead in the trenches.

By 5TH February, the Turkish attack on Suez Canal had failed, and they retreated across the Sinai. Naiks Karam Singh, Dalip Singh, Sepoys Dharam Singh and Joginder Singh were awarded the I.D.S.M., for the gallantry against the Turks on the Suez Canal.

8TH Punjab Regiment

92ND Punjabis (4/8TH)

The regiment having spent a year guarding the Suez Canal arrived at Basra in Mesopotamia on 24TH December 1915. Next day, they proceeded to Ali Gharbi to join the 19TH Brigade of the 7TH Division. On 4TH January 1916, The 19,000 troops of the Tigres Corps arrived at Shaikh Saad. The town was situated in a loop of the River on the right bank, with Turkish trenches running out from both sides of the River. It was defended by about 4,000 troops, who were later reinforced by several thousand more. On 6TH January, the attack commenced on both banks, but could make no headway as the well dug in Turks swept the open ground with lethal fire. The 92ND Punjabis, who had moved to support of the 51ST Sikhs, suffered 24 casualties and retired to the nullah in the rear.

The next day the 92ND Punjabis advanced to the firing line with the 28TH Brigade, charged over 300 yards of open country, carrying the Turkish frontline trenches. Soon, the second line trenches were also taken, but then came under fire both from the third line trenches as well as from the flank. The brigade was ordered to consolidate its gains and resume the attack next morning. The attack, which began in the early afternoon of 13TH January, postponed from the morning because of a persistent mist and a slow advance by artillery across the River, quickly lost the intended element of surprise, as the outnumbered British forces on both sides of enemy lines struggled to assert themselves against a robust Turkish defence. Kemball made a frontal advance, while Younghusband, with the bulk of the British force, attempted a wide turning movement. The delay seriously affected the chances of success, as small-arms and artillery fire from the alerted Turkish forces began to halt the British infantry movements. Lacking proper maps, the leading British column became lost. Seizing the opportunity, the Turkish units began to wheel around from a north-south orientation to an east-west, to face the British flanking manoeuvre. The resulting frontal attack by the 28TH Brigade was repulsed with heavy casualties. By dusk, it became clear that the attempt had failed. British troops, attempting to manoeuvre around the Turkish flanks, failed to reach the River, and the mouth of the Hanna Defile was still strongly held by the entrenched Turkish troops. General Aylmer called off the attack by the end of the day and ferried most of his remaining troops to the right bank of the Tigris. By this time, Aylmer's troops had gained control of the Wadi, but it was a small advance that was unworthy of the 1,600 men killed or wounded in the attack. The 92ND Punjabis had sustained 179 casualties during the battle of the Wadi. The provision of adequate medical capacity and supplies had not improved significantly since the appalling debacle at Sheikh Saad, so again many casualties suffered without treatment or evacuation for several days. Having failed twice earlier in the month of January 1916 to relieve Sir Charles Townshend's beleaguered force at Kut-al-Amara, General Aylmer was nevertheless continued with his increasingly unsuccessful operation. Aylmer's force of 10,000 men, in order to reach Kut, was travelling upstream on the River Tigris.

8TH Punjab Regiment

92ND Punjabis (4/8TH)

Blocking his way were some 30,000 Turkish troops commanded by the increasingly confident Khalil Pasha. With the Turks sited on the Hanna Defile slightly upstream from the Wadi, now in British hands, Aylmer could not hope to relieve Townshend without first defeating Khalil's force. Thus on 21ST January 1916 Aylmer launched a fresh attack. Aylmer' setback began with an advance by 4,000 troops on 20TH January and on the morning of 21ST January. The sole effect of the weak bombardment was to warn Khalil of an approaching attack. Consequently around 60% of the attacking British force was cut down by carefully sited machine gun positions. No ground was gained. Intending to resume the attack on the following day General Aylmer called off operations once he witnessed at first hand the critical condition of his forces injured and sick. The failed attack had resulted in a further 2,700 British casualties. Medical supplies were, as ever during the Mesopotamian campaign, pitifully under-provided. His force of less than 10,000 was now outnumbered by at least five-to-one in the area; he therefore saw no possibility of success. Incoming regional Commander-in-Chief Sir Percival Lake, nevertheless ordered Aylmer to try again, at the Battle of Dujaila. The regiment went on to take part in the Battles of Dujaila, three Battles of Sannaiyat, Beit Isa and the Actions of Shawa Khan, Istabulat, Daur and Tikrit. On 31ST October, the Turkish commander in Mesopotamia made an unconditional surrender to the British.

The regiment fought with great gallantry and suffered grievous losses in the long and bloody campaign in Mesopotamia. Subedar Sher Singh, Jemadar Partab Singh, Jemadar Hazara Singh, and Sepoy Mihan Singh of the regiment were awarded the I.O.M. while Jemadar Kishan Singh, Havildar Sapuran Singh, Havildar Wasakha Singh, Havildar Harnam Singh, Naik Hari Singh, Naik Basant Singh, Naik Harnam Singh, Naik Chanan Singh, Lance-Naik Dalip Singh, Sepoy Sapuran Singh, Sepoy Sohan Singh, Sepoy Kishan Singh and Sepoy Jhanda Singh, were awarded the I.D.S.M. for their conspicuous gallantry in Mesopotamia.

In 1918, the 92ND Punjabis were ordered to proceed to Palestine. By April they were in the frontline in Palestine. The objective given to the 7TH Division was the western portion of the El Tireh defences. The leading waves of 92ND Punjabis swarmed into Turkish trenches after tearing their way through the enemy's wire with cutters, hands and feet. Dozens of Turks were killed or captured. Naik Dalip Singh and his section charged a machine gun, killing its crew and capturing the gun. Leaving parties to mop up the remaining Turks, the regiment continued its rapid advance, the leading troops having to halt several times as they outpaced their own artillery barrage. Having overrun the Turkish trenches, the 92ND Punjabis concentrated with the rest of the brigade for the next phase of operations. Then 7TH Division advanced towards El Tireh, moving into the hilly country towards the east of the coastal plain.

8TH Punjab Regiment

92ND Punjabis (4/8TH)

The advance was led by the 92ND Punjabis, after passing through the northern outskirts of El Tireh, they were ordered to occupy hill west of El Majdal. As the regiment advanced, it faced considerable resistance from the Turkish rearguard, which was occupying both sides of Wadi al Ayun. The Turks were driven from their positions and El Majdal was occupied. The regiment's casualties during the operations were eight men killed, including a British and an Indian officer, and 58 wounded. The day's operations had been a spectacular success for the Indian Army. The Turks finally gave in and sued for peace. The armistice came into force on 31ST October, bringing to an end the Indian Army's brilliant campaign. In February 1919, the 92ND Punjabis embarked at Beirut for Cilicia in Turkey to assist French troops occupying Turkish territory. It sailed for India in May 1920. For their exceptional bravery and excellent performance in the war, the 92ND Punjabis were made Prince of Wales's Own and on 1ST January 1922, Edward; the Prince of Wales was gazetted as their Colonel-in-Chief.

Naik Karam Singh, Naik Dalip Singh, Sepoy Dharam Singh and Sepoy Dalip Singh were awarded the I.D.S.M. for their conspicuous gallantry in Egypt. The 92ND (Prince of Wales's Own) Punjabis were grouped with the 90TH Punjabis, 91ST Punjabis (Light Infantry), 93RD Burma Infantry and 89TH Punjabis to form the 8TH Punjab Regiment in 1922. The Battalion was redesignated as the 4TH Battalion (Prince of Wales's Own) 8TH Punjab Regiment.

At the outbreak of Second World War, 4TH Battalion, 8TH Punjab was serving on the North-West Frontier. In April 1941, the regiment moved to Basra in Iraq. The Battalion remained in Iraq and Iran throughout the war. The battalion returned to India in January 1946. At the time of independence, and the creation of Pakistan, the battalion was allocated to the newly formed Pakistan Army. The new designation of the battalion became, 4TH Battalion, The Baluch Regiment. The Sikh soldiers from the battalion were transferred to the Indian Army.

93RD Burma Infantry (5/8TH)

The regiment was raised on 1ST January 1800 at Madura as the 2ND Battalion 16TH Regiment of Madras Native Infantry. In 1890, it was reconstituted with Sikhs, Punjabi Mussalmans and permanently based in Burma. Its designation was changed to the 3RD Regiment of Burma Infantry, and in 1891, to the 33RD Regiment of Madras Infantry. In 1901, its title was changed to the 33RD Burma Infantry. From 1891 to 1893, the regiment operated in the Kachin State in northern Burma, quelling various outbreaks of rebellion. During the operations Subedar Prem Singh was awarded the Order of British India (OBI) while Sepoy Jawand Singh, Sepoy Badhawa Singh and Sepoy Narain Singh were awarded the I.O.M. for conspicuous bravery. As part of the reforms brought about in the Indian Army in 1903, the regiment's designation was changed to 93RD Burma Infantry.

8TH Punjab Regiment

93RD Burma Infantry (5/8TH)

On the outbreak of the First World War, the regiment was deployed to defend the Suez Canal against the Turks in November 1914. On their arrival at Suez, the 93RD Burma Infantry moved to Qantara on the east bank of the canal, where it stayed till 9TH January 1915, when on joining the 31ST Brigade of 11TH Division, it moved to Moascar near Ismailia. During its stay in Egypt, the regiment served at Port Said and again at Qantara, but was not engaged in any fighting.

In September 1915, they left for France, and reached Marseilles on 18TH September and entrained the same evening for Merville, arriving there three days later, just in time to take part in the Battle of Loos about to get underway. The Battle of Loos opened on September 25TH. In many areas, the British artillery had not succeeded in cutting the German wire in advance of the attack. While advancing over open fields within the range of German artillery and guns, the British suffered heavy losses.

However, due to numerical superiority, the British were finally able to break through the weak German defences and capture the town of Loos. The battle resumed the following day and the Germans were very prepared and held back any attempts to continue the opposing side's advance. All the reserves were committed against the strengthened German positions. The twelve attacking battalions suffered 8,000 casualties out of 10,000 men in just four hours. On September 28TH, the fighting subsided with the British having retreated to their starting positions, and the offensive was finally abandoned. The British casualties at Loos were 48, 267 men, 4000 of them in the Indian Corps, while the French and the German losses were almost 2,000 each. The battle of Loos was the last major engagement of the Indian Corps in France. In January 1916, the last Indian infantry left France for other battlefields.

In January 1916, the regiment arrived in Mesopotamia. On 18TH January, during the Battle of Hanna, the 93RD Burma Infantry had kept up an intense fire on the Turks, killing a number of them as they retreated during the first onslaught by the 7TH Division. But on the counter-attack, the Turks turned their attention on the 93RD Burma Infantry, and they came under heavy fire. The regiment sustained heavy casualties, and had to retreat to the other side of the River.

In February, the 93RD Burma Infantry was transferred to the 9TH Brigade. On 8TH March, the 9TH Brigade launched its attack on Dujaila Redoubt with the 93RD Burma Infantry and 1ST Gurkhas in the lead. They were supported by two brigades on their flank. The 9TH Brigade came under heavy machine-gun and rifle fire, while their own artillery was shelling the redoubt instead of the Turkish trenches in front of them. The attack was continued over open ground with utmost gallantry and 93RD Burma Infantry suffered heavy losses. A little progress was made as all the brigades had been checked. Aylmer decided to withdraw his force. The British had suffered almost 3,500 casualties, while the losses in 93RD Burma Infantry were 190, almost half of those engaged.

8TH Punjab Regiment

93RD Burma Infantry (5/8TH)

Another, causality was General Aylmer, who was sacked soon after, his place being taken by General Gorringe. During the Battle of Beit Isa, on 17TH April, the 93RD Burma Infantry had been reduced to 154 men out of 300, who had gone into action earlier in the day. During the chaos of the battle, the officers made desperate efforts to rally their men. Amongst these was Jemadar Indar Singh of 93RD Burma Infantry, who was awarded the I.O.M., for his courage and initiative. Although all major operations of the Tigres Front had ceased, more misery was in store for the 93RD Burma Infantry. On 23RD April, the 9TH Brigade was ordered to capture an isolated Turkish trench system called the Apex. The advance was led by the 93RD Burma Infantry and the Highland Light Infantry before dawn on 24TH April. When day broke, the leading Battalions had advanced 1,500 yards but were still some 800 yards short of their objective, and encountering heavy enemy fire. By evening, the entire position was clear of the enemy. The 93RD Burma Infantry suffered 40 casualties during the action.

The Turks had waged a skilful campaign and their troops had shown great courage and determination in fighting the British to a standstill. The Tigres Force was a spent force and the British finally decided to give up further attempts at relief of Kut-al-Amara. On 29TH April, General Townsend surrendered his starving garrison to the Turks. The Tigres Force had suffered 23,000 casualties trying to rescue him, but he never made any attempt to breakout to assist the relieving force. The General and his officers went into comfortable captivity, where more than 4000 died of starvation and neglect.

The Punjabis had suffered great deal during the fighting on the Tigres Front. The 92ND Punjabis and the 93RD Burma Infantry had been reduced to less than a hundred men each, while the total strength of 89TH Punjabis was 164.

During the eleven day's fighting in the Khudaira Bend, in January 1917, the 3RD Division had suffered 1,693 casualties including 188 in the 93RD Burma Infantry. Subedar Lachman Singh received the I.O.M., for stopping and rallying men of the Manchester Regiment during their retreat. Between 20TH January and 15TH February, the Turks were also driven out of the Hai Salient and their position in the Dahra Bend, thus clearing the entire right bank of the Tigris of all Turkish forces.

In the battle of Jabal Hamrin, as soon as they had crossed the forward crest, the Battalions came under intense fire from concealed Turkish positions. A series of Turkish counter-attacks pushed the British front line back. As the company of 93RD Burma Infantry moved in to support the Gurkhas, the situation had become so precarious the General Campbell ordered the brigade back. The remaining three companies of 93RD Burma Infantry and the two Battalions of 8TH Brigade were ordered to cover the retirement. During the disastrous battle of Jabal Hamrin the force had suffered 1,165 casualties, 153 of them in 93RD Burma Infantry.

8TH Punjab Regiment

93RD Burma Infantry (5/8TH)

General Maude had been contemplating a move against the Turks on the Euphrates Front since March 1917. In July, he decided to attack Turkish garrisons at Ramadi despite the intense heat. The task was given to 7TH Brigade which had been deployed on the Euphrates since March. The 93RD Burma Infantry at Baghdad was ordered on 6TH July to join 7TH Brigade for the operations. The Battalion marched out the same evening, arriving at Fallujah early on 8TH July. On 10TH July, two companies of 93RD Burma Infantry occupied Madhij, driving out the Turkish garrison there. The 7TH Brigade with the rest of the force then concentrated on the enemy positions. The Turks started surrendering to the attacking force, all along the front. The Second Battle of Ramadi resulted in complete destruction of the Turkish 'Euphrates Group' and opened up the River to the British. The British killed or captured almost 3,600 Turks, besides seizing a large amount of war material. Their own losses amounted to about thousand men. The 93RD Burma Infantry had fought with great gallantry and suffered heavy losses in this long and bloody campaign in Mesopotamia.

Subedar Indar Singh and Subedars Lachman Singh and Lal Singh, were awarded the I.O.M for their conspicuous gallantry against the Turks in Mesopotamia in 1916 and 1917. Havildar Sahib Singh, Lance-Naik Bhan Singh and Sepoy Bhan Singh were awarded the I.D.S.M. for their conspicuous gallantry against the Turks in Mesopotamia in 1916.

In 1918, the 93RD Burma Infantry proceeded to Palestine and took part in the Battle of Megiddo, which led to the annihilation of Turkish Army in Palestine. Subedar Harnam Singh of the regiment was awarded the Military Cross for his gallant leadership in 1918 in Palestine. During the war, the 93RD Burma Infantry suffered 1157 casualties including 235 killed.

The 93RD Burma Infantry was grouped with the 90TH, 91ST and 92ND Punjabis and 89TH Punjabis to form the 8TH Punjab Regiment, and was designated as the 5TH (Burma) Battalion 8TH Punjab Regiment in 1922.

Since December 1923, 5/8TH Punjab Regiment had seen continuous service in Baluchistan and the North-West Frontier Province. They arrived at Jamrud in 1935, and in 1937, they were posted to Kohat, yet another frontier station. In April 1938, the battalion moved to Spinwam in Tori Khel country in support of *Tochi Scouts, who were having some trouble with the tribesmen. From June to November, it was employed on road protection duties on the Bannu-Kohat road during operations against Mehr Dil and his band of outlaws, who had been raiding around Bannu.

*The Tochi Scouts operated in North Waziristan, with their headquarters at Miranshah. They were part of the Frontier Corps which consisted of a number of scout units stationed in and the tribal territories, to keep the peace and police the territory.

8TH Punjab Regiment

93RD Burma Infantry (5/8TH)

In early 1940, the 5/8TH Punjab Regiment were again engaged in operations against Mehr Dil in the Ahmedzai Salient. By May, the outlaw band was dispersed and the Battalion moved back to Kohat. In October 1940, 5/8TH Punjab Regiment moved to Razmak. On 7TH December, the Razmak Brigade was despatched to deal with a band of troublesome Mahsuds in the inaccessible mountain country south of Razmak. As the rearguard of the column passed the Pakalita Star feature, where three Piquets were posted, signal was given the Piquets to withdraw. The first Piquet was descending into a gorge, however, the Piquet failed to reappear and a Gun Position Officer reported that he had seen tribesmen moving about Pakalita Star. The Commanding Officer decided to go up himself to investigate. Apparently the Piquet was ambushed as it descended into the gorge, and all were killed. In the meantime, Colonel Faulkner had arrived at the other two Piquets and gave the order to take up defence for the night. However, the tribesmen attacked the position and the colonel was shot through the head. As their casualties started to mount, the men panicked and tried to flee, but were skilfully cut down by the tribesmen. During the night, a few exhausted survivors were able to reach the brigade camp. The next morning relief column was despatched, only to find dead and mutilated bodies of the soldiers. The tribesmen had melted away after collecting the weapons of the dead men. During the action, the battalion suffered casualties of two officers and 53 Other Ranks killed, and one officer and 40 Other Ranks wounded. It was the worst disaster for the Battalion during its long stay on the Frontier.

On 31ST January 1941, the battalion moved to Ahmed Khel in the Tochi Valley, where it was engaged operations against the Datta Khel tribesmen. This was the last operation of 5/8TH Punjab on the Frontier during which they suffered several casualties. Subedar Dhana Singh was awarded the I.D.S.M., for gallantly leading his platoon in capturing a spur on the Kani Rogha under heavy hostile fire. Sepoy Tara Singh also won the I.D.S.M. the same day, when he rescued a wounded comrade while exposed to fire. On 29TH August, the battalion returned to Razmak, and in October, it left the Frontier for Secunderabad.

During the Second World War, 5/8TH Punjab Regiment arrived in the Burmese Theatre and joined the 14TH Indian Division in March 1942, as part of the 47TH Indian Infantry Brigade. The 14TH Indian Division was to capture the entire Mayu Peninsula, which was to be followed by a short-range seaborne assault on Akyab Island from the tip of the Peninsula by the 6TH British Brigade. On 17TH December the leading troops of the 14TH Division arrived at Maungdaw and found the town abandoned by the Japanese. The British then occupied the line Maungdaw-Buthidaung. The 5/8TH Punjab Regiment, operating in the area of Maungdaw suffered few casualties in minor engagements with enemy patrols. During one such encounter, a patrol sent to reconnoitre the eastern entrance to the Sangan Chaung was ambushed by the Japanese.

8TH Punjab Regiment

93RD Burma Infantry (5/8TH)

On 22ND December, the 47TH Brigade was ordered to advance on both sides of the Mayu Range and clear it of the enemy. The 5/8TH Punjab Regiment moving along the coast reached Indin without any opposition. The Kondan area east of the Mayu Range was held in strength by the enemy, and the Battalion was ordered to cross the ridge and capture it. Leaving its carrier platoon on the coast, the Battalion crossed the range with great difficulty after cutting its way through the thick jungle. The attack was launched on 4TH January 1943, only to find the enemy had withdrawn towards Rathedaung. In the meantime, the Japanese hurriedly despatched a battalion form Akyab with orders to hold Laungchaung and Donbaik, about ten miles north of Foul Point, at all cost.

The 5/8TH Punjab Regiment was then ordered to move south and occupy Foul Point. But the Battalion's move was delayed due to reports of Japanese landings, and when it arrived at the outskirts of Laungchaung on 6TH January, the village was already occupied by the Japanese, who were also dug in at Donbaik. The Battalion was without its mortars and despite repeated attacks, was unable to dislodge the enemy from his well-fortified bunkers. This was the first time that the British had come across the famous Japanese 'Bunkers'. These were cleverly camouflaged strong-points made of heavy logs covered by several feet of earth, making them impervious to bombardment. For the attacking infantry, it was like entering a killing zone, where it came under fire from at least three directions. Having failed to dislodge the enemy, 5/8TH Punjab Regiment took up defensive position at Thayetpyin on 8TH January.

In the meantime, the carrier platoons of 47TH Brigade had been operating freely on the coast. A few enemy patrols were encountered, but these were easily driven off. But on 6TH January, the carrier platoon of 5/8TH Punjab Regiment was attacked by a strong Japanese patrol near Donbaik. Captain Causey, the Platoon Commander was wounded by a grenade splinters and was forced to retire, handing over the command of the platoon to Havildar Parkash Singh. Parkash Singh noticed two other carriers bogged down in a Chaung, and under heavy Japanese fire. Havildar Parkash Singh immediately rushed to the rescue of the stricken carriers, calling on their crews to abandon the vehicles and run for safety while he provided covering fire. When his Bren gunner was wounded, he took control of the gun from him, and charged towards the enemy, driving with one hand and firing the Bren gun with the other. The astonished Japanese scattered to take cover. Havildar Parkash Singh continued to follow the Japanese and drove them out of their fixed positions. As he returned to pick the crews of the stranded carriers he came under heavy Japanese fire, but calmly rescued all eight men. On 19TH January, while the Battalion was making yet another attempt to take Donbaik, the brigade carriers were ordered to advance along the beach in order to draw enemy fire. The carriers were met with anti-tank fire, and several of them were destroyed including that of Captain Causey. The crews of the destroyed vehicles were given up for dead, and the rest of the carriers withdrew.

8TH Punjab Regiment

93RD Burma Infantry (5/8TH)

But Havildar Parkash Singh was not ready to abandon them and wanted to see if there were any survivors among the burning recks. Driving down the beach under intense enemy fire, he found Captain Causey and his driver in their badly damaged carrier. Both were seriously wounded, with the driver having lost both legs. The men were too badly injured to be moved, so Parkash Singh decided to tow their vehicles to safety. Despite the order of his Platoon Commander to go back and save himself, the fearless Parkash Singh rigged a makeshift tow chain and secured it to the damaged carrier, all the time exposed to the enemy fire. As he tried to tow the vehicle, he found that it would not budge. He again went out to put the vehicle in neutral gear, and then towed it back to safety over broken ground. Both carriers were hit by anti-tank rounds but Parkash Singh remained unperturbed. During the last hundred yards he got out, and oblivious to the bullets flying around him, sat on top of his carrier with his arms folded, one more act of defiance for the Japanese. For his incredible feats of courage and selfless devotion on 6TH and 19TH January, Havildar Parkash Singh was awarded the Victoria Cross.

Having failed to breakthrough at Donbaik and Rathedaung the British were getting desperate. Fresh reinforcements were rushed south. The 55TH Brigade relieved 47TH Brigade on the frontline, taking 5/8TH Punjab Regiment at Laungchaung under its command. A troop of tanks was moved in support of 55TH Brigade and the attacks were renewed but the Japanese tenaciously held on to their positions.

The last attack on Donbaik was carried out on 19TH March, which ended up in failure. The 5/8TH Punjab Regiment reverted to its own brigade and moved towards Atet Nanra in the Mayu Valley. By now, the 4TH and 71ST Brigades of the 26TH Indian Division had also arrived in the theatre to reinforce the beleaguered 14TH Division. On 25TH March, a Japanese force of about two battalions crossed the Mayu River and fell on the 47TH Brigade's flank. The brigade was strung out over eleven miles and was unable to concentrate for a counter-attack. The 'C' Company of 5/8TH Punjab Regiment at Atet Nanra was attacked from the rear and badly mauled. The Battalion Headquarters and 'B' Company moved in its support and heavy fighting took place. But on the 27TH March, the Japanese occupied the crest of the range west of Atet Nanra, thus cutting off 47TH Brigade's line of communication. The 5/8TH Punjab Regiment, reinforced by 'A' Company and a company each of the Inniskillings and the Rajputs, launched a counter attack and gained some ground but again was pushed back in the face of determined Japanese attacks. On 31ST March, the 5/8TH Punjab Regiment was ordered to withdraw south towards Sinoh with the rest of the brigade. The position of 47TH Brigade had become extremely precarious. In the meantime, the 4TH Brigade was ordered to concentrate at Hparabyin and attack the Japanese force from the north.

8TH Punjab Regiment

93RD Burma Infantry (5/8TH)

By 5TH April, the British situation had become critical. The 4TH Brigade was moved to Gwindow on the western side of Mayu Range to cover the withdrawal of the 6TH Brigade. The two brigades were then ordered to breakout. However, during the night, the Japanese attacked both brigades. Although HQ 6TH Brigade was overrun, most of the troops were able to escape by moving along the beach. This left the Japanese in control of the western approaches of the Sino-Indin track, thus isolating the 47TH Brigade east of the range. By 7TH April, the brigade was completely surrounded. A British Battalion defending a hill gave way, allowing the Japanese to cut the Maungdaw-Buthidaung road. Counter-attacks failed and the British and Indian troops in Buthidaung and the Kalapanzin valley were cut off. As there was no other route for motor vehicles across the Mayu Range, they were forced to destroy their transport before retreating north up the valley, and back into India. The remnants of 5/8TH Punjab Regiment were withdrawn to Chittagong, where the battalion was reformed. During the ill-fated campaign in the Arakan, the battalion had suffered more than 250 casualties including 119 killed and 102 taken prisoners. After a short stay at Ranchi, the Battalion moved to Pashawar in May, where it was converted into a Reconnaissance battalion. At the end of the Burma campaign, the battalion was employed in Malaya in dis-arming the Japanese forces, before moving on to Dutch East Indies, to take control of the former Dutch colony.

1942 Java had been a Dutch colony, after the Japanese invasion in 1942, the Indonesians were not unhappy to see their former masters being imprisoned. Thus by the time the Punjabis arrived, Java was in the throes of popular uprising. The 5/8TH Punjab sailed for Java on 15TH October and its companies were dispersed all over the island. The Battalion was considerably hampered in its efforts to disarm the Japanese due to frequent attacks by the Indonesians. In December, the Battalion concentrated at Buitzenborg under 36TH Indian Brigade. It was a period of increasing violence, and on 15TH December, the Battalion had to open fire on a violent mob, killing sixty of them. On 17TH December 1945, Major Rawind Singh Grewal's company was suddenly confronted with a roadblock manned by 400 Indonesians whom he immediately attacked killing 80. Major Rawind Singh was awarded the Military Cross on 6TH February 1946. He eventually attained the rank of Major General in the Indian Army. The 5/8TH Punjab Regiment saw frequent skirmishes with the Indonesians until March 1946, when the situation eased considerably. In late October, the battalion left Java for India, and was garrisoned at Pulgaon in Central India.

In July 1947 partition of India imminent, the battalion moved to North-West Frontier Province and was stationed at Wana at the time of independence. At the time of independence, and the creation of Pakistan, the battalion was allocated to the newly formed Pakistan Army. The new designation of the battalion became the 5TH Battalion, The Baluch Regiment. The Sikh soldiers from the battalion were transferred to the Indian Army.

12TH Frontier Force Regiment

51ST Sikhs (1/12TH)

The regiment was raised on 14TH December 1846 at Hoshiarpur as the 1ST Regiment of Infantry, The Frontier Brigade by Major J.S. Hodgson. It was composed of Sikhs, Punjabi Mussalmans, Pathans and Dogras, mostly recruited from the disbanded regiments of the Sikh Empire following the First Anglo-Sikh War. In 1847, it was designated 1ST Regiment of Sikh Local Infantry, becoming the 1st Regiment of Sikh Infantry in 1857. It was designated as the 51ST Sikhs (Frontier Force) in 1903.

The 1ST Sikh Infantry took part in numerous frontier operations besides the Second Sikh War of 1848-49. In 1852, it took part in the expedition directed against the Hasanzais, one of the clans inhabiting the western slope of the Black Mountain. The casus belli was the unprovoked murder by the Hasanzais of two British officers of the Customs Department, employed in connection with the prevention of the importation of trans-Indus salt into the Punjab. The tribesmen refused to surrender the murderers, and seized the two forts of Chamberi and Shanglai, which belonged to a friendly Khan, who tried to bring about a peaceful compliance with the British demands. No alternative remained, therefore, but to send a punitive expedition into Hasanzais territory. Before advancing Colonel Mackeson, the Commissioner of Pashawar, made one more attempt to induce the Hasanzais to comply with the demands already communicated to them. The tribesmen, however, maintained a defiant attitude, and were found to be so strongly posted in the hills, that Colonel Mackeson determined to transfer his reserve to the Indus Valley, and so take the enemy in rear before committing his other three columns to the frontal attack of the formidable position before him. He ordered Lieutenant-Colonel Butler to march to Darband, and send four companies to Chamberi, to demonstrate on the heights to the south of the enemy's position facing Shanglai, and to march the remainder to Bruddur. Colonel Butler's dispositions were completed on December 28TH, and on the next day the advance into Hasanzai territory began. The right column, with the Sikhs, the most opposition; but the Sikhs, covered with the fire of the guns, carried everything before them, and in spite of the abatis constructed by the tribesmen in front of their position, a heavy matchlock fire, and a series of desperate charges by the enemy, turned the hostile left flank and insured the success of the whole attack. The Hasanzais then took up another strong position, but, finding their retreat threatened, soon evacuated it, and took to flight. The three following days were devoted the destruction of the Hasanzai villages. At the end of the Hasanzai expedition, the Sikhs proceeded to Kotla against the Hindustani fanatics.

The individuals known as the Hindustani fanatics were the followers of a mullah named Ahmad Shah, a native of Bareilly. The man had been to Mecca and returned to India by the way of Kandahar and Kabul. Establishing on the Pashawar border in what was then the Sikh Kingdom; he proceeded to attract to his side a large following of co-religionists from among the Pathan tribes of the frontier hills.

12TH Frontier Force Regiment

51ST Sikhs (1/12TH)

It was not long before the Hindustani's and Sikhs came to blows, till finally, in 1829, in a series of encounters the forces of Maharajah Ranjit Singh, the Mullah was slain, together with the greater part of his followers. The remnants of the Hindustani fanatics, some 300 in number, escaped to the hills on the right bank of the Indus, and took refuge with one Syad Akbar Shah, a man of considerable influence in the neighbourhood, who had been a follower of Ahmad Shah, and known to be an enemy of the Sikhs. Akbar Shah's stronghold was at Sittana, a village about a mile from the right bank of Indus, where the fugitives from the Sikhs constructed a fort which they called Mandi. With the annexation of the Sikh Kingdom, British had to police all the frontier regions and deal with the fanatic tribes.

During the disturbances of 1852, the Hindustani fanatics sided with the Hasanzais, even seized a small fort at Kotla belonging to the Khan of Amb, who was friendly to the British Government. Accordingly, after the conclusion of the operations against the Hasanzais, Lieutenant-Colonel Mackeson moved down the left bank of the Indus to Kirpilian on the opposite side of the river to Kotla. The day before, the Khan of Amb's men had ascended the hills to the west of Kotla and establish themselves in a position from which the interior of the fort could be commanded. The place was soon in the hands of the attacking troops, for as soon as the Sikhs and mountain guns began to climb the hill, the defenders, numbering between 200 and 300, took to flight.

After the events of 1852, the Mohmands remained quiet for a short time, but then fell into arrears with the tribute due from them, and one of their chiefs, Rahim Dad, had been summoned to Pashawar in connection with the matter fled before the settlement had been reached. An expedition that included the 1ST Sikh Infantry, then left Michni on August 31ST, 1854, and captured the Rahim Dad's cattle in payment of the sum due. Some frontier villages were destroyed. After the expedition of 1854, fresh Mohmand outrages occurred, but owing to the political situation of the time the Government of India were unwilling to undertake any military operations.

Events near the southern end of the frontier line now claim a brief description. Expeditions against the predatory tribes inhabiting the district lying to the north-west of Dera Ghazi Khan were undertaken in 1853 by Brigadier General J.S. Hodgson, with a portion of the force employed against the Shiranis. The force assembled at Taunsa, a place about fifty miles north of Dera Ghazi Khan, and had sharply contested engagement on March 7TH with the enemy at a point called Khan Bund, in a pass giving access to the territory of the Bozdars. The enemy was found barring the way in a strong position, but a combined flank and frontal attack, well supported by artillery fire, had the effect of causing its speedy evacuation. After considerable loss of property had been inflicted on the tribesmen, satisfactory terms were arranged without further fighting.

12TH Frontier Force Regiment

51ST Sikhs (1/12TH)

During the Sepoy Mutiny of 1857-58, the Regiment fought in Rohilkhand and Oudh. The Mutiny brought to an end the rule of East India Company. Its army was incorporated into the British forces.

Dera Ghazi Khan was undertaken in 1857, by Brigadier General Chamberlain with a force that included the 1ST Sikh Infantry. The force assembled at Taunsa, a place about fifty miles north of Dera Ghazi Khan, and had a sharply contested engagement on March 7TH, with the enemy at a point called Khan Bund Pass, giving access to the territory of the Bozdars. The enemy were found barring the way in a strong position, but a combined flank and frontal attack, well supported by artillery fire, had the effect of causing its speedy evacuation. After considerable loss had been inflicted on the tribesmen, satisfactory terms were arranged without further fighting.

In 1872, the Dawaris lent their assistance to the Waziris in acts hostility towards the Indian Government. As a punishment for their complicity in these outrages the Dawaris were ordered to pay a fine, but half of the tribe refused to comply with this demand. The Punjab Frontier Force with the 1ST Sikh Infantry was ordered to chastise the refractory section of the Dawari tribe. The force, covered by the skirmishers of the 1ST Sikh Infantry advanced to within matchlock range of the enemy without firing a shot. When the skirmishers had arrived within 200 yards of the Dawaris a shot was fired, apparently as a signal, which was followed by a volley from the rest of the enemy, who at once took shelter behind the walls and in the ditches. The guns were promptly brought into action on the village, while the 1ST Sikh Infantry made a spirited advance on the enemy. The wing of the 4TH Sikh Infantry was at the same time sent round to the left flank of the village, and the cavalry to its right and rear, to cut off any attempt to escape. The 1ST Sikh Infantry stormed the closed gates of the village, and affected an entry, driving the inhabitants to the north corner, where for some time they made a stand behind some high-walled houses. The 1ST and 4TH Sikh Infantry, having obtained entire possession of the left portion of village, set it on fire. The fire, and the determined bearing of the two Sikh regiments, was soon too much for the defenders of the village, and abandoning their position, they fled towards the plain, only to find surrounded by the cavalry on the left, dark coats of the Punjab Infantry in their front, the guns on their right, and behind them the deadly Enfields of the two Sikh regiments. The cavalry was speedily down upon them, and sabred ten of their number, when the rest, seeing that all was lost, made rush for the guns and headquarters, and, throwing down their arms as they ran, surrendered as prisoners. Aipi was surrounded in a similar manner, and the inhabitants of Hassu Khel sent in an unconditional surrender whereupon the troops returned to camp un-molested, having been under arms for eighteen hours.

12TH Frontier Force Regiment

51ST Sikhs (1/12TH)

In 1877, when affected by the general unrest prevalent among the neighbouring clans, the Jowakis committed a series of raids on the main road connecting Kohat with India. In August 1877, therefore, a punitive expedition was organized which included the 1ST Sikh Infantry and its sister regiments of the 3RD and 4TH Sikh Infantry, to carry out punitive measures against the refractory clan. After bringing the Jowakis to heal, the regiment took part in the Second Afghan War of 1878-80, where it took part in the capture of Ali Masjid and the advance to Jalalabad. At the conclusion of the war, the Afghans were permitted to maintain internal sovereignty but they had to cede control of their nation's foreign relations to the British. Most of the British and Indian soldiers withdrew from Afghanistan.

After the conclusion of the Afghan war, sanction was accorded for an expedition against the Mahsuds. The object of the expedition was to exact punishment for a long list of outrages committed before and during the Second Afghan War. The expedition included the 1ST Sikh Infantry and its sister regiments the 4TH Sikh Infantry, with all the Punjabi regiments of the Punjab Frontier Force. A column of the force left Tank on April 18TH, 1881, and reached Jandola without incident four days later. The advance was continued up the difficult Shahur Gorge on April 24TH, and then into the Khaisora Valley. Very few of the enemy were seen, property of all kinds was devastated, and submission of some of the neighbouring clans received. On May 4TH, an engagement occurred at Shah Alam, where the enemy had taken up a strong position on some wooded hills. Three battalions were detailed for the attack, supported by the guns and another battalion in the centre; but, just as the infantry had got into position, the tribesmen charged down on the left battalion, who stood firm, and following close on the enemy's heels, when the latter fell back, rapidly gained possession of the position. General Gordon left Bannu on April 16TH, and marching west up the Khaisora Valley without opposition reached Razmak on May 9TH, and returned to Bannu by the unexplored Shaktu Valley. General Kennedy marched back to Tank and reached it on May 18TH Bannu four days later. Neither column was molested during the withdrawal, the tribesmen were submissive. Much valuable survey work was done during these operations, and the tribesmen overawed, but without any decisive military success somewhat discounted the value of these results.

The Mahsuds failed to comply fully with the British terms, so it was necessary to blockade their territory, which lasted till September 7TH, 1881, when despairing of outside assistance the Mahsuds finally complied with the British demands.

The regiment continuously mounted punitive expeditions against the various clans, on the North-West Frontier. The main actions were fought against the Shiranis (1883), The Zhob Valley (1890), Mahsuds (1894), and the Tochi Valley (1897). During the Tochi Valley expedition, the troops had arrived in Maizar as an escort to the Political Officer, to settle a tribal dispute when a major mishap happened to the escorting troops.

12TH Frontier Force Regiment

51ST Sikhs (1/12TH)

A political agent with a military escort of British officers and Indian Sepoys rode out to Maizar in 1897, to settle a dispute between the tribal Maliks. As the escort rested under some trees, the tribals suddenly attacked them. Being outnumbered the escort had to make a quick retreat, during which all the British officers were soon wounded. The Sikh officers nobly rose to the occasion. Subedars Naryan Singh and Sundar Singh covered their retreat, in the course of which the latter and ten of his Sepoys sacrificed their lives to enable the remainder to get clear of the village. Ten Sikh officers and men of the Mountain Batteries were awarded the I.O.M. for their conspicuous gallantry in operating their guns to keep the tribesmen at bay.

Subedar (Hon. Captain) Naryan Singh of the regiment was awarded the I.O.M. for his gallant leadership and following Sikh soldiers, who had sacrificed their lives, was awarded the posthumous I.O.M. and their widows granted pensions. Subedar Sundar Singh, Naik Bur Singh, Naik Assa Singh, Lance-Naik Kanhaiya Singh, Lance-Naik Bela Singh, Sepoy Indar Singh, and Bugler Ishar Singh.

As soon as news of the Maizar outrage reached the Government of India, it was decided that a force consisting of two brigades, should be despatched with as little delay as possible into the Tochi Valley, to exact punishment from the treacherous tribesmen.

It was the most formidable outbreak the British arms have ever been called upon to suppress on the North-West Frontier of India. From earliest times political agitators had found the surest way to gain the support of wild impressionable tribes is through medium of their religious beliefs. By the end of July 1897, the Mullahs had done their work, and the whole frontier rapidly burst into a blaze. The conflagration moved from north to south and the whole of the Tochi Valley right up to the Afghan border had to be overrun systematically before the clans were subdued.

In 1900, the regiment went to China to suppress the Boxer rebellion. The Boxers, was a xenophobic movement, which carried out series of attacks on foreign missionaries, merchants and property. The Chinese government did little to remedy the situation, and in June 1900 issued an edict, which amounted to support for the Boxers. The foreign legations in the Imperial capital Peking (Beijing) were besieged by the Boxers, and held out for three months despite having a small garrison. An international relief force was organised by seven nations, and in June 1900 the Taku Forts were captured. The force then moved on Peking, which was captured in August. Eventually peace was concluded in January 1901.

Subsequent to the reforms brought about in the Indian Army in 1903, the regiment's designation was changed to 51ST Sikhs (Frontier Force). In 1914, the regiment's class composition was four companies of Sikhs, two of Pathans, and one each of Punjabi Mussalmans and Dogras.

12TH Frontier Force Regiment

51ST Sikhs (1/12TH)

During First World War it served in Egypt and Aden, moving to Mesopotamia in December. Here, it fought with great gallantry in the bloody battles on the Tigris Front in 1916-17, the capture of Baghdad and in operations north of Baghdad at Istabulat, Daur and Tikrit. In 1918, the regiment moved to Palestine and took part in the Battle of Megiddo, which led to the annihilation of Turkish Army in Palestine. It returned to India in 1920. For their excellent performance in the war, in which they suffered heavy losses, the 51ST Sikhs were made Prince of Wales's Own in 1921.

Subedar Arjan Singh and Havildar Suhel Singh were awarded the I.O.M. for conspicuous gallantry and devotions to duty on 22ND April in Mesopotamia.

Subedar Labh Singh, Subedar Ujagar Singh, Subedar Arjan Singh, Jemadar Sundar Singh, Jemadar Prem Singh, Havildar Hira Singh, Havildar Mangal Singh, Naik Labh Singh, Lance-Naik Gurdit Singh, Lance-Naik Jowala Singh, Sepoy Bhola Singh, Sepoy Sundar Singh, Sepoy Dalip Singh, Sepoy Kishan Singh, and Sepoy Ishar Singh were awarded the I.D.S.M. for their conspicuous gallantry against the Turks in Mesopotamia in 1916, 1917 and 1918.

In 1922, 51ST Sikhs were grouped with the 52ND, 53RD and 54TH Sikhs, and the two Battalions of Guides Infantry to form the 12TH Frontier Force Regiment in 1922. The 51ST Sikhs became 1ST Battalion (Prince of Wales's Own Sikhs) of the new regiment.

Iraq had been officially granted independence by the United Kingdom in 1932, under a number of conditions, including the retention of British military bases. This caused resentment within Iraq and a pro-Axis prime minister, Rashid Ali, assumed control. In early 1941, Ali ordered British forces to withdraw. The events in Iraq had crucial strategic consequences. The country's oil reserves were a highly coveted prize for the Axis powers, and its location provided a corridor in the defence of Palestine and the Suez Canal. Had Iraq fallen to the Axis powers, Britain could have lost its foothold in the Middle East and the Mediterranean and risked losing World War Two.

The Middle East Command hastily assembled a formation known as Iraq Force which included the 1/12TH Frontier Force Regiment. There were two main British military bases in Iraq, at Basra and at Habbaniya, north east of Baghdad. On April 30TH, the Iraqi Army surrounded and besieged the isolated and poorly defended Royal Air Force base at Habbaniya. Although the base had no offensive aircraft, RAF personnel converted training aircraft to carry weapons, and attacked the Iraqi forces. Habbaniya was soon relieved by Iraq Force, which defeated the larger but poorly trained Iraqi Army in a series of battles. Rashid Ali and his supporters fled the country and an armistice was signed. In matter of 30 days British had initiated and won the war that was forced on them by a nationalist political clique determined to remove British influence from Iraq and replace it with that of Germany.

12TH Frontier Force Regiment

51ST Sikhs (1/12TH)

A Luftwaffe aircraft was shot down over Iraq during the advance on Baghdad. Since the nearest Axis bases were on Rhodes, the Allies realised that the plane had refuelled in Vichy French controlled Syria or Lebanon. British and Indian units invaded Syria and Lebanon from Palestine in the south on 8TH June 1941. Vigorous resistance was put up by the Vichy. However, the Allies' better training and equipment, as well as the weight of numbers eventually told against the Axis. By 8TH July the whole of north east Syria had been captured and elements of Iraq Force advancing up the River Euphrates were threatening Aleppo and as a consequence the rear of the Vichy forces defending Beirut from the advance from the south. Negotiations for an armistice were started on 11TH July and surrender terms signed on 14TH July 1941. After serving in the Middle East, the regiment was ordered to Italy in 1943, where it again served with distinction.

On 24TH September 1943 the 8TH Indian Division with 1/12TH Frontier Force Regiment landed in Taranto (Italy), to take its part in the Italian Campaign, and for 19TH months was almost continuously in action advancing through mountainous country, crossing River after River. The formation later adopted the motto 'One more River'.

From October 1943 to April 1944 the Division was part of the Allied thrust by British 8TH Army up the Adriatic front on the Eastern side of Italy. This involved opposed River crossings of the Biferno, Trigno (October 1943), Sangro (November 1943) and Moro (December 1943). The following three months proved almost as arduous for, although there was no formal offensive, the period was characterised by patrolling and vicious skirmishes in very difficult terrain and abominable winter weather which proved physically hugely demanding and stressful.

On 17TH March 1944, the Company commanded by Major Amar Singh took over the left forward Company position of 'B' sector of the 8TH Indian Division front, very close to strong German position in Orso area. The enemy was very aggressive with shelling, mortar fire and Machine Gun fire and his strong fighting patrols were very active. The Company's forward platoon, situated in a very exposed position in a cave and completely isolated, was particularly an enemy objective. By day no movement was possible and by night it was very difficult. The night after the Company's arrival, the enemy launched an attack on the platoon in the caves, supported by heavy covering fire. All communications were quickly cut. Major Amar Singh went forward immediately under heavy fire to control the situation, taking an NCO and three soldiers with him. After encouraging his isolated platoon and taking necessary measures to meet the situation, he returned to his Headquarters and directed the fire of his mortars so successfully that the attack was repulsed with loss. He was the only survivor of the party he took forward with him and had he not acted as he did, his platoon would have been overrun.

12TH Frontier Force Regiment

51ST Sikhs (1/12TH)

During his Company's tenure of this exposed forward position, in close contact throughout with and aggressive enemy, Major Amar Singh set a magnificent example of courage and coolness under fire and of cheerful acceptance of the hardships involved in the appalling winter weather conditions. His offensive spirit and sound leadership quickly resulted in his Company dominating the caves area, a complete reversal of the previous position. Major Amar Singh was awarded an immediate Military Cross.

When the spring came the Division was switched 60 miles west across the Apennine mountains to concentrate along the River Garigliono at a part of the River better known as the Rapido. They were heavily opposed during night crossing of River Gari in May 1944. Major Himmat Singh Sandhu was in command of the Company supplying boatmen for ferrying across personnel during the crossing of the River Gari in Italy on the night of 11/12TH May 1944, where his men were exposed to machine gun and mortar fire from enemy posts. On completion of their task the Company proceeded towards the enemy positions and ran into three machine gun posts. On each occasion, in spite of the continuous fire from the posts, Major Sandhu personally organised and led a series of charges against the posts. Visibility being such, that their exact positions could not be located, and Major Sandhu was forced to shout his commands and drew much of the fire on himself. His relentless attack on these posts under almost continuous fire from grenades and machine guns and smoke resulted in two enemy posts being withdrawn and the third destroyed. Throughout the action Major Sandhu was conspicuous in his complete indifference to danger and his fearless leadership. His personal example was outstanding. Major Himmat Singh Sandhu was awarded an immediate Military Cross on 12TH May 1944.

Following this, the Division advanced some 240 miles in June across mountainous country fighting many actions against rearguards and defended strong points. Florence was occupied on 12TH August where they had the unusual task to recover some of the world's greatest art treasures and arrange safe custody. By mid September the Division was in the mountains again, breaking through the Gothic Line and then spending two months of grim battling in foul weather towards the plains of Northern Italy.

During the battle for the Castelnuovo feature North of Tavaletto, Jemadar Santa Singh was commanding the leading platoon of 'A' Company. On the morning of 6TH September his platoon assisted the tanks in their advance over an exposed ground, which was under heavy mortar and machine gun fire. On the afternoon of 6TH September Jemadar Santa Singh was ordered to cooperate in the attack on Point 419. The approaches to this objective were over open ground, which was under fire from enemy mortars and machine guns. Jemadar Santa Singh placed himself at the head of his men and led them forward within hundred yards of the objective where a low bank offered them some cover.

12TH Frontier Force Regiment

51ST Sikhs (1/12TH)

Jemadar Santa Singh made an extensive reconnaissance during which he was under constant fire and eventually found a small drain, which gave cover of advance. Posting two of his sections to give covering fire from the low bank, he then led the third section up this drain and rushed an enemy machine gun post in a surprise attack and captured four of the gun crew with their gun. The enemy from the second post panicked and fled leaving their gun behind them, while the assaulting section suffered no casualties at all. 'D' Company was then able to capture Point 419 without further trouble. That night 6/7 September the enemy counter attacked the whole Battalion position with great determination Jemadar Santa Singh rallied his exhausted platoon, he ran from one section to another shouting words of encouragement and praise to his me, many of whom were raw recruits and were in battle for the first time, and had been continuously in action for twenty-four hours. Later the same night the platoon ran short of ammunition, Jemadar Santa Singh distributed the captured German machine guns to them and kept his men firing them until reserve ammunition was brought forward the next morning. The Company had lost their Commander on the first night of the operations, but through bold initiative, resourcefulness and above all magnificent example of personal courage, Jemadar Santa Singh was able materially to contribute to the success of the whole battle. Jemadar Santa Singh was awarded an immediate Military Cross.

On the 11TH April 1945, during the assault across the River Santerno in the area of Ca Lugo, Jemadar Mohinder Singh commanded a platoon and had the task of securing the houses beyond the West Flood bank. His first attempt to cross the Flood bank was met with heavy Spandau fire, three men being killed instantly and others wounded. Jemadar Mohinder Singh led the remainder of the platoon through the enemy fire and attacked and captured three houses and went on to mop up two further enemies occupied houses, capturing between twenty and thirty prisoners. Jemadar Mohinder Singh secured the important bridgehead, which enabled the rest of the Company to fan out behind the enemy positions and capture twenty more prisoners. Jemadar Mohinder Singh was awarded an immediate Military Cross.

Jemadar Dhana Singh has commanded the Pioneer Platoon throughout the Italian campaign. During this period well over two thousand mines have been lifted by the Platoon, a large proportion by Jemadar Dhana Singh himself, he was strongly recommended for and awarded the Military Cross on 14TH June 1945. The campaign ended on 2ND May 1945, and the regiment proceeded back to India. Havildars Kuldip Singh, Mehar Singh, Karam Singh, Dilwar Singh, Naik Ujagar Singh and Sepoy Avtar Singh were awarded the I.D.S.M. for their conspicuous gallantry in Italy.

After the independence of the subcontinent in 1947, and the creation of Pakistan, the battalion was allotted to the new Pakistan Army. The Sikh soldiers from the battalion were transferred to the Indian Army.

12TH Frontier Force Regiment

52ND Sikhs (2/12TH)

The regiment was raised on 22ND December 1846 at Kangra as the 2ND Regiment of Infantry. It was composed mostly of Sikhs, Dogras, with some Pathans and Gurkhas. In 1851, the regiment became part of the Punjab Irregular Force. Their mission was to maintain order on the Punjab Frontier, and the regiment took part in numerous frontier operations. It took part in the Sepoy Mutiny of 1857-58, and dealt with the Hindustani Fanatics during the Mutiny.

During the Second Afghan War of 1878-80, the regiment fought in the Battles of Ahmad Khel and Kandahar. Subedar Major Gurbax Singh and Sepoy Alan Singh Sepoy Jai Singh, Sepoy Hira Singh and Sepoy Pertab Singh were awarded the I.O.M. for their gallantry against the enemy in this war.

In 1902, it went to British Somaliland to suppress the resistance movement led by the Somali religious leader Sayed Mohammed Abdullah Hassan. His followers were known as the Dervishes. The regiment took part in a series of military expeditions that took place against the Dervishes. They were assisted in their offensives by the Ethiopians and Italians. During the First World War, Hassan received aid from the Turkish, Germans and, for a time, from the Emperor Iyasu V of Ethiopia. The conflict continued until well after the First World War.

Subsequent to the reforms brought about in the Indian Army in 1903, the regiment's designation was changed to 52ND Sikhs (Frontier Force).

During war, the regiment joined the 18TH Indian Division in Mesopotamia in 1917. It remained in Mesopotamia for the rest of the war, taking part in the Action at Fat-ha Gorge on the Little Zab (23–26 October 1918) and the Battle of Sharqat (28–30 October 1918) under the command of I Corps. Havildar Indar Singh, Havildar Mit Singh and Naik Sundar Singh were awarded the I.D.S.M. for their conspicuous gallantry in action against the Turks in Mesopotamia.

At the end of the war, the 18TH Division was chosen to form part of the occupation force for Iraq. It took part in the Iraq rebellion in 1920. Erupting on June 30TH in the town of Rumaitha, the rebellion had spread by August to all agricultural regions inhabited by Arabs and to several Kurdish areas. The British retained Baghdad, Mosul, Basra, and the middle Tigris region. The peasantry, especially the semi settled tribes of the middle Euphrates, constituted the main force of the uprising. Tribal sheikhs and Shiite theologians headed the rebellion. Organs of revolutionary power were formed in the liberated regions, but these regions were isolated from each other. The insurgents dealt the British occupation forces a number of defeats. In October 1920 a British army of 65,000 men defeated the main rebel forces.

The rebellion had a great influence on the future development of the country. The British now wanted to control Iraq through more indirect means, mainly by installing former officials friendly to the British government. They eventually decided to install Faysal ibn Hussain as King of Iraq, and were forced to renounce plans to establish an outright colonial regime in Iraq.

12TH Frontier Force Regiment

52ND Sikhs (2/12TH)

During the Second World War, the 2/12TH Frontier Force Regiment was part of the 9TH Indian Division and was sent to Malaya in 1941. The Division was the main defending force at Kota Bharu. Japanese Zero fighters began bombing the airfield in Kota Bharu and other airfields in northern Malaya, namely those at Sungei Patani, Butterworth, Penang, Gong Kedah and Machang. The air attacks seriously destroyed British installations and weakened the Allied air force.

The Japanese invasion of the coast in north Malaya began on 8TH December. The landing was carried out between Sabak and Badang. The invading troops suffered loss from artillery fire, and had difficulty in dealing with the determined defence offered by the 17TH Dogras. After severe fighting and with considerable losses on both sides, the Japanese succeeded in capturing the strong points. Since the Japanese landings clearly represented a serious threat to the airfield at Kota Bharu barely two miles inland, The 2/12TH Frontier Force Regiment was moved to Kota Bharu to protect it. At the Japanese gradual advance, Brigadier Key ordered the 1/13TH Frontier Force Rifles to counter attack eastwards along the beaches from Badang, and 2/12TH Frontier Force Regiment to attack westwards from Sabak, to join hands and destroy the enemy troops who had landed. Both these attacks failed to achieve their object. Further efforts also failed and the situation in the beach area remained very confused. In view of the general air situation, and since raids on airfields in Kelantan had caused much damage, the airfield at Kota Bharu was abandoned and the withdrawal became necessary.

In heavy rain, the 22ND Brigade with 2/12TH Frontier Force Regiment tried to hold the enemy at bay, but was forced to withdraw to Kuantan. The Brigade had the task of defending the Kuantan airfield. The airfield lay west of the River close to the main road some nine miles from the coast. The Japanese wasted no time and on the 1ST and 2ND crossed the River and infiltrated towards the airfield. It soon became clear that 22ND Brigade would be unable to hold the airfield, it had to be abandoned and the Brigade was withdrawn to Jerantut.

Buildings and installations at the airfield were accordingly demolished and preparations were made to withdraw the Brigade. While the final withdrawal was in progress, the Japanese, who had been closing all day, attacked the 2/12TH Frontier Force Regiment, which was acting as rearguard, just it was about to leave the airfield and, getting it behind it, formed road blocks between it and the main body of the Brigade. Very fierce fighting at close range ensued. Eventually forty men of the regiment fought their way back through two road blocks. The next day the retirement continued through Maranm, and the 22ND Brigade reduced to two-thirds of its original strength, crossed the Jerantut Ferry and moved to the Raub area. On 26TH January the Brigade was ordered to withdraw to Singapore. With the Japanese relentless attacks only some sixty officers and men of 5/11TH Sikhs and 2/12TH Frontier Force Regiment, eventually found their way to the coast and thence to Singapore Island.

12TH Frontier Force Regiment

52ND Sikhs (2/12TH)

By the morning of the 13TH February the battle for Singapore Island was irretrievably lost and it was only a question of time before capitulation would become investable. By the morning of 15TH February, the Japanese had broken through the last line of defence; the Allies were running out of food and ammunition. The anti-aircraft guns had also run out of ammunition and were unable to disrupt Japanese air attacks which were causing heavy casualties in the city centre. Little work had been done to build air raid shelters and looting and desertion by Allied troops further added to the chaos in this area

General Percival held a conference at Fort Canning with his senior commanders. He proposed two options: either launches an immediate counter-attack to regain the reservoirs and the military food depots in the Bukit Timah region, or surrender. After heated argument and recrimination, all present agreed that no counterattack was possible. Percival opted for surrender,

General Percival reported the situation fully to General Wavell and indicated that it was unlikely that the resistance could last more than day or two, He said there must come a stage when, in the interest of the troops and the civil population, further bloodshed would serve no further useful purpose and asked that he might be given wider discretionary powers. Informed by his senior officers that no counterattack was possible, Percival saw little choice other than surrender. Dispatching a messenger to Yamashita, Percival met with the Japanese commander at the Ford Motor Factory later that day to discuss terms. The formal surrender was completed shortly after 5:15 that evening. The worst defeat in the history of British arms, the Battle of Singapore, and the preceding Malayan Campaign saw Percival's command suffer around 7,500 killed, 10,000 wounded, and 120,000 captured.

After the fall of Singapore on February 15, 1942, 40,000 men of the Indian Army became prisoners of war Some 30,000 of them joined the Indian National Army. (Indian National Army, also known as the Azad Hind Fauj, was formed for the liberation of India from the British rule).

Those who refused were destined for torture in the Japanese concentration camps. They were first sent to transit camps in Batavia (now Djakarta) and Surabaya from where they were packed off to New Guinea, New Britain and Bougainvillea.

The surrender of the Japan was announced by Imperial Japan on August 15TH and formally signed on September 2, 1945, bringing the hostilities to a close.

With the influx of new recruits and the remnants of the solders that had survived the war the battalion was re-raised in 1946. After the independence of the subcontinent in 1947, and the creation of Pakistan, the battalion was allotted to the new Pakistan Army. The Sikh soldiers from the battalion were transferred to the Indian Army.

12TH Frontier Force Regiment

53RD Sikhs (3/12TH)

The regiment was raised on 1ST January 1847 at Ferozepore as the 3RD Regiment of Infantry the Frontier Brigade by Captain D.F. Winter. It was composed of Sikhs, Punjabi Mussalmans, Pathans, Dogras and Hindustanis. In 1847, it was designated 3RD Regiment of Sikh Local Infantry, becoming the 3RD Regiment of Sikh Infantry in 1857.

In 1851, it became part of the Punjab Irregular Force. Their mission was to maintain order on the Punjab Frontier and took part in the punitive expeditions against Bozdars in 1857. At the outbreak of the Sepoy Mutiny the regiment took part in the mopping operations against the mutineers in north India. At the conclusion of the Sepoy Mutiny the regiment was back on the frontier, subduing the tribal clans. The regiment took active part in the expeditions of Ambela (1863), The Black Mountain (1868), Jowakis (1877), before taking part in the Second Afghan War of 1878-80, where the regiment took part in the defence of Sherpur Cantonment and the Battle of Kandahar. During the Second Afghan War Havildar Gurdit Singh, Naik Sham Singh and Sepoy Punjab Singh were awarded the I.O.M. for their conspicuous gallantry against the Afghans.

Back on the frontier again it participated in the following expeditions, Maris (1880), Miranzai (1891), Mahsuds (1894), Tirah (1897), Waziris (1901), Zakha Khel (1908), and Mohmunds (1908). During the operations on the North-West Frontier in 1908 Naik Teja Singh, Sepoy Hira Singh and Sepoy Basant Singh were awarded the I.O.M. for their gallantry against the tribals at Gomal Pass.

During the First World War, the regiment served with the 28TH Frontier Force Brigade. In 1915, it served in Egypt and Aden (Yemen), moving to Mesopotamia in December. Here, it fought with great gallantry in the bloody battles for the relief of Kut-al-Amara, on the Tigris Front in 1916-17, the capture of Baghdad, and in operations north of Baghdad at Istabulat, Daur and Tikrit. In 1918, the regiment moved to Palestine and took part in the Battle of Megiddo, which led to the annihilation of Turkish Army in Palestine. It returned to India in 1920.

During the First World War Subedar Molar Singh, Subedar Buta Singh, Jemadar Chanan Singh, Havildar Shingar Singh, Naik Kehar Singh, Lance-Naik Dalel Singh and Sepoy Shingar Singh were awarded the I.O.M., while Havildar Harnam Singh, Havildar Arjan Singh, Havildar Hari Singh, Havildar Mangal Singh, Jemadar Hazara Singh, Jemadar Gurdial Singh, Lance-Naik Bhola Singh, Lance-Naik Ram Singh;

Lance-Naik Bahadur Singh, Sepoy Jowahir Singh, Sepoy Mehr Singh, Sepoy Jiwan Singh and Sepoy Pala Singh were awarded the I.D.S.M. for their conspicuous gallantry against the Turks in Mesopotamia and Egypt in 1916-18.

In 1922, the 53RD Sikhs were grouped with the 51ST, 52ND and 54TH Sikhs, and the two Battalions of Guides Infantry to form the 12TH Frontier Force Regiment. The 53RD Sikhs became 3RD Battalion (Sikhs) of the new regiment.

12TH Frontier Force Regiment

53RD Sikhs (3/12TH)

During the Second World War, on July 4TH, 1940, Italian forces in Eritrea crossed the Sudanese border and forced the small British garrison holding the railway junction at Kassala to withdraw. The Italians also seized the small British fort at Gallabat, just over the border from Metemma. General Platt had a 1200-mile frontier with Abyssinia to watch with his meagre forces.

The arrival at Port Sudan in September of 5TH Indian Davison, transformed his position. The Division's two Brigades were made up to three, 9TH, 10TH and 29TH, each of one British and two Indian Battalions. The 9TH Brigade's two Indian battalions were, 3/12TH Frontier Force Regiment and 3/5TH Mahratta Light Infantry.

The Division also provided most of 'Gazelle Force', one of those piratical semi-private armies that consisted of the motor-machine-gun batteries of the 'Sudan Defence Force', a 5TH Indian Divisional Cavalry Regiment mounted in 15cwt trucks, a Field Regiment, and one or two companies of Infantry whenever they could be spared. On November 6TH, a small mixed force attacked the enemy position at Gallabat, and had the privilege of instituting the first British offensive in Africa. The fort was thoroughly bombed, while the Artillery put down a heavy concentration on it. The Infantry followed up tanks in a direct assault. The fort was reached and fierce hand-to-hand fighting ensued. The enemy fought well. Some very stout hearted Italians and Eritrean, who had remained to fight in spite of the severe bombing and shelling, took a deal of evicting. After this action constant offensive patrolling was maintained, shaking the enemy's morale and inflicting further casualties. British Gunners forced the Italians to evacuate the town and fort of Metemma. The troops which took part had been blooded and in their patrolling were so fierce, the enemy feared to stir out of their trenches behind barbed wire.

Soon after leaving Metemma, camps were passed, previously occupied by the retreating enemy and now littered with refuse, food, dead mules and lumps of raw meat, alive with flies.

The Gandwa River was reached on February 3RD, proved a real obstacle, covered as it was by the fire of an Italian rearguard and by well-placed minefields. Neither carriers nor trucks could be manoeuvred in the dense bush or across the River and its tributaries. To disperse the rearguard and clear the mines took two hours. The next twenty miles to Wahni were rapidly covered, despite an ambush and two attacks on the advanced camp by native troops. Early on the 7TH Wahni was occupied, the enemy being withdrawn during the night and number of prisoners and stragglers been left behind.

Early in February Colonel Messervy, who had replaced Mayne, withdrew his troops to Gedaref, leaving behind two companies of the 3/12TH Frontier Force Regiment to keep watch at Wahni and by the Gandwa crossing. After nearly three month's hunting the enemy, the 3/12TH Frontier Force Regiment prepared to rejoin the main Division pack on the Kassala front.

12TH Frontier Force Regiment

53RD Sikhs (3/12TH)

On the night of January 17TH, the enemy slipped out of Kassala. Kassala, a town of some 25,000 inhabitants, consisted largely of mud buildings, the old fort, and certain government buildings and gardens.

The two battles, 4TH Division at Agordat and 5TH Division at Barentu, were fought simultaneously. The 4TH Indian Division, in a frontal attack captured the four hills astride the road just outside Agordat, which were fortified with concrete emplacements, trenches and wire. Resistance died away in the face of this attack and the Italians bolted away before they were captured. Next day the Division went into town, which was found to be abandoned and the enemy had slipped away, leaving his guns, vehicles, and huge quantities of stores. About a thousand prisoners had been taken and this number was doubled when the pursuing forces overtook stragglers.

Barentu is another town similar to Agordat, lying on a small plain surrounded by steep, scrub-covered hills. One Brigade of 5TH Division was advancing from Aicota, the other from Agordat; the only possible line of retreat left to the Italians was by a road running westward. Retirement would mean the loss of all guns, vehicles and stores, so the Italians had no alternative but to stand and fight it out. Fighting round Barentu was a grim soldier's battle in which the better men won by sheer fighting ability. On the morning of February 2ND the Italians abandoned their defences and Barentu fell.

The battle at Keren began on 3RD of February 1941. Over 90,000 men in total were engaged in the battle. The Italians, knowing the loss of Keren would mean the loss of their East African empire, were determined to hold their positions, and managed to defend the area for two months of fierce fighting. The battle finally ended on the 27TH March 1941, after the British assaulted and took Mount Sankil, home to an Italian fortress. During the whole battle they used over thirty thousand Infantry and one hundred and forty-four guns. Many of these were fresh troops.

The total Italian losses probably were about ten thousand. The fall of Keren had finally shattered the morale of the Italian Army. At the end of the battle of Keren there were only three battalions and a few batteries uncommitted between Keren and Asmara. Practically all had been staked on holding Keren. The British and Indian troops had fought hard and won.

The battle was described by General Platt as "a ding-dong battle, a soldier's battle, fought against an enemy infinitely superior in numbers, on ground of his own choosing which gave him every bit of observation against the movement of our troops, the positions of our guns and the approaches of our transport". And it was won by "the tenacity and determination of Commanders and troops, by whole-hearted cooperation of all ranks, whether forward or back, of whatever race or creed, and by the continuous support given to Infantry by the Royal Artillery." The British casualties were not light. Some 500 Officers and 3,000 men had been killed and wounded.

12TH Frontier Force Regiment

53RD Sikhs (3/12TH)

The 4TH Indian Division was particularly hard hit. Yet the determination of the British and Indian troops to fight to victory was to leave its mark upon the Italians and to affect their conduct in the subsequent operations. They were never really to stand to fight again in the same spirit. The outcome of the contest in Italian East Africa was no longer in doubt. There were to be more battles and more victories before Italian East Africa was conquered, but Keren had broken the back of Italian resistance and subsequent operations were easier.

The conduct of 4TH and 5TH Indian Divisions won them ready applause from several quarters. "The whole Empire", wrote the British Prime Minister to the Viceroy of India shortly after the victory at Keren, "has been stirred by the achievement of the Indian forces in Eritrea." At the fall of Keren the 4TH Indian Division went off to gain further laurels in Syria and the Western Desert.

From now onwards 5TH Indian Division carried out the campaign alone. It was sad for these two Divisions of the Indian Army thus parted after fighting side by side through this arduous campaign. The Italians had destroyed the road in many places in order to delay the advance and in consequence these operations followed almost a stereotyped form. The mobile troops ran up against the demolition and carried out reconnaissance to discover the extent of the enemy position; the Infantry then arrived and assisted by the Artillery, forced the enemy from the hills on either side; the Sappers and Miners cleared the road block and the tanks and guns went through. There was some hard fighting along the road in which the 3/12TH Frontier Force Regiment particularly distinguished itself. The Italians were, however, very disorganized and their morale shattered. In the face of these determined attacks, they gave way easily. When finally 5TH Indian Division broke through at Asmara, the emissaries came out with white flags. Asmara was declared an open town and was occupied on April 1ST. Thus, after two and a half months intense fighting, the capital Eritrea surrendered.

When finally 5TH Indian Division broke through at Asmara, the emissaries came out with white flags. Asmara was declared an open town and was occupied on April 1ST. After the fall of Asmara, 5TH Indian Division was split up. Part went to Massawa; part remained in Asmara sorting out the very difficult problems that arose in taking over this large town, and a small force pursued the Italians down the road towards Addis Ababa. They captured some 2,000 prisoners, who were frequently only too glad to surrender, owing to the activities of the Abyssinian patriots. They secured large dumps of stores and on one occasion captured a complete Battalion in Lorries. The Lorries were turned round and the Battalion moved North under escort. The Italians decided to defend the area around Amba Alagi in force. In this mountain fortress, the defenders, thought themselves to be impregnable. In the early hours of 4TH May, the main attack was made from the Northwest and Amba Alagi was surrounded. The 7000 Italian troops of Amedeo, Duke of Acosta, were directly attacked by 9000 British troops and more than 20000 Ethiopian irregulars.

12TH Frontier Force Regiment

53RD Sikhs (3/12TH)

A final assault was planned for 15TH May, but a fortuitous Artillery shell hit an Italian fuel dump and ruptured a vessel containing oil. This caused oil to flow into the remaining drinking water of the Italian defenders. On 18TH May, Amedeo, Duke of Acosta, surrendered his embattled forces at Amba Alagi. General Mayne agreed to surrender with 'full military honours' (allowing the troops to march off the battlefield in formation and then surrender their arms).

While the victorious troops watched from the hill tops, the defeated army came down in ling column, eight abreast past the point where General Mayne took their salute. A few hundred yards further on was a guard of honour, composed of one platoon from each battalion, British, Indian and South African, which presented arms as the tired Italians marched by. 'The flowers of the Forest' added to the pathos of the scene, as the vanquished troops filed into the village of Medani Alem and laid down their arms. It had been a very complete victory and a glorious end to a campaign, which will remain famous for its speed and the magnificent fighting of always outnumbered Imperial forces. The 5TH Indian Division with 3/12TH Frontier Force Regiment, had advanced 500 miles across deserts, up mountains, in burning heat and drenching rain, had taken part in the fearful battle of Keren, had won the fights at Barentu, Ad Teclesan and Massawa, and had taken prisoner more than twice its own numbers. Although there was mopping up to be done, this campaign was over for the frontiersmen.

In July 1941, the 3/12TH Frontier Force Regiment left Eritrea for Egypt. Three weeks were spent in dusty camps of the Suez Canal, Qassassin and Tahag, where the battalion was re-equipped and trained. Then they were ordered to move westward to the Desert, for a period of training in mobile desert warfare, combined with the task of preparing defence positions on the Alamein Line. In August 22ND, the digging of fortifications was interrupted quite suddenly.

The regiment was to move next morning. The regiment was hurried from the Desert to Iraq to reinforce the Eighth and Tenth Indian Divisions for operations against Persia, and to take share in maintaining the internal security of Iraq, where the uprising of Rashid Ali and his followers was quelled in Baghdad. The battalion passed through the towns of Ramadi, Fallujah, to Habbaniya with its Royal Air Force station. It was here that the news was brought the disturbances of the Rashid Ali revolt bad already been quelled by the Household Cavalry and other troops who had hurried to Baghdad. The battalion was sent further north to the oilfields of Kirkuk, in case of renewed trouble. After three weeks in Kirkuk, the battalion was heading towards Egypt once again by the same route. The battalion settled down at Kabrit on the shores of the Bitter Lakes. Then suddenly again the battalion was ordered to Cyprus. After four months in Cyprus, the battalion sailed away direct to Alexandria. During this crossing to Egypt the ships, escorted by a destroyer, were bombed by a German plane, fortunately without damage or casualties. The battalion went on to form part of the Tobruk garrison.

12TH Frontier Force Regiment

53RD Sikhs (3/12TH)

The battalion was newly stationed around Tobruk when Rommel's offensive against the Gazala Line commenced at the end of May 1942. Fresh to the desert, just recently equipped with obsolete anti tank guns and poor transport, they were ordered to counterattack (Operation Aberdeen) the German breakthrough. The operation was badly mismanaged by the Corps commander, tank and artillery support failed to materialise, and casualties were crippling. The 3/12TH Frontier Force Regiment, was all but destroyed at El Adem on 15TH June 1942. It was reformed in Egypt before transferring to the 11TH Brigade, 4TH Indian Infantry Division.

The 4TH Indian Infantry Division moved to Italy in January 1944, and entered the line near Orsogna. At dawn on May 14TH, a sharp shoot descended on 11TH Brigade's front between Arielli and Orsogna, where the right forward company of 3/12TH Frontier Force Regiment was stationed on a neck land between three convergent valleys. Emerging from these valleys, a substantial German force, supported by tanks, overran the Frontiersmen. A counter-attack by a reserve company failed to eject the enemy, and it was not until evening that the intervention of 2ND Camerons restored the situation. In view of the possibility of an enemy withdrawal on the Adriatic front, both Indian Divisions undertook to pin down their adversaries and to keep them under strict observation. During the last days of May, heavy German transport movements to the north were reported. Attempts to explore the enemy positions, however, led to clashes with proved the enemy still to be holding in force. Both Camerons and 3/12TH Frontier Force Regiment on 11TH Brigade's front, ran into trouble when they attempted to probe too intimately. At the end of May, a regrouping of forces in the Adriatic sector occurred. The Italian Utili Division arrived to relieve Fourth Indian Division on the Orsogna front.

Their advance parties came forward with bands playing and with flags flying. The German greeted such advertisement of intention with a heavy shoot which interfered to some extent with relief. Fourth Indian Division side-slipped on to the coastal sector, and on June 4TH, relieved Tenth Indian Division, which left at once for Central Italy. Fourth Divisional Artillery remained behind Orsogna in support of the Italians, while the guns of the Third Carpathian Division covered the Indians on the coast. From time to time, the Indian Divisions were relieved on the Adriatic coast and disappeared. All took the roads to Central Italy, where in turn they were committed to the epic struggle for Cassino. This battle stands in the heroic category of Dunkirk, Stalingrad and Caen.

As darkness deepened on July 23RD, 3/12TH Frontier Force Regiment, until now in 11TH Brigade Reserve, moved forward to attack Caampriano, on the crest of a ridge two and a half miles east of the road to Florence. Tanks of Warwickshire Yeomanry accompanied the three assault companies.

12TH Frontier Force Regiment

53RD Sikhs (3/12TH)

An observer describes the weird effect of the afterglow of the setting sun reflected on the white smoke screen, intermingled with columns of brown dust from the German counter-barrage.

Night closed in with signal lights soaring to denote positions gained or calls for aid. The Frontiersmen had disappeared into the cauldron of battle; hour by hour the artillery thundered on. At dawn the Indians held both flank objectives but had been unable to prise the centre from the grip of the enemy. Casualties had been heavy, and 'A' and 'B' Companies of the Frontiersmen had been merged. Heavy counter-attacks swept against the Indians, to be thrown back again and again.

Towards the evening the enemy intensified his efforts and the forward companies were obliged to withdraw to the south of the ridge. After the withdrawal from Caampriano two companies of the Frontier Force Regiment had dug in on the approaches to the ridge. They next gave attention to a monastery a half mile further west, on a pinnacle a few hundred feet higher than Caampriano. This hospice was employed by the enemy as an observation post from which t direct fire on to all parts of the Brigade front. After nightfall on July 27TH, a company of the Frontiersmen crossed the valley and chased the enemy artillerymen from the chapel tower. As if expecting ejection, the chancellery was found to be abundantly booby-trapped.

On the night of September 5/6TH, 11TH Brigade launched its attack on Pian di Costello, with 3/12TH Frontier Force Regiment on the right and the Camerons on the opposite flank. The enemy had an uninterrupted view of the slopes down which attacking troops must move to the River. Anti-personnel mines were strewn in cunning patterns on both banks. On the slopes above the River, scattered farmhouses and cemeteries had been transferred into strong-points. Under the handicap of rain and mud, the advance became a slow and expensive slogging match. At dawn the enemy threw in a counter-attack which the Frontiersmen smashed.

During the day, tanks of the 6TH Royal Tank Regiment negotiated the floods and moved in close support. Their intervention turned the tide of battle, and 11 Brigade consolidated its objectives. At the end of a stiff night's fighting the Indians were firmly ensconced on the crest of the ridge on Castel Nuovo.

It was now thirty-five days since the Fourth Indian Division had moved out of Fossato, and thirty-one days since its committal to continuous battle, during this period the Indians had advanced over sixty miles, the last twenty-five miles through defensive zone heavily massed by first line troops with a great weight of artillery and armour in support. Mile by mile the wearers of Red Eagles has smashed, probed, and infiltrated through the strongest defences. The 3/12TH Frontier Force Regiment moved to rest in Umbria in anticipation of rejoining Eighth Army for the final overthrow of the enemy in Italy.

12ᵀᴴ Frontier Force Regiment

53ᴿᴰ Sikhs (3/12ᵀᴴ)

At Lake Trasimeno dramatic news arrived. Greece was about to be liberated, and the Fourth Indian Division would to proceed that theatre at once. In November 1944 the division was shipped to Greece to help stabilise the country after the Axis withdrawal. The plan called for 4ᵀᴴ Indian Division to be dispersed in three widely scattered areas. 11ᵀᴴ Indian Brigade with 3/12ᵀᴴ Frontier Force Regiment would garrison the towns of Western Greece and the Ionian islands.

In their introductory sweeps through the countryside the officers and men discovered the magnitude of their task in the Macedonian hinterland. Living had sunk to brute level. The scorched earth policy and the Bulgarian influx had left the inhabitants starving, houseless and naked. Communications had broken down. Authority had disappeared of if maintained was engrossed with reprisals against neighbours. The hungry wasted for want of a handful of grain; sick died for the lack of simple remedies. The mountains were devil's cauldrons in which hate stewed, in which violence and disorder represented the normal routine. The political fanatics drew support in their feuds from gang's intent upon plunder. Every man was a partisan who regarded the occupation forces either as partners or as enemies. A moderate directive established the British/Indian forces of occupation not as an umpire but rather as a buffer between two groups determined to have each other's blood.

Week by week the situation in Greece improved. The easy tolerance, good humour and impartiality of British and Indian troops brought quiet to a tormented country. All in all the Fourth Indian Division had set the feet of Greeks in the path of rehabilitation.

The 3/12ᵀᴴ Frontier Force Regiment returned to India in 1945, after five years of overseas service, in the midst of communal strife. The tragic expedient of the partition of the Indian subcontinent became inevitable.

At the independence of the subcontinent in 1947, and the creation of Pakistan, the battalion was allotted to the new Pakistan Army. The Sikh soldiers from the battalion were transferred to the Indian Army.

Lieutenant Karamjeet Singh Judge VC

12TH Frontier Force Regiment

54TH Sikhs (4/12TH)

The regiment was raised on 1ST January 1846 at Ludhiana as the 4TH Regiment of Infantry, by Captain C Mackenzie. It was composed of Sikhs, Punjabi Mussalmans, Pathans, and Dogras. In 1847, it was designated 4TH Regiment of Sikh Local Infantry, becoming the 4TH Regiment of Sikh Infantry in 1857. Subsequent to the reforms brought about in the Indian Army in 1903, the regiment's designation was changed to 54TH Sikhs (Frontier Force). In 1851, it became part of the Punjab Irregular Force. Their mission was to maintain order on the Punjab Frontier.

In 1852, the regiment volunteered for service in the Second Burmese War 1852. In 1852, Commodore George Lambert was dispatched to Burma over a number of minor issues related to the Treaty of Yandaboo between the countries. The Burmese immediately made concessions including the removal of a governor whom the Company made their casus belli. Lambert, eventually provoked a naval confrontation in extremely questionable circumstances by blockading the port of Rangoon and seizing the King Pagan's royal ship and thus started the Second Anglo-Burmese War which ended in the Company annexing the province of Pegu and renaming it Lower Burma. At the conclusion of the Burmese war the regiment returned to India in 1854.

On the outbreak of the Sepoy Mutiny in 1857, the regiment marched from Abbottabad to Delhi; 560 miles in thirty days in an Indian June, going into action soon after their arrival. At the fall of Delhi, the regiment was employed in pursuing and apprehending the mutineers, who were trying to escape to the countryside around Delhi. At the conclusion of the Sepoy Mutiny the regiment was back on the frontier, subduing the tribal clans. The regiment took active part in the expeditions against the Waziris (1859), Mahsuds (1860), Mohmands (1864), Tochi (1872), Jowakis (1877), Mahsuds (1881), Black Mountain (1891), Chitral (1895), Mahsuds & Waziris (1901, Zakha Khel (1908) and the Mohmands in 1908. The Mahsud raids rendered life and property in the Tochi and Gomal Valleys so insecure, and the perpetrators of these outrages established such terrorism over the inhabitants of British villages that retaliatory measures became absolute necessary. Sepoy Bishan Singh was awarded the I.O.M. for his conspicuous gallantry in the action against the Mohmands.

During the First World War, the regiment remained deployed on the North West Frontier of India. In 1918, it moved to Egypt to take part in the Palestine Campaign. During this time, two unsuccessful attacks were made to capture Amman and to capture Es Salt in March and April 1918, before Allenby's force resumed the offensive during the manoeuvre warfare of the Battle of Megiddo. In the process it destroyed three Turkish armies during the Battle of Sharon, the Battle of Nablus and the third Transjordan attack, capturing thousands of prisoners and large quantities of equipment.

12TH Frontier Force Regiment

54TH Sikhs (4/12TH)

Damascus, and Aleppo, was captured during the subsequent pursuit, before the Turkish Empire agreed to the Armistice of Mudros on 30TH October 1918, ending the Sinai and Palestine Campaign. The British Mandate of Palestine was created to administer the captured territories.

Jemadar Bikham Singh was awarded the Military Cross while Subedar Kesar Singh, Havildar Bachant Singh, Sepoy Delair Singh, Sepoy Darbara Singh and Sepoy Jhanda Singh were awarded the I.D.S.M. for their conspicuous gallantry against the Germans and the Turks during the Sinai and Palestine Campaign. After serving in the Russian Transcaucasia in support of the Russian Empire and its fall to the Bolsheviks in 1918, the regiment moved to Turkey, on occupational duties. It returned to India in 1920.

1922 the 54TH Sikhs were grouped with the 51ST, 52ND and 53RD Sikhs, and the two Battalions of Guides Infantry to form the 12TH Frontier Force Regiment. The 54TH Sikhs became 4TH Battalion (Sikhs) of the new regiment.

In August 19414, the Commander-in-Chief, Far East, having reviewed the state of defence of Burma, told the War Office it was essential that with eleven days of a Japanese attack on the country, Burma should be reinforced by an infantry brigade. In view of the importance of Burma to the defence of India, and grave risks involved in reinforcing it after the war had broken out, it was advised that a brigade should be sent as soon as possible. The advice was accepted and 16TH Indian Brigade, including the 4/12TH Frontier Force Regiment, began to move to Burma at the end of November 1941, and brigade was still arriving on the outbreak of war. It was sent to Mandalay, and remained as a general reserve under the command of General Officer Commanding. The Japanese attacked Burma on January 22ND, 1942. It was soon apparent that the British and Indian troops in Burma were too few in number, wrongly equipped and inadequately trained for the terrain and conditions. To meet the Japanese advance they were hurriedly thrown together and widely dispersed under the 17TH Indian Division. The 2ND Burma Brigade, mainly composed of untried Burma Rifle battalions and consisted at this time also the 4/12TH Frontier Force Regiment, was disposed for the defence of Moulmein. Only four battalions were available to defend the perimeter of about twelve miles, whereas at least two infantry brigades were needed for a protracted defence.

The 2ND Burma Brigade was disposed with 7TH Burma Rifles holding the northern sector, 3RD Burma Rifles the west bank of the Ataran River and 8TH Burma Rifles the southern sector. The 4/12TH Frontier Force Regiment was in reserve. Early on the 30TH the Japanese attacked the perimeter from the south and east. The 8TH Burma Rifles in the southern sector had repulsed all the Japanese attacks, but the Japanese had succeeded in crossing the Ataman River and had occupied Ngante and Hmyawlin, overrunning the forward posts of 3RD Burma Rifles.

12TH Frontier Force Regiment

54TH Sikhs (4/12TH)

The Burma Rifles were ordered to withdraw to a north-south line through Myenigon and moved the 4/12TH Frontier Force Regiment into a position along the ridge. During the afternoon 3RD Burma Rifles disintegrated in face of further attacks and the 4/12TH Frontier Force Regiment was closely engaged with the enemy along the whole length of the ridge, defied all enemy efforts break into its position. The defence of Moulmein might well end in disaster, since the defenders had their backs to a wide river estuary. Many units, such as 12TH Mountain Battery, 4/12TH Frontier Force Regimen and 8TH Burma Rifles, for all of whom it was a first experience of war, put up a stubborn defence and the withdrawal was brilliantly handled in exceptionally difficult circumstances.

After failing to hold the Kawkareik Pass and Moulmein, the 17TH Division with 4/12TH Frontier Force Regiment, fell back to the Bilin River. General Hutton had ordered one company to move the Sittang Bridge for its protection and reported the 17TH Division had checked the enemy on the Bilin River, but the troops were tired and had suffered a good many casualties. In the event of an enemy offensive with fresh troops, which appeared possible in the near future, he could not be certain of holding the position on the Bilin River. The Bilin was not a proper defensive position, and the division tried to retreat over the Sittang River. Air attacks, poor organization and vehicle breakdowns delayed the division, and Japanese parties infiltrated around them to threaten the vital bridge over the Sittang. The division's commander, Major General "Jackie" Smyth VC, was forced to order the bridge to be destroyed, with most of the division cut off on the far side of the river. Only a few thousand men without equipment succeeded in crossing the river. Smyth was dismissed and replaced by Major General Cowan. The division was reinforced with 63RD Indian Infantry Brigade, and narrowly escaped being trapped in Rangoon. After trying to hold a front in the Irrawaddy River valley, it subsequently retreated north into Assam just before the monsoon broke, fighting off a Japanese attempt to trap it at Kalewa. For the campaigning season of 1943, the division was reorganised as a 'Light' formation, with two brigades only (48TH and 63RD), supported by mountain artillery, and with mules and jeeps only for transport.

It disputed the mountainous and jungle-covered region around Tiddim, with mixed success. The division was at the end of a long and precarious supply line, and the "light" establishment was found to be inadequate in some respects. Some heavier equipment and transport was restored.

In 1944, the Japanese launched a major invasion of India. During the long Battle of Imphal, 17TH Division first successfully fought its way out of encirclement at Tiddim, and then disputed the vital Bishenpur sector south of Imphal. In July, the Japanese were broken by heavy casualties and starvation, and retreated. Some units of 17TH Division had suffered nearly 100% casualties.

12TH Frontier Force Regiment

54TH Sikhs (4/12TH)

On 8TH July 1944, a Japanese force of some 500 strong, supported by Artillery, Mortars and Medium Machine Guns, attacked positions in the village of Chepu held by 4/12TH Frontier Force Regiment. Major Kehar Singh Rai was ordered to take his company forward into these positions to reinforce the Company already there. On arrival in the positions, Major Rai found that both the Company Commander and the Company Officer of this Company had been killed and that the Company had suffered heavy casualties. He at once rallied the men and reorganized the defence of the area. Later in the afternoon, two platoons of another Company were despatched to strengthen Major Rai's position. The Company Commander was seriously wounded immediately after arrival in the position. Major Rai at once took command of these men and personally led them to their positions, despite heavy fire from Medium Machine Guns. Throughout the many attacks made upon his position by the Japanese during the day and despite heavy Mortar, Artillery and Medium Machine Gun fire, Major Rai remained completely unperturbed and was always in complete control of the situation. His personal gallantry and determination in the hand-to-hand fighting which accompanied these attacks was a great source of inspiration and encouragement to his men. Major Rai displayed complete contempt for personal safety at all times and was always in the thick of the fight, encouraging his men by both word and deed to even greater efforts. Major Rai's sustained offensive spirit and refusal at any time to permit the initiative to remain in the hands of the attacking Japanese largely contributed to the success of the defence of that day, and the infliction of very heavy casualties upon the Japanese. Major Kehar Singh Rai was awarded the Military Cross on 7TH August 1944.

Subedar Karam Singh has commanded a Machine Gun platoon for eighteen months in the forward area of the Arakan front in Burma. On 9TH October 1944, in the area south of Maungdaw, one his sections was preparing to take up position on the Sausage feature when it came under concentrated artillery fire from a Japanese 75m.m. gun. One of his Sepoys was badly wounded, and Subedar Karam Singh, ran out into the open and brought him back into a trench. In the afternoon of the same day, one of his Sections was giving a supporting fire on to Point 305 feature, and shortly after opening fire; its guns came under direct fire from an enemy 75m.m. gun, but encouraged by Jemadar Karam Singh's presence the Section maintained its concentrated fire. The platoon thus neutralized the enemy's small arms fire and enabled the operation to be carried out successfully with few casualties. For a further month until its withdrawal in November, Subedar Karam Singh was responsible for the many successful attacks carried out by his Platoon against the enemy. For his courageous leadership, Subedar Karam Singh was awarded the Military Cross on 26TH December 1944.

12TH Frontier Force Regiment

54TH Sikhs (4/12TH)

During the late monsoon season, the division was temporarily withdrawn to India and reorganised once again. 48TH and 63RD Brigades were fully equipped with vehicles to become Motorized infantry. 99TH Indian Infantry Brigade was added to the division, equipped to be transported by Douglas DC-3 aircraft. In late February, 1945, the motor elements of the division, with the bulk of 255TH Indian Tank Brigade under command, crossed the Irrawaddy River and advanced on the vital Japanese communications centre of Meiktilla.

On the 8TH March 1945, Major Harbans Singh Virk was in command of 'C' Company, 4/12TH Frontier Force Regiment, and with Royal Deccan Horse in support, was ordered to attack and capture the village of Sadaung. The village was known to contain a strong force of the enemy with 75mm guns, Medium Machine guns and Mortars. He went in from the North at 1315 hours, and in spite of heavy enemy fire, secured a firm base well inside the village. At 1430 hours, however, his company was held up by heavy mortar fire from South of the village, and very accurate Medium Machine Gun fire from the front and a pagoda to the left flank. Discharger Grenades were also being showered in to his position. He extricated his other two platoons, with the object of putting in and attack from the Eastern Flank. The country here was very boggy but relying on swift and decisive action to achieve success he ordered the tanks away to high ground on the left to give covering fire, and formed his men for the attack. At 1600 hrs, he rose, and with great shout to his men dashed into the centre of the enemy position, which was quickly overrun. He then led his men in a further magnificent charge, to clear the southern portion of the village, and finally reported at 1700 hrs that the enemy was beaten and running. The tanks then came to their own and demoralized the running Japanese. The enemy killed by Major Virk and his company on this afternoon, amounted to over one hundred and the booty included two 75mm guns, five Medium Machine Guns, two 81 mm Mortars and quantities of small arms and equipment. Throughout the action, under extremely heavy fire, he was ubiquitous, climbing on to the tanks to give orders under hail of bullets. He so inspired his men with his indomitable spirit, that when he gave the order for the charge, they followed him with the utmost dash and the battle was won. This officer has shown highest qualities of courage and leadership throughout the present operations, and has led and inspired his men on the victory on several previous occasions. It was the faith in their leader, inspired and bred from previous actions that gave the great impetus to the company to achieve what they did on this day. His personal count of dead Japanese had been considerable. Major Harbans Singh Virk was awarded an immediate Military Cross followed by the DSO on 27TH May 1945.

17TH Division had joined by 99TH Indian Infantry Brigade which was flown into the captured airfield at Thabutkon; they captured Meiktilla in only four days. The Battle of Meiktilla largely destroyed the Japanese armies in Central Burma.

12TH Frontier Force Regiment

54TH Sikhs (4/12TH)

On the 2ND March 1945, Jemadar Phaga Singh was a Platoon Commander in 'A' Company, which was part of an attacking force ordered to capture and clear the area of Meiktilla town in Burma. The attack was supported b a troop of tanks. Shortly after crossing the starting line, Jemadar Phaga Singh's platoon came under very heavy automatic, mortar, and grenade and rifle fire, and was pinned to the ground, suffering casualties. The whole area was a mass of bunkers and foxholes, and infested with cunningly concealed snipers. Without hesitation Jemadar Phaga Singh ran forward to his leading Sections, pin-pointed the opposition in front of each, and then rushed back to the tanks, giving them instructions, led them up to positions from which they could bring fire to bear on the enemy. Throughout the action he was under heavy fire, and his complete disregard for his own life, and the devotion with which he calmly directed the fire of the tanks, thus enabling his men to advance and mop up. His indomitable courage and determination to exterminate every Japanese soldier, throughout eight gruelling hours of stiff hand-to-hand fighting was worthy of the highest standards of the Indian Army, and his personal count of enemy dead was considerable. As part of the same operations, Jemadar Phaga Singh's platoon was ordered to form part of Road Block on the Mandalay Road. On the morning of the 14TH March the enemy attacked the position, but was driven off with heavy casualties. Thereafter supported by armoured cars, Jemadar Phaga Singh's platoon was ordered to go forward and capture a Japanese gun that had been located the previous day. When hearing the advance the enemy opened up with concentrated fire, and made determined attempts to destroy the armoured cars with magnetic mines. In this they were frustrated, but the cars were forced to withdraw to a safer distance. Jemadar Phaga Singh then went in to the attack, and under his inspiring leadership the Frontiersmen overran the enemy position, killing 20 Japanese in hand-to-hand fighting and completely routed the enemy force, considerably superior in numbers to their own. In the two actions detailed above Jemadar Phaga Singh showed the highest qualities of courage and true leadership, and the great success achieved against determined enemy are due to the outstanding qualities as a great leader in the Field. Jemadar Phaga Singh was awarded an immediate Military Cross at the conclusion of the above fighting.

On 10TH March 1945, Jemadar Udham Singh was the platoon commander of No.3 Platoon, 'A' Company, detailed to attack and clear up an enemy position astride the road Meiktilla-Mahlaing in Burma. A troop of tanks was operating in support of his platoon. The platoon deployed and went into action with the tanks on the left of the road and at once came up against fanatical Japanese resistance. The country here was broken, and covered with thick scrub, and a network of defences and foxholes, which proved more than usually difficult to locate. Jemadar Udham Singh, however, resolved to deal harshly with the enemy, and led his section in with great dash and vigour.

12TH Frontier Force Regiment

54TH Sikhs (4/12TH)

Jemadar Udham Singh led his men in this close and difficult country, in the most exemplary manner, without thought of personal danger, being always to the fore and quick to expose himself whenever it became necessary to direct the fire of the tanks. He took his platoon into action at 25 strong and after magnificent fighting on the part of all, he had only 12 men left, the remainder either being killed or wounded. The troop of tanks then went off leaving his small force to carry on without them, and surrounded by snipers on all sides.

This situation, however, merely goaded this gallant leader to redouble his efforts, rallying his men he went forward again, clearing up trench after trench, and inflicting great slaughter amongst the enemy. It was not until 1400 hours that a fresh company supported by tanks could be sent forward to relieve him on the ground to carry on the fight. Jemadar Udham Singh had killed many Japanese both with grenades and Sten gun, and it was his gallantry and inspiring leadership that spurred on the remnants of his gallant band of men to fight with frenzy, until finally ordered to withdraw and reorganize. Jemadar Udham Singh's conduct in the evacuation of all his casualties under heavy fire, both small arms and artillery, was of the highest order. Jemadar Udham Singh was awarded an immediate Military Cross on 10TH March 1945.

On the 10TH April 1945, Jemadar Narain Singh was a platoon commander of 'B' Company, when the Battalion was ordered to attack and consolidate the Frontier Force lines area of the main Pyawbwe-Meiktilla Road, as there was a strong enemy presence there. The 'B' Company had to advance across 1000 yards of bullet-swept, open country. Jemadar Narain Singh was in the vanguard of the advance, and kept the platoon under perfect control in spite of casualties from the enemy's Light Machine Guns. On arrival it was found that contrary to reports, the Frontier Force lines area was very strongly held by the enemy. The attack went in on a two Company front, with 'B' Company on the right. Jemadar Narain Singh's platoon at once came under heavy mortar and automatic fire, and the platoon suffered casualties. Holding his ground, however, Jemadar Narain Singh arranged, at great personal risk to himself, the evacuation of his wounded and then personally directed the artillery fire, preliminary to his further advance. He then led his platoon forward, but the enemy once again replied with everything he had and the attacking platoon suffered more casualties. Time was precious however, and without further ado, Jemadar Narain Singh led the charge, and rushed in at their head to capture the first objective. Inspired by his leadership his men fought magnificently, and the area was soon under control. There remained the wooded area, round the church and up to the railway line to be captured. Again 'B' Company was on the right, and Jemadar Narain Singh urgently requested that his platoon lead the attack. His request was granted and the men went in at the head of the tanks. The enemy fought back bravely and tenaciously, as the platoon cleared the whole area yard-by-yard.

12TH Frontier Force Regiment

54TH Sikhs (4/12TH)

Throughout this day, Jemadar Narain Singh led his men with utmost gallantry. His fierce cries of "Sat Siri Akal", and the encouragement he gave his men, going from section to section and personally directing the attack and his imperturbability under heaviest fire was beyond praise. On this day, Jemadar Narain Singh personally killed six Japanese and his platoon added another 133 to very substantial Battalion total. Within Company he has earned for himself the name of 'Sher' (Lion). Jemadar Narain Singh was awarded a Military Cross on the 10TH April 1945.

Major Amrik Singh fought and led his Company with great distinction at Meiktilla in Burma. On the second day of the attack on the town, and though wounded himself, in the shoulder, he refused to be evacuated, and by evening had cleared the enemy from whole of the built-up area from North to South. In the process his Company suffered heavy casualties, but his determination to defeat the enemy, and his fine personal example, inspired his men to win through bitter and difficult hand-to-hand fighting. A few days later he organised a most successful roadblock on the Mandalay Road, when his Company killed 40 Japanese and captured several guns. Again on the Meiktilla–Mahlaing road he led his Company in to attack and capture the high ground against numerically superior enemy forces over most difficult and broken country thickly entrenched and bunkered. In two days fighting the infantry with the Tanks in support, and despite their own heavy casualties killed over 200 of the enemy. Major Amrik Singh distinguished himself again at Kandaung and at the battle of Pyawbwe, numerous Japanese being killed and much equipment captured on both occasions. Finally it was Major Amrik Singh and his Company, which after a day and night of tough, close quarter fighting, secured the bridgehead over the Pegu River, thus enabling the Division to continue its advance southwards. This gallant and capable officer has been an inspiration and example to his men, throughout these operations, and has shown a high standard of personal skill and bravery. Despite very heavy casualties amongst his command, he has maintained a magnificent fighting spirit in his Company. The Company bears the proud record of never having failed to win all objectives given to them. No praise can be high enough for the way Major Amrik Singh has led and commanded his Company throughout these operations. Major Amrik Singh was awarded the Military Cross on 15TH May 1945.

After the war ended, elements of it formed part of the Commonwealth Occupation force in Japan. At the independence of the subcontinent in 1947, and the creation of Pakistan, the battalion was allotted to the new Pakistan Army. The Sikh soldiers from the battalion were transferred to the Indian Army.

12TH Frontier Force Regiment

Guides Infantry (5/12TH)

Corps of Guides was raised on 14TH December 1846 at Pashawar. It was raised from the veterans of the Sikh army at the conclusion of the First Sikh War. Sikhs, Pathans, Punjabi Mussalmans, and Dogras formed the bulk of its manpower. Initially composed of a troop of cavalry and two companies of infantry mounted on camels, the Guides were organized as a highly mobile force. The corps was ordered to recruit, trustworthy men, who could, at a moment's notice, act as guides to troops in the field; men capable, too, of collecting trustworthy intelligence beyond, as well as within, our borders; and, in addition to all this, men, ready to give and take hard blows, whether on the frontier or in a wider field. These were qualities that would become the hallmark of the Guides. During more than a hundred and fifty years of glorious military service, the regiment has earned the reputation of one of the most glamorous military units in the world. In 1851, the Guides established themselves at Mardan, near the border in the Yuzufzai country. In 1851, The Corps of Guides became part of the Punjab Irregular Force, which later became famous as the Punjab Frontier Force or Piffers. The Piffers consisted of five regiments of cavalry, eleven regiments of infantry and five batteries of artillery besides the Corps of Guides. Majority of the soldiers of these units were veterans of the Sikh armies. Their mission was to maintain order on the Punjab Frontier where they quickly made a name for themselves in numerous operations against the turbulent frontier tribes. Between 1847 and 1878, the corps participated in fifteen major frontier expeditions and operations.

In 1853, Subedar Kor Singh and Sowar Dal Singh were awarded the I.O.M. in the action against the Afridis in Borer Valley.

During the Sepoy Mutiny in 1857, 153 sabres and 349 rifles, in the hottest season of the year, after seizing Attock Fort from its garrison of Bengal Infantry, till replaced by a detachment from Kohat, halting two days, they marched on the 16TH on the first stage to Delhi, thirty-two miles in a dust storm, and on the 9TH June reached the camp on the Ridge, having come the 586 miles from Mardan in twenty-six days. The moral effect of the arrival of the Guides in Delhi was perhaps in some measure greater even than the actual fighting strength thus brought into line. The fame of the march from the far distant frontier, the fine physique and martial bearing of soldiers new to the eyes of their British comrades, all tended to give the approach of the travel-stained Guides a high significance. Marching in strength of the Guides Infantry was 423 all ranks. The Guides Infantry went into action the same day, in support of the Piquets; they engaged the enemy in hand-to-hand combat and drove them back to the city. The Guides Infantry then was permanently posted on the right of the Ridge, and, besides taking their share in the general operations with the Sirmur battalion; they held the position and furnished the outposts round the Hindu Rao's house.

12TH Frontier Force Regiment

Guides Infantry (5/12TH)

On 12TH June the enemy made an attempt to turn this flank, occupying Sabzi Mandi in great numbers, whereupon the Guides Infantry were ordered to turn them out; and this was successfully accomplished with a loss to the Guides five killed and six wounded after two hours fighting. During the course of the siege the enemy delivered no fewer than twenty six separate attacks upon this part of the line, and these occurred almost daily.

On the 13TH the enemy again got into the Sabzi Mandi, and again they were ejected by the Guides Infantry. They had some ten men killed and wounded in this action, and on the 14TH there was another attack by the enemy in which Subedar Mehr Singh was killed.

On the morning of 9TH July the Guides Infantry greatly distinguished themselves, when seventy eight men only held a breastwork against far superior numbers of the enemy advancing to very close quarters. They had run out of ammunition, of which the enemy appeared to be equally short, and the fight carried on with stones, until reinforcement of fifty bayonets, charged the enemy on the flank, so bewildered them that they broke and fled leaving ninety dead on the breastwork. They continued to fight gallantly throughout the summer and took part in the final assault and capture of Delhi.

Subedar Bhup Singh, Havildar Jai Singh and Bugler Gurdit Singh, of the Guides Infantry, were awarded the I.O.M for their conspicuous gallantry against the mutineers at Delhi. Thirty three of the Infantry were specially promoted for gallantry in the field.

When Delhi fell the Guides Infantry went home to the frontier. Sayed Ahmad Shah was a Wahabi preacher who came into the Yusafzai territory in 1824 when it was part of the Sikh Empire. He stirred the Pathan tribes into rebellion but was defeated by the Sikh army. He then increased his support and by 1829 gained control of Yuzufzai and occupied Pashawar. His 'Hindustani Fanatics' were once again defeated by the Sikhs and Sayed Ahmad was killed. His disciples retreated to Sittana under the leadership of Sayed Akbar. A further confrontation with the Hindustani Fanatics took place in 1863, this time by the British. Much severe fighting occurred against the fanatics and their tribal allies, during which the Guides Infantry took a leading part in crushing the fanatics. Sepoy Sobha Singh was granted the I.O.M for his conspicuous gallantry against the Fanatics in 1863.

In 1876, HM Queen Victoria was pleased to make them a royal regiment, and they became The Queen's Own Corps of Guides.

In 1878 a Russian Mission had been received in Kabul and a British Mission, led by General Sir Neville Chamberlain, was refused admission at the mouth of the Khaiber by the Afghan commander. His escort was found by the Guides, under Lieutenant Colonel Jenkins, with 100 sabres of the Cavalry and 50 bayonets of the Infantry. Consequently the British Government invaded Afghanistan.

12TH Frontier Force Regiment

Guides Infantry (5/12TH)

General Roberts gained a victory at the Peiwar Kotal and General Sam Browne took Ali Masjid and advanced on Kabul, and General Donald Stewart occupied Kandahar. The Guides Cavalry formed part of the cavalry brigade of Sam Browne's force and the Guides Infantry were in his 2ND Infantry Brigade. Amir Sher Ali fled at the British advances and soon after died, and the British acknowledged his son, Yaqub Khan, as Amir, making with him the treaty of Gandamak, which rectified the frontier, so far as the protection of India against Russia.

Subedar Jowala Singh, Subedar Jiwand Singh, Subedar Attar Singh, Sepoy Wariam Singh, Guides Infantry, was awarded I.O.M for their conspicuous gallantry in the capture of the Afghan capital Kabul.

The new Amir ascended his throne and sent to meet the new Agent, Major Sir Louis Cavignari the son of an Italian aristocrat who had served for several years in the British colonial administration, in particular as District Commissioner of Peshawar. Despite his experience of the region and his qualities as a diplomat, Cavignari's appointment was viewed with some misgivings by British observers who knew his arrogant manners.

Sir Louis Cavignari accompanied by his secretary, Mr. Jenkins, and medical officer Dr. Kelly, escorted by a detachment of 25 cavalry and 52 bayonets of Guides, under command of Lieutenant Hamilton V.C., arrived at Kabul on 24TH July1879, and was lodged in a spacious building in the Bala Hissar, 250 yards from the Amir's palace. A few days later, six Afghan regiments, due for disbandment, arrived in Kabul from Herat, loudly abusing the Mission.

On 3RD September without any warning, these Afghan soldiers attacked the Residency. British officers and Indian troops of the Guides faced countless Afghan soldiers and civilians. Soon all the British officers were dead. The Guides fought desperately, even charging out of the Residency to bayonet the crews of Artillery brought against them, The Afghans set the Residency of fire and the buildings started to collapse. All day the Afghans called upon the Guides to surrender, promising them their lives. Guides rejected the offer and after 12 hours of fighting the few remaining men commanded by a Sikh Jemadar, Jiwand Singh, fixed bayonets and charged out to their deaths. Twenty six of the Guides Infantry sacrificed their lives. Over 600 Afghans dead bore witness to the heroic sacrifice of this small force.

The sacrifice of these gallant men is commemorated in the impressive Guides Memorial at Mardan with the following words: 'The annals of no army and no regiment can show a brighter record of devoted bravery than has been achieved by this small band of Guides. By their deeds they have conferred undying honour not only on the regiment to which they belonged but on the whole British Army,' Double pensions were granted to the widows and heirs of the escort.

12TH Frontier Force Regiment

Guides Infantry (5/12TH)

Following are the names of the fallen, given for Infantry, so all may remember the richness of their inheritance:-

Jemadar Mehtab Singh, Havildar Hazara Singh, Havildar Kharak Singh, Sepoy Devi Singh, Sepoy Jai Singh, Sepoy Amar Singh, Sepoy Fateh Singh, Sepoy Wariam Singh, Sepoy Mith Singh, Sepoy Hira Singh, Sepoy Chanda Singh, Sepoy Gurdit Singh, Sepoy Gaja Singh, Sepoy Waryam Singh, Sepoy Ajaib Singh, Sepoy Nidham Singh, Sepoy Tahil Singh, Sepoy Ranju Singh, Sepoy Bhagat Singh, Sepoy Esa Singh, Sepoy Narain Singh, Sepoy Hari Singh, Sepoy Udin Singh, and Sepoy Gurdit Singh.

The massacre at Kabul led to the resumption of hostilities. Sir Roberts led the Kabul Field force on Kabul via the Peiwar Kotal, defeating the Afghan force at Charasiab, and reached Kabul on 8TH October. The Amir came to meet him to surrender. In the meantime another force was moving up the Khyber, led by the Guides Cavalry and Infantry. Eventually the two units marched through to join Roberts, who was faced with a national rising around Kabul. This after some fierce fighting round the city drove Roberts into the entrenched camp of Sherpur Cantonment outside Kabul, on which the tribesmen made fierce attacks. To relieve him, General Stewart marched from Kandahar, fighting the battle of Ahmed Khel en route; while another force was also pressing up from the Khyber, and this put an end to the struggle around Kabul. In these operations the Guides Infantry took an ample share. Havildars Jowala Singh, Jiwand Singh, Attar Singh and Wariam Singh, were awarded the I.O.M. for their conspicuous gallantry in capture of the Afghan capital, Kabul.

Throughout the 1890's the Guides Infantry was more or less continuously engaged in frontier actions. In 1895, a coup d'état in Chitral cost the life of the ruling chief. The victors attempted to destroy the Indian troops in Chitral, who were besieged in the Chitral fort. To rescue them, a couple of hundred miles of continuous frontier hills or as much by almost non-existent precipitous roads from Gilgit, was a very great problem.

When reports became more serious they ordered Colonel James Kelly at Gilgit to act. He gathered what troops he could: 400 Sikh Pioneers - mostly road-builders, 40 Kashmiri sappers with 2 mountain guns, 900 Hunza irregulars, all hearty mountain men, and a number of hired coolies to carry the baggage. Although his force was small he had the advantage that the Chitralis did not think that anyone would be fool enough to cross 150 miles of mountains in late winter. He left Gilgit on March 23RD, probably up the valley of the Gilgit River, and by March 30TH had crossed the snowline at 10,000 feet. Seeing what they were in for, the coolies deserted with their laden ponies, but were soon rounded up and kept under guard. The main problem was the 12,000 foot Shandur Pass at the head of the Gilgit River which was crossed in the waist-deep snow dragging mountain guns on sledges. Fighting began the next day when the Chitralis became aware of them.

12TH Frontier Force Regiment

Guides Infantry (5/12TH)

By April 13^{TH,} the Sikhs had driven the enemy from two main positions and by April 18TH the enemy seemed to have disappeared. The story of the relief of Chital Fort, by 32ND Sikh Pioneers, who set out from Gilgit on a epic march to cover 220 miles of poor road to Chitral was never fully recognised most of the publicity and fame for the relief being lavished on the well-known British regiments!

Meanwhile, the British had assembled 15,000 men at Pashawar which included the Guides Infantry. On April 3RD they stormed the Malakand Pass, which was defended by 12,000 local warriors who lost more than 500 men before giving up control of the pass. The British fought significant engagements later. On April 17TH Umra Khan's men prepared to defend his palace at Munda, but finding themselves greatly outnumbered, they slipped away. Umra Khan fled with eleven mule-loads of treasure and reached safety in Afghanistan. Sher Ali ran into one of the British forces and was sent into exile in India.

Dafadar Sham Singh, Jemadar Bahadur Singh, Sowar Gurdit Singh, Sepoy Jowahir Singh and Sepoy Bishan Singh of the Infantry, were awarded the I.O.M. for their conspicuous gallantry at the Malakand Pass.

However, after the successful actions of the Malakand Pass and ridge, the Guides Infantry carried out various operations against the tribals including the punitive actions during the Pathan Revolt of 1897-98.

The conflagration began in Waziristan and then spread along the whole length of the frontier from Gomal up to the hills near Mardan. The summer of 1897 found the North-West Frontier border in an inflammable condition. The prevalent excitement soon sprang into flame. The tribes in the Swat Valley, with whom peaceable arrangements had been made, and to whose chiefs large subsidies had been promised and paid, commenced an outbreak. In Tochi, an unexpected visit from the Political officer, accompanied by an unusually strong escort, on June 10TH, to the village of Maizar, of which the inhabitants were already in disgrace for the murder of a Hindu, caused the explosion. After being hospitably entertained, the troops were treacherously attacked. All the British military officers were killed or wounded, but the escort, with the Political officer, withdrew in good order to Datta Khel.

The news spread rapidly and everywhere formed the text of fanatical harangues by the Mullahs The numbers, which at first had barely reached 1,000 men , were rapidly swollen to 12,000 at Malakand and 8,000 at Chakdara. The extent and character of this attack were of such a nature that two brigades, one containing four and the other three regiments, with three mountain batteries, were sent forward to support the garrison. After five days' fighting, the force under the command of Sir Bindon Blood, about 5,000 men, completely defeated the tribes. By this victory the attack on the Malakand Fort the principal fort on the road by an army of 6,000 men was prevented.

12TH Frontier Force Regiment

Guides Infantry (5/12TH)

A week later several thousand men of another tribe attacked one of our forts only 15 miles from Pashawar. That attack was, after fierce fighting, brilliantly repulsed. Heavy fighting continued at both places, until the Malakand was relieved on August 1ST and Chakdara on the 2ND. The assailants then drew off with a loss of not less than 3,000 men, while the British losses had amounted to 33 killed and 188 wounded. On the relief of Chakdara the gathering quickly dispersed, and the task of punishment and prevention of further combination was taken in hand at once.

Sepoy Jowahir Singh and Sepoy Bishan Singh of the Guides Infantry were awarded the I.O.M. for gallantry in connection with the operations of 2ND August.

The next to rise were the Mohmands. Animated by the discourses of Hadda Mullah, a gathering of about 5,000 armed men from all sections advanced on August 7 into the Pashawar valley, and attacked the village of Shankargarh, in which there is a large Hindu element, and the adjoining police post of Shabkadar. Troops were dispatched from Pashawar, and the tribesmen were driven back into the hills.

Meanwhile, throughout Afridi and Orakzai Tirah the excitement had been growing; and frequent rumours reached Pashawar, Kohat, and Kurram of the reconciliation of intertribal feuds and the gathering of clans for jihad, at the bidding of Mullah Sayed Akbar, Aka Khel Afridi. The trouble began with desultory firing by the Orakzai at the troops on the Samana on August 15TH. The Government of India promptly poured troops into the district, and by the middle of August British forces had increased to about 37,000 men including the Guides Infantry. By the 23RD and 24TH the whole of the posts in the Khyber, held only by the Khyber Rifles, whose British officers had been withdrawn, fell before a strong combination of Afridis. By the end of the month the Orakzai and Afridis had collected 15,000 men, all the posts on the Samana were closely invested, Shinwaris (a police post at the juncture of Upper and Lower Miranzai) had fallen, and Hangu was threatened.

Then came the treacherous outbreak of the Afridis, a tribe hitherto loyal to the Government, they had been entrusted for nearly 20 years the guardianship of the Khyber Pass. In September the British were attacked at Nawagai. The Khan of that tribe was the chief who openly declared himself a friend of the Government on receipt of the proclamation. His tribe attacked British forces with 3,000 men. These tribal risings have necessitated military operations on a most gigantic scale. The siege of the Samana posts continued till September 14TH, when Fort Lockhart and Fort Cavagnari (Gulistan) were relieved, the small post of Saraghari with the Sikh garrison of twenty two, having fallen on September 12TH. On the approach of the relief force the enemy withdrew from the Samana ridge into the Khanki valley.

12TH Frontier Force Regiment

Guides Infantry (5/12TH)

The operations began again with the dispatch of two brigades (7,000 men) to Datta Khel in the Tochi valley, which caused the submission of the Madda Khel, who agreed to give up seventeen ringleaders, make compensation for the property taken at Maizar, and pay a fine. The final submission was, however, not concluded till 1901, after further operations. In Swat a quicker settlement was made.

Before the end of the year Upper Swat, Bajour, Chamla, and the Uthman Khel country had been penetrated by British troops, and the fines imposed had been realized. In January, 1898, an expedition was sent through Buner, fines were realized from the Khuda Khel and Gaduns of the Yuzufzai border, and the Mullah Mastan was expelled by political pressure from Dir and Swat. The Malakand Field Force consisted of three brigades with the usual complement of divisional troops, in all 10,000 men.

The punishment of the Mohmands was effected by two brigades (7,000 men) advancing from Pashawar, in co-operation with two others detached from the Malakand Field Force. Difficulties were encountered in the advance of the latter, during which the affair at Inayat Killa took place. After the destruction of Badalai, active operations against the Mohmands came to an end, and before the end of October the Mohmands had been punished, and the Hadda Mullah fled to Afghanistan. On his departure a fine was paid by the clan and weapons were surrendered, and settlement was made on October 18^{TH,} after which the troops were withdrawn. Between November 23RD and December 6TH an expedition was made against Uthman Khel, living on the left bank of the Swat River, and the surrender of the clan was received without a shot being fired.

Tirah was invaded from Miranzai by the route passing from Shinwaris over the Chagru Kotal, between the cliffs of Dargai and the Samana Sukh. The army consisted of two divisions, under Sir W. Lockhart, supported by columns at Pashawar and in the Kurram. The advance began on October 18TH, and on the 21ST was fought the severe action of Dargai, in which the British loss was 38 killed and 191 wounded. The troops then penetrated to Maidan and Bara. By December 20TH, the Orakzai had completely fulfilled their obligations, but the Afridis, who had as yet received little punishment, held out. Their territories were, therefore, still further harried; but the demands of the Government were not complied with till April 1898, and the posts in the Khyber were held by regular troops till December 1899, when they were made over to the Khyber Rifles. About 30,000 men were employed in the Tirah campaign, which had taken place in a difficult and unknown country, with an enemy who gave the troops no rest and pressed close on the heels of every retirement, while cleverly avoiding resistance in strength to an advance. The Guides Infantry was in the van of these operations and were highly praised for their achievements and their gallantry in action,

12TH Frontier Force Regiment

Guides Infantry (5/12TH)

Minor frontier operations brought the Guides Corps to the days of the First World War. From this time on this history will chronicle separately the services of the Cavalry and of Infantry Battalions of the Guides. At the outbreak of World War I, the Guides Infantry initially remained in India for service on the Frontier. On 8TH January and called upon to furnish reinforcement for the 24TH Punjabis in Mesopotamia. On 9TH March draft of fifty rank and files to reinforce 53RD Sikhs; and this was followed on January of second draft of equal strength to the same regiment. Later on 9TH October, a draft of 101 of all ranks proceeded to join the same regiment.

The people of Buner remained quiet until 15TH August, when information was received that a certain mullah, known as the Haji Sahib of Turangzai, was in the neighbourhood of the Ambela Pass, with several thousand men, including a number of those perennial firebrands, the Hindustani Fanatics, and was preparing to invade British territory. Accordingly, 270 rank and files of the Guides Infantry, under Major Buist, moved out to Rustam on the Buner border. On reaching Rustam on 16TH August the troops entrenched and were joined later in the evening another 163 men of the Guides Infantry marched in under Lieutenant Erskine. Next day after the action that ensued, the tribesmen were defeated with seventy killed and seventy wounded.

Major Buist made the following report on Havildar Kishen Singh was awarded the I.O.M. for gallantry in action at Rustam:

"On the 17TH of August during the Guide's retirement from the foothills east of Rustam, Havildar Kishen Singh, Guides Infantry, whilst carrying out the retirement of his section across a nullah was suddenly attacked by three ghazis. He turned and closed with them. Having bayoneted two, although severely wounded by sword-cuts in four places, he succeeded in killing the third ghazi with a downward blow of his rifle on the man's head, smashing his rifle in the act. His wounds are such as to make it very probable that he will be invalided out of the Service."

In 1915, the Mohmands announced Jihad against the British and their Lashkar invaded Pashawar district near Shabkadar and were defeated with great losses. Another Lashkar came down from the hills to join the Jihad. The Mohmand Blockade line then was instituted. It began in late September 1916 and continued on to July 1917. The Blockade was made of a series of blockhouses and barbed wire defences manned by the men of the Indian Army, along the British border of Mohmand territory. Blockade began in response to excessive Mohmand attacks. The most important engagement occurred on 15TH November 1916, at Hafiz Kor, when a large number of Mohmands were defeated. The blockade was eventually lifted in July 1917, when the Mohmands finally submitted to British demands. The military report on Mohmand country recommended the temporary occupation of country and destruction of crops and villages.

12TH Frontier Force Regiment

Guides Infantry (5/12TH)

On 6TH February 1917 orders were received for the Guides Infantry to proceed on active service to Mesopotamia. The 1ST Guides Infantry reached Basra on the 4TH March where it joined the 7TH (Meerut) Division, Tigres Corps.

Just before the regiment reached Aziziya, Baghdad had been captured and as the result of the fighting during the month of April, the enemy's 13TH and 18TH Corps was driven back into the Jebel Hamrin and to Tikrit respectively. Early in May the regiment received orders to proceeded up-River to Samara. At Samara the regiment remained throughout the summer, carrying on a vigorous system of training, and working on the Samara defences on both banks of the River. On the 5TH November the regiment fought in the Action at Tikrit, in which the Turkish army suffered 2,000 casualties with 300 killed.

On the 7TH December 1918, the regiment was ordered to proceed to Palestine. On 24TH March the move to Palestine began, it marched in two stages to Qantara on the Suez Canal, then the base of the Palestine Expeditionary Force. On 1ST April it marched to Sarona, and on the evening of the following day went up to the front line, and took over the sector near the village of Jelil.

The regiment captured 'North Sister' and 'South Sister' Hills on 8TH June, and raided 'Piffer Ridge' on 27TH June. Several remmendations were put forward for the repeated gallantry during the three days the Regiment was in action and the latter the part it played in dislodging the enemy from the trenches. Enemy's losses were considerable and 4 officers and 101 other ranks were captured.

The capture of these positions not only prevented the enemy from overlooking a considerable length of the defences and the ground in rear, but secured observation of the approaches to the enemy's position, with the result that his movements by day had been considerably restricted. During this tour of twenty-five days in the frontline the Guides put in much hard work at the further consolidation of the trenches and lost men at the rate of two a day. At dawn on 19TH September the attack was launched by the five divisions and the great offensive had begun. The 19TH Brigade, with two regiments attached, the 1ST Guides Infantry and 20TH Punjabis, formed the main 7TH Division column of attack on a front of 400 yards facing the Turkish position in the coastal area at Tabsor. On reaching the position of deployment on a very misty morning, the Guides formed up in the rear of the 1ST Seaforth Highlanders in four lines of platoon a fifty yards interval and distance. The advance began, with the Seaforth Highlanders on reaching their first objectives, the Guides passed through to their own objectives beyond, finding the Turkish trenches terrible battered by the British barrage which crept forward at an average rate of a hundred yards in two minutes. The Turks were taken completely by surprise, and practically no opposition was met with except from Turkish barrage, where Lieutenant Arnot, Jemadar Mangal Singh and some twenty men became casualties.

12TH Frontier Force Regiment

Guides Infantry (5/12TH)

The Guides and the Seaforth Highlanders now pushed on to the second objective, the main El Tireh position, consisting of newly-dug and unused trenches. This was occupied without much opposition, and the advance continued for another mile when the outpost line was put out and a halt called until the 7TH Division came up on the right.

The 7TH Division was now ordered to march northwards via the coast on Beirut and Tripoli. Starting on the 24TH and marching via Hudera and Zimmerarin, it reached the coast at Athlit on the 26TH, total march of thirty-seven miles. From Athlit the 1ST Guides Infantry was pushed on in advance of the rest of the 21ST Brigade to Haifa, and there took over from Cavalry the outposts on Mount Carmel, al line of some three miles. At Haifa the Regiment met two Sepoys of the 2ND Guides Infantry, who had become separated from their regiment during the attack on the 19TH and had been wandering about the country for over a week looking for it. The 2ND Guides were at that time some sixty miles farther south! The 21ST Brigade remained in bivouac at Haifa until 4TH October, and the rest was greatly appreciated, for the march had been arduous on the men had suffered much for the lack of water.

The Division then marched on and the first days march round the Bay of Acre. From Acre they marched to Musheirafeh and Ras-el-Ain, crossing here the famous 'Ladder of Tyre'. The Brigade carried on its march by Saida and El Damur, reaching Beirut on 10TH October. During this long and strenuous march of ninety- six miles, the troops bivouacked at each halting place en route. The Brigade remained for twelve days in Beirut, during which one and half companies of the Guides were on outpost duties, billeted in villages on the Lebanon mountains some 4,000 Feet above and overlooking the town.

On 22ND October the advance continued by Dabaye, Junie, Jebeil, Batrum, Beshmezzin to Ras-el-Lados, a camp some four miles north of Tripoli town, the last part of the march being made in heavy rain. Here ended, as far as the 1ST Guides Infantry was concerned, the long pursuit which had taken them 270 miles of marching in twenty-two marching days since 19TH September; for on 31ST October, the day after their arrival at Tripoli, news was received of the conclusion of the armistice with Turkey.

In January the regiment was sent north to Jisi Ayash, working on the main road from Tripoli to Homs, which was the only communication with north Syria. On 18TH the Regiment marched back to Tripoli. In November orders were received the Syria was to be evacuated by British troops and handed over to the French. The 1ST Guides Infantry embarked for Port Said and proceeded to Qantara. The time had come now for the 1ST Guides Infantry to return to India, reaching Karachi on the 19TH December 1920. Subedar Bishan Singh, Subedar Fauja Singh, Naik Mian Singh and Sepoy Bhan Singh were awarded the I.D.S.M., for their gallantry during the First World War.

12TH Frontier Force Regiment

Guides Infantry (5/12TH)

In 1922, 1ST Guides Infantry was grouped with the 51ST Sikhs, 52ND, 53RD and 54TH Sikhs, and the 2ND Guides Infantry to form the 12TH Frontier Force. The 1ST Guides Infantry became 5TH Battalion (QVO Corps of Guides) 12TH Frontier Force Regiment.

The 1ST Guides Infantry arrived in Mardan in December 1920 from Syria, and as 5/12TH Frontier Force Regiment it went to Aden in 1924. During 1924 the Yemen was considerably disturbed, and in September the only incident that affected the 5/12TH Frontier Force Regiment during their tour on the Barren Rock. The island of Perim at the entrance to the Red Sea, 100 miles west of Aden itself, was occupied by a detachment of the Yemen Infantry, under Lieutenant Lawrence; on 3RD September Lieutenant Lawrence was stabbed to death at night by the guard of the unit in his bungalow. The N.C.O., bugler and six men of the guard fled to the mainland with several thousands of Government rupees that had been in the island commander's safe. A political officer and the commandant of Yemen Infantry, with an escort of twenty men of the 5/12TH Frontier Force Regiment under Subedar Jaimal Singh, were sent to the scene. Orders came shortly afterwards for a British officer and suitable party to occupy Perim and disarm the Yemen Infantry detachment and another to go to the island of Kamaran, a British possession near the coast of the Yemen some 150 miles north of Perim. Lieutenant Coleman left on the 14TH for Kamaran, and on the 16TH Lieutenant Barlow, took a company to Perim and the Yemen detachment laid down their arms. The Yemen battalion was shortly after disbanded, and during the next two years five of the eight criminals were brought to justice. The British officer's detachments on both islands were maintained by the Battalion the whole of its tour at Aden.

The 5/12TH Frontier Force Regiment returned from Aden in 1926, to a long period that was to see several years of severe fighting on the Frontier. The trouble began with the Red Shirt movement, by name of Khudei Khitmatgar (Persian: 'Servants of God'), in support of the Indian National Congress, an action started by Abdul Ghaffar Khan of the North-West Frontier Province of India. Abdul Ghaffar Khan was a Pakhtun and was called the Frontier Gandhi. It was a semi-rebellious body with vast following in semi-military guise, and was involved in series of troubles which were to involve the Frontier troops, including of course the 5/12TH Frontier Force, in seven years of trouble and war. Both the Mohmand and the Waziristan troubles were to keep the Battalion extremely busy for some years. During the these operations Subedar Rur Singh was awarded the I.O.M., while Havildar Sadhu Singh, Naik Sarban Singh and Sepoy Gurdial Singh were awarded the I.D.S.M.

12TH Frontier Force Regiment

Guides Infantry (5/12TH)

During the Second World War, British command formed Paiforce to invade and subsequently occupy Iraq and Persia. In 1941 the British sent a force to Iraq to suppress a coup d'etat by elements sympathetic to Nazi Germany and then invaded Persia in conjunction with Soviet forces from the north to safeguard the oil fields.

Most of the troops of Paiforce (Persia and Iraq Force) were Indian. The 5/12TH Frontier Force Regiment was ordered to join Paiforce. With a brief spell in Lebanon, the Battalion and served throughout the Second World War in Iraq and Iran, guarding against the German threat from the north. After the battalion moved into camp in Persia to train for jungle warfare, it received the news that the Second World War was over. That was the end of four years of very hard work, and only 'well done' to show for it. In 1945, the 5/12TH Frontier Force Regiment returned to India after long and faithful but non-eventful sojourn in Persia and Iraq.

Havildar Gurdial, Havildar Bhghel Singh, Havildar Karam Singh, and Naik Kehar Singh were awarded certificates by G.O.C.-in-C., in recognition of their outstanding good service in Iraq and Persia in 1945.

At the independence of the subcontinent in 1947, and the creation of Pakistan, the battalion was allotted to the new Pakistan Army. The Sikh soldiers from the battalion were transferred to the Indian Army.

Guides Infantry (10/12TH)

The 2ND Battalion was raised on 15TH January 1917, by Captain Pollock at Mardan. The Class composition was Sikhs, Yusafzai, Punjabi Mussalmans, Gurkhas and Dogras. The regiment was ordered for service in Egypt in 1918. It arrived at Suez on 9TH June, and proceeded to Tel-el-Kebir, where it was allotted to 180TH Brigade of 60TH Division. The Division was with General Allenby's force on the Jordan River. Between 17TH and 25TH July the regiment took over the sector near Juljilia. The sector was handed over to the 30TH Punjabis, between 13TH and 15TH August; and on the 18TH preparations was made for a move to Beit Nuba which took place on 19TH and 20TH August. While the regiment was Beit Nuba Lance-Naik Gujar Singh won the Corps Commander's Lewis Gun Competion. On 14TH September orders were received for the regiment to march from Beit Nuba to take part in General Allenby's great offensive. The 60TH Davison was placed on the extreme left of the line with the sea-shore on its left. On its right was the 7TH Division containing the sister regiment of 1ST Regiment Guides Infantry.

On the 18TH orders were received to prepare to attack the Turkish trenches, and the day was spent reconnoitring the line with a view to finding the best places to get through the wire and to deploy preparatory to the attack. The Turks occupied an intricate system of trenches of sandy hillocks with their right resting on the sea.

12TH Frontier Force Regiment

Guides Infantry (10/12TH)

The strength of the enemy opposed to the Guides was not exactly known, but there were many machine-gun opposing them and trench-mortar battery manned by a detachment of Germans.

In the early hours of 19TH September the British barrage opened from the Jordan to the sea. Three minutes later the Turkish barrage brought down the sides of the wadi in an avalanche. Thus at the very outset of the attack all communications were dislocated and Battalion Headquarters was completely cut off from the companies.

A platoon of 19TH Londons was wiped out, and all the men of the machine-gun section attached to the Guides were killed or wounded except one, thus leaving no guns in action. Luckily the aid post escaped, though it was nearly buried by falling earth, and the Medical Officer, Lieutenant Sher Singh, did fine work in attending to the wounded, while the N.C.O., of the 19TH London Regiment bandaged at least forty of the injured Guides.

The advance of the Guides began simultaneously with the opening of the barrage. 'D' Company suffered heavily both from the enemy shells and from short bursts of their own Guides, fifty-six men dropping as they advanced. The survivors, however, advanced steadily, a gap in their line being promptly filled with 'C' Company. Together the Companies charged through the wire into the first position. On the right of the regiment, the companies went straight on to the second objective without a pause, the companies charged through the wire into the first position. On the right of the regiment the companies went straight on to the second objective without a pause. One left, the companies were momentarily checked by a deep ravine, topped on the enemy's side with wire. These companies at once went down into the ravine and scaled the far side just in time to escape the fire of Turkish machine-guns which could not be sufficiently depressed to engage the attackers, and which were now captured.

179TH Brigade passed through and the cavalry coming on the scene carried on the pursuit of the fleeing Turks. The 180TH Brigade now halted for an hour and then advanced towards Tul Keram, the regiment bivouacking that night at Burin Wells, two miles west of Tul Karam. During the action the captures made by the 2ND Guides Infantry totalled 250 prisoners, including thirty Germans, five machine-guns and three trench mortars. While the Guides had seventeen other ranks killed and 109 other ranks wounded including Jemadar Tarlok Singh.

On the 20TH, the 180TH Brigade moved to a point about a mile west of Tul Keram, and on the following day marched up a valley which was a veritable shambles, strewn with dead Turks and animals, to Anebta where it bivouacked, while the 2ND Guides Infantry Piqueted the ridge between the bivouac, and Kefr-el- Lebad, to intercept Turkish fugitives. On the 23RD the regiment moved south with the Brigade, camping at Kaikileh and the next day and night at Feijja, where there was a welcome two-days halt.

12TH Frontier Force Regiment

Guides Infantry (10/12TH)

On 31ST October news was received that an armistice had been concluded with Turkey. On 7TH November the regiment learnt that it was shortly to proceed to Qantara, and on the 10TH this move was made in two trains. Next day came the news of the conclusion of the armistice with Germany and that the Great War was at an end. On 16TH November the regiment arrived at Alexandria and encamped at Sidi Bishr. On 3RD December they lined a portion of the road from Sidi Gaber railway station to the racecourse on the occasion of the arrival of the Commander-in-Chief, General Allenby, and then marched past with the rest of the Division. They were congratulated on their steadiness and smartness.

On 20TH November, bar to the I.D.S.M. to Subedar Fauja Singh, was announced. The time had now come for the 2ND Guides Infantry to leave Lower Egypt and take their turn of garrison duty in Syria, and on 2ND April the Regiment, having called in all outlying detachments, embarked at Alexandria. Beirut was reached on 4TH April, and here two British officers, three Indian officers and 179 men were disembarked and remained on detachment, while the rest of the regiment proceeded to Tripoli on the 6TH, where it marched to a summer camp where it was brigaded with the 1ST Guides Infantry.

On 4TH January 1920, the regiment entrained at Qantara West for Kom Abu Rade. The stay at Kom Abu Rade was not very long one, for on 9TH February the Headquarters Wing marched to Beni Suef, where one of the companies rejoined the next day form Fayoum, the other proceeding to Minia, very much farther up the Nile. In the spring of 1921, the regiment was again moved to Palestine. They had their headquarters at Roshpins, north of the Sea of Galilee, and furnished detachments at Nazareth, Beisan and Samakh. The Regiment was moved again to Egypt, where it was hurriedly moved from Qantara to Cairo, in view of the unsettled state of the country, and once again come under the 10TH Division at Camp Helmeih, seven miles from Cairo. On more than one occasion they were called out in aid of the Civil Power and had been in a state of constant readiness.

In April 1922, the regiment left Egypt, and arriving at Mardan the 2ND Regiment Queen Victoria's Own Corps of Guides, Frontier Force, became the Training Battalion of the 12TH Frontier Force Regiment, with effect from 1ST July 1922, with the designation 10TH Battalion, 12TH Frontier Force Regiment (Queen Victoria's Own Corps of Guides). So ends the history of the 2ND Guides Infantry, a regiment which, though hastily raised and trained in time of war, maintained during the six years of its existence the highest traditions of the Corps of Guides and proved it to be a thoroughly efficient regiment both in peace and war. These traditions it carried out as a Training Battalion during the Second World War.

At the independence of the subcontinent in 1947, and the creation of Pakistan, the battalion was allotted to the new Pakistan Army. The Sikh soldiers from the battalion were transferred to the Indian Army.

13TH Frontier Force Rifles

55TH Coke's Rifles (1/13TH)

The regiment was raised in 1849 as the 1ST Regiment of Punjab Infantry. It was designated as the 55TH Coke's Rifles (Frontier Force) in 1903. It was one of five such regiments raised to form the infantry element of the Frontier Brigade. The men were recruited from veterans of disbanded forces of the Sikh Army, and comprised companies of Sikhs, Afridis and, Punjabi Mussalmans.

From the time of its enrolment the regiment was engaged in imposing law and order among the turbulent border clans on the North-West Frontier of India; the Kohat Pass Afridis, the Uthman Khel, the Wazirs and the Shiranis.

During the Sepoy Mutiny in 1857, the regiment joined the force on the famous Ridge overlooking the rebel-held Delhi. The force was tasked with storming the Kashmiri Gate, a part of the walled defences of Delhi, which it successfully achieved. Fierce fighting, however, ensued and Delhi was not fully retaken until 20TH September. The rebellion was finally quelled by July 1858. The regiment had arrived on the Ridge 664 strong, in the course of the siege it had lost three British officers three Indian officers, and seventy-one other ranks killed and five British officers, five Indian officers and 141 other ranks wounded. Among who fell on in the assault was the veteran Subedar Ratan Singh, who had been pensioned off after losing an arm in the Bozdar expedition, but had rejoined when he heard the outbreak of Mutiny, bringing his son with him.

During the operations which eventually resulted in the capture of Bareilly, the capital of Rohilkhand and a rebel stronghold, the 1ST Punjab Infantry played a prominent part. The operations being completed the regiment was ordered to the North-West Frontier Province.

In November 1859, a punitive force, which included the 1ST Punjab Infantry was dispatched to chastise the Kabul Khel Wazirs, The Davesta Star, a mountain stronghold deemed impregnable, was captured, and the tribe submitted. In the following year another column which included the 1ST, 2^{ND,} and 3RD Punjab Infantry was sent against the most powerful marauding tribe of the Mahsuds in Waziristan, and encountered stubborn resistance. More than any other tribe they have shown implacable hostility and opposition to all attempts to penetrate their country or subdue or civilize them. They have remained collectively and individually unreliable and unruly. Some villages were burnt and towers blown up by the column as punitive measures before the force returned to Kohat.

On 29TH October, 1863, a determined attack was made on Crag Piquet, which was indeed a weak position in itself, but had to be held for the safety of the lower Piquet which it commanded. It was now lightly held by twelve men of the 1ST Punjab Infantry under a Havildar. The attackers, a body of Hindustani Fanatics led by an Indian officer of the Bengal Infantry, (a mutineer from the 55TH Bengal Infantry) succeeded in rushing the post in darkness. The position was recaptured with the reinforcements from the Battalion. The severity of the fighting is evidenced by the fact that the enemy left behind fifty-four dead and seven wounded on the ground.

13TH Frontier Force Rifles

55TH Coke's Rifles (1/13TH)

In 1865 the Punjab Irregular Force was renamed the Punjab Frontier Force and the regiment's title was consequently changed to become the 1ST Regiment of Infantry, Punjab Frontier Force.

In 1878, during the Second Afghan War the 1ST Punjab Infantry cleared the enemy from the heights commanding the line of advance of a column at the point of the bayonet, killing over a hundred and capturing seventy-two, with only seven casualties. The force captured the city of Kandahar on 8TH January 1879. The Amir Shere Ali fled to Russian Turkestan, where he died two months later. A treaty of peace was signed with Yakub Khan the new Amir.

In 1886, The Punjab Frontier Force was transferred from the Punjab Government to the direct control of the Commander-in-Chief. In the forty three- years since its foundation, the Punjab Frontier Force had expanded from a brigade, consisting of a field battery, four infantry regiments and the Corps of Guides, to a body of troops consisting of four mountain batteries, one company of garrison artillery, five regiments of cavalry, the Corps of Guides, four regiments of Sikh infantry, five regiments of Punjab infantry and a regiment of Gurkhas.

1890s saw the 1ST Punjab Infantry involved in several major operations against the hostile tribes on the North-West Frontier. These included Maizar, and Waziristan, on 10TH June 1897, when the regiment was ambushed in an action that signified the beginning of a large tribal uprising against the British.

In 1901 it became, simply the 1ST Punjab Infantry. In a punitive expedition in 1901, the regiment encountered and overcame heavy opposition as it destroyed Kot Shingi. Sepoy Badan Singh was most forward in the attacks and was awarded the I.O.M. for his conspicuous gallantry.

In 1903, the regiment was designated a rifle regiment and retitled as the 55TH Coke's Rifles (Frontier Force). The 55TH Rifles did not serve abroad during the First World War but saw active service on the North-West Frontier, fighting many of the numerous marauding tribes that populated the area.

Many men of the regiment did, however, see service abroad during the war while attached to other units.

The following Sikh soldiers of the regiment were awarded a collective gallantry award of I.O.M. for their outstanding performance in Waziristan against the Mahsuds in 1916; Jemadar Kishan Singh, Jemadar Kehar Singh, Lance-Naik Ishar Singh and Sepoy Ram Singh. And Havildar Chanan Singh and Sepoy Bagga Singh were awarded the I.D.S.M.

On 9TH August, 1917, the regiment was ordered to proceed to East Africa. On 28TH August, they arrived off Dar-es-Salaam and then steamed 160 miles south to Kilwa Kisswani, where they disembarked on the 30TH and made two marches to Kilwa camp. The regiment remained in this area until 10TH September, training for bush warfare. On the 17TH, the regiment moved out with the 2ND Kings African Rifles, to secure and develop water supply at Bakari.

13^(TH) Frontier Force Rifles

55^(TH) Coke's Rifles (1/13^(TH))

At Bakari they met some enemy, who were driven off, and the water-hole secured. On 8^(TH) November, during the advance to Chiwata, Coke's Rifles staged an attack on Miwale Hill, a forest-clad position, precipitous on one flank. In this fighting, the Battalion lost one Havildar and four sepoys killed; while one Jemadar and five sepoys were wounded, one of whom died of wounds. On 25^(TH) November, Tafel a colleague of the German commander Von Lettow, who, unable to escape surrendered unconditionally three days later. On the 28^(TH), Coke's Rifles accepted the surrender of 111 Germans, 1,200 Askaris and 2,200 porters. It had been decided that Indian units should not be used in the subsequent operation against Von Lettow in Portuguese East Africa. On the 29^(TH), the Indian units began their return march to the sea with Tafel's surrendered force. After halt from 10^(TH) to 20^(TH) December at Matama, the Coke's Rifles arrived at Lindi on 2^(ND) January, 1918, having covered 688 miles since their arrival in East Africa four months before. The regiment embarked in the Royal George on 13^(TH) February and disembarked at Karachi nine days later. Subedar Hardit Singh was awarded the I.D.S.M. for his conspicuous gallantry against the Germans in East Africa.

On 26^(TH) February the regiment at Multan, but within a week it was ordered off on yet another Frontier expedition. The Marri tribesmen of Baluchistan had since February 1918, been committing hostile acts even to the extent of assaulting British fort and outposts. It had therefore been decided to send a punitive expedition against them. Coke's Rifles received orders to move to Fort Munro, some fifty-five miles away at the summit of a 6,000-foot escarpment. On 15^(TH) March a large hostile force of tribesmen, numbering two to three thousand, began an assault of Fort Munro; and Coke's Rifles, arriving in the nick of time, drove them off in confusion. In this action Coke's Rifles had four men wounded (one mortally), all with sword cuts inflicted in hand-to-hand fighting. On 16^(TH) March more troops arrived, and next the Force moved on to Rakhni. From here, parties of the Battalion were sent out on punitive columns to destroy neighbouring villages. They captured many prisoners and large number of cattle. By the end of March most of the tribal sections had surrendered, but it was not until 7^(TH) May that final terms were made known to the tribal headmen. On 9^(TH) May Coke's Rifles began their move back to India, reaching Multan four days later.

Early in 1918 a British mission had been sent to South Persia, with the approval of the Persian Government, to restore and maintain order. The Persian Government soon changed its tone and whole of South Persia began to show hostility, which aimed at the complete expulsion of the British from South Persia. It was therefore decided to send reinforcement from India to Bushire. Coke's Rifles were selected to form part of these reinforcements.

13TH Frontier Force Rifles

55TH Coke's Rifles (1/13TH)

On 20TH December, Coke's Rifles fought and action at Kamarij, in which they advanced in a most gallant manner up precipitous slopes commanded by the fire of the enemy's Sangars; but the covering fire was so accurate that the enemy was unable to use his rifles with any effect, and the summit of the range was reached after difficult climb with slight loss two hours the attack commenced. The Coke's Rifles then occupied Kamarij village. By the middle of March it was considered that the objects of the expedition had been achieved and on the 29TH of that month orders for the withdrawal to Bushire were received. In due course Coke's Rifles completed their march to Bushire, where it embarked for Bombay, and disembarked at that port on 21ST April. Thus ended the operations carried out by Coke's Rifles from its inception to 1919.

In 1922, a major reorganization was undertaken in the British Indian Army leading to the formation of large infantry groups of four to six Battalions. Among these was the 13TH Frontier Force Rifles. The Coke's Rifles new designation was 1ST Battalion (Coke's) 13TH Frontier Force Rifles.

During the Second World War, the 1/13TH Frontier Force Rifles was part of the 9TH Indian Division based on the west coast of Malaya. Japanese Zero fighters also began bombing the airfield in Kota Bharu and other airfields in northern Malaya, namely those at Sungei Patani, Butterworth, Penang, Gong Kedah and Machang. The air attacks seriously destroyed British installations and weakened the Allied air force. In heavy rain, the Allied forces tried to hold the enemy but were forced to withdraw pursued by them. The retirement continued. On the 26TH a Sikh Company of the 1/13TH Frontier Force Rifles came into contact with the Japanese who were blocking their retreat. A fierce encounter took place and the Sikhs with cry of 'Sat Sri Akal' charged home with the bayonet, some thirty Japanese were killed, and a small mortar and a number of light automatics were captured.

Subsequently, fighting continued the Allied troops put up a strong resistance and were able to hold up the Japanese for a week despite the lack of air and tank support. Between 16TH and 22ND January 1942, the Japanese lost a company of tanks and the equivalent of a Battalion of troops. The Allied forces also suffered heavy losses. The disastrous Malayan Campaign ended on 31ST January 1942, when the last Allied troops crossed the Causeway linking Johor to Singapore. The Battalion was captured by the Japanese on Singapore Island in February 1942.

Story of the Indian prisoners was a long tale of intimidation and cruelty. The Sikhs and Dogras were sent to New Guinea, where most of them perished.

At the Japanese defeat the battalion was re-raised in 1946. On the Partition of the subcontinent in 1947 into India and Pakistan, the battalion was allotted to the newly formed Pakistan Army. The Sikh soldiers from the battalion were transferred to the Indian Army.

13TH Frontier Force Rifles

56TH Punjabi Rifles (2/13TH)

The regiment was raised in 1849 as the 2ND Regiment of Punjab Infantry. It was designated as the 56TH Punjabi Rifles (Frontier Force) in 1903. It was one of five such regiments raised to form the infantry element of the Frontier Brigade. The men were recruited from veterans of disbanded forces of the Sikh Army, and comprised companies of Sikhs, Afridis, Punjabi Mussalmans, and Yuzufzai.

In 1851, the Frontier Brigade was expanded and redesignated as the Punjab Irregular Force. Their mission was to maintain order on the North-West Frontier of India. From the time of its enrolment the regiment was engaged in imposing law and order among the turbulent border clans; the Kohat Pass Afridis, the Uthman Khel, the Wazirs and the Shiranis.

In 1857, the 2ND Punjab Infantry had to force the Khan Band defile to take action against the Bozdar tribe. Sepoy Bux Singh and Sepoy Jowahir Singh were awarded the I.O.M. in consideration of their conspicuous gallantry against the Bozdar tribe at Khan Band.

On the outbreak of the Sepoy Mutiny, the regiment was moved to Multan, where it was employed in watching the suspected units of the Bengal Army. On 14TH September in the assault on Delhi, 480 men of the regiment stormed the breach between the Kashmir Gate and the Water Bastion. After the assault the attackers became mixed up with a part of the 1ST Punjab Infantry, and penetrated far into the city. Their losses were severe. One Indian officer and forty other ranks were killed, and one Indian officer and twenty-two other ranks were wounded.

The regiment then became part of the force which was sent to join the units concentrated for operations in Oudh. On 10TH October they proceeded to Agra, where they fought a pitched battle with the mutineers outside the city, the enemy cavalry charging the Infantry the whole length of the parade ground and forcing them to form squares. The conflict ended in the complete rout of the rebels, who were pursued for seven miles, losing their guns, baggage and ammunition. After the battle, the regiment was commended by General Greathed for "the gallant manner in which the Punjab Regiment behaved, and their untiring exertions after a march, without a halt, of thirty miles, deserves the highest admiration".

The regiment reached Cawnpore at the end of October and was attached to the army which was being organized at Almanbagh for the relief of the Lucknow Residency. It then took part in the reduction of the various fortified buildings which barred the way, the capture of Dil Kusha and La Mariniere and the epic struggle for the Sikander Bagh on 16TH November.

Another daring exploit was the seizure of a key point known as Bank's House. This was carried out by fifty Sikhs, who crept unobserved through the enemy's Piquets. They held the position until the completion of the operation, though they were completely isolated and might at any moment have been overwhelmed before aid could reach them. The besieged garrison of the Residency was successfully withdrawn to Dil Kusha on 23RD November in an operation which involved the greatest hazard.

13TH Frontier Force Rifles

56TH Punjabi Rifles (2/13TH)

Sir James Outram was left to hold the Residency with 4,000 men. This important task of the evacuation was entrusted to the 2ND Punjab Infantry, and indeed had there been any failure the whole security of the Force would have been at stake. Reaching Cawnpore on 29TH November, the enemy was attacked on 6TH December and defeated with a loss of their guns, equipment and baggage. In this action the 2ND Punjab Infantry and the 4TH Punjab Infantry had a leading role in the attack. Moving with the Force towards Fatehgarh as its next objective, the Battalion took part in the battle of Kali Nadi on 2ND January, in which the enemy was again completely defeated, and Fatehgarh occupied the next day. Thereafter, during the first few weeks of 1858, the Battalion was employed in mopping-up operations in Rokiland. On 4TH February, 1858, it marched with the Rifle Brigade from Fatehgarh towards Lucknow, rejoining the army there on 2ND March. During the subsequent operations for the final capture of Lucknow, the 2ND Punjab Infantry formed part of the 3RD Infantry Brigade, which crossed the Goomtee as part of a mixed force advancing on the city from the north. The final capture of the city was completed on 15TH March, and on the 8TH May the Battalion took part in the capture of Bareilly, which was its final operation in the campaign of the Sepoy Mutiny. On 10TH May the regiment commenced its journey to the Punjab. It reached Ferozepore on 10TH June and Bannu on 8TH December.

In 1860 a column which included the 1ST, 2^{ND,} and 3RD Punjab Infantry was sent against the most powerful marauding tribe of the Mahsuds in Waziristan, and encountered stubborn resistance. Some villages were burnt and towers blown up by the column as punitive measures before the force returned to Kohat.

During the Second Afghan War of 1878-80, the 2ND Punjab Infantry was heavily engaged in driving the enemy from the wooded heights in the direction of Peiwar Kotal, and in a fierce encounter took place for the possession of the Signal Hill. The Regiment was ordered to hold it at all costs. The troops bivouacked on the captured ground, and the cold at 7,000 feet was intense. The following evening the 2ND Punjab Infantry rejoined the main body in the Hariab Valley. For some years there was little to record of the doings of the Battalions of the Punjab Frontier Force, but in 1890 trouble with Orakzais which had been brewing for twenty years came to a head. The first Miranzai Expedition followed, which penetrated the Orakzais country with three columns in January, 1891. The 1ST, 2^{ND,} 4TH and 5TH Punjab Infantry were all included in these columns. The expedition was noteworthy for the extreme severity of the conditions. There were twenty degrees of frost and numerous cases of frostbite occurred in the force. The punitive measures adopted caused the hostile tribesmen to submit within a month and the columns withdrew in February, 1891. Scarcely was this hostility dealt with when trouble once more arose farther north in Tirah, and led to the expedition that year that traversed in the entire Afridi country.

13th Frontier Force Rifles

56th Punjabi Rifles (2/13th)

At the outset the 2nd Punjab Infantry formed part of a force for the support of the garrison of the Kohat-Kurram line. On the evening of 26th August, 1897, a detachment including 2nd Punjab Infantry moved out to Muhammadzais in consequence of an attack on the police post there. The 2nd Punjab Infantry was ordered during the advance to occupy the Ublan Kotal, a precipitous mountain pass overlooking the line of advance on the right flank and this was carried out under very difficult conditions. The regiment suffered severely from the great heat and lack of water, and lost two killed and seven wounded. On 9th September the regiment formed part of a column which was conveying supplies to the posts on the Samana, which was closely besieged by the Afridis. After defeating severe opposition, the column relieved the posts, and the regiment returned to Kohat. 2nd Battalion is the only one in the Regiment of Frontier Force Rifles to bear the name 'Tirah' on its battle honours.

In 1900 the Mahsuds once more began to give trouble in Waziristan, and blockade was enforced to bring them to terms. The 1st and 2nd Punjab Infantry were concerned in this enterprise, which was followed by punitive expeditions into tribal territory. One of these columns, of which 2nd Punjab Infantry formed part, and known as Tonnochy's raid was a notable feat. Starting from Data Khel, it traversed the most difficult territory in Waziristan, destroying the Mahsud centre of Makin and many other hostile villages. It withdrew having carried out a difficult and dangerous mission with trifling loss, great rapidity and complete success.

In 1903, the regiment's designation was first changed to 56th Infantry (Frontier Force) and then in 1906, to 56th Punjabi Rifles (Frontier Force). In 1914, the regiment's class composition was two companies each of Sikhs, Dogras, Pathans, and Punjabi Mussalmans.

During the First World War, the regiment served with the 28th Brigade. In 1915, the Brigade was sent to Ismailia for the defence of the Suez Canal. On 31st January reconnoitring patrols made a contact with the enemy, and there were constant skirmishes. At dawn on 3rd February the Turks were seen advancing on the post held by the 56th Punjabi Rifles, and their artillery opened fire on the shipping in Lake Timsah. They advanced with 1,000 yards of the position, but withdrew during the night. This turned out to be a feint, and the main attack was delivered, without success, at Tussum, south of Ismailia. It was afterwards learnt the Turkish force was 20,000 strong, and suffered 1,300 casualties. On one occasion a Piquet of nine men under Havildar Suba Singh ran into a Turkish detachment of 1,000 men and two guns. The Turks tried to capture Suba Singh's party. The latter, nearly surrounded, put up a gallant fighting withdrawal. The noise caused Major Browne, who commanded the post, to send reinforcements, The Turks seeing the game was up, beat a hasty retreat, leaving a number dead.

13TH Frontier Force Rifles

56TH Punjabi Rifles (2/13TH)

On 9TH July the 28TH Brigade received orders to proceed to Aden, where the situation had become serious. The Turks had attacked, the Sultan of Lahej, and a British force sent to drive them had suffered severely during the forced march of thirty miles at the height of hot weather. The Turks had since advanced beyond Shaikh Othman to within few miles of Aden. The Brigade embarked at Port Tewfik (Suez), reaching Aden on 18^{TH,} July. Shaikh Othman is separated from Aden by a narrow isthmus, beyond which are salt-pans, intersected by narrow banks which could only be crossed with safety under cover of darkness. A column including 56TH Rifles was ordered to capture Shaikh Othman. It moved out on the night of 20TH July, the 53RD Sikhs and 56TH Punjabi Rifles leading the advance. An encircling movement carried out by these two Battalions caused the enemy to retire in a northerly direction to Dar Amir, and Shaikh Othman was occupied and put in a state of defence. The men suffered from thirst and the great heat. The water was brackish and caused much sickness. For the next three months there was almost continuous skirmishing in the 'No man's land' between Shaikh Othman and Lahej.

On 11TH October the regiment was withdrawn to Aden on relief by the Sikhs of Malay States Guides. Few days later the regiment embarked for Suez, whence it proceeded by train to Port Said.

On 9TH November the 28TH Brigade was ordered to Mesopotamia. On 20TH November the regiment embarked for Basra and was reached on 4TH December in bitter cold. By the beginning of January,1916, a force of four brigades had been concentrated at Ali Gharbi, and was disposed for the attack on Sheikh Saad position with 28TH Brigade on the right bank. The advance began on 4TH January and contact was made with the enemy outposts two days later, and they were driven in some sharp fighting. On the 7TH January the assault failed to carry the Turkish position and the losses were very severe, amounting in all to 246. The Turks evacuated Sheikh Saad on the night of the 9TH, and took up a new position in rear of the left bank of the Tigres. The 28TH Brigade was ordered to deliver a frontal attack. About 800 yards from the enemy's position, very heavy gun and rifle fire was encountered, but nothing would stop the 56TH Punjabi Rifles as they fell on the Turks. In spite of the most gallant attempts to advance the attack was held up with severe losses. Throughout the action the men had displayed conspicuous gallantry, regardless of loss.

On the 8TH March the ill-fated attempt was made to surprise the Dujailah Redoubt, the key point in the Turkish lines surrounding Kut. The regiment, which had been much depleted by sickness, had gone into action 300 strong, and of these, forty-one were killed and 117 wounded and missing. The survivors were rallied by Subedar Harnam Singh, and withdrawn after night fall. The failure of the attack on the Dujailah Redoubt left the attacking force in a dangerous position.

13TH Frontier Force Rifles

56TH Punjabi Rifles (2/13TH)

An immediate withdrawal was necessary and the 28TH Brigade acted as rearguard, and its chief duty was to deal with the prowling Arabs who murdered and pillaged the disabled and stragglers without mercy. The operations for the relief of Kut-al-Amara ended in stalemate, and on the 29TH April, after siege of 146 days, General Townshend, his food at an end, surrendered. The total casualties of the 56TH Punjabi Rifles during the previous three and have months amounted to nineteen British officers and sixteen Indian officers and 708 other ranks; of these 164 were killed. During the rest of the year one brigade held the trenches, while one was in close support and did minor training, and the third in reserve did more advanced training. General Sir Stanley Maud, now took command, commenced the preliminaries to an offensive that was destined to drive the Turks out of Mesopotamia.

At Sannaiyat the 7TH Division that included the 28TH Brigade delivered a frontal attack. On the 23RD the formidable Sannaiyat position, which had defied all efforts for a year, was breached, and the enemy was in full retreat. The casualties to the 56TH Rifles amounted to eighty. The pace of the advance was now very rapid, each formation being very anxious to have the honour of being the first to enter Baghdad. The Turks made their final stand along the line of the Diala River, which enters the Tigres below the city, and the 111 Corps made an unsuccessful attempt to force the passage. The 28TH Brigade now crossed the right bank of the Tigres on 8TH March, and after marching all night found themselves opposite the Shawa Khan ruins, a distance of twelve miles. The 56TH Punjabi Rifles were ordered to turn the enemy's right. The advance was made for about 2,000 yards over flat plain, devoid of cover. The troops advanced with great dash. The advance was checked for a time, mainly due to enfilade machine – gun fire from some low mounds on the left. As dusk fell it was established that the Turks had withdrawn. The regiment's casualties were one British officer, eight Indian officers and 187 other ranks, over 40 per cent.

On 11TH March the Turks had evacuated Baghdad and retired to the north. On the 14TH pursuit of the retreating enemy was continued along the right bank of the Tigres, the 28TH Brigade leading. After a night march of fourteen miles, the Turks were located in a position near Mushahida. The attack was made by the 21ST and 28TH Brigades and the 56TH Punjabi Rifles was ordered up to fill a gap between the 53RD Sikhs, and the Black Watch. The three Battalions fought side by side, clearing the enemy out of Mushahida railway station. In April the advance was renewed. The enemy was now fighting a series of rear-guard actions, but stood at Istabulat ruins near Samara and fought determined defensive battle. During the fierce battle of Istabulat, the Battalion compelled the Turks to retreat at a very high cost; Subedar Harnam Singh lost his life. The regiment had gone into action with seven British and seven Indian officers and 473 other ranks. Its losses were three British officers killed and one wounded, three Indian officers killed and two wounded, and thirty-one other ranks killed and 144 wounded.

13TH Frontier Force Rifles

56TH Punjabi Rifles (2/13TH)

Operations resumed at the end of October, 1917, when three brigades were detailed to attack an enemy position at Duar. The 28TH Brigade was advanced guard and the 56TH Punjabi Rifles were vanguard in the advance. Everything was staked on the speed of the advance; the enemy flank outposts were overrun, and the Turks fled. One hundred prisoners were taken and a quantity of stores. The 56TH Rifles suffered 107 casualties. This was the last action that the Battalion fought in Mesopotamia, and on the 7TH December orders were received that the 7TH Division was to leave for Palestine. The total casualties suffered by the Battalion during the campaign were 1,564, including ten British and nine Indian officers and 335 other ranks killed. The withdrawal was conducted by stages and Basra was reached on 30TH December. The troops were embarked on the S.S. Chakdara, and sailed next day for Palestine, where General Allenby was preparing the offensive that proved to be the knock-out blow to the Turkish army. The strength of the regiment was now twelve British and seventeen Indian officers and 1,059 other ranks.

The battle opened on 19TH September and was completely successful, the enemy's line being driven back all along the front. The 28TH Brigade took up the pursuit, with the 56TH Punjab Rifles as advance guard, and carried on until the men were obliged to halt owing to exhaustion and lack of water. On 21ST September they captured the important railway junction of Messudie, completely blocking the enemy's retreat, and capturing 400 prisoners and a quantity of stores and rolling stock, including a train which was in the station. Since leaving its bivouac the Battalion had covered forty miles in forty-eight hours over very rough country. On 31ST October the Turks asked for an armistice. The regiment was detained by an outbreak of unrest in Egypt, where it had to act in support of the civil government until 1920. It landed in Bombay on 1ST August and entrained for Jullundur, where the demobilization began. In 1917, the 56TH Punjabi Rifles raised a second Battalion, which served in the Third Afghan War of 1919. The regiment's total casualties during the war were 1679; including 389 killed or died of wounds.

After the First World War, the two Battalions of 56TH Punjabi Rifles were grouped with the 55TH, 57TH, 58TH and 59TH Scinde Rifles (Frontier Force) to form the 13TH Frontier Force Rifles in 1922. The 1ST Battalion 56TH Rifles became the 2ND Battalion, while 2ND Battalion 56TH Punjabi Rifles became the 10TH (Training) Battalion of the new regiment.

At the time of the outbreak of the Second World War, the 2/13TH Frontier Force Rifles was at Wana in Southern Waziristan. The Battalion suddenly received orders to go to Burma as part of the 63RD Infantry Brigade of the 17TH Indian Division. The Battalion was woefully short of weapons and transport and the only mortars they had were two given to the Battalion for the men to learn on during the voyage

13TH Frontier Force Rifles

56TH Punjabi Rifles (2/13TH)

Singapore had fallen on 15TH February, and the Japanese invasion of Burma from Siam had pressed back the ill-prepared forces till by 3RD March the Japanese threat to Rangoon was imminent. The evacuation of Rangoon was ordered on 7TH March and the only feasible plan of campaign now was to retire northward and try to hold Upper Burma with possibly Chinese aid. The attempt to hold Upper Burma with the Chinese aid of two Chinese armies failed, and the successful withdrawal of the forces to India was an epic in which the 2/13TH Frontier Force Rifles fought a staunch and enduring campaign.

The Brigade now withdrew across the Ava Bridge at dusk, and entrained on 1ST May to take up a position to assist the 1ST Burma Division, which was moving north parallel with the 17TH Indian Division. After marching six miles they occupied Mau station without incident, and located the enemy in some woods on the edge of the rice-fields about a mile away. A hail of fire enemy fire broke out and the Battalion lost about seventy-five men in first ten minutes. Subedar Mula Singh, commanding the Sikh Company, was shot through the face, but continued to carry on by signs, though unable to speak. For this and his previous bravery at Shwedaung he was awarded the I.O.M.

The 2/13TH Frontier Force Rifles was then sent back in reserve to hold Mau station. The men had fought for over twelve hours on empty stomachs and were utterly exhausted, but had no respite. Four attacks were launched by the enemy during the night and were only beaten off by the Sikh and Pathan Companies with great difficulty. Heavy fighting continued throughout 2ND May. Four Brigades repeatedly assaulted Monywa from three sides, and the town was raked with artillery fire without dislodging the Japanese; finally at dusk the Division was ordered to make its way by a detour over rough tracks to the north of the town. Determined counter attacks held off the Japanese and all the troops were safely withdrawn across the Chindwin. After this the 2/13TH Frontier Force Rifles formed the rear-guard as the force made its way to Palel, and marched in stages up the Kubaw Valley to Tamu and Lokchau. ON 22ND May the battalion, the last out of Burma, and had managed to keep the Japanese from the borders of India. Mula Singh returned from convalescent leave after his wound had healed and became the new Subedar Major. To him more than anyone else is due the credit of rebuilding a largely new battalion into the fine and forceful unit that, in its next campaign, remained longer in close contact with the enemy than any other unit in the Corps.

The battalion was now entering on a period which has been described as one of the heaviest fighting of any period of hostilities anywhere in Burma in the Second World War. In so far that the 2/13TH Frontier Force Rifles was concerned, it was in contact with the enemy from this time onward, night and day. In Arakan during 1944, the battalion had inflicted known casualties on the Japanese of seventy-five killed and a conservative estimate of 150 wounded. Its own losses were ten killed and one officer and seventy-five other ranks wounded.

13TH Frontier Force Rifles

56TH Punjabi Rifles (2/13TH)

The Ticker Ridge was a formidable and strongly held position, which had defied all efforts to capture in the early phase of the campaign. The 2/13TH Frontier Force Rifles was to make a frontal assault on Ticker Ridge, and this was to be yet another outstanding success, for the great bastion fell to the Battalion at its first major assault.

During a major assault on 17TH March, Subedar Bhajan Singh one of the best of Battalion's V.C.Os., was killed. The 2/13TH Frontier Force Rifles was now embarking on the period of its most severe and strenuous fighting in the Arakan Campaign if not the whole of the Second World War. 4TH May was the end of the Arakan campaign. For their services in the course of it, Subedar Sant Singh was awarded an immediate Military Cross on 14TH February, 1944. Subedar Major Mila Singh was awarded the I.O.M. for conspicuous gallantry against the enemy. Havildar Bachan Singh, Naik Tara Singh, Lance-Naik Gurbachan Singh, and Sepoy Amar Singh, were awarded the I.D.S.M., for their gallantry in Burma. Naik Jhanda Singh (Bar to Military Medal) and Tara Singh were awarded the Military Medal for their conspicuous gallantry in Burma.

On 18TH October, 1945, the 2/13TH Frontier Force Rifles received orders to move to Sumatra. The British military presence on Sumatra was limited to the cities of Medan, Padang and Palembang. The Polonia camp in Medan was initially guarded by Japanese soldiers. Large parts of the city were in republican hands. The situation outside Medan was very unsafe, but murder, abduction and shootings were also regular occurrences within the city. The British managed to calm the situation down and in the process the 2/13TH Frontier Force Rifles was to lose many good men, the veterans that had defeated the Japanese in Burma, in fighting against the Indonesians, who were fighting to gain the control of their own country! There was no heavy fighting, there were mainly small-scale skirmishes. In the first weeks of 1946 the British managed to calm the situation down somewhat. Thousands of Dutch nationals left for the Netherlands in the first half of 1946. In November 1946 Dutch troops took over from the British. Many planters were to return to their former positions after the first 'Police Action', when the companies were partly recaptured. On 19TH November the Battalion let Medan for the last time, and embarked on the troopship Antenor two days later. It had spent one year and three weeks in Sumatra, in the course of which it had sustained the following casualties:-

One British officer, one Indian officer and thirteen other ranks killed. Three British officers, three Indian officers and 74 other ranks wounded, and one other rank missing.

After the independence of the subcontinent in 1947, and the creation of Pakistan, the battalion was allotted to the new Pakistan Army. The Sikh soldiers from the battalion were transferred to the Indian Army.

13TH Frontier Force Rifles

57TH Wilde's Rifles (4/13TH)

The regiment was raised on 18TH April 1849 as the 4TH Regiment of Punjab Infantry. It was designated as the 57TH Punjab Rifles (Frontier Force) in 1903. It was one of five such regiments raised to form the infantry element of the Frontier Brigade. The men were recruited from veterans of disbanded forces of the Sikh Army, and comprised companies of Sikhs, Afridis, Punjabi Mussalmans, and Yuzufzai.

In 1851, the Frontier Brigade was expanded and redesignated as the Punjab Irregular Force. Their mission was to maintain order on the North-West Frontier of India. From the time of its enrolment the Regiment was engaged in imposing law and order among the turbulent border clans; the Kohat Pass Afridis, the Uthman Khel, the Wazirs and the Shiranis. From the time of its enrolment the Regiment was engaged in imposing law and order among the turbulent border clans.

At the outbreak of the Sepoy Mutiny in 1857, it was employed to disarm disaffected Bengal regiments at Nowshera, Rawalpindi, and Amritsar. After the fall of Delhi, the Regiment it took part in the successful action outside the walls of Agra Fort. The regiment then formed part of the column marching to the relief of the beleaguered Residence at Lucknow. On November, 1857, the regiment took in the storming of Sikander Bagh. Sikander Bagh was large loop-holed enclosure with massive walls and square bastions which was held by 2,000 mutineers. After desperate struggle the defenders were overpowered and killed to a man. The total casualties sustained by the regiment were seventy-two. After the relief of the Residency in Lucknow and the withdrawal of its garrison on the night of 22ND November, 1857, the whole force moved to Cawnpore, which was besieged by Nana Sahib's army. The regiment was responsible for the capture of its guns on 6TH and 8TH December. The regiment lost two killed and nine wounded in this battle. The regiment was now posted with the rest of the 4TH Brigade to the 2ND Division, destined to the final capture of Lucknow. In this, the regiment led the assault which resulted in the capture of La Martinere College on 9TH March and the Begum's palace on 14TH March. During the severe fighting inside the palace the enemy lost over 800 men and the regiment sustained twenty-five casualties. After the Palace had been carried, some of the men of the regiment proceeded up a street, where a sharp opposition was met, and the men were temporarily driven back. Here Sepoy Munah Singh remained alone, helping the wounded, until the remainder of the men rallied and counter-attacked the mutineers. He was awarded the I.O.M. for his bravery

In the course of the operations in Rohilkhand, Subedar Hira Singh was killed, and Jemadar Jowala Singh was awarded the I.O.M. for helping the wounded to safety. Last action in which the regiment was engaged in Rokiland was the capture of Bareilly, the chief rebel centre, by which the back of resistance was broken. However, the fighting strength of the regiment had been reduced to 103 of all ranks.

13TH Frontier Force Rifles

57TH Wilde's Rifles (4/13TH)

Just eight months before, it had joined the army before Delhi about 1,000 strong, but now could only parade one-tenth of that number. During the Sepoy mutiny, the following Sikh soldiers of the regiment were awarded the I.O.M. for their gallantry during the Sepoy mutiny; Subedar Hira Singh, Havildar Lachman Singh, Naik Gurmuck Singh, Naik Bir Singh, Sepoys Mangal Singh, Chuba Singh, Nand Singh, Gulab Singh, Mehtab Singh, Chatar Singh, Suba Singh and Essur Singh.

In 1885 the 4TH Punjab Infantry took part in operations against the turbulent of the Black Mountain district. The regiment scaled some difficult heights commanding the right flank of the advancing column, driving the enemy from every point of vantage in a most spirited manner.

In 1887 Subedar Major Sher Singh received the Order of British India as a reward for his long service of forty-two years. He was the very type of an old Sikh soldier, tall, handsome and gallant. He left the service the following year full of years and honours, having fought with the regiment through the Mutiny and in all its subsequent expeditions.

On the 9TH October the regiment crossed the Indus to test the capacity of the boats, and to establish heliographic communication with Divisional Headquarters. When the regiment was withdrawing to Kotkai, the rear guard of the regiment was attacked in a determined manner by the Chagarzis. Two Sepoys of the regiment were wounded, and the enemy sustained six casualties. For his gallantry in this action Sepoy Mehtab Singh was awarded the I.O.M., for conspicuous gallantry in having on the 10TH October, 1888, near the trans-Indus village of Garhi, he successfully held, with the aid of a few comrades, a considerable body of the enemy in check, whilst the main body of the regiment retired to a ferry to cross the Indus.

For some years there was little to record the doings of the regiment, but 1890 was trouble with Orakzais. The Miranzai expedition followed, which penetrated the Orakzai country in with three columns in 1891. The 4TH Infantry Regiment was included in these columns. The punitive measures adopted caused the hostile tribesmen to submit within a month and the columns withdrew in February.

In 1900 the 4TH Punjab Infantry went with the 3RD Brigade to China for the suppression of the Boxer Rebellion. Leaving Kohat in August it disembarked at Wei-Hai-Wei in the following month. From there it proceeded to Shan-hai-Khwan. In consequence of a threatened incursion of Manchurian brigade and ex-Chinese soldiery, the magistrate of Funing, a town of some importance some miles to the north-west of Shan-hai-Khwan, sent in urgent appeals for assistance. The regiment carried out operation against a large party of brigands, estimated at a thousand strong, holding the village. In endeavouring to turn them out, Major Browning was killed, his orderly, seeing him fall, went immediately to his assistance, and was also shot dead.

13TH Frontier Force Rifles

57TH Wilde's Rifles (4/13TH)

Lance-Naik Lehna Singh then ran forward to where the bodies lay, and was shot down with a bullet through his thigh. Lance-Naik Dial Singh then went forward and succeeded in reaching the bodies and tried to carry Major Browning's body. In the meantime, Lieutenant Stirling and four Sepoys were wounded. Next day a force the including the 4TH Punjab Infantry, went out to attack the position. The result was completely successful, compelling the brigand's in full flight pursued by the Lancers. The 4TH Punjab Infantry then returned to Kohat in July, 1902. Lance-Naik Lehna Singh, and Lance-Naik Dial Singh, was awarded the I.O.M., for conspicuous gallantry while Subedar Lakha Singh was mentioned in dispatches.

In 1903 the 5 regiments were renumbered 55 to 59 and afforded the crack status of 'Rifle Regiments'. Each was named after a notable early commanding officer. The 4TH took the appellation '57TH Wilde's Rifles (Frontier Force)' in honour of its gallant commanding officer.

The only important event of the period was the Mohmad campaign of 1908. A punitive force including 200 men of the 57TH Rifles and 150 of the 59TH Rifles, moved out in April, on the onset of the hot weather, fought a brisk engagement at Matta, the enemy's Sangars being cleared at the point of the bayonet. After this the column penetrated deep into the heart of the tribal territory and the Mohmands submitted and paid the fine imposed on them.

Havildar Jagat Singh, Jemadar Bhagat Singh, and Sepoys Gian Singh, Mangal Singh, and Nihal Singh, were awarded the I.D.S.M. for their conspicuous gallantry on the in 1908 at the North –West Frontier of India.

During the First World War, the regiment served on the Western Front in France and Belgium, where they fought in battles of La Bassée, Messines, Givenchy, Neuve Chapelle, and the Second Battle of Ypres. The total casualties suffered by the 57TH Rifles in their thirteen months in France were seven British and seven Indian officers killed eight British and eight Indian officers wounded, and 148 other ranks killed and 536 wounded. In addition, three British and one Indian officer and sixty-eight other ranks attached to the Regiment were killed.

In an action on the 24TH April, 1915, that Jemadar Mir Dast of the 55TH Coke's Rifles, who had joined the 57TH Rifles with the draft from that regiment, had won the Victoria Cross. This was the first Victoria Cross won by an Indian rank of the Frontier Force. In fact he was the first Indian to be awarded the Victoria Cross. On 23RD November the dressing station at Festubert was hit by two shells of large calibre and completely wrecked. The medical officer Captain Kunwar Indarjit Singh was killed, and his loss was keenly felt, as he was very popular with all ranks. Captain Kunwar Indarjit Singh was awarded a posthumous Military Cross. Jemadar Mangal Singh and Sepoy Atma Singh were awarded the I.O.M., and Havildar Bur Singh and Naik Sohan Singh, were awarded the I.D.S.M., for their conspicuous gallantry on the Western Front.

13TH Frontier Force Rifles

57TH Wilde's Rifles (4/13TH)

Leaving Marseilles on 4TH December, 1915, after one year and twenty-seven days in France, the 57TH Rifles disembarked at Port Said, and became part of the force guarding the Suez Canal. On 26TH June the regiment received orders to proceed to East Africa. In East Africa, the regiment was constantly employed in the pursuit of General Von Lettow-Vorbeck's forces. On the night of 9TH August a company of the 57TH Rifles, commanded by Major Buller, was sent forward to reconnoitre the enemy's position. They encountered the Germans strongly entrenched with six machine guns at the village of Matomondo. A sharp encounter followed. Major Buller, seeing that the situation was critical, personally led his men in an attempt to turn the enemy's flank. He was wounded and all the detachment with him wipe out. Lieutenant Taylor, who tried valiantly to come to Major Buller's assistance, was unable to get through, owing to intense fire. The action was fought in dense jungle where visibility was reduced to practically nil. The enemy eventually fell back owing to threat to their flank by the cavalry brigade which suddenly appeared from the west. The regiment continued in the pursuit of General Von Lettow-Vorbeck's forces.

10TH September an advance of the regiment met with considerable resistance on the Duthum River, which resulted in heavy fighting during the next three days, after which the enemy again withdrew. Among regiment's casualties was Sepoy Bhan Singh, I.O.M., who had been decorated for gallantry at the second battle of Ypres, on the Western Front. Finally with the enemy still farther, the regiment reached Chemera, forty-miles farther south on the Matandu River. This was accomplished after series of marches over waterlogged ground, deep ravines and Rivers in flood, generally in tropical rain. At Chemera there was little rest, for patrolling and skirmishes with the enemy was order of the day. On 2ND September, 1917, the regiment embarked at Kilwe Kisswani en-route for Dar-es-Salaam and reached Bombay on 30TH September

Havildars Kapur Singh, Bhagwan Singh, Udham Singh, Sundar Singh and Jemadar Hira Singh, Naiks Amir Singh and Amar Singh, were awarded the I.D.S.M., for their conspicuous gallantry in East Africa.

After their return form East Africa, 57TH Rifles were stationed for some months for quarantine in the Murree Hills. In 1918 they were transferred to Kohat, with two companies on garrison duty at Thal Fort. On 5TH May, 1919, came the news of the outbreak of the Third Afghan War. Battalion Headquarters of the regiment and the remaining half of the regiment were entrained to Thal, and from there set off on a forced march to Parachinar, a distance of fifty-six miles with a climb of over 3,000 feet. This was covered in the remarkably short time of forty-eight hours. Nadir's main force, advancing via Spinwam, laid siege to Thal. His artillery outranged the guns of Thal Fort, and petrol dumps and stacks of bhoosa were set on fire. The Fort was relieved by brigade from Kohat, and the enemy beat a hasty retreat.

13TH Frontier Force Rifles

57TH Wilde's Rifles (4/13TH)

On 2ND June the 57TH Rifles from Parachinar, moved out to the Peiwar camp. Here they remained for about ten days, without tents, until relieved by the Guides. The area of ten miles, were plainly visible at night, and there was much singing and shouting and blowing of bugles. The Afghans signed a peace treaty at Rawalpindi on 8TH August, but much harm to British prestige had been done by the evacuation of the posts in the Tochi Valley, and numbers of South Waziristan Militia deserted, taking their arms and accoutrements with them. Five British officers were killed and two wounded. Major Russell, who was afterwards posted to the regiment, with 300 loyal Sepoys made a remarkable withdrawal to Mir Ali Khan in the Zhob Valley, right through the enemy lines.

In 1922, the 57TH Rifles became the 4TH Battalion, 13TH Frontier Force Rifles. On 9TH November the Wazirs capitulated, but the Mahsuds remained defiant in spite of air attacks, and the 4/13TH Frontier Force Rifles was ordered to join the Derajat Column at Tank, which entailed a march of 140 miles. This was accomplished in eight days. The 4/13TH Frontier Force Rifles took part in the heavy fight on 17TH December, when the Mahsuds made an attack on the Piquets at Palosina camp, which was pressed home with great determination. Parties of the enemy dashed in, shouting and waving swords, regardless of rifle and machine-gun fire. The Piquet on Mandanna Hill was surprised, and the British officer in charge and a number of men were killed. These small actions resulted in such heavy casualties to British officers; it was ordered that only half should in future accompany the troops in future. The battalion continued to take a large part in fighting of the Derajat Column at Palosina.

The next task before the column was the capture of the Ahnai Tangi. The objective assigned to the battalion was the portion of the Spin Gara heights designated as Ahnai Right. It was severe undertaking, as the ascent was barred by precipitous cliffs. The assault was an inspiring sight; the Mahsuds were beating their drums and shouting defiance. A mountain battery gave such covering fire as it could, and two unarmed aircraft endeavoured to distract the enemy. The heights were at length taken by storm, and two companies were left to build Sangars, while the rest were withdrawn. On 14TH January the day's fighting at Ahnai Tangi was the most stubbornly contested of the campaign, and the casualties to the force amounted to fifteen British officers and 365 Indian ranks killed and wounded. On 28TH January the battalion took a prominent part in storming Barari Tangi.

During the Second World War, the 4/13TH Frontier Force Rifles took part in the British invasion of Iraq in May 1941. The battalion arrived in Basra on 6TH May, 1941; it became part of the 21ST Brigade of the 10TH Indian Division. While the Battalion in company with the rest of 10TH Indian Division remained in the Basra Bridgehead, the short campaign to secure Iraq form Axis domination was completed by the end of May.

13TH Frontier Force Rifles

57TH Wilde's Rifles (4/13TH)

There remained problem with Syria, which was under French mandate. After the fall of France, Syria had remained in the administration of men of Vichy. Syria began to fill with Germans and Italians. It then participated in the Syria-Lebanon Campaign against the Vichy French and fought in the Battle of Deir-ez-Zor on 3 July 1941.

The next point of importance was Raqqa, seventy-five miles North West of Deir-ez-Zor. This fell on the 8TH July. The Sikh Company were accordingly ordered to escort a convoy of supplies and petrol to Raqqa. The Sikhs was now suddenly attacked from a quite unexpected quarter. The Arab freebooter Fawzi el Kawuckji launched a night attack on Raqqa. He was driven off after heavy fighting all night in which one platoon made two bayonet charges. The Syrian campaign was now at an end. The heavy calibre naval bombardment of Tyre and Sidon had loosened the French defensive hold in the south, and enabled the main forces to roll forward where the enemy was strongest. General Dentz, who had been at the heart of the French resistance surrendered. The armistice convention was finally signed on 14TH July at Acre. By it the British acquired the right to occupy all Syria and the Lebanon. The Syrian campaign of five was one of the most brilliant of the minor successes of the war. This was an affair of small forces, in modest but hard-fought engagements, that had prevailed. In these matters it was the happy lot of the 4/13TH Frontier Force Rifles.

The armistice concluded the campaign and the forces moved forward to occupy Syria, as was the clearly a military necessity so long as the German menace to the East persisted.

Diplomatic advances having failed the British invaded Persia, moving on Kermanshah from Khaniqin. On 22ND September the 4/13TH Frontier Force Rifles handed over to 2/11TH Sikh Regiment and left by road for Persia to rejoin the 21ST Brigade, which had preceded it there. A Persian force made a show of opposition to the advance on the magnificent defensive position of the Pai Taq Pass, then broke and disintegrated. The old Shah abdicated and fled, and his son Mohamed Reza assumed the Peacock Throne as an Allied nominee. The Battalion was ordered back to Iraq, and arrived at Habbaniya on 16TH October. On 14TH May 21ST Brigade was ordered to the North Africa.

Fighting began in North Africa on September 13TH, 1940, when Marshal Rodolfo Graziani's Italian 10TH Army launched an attack from its bases in Libya on outnumbered British forces in western Egypt. A successful British counterattack initiated on December 9TH, 1940, led by General Sir Archibald Wavell, resulted in Italian defeat at Tobruk (Tobruk) in eastern Libya on January 22ND, 1941. On February 12TH, 1941, German General Erwin Rommel arrived in Libya to take command of troops sent to reinforce Germany's Italian allies. The Eighth Army had begun the battle with five infantry divisions and two infantry brigade groups. Gradually these forces were depleted

13TH Frontier Force Rifles

57TH Wilde's Rifles (4/13TH)

In the event a withdrawal to the Egyptian frontier was ordered, and Tobruk was left with as garrison lacking in sufficient anti-tank artillery, unsupported by air and with the command of the sea now in enemy hands. On March 24TH, 1941, Rommel launched an offensive, and, bypassing Tobruk reached the Egyptian border on April 14Th. There, the opposing British and German-Italian armies remained stalemated until November 1941, a reorganized British Eighth Army attacked Rommel's positions in what was known as Operation 'Crusader'. After early reverses, the British drove the Axis armies back into Libya, relieved the garrison in Tobruk, and forced Rommel to pull back on January 6TH, 1942, to El Agheila.

Subedar Major Sohan Singh O.B.I., Havildar Natha Singh, Sepoy Saudagar Singh, was awarded the I.O.M., and Jemadar Jiwan Singh was awarded the Military Cross for his gallant leadership in North Africa. Havildar Babu Singh, Havildar Kehar Singh, Naik Indar Singh, and Naik Nika Singh Havildar Partap Singh, Havildar Ishar Singh and Lance-Naik Rattan Singh were awarded the I.D.S.M., for their conspicuous gallantry against the enemy in North Africa.

While the German main armies in France had suffered shattering defeat, their opposition to the Allied advance in Italy stood firm on a defensive system across Northern Italy known as the Gothic Line. It was in the fighting to break this defence and drive the Germans out of Italy which took place during the autumn of 1944 and spring of 1945 that the 4/13TH Frontier Force Rifles became heavily involved and rose to the heights of military achievement excelled or indeed equalled by few in the Second World War. The Battalion arrived in Italy on 29TH August, 1944. During the action of on Monte Alto on 17TH and 18TH September, six enemies L.M.G's (Spandau) were captured, fifteen prisoners were taken and number of enemy killed and wounded. For their gallantry on Monte Alto, as well as previously on Monte Acuto, Subedar Chanan Singh, and Jemadar Karnail Singh was awarded the Military Cross and Havildar Partap Singh the I.D.S.M., for bravery on Monte Acuto, whilst Havildar Ishar Singh was awarded the I.D.S.M., for Monte Alto. On 12TH December the enemy launched a company-strength attack under cover of mist on Point 431. No 1 Platoon fought magnificently, repulsing every enemy attempt to dislodge them during two and half hours. Balwant Singh had been wounded very early, but continued to command. Jemadar Balwant Singh and Sepoy Gurdial Singh gained immediate awards of the Military Cross and Military Medal respectively for their gallantry. On 29TH April 1945, the Germans signed an instrument of surrender, and hostilities in Italy formally ceased on 2ND May 1945. The 4/13TH Frontier Force Rifles embarked for India on 15TH October 1945.

After the independence of the subcontinent in 1947, and the creation of Pakistan, the battalion was allotted to the new Pakistan Army. The Sikh soldiers from the battalion were transferred to the Indian Army.

13TH Frontier Force Rifles

58TH Vaughan's Rifles (5/13TH)

The 5TH Punjab Infantry was raised in 1849, from the men who had served in the Sikh Army. It was designated as the 58TH Vaughan's Rifles (Frontier Force) in 1903.Their mission was to maintain order on the Punjab Frontier.

The 5TH Punjab Infantry was engaged in the Miranzai Valley expedition of 1856, and the expedition against the Hindustani Fanatics of Narinji. It did not play a very prominent part in the fighting during the Sepoy Mutiny of 1857, as it was employed in the important if less spectacular duties of guarding the Frontier and dealing with mutinous regiments of the Bengal Army in the Punjab. On 22ND May, 1857, it was ordered from Attock to Nowshera, where the 55TH Bengal Native Infantry was reported to have mutinied. The regiment took over the fort of Attock from a unit suspected of disaffection, and acted against an incursion on the part of the Yuzufzai tribe. In January 1858, the 5TH Punjab Infantry took a prominent part in cleaning up the rebels in Oudh, and in one action Sepoy Fateh Singh killed a notorious ringleader Bakht Khan of the Bareilly Brigade. For this he was awarded the I.O.M. The regiment then assisted in the pursuit of the flying enemy in the rough and pathless jungles on the Nepal border. It returned to the Punjab on 26TH December. An expedition against the Hindustani Fanatics, that included 5TH Punjab Infantry, was organized in October, 1863. On 20TH October the Regiment pushed on to a plateau known as Keyes' Piquet, where it encamped. The position was commanded by two lofty spurs, the Eagle's Nest on the left and Crag Piquet on the right, both of which were seized and fortified. The Hindustani Fanatics reacted at once and heavy fighting ensued which centred round these two points. On 26TH October an attack was launched on the Eagle's Nest, and a Company of the 5TH Punjab Infantry did excellent service in assisting the 6TH Punjab Infantry to regain position which was lost in the initial fighting.

During the Second Afghan War of 1878-80, the regiment fought in the Battles of Peiwar Kotal, Charasia, and took part in the defence of Sherpur Cantonment at Kabul. The 5TH Punjab Infantry, on 6TH October they took a prominent part in the decisive battle of Charasia, eleven miles outside the Afghan capital. This assault was carried out in gallant style by the Sikh Company under Subedar Budh Singh, who received the I.O.M. for his services in this battle. Havildar Sham Singh, Naik Sarwan Singh, and Sepoy Man Singh were awarded the I.O.M. for their conspicuous gallantry in the capture of the Afghan capital Kabul.

Subsequent to the reforms brought about in the Indian Army in 1903, the regiment's designation was changed to 58TH Vaughan's Rifles (Frontier Force. In 1914, the regiment's class composition was three companies each of Sikhs, Pathans and one company each of Dogras and Punjabi Mussalmans.

During the First World War, the regiment served on the Western Front in 1914-15. During this time the regiment was engaged in three defensive actions and three major offensive battles.

13TH Frontier Force Rifles

58TH Vaughan's Rifles (5/13TH)

In an action near Givenchy on 30TH October, the regiment was ordered forward to recover trenches taken by the Germans. An attack by two half-battalions of British troops had failed to restores the situation, and on the 31^{ST,} the leading companies of the regiment bayoneted the Germans and re-took the captured trench. The position was then consolidated. On 23RD November near Givenchy, the Germans had driven from their trenches the battalion on the left of the 58TH Rifles. In consequence a part of the 58TH Vaughan's Rifles front-line trench was enfiladed and rendered untenable. To meet the threat from the left, a Sikh Company was ordered to form the line in the open facing left. In doing so the Sikh Company suffered heavy casualties, and withdrew to the reserve trenches. Two platoons of the next company, seeing the Sikhs moving back, conformed and themselves took up a position in the rear. The remaining two platoons made a block in the front-line trench and held up the enemy, by bombing and rifle fire. A counter attack, preceded by a very effective artillery bombardment, swept forward to the lost trenches with few casualties, taking a number of prisoners and recovering a British officer.

In an action at La Quinque Rue on 22ND December the regiment was ordered forward from reserve to fill a gap on the left of the Seaforth Highlanders caused by a regiment being driven from its trenches by a German bombing attack supported by artillery and machine-guns. The attacks were excellently supported by the remaining companies especially by the machine-guns under Harchand Singh, in spite of the fact that the enemy by accurate shell fire demolished the recesses on either side of that in which the machine guns were in action. The Germans were finally driven back to their own trenches by an attack made after dark by units of the 2ND Brigade supported by the fire of the 58TH Vaughan's Rifles. The gap now being filled by portions of two British battalions, the 58TH Vaughan's Rifles were ordered to withdraw. In this action the fighting had been for thirty-six hours at hand-bombing distance. The Seaforth Highlanders spoke highly of the élan and initiative shown by the 58TH Vaughan's Rifles in protecting their left and rear.

During the battle of Neuve Chapelle the trenches held by the 58TH Vaughan's Rifles were heavily shelled during the four days and a number of casualties occurred. On the 12TH March an attack made by the Germans in misty weather was easily beaten off and about seventy prisoners taken. During the battle of Loos the casualties had been very severe and no reinforcements or supplies of ammunition or bombs had come up from the rear, what was left of the Battalion was withdrawn to the original front line. The memory of the last stand of 58TH Vaughan's Rifles was a noble example of high courage and self-sacrifice. Among the many that fell this day was Subedar Sohel Singh, I.O.M., who had risen from being Adjutant's clerk and proved himself a true Sikh, a leader of the highest quality and example of the greatest bravery.

13TH Frontier Force Rifles

58TH Vaughan's Rifles (5/13TH)

Mauquissart was to be the 58TH Rifle's last battle in France, and the usual routine of billets and trenches came to an end on 6TH November.

New British Divisions were now in France, the chance of further offensive had passed with the summer, and the Indian Corps, less the Cavalry, was to be transferred to fronts for which it was better suited; Mesopotamia, East Africa, Egypt and Palestine.

Subedar Sohel Singh, who had on 31ST October, 1914, in his first action, been awarded the I.O.M. for bravery and fine leadership, was on 10TH March was awarded the Bar of this order for leading a party which three times carried forward bombs and ammunition after the men of another unit bad put down their loads. Subedar Sohel Singh was killed on 25TH September, 1915 (Loos). Subedar Karam Singh, Subedar Harchand Singh, Havildar Santa Singh, Naik Phangan Singh, Sepoy Diwan Singh and Sepoy Ishar Singh were awarded the I.O.M., for their conspicuous gallantry against the Germans on the Western Front.

On November 23^{RD,} 1914, on the Western Front, when all the British officers had been killed, Havildar Indar Singh took command of the Company, and held the position against heavy attacks until relieved next morning for which he was promoted to Jemadar and awarded the Military Cross. Subedar Indar Singh M.C., Subedar Phuman Singh, Havildar Sundar Singh, and Naik Dewa Singh were awarded the I.D.S.M., for their conspicuous gallantry against the Germans on the Western Front.

In 1916, 58TH Vaughan's Rifles served in Egypt, where form January, 1916, to September, 1917, it was on the Suez Canal defences, mainly on the south end of the Canal. The Turks, after their unsuccessful attempt in 1915 to cross the Canal, had withdrawn beyond the Sinai Desert, leaving only very light irregular forces in the waterless hills twenty miles east of the Canal. On 12TH September, 1917, the 58TH Vaughan's Rifles left the Canal to join the 7TH Division in Palestine. During the Palestine campaign the regiment fought in the Third Battle of Gaza, the Battle of Nebi Samwil and the Capture of Jerusalem. In 1918, it fought in the Battle of Megiddo, which led to the annihilation of Turkish Army in Palestine. During the remainder of 1918 the regiment was engaged on salvaged work until on 5TH December, it left Palestine for Qantara on the Suez Canal.

In March, 1919, a rebellion flared up in Egypt. This resulted in the regiment moving first to Cairo, then Upper Egypt, and later to the Delta. The duties which the 58TH Vaughan's Rifles were called on to carry out included the protection of railways, the trial of rebels, show the flag, marches, patrols by a Mounted Infantry Detachment, and sending detachments to many different isolated places. Acting Subedar Major Indar Singh M.C., I.D.S.M., went to London to attend the Peace Celebrations. Indar Singh received his decoration form the hands of His Majesty King George V. The regiment arrived at Karachi on 9TH February, 1920, after five years and five months overseas.

13TH Frontier Force Rifles

58TH Vaughan's Rifles (5/13TH)

They were soon called on for active service and moved to South Waziristan in the middle of June, 1920. Anyone who has experienced Waziristan hot weather will know what this entailed for the men not fully recovered from the strain of five and a half year's campaigning. After various moves between June and September, 1920, the regiment was selected to join the column assembling at Jandola. The objective of this column was the reoccupation of Wana Fort, empty since 1919, when the trans-border personnel of the South Waziristan Scouts had mutinied, and the subjugation of the Wana Wazirs. The column began its advance on 12TH November, and arrived in Wana on 22ND December. The column remained till the end of January in passive occupation of Wana Fort. This resulted in the tribesmen becoming more and more aggressive and truculent. Attack on convoys and sniping of the camp became frequent. On 17TH March, 1921, a Convey escorted by the 58TH Vaughan's Rifles was attacked at close range by a strong body of enemy.

Sepoy Kartar Singh moved into the open, the only position from which he could send a message, but was almost immediately killed. Sepoy Kartar Singh's widow received the pension of the I.D.S.M. On 5TH April the convoy was again attacked and Subedar Kehar Singh gained the I.D.S.M. for conspicuous coolness and gallantry in command of his platoon on the exposed flank. On the following day there was an action of a more important character in which a platoon under Havildar Jiwan Singh was attacked at close quarters with heavy rifle and a knife rush. Supported by the platoon under Havildar Lal Singh, this attack and another from the other flank were beaten off with rifle fire and grenades and a punishing loss was inflicted on the enemy. On 20TH December, 1921, the Wana column was broken up after being in operation for twelve months.

In addition to the awards mentioned above, the following decorations and awards were gained for the operations in Waziristan: Havildar Jiwan Singh was awarded the I.O.M., Havildar Lal Singh the I.D.S.M. and O.B.I. to Subedar Thakur Singh.

The 58TH Rifles took part in numerous frontier operations which included six years in Kohat. After which it served at Bannu, Multan, Thal, Samana and finally in the Ahmedzai Salient, where it rounded up the gangs operating under Meher Dil and established control of the area by building roads and Frontier Constabulary posts within the area.

In 1922, the 58TH Rifles was grouped with the 55TH, 57TH, 59TH, and the two Battalions of 56TH Punjab Rifles (Frontier Force) to form the 13TH Frontier Force Rifles. The 58TH Rifles became 5TH Battalion of the new Regiment.

The 5/13TH Rifles was stationed at Delhi Cantonment when, in April 1941, orders were received to mobilize in readiness to proceed overseas by 24TH May. The day before mobilization was completed Subedar Major and Honorary Captain Kehar Singh retired on pension, having completed twenty-nine year's service and five years as Subedar Major of the Battalion. He was a loss but, a veteran of the First World War, had had well earned his rest.

13TH Frontier Force Rifles

58TH Vaughan's Rifles (5/13TH)

In the intense heat of Delhi in May, mobilization was completed; and the Battalion embarked at Bombay for Basra on 1ST July and reaching the destination fifteen days later. At the time when the 5/13TH Frontier Force Rifles moved up to the northern corner of the Iraq-Syria frontier at Tel Alo, this campaign had just come to an end; so that the battalion missed taking part in such fighting as there was. Unfortunately, this was in the nature of an unhappy augury of its future fortunes as a Battalion throughout the Second World War. It just missed taking part in the campaign of the Western Desert in 1942, and after continuous efforts to get into battle only reached the 8TH Indian Division in Italy just as the enemy surrendered in May, 1945.

The period 1943-1945 had been one during which irksome and exacting duties were accompanied by repeated disappointments. Throughout this period the 5/13TH Frontier Force Rifles never lost heart and at all times gave it best. There were no thrills, no distractions, no honour and glory and no promotions to compensate for hardship and privation. A more severe test of discipline and esprit de corps could not have been thought out. All ranks realized that their luck was out and made the best of it. On its arrival at Tel Alo, the Battalion's role was to maintain order in a countryside where the French administration had ceased to exist, and for this purpose it was split up into a number of detachments stationed in the areas from which the French administration had been recently withdrawn. The only event of note at this time was a serious outbreak of fire in the petrol, oil and lubricant store, which resulted in injuries to seven Sepoys. Havildar Gulab Singh showed commendable bravery in rescuing the trapped men from the flames. Early in March the posts were taken over by Transjordan Frontier Force, and the 5/13TH Frontier Force Rifles was concentrated at Dier ez Zor. It was not long before orders arrived to be ready to move to Egypt, and on 18TH March it left for Damascus in Lorries. From Damascus the 5/13TH Frontier Force Rifles went by rail to Egypt. It was stationed at various localities in the Cairo area, guarding R.A.F. landing grounds, and remaining in readiness to repel enemy raids on lines of communications. On 14TH September, the Battalion was ordered to proceed to Persia. The battalion then commenced its long journey across the desert soon afterwards. All troops in Iraq and Persia (Iran) at that time were there for two reasons, to ensure that very large Allied organization aid to Russia was in no way interfered with, and to protect the vital oilfields and their pipelines to the Mediterranean Sea. The 5/13TH Frontier Force Rifles did its share of both duties. The fighting was virtually over in all theatres, so after brief spells in Lebanon, Egypt and Italy, the battalion sailed back to India on 17TH July 1945.

After the independence of the subcontinent in 1947, and the creation of Pakistan, the battalion was allotted to the new Pakistan Army. The Sikh soldiers from the battalion were transferred to the Indian Army.

13TH Frontier Force Rifles

59TH Royal Scinde Rifles (6/13TH)

The Scinde Camel Corps was raised at Karachi in 1843 after the conquest of Sind by Lieutenant R. Fitzgerald, for the purpose of keeping order among the wild desert tribes. It was a corps of mounted infantry. It was entirely self-supporting as it carried its own provisions and bedding. In 1853 the Camel Corps was transformed into the Scinde Rifles Corps. It became 6TH Punjab Infantry in 1856.

Shortly after the outbreak of the Sepoy Mutiny, the Regiment, which was stationed at Kohat was ordered to send two companies to Pashawar, where it formed part of the column which dispersed the mutineers of the 55TH Bengal Native Infantry, while a detachment defeated the mutineers from the 46TH Bengal Native Infantry and the 9TH Cavalry at Tammu Ghat, capturing the Regimental Colours of the former. Other detachments were employed in dealing with the Hindustani Fanatics who, aided by the funds from India, were trying to foment trouble among the border tribes.

From the end of the Sepoy Mutiny to the First World War the regiment was continuously involved in the punitive operations against the tribesmen on the North-West Frontier of India and the Afghan War; The Mahsud Expedition, 1860, The Hindustani Fanatics, 1863, The Second Afghan War, 1878, Miranzai, 1891, Tirah, 1897, and Tonnochy, 1900.

Subsequent to the reforms brought about in the Indian Army in 1903, the regiment's designation was changed to 59TH Rifles.

During the First World War, the Regiment served in France, and fought its first action on the 24TH, when they repulsed an overwhelming enemy attack. For the next five weeks of static warfare the regiment was almost continuously under fire, and casualties mounted steadily. On 18TH December the 59TH Rifles was attached to the Ferozepore Brigade in the bloody and indecisive struggle at the battle of Givenchy, where a Sikh platoon was annihilated by the point-blank enemy fire.

On 8TH March, the regiment was called upon to take part in the battle of Neuve Chapelle. It failed with very heavy losses. On 12TH March the regiment was ordered to take part in the assault on the Bois du Biez. The attack on Bois du Biez had to be made across the open in broad daylight, and the 59TH Rifles suffered heavily. The regiment was entirely without British officers; a Subedar-Major took command, and ultimately brought the Regiment out of action. The 59TH Rifles had suffered very heavily and was complimented for its behaviour and mentioned in an Indian Army Order as having particularly distinguished itself in the fighting.

On 26TH April the 59TH Rifles was ordered to assault the German trenches at Ypres. The regiment, deployed as steadily as on parade, and advanced at a great pace under a terrific cross-fire, the enemy using gas shells, which the Regiment experienced for the first time. At length it was realized that further progress was impossible, and the troops dug in.

13TH Frontier Force Rifles

59TH Royal Scinde Rifles (6/13TH)

On 27TH April they were relieved by the Sirhind Brigade. For the remainder of their stay in France, the regiment was continually in the front line, but did not take part in any major offensive. On 10TH December the regiment entrained for Marseilles and embarked for Mesopotamia, four days later. During its fifteen months in France it had suffered 813 casualties of all ranks.

Havildar Buta Singh was awarded the I.O.M., while Subedar Bishan Singh was awarded the I.D.S.M for conspicuous gallantry fighting the Germans in France.

From France the 59TH Rifles proceeded to Mesopotamia on 4TH January, 1916. They fought in the battle of Dujailah, the key position protecting the Turkish lines of circumvallation surrounding Kut-Al-Amara, where it suffered heavily. The next action was fought at Beit Aissa on 18TH April, where the Turks left no fewer than 2,000 dead in front of the 47TH Sikhs and 59TH Rifles. Beit Aissa was subsequently described as the regiment's finest performance in the First World War. On 23RD October the regiment was in action against the Turks at Duar, and on 5TH November took a leading part in the action at Tekrit. The Regiment and the 47TH Sikhs captured three lines of enemy trenches in twenty minutes, but the Indian losses were very heavy. This was the last major action which the Regiment fought in Mesopotamia.

Subedar Tola Singh was awarded the I.O.M., while Naik Phuman Singh was awarded the I.D.S.M., for conspicuous gallantry fighting the Turks in Mesopotamia.

On the 27TH March, 1918, the regiment disembarked at Ismailia, their destination was the Palestine front. Here the Turks, having lost Jerusalem, were holding front stretching from the Jordan, north of Jericho, to a point north of Jaffa on the sea coast, covering their main line of communications with Damascus. Static warfare followed until September, when General Allenby had completed his preparations for the break-through which was destined to drive Turkey out of the war. On the 19TH an intensive bombardment was opened by massed artillery, in which monitors joined from the sea.

The 59TH Rifles received orders to advance, and every officer and man charged out on the enemy. On 20TH September the regiment found itself in broken and hilly country, completely exhausted. In spite of this, they pushed on to Samaria, astride the main road connecting Damascus with Jerusalem, and the main line of the enemy's retreat. It was now bitterly cold, and the rapidity of the advance had far outstripped the baggage. The regiment saw no more fighting after this. The enemy was now in disorderly retreat, with the cavalry at their heels and the R.A.F. bombing them relentlessly from air. The Turks asked for an armistice on 31ST October. The 59TH Rifles, however, was detained in Egypt by internal disorders, and subsequently returned to Palestine on garrison duty. It eventually embarked for India on 5TH May, 1920, and reached Jullundur on 23RD after five year's warfare overseas.

13TH Frontier Force Rifles

59TH Royal Scinde Rifles (6/13TH)

In recognition of its distinguished services and gallantry during the First World War, His Majesty the King Emperor George V was graciously pleased to confer the title 'Royal' on the 59TH Scinde Rifles (F.F.).

It is impossible to close this account without reference to the close comradeship which sprang up between the 59TH Rifles, The Manchester Regiment, and the 47TH Sikhs, who were brigaded together from 1912 to 1919, and shared the trials and hardships of the campaigns in France, Mesopotamia and Palestine.

In 1922, the 59TH Scinde Rifles (Frontier Force) was grouped with the 55TH, 57TH, 58TH, and the two Battalions of 56TH Punjabi Rifles (Frontier Force) to form the 13TH Frontier Force Rifles. Hence 59TH Scinde Rifles (Frontier Force) becoming 6TH Royal Battalion (Scinde) 13TH Frontier Force Rifles.

During the Second World War the 6/13TH Frontier Force Rifles served in Italian East Africa, Persia, Iraq, Syria, Palestine and Italy. On 7TH September, 1940, the Battalion disembarked at Port Sudan and was entrained for Derudeb, 140 miles north of Kassala, where it came under the orders of the 29TH Brigade. Derudeb was a desolate spot in the midst of the desert, but the battalion was soon busy with training and motor reconnaissance, and preparing a defensive position at Tahilla gap, to prevent the enemy from attempting to move from Kassala in the direction of Haiya. Towards the end of October the battalion was relieved at Derudeb and Tahilla, and moved to Sennar by the way of Atbara. On 14TH January orders were received by the Battalion to move to Khashm el Girba.

On the 18TH it was ordered to Eritrea in pursuit of the enemy, who were reported to be evacuating Kassala. The pursuit was too fast for the Italians, who were forced to fight a rear guard action near Gogni. The battalion was ordered to capture the position. As the attack was launched, the Italians broke and fled, abandoning two pack guns, six machine guns, and 180 mules. In this their first action, they inflicted over 200 casualties while they suffered only four. On the 28TH the Battalion, advancing from southerly direction from Eimasa, again came into action against strongly posted force, which was disposed at great depth and in considerable strength. The enemy counter attacked without success, and withdrew the next day. The advance was continued despite opposition along the whole front of the Brigade until 2ND February, when it was found that Barentu had been evacuated. During its first two weeks in Eritrea the 6/13TH Frontier Force Rifles, had advanced for 130 miles and been in action twice against enemy rear-guards sited in well-concealed positions.

The Italians had good reason to believe Keren to be impregnable, as it might well have been to troops not inured to warfare on the North-West Frontier of India. The road runs up a narrow, rocky valley, overlooked by towering mountains. To the east is Fort Dologorodoc, 1,475 metres high, a pinnacle with almost perpendicular sides, while to the west, the great massif of Sanchil to a height of 1,786 metres. Behind them again were the towering heights of Zeban and Falestoh. Besides these was a group of peaks.

13TH Frontier Force Rifles

59TH Royal Scinde Rifles (6/13TH)

The forces holding them were the flower of the Italian army, the Savoy Grenadiers, the Bersagliery and the Alpini, besides fully trained native levies, well supplied with artillery and mortars. At Keren the flower of the Italian army fought with a bravery and determination second to none. In the initial advance of the troops in early February, the gallant men who seized a number .of the outlying positions were too few to hold them, and it became evident that the great escarpment would only fall to a combined assault on a grand scale.

During the next few weeks the 4TH and 5TH Divisions were busy making preparations, and finally amassed a force of nineteen Battalions and 120 guns, but even then the enemy in their mountain fastnesses outnumbered them two to one. On 15TH March, after an intense bombardment, the men of the 4TH Division went forward to scale the cliffs of the Sanchil position, but by the end of the day they still had not succeeded. In the valley below, the 5TH Division, whose allotted task was the capture of Fort Dologorodoc to the east of Keren gorge, were pinned down by heavy cross-fire. As dusk set in units of the 9TH Brigade managed to get a footing on the northern slopes, and the following morning, after twenty hours desperate fighting, the fort was in their hands. The 29TH Brigade was now ordered to pass through and attack the precipitous Falestoh and Zeban positions. At daybreak on the 17TH, a counter-attack came in from the left rear of 2ND Punjab Regiment, and a Company under Captain Anant Singh Pathania was sent up to reinforce. The company rushed across an area swept by fire and beat off the attack with the loss of three dead and five wounded. They made forty prisoners and inflicted heavy casualties. Later they were again counter-attacked by a force estimated at about a Battalion, but in spite of suffering 35 per cent casualties, they beat back the enemy with heavy loss. In this engagement, Captain Anant Singh displayed outstanding qualities of leadership. Although wounded in the face and both legs, he collected his company headquarters and all the other men he could get hold of and drove off, at the point of the bayonet, the enemy who had penetrated the position. He only handed over to Lieutenant Sadiqullah when ordered to do so by a senior officer. Captain Anant Singh Pathania was awarded an immediate Military Cross for his leadership and gallantry in this action.

On the 26TH March the Brigade was ordered to capture Zaban, and did so without meeting any opposition. It was evident now that Keren had been evacuated, and the 6TH Royal Battalion, pressing forward at top speed to intercept the retreating enemy, had the honour of being the first to enter the town. On 28TH March the 6/13TH Frontier Force Rifles took part in the pursuit of the retreating enemy, and the Italian main rear-guard position, which they were holding in strength, was contacted at Ad Teclesan. It was formidable position overlooking a road-block, and the 29TH Brigade was ordered to consolidate their own position while the 9TH Brigade came through and attacked the enemy. During this process the Battalion came under heavy artillery fire, and it was found that the enemy were in strength on the hills to the Battalion's left.

13TH Frontier Force Rifles

59TH Royal Scinde Rifles (6/13TH)

On the 31ST an attack by the Worcestershire Regiment was held up. A company of the 6/13TH Frontier Force Rifles was sent to help the Worcesters and was given the task of attacking the high features, fire from which had held up the advance. A company under Lieutenant Bharat Singh, with artillery support, put up a fine performance, capturing the right hand feature, including a very important enemy observation point, within an hour. Two platoons of the company, however, ran into heavy mortar and machine-gun fire, without artillery to support them, and were ordered to stop their attack. The company lost seven killed and twenty-eight wounded in this action, but inflicted many casualties and captured two officers and sixty men besides several machine guns. During the night the enemy evacuated the position. Havildar Natha Singh who was killed in this action was awarded a posthumous I.O.M.

On the 4TH May, the 6/13TH Frontier Force Rifles lead an attack on Amba Alagi. A company made a frontal assault; the speed with which the men scaled the rocky slopes was amazing, and they moved so closely behind the artillery barrage that several were wounded by splinters. The enemy was completely overwhelmed, the commanding officer of the left centre of the Italian defences, with all his staff and 110 men surrendered. The enemy had established his left flank defences on a chain of hills, situated on the south-west of Amab Alagi and covering the main road to the south. On the 7TH the 6/13TH Frontier Force Rifles was ordered to capture these points. The positions were taken, but the enemy counter-attacked under the cover of heavy machine-gun and mortar fire, and finally the company suffering 70 per cent losses and exhausting its ammunition, was withdrawn to Centre Hill. Many gallant deeds were performed during these operations at Amba Alagi, but none braver that of Sepoy Saudagar Singh in the attack on Castle Hill on 8TH May. He was with the leading section of his platoon which, after descending all night a steep drop of 2,000 feet, were confronted with a ridge 1,500 feet above them. While clambering up, the men were met with heavy small-arms and grenade fire from a Sangar at the summit. The section commander, Saudagar Singh, and another Sepoy were wounded, but Saudagar Singh took over command and led the assault on the Sangar. He bayoneted two of the enemy and closing on a third was shot dead. Brigadier Marriot, who witnessed the episode through his glasses, recommended him for a posthumous Victoria Cross, and he was eventually awarded the I.O.M. Seldom has the decoration been more richly earned.

The Italians did not wait for the final assault, and on 11TH May an envoy came to ask for terms of surrender. These were accepted, and on 18TH May the remnants of the Italian Army of Eritrea were allowed to march out, headed by the Duke of Acosta, with the full honours of war, passed a guard of honour composed of representative of all units of the Division.

6/13TH Frontier Force Rifles was now ordered to Massawa, which was reached on 29TH July, and proceeded to embark for Egypt.

13TH Frontier Force Rifles

59TH Royal Scinde Rifles (6/13TH)

The 6/13TH Frontier Force Rifles disembarked at Suez on 5TH August, 1941. On 1ST February the battalion had orders to rejoin the 29TH Brigade at Tobruk in the Western Desert, and reached its destination and took over section of the eastern defences. Its stay at Tobruk was uneventful, save for daily tip-and-run raids on the harbour by Stuka aircraft. On 27TH March the 6/13TH Frontier Force Rifles left Tobruk for Hamra on the Egyptian frontier, a strong base from which a striking force could operate in any direction at short notice. The battalion's stay in the Western Desert now came to an abrupt end, as on 11TH April it was ordered to Iraq; it seemed that some seasoned units with battle experience were needed to stiffen up the Tenth Army in Iraq. At the end of 1ST June 1/12TH Rifles and 6/13TH Frontier Force Rifles were detached from 17TH Brigade to join two Battalions from 20TH Indian Infantry Brigade (part of 10TH Indian Infantry Division) to take part in the Syria-Lebanon campaign and capture the Duck's Bill area in north east Syria and secure the Mosul to Aleppo railway. This was achieved without a shot being fired as the Vichy French forces retired westwards. After a short spell in Iraq, and Palestine the battalion was ordered to Italy. The Battalion landed in Italy 24TH September 1943 and served in the 8TH Indian Division. The Division was operating on the Adriatic front as part of the right wing of the Allied armies forcing their way northward. On 23RD October it moved forward to take part in forcing the passage over the Trigno River, which the enemy were holding in strength. The 8TH Indian Division's continuous attacks on the Trigno had their effect, and early in November, 1943, the Germans withdrew to their main position on the Sangro River. The pursuit of the retreating Germans was resumed over terrible country in torrents of rain. The Battalion went on to advance on the town of Archi. All the way to Archi the ground was stubbornly contested. Every house was a strong-point, and the troops advanced up narrow defiles swept by artillery, mortar and machine-gun fire; there was particularly fierce struggle for the commanding position of Monte Torreto, which was occupied on the night of the 16TH. Led by the Sikhs of 'A' Company, they attacked and took Archi by midnight. The 6/13TH Frontier Force Rifles were now withdrawn to San Marco. However, the Division was given the Villa Grande as its next objective. When moving forward to its task in the attack on 17TH December, the battalion pushed on towards the main German position behind the Ortona-Orsogna lateral road. The attack all along the line was now held up on the brink of a ravine by withering fire from groups of houses on the far side which were nicknamed 'Stalingrad'. The troops had to dig in, while the tanks were literally plastered with shells and were forced to withdraw to their leaguer till nightfall. Throughout the 18TH December attempts were made without success to cross the ravine. Finally, just as the dusk was setting in, an artillery concentration with smoke was brought down which blinded enemy observation, and the Sikhs assaulted and captured a village immediately in front of them, taking several prisoners, including a German officer.

13TH Frontier Force Rifles

59TH Royal Scinde Rifles (6/13TH)

During the action at Ortona-Orsogna Sepoy Darshan Singh was awarded the I.O.M. for his gallantry.

The battalion continued its assault and brilliantly captured the left group of the farmhouses comprising 'Stalingrad'. The fighting was desperate, only the utmost bravery and determination brought success. Every door and window was sand-bagged, and the Germans fought to the last. The 8TH Division moved over the Cassino sector of the Allied front in Italy early in April. In the next task the 6/13TH Frontier Force Rifles probably did more for the Allied cause than any other action in which it fought in the Second World War; the forcing of the Gari River, which broke the Gustav Line. This river was a rapid mountain stream with lofty banks which runs directly under the historic Monte Cassino. The enemy defence of this river line had proved too much for the American troops, and the countryside was still littered with discarded guns and vehicles and decomposing bodies, grim relic of their gallant but unsuccessful attempts. The two Indian Divisions were to attack together, the 8TH Indian Division on the left, while at a given moment the Polish Corps would assault the famous Monastery Hill. The River Gari separated the adversaries on the entire front of the 8TH Indian Division. It was about forty feet wide, six to eight feet deep, swiftly flowing. The crossing of the Gari River and the subsequent fighting was, perhaps, the finest feat of the 6/13TH Rifles during the whole of this hard-fought campaign. An advance then was made on Pignataro, and it was taken by the 6/13TH Frontier Force Rifles after a fierce struggle. This town was of great importance, and its capture was essential to complete the break-through of the Division. Following this, the Division advanced some 240 miles in June across mountainous country fighting many actions against rearguards and defended strong points. In late June they had reached Assisi and the Division was rested. By the end of July 1944 the Division was back in the line with 1ST Canadian Armoured Brigade in front of Florence pushing towards the River Arno. Florence was occupied by 21ST Brigade on 12TH August where they had the unusual task to recover some of the world's greatest art treasures and arrange safe custody. By mid September the Division was in the mountains again, breaking through the Gothic Line.

On the 12TH December after a night of continuous patrol movement on the front, a heavier than usual artillery and mortar concentration fell on the 6/13TH Frontier Force Rifles area, and shortly afterwards a forward post of a Company reported that the enemy was attacking in large numbers and the attack had been beaten off and eleven prisoners taken. The forward post was attacked again, this time with the aid of flame-throwers and after fierce hand to hand struggle, the enemy completely overran it. The last report from the post commander was that he had only a few wounded men left and that he estimated the enemy to be at least two companies strong. After this, general infiltration by the enemy took place.

13TH Frontier Force Rifles

59TH Royal Scinde Rifles (6/13TH)

The German paratroops worked their way forward in groups, bombing and firing in bursts from their automatic weapons, and completely overran the company's right-hand post. At this stage thirty men from the Company's reserve platoon were ordered to recapture the vital ground ahead on which the paratroops had begun to consolidate. They charged up and over the slope and hurled back the surprised Germans off their newly won positions. Mortar defensive fire was called for, while the M.M.Gs., firing on fixed lines across the front, did great execution among the enemy. Meanwhile on company's right another enemy attack had surged over the left-hand post at Casa Nuova. Having done this, the enemy turned and threw themselves on and overrunning two sections posts before being stopped. The Germans suffered many casualties from one of the 6/13TH Frontier Force Rifle's M.M.Gs. This M.M.Gs manned by Havildar Tara Singh, was vitally effective in the part it played in this action. The attack having failed, the enemy suffered more casualties as they withdrew. During the counter-attack Havildar Tara Singh once more pumped lead form the flank into the enemy into the enemy occupying Casa Nuova and greatly contributed to restoring the position.

By 11TH April the Division reached and crossed the River Santerno breaking open a hole in the German line for the 78TH Division and elements of British 56TH Infantry Division to engage the enemy and defeat them in the Argenta Gap. This opened the way to Ferrara and the Po River and for 6TH Armoured Division to pass through, veer left and race westward across country to link with the advancing U.S. 5TH Army and complete the encirclement of the divisions of the German 10TH and 14TH Armies defending Bologna. In the aftermath of the Argenta fighting, the Division drove on rapidly through to Ferrara and across the Po and shortly thereafter to their last river crossing of the war, the Adige. The campaign ended on 2ND May 1945.

Apart from the gallantry awards already mentioned the following awards were made to the Sikh soldiers of the 6/13TH Frontier Force Rifles:
Jemadar Amar Singh, Jemadar Chuhar Singh and Jemadar Thakar Singh were awarded the Military Cross. Subedar Chuhar Singh and Subedar Santa Singh, and Subedar Pritam Singh, were awarded the OB.I., Naik Gian Singh, Naik Jagir Singh, Naik Teja Singh, Lance-Naik Bachan Singh, Lance-Naik Mehar Singh, Lance-Naik Ram Singh, Sepoy Dalip Singh, and Sepoy Saran Singh were awarded the Military Medal, for their conspicuous gallantry against the Germans in Italy.

Early in May, 1947, the 6/13TH Frontier Force Rifles returned to India, and soon afterwards the Independence and partition of the Indian Subcontinent took place. After the independence of the subcontinent in 1947, and the creation of Pakistan, the battalion was allotted to the new Pakistan Army. The Sikh soldiers from the battalion were transferred to the Indian Army.

14TH Punjab Regiment

19TH Punjabis (1/14TH)

The 19TH Punjabis was raised in 1857 and designated as the 19TH Punjabis in 1903. The regiment was formed during the upheaval of the Indian Mutiny in 1857 on the orders of John Lawrence, the British Chief Commissioner of the Punjab, and saw service in North India.

In 1864, the 19TH Punjabis participated in the Bhutan war fought between British India and Bhutan in 1864–1865. Britain sent a peace mission to Bhutan in early 1864, in the wake of the recent conclusion of a civil war there. Bhutan rejected the peace and friendship treaty it offered and Britain declared war in November 1864. The war lasted only five months and, despite some battlefield victories by Bhutanese forces, resulted in Bhutan's defeat, loss of part of its sovereign territory, and forced cession of formerly occupied territories. Havildar Prem Singh and Naik Hira Singh were awarded the I.O.M. in 1865, in consideration of their conspicuous gallantry against the Bhutanese army.

During the Second Afghan War of 1878-80, the 19TH Punjabis fought with distinction in the Battle of Ahmed Khel. The Battle occurred during General Donald Stewart's march from Kandahar to Ghazni, then on to Kabul. The British forces consisted of 7,200 British and Indian troops, on the side of the Afghans were 15,000 tribesmen mounted and on foot of the Andarees, Tarkees, Suleiman Khels and other Afghan tribes. Despite the fierce efforts from the forces of Afghanistan, the battle ended in a British victory.

In 1891, 19TH Punjabis took part in the Black Hill Expedition and the 2ND Miranzai Expedition on the North West Frontier of India, which it guarded over the years. In 1903, the 19TH Punjabis took part in the British expedition to Tibet which began in December 1903 and lasted until September 1904. The expedition was effectively a temporary invasion by British Indian forces under the auspices of the Tibet Frontier Commission.

Subsequent to the reforms brought about in the Indian Army in 1903, the regiment's designation remained as 19TH Punjabis, with the class composition of Sikhs, Punjabi Mussalmans, Dogras and Pathans.

On the outbreak of the First World War, the regiment initially remained in India guarding the North West Frontier. In February 1916, it moved to Persia, where it had the unique distinction of being actively engaged against the Bolsheviks in Trans-Caspia. The actions were primarily undertaken against Turco-Germans, to block their advance through the Caucasus towards India and Afghanistan. The Intervention brought British troops into conflict with Soviet Russian military forces on the Caspian and in Trans-Caspia. The British force was led by General Wilfred Malleson.

The detachment from Meshed, consisting of 25 sabres 28TH Light Cavalry and 175 rifles and two machine guns 19TH Punjabis, reached Muhammadabad (near the Perso-Russian frontier) on 2ND August 1918.

14TH Punjab Regiment

19TH Punjabis (1/14TH)

On 8TH August General Malleson learnt the Trans-Caspian force had been driven back by the Bolsheviks to Bairam Ali, on the Eastern edge of the Merv oasis. The two machine guns of 19TH Punjabis left Muhammadabad on 11TH August and reached Bairam Ali on 12TH. Next day the Bolsheviks attacked. The Trans-Caspian force consisting of about 1,000 men, largely Turkomans, was defeated by the Bolshevik attacking force. The Trans–Caspian force's retirement would have resulted in a decisive disaster, but for the gallant behaviour of the Punjabi Machine Gun Detachment. These men fired their guns till they became too hot to handle and, inflicted 350 casualties on the enemy. Two of the Punjabi Detachment was wounded and one of its machine guns had to be abandoned after two men had been burnt in trying to carry it out of action. The Trans-Caspian force, thoroughly demoralised, fell back to Merv on 14TH August, after damaging the bridge over the Murghab River. They retreated before a Bolshevik advance without attempting resistance past Tejend to Dushak.

There was further action at Kaahka on 28TH August, 11TH and 18TH September. The village of Kaahka was grouped round the railway station. On 28TH September, the Bolshevik's opened with an Artillery bombardment, and the Infantry advanced forward till they reached the orchards immediately North of the station. Here they were checked for some time by the gallant resistance offered by a few Punjabis, who had been left in camp on various fatigue duties. Meanwhile, a Company of Punjabis, arriving almost simultaneously with the enemy, charged with the bayonet and drove Bolshevik's back, eventually putting him to flight and capturing five of his machine guns. This ended the fighting, which had been confined to the area north of the station, for the Bolshevik force all withdrew.

On the 14TH October, the British detachment from Kaahka found the Bolshevik force some distance to the North of Dushak; and was met by a heavy gun and machine gun fire. The Punjabis pushed on with speed and determination, but suffered heavy casualties. The British guns, firing with great accuracy, did much damage to the enemy trains and to the station. When the Punjabis reached the station it was totally wrecked by an explosion of some trucks full of munitions. Having lost the station, the Bolsheviks started a counter-attack which was met by about 150 Punjabis and 120 dismounted Indian Cavalry. A retirement became necessary and withdrawal was ordered. The British casualties had been considerable. Those in 28TH Light Cavalry amounted to 6 killed and 12 wounded, while the Punjabis, with 47 killed and 139 wounded, and had lost about 50 percent of their strength. The 19TH Punjabis were led out by Subedar Bal Singh. As the Chief of Staff of Trans-Caspia forces said in his official report, only the disgraceful action of their own troops had prevented them from obtaining a decisive victory, and only the heroic conduct of the Punjabis had saved them from complete disaster.

14TH Punjab Regiment

19TH Punjabis (1/14TH)

General Malleson also reported that Russian circles were filled with the greatest admiration for the part played by the Indian troops, whom they regarded as being equal to ten times their own number of any of the other combatants.

On 16TH January a Bolshevik force made a sudden attack on the Trans-Caspian position at Annenkovo. Besides the Trans-Caspian force, there were at Annenkovo a half-Squadron 28TH Light Cavalry and a Company (150 rifles) 19TH Punjabis. The Punjabis experienced little difficulty in maintaining their position, but the Armenians were greatly outnumbered and had to be reinforced by a Punjabi Platoon. The enemy, however, continued to push in fresh troops and, under a heavy enfilading machine gun fire, the Armenians broke and fled. Fortunately, at this critical juncture, the train carrying a Company of Punjabis from Bairam Ali steamed up and came on right into the hail of bullets. The Bolsheviks held their ground till the Punjabis were within 50 yards and then broke and fled in disorder, losing heavily as they crossed the front of the other Punjabi Company. By this time the main Bolshevik force was in full flight across the desert and, seeing this, those attacking the Trans-Caspian right also broke and fled. Bolshevik casualties had been severe, nearly 200 corpses being found next morning, his total losses being subsequently estimated at 600. However, the Bolshevik had inflicted 70 casualties on the Trans-Caspian force and 46 among the Punjabis. It was subsequently ascertained that the Bolshevik plan had been to cut the railway and telegraph communications and then immediately surprise and overwhelm the Annenkovo detachment by simultaneous attacks against both flanks; that against the left being carried out by 2,500 Infantry and the one against the other flank by 1,500 Infantry.

The Indian troops evacuated Trans-Caspia on 14TH April 1919, leaving behind them a reputation for discipline and gallantry which any troops might be proud of and which they well deserved.

Subedar Bal Singh, Sepoy Dalel Singh and Subedar Hukam Singh (Posthumous award) were awarded the I.O.M. for their conspicuous gallantry in the fighting at Dushak.

Jemadar Nihal Singh, Havildar Asa Singh, Naiks Karam Singh, Jowala Singh, Sher Singh, Lance-Naiks Gurdit Singh, Sohan Singh, Gian Singh, Asa Singh, Sepoys Waryam Singh, Surjan Singh, Udham Singh, Ganga Singh and Bal Singh, were awarded the I.D.S.M., for their conspicuous gallantry in Trans-Caspia.

In 1921-22, a major reorganization was undertaken in the British Indian Army leading to the formation of large infantry groups of four to six battalions. Among these was the 14TH Punjab Regiment, formed by grouping the 19TH Punjabis with the 20TH, 21ST, 22ND and 24TH Punjabis, and the 40TH Pathans. The regiment's new designation was 1ST Battalion, 14TH Punjab Regiment.

14TH Punjab Regiment

19TH Punjabis (1/14TH)

During the Second World War, the battalion fought in the Malayan Campaign. In December 1941, a small mechanized force advanced into Siam from north of Kedah to harass and delay the advance of the Japanese forces from Singora. An armoured train was also sent into Siam from Padang Besar on the frontier of Perlis. By dusk on the 9TH January, 1942, the mechanized force halted at Sadao, ten miles north of the frontier on the Jitra-Singora road. A Japanese column, headed by tanks and moving in close formation with full headlights, was seen approaching. The leading enemy tanks and a convoy of some thirty motor vehicles behind them were engaged and brought to a standstill; but the Japanese Infantry quickly debussed and started and enveloping movement. Thereupon, the mechanized force withdrew southwards towards the frontier, destroying Road Bridge as it went. It passed through 1/14TH Punjab Regiment, who had been detailed both to provide the covering troops on the frontier and to hold an outpost position three and half miles north of Jitra.

Early on the morning of the 10TH, Japanese crossed the frontier and made contact with forward detachments of 1/14TH Punjab Regiment, which had been providing both the covering and outposts, troops of this sector. The Punjabis withdrew slowly southwards. Meanwhile, to give sufficient time for 15TH and 6TH Brigades to prepare and occupy their allotted sectors, General Murray- Lyon instructed Brigadier Garret to delay the enemy north of Jitra till dawn on the 12TH, and gave him 2/1ST Gurkha Rifles to assist him. Garret ordered this unit to take over the outpost position at Asun, and concentrated the whole of 1/14TH Punjab Regiment forward. By the evening of the 10TH the Punjabis were occupying a defensive position at Changlun. On the 11TH, enemy infantry attacked and, in the fighting, the defence lost some ground and the two Breda anti-tank guns. Since the whole of the battalion was to delay the enemy without becoming too involved, Garret had decided to withdraw it during the afternoon through the outpost position at Asun, but Murray-Lyon ordered him to occupy and intermediate position near Nangka, some two miles north of the outpost position and to hold it overnight. The Punjabis were moving to this position in heavy rain and in poor visibility when a Japanese mechanized force, led by medium tanks followed by lorried infantry, suddenly attacked the rear of the column. Firing indiscriminately ahead and to both sides, the tanks broke through the rearguard and drove through the column, overrunning the section of 2ND Anti Tank Battery which was limbered up and not in action. They caused utter consternation among the Indian troops, most of whom had never seen a tank.

The Punjabis were thrown into confusion by this attack and forced off the road. Only some 200 men, succeeded in joining the division the following day. Small parties made their way back later but, for the time being, the 1/14TH Punjab Regiment could not be regarded as a fighting unit. The British-Indian troops were compelled to withdraw from the State of Perlis.

14TH Punjab Regiment

19TH Punjabis (1/14TH)

On the 24TH December, General Heath had selected two main positions suitable for defence south of Ipoh, the first at Kampar and the second north of Janjong Malim. He decided that the reconstituted 15TH Brigade, which included the 1/14TH Punjab Regiment, should occupy the Kampar position. In accordance with this plan 15TH Brigade, now rested and partly re-equipped, had moved to Kampar position on the 23RD and had begun preparing defences. The 15TH Brigade, with 88TH Field Regiment and 273RD Anti-Tank Battery under command, was disposed in considerable depth astride the trunk road at Kampar Village.

The Japanese lost no time in attacking the Kampar position. The 11TH Indian Division managed to delay the Japanese advance at Kampar for a few days, in which the Japanese suffered severe casualties, in terrain that did not allow them to use their tanks or their air superiority, to defeat the British. However, the British were compelled to withdraw their troops, and the 15TH Brigade withdrew to Sungai. Apart from the air reconnaissance on both coasts of the Peninsula, little direct air support was available for British troops throughout this critical period. By contrast, the Japanese air force was constantly attacking forward troops and communications. The casualties and damage they inflicted was considerable, and their unopposed bombing and machine-gunning undoubtedly affected the morale of both British and Indian troops. Allied air resources were quite inadequate in meets their many commitments. The relentless Japanese advance compelled the remnants of the 1/14TH Punjab had retreated to Singapore, On 31ST January, the last organised Allied forces left Malaya, and Allied engineers blew a 70 ft (21 m)-wide hole in the causeway that linked Johor and Singapore; a few stragglers would wade across over the next few days. Japanese raiders and infiltrators, often disguised as Singaporean civilians, began to cross the Straits of Johor in inflatable boats soon afterwards.

In less than two months, the Battle for Malaya had ended in comprehensive defeat for the Commonwealth forces and their retreat from the Malay Peninsula to the fortress of Singapore. Nearly 50,000 Commonwealth troops had been captured or killed during the battle.

The Japanese Army invaded the island of Singapore on 7TH February and completed their conquest of the island on 15TH February, capturing 80,000 more prisoners out of the 85,000 allied defenders. Story of the Indian prisoners was a long tale of intimidation and cruelty. The Sikhs and Dogras were sent to New Guinea, where most of them perished.

The battalion was re-raised in 1946 with remnants and the reinforcements. After the independence of the subcontinent in 1947, and the creation of Pakistan, the battalion was allotted to the new Pakistan Army. The Sikh soldiers from the battalion were transferred to the Indian Army.

14TH Punjab Regiment

20TH DCO Infantry (2/14TH)

The 20TH DCO Infantry (Brownlow's Punjabis) was raised in 1857, as the 8TH Regiment of Punjab Infantry, from the veterans of the Sikh armies. It was designated as the 20TH Duke of Cambridge's Own Infantry (Brownlow's Punjabis) in 1904.

The regiment was raised at Nowshera on 1ST August 1857 by Lieutenant Charles Henry Brownlow from drafts provided by 4TH and 5TH Punjab Infantry on the orders of John Lawrence, the British High Commissioner of the Punjab. It was one of several regiments raised by Lawrence to suppress the Great Sepoy Mutiny of 1857. Brownlow, who became their first commanding officer, remained associated with the regiment for more than half a century; becoming their Honorary Colonel in 1904.

The regiment's first overseas service came during the Second Opium War against China. During 1856–1860, British forces fought towards legalization of the opium trade, and to open all of China to British merchants, and to exempt foreign imports from internal transit duties. Soon after landing there, it took part in the successful assault on Taku Forts on 21ST August 1860. The regiment then advanced with the rest of the British force, arriving at Peking (Beijing) in late September, which was captured on 6TH October.

In 1861, the regiment was brought into the line as the 24TH Regiment of Bengal Native Infantry, replacing the previous 24TH which had mutinied in 1857. It was renumbered as the 20TH Regiment later in the year.

In 1863, it took part in the Umbeyla Campaign on the North-West Frontier of India. During the fierce fighting at Crag Piquet in October and November, the 20TH Punjabis retook the position, which had been captured by the tribesmen on 30TH October. It then successfully defended the post from repeated attacks by the tribal forces. It was the first of many such engagements against the hostile Pakhtun tribes of the Afghan frontier.

In 1864, the regiment, now designated as the 20TH (Punjab) Regiment of Bengal Native Infantry, took part in the Black Mountain Expedition, and in 1877, it operated against the Jowaki Afridis. Next year, the regiment advanced into the Khyber Pass to clear Afghan forces at Ali Masjid during the Second Afghan War, as part of the 1ST Brigade of the Pashawar Field Force. Ali Masjid, an imposing fortress, was the first engagement of the war. After the capture of the fort, the Pashawar Field Force advanced into Afghanistan and captured Jalalabad.

In 1882, the regiment was dispatched to Egypt as part of an expeditionary force to suppress the revolt by Arabi Pasha against the Egyptian Government. In a surprise dawn attack on 13TH September, the Egyptian forces at Tel-el-Kebir were completely routed by the British. The 20TH Punjabis fought on the left flank of the Indian Brigade. In honour of their service in Egypt, the Duke of Cambridge was appointed as their honorary colonel in 1883, and the regiment was retitled as the 20TH (Duke of Cambridge's Own) (Punjab) Regiment of Bengal Native Infantry.

14TH Punjab Regiment

20TH DCO Infantry (2/14TH)

In 1897, during a general uprising of Pakhtun tribes, the regiment operated as part of the Mohmand Field Force. The regiment, under the command by Lieutenant-Colonel J.B. Woon, fought in a fierce engagement against a force of about 6,000 Mohmands at Shabkadar.

In 1900, the 20TH Punjabis were sent to China to suppress the Boxer Rebellion. Beginning in 1898, groups of peasants in northern China began to band together into a secret society known as I-ho ch'üan ('Righteous and Harmonious Fists'), called the "Boxers" by Western press. At first, the Boxers wanted to destroy the Ch'ing dynasty and wanted to rid China of all foreign influence. When the Empress Dowager backed the Boxers, the Boxers turned solely to ridding China of foreigners. By late 1899, bands of Boxers were massacring Christian missionaries and Chinese Christians. By May 1900, the Boxer Rebellion had come out of the countryside and was being waged in the capital of Peking (now Beijing). To help their fellow countrymen and to protect their interests in China, an international force of 2,100 American, British, Russian, French, Italian, and Japanese soldiers were sent to subdue the 'rebellion'. On June 18, 1900, the Empress Dowager ordered all foreigners to be killed. Several foreign ministers and their families were killed before the international force could protect them. On August 14TH, 1900, the international force took Peking and subdued the rebellion. The Boxer Rebellion weakened the Ching dynasty's power and hastened the Republican Revolution of 1911 that overthrew the boy emperor and made China a republic.

Subsequent to the reforms brought about in the Indian Army by Lord Kitchener, the regiment's designation was changed to 20TH Duke of Cambridge's Own Punjabis in 1903 and then 20TH Duke of Cambridge's Own Infantry (Brownlow's Punjabis) in 1904.

During the First World War, the regiment saw active service in Mesopotamia and Palestine against the Turkish Empire. On 11TH November, the regiment was actively involved in repulsing a Turkish attack near Sanniya. The regiment then took part in the successful attack on the Turkish force at Sahilan on 15TH November, and Zain on 19TH November. After the Turks retreated northwards, the regiment took part in the capture of Basra, which was occupied on 23RD November. In April 1915, the regiment fought at the Battle of Shaiba, where the Turkish attempt to retake Basra was foiled. The 20TH Punjabis subsequently took part in the British advance northwards, which led to the capture of Kut-al-Amara in September 1915. For the next two years, the regiment remained engaged in a number of actions against the Turks including the Battle of Istabulat. Havildar Mewa Singh and Bugle Major Surain Singh were awarded the I.O.M. for their conspicuous gallantry in Mesopotamia in 1914. However, Sepoy Hazara Singh was awarded a posthumous I.O.M in 1917.

14TH Punjab Regiment

The 20TH DCO Infantry (2/14TH)

After spending a few months in Egypt, it was dispatched to Palestine in March 1918. The regiment took over trenches north of Jaffa during the Second Battle of Gaza. The Second Battle of Gaza in April 1917 was an attack planned by Lieutenant General Dobell, who was disappointed with the defeat of the First Battle of Gaza. The British Egyptian Expeditionary Force used tanks and gas shells to attack the Turkish troops. The Turkish troops had, however, received reinforcements since the initial attack and were better prepared. This attack also ended in a failure for the British troops. The regiment returned to India in May 1918, as the British prepared for the third and final attack on Beersheba.

In 1921-22, a major reorganization was undertaken in the British Indian Army leading to the formation of large infantry groups of four to six Battalions. Among these was the 14TH Punjab Regiment, and the Battalion's new designation was 2ND Battalion (Duke of Cambridge's Own) 14TH Punjab Regiment.

During the Second World War, the battalion was part of the British garrison of Hong Kong. In 1940 the Chiefs-of-Staff in London had described Honk Kong as 'an undesirable military commitment'. However, Britain could not withdraw from it simply because this would undermine her prestige in the region. The Japanese began their attack from the Chinese mainland early on 8TH December 1941. By 15TH December, they began systematic bombardment of the island's North Shore. The Allied defenders had been forced back to the 'Gindrinkers Line', massively outnumbered by Japanese troops, artillery and aircraft, by 9 Line' on the Kowloon Peninsula. Two demands for surrender were made on 13TH and 17TH December. When these were rejected, Japanese forces crossed the harbour on the evening of 18TH December and landed on the island's North-East. By the afternoon of 25TH December 1941, it was clear that further resistance would be futile and British colonial officials headed by the Governor of Hong Kong, Sir Mark Aitcheson Young, surrendered in person at the Japanese headquarters on the third floor of the Peninsula Hong Kong hotel. This was the first occasion on which a British Crown Colony had surrendered to an invading force.

The Japanese had taken Hong Kong in under three weeks at the cost of around 3,000 casualties, and had taken about 12,000 prisoners. The Battalion had heroically resisted the enemy for 18 days but was forced to surrender and spent the rest of the war in Japanese captivity. Story of the Indian prisoners was a long tale of intimidation and cruelty. The Sikhs and Dogras were sent to New Guinea, where most of them perished.

At the end of the hostilities the battalion was re-raised in 1946 with the remnants of the soldiers that had survived Japanese captivity.

After the independence of the subcontinent in 1947, and the creation of Pakistan, the battalion was allotted to the new Pakistan Army. The Sikh soldiers from the battalion were transferred to the Indian Army.

14TH Punjab Regiment

22ND Punjabis (3/14TH)

The regiment was raised at Multan on 1ST August 1857, during the upheaval of the Indian Mutiny, as the 11TH Regiment of Punjab Infantry from the men of the 1ST Sikh Infantry and the 3RD Punjab Police Battalion. They were all veterans of the disbanded Sikh army.

The regiment's first overseas service came during the Second Opium War against China. During 1856–1860, British forces fought towards legalization of the opium trade, and to open all of China to British merchants, and to exempt foreign imports from internal transit duties. During the war, the Punjabis took part in the successful assault on Taku Forts on 21ST August 1860. The regiment then advanced with the rest of the British force, arriving at Peking (Beijing) in late September, which was captured on 6TH October. The War resulted in a second group of treaty ports being set up; eventually more than 80 treaty ports were established in China, involving many foreign powers. All foreign traders gained rights to travel within China.

Then the Regiment took part in the Lushai Expedition of 1871 to 1872. The objectives of the expedition were to rescue British subjects who had been captured by the Lushais in raids into Assam and to convince the hill tribes of the region that they had nothing to gain and everything to lose by placing themselves in a hostile position towards the British Government. The expedition was a success, twenty Lushai villages were destroyed, the prisoners were freed, and the hill tribes agreed to negotiated peace terms.

The regiment with its sister regiment, 24TH Punjabis, then took an active part in the Second Afghan War of 1878. June 1878 Russia sent a diplomatic mission to Kabul. British demanded that Sher Ali accept a British mission too. The Amir not only refused to receive a British mission, but threatened to stop it if it were dispatched. Lord Lytton, the viceroy, ordered a diplomatic mission to set out for Kabul in September 1878. The mission was turned back as it approached the eastern entrance of the Khyber Pass, triggering the Second Anglo–Afghan War. The war ended after the British emerged victorious and the Afghans agreed to let the British attain all of their geopolitical objectives from the Treaty of Gandamak. The Afghans were permitted to maintain internal sovereignty but they had to cede control of their nation's foreign relations to the British.

During the Second Afghan War, the Orakzai had proceeded to harass the line of communication of the British force operating in Afghanistan. Early in the 8TH December a force which included the Punjabis, invaded the Orakzai territory. Having destroyed villages on the way the force continued its advance on Zawo, the chief Zaimukh stronghold. The pass leading to Zawo was gained after a short fight. As soon the heights around Zawo had been crowned, a detachment was sent down from the pass to destroy the place, while the main body waited on the Kotal. The Orakzai tendered their submission six days after the destruction of Zawo.

14TH Punjab Regiment

22ND Punjabis (3/14TH)

Subsequent to the reforms brought about in the Indian Army by Lord Kitchener in 1903, the regiment's designation was changed to 22ND Punjabis.

During the First World War, the regiment served in Mesopotamia Campaign. British and Indian troops, sent to the Persian Gulf in early November to protect British oil interests at Abadan, made rapid progress inland against weak Turkish resistance. In less than a month, they had occupied the towns of Basra and Kurna, capturing more than 1,000 Turkish prisoners and losing just 65 of their own men. British forces continued to march steadily up the River Tigris in 1915. By 28 September, they had taken the town of Kut-al-Amara just 120 miles south of Mesopotamia's major city, Baghdad. The tide turned quickly, however, at the Battle of Ctesiphon was a bloody affair, in which Turkish troops withstood heavy casualties to defeat the British attacking forces. More than half of the 8,500 British and Indian troops who fought at Ctesiphon were killed or wounded and 22ND Punjabis suffered 396 casualties out of strength of 814.

Bolstered by 30,000 reinforcements, Turkish troops besieged Kut-al- lasted 147 days, before the 11,800 British and Indian troops inside the garrison town finally surrendered on 29 April 1916.

Despite the setback at Kut-al-Amara, the British position in Mesopotamia was far from hopeless. Indeed, with reinforced troop divisions advanced rapidly up the Tigris in early 1917. Kut-al-Amara was recaptured on 24TH February, and Ctesiphon where the previous British advance had been checked in November 1915, was taken soon afterwards. On 11TH March, British troops finally entered Baghdad. The path was cleared for an advance into northern Mesopotamia, towards the heart of the Turkish Empire in Anatolia.

The British and the Indian Army forces lost 92,000 soldiers in the Mesopotamian campaign. Turkish losses are unknown but the British captured a total of 45,000 prisoners of war. By the end of 1918 the British had deployed 350,000–410,000 men into the area. 112,000 of them were combat troops. The vast majority of the British Empire forces in this campaign were recruited from India.

After the hard fought battles in Mesopotamia the 22ND Punjabis, went on to serve in the Persia Campaign. During the War, Persia declared strict neutrality but was powerless to prevent the two warring sides from operating in their land. The Indian Army units fought a series of actions against the Turks at northern Persian Azerbaijan and western Persia ending with the Armistice of Mudros on October 30TH.

Havildar Lal Singh was awarded the I.OM. while the following Sikh soldiers were awarded the I.D.S.M. for their gallantry during the Great War against the Turks: Havildars Roda Singh, Ganga Singh, Jowala Singh, Hari Singh, Naik Solakhan Singh, Sepoys Mela Singh, Dalip Singh, Mangal Singh, Joga Singh, Partab Singh, Jawala Singh, Jiwan Singh, Narian Singh, and Dhana Singh.

14TH Punjab Regiment

22ND Punjabis (3/14TH)

In 1919, the 22ND Punjabis t fought in the Third Afghan War. The war began on the 6TH May, 1919, and ended with an armistice on 8TH August, 1919. It was essentially a minor tactical victory for the British; in so much as they were able to repel the regular Afghan forces. The Durand line was reaffirmed as the political boundary between British India. The Afghans agreed not to formant trouble on the British side.

In 1921-22, a major reorganization was undertaken in the British Indian Army leading to the formation of large infantry groups of four to six Battalions. Among these was the 14TH Punjab Regiment, formed by grouping the 20TH Punjabis with the 19TH, 21ST, 22ND and 24TH Punjabis, and the 40TH Pathans. The Battalion's new designation was 3RD Battalion, 14TH Punjab Regiment.

During the Second World War, the Battalion fought the Italians in Eritrea. In Eritrea and Abyssinia were a quarter of million Italian and colonial troops, many of excellent quality, two hundred military aircraft, sixty tanks, a hundred armoured cars, ten regiments of Field Artillery and fifty- eight batteries of Pack-Artillery. On July 4TH, the Italian forces in Eritrea crossed the Sudanese border and forced the small British garrison to withdraw. In January 1941, two Indian Divisions, the 4TH and the 5TH launched a counter offensive. From Sudan in the north, they advanced into Eritrea on 19TH January. Battling through mountainous territory, the Indians reached the heavily garrisoned town of Agordat, 160km (100 miles) from the border. On 28TH January it fell after two days of hard fighting. They now made for Keren, Agordat, Barentu, As Teclesan, Asmara, Massawa, pursued and cornered the Italians to Amba Alagi. The Italian troops were attacked by 9000 Indian troops. On 18TH May, Amedeo, Duke of Acosta, surrendered his embattled forces at Amba Alagi.

The 3/14TH Punjab Regiment took active part in the fighting in North Africa. The North African Campaign was fought in the Libyan and Egyptian deserts. The Axis powers aimed to deprive the Allies of access to Middle Eastern oil supplies, to secure and increase Axis access to the oil, and to cut off Britain from the material and human resources of its empire in Asia and Africa During the entire North African campaign, the Germans and Italians suffered 620,000 casualties, while the British Commonwealth lost 220,000 men. The Allied victory in North Africa destroyed or neutralized nearly 900,000 German and Italian troops, opened a second front against the Axis, permitted the invasion of Sicily and the Italian mainland in the summer of 1943, and removed the Axis threat to the oilfields of the Middle East and to British supply lines to Asia and Africa. It was critically important to the course of World War II.

Jemadar Kartar Singh of the 3/14TH Punjab Regiment was awarded the I.O.M. while Havildar Sham Singh, Naik Bela Singh, Sepoys Puran Singh and Tara Singh the I.D.S.M., for gallantry in North Africa in July 1942.

14TH Punjab Regiment

22ND Punjabis (3/14TH)

Finally the 3/14TH Punjab Regiment was ordered to Burma. There were two reasons for the Japanese invasion of Burma. Firstly the Japanese knew it would serve them well if they cut overland access to China from Burma via the famed Burma Road. Along this road a steady stream of military aid was being transported from Rangoon, over the mountains of the 'Hump' and into Nationalist China, but if this supply route was closed, the Japanese could deprive Chiang Kai Shek's Kuomintang (Nationalist Chinese) armies of their life-blood, permitting the Japanese to conquer all China. Furthermore, possession of Burma would place the Japanese at the gate of India, where they believed general insurrection against the British Raj would be ignited once their troops had established themselves in Assam, within reach of Calcutta.

The campaign had a number of notable features. The geographical characteristics of the region meant that factors like weather, disease and terrain had a major effect on operations. The lack of transport infrastructure placed an emphasis on military engineering and air transport to move and supply troops, and evacuate wounded. It was also the only land campaign by the Western Allies in the Pacific Theatre which proceeded continuously from the start of hostilities to the end of the war. By extending from Southeast Asia to India, its area included some lands which the British lost at the outset of the war, but also included areas of India wherein the Japanese advance was eventually stopped. In 1944 Japanese invasion of India ultimately failed following the battles of Imphal and Kohima; and, finally, the successful Allied offensive which reoccupied Burma from late-1944 to mid-1945.

Havildar Arjan Singh awarded the I.O.M, for his gallantry against the Japanese and the citation reads:

"Havildar Arjan Singh was Platoon Havildar of the leading platoon of a Company in its attack on the enemy positions on 15TH January 1944. In the preliminary advance the leading Section Commander was killed and the Company Commander of the flank of the platoon was seriously wounded. Realizing that there was only one feasible quick approach to the enemy's position in the jungle, Arjan Singh, although badly wounded in the arm, led the remainder of the section up a steep track to the final assault. When still short of the enemy position he was killed by a grenade, but by then his leadership had taken the section into the assault and the enemy was routed. He showed complete disregard for his personal safety and by his example the section captured the enemy position without suffering further loss."

Havildars Faqir Singh, Jogindar Singh, Naiks Puran Singh, Gurbaksh Singh and Sepoy Jaimal Singh the I.D.S.M., for his gallantry against the Japanese in 1944.

After the independence of the subcontinent in 1947, and the creation of Pakistan, the battalion was allotted to the new Pakistan Army. The Sikh soldiers from the battalion were transferred to the Indian Army.

14TH Punjab Regiment

24TH Punjabis (4/14TH)

The 24TH Punjabis was raised in 1857, as the 16TH Regiment of Punjab Infantry. It was designated as the 24TH Punjabis in 1903. The regiment was raised on 5 June 1857, during the upheaval of the Indian Mutiny. The class designation of the regiment at the time was Sikhs, Punjabi Mussalmans, Pathans and Dogras. During the Indian Mutiny the only quarter in which trouble arose with any of the border tribes was to the north-west of Rawalpindi beyond the Indus. The Hindustani Fanatics, sustained by assistance in men and money from India, were at the bottom of the outbreak. On July 14TH an outbreak instigated by the Hindustani Fanatics occurred at Narinji. In a surprise attack on July 21ST, 1857, against several attacks by the enemy, the destruction of lower part of the village was carried out. The enemy suffered severely, fifty of mainly Hindustani Fanatics being killed, before the force withdrew. It was not long before another expedition to Narinji had to be undertaken, with a composite force which included the 150 bayonets of the 24TH Punjabis. As soon as the destruction of the village was complete the force was withdrawn without molestation. Three prisoners were taken and they were all subsequently executed. The regiment continued to police the frontier region. In 1868 trouble arose with the Black Mountain tribes. Early on the morning of July 30TH, about 500 tribesmen, attacked a police post, but after a sharp fight were driven off successfully. Reinforcements were sent up immediately, which included the 24TH Punjabis. After the conclusion of the expedition, in which the tribesmen were severely dealt with, the usual raids common on the Indian frontier continued for some years, but punishment was inflicted without difficulty.

The regiment participated in the Second Afghan War of 1878-80, and after taking part in Lord Roberts' 'Kabul to Kandahar' march, fought at the Battle of Kandahar. The Battle of Kandahar was the last major conflict of the Second Anglo-Afghan War. It ended with a decisive British victory, having inflicted nearly 3,000 casualties in total. The Afghans agreed to let the British attain all of their geopolitical objectives from the Treaty of Gandamak. Most of the British and Indian soldiers withdrew from Afghanistan. The Afghans were permitted to maintain internal sovereignty but they had to cede control of their nation's foreign relations to the British.

In 1897 occurred the most formidable outbreak the British arms have been called upon to suppress on the North-West Frontier of India. During a general uprising of Pakhtun tribes, 24TH Punjabis was stationed at Malakand Fort with 45TH Sikhs. The Guides arrived at Malakand on July 27TH, having accomplished a remarkable march under trying conditions of intense heat. The dispositions made for the defence of the post were now as follows: - the 45TH Sikhs and the Guides Infantry, held the interval between the crater and the fort; the 24TH Punjabis were posted to the west of the crater, and remainder of the force guarded the camp in the centre. The serai was garrisoned by twenty-five men of the 31ST Punjab Infantry.

14TH Punjab Regiment

24TH Punjabis (4/14TH)

On the 27TH the tribesmen attacked all along the line, but were repulsed everywhere, except at the serai, which was held with great gallantry, till the enemy succeeded in setting it on fire, and so compelled the garrison to fall back on the main position. At dawn on the 28TH a successful counter-attack was made by the 24TH Punjabis, which not only inflicted a loss of about 100 men on the enemy, but produced a most salutary moral effect on the attacking troops. During the 29TH, the enemy attacked again, where the 24TH Punjabis were stationed. The fighting was of a most desperate character, but the Punjabis stood firm and repulsed all attacks. The relief of Malakand garrison was accomplished on July 31ST. Subsequent to the reforms brought about in the Indian Army in 1903, the regiment's designation was changed to 24TH Punjabis.

During the First World War the regiment served in Egypt and then in Mesopotamia, Salonika and the Russian Transcaucasia. Great Britain declared was against Turkey on 5TH, 1914. Egypt's strategic importance lay in its possession of the Suez Canal, a waterway regarded with good reason by the Turks as the jugular vein of the British Empire. The Indian army regiments took over the first-line defence of the Suez Canal.

After the 24TH Punjabis carried out their defensive duties on the Suez Canal, they were ordered to Mesopotamia. The Turkish Commander Suleiman Askeri had about 4,000 regular soldiers, including a large number of irregular Arabs and Kurds, numbering maybe 14,000, for a total of 18,000 personnel. He chose to attack the British positions around Shaiba, Southwest of Basra. The British garrison at Shaiba consisted of about 7,000 men in a fortified camp. On 12TH April, the Turkish attack on the British camp was repulsed. Next day 2ND Dorset and 24TH Punjabis routed the Arab irregulars, capturing 400 and dispersing the rest. The Turkish regular troops fell back on Barjisiya Wood. The Dorset and the Punjabis then launched a bayonet charge that overwhelmed the rest of the Turks. The enemy was forced to retire on Nasiriyah, with a loss of 3,000 killed and wounded and 700 prisoners.

Following the successive defeats of their forces and their continued withdrawal further up country, the Turks concentrated around the town of Kut-al-Amara, with extensive defence lines on both sides of the Tigres around Es Sinn. The battle to take Kut-al-Amara from the Turks began on 27TH September and lasted for two full days, and successively drove them out their positions, forcing them back on Ctesiphon. British casualties amounted to 1,233 men, including many slightly wounded, while the Turks lost over 4,000, including 1,153 prisoners. Distinctions were won by the Sikh soldiers of 20TH, 22ND, 24TH, 76TH Punjabis, 7TH Hariana Lancers, 16TH Cavalry, the Sappers and Miners, and 34TH Signal Company. "The battle of Kut-al-Amara will be remembered as one of the most brilliant actions, possibly the most brilliant fought by the Indian Army." (Chandler)

14TH Punjab Regiment

24TH Punjabis (4/14TH)

Turks were driven back across the Diala, but at a very heavy cost. The Infantry lost 4,000 out of the 8,500 engaged, and even the Cavalry lost 200 out of 1,200. The, who had been strongly re-inforced, counter attacked strenuously on the night of 23RD, but was resolutely repulsed with heavy loss. Exhausted and outnumbered the British retreated to Kut-al-Amara on 2ND December. Thus began the siege of Kut-al-Amara. The failure of the attempt to break through and reach Kut-al-Amara spelled the end for the garrison, strained to the limits of its endurance by hunger and disease the garrison surrendered after siege of 147 days. The 24TH Rifles were captured and went into captivity. The 24TH Punjabis returned to Mesopotamia in April 1917, after reforming, and fought in the Battle of Khan Baghdadi.

Subedar Sohan Singh, Subedar Ujagar Singh, Havildar Sundar Singh (Posthumous), Jemadar Mangal Singh, Jemadar Lachman Singh, Naik Labh Singh I.D.S.M., Naik Bhag Singh, Lance-Naik Lal Singh, Lance-Naik Parmodh Singh, Lance-Naik Pal Singh (Posthumous) were awarded the I.O.M. Jemadar Sohan Singh was awarded the Military Cross and Subedar Ujagar Singh, Havildars Bhagwan Singh, Mangal Singh, Kesar Singh, Tahl Singh, Naiks Labh Singh, Kharak Singh, Bhagat Singh, Lachman Singh, Lance-Naiks Pal Singh, Ganda Singh, Lala Singh, Sepoys Vir Singh, Ram Singh, Jiwan Singh, Thakar Singh, Kishen Singh, Pal Singh, Lal Singh, Amar Singh, Kishen Singh, Kartar Singh and Labh Singh, were awarded the I.D.S.M., for theirs conspicuous gallantry in battle against the Turks in Mesopotamia.

In 1921-22, a major reorganization was undertaken in the British Indian Army leading to the formation of large infantry groups of four to six Battalions. Among these was the 14TH Punjab Regiment, formed by grouping the 20TH Punjabis with the 19TH, 21ST, 22ND and 24TH Punjabis, and the 40TH Pathans. The Battalion's new designation was 4TH Battalion, 14TH Punjab Regiment.

During the Second World War, the Battalion saw service in Burma. The Burma Campaign was fought primarily between the forces British Indian forces and the forces of the Japanese Empire. The campaign had a number of notable features. The geographical characteristics of the region meant that factors like weather, disease and terrain had a major effect on operations. The lack of transport infrastructure placed an emphasis on military engineering and air transport to move and supply troops, and evacuate wounded. It was also the only land campaign by the Western Allies in the Pacific Theatre which proceeded continuously from the start of hostilities to the end of the war. By extending from Southeast Asia to India, its area included some lands which the British lost at the outset of the war, but also included areas of India wherein the Japanese advance was eventually stopped. In 1944 Japanese invasion of India ultimately failed following the battles of Imphal and Kohima; and, finally, the successful Allied offensive which reoccupied Burma from late-1944 to mid-1945. The 4TH Battalion fought with great distinction against the Japanese in Burma.

14TH Punjab Regiment

24TH Punjabis (4/14TH)

On the Japanese advance towards India, the 4/14TH Punjab Regiment fought an action, to delay their advance, during which Subedar Gurbux Singh was awarded the Military Cross, on 19TH January 1944, .the citation for the award reads:

"Subedar Gurbux Singh was second in command of 'A' Company, when the Company carried out an attack on the enemy position on the Windwin feature 5648 0n 15TH January 1944. Early in the action the Company Commander, with two platoons, carried out an encircling attack on the enemy and was seriously wounded. On receiving the information Subedar Gurbux Singh went forward from the covering platoon and on arrival he found that with the Company Commander the Leading Platoon Commander was also wounded and the Platoon Havildar killed. He reorganized these two platoons, under heavy grenade fire, and pressed home the attack. This was carried out with great dash, largely through Subedar Gurbux Singh's leadership, and the position was taken. On 17TH January 1944, the Company was attacked from the rear by approximately one platoon of the enemy. The attack lasted for two hours and was repulsed. Subedar Gurbux Singh again showed great coolness in the control of his Company. During these actions Subedar Gurbux Singh has shown personal courage and powers leadership of high order."

March 1944, the Imperial Japanese Army invaded India. As the available British and Indian forces were besieged in Imphal, there was a danger that Japanese units would infiltrate through the Lushai Hills, which were rugged and heavily forested, but not guarded other than by lightly armed levies. To guard against this threat, the commander of the British Fourteenth Army, Lieutenant General William Slim, formed four independent Indian infantry battalions into an ad hoc brigade, the Lushai Brigade, which included the sister battalion the 7/14TH Punjab Regiment. The Japanese did not try to cross the Lushai Hills, instead concentrating their force in this sector at Bishenpur, south of Imphal. Their lines of communications ran along a rough track from Tiddim. In July, Slim ordered the Lushai Brigade to interfere with these Japanese communications. As the monsoon ended, the brigade began moving south along the Gangaw Valley, to cover the right flank of Fourteenth Army. As the Lushai Brigade was thus employed the 4/14TH Punjab Regiment was rushed to deal with considerable enemy force confronting the Chin Levies in the hills north of Saw. The 4/14TH Punjab Regiment helped to successfully block the Japanese advance towards Bishenpur. On the 7TH February 1945, as the 7TH Indian Division started to cross the Irrawaddy, and the leading battalion of 114TH Brigade in hand-to-hand fighting cleared the way, allowed the 4/14TH Punjab Regiment, which had rejoined its brigade after dealing with a Japanese detachment in the hills north of Saw, to by-pass Kanha. The brigade, with 4/14TH Punjab, then pushed eastwards, and closed on Pakokku; the village was found resolutely defended by the Japanese 214TH Regiment, whose rearguard had caused the delay at Kanha.

14TH Punjab Regiment

24TH Punjabis (4/14TH)

The 1/11TH Sikhs had meanwhile found Myitche clear and had moved south-west to collect country boats and find a place from which it could cross to Pagan. The capture of Kanha on the 10TH was the signal for Slim to order 14TH Army's general advance to begin.

The 7TH Division had begun operations to clear the Nyaungu-Myingyan-Taungtha- Welaung area and the task of protecting 1V Corp's right flank against counter-attack from the Chauk and Saw areas. The 114TH Brigade, which had completed the clearance of Pakokku on the 21ST, was ordered to send 4/14TH Punjab Regiment to help 28TH (E.A.) Brigade at Letse, where it had dug itself in after being driven back from Seikpyu, and take over the left sector of Nyaungu bridgehead to release 33RD Brigade for operations to clear Myingyan and Taungtha. The 89TH Brigade, holding the right sector, had meanwhile steadily increased pressure towards Chauk to prevent any forces from the oilfield area moving towards Meiktilla.

By 28TH February the operations of 4/14TH Punjab Regiment and a squadron of tanks against the flank and communications of the enemy force attacking the East Africans at Letse had restored the situation on the right flank. The 89TH Brigade in a series of hard fought actions had driven the Japanese from strong positions, which ran from the Kyaukpadaung road to Irrawaddy at Monatkon.

The 4/14TH Punjab Regiment had taken part in the second phase for the battle for Meiktilla, when it took pressure off the 28TH Brigade, by coming to its assistance. On the 11TH the battalion while acting as a floater battalion outside the defended area successfully attacked a strong Japanese position at Saka covering Myingyan. On the 17TH March enemy pressure in both the Letse and Chauk sectors increased considerably. At Letse, a heavy attack was made on the 21ST, after five hours bombardment of the defences held by the East Africans. Two posts were overrun and some Japanese reached the supply area. The enemy was eventually driven back with the help of 4/14TH Punjab Regiment, leaving behind 251 dead. About half of these lay in the barbed wire entanglement on to which they had hurled themselves regardless of whether or not it had been cut.

Early in 1945, 14TH Army continued to advance, no longer in the jungle but in the open plains of upper Burma. Mandalay fell in March, and Slim conducted a brilliant crossing of the mighty Irrawaddy before heading south. In the Arakan, the Japanese had to be winkled out of strong positions before Rangoon was taken on 3RD May. The 4/14TH Punjab Regiment had fought the fanatical enemy throughout the Burma campaign. The Punjabis went back to the Punjab and had to contend with the butchering of their homeland. The policy of divide and rule had prevailed!

After the independence of the subcontinent in 1947, and the creation of Pakistan, the battalion was allotted to the new Pakistan Army. The Sikh soldiers from the battalion were transferred to the Indian Army.

14TH Punjab Regiment

21ST Punjabis (10/14TH)

The regiment was raised in 1857, during the upheaval of the Indian Mutiny, as the 9TH Regiment of Punjab Infantry, from the men of the 3RD and 6TH Punjab Infantry. The class designation of the regiment at the time was Sikhs, Punjabi Mussalmans, Pathans and Dogras. During the Indian Mutiny the only quarter in which trouble arose with any of the border tribes was to the north-west of Rawalpindi beyond the Indus. The Hindustani Fanatics, sustained by assistance in men and money from India, were at the bottom of the outbreak.

Three months had elapsed since the destruction of Narinji, in which the Punjabis had taken part, when an attack on the British Assistant Commissioner of the district encamped at Shekh Jana, rendered another punitive expedition necessary. The force which included the Punjab Infantry assembled in the following spring near Nowshera. On April 26TH the first column started via Daran Pass, for Chinglai, which was occupied and destroyed almost without opposition. Another hostile stronghold at Mangal Thana was destroyed on April 29TH. On May 3RD the force proceeded against the last remaining Hindustani stronghold at Sittana; the enemy was caught by a cross-fire and after a short hand-to-hand struggle, every Hindustani in the position was either killed or taken prisoner. Before the troops left the neighbourhood an ultimatum was sent to the clans inhabiting the hilly country west of Sittana, requiring them to into an agreement not to assist the Hindustani fanatics in any way. The British terms were complied with, and the force marched back to Nowshera.

Then the regiment took part in the Abyssinian Campaign of 1867-68. Emperor Tewodros II of Ethiopia, then known as Theodore imprisoned several missionaries and two representatives of the British government in an attempt to get the attention of the British government, which had decided against his requests for military assistance. The punitive expedition launched by the British in response required the transportation of a sizable military force hundreds of miles across mountainous terrain lacking any road system. The formidable obstacles to the action were overcome; the Ethiopian capital captured and rescued all the hostages.

The regiment with its sister regiments then took an active part in the Second Afghan War of 1878. The war ended after the British emerged victorious against the Afghan rebels and the Afghans agreed to let the British attain all of their geopolitical objectives from the Treaty of Gandamak. The Afghans were permitted to maintain internal sovereignty but they had to cede control of their nation's foreign relations to the British. Most of the British and Indian soldiers withdrew from Afghanistan. After the conclusion of the Afghan War, an expedition that included the Punjab Infantry was mounted against the Mahsuds to exact punishment for a long list of outrages committed before and during the Second Afghan War. The force left Tank on April 18, 1881, and reached Jandola four days later.

14TH Punjab Regiment

21ST Punjabis (10/14TH)

The advance continued up the difficult Shahur Gorge on April 24TH, and thence into the Khaisora Valley. Very few of the enemy were seen, property of all kinds was devastated, and the submission of some of the neighbouring clans received. On May 4TH a small engagement occurred at Shah Alam, where the enemy had taken up a strong position on some wooded hills. Three battalions were detailed for the attack, supported by guns and another battalion in the centre; but just as the assaulting infantry had got into position, the tribesmen charged down the left of the battalion, who, however, stood firm, and following close the enemy's heels when the latter fell back, rapidly gained the possession of the position. During these operations the purdah had been effectively lifted and the tribesmen overawed, but the absence of any decisive military success somewhat discounted the value of these results. The Mahsuds failed to comply fully with the British terms, so it was necessary to continue the blockade, which lasted till September 7^{TH,} 1881, when despairing of outside assistance; the Mahsuds finally complied with the last demand.

The summer of 1897 found the Northwest Frontier border in an inflammable condition. The tribes in the Swat Valley, with whom peaceable arrangements had been made, and to whose chiefs large subsidies had been promised and paid, commenced an outbreak. The Malakand Field Force that included the Punjab Infantry was assembled at Nowshera. The post at Malakand was reached on 1ST August, and on the following day Chakdara was relieved.

The Mohmands was immediately dealt with, and against them the two brigades of Sir Bindon Blood's division advanced from Malakand simultaneously with the movement of another division under Major-General Edmond Elles from Pashawar; it was intended that the two columns should affect a junction in Bajour. About 6TH September the two forces advanced, and Major-General Blood reached Nawagai on 14TH September, having detached a brigade to cross the Rambat Pass. This brigade being sharply attacked in camp at Markhanai at the foot of the pass on the night of the 14TH was ordered to turn northwards and punish the tribesmen of the Mamund valley. On the 15TH a retirement was ordered, the tribesmen following, and when darkness fell, the general, with a battery and a small escort, was cut off, and with difficulty defended some buildings until relieved. The casualties in this action numbered 149. This partial reverse placed General Blood in a position of some difficulty. He determined, however, to remain at Nawagai, awaiting the arrival of General Elles, and sent orders to General Jeffreys to prosecute the operations in the Mamund valley.

From the 18TH to the 23RD these operations were carried on successfully, several villages being burned and the Mohmunds were disheartened. Meanwhile, the camp at Nawagai was heavily attacked on the night of the 20TH by about 4000 men belonging to the Hadda Mullah's following. The attack was repulsed with loss and on the 21ST Generals Blood and Elles met at Lakarai.

14TH Punjab Regiment

21ST Punjabis (10/14TH)

After marching into Buner, and revisiting the scenes of the Umbeyla Campaign of 1863, the Malakand Field-Force was broken up on the 21ST of January. The objects of the expedition were completely attained, in spite of the great natural difficulties of the country. The employment of imperial service troops with the Pashawar column marked a new departure in frontier campaigns.

Subsequent to the reforms brought about in the Indian Army in 1903, the regiment's designation was changed to 21ST Punjabis.

On April 20TH, 1908, news was received the Mohmands were preparing to attack the border posts, that the shots had already been exchanged already, and that casualties to British troops had occurred at Matta. Mohmand Field Force, that included the 21ST Punjabis, was mobilised to deal with the uprising. The tribesmen received severe a rude shock as almost the whole country was overrun by the force under Sir James Wilcocks. The Mohmand Expedition of 1908 was thus brought to a close. Twenty days sufficed since the invasion of their country began to reduce this important tribe to submission. The cost of the Expedition was estimated at £10,000, and the total casualties of British and Indian troops were 97 dead and 218 wounded.

During the First World War, the regiment served in Egypt and Palestine. In Egypt it became part of the force guarding the Suez Canal. At this time the Canal was threatened by a Turkish force which, having crossed the Sinai Desert, was defeated in an attempt to cross the Canal and invade Egypt, and had withdrawn into Sinai. The regiment's chief was to protect the Canal and prevent the enemy from laying mines in it under cover of darkness. Reconnaissance patrols were pushed forward to the Milta Pass, and every effort was made to improve the Canal defences. Detachments were employed on garrison duty at posts in the Sinai Peninsula.

In 1918, it took part in the final triumph in the Palestine Campaign at the Battle of Megiddo. General Allenby by series of carefully concealed moves had concentrated his infantry on the coast quite unperceived by the Turks. He now planned to break through to the rear of the Turks, surround them, and destroyed them. He achieved complete success. On 19TH September, the big attack commenced with six divisions on a very short front, and over 300 guns putting down a huge barrage. Thereafter, all resistance had ceased and victory was complete. The brilliant attack had led to the annihilation of Turkish Army in Palestine. Subsequently, in February 1919 the regiment was ordered back to India.

In 1922 the 21ST Punjabis were grouped with the 19TH, 20TH, 22ND, 24TH Punjabis, and 40^T Pathans to form the 14TH Punjab Regiment. The battalion was redesignated as 10TH (Training) Battalion of the 14TH Punjab Regiment. During the Second World War, 10/14TH Punjab was converted into the 14TH Punjab Regimental Centre. In 1947, the 14TH Punjab Regiment was allocated to Pakistan Army. The Sikhs were routed to India, to join the India Army.

15TH Punjab Regiment

25TH Punjabis (1/15TH)

25TH Punjabis was raised in 1857, as the 17TH Regiment of Punjab Infantry. It was designated as the 25TH Punjabis in 1903. The regiment was raised by Captain R Larkins at Mian Mir, Lahore on 8TH June 1857, during the upheaval of the Indian Mutiny. The recruits were mostly Sikhs, Punjabi Mussalmans, and Dogras. The regiment's opportunity for active service came in 1878, when it took part in the Second Afghan War, where it fought in the Battles of Ahmad Khel and Kandahar. The war ended after the British emerged victorious against the Afghan rebels and the Afghans agreed to let the British attain all of their geopolitical objectives from the Treaty of Gandamak.

In 1895 the 25TH Punjabis formed a part Chitral Relief Force. The Chitral Relief Force was sent by the British authorities to relieve the fort at Chitral which was under siege after a local coup. After the death of the old ruler, power changed hands several times. An intervening British force of about 400 men was besieged in the fort until it was relieved by two expeditions, a small one from Gilgit and a large one from Pashawar. 25TH Punjabis formed part of the British force assembled at Pashawar under Major-General Sir Robert Low. On April 3RD they stormed the Malakand Pass which was defended by 12,000 local warriors. There were significant engagements and 10 days later. Low was still crossing the Lowarai Pass on the day Kelly entered Chitral. Although Kelly got to Chitral first, it was the massive size of Low's force that forced the enemy to withdraw.

In 1897 occurred the most formidable outbreak the British arms have ever been called upon to suppress on the North-West Frontier India. The rebellion started with an attack by the Madda Khel section of the Waziris in June 1897. The Tochi Valley Field Force was assembled and included 25TH Punjabis. The rebellion was finally put down in October 1897.The record of the operations of the Tochi Field Force, was one of struggles against climate and nature rather than the human enemy. The swollen Indus River, the heat, and the scarcity of water, were typical of the chief difficulties to be overcome by the troops.

Subsequent to the reforms brought about in the Indian Army in 1903, the regiments' designation remained as 25TH Punjabis.

In 1908, the Zakha Khel Afridis began raiding from the Bazaar Valley in the Tribal areas across the North West Frontier of India. This encouraged raids by the Mohmunds, who threatened Shabkadar Fort. By using surprise and rapid movement, a force that included the 25TH Punjabis, subdued the Afridis and the Mohmunds within a fortnight in February 1908.

Subedar Indar Singh and Havildar Sadhu Singh were awarded the I.D.S.M., for their gallantry in action against the tribesmen on the North-West Frontier.

As result of the First Opium War, and Chinese fear of British military threats, Hong Kong was awarded to the British in January 1841. In China the success of the Wuchang Uprising on 10TH October 1911, started a chain reaction, and in less than two months 14 out of the 18 provinces within China's main borders had declared independence.

15TH Punjab Regiment

25TH Punjabis (1/15TH)

The imperial regime had been overthrown and replaced by a republican system, signifying a new era of modern China. During this period in 1911, the 25TH Punjabis moved to Hong Kong to protect British interests.

On the outbreak of the First World War, the regiment returned from Hong Kong to India. In December 1917, it moved to Mesopotamia as part of the 54TH Indian Brigade of 18TH (Indian) Division. The brigade was formed from the regiments transferred directly from India, so time was needed for them to become acclimatized. 25TH Punjabis remained with the brigade at the Iron Bridge near Baghdad, until September, 1918. In the vicinity of Baghdad they did much useful work on the railway embankments at Diala, Bawi, and Bustan. While in Mesopotamia the 25TH Punjabis were involved in hard marches up the Tigres to Daur and again from Tigres to Tekrit; and fought actions at Daur and Nejef; during which Havildar Sawan Singh and Lance-Naik Arjan Singh were awarded the I.D.S.M., for their conspicuous gallantry in battle.

At the beginning of September 1918, the regiment moved to Salonika in Greece and then to Turkey as part of the Allied occupation forces. It returned to India in 1921 and was ordered for immediate service in Waziristan.

Havildar Hari Singh, Jemadar Bhagwan Singh, Lance-Naik Harnam Singh and Sepoy Bishan Singh were awarded the I.D.S.M., for their gallantry in action in Waziristan.

In 1921-22, a major reorganization was undertaken in the British Indian Army leading to the formation of large infantry groups of four to six Battalions. Among these was the 15TH Punjab Regiment, formed by grouping the 25TH Punjabis with the 26TH, 27TH, 28TH and 29TH Punjabis. The Battalion's new designation was 1ST Battalion, 15TH Punjab Regiment.

During the Second World War, the battalion fought in the Burma Campaign with great distinction. During 1941 and early 1942, the Japanese army had driven Allied troops (British and Indian) from Burma. During 1943, the Allies had tried a limited offensive into Arakan, the coastal province of Burma. The aim had been to secure Akyab Island at the end of the Mayu Peninsula. The island possessed an important airfield, which featured prominently in Allied plans to recapture Burma. This offensive had failed disastrously. During the following months, the Allies reorganised, engaged in extensive jungle training, and prepared for a renewed effort in 1944.

1/15TH Punjab Regiment as part of the 19TH Division took part in an offensive in Arakan. During the period 16TH November 1944 to 15TH February 1945, Subedar Hari Singh, a Platoon Commander of 'A' Company, has shown initiative and personal courage of the highest order on several occasions. On 25TH January at the Ngapyin Bridgehead, in Burma, 'A' Company was sent out to investigate the result of an air strike, which had been made about 200 yards outside the Brigade perimeter. Subedar Hari Singh's platoon was leading and had completed its first bound.

15TH Punjab Regiment

25TH Punjabis (1/15TH)

Subedar Hari Singh was between the two leading sections and had signalled his right hand section Bren gun to move forward slightly. As the Bren gun section moved forward the enemy opened fire and the No 1of the Bren gun was killed. At the same time fire was opened on the Subedar from his right and front. With great coolness Hari Singh ordered his Platoon Havildar to man the right hand Bren gun and engage the enemy's Light Machine Guns. Four enemies were killed but the Light Machine Guns were not silenced. Simultaneously a party of about 20 Japanese charged the Platoon position and was engaged by the left hand section, 7 enemies being killed. The Platoon was then was ordered to withdraw and Subedar Hari Singh carried out the withdrawal with exceptional ability. Under cover of 2-inch Mortar and Light Machine Gun fire he withdrew the Platoon group by group without suffering further casualties and bringing back his dead. On several previous occasions Subedar Hari Singh's Platoon had borne the brunt of strong enemy attacks during the establishment of the Bridgeheads. The excellent control and personal example displayed by Subedar Hari Singh enabled the Platoon to inflict many casualties on the enemy, with little loss to the platoon. At all times Subedar Hari Singh has been an outstanding example to his fellow Viceroy's Commissioned Officers. Subedar Hari Singh was awarded the Military Cross.

A company of the 1/15TH Punjab Regiment was attached to the 62ND Brigade, of 19TH Division, when it relieved the 64TH at Kyaukmyaung on the 27TH March 1945, and the infantry in the Kabwe bridgehead was increased to five battalions. No sooner had this relief been completed than an enemy counter-attack supported by artillery, including heavy field guns, nearly reached the brigade headquarters before it was finally thrown back. The pursuit by part of the brigade reserve ended in hand-to-hand fighting far outside the bridgehead perimeter.

On 11TH May at Seitpudaung in Burma, Jemadar Kesar Singh was in command of a fighting Patrol, which suddenly encountered the Japanese in considerably great strength. The Patrol came under heavy fire from Japanese automatic fire and four of the platoon was wounded immediately, including Jemadar Kesar Singh. As a large party of enemy move round the right flank, ignoring his own wounds Jemadar Kesar Singh fought back inflicting losses on them, and by skilful disposition and his own example of steadiness under fire, extricated his platoon, taking his casualties to Paddaukon Village. The Japanese in greatly superior numbers again attacked and attempted to surround him, but Jemadar Kesar Singh again fought back hard inflicting casualties and skilfully extricating his platoon again. He made repeated contact with the enemy and finding all routes blocked by superior numbers of the enemy took up a defensive position for the night. Next day he continued to encounter superior numbers of Japanese and continued to fight back stoutly, inflicting more casualties on the enemy and succeeding in safeguarding his own increasing casualties.

15TH Punjab Regiment

25TH Punjabis (1/15TH)

By ignoring his own wounds and by his cheerfulness and personal example, the Jemadar heartened the wounded that they too made light of their wounds. On the third day Jemadar Kesar Singh although in pain so inspired his platoon that they continued in excellent fighting spirit, fought their way back to their Company line and brought in all their wounded and identifications of enemy killed. The platoon had been out for 56 hours surrounded by enemy, and, though short of food, had covered many miles in thick jungle and fought with conspicuous success, inflicting many casualties on the enemy. It was Jemadar Kesar Singh's high standard of military skill and leadership, his complete disregard of personal safety, his steadiness, determination and example that inspired his men to such heights of endurance. Jemadar Kesar Singh was awarded Military Cross.

Lieutenant Sucha Singh was commanding 'D' Company, 1/15TH Punjab Regiment during the Kama Bridgehead operations near Prome in Burma. On the 27TH May 1945, the Company was ordered to move its position to the right in order to close up with the next Company and block a possible escape route of the Japanese in the Bridgehead. Owing to late receipt of the orders only two platoons of the Company had reached the new position and were not dug in when the Japanese put in their first attack. This was repulsed with heavy loss to the enemy. The third platoon came up before dusk and the defensive position was dug, but not wired, as none could be brought up. A further attack by the Japanese was also beaten off. During the night and altogether seven attacks were put in by the Japanese on this position, which proved that it lay across and important Japanese escape route. Twice during these attacks, the direction of which was from three sides, the Japanese penetrated the position but were driven out by grenades and the bayonet. Throughout the engagement Lieutenant Sucha Singh directed the defence with utmost coolness and determination, encouraging the Company with cheering remarks. During one attack he killed a Japanese soldier who was creeping up unnoticed along a covered approach. His communications throughout the night was only by 48 set to the next Company, and his N.C.O.'s set did not work. Nevertheless he passed all orders through his set with complete coolness and caused most accurate artillery defensive fire to be brought down in front of his position. The Company counted forty-eight dead Japanese bodies' around the position the next morning and the Company had suffered four killed and seven wounded. The leadership of Lieutenant Sucha Singh throughout the whole engagement was of the highest order and contributed very largely to the successful defence of the position and the blocking of one important Jap escape route. In view of the fact that the officer was a subaltern commanding a Company for the first time in action, his performance is considered especially outstanding." Lieutenant Sucha Singh was awarded Military Cross.

The immediate task given to the Corps was to capture Mandalay and destroy all enemy forces defending it. On the day these orders were issued 19TH Division had the 98TH Brigade on the north bank of Chaungmagyi Chaung.

15TH Punjab Regiment

25TH Punjabis (1/15TH)

The 'Stiletto Force' with 1/15TH Punjab Regiment standing ready to strike south as soon the engineers reported the tanks crossing ready. During the 7TH 'Stiletto Force' advanced to within a few miles of Kabaing. The Force passed through the village unopposed that night and on the 8TH burst through the northern outskirts of Mandalay, scattering small parties of surprised Japanese and seeing the northern slopes of the pagoda-crowned Mandalay Hill.

"During 16TH November to 15TH February 1945, Jemadar Kapur Singh has been an outstanding example to his fellow Viceroy Commissioned Officers for his courage and initiative. On several occasions his Platoon was heavily attacked by the enemy and in particular on the night of 22/23RD January 1945 in the Ngapyin Bridgehead. Attacks started at 1230 hours and immediately his Platoon suffered casualties. One section was completely disabled having four men killed and 2 wounded, leaving a dangerous gap. With a composite section drawn from his Platoon Headquarters and remaining two sections he continued to deny the ground to the enemy until he was reinforced. The attacks continued throughout the night and Jemadar Kapur Singh, under heavy fire moved amongst his section posts, exhorting his men with complete disregard for his own safety. In a later action a few days later Jemadar Kapur Singh was wounded while leading his Platoon. Throughout the operations Jemadar Kapur Singh has set a high example of courage and determination." Jemadar Kapur Singh was awarded the Military Cross on 28TH August 1945.

On the 8TH the 2ND British and 20TH Indian Divisions begin to break out of the bridgeheads over the Irrawaddy to the west of Mandalay. On the 9TH, 19TH Indian Division reaches the outskirts of Mandalay. On the 11TH Mongmit is captured by a converging attack by the two brigades of the British 36th Division which moved in from the west. On the 12TH Myotha, falls to the 20TH Indian Division. On the 14TH Maymo, to the east of Mandalay is taken by the 62ND Indian Brigade. The last rail line to Mandalay is therefore cut. Other units of the 19TH Indian Division are still fighting in Mandalay but have captured much of the city in a bitter house to house engagement. On the 17th the heavy fighting in Mandalay and around Meiktilla continues. On the 19TH the 19TH Indian Division completes the capture of Mandalay. The 1/15TH Punjab Regiment went on to fight at the battles of Taungtha, The Irrawaddy, Yenangyaung, Kama, Taungoo and Sittang. In the Arakan, the Japanese had to be winkled out of strong positions before Rangoon was taken on 3RD May. Jemadar Chanan Singh, Jemadar Kartar Singh, and Naik Amar Singh were awarded the I.D.S.M., for their gallantry in action during the Burma Campaign. The 1/15TH Punjab Regiment went back to India at the end of the Burma Campaign.

After the independence of the subcontinent in 1947, and the creation of Pakistan, the battalion was allotted to the new Pakistan Army. The Sikh soldiers from the battalion were transferred to the Indian Army.

15^(TH) Punjab Regiment

26^(TH) Punjabis (2/15^(TH))

The 26^(TH) Punjabis was raised in 1857, as the 18^(TH) Regiment of Punjab Infantry. It was designated as the 26^(TH) Punjabis in 1903. The regiment was raised by Captain HT Bartlett at Pashawar in June 1857, during the upheaval of the Indian Mutiny. The manpower consisted of Sikhs, Pathans, Punjabi Mussalmans, and Dogras.

Barely two months after the first recruit had been enlisted; the regiment had been called out to help against the 51^(ST) Bengal Native Infantry, who mutinied. On August 28^(TH) the lines of the 51^(ST) Bengal Native Infantry were overhauled by some Afridi levies of the 18^(TH) Regiment of Punjab Infantry, who freely taunted and abused the unarmed Hindustani Sepoys. The work over, the Sepoys were ordered to move out to a camp on the British side of the cantonment. Thinking they were to be killed, and seeing the piled arms of a newly-raised Sikh regiment within reach, in a mad rush for self-preservation they made for the arms, fought desperately for few minutes, then broke and fled towards the Khyber Pass. Then followed a wild chase by Sikhs and Afridis, and before Jamrud was reached, the last of the 700 panic-stricken Sepoys had been shot down.

In April 1858, the regiment joined the Yuzufzai Field Force near Nowshera. They took part in the capture of Chinglai and Mangal Thana on April 26^(TH) and 29^(TH), and in the subsequent attack of May 4^(TH), upon the headquarters of the colony of the Hindustani fanatics at Sittana. The regiment in a hand-to-hand struggle of several minutes either killed or took prisoner every Hindustani Fanatic in the position. Subedar Sahib Singh was awarded the I.O.M., for gallantry on this occasion.

In 1859, a detachment of 500 strong, joined part of the Trans-Gogra Brigade under Brigadier Holdich on the Nepal Frontier. They were tasked with shutting up the Nepal Passes, while the Gurkha Force under the Maharajah Jung Bahadur captured or dispersed the last remnant of the Sepoy mutineers, who fled into Nepal. This duty was most effectively done, and Brigadier Holdich has had the satisfaction of transferring to the Civil authorities a very considerable number of rebel chiefs who were captured by the Maharajah, and the precaution taken by the Brigadier to prevent their escape when they were pursued by the Gurkhas, having been eminently successful. In 1860 the regiment stayed at Gondah for the whole year. In December on being called upon to volunteer for China, almost the whole regiment came forward, but they were not sent.

In August 1865, the regiment received orders for service in Bhutan, during the ensuing cold season. They were to provide their own transport train of mules and ponies. They arrived at Dewanigiri in Bhutan on December 12^(TH.) On February 4^(TH) 1866, three companies advanced to Saleeka, where the enemy showed some resistance; and the force subsequently pursued the enemy to the chain bridge over the River Monass, which was taken and held by the force. A couple of day's later headquarters and the remainder of the Punjabis followed this wing, and the whole advanced to Monass Bridge.

15TH Punjab Regiment

26TH Punjabis (2/15TH)

On February 23RD, the Punjabis were ordered to move to the front across the Monass Bridge. This movement, however, was hardly completed when the British guns which had been captured by the enemy in the previous year were brought into camp. As the recovery of these was the whole object of the campaign, the troops were ordered to return to Dewanigiri, and the regiment then proceeded to Aliport where they encamped. For the next few years nothing of much importance happened to the Regiment. During the Second Afghan War, the Regiment garrisoned the city of Kandahar, and marched back to Sialkot on April 1879.

On March 4TH 1886, the regiment was ordered to go to Burma and join the Burma Field Force. It arrived at Rangoon on March 15TH, and was ordered to assist in the operations against the dacoits, and was sent to scour the country under several officers. Immediately on the regiment's arrival at Mandalay, a column was dispatched to Mausi against a refractory tribe of Kachin. The expedition, being unsuccessful, had to retire, and Subedar Raja Singh, who covered the retirement, was very highly spoken of by Captain Wace for the manner in which he behaved.

On December 8TH a detachment of about 60 men at Shwekee Gee, was attacked by dacoits, but after six hours' heavy fighting the dacoits were driven off with much loss. Subedar Lakhmir Singh, who headed two sorties, behaved with great coolness and judgement on this occasion, and was admitted to the Order of British India. Two companies of the Regiment took part in the expedition against the Wuntho Swaha, and were well spoken of. The Regiment returned to Meerut in March 1887. Thirty-six Sikhs of the regiment had volunteered for and been transferred to the Burma Police, and were formed into Mounted Infantry. The detachment under Havildar Atma Singh did splendid service. Atma Singh and his troopers had only carbines, and they showed wonderful pluck in their gallant charge. In this fight Naik Rur Singh fought with great gallantry.

On May 11TH 1896, the regiment was mobilised for service in Egypt. The regiment reached Suakin on May 30TH, but was then ordered to form the garrison of Tokar, where it was destined to spend five long months. They were employed on the unattractive, but important duty of holding Suakin, and the surrounding country, during the operations in Sudan. The regiment left Tokar on November 7TH, and arrived at Jullundur on December 1ST.

In 1897; the regiment operated with the Mohmand Field Force during the great tribal uprising on the North West Frontier. Subsequent to the reforms brought about in the Indian Army by Lord Kitchener in 1903, the regiment's designation was changed to 26TH Punjabis.

On January 15TH 1912, the 26TH Punjabis were ordered to embark at once for Hong Kong. In China the success of the Wuchang Uprising on 10TH October 1911, started a chain reaction, and in less than two months 14 out of the 18 provinces within China's main borders had declared independence.

15TH Punjab Regiment

26TH Punjabis (2/15TH)

The imperial regime had been overthrown and replaced by a republican system, signifying a new era of modern China. During this period in 1912, the 26TH Punjabis moved to Hong Kong to protect British interests.

On the outbreak of war on August 4TH, 1914, the 26TH Punjabis found themselves still in Rennie's Mill at Kowloon, near Hong Kong. They had been there for two and half years. In December 1915, the regiment sailed for Mesopotamia. During 1916, it fought on the Tigris Front in the Battle of Dujaila. The attempt to capture Dujaila by a surprise attack failed, and it was found to be impossible to complete a deliberate attack that day. The British force was obliged to withdraw all the way back to the place where it had started. About 150 men who had become separated from their units were able to fall back to this position, over rifle and machine-gun fire driving back the swarms of Arabs who were trying to cut them off. Thus ended what seemed a most promising operation for the relief of the beleaguered garrison at Kut-al-Amara.

On April 5TH, the Turkish position at Hannah was attacked by the 18TH Division under cover of artillery bombardment from both banks of the River, under cover of overhead indirect machine-gun fire. This latter was provided by the brigaded machine-guns of the 36TH Brigade, in which the 26TH Punjabi's machine guns were included. After the attack had been successfully pushed through, the machine-gun section rejoined the regiment at Sanna position to hold, for which the regiment had been pushed up.

In May 1916, the brigade with the 26TH Punjabis joined the newly formed 14TH Indian Division and remained with it until June 1918. It took part in a large number of small actions: the Advance to the Hai and Capture of the Khudaira Bend (14TH December 1916 – 19TH January 1917), the Capture of the Hai Salient (25TH January – 5TH February 1917). On January 26TH, for his gallant behaviour Lance-Naik Chanan Singh was awarded the I.D.S.M. The regiment took part in the Capture of the Dahra Bend (9TH – 16TH February), the Capture of Sannaiyat (17TH – 24TH February), the Passage of the Tigris (23RD – 24TH February), the Second Action of Jabal Hamrin (16TH – 20TH October), and the Third Action of Jabal Hamrin (3RD – 6TH December 1917). The results of these battles were far reaching. The Turks, with their line of retreat threatened retired halter-scelter from their positions and not only abandoned large quantities of ammunition, equipment, and stores, but also surrendered in great numbers. The whole Turkish Army was now in full retreat to Baghdad. The whole British force followed hard on the Turkish heels, and the 26TH Punjabis took part with the rest of the 14TH Division in this pursuit. During this period the Turkish forces were very careful to keep at arm's length. They left no garrisons or posts within reach which could be surrounded or destroyed by a sudden advance from the British side.

On April 8TH, 1918, the regiment was ordered to march to Qasr-i-Shirin over the Persian Frontier, and was to garrison certain detached posts at Sar-i-Pul, Pa-i-Taq, and Taq-i-Girrah.

15TH Punjab Regiment

26TH Punjabis (2/15TH)

This extension of the line into Persia was due to despatch into that country of 'Dunsterforce.' Its despatch and maintenance over a country proved so difficult that delays were unavoidable, and 'Dunsterforce' never reached its original destination. Its lines of communication up to the north of Persia constituted a problem that taxed the resources of the Mesopotamian Expeditionary Force to its utmost. It was on this duty that the 26TH Punjabis were employed for the remainder of the war until June 1921, when it returned to India. During the First World War, the following Sikh soldiers were awarded the I.D.S.M. for their gallantry against the Turks in Mesopotamia. Lance-Naik Channan Singh, Lance-Naik Bawa Singh, Sepoy Hazara Singh, Sepoy Waryam Singh and Sepoy Sher Singh.

After the First World War the Regiment was based in the North-West Frontier, where it was continually in action against the various tribal clans. In 1921-22, a major reorganization was undertaken in the British Indian Army leading to the formation of large infantry groups of four to six Battalions. Among these was the 15TH Punjab Regiment, formed by grouping the 26TH Punjabis with the 25TH, 27TH, 28TH and 29TH Punjabis. The Battalion's new designation was 2ND Battalion 15TH Punjab Regiment.

During the Second World War, the 2/15TH Punjab Regiment fought in Borneo. The Island was partly Dutch and partly British. The British Borneo comprised of two states of North Borneo and Sarawak, the small protected state of Brunei and the Crown Colony of Labuan Island.

To gain control of the oilfields and as a subsidiary operation to their Malayan campaign, the Japanese decided to seize British Borneo. With the forces available, there was no possibility of defending the oilfields against determined attacks. It was decided that no attempt should be made to defend British North Borneo, Brunei or Labuan, and the Governor of North Borneo was informed that the police were to be used solely for the maintenance of internal security.

It was however decided to defend Kuching because of its airfield, and because its occupation by the enemy would give access to the important Dutch airfield at Singkawang. In May 1941, therefore, the rest of 2/15TH Punjab Regiment was sent there to provide garrison. On the 29TH, at the Japanese advance, and after series of rearguard actions, the Punjabis withdrew to Ngabang and two days later to Nangapinoh. By this time further resistance was useless, and on the 4TH February the Punjabis with Dutch agreement set out in two columns for Samlpit and Pangkalanboeoen on the south coast in the hope of finding ships to take them to Java.

At the Japanese surrender, with the remnants of the battalion, it was re-raised in 1946, as a Machine-Gun Battalion. After the independence of the subcontinent in 1947, and the creation of Pakistan, the battalion was allotted to the new Pakistan Army. The Sikh soldiers from the battalion were transferred to the Indian Army.

15TH Punjab Regiment

27TH Punjabis (3/15TH)

The 27TH Punjabis was raised in 1857, as the 19TH Regiment of Punjab Infantry. In 1860, the regiment was sent to China to fight in the Second Anglo-China War. In the summer of 1860, London dispatched Lord Elgin with an Anglo-French force of 11,000 British troops and 6,700 French troops to China. They pushed north with 173 ships from Hong Kong and captured the port cities of Yantai and Dalian to seal the Bohai Gulf. On 3RD August they carried out a landing near at Beitang some 3 kilometres from the Dagu Forts, which they captured after three weeks on 21ST August. After taking Tianjin on 23RD August, the Anglo-French forces marched inland toward Beijing.

The Xianfeng Emperor then dispatched ministers for peace talks, but the British diplomatic envoy, Harry Parkes, insulted the imperial emissary and word arrived that the British had kidnapped the prefect of Tianjin. Parkes was arrested in retaliation on 18TH September. Parkes and his entourage were imprisoned and interrogated. Half were reportedly executed by slow slicing, with the application of tourniquets to severed limbs to prolong the torture; this infuriated British leadership when they recovered the unrecognizable bodies. The Anglo-French forces clashed with Sengge Rinchen's Mongol cavalry on 18TH September near Zhangjiawan before proceeding toward the outskirts of Beijing for a decisive battle in Tongzhou. On 21ST September, at Baliqiao, Sengge Rinchen's 10,000 troops, including the elite Mongol cavalry, were annihilated after doomed frontal charges against concentrated firepower of the Anglo-French forces, which entered Beijing on 6TH October.

The British and the French were granted a permanent diplomatic presence in Beijing. The Chinese had to pay 8 million taels to Britain and France. Britain acquired Kowloon (next to Hong Kong), and the opium trade was legalized.

In 1877, the Jowakis committed a series of raids on the main road connecting Kohat with India. In August, 1877, an expedition that included the 19TH Punjab Infantry was ordered to penetrate the Jowaki Hills, and carry out punitive measures against the refractory clan. The expedition carried out the necessary measures before withdrawing from the Turkai Valley.

During the Second Afghan War of 1878-80, as part of the Pashawar Valley Field Force, the regiment advanced into the Khyber Pass to clear Afghan forces at Ali Masjid. The war ended after the British emerged victorious and the Afghans agreed to let the British attain all of their objectives from the Treaty of Gandamak. The Afghans were permitted to maintain internal sovereignty but they had to cede control of their nation's foreign relations to the British.

Havildar Gurdit Singh, Havildar Dyal Singh and Sepoy Asa Singh were awarded the I.O.M., for conspicuous gallantry in the action on 21ST November, 1878, at Ali Masjid.

1885, the regiment participated in the Third Burma War. End of the war saw the loss of sovereignty of an independent Burma under the Konbaung Dynasty, whose rule had already been reduced to the territory known as Upper Burma.

15TH Punjab Regiment

27TH Punjabis (3/15TH)

Following the third war, Burma came under the rule of the British Raj as a province of India.

In 1888, after signing successive treaties with the then ruling Somali Sultans such as Mohamoud Ali Shire of the Warsangali Sultanate, the British established a protectorate in the region referred to as British Somaliland. Beginning in 1899, the British were forced to expend considerable human and military capital to contain a decades-long resistance movement mounted by the Dervish State. The polity was led by Sayed Mohammed Abdullah Hassan. In 1901, the 19TH Punjab Infantry was dispatched to British Somaliland suppress the Somali resistance. Repeated military expeditions were unsuccessfully launched against Hassan and his Dervishes before World War I.

Subsequent to the reforms brought about in the Indian Army in 1903, the regiment's designation was changed to 27TH Punjabis.

During the First World War, the 27TH Punjabis were initially sent to Egypt to protect the Suez Canal. The Turkish infantry approached the east bank on 3RD February 1915. The Punjabi machine-gunners cut swathes through those on the water, and through men now massing in the gullies on the east bank. Much panic began, and many Arab troops on the Turk side surrendered. The entire Turk force withdrew, unmolested by the British who did not follow them in any force, back across the Sinai towards Beersheba. The Turks lost 1,500 troops in this action. Havildar Partab Singh was awarded the I.O.M., for gallantry in this action. On the 19TH September 1918 his platoon commander has been wounded, he took charge of the platoon and very ably led the men when the order was given to charge a battery of four guns firing at point blank range. He was the first to come forward, and charging a few yards ahead of his men, assisted in the capture of the whole battery

The 27TH Punjabis from Egypt were rushed to the Western Front. The Indian Army, 161,000 strong, seemed an obvious source of trained men, shortly after they arrived; they were fed piecemeal into some of the fiercest fighting around Ypres. Losses were heavy. The average Indian battalion had 764 men when it landed; by early November the 47TH Sikhs had only 385 men fit for duty. The troops were taken out of the line and rested in early 1915, but were soon back in the trenches and involved in the heaviest fighting. The Indian Corps provided half the attacking force at the Battle of Neuve Chapelle in March, and they were thrown into the counter-attack at the Second Battle of Ypres in April. The Indians again took heavy losses at the Battle of Loos in September. The two Indian infantry divisions with the 27TH Punjabis were withdrawn from France, and sent to Mesopotamia in 1915.

Subedar Bhagat Singh MC, Subedar Kahn Singh and Jemadar Nand Singh were awarded the I.O.M., while Havildars Hira Singh, Bela Singh, Bhagat Singh, Jemadar Basawa Singh, Lance-Naiks Natha Singh and Santa Singh were awarded the I.D.S.M., for gallantry against the Turks in Mesopotamia.

15TH Punjab Regiment

27TH Punjabis (3/15TH)

In 1921-22, a major reorganization was undertaken in the British Indian Army leading to the formation of large infantry groups of four to six Battalions. Among these was the 15TH Punjab Regiment, formed by grouping the 27TH, 26TH Punjabis with the 25TH, 28TH and 29TH Punjabis. The battalion's new designation was 3RD Battalion, 15TH Punjab Regiment.

During the Second World War, the battalion served in British Somaliland. The defection of the French in French Somaliland left the position of British Somaliland very precarious. At first it was considered that the country was not worth fighting for; it is practically all deserts with no industries or products and could be a liability to the Italians. Then it was decided that although there were insufficient forces to hold the country it would be worth while making the Italians fight for it and so use up their carefully husbanded supplies. A small force consisting of battalions of Black Watch, 2ND Punjab Regiment and the 3/15TH Punjab Regiment, from Aden, was therefore sent to meet the large Italian forces being massed across the frontier. The Italians had brought more than two divisions with tanks, aircraft and heavy artillery in support. The small force against them had little equipment, and was quite insufficient to hold a continuous line.

In the ring of hills surrounding Berbera the Imperial troops took up positions covering the passes, the most famous of which is the Tug Argan Gap. Patently over-confident under cover of their tanks, artillery and air support, the Italians attacked the thinly defended posts in massed formation and were time and again mown down by withering fire. Their opponents took full advantage of darkness of effect retirement from one position to another, and as a result the enemy often lost contact only to find themselves up against stolid opposition from new and unexpected directions. Even the most audacious defence could not, however, prevent infiltration; the enemy's steady advance was recognised to be an inevitable as it proved costly to them.

The withdrawal to the port now began. One company of the 3/15TH Punjab Regiment, holding out against a concentrated enemy assault, became isolated and was feared to be lost, but by a skilful night march it evaded the enemy and rejoined the rearguard two days later. Such losses had been inflicted on the enemy that re-embarkation to Aden was carried out unopposed. During this period, the British rounded up soldiers and governmental officials to evacuate them from the territory through Berbera. In total, 7,000 people, including civilians, were evacuated and British Somaliland was briefly occupied by Italy.

In March 1941, the British forces from Aden, which included the 3/15TH Punjab Regiment, recaptured the Somaliland Protectorate, after a six month's Italian occupation. Berbera was soon occupied, the enemy streaming away down the road towards Hargeisa, and the search for booby traps, stores and weapons began. The enemy had been completely surprised and fled without doing any damage, though the town was in a disgusting state.

15TH Punjab Regiment

27TH Punjabis (3/15TH)

Sanitation had been completely neglected; the town stank to heaven. About 120 prisoners with ten guns were captured, while the Punjabi casualties were one man wounded. The most difficult operation of war had been carried out against an admittedly not very determined foe, with complete success, inflicting heavy losses on the enemy and recapturing the town which was to provide a base for future operations. The Italian venture in British Somaliland had been an expensive luxury. Towards the end of April, a small military force was embarked and the ships moved down the coast to Cape Guardafui, the most easterly point of Africa. On landing the Punjabis had rounded up the enemy, and thirty Italian officers and 154 other ranks were taken away as prisoners from this inhospitable stretch of coast.

The battalion then moved to Egypt and came under command British Eighth Army between July and November 1942. It returned to Iraq, assigned to the 8TH Indian Infantry Division, in November 1942 and moved with to Damascus in March 1943. In September 24TH, 1943, it arrived in Taranto in southern Italy and remained with 8TH Indian Division throughout the rest of the Italian Campaign.

On 24TH September 1943, 8TH Indian Division, consisting of 17TH, 19TH, and 21ST Brigades, landed unopposed at Taranto and for 19 months was almost continuously in action, advancing through mountainous country, crossing River after River. The formation later adopted the motto 'One more River'. The Division concentrated to the East of Taranto and immediately began to follow North in the path of 8TH Army. At Trigno, the Division was committed to its first action in Europe. The 19TH Brigade, with sharp skirmishes against the most skilful and belligerent German formations, took a firm grip on the South bank of the River Trigno through occupation of Monte Mitro and Monte Falcone. The Brigade immediately prepared to force the Trigno, in order to seize Tuffilo village and Monte Farano on the high ground. The Brigade established a bridgehead over the River Trigno as a result of heavy fighting during the periods 22ND October–5TH November. A decisive event was the capture of the enemy positions on the San Salvo Ridge, which dominated the area north of the River.

Subsequently the 8TH Indian Division advanced on the fortified village of Mozzagrogna. Corps Artillery concentrated a terrific shoot on the village as the bombardment held the enemy garrison in the dugouts and once it lifted, the Germans rushed to their surface posts. The battle resolved into dozens of sudden deadly encounters in cellars, on rooftops, in alleys, and behind the angles of broken walls. With the arrival of the British Armour the defences of Mozzagrogna collapsed and essential crossroads to the Northwest of Mozzagrogna were secured. One thousand prisoners had been taken and a number of German Units had been decimated. All anchor positions of the Gustav Line were now in British hands. To sustain the momentum of the advance, 21ST Indian Brigade turned west from Mozzagrogna along the top of the ridge with Romagnoli.

15TH Punjab Regiment

27TH Punjabis (3/15TH)

The next objective was a line of trenches concealed behind hedges on the outskirts of the village. Pinning down the defenders, the village was stormed. Three counter–attacks which were shattered in quick succession convinced the enemy that Romagnoli could not be regained.

On December 2ND, the town of Lanciano was closely invested on three sides. That night the enemy cleared out. The next objective was to take Caldari beyond the River Moro. 8TH Indian Division was told to cross the River and capture Caldari as the other two Divisions on the flanks failed to cross the River. It was impossible to build a bridge from the near bank, so it was decided to build it backwards from the enemy's bank. 'The Impossible Bridge‖' over the River Moro came to be a legend in the annals of combat engineering, when the Indian Engineers crossed over to the enemy side and built a bridge in reverse direction, to overcome the technical difficulty arising out of lack of construction space on the home bank. The area surrounding the bridge site was extremely active with German fighting patrols and they reacted violently to this incursion. The Frontiersmen of 1/12TH Frontier Force Regiment cleared the enemy patrols with the bayonet.

The next objective was to take Caldari beyond the River Moro. 8TH Indian Division was told to cross the river and capture Caldari as the other two Divisions on the flanks failed to cross the river. It was impossible to build a bridge from the near bank, so it was decided to build it backwards from the enemy's bank. The Impossible Bridge‖ over the River Moro came to be a legend in the annals of combat engineering, when the Indian Engineers crossed over to the enemy side and built a bridge in reverse direction, to overcome the technical difficulty arising out of lack of construction space on the home bank. The area surrounding the bridge site was extremely active with German fighting patrols and they reacted violently to this incursion. The Frontiersmen of, 1/12TH Frontier Force Regiment cleared the enemy patrols with the bayonet.

At the opening of the Impossible Bridge‖ 8TH Indian Division advanced against Caldari. 1/12TH Frontier Force Regiment stormed the village after some fierce fighting and seized positions along the road, which ran parallel to the Moro. An enemy tank force, which included flame-throwers, charged the consolidation group and cut off the Dogra Company. At dawn the Sikh Companies of Frontiersmen hurled back the enemy in headlong flight and captured two disabled tanks.

The 3/15TH Punjab Regiment joined the fray and seized fresh positions along the lateral road joined the fray and seized fresh positions along the lateral road. General Russell planned to lead off with 21ST Brigade in an assault upon Monte Citerna and Monte Stiletto, two feeder ridges intruding into the Alpe di Vitiglano buttress. At dusk on September 12TH, 3/15TH Punjab Regiment began their arduous advance. Just before dawn they made contact with the enemy at Point 632, South-West of Monte Citerna.

15TH Punjab Regiment

27TH Punjabis (3/15TH)

Jemadar Chattar Singh was commanding a Platoon of 'B' Company, which had been ordered to capture Alpe di Vitiglano. While the Company was forming up for the attack on a narrow ridge, the enemy brought down heavy artillery fire on the forming up area, causing casualties and considerable confusion in the darkness. In spite of the heavy fire Jemadar Chattar led the assault up an exceptionally steep hillside, covered with thick scrub, and in pitch darkness against strongly prepared enemy positions on the crest of the ridge 350 feet above the forming up place. On reaching the crest, Jemadar Chattar Singh led the assault on the enemy trenches. During this assault he saw that one of the enemy, who had been captured, was about to throw a stick grenade; he at once attacked the man, and after a hand-to-hand struggle, overcame and dis-armed him.

As the day broke the Punjabis scaled an almost vertical cliff and cut through a belt of wire. Machine gun fire pinned them down on two occasions, but thrusting with splendid dash they swept over Monte Citerna and destroyed the garrison. Without pause the Battalion drove for the central buttress of Alpe di Vitiglano, and shortly after noon, after climbing along the reverse slope of the spur in a great-hearted effort, routed the garrison on Point 1015, about half-way between Citerna and the main objective. The Punjabis had climbed one thousand feet since dawn and had stormed two positions. They were now halted by concentrated fire from Monte Stiletto on their right rear and Le Scalette on their left front. It was impossible to run the gauntlet of two flanking fires by daylight so the doughty Punjabis dug in and waited for night.

An Officer wrote truly: "The Punjabis have opened with a magnificent innings." After bitter resistance on the lower slopes of Alpe di Vitiglano the Punjabis had spent the day in reorganization. The assault was renewed at 2230 hours that evening. Enemy Artillery and mortar fire searched their line of advance, and when they closed upon their objective at midnight it was in anticipation of a grim struggle. The narrow approach compelled attack on a single Company frontage. As the leading Platoons clambered towards the black skyline they were greeted by heavy small arms fire. Dauntlessly they flung themselves at the crest. A few enemies remained to die in the weapon pits, but more scuttled to safety in the dark. The emplacements were mopped up, and a second bastion of the Gothic Line had fallen. Throughout the action Jemadar Chattar Singh's gallantry and leadership was quite exceptional, for which he was awarded the Military Cross.

On the night of 17/18TH October 1944, during the attack on Groce Daneie in Italy, Jemadar Dharam Singh was commanding a platoon of a Company. As the Company moved forward heavy and concentrated fire was experienced, and most of the Company was thrown into confusion. The advance was held up by heavy Machine Gun fire. Jemadar Dharam Singh's coolness and confidence and his immediate offer to lead the advance restored morale and put new life into all ranks.

15TH Punjab Regiment

27TH Punjabis (3/15TH)

Finally against all enemy resistance the objective captured. For his courage and outstanding leadership, Jemadar Dharam Singh was awarded the Military Cross. Subedar Arjan Singh, Havildar Kartar Singh and Lance-Naik Gurdas Singh were awarded the I.D.S.M., while Subedar Major Chattar Singh and Sepoys S. Singh and Ujagar Singh were awarded the Military Medal for their gallantry during the Italian campaign.

The Punjabis distinguished themselves for courage and tenacity in the battles of the Sangro, Cassino, and the Liri Valley, the Gothic line, the Senio and several other engagements.

After the independence of the subcontinent in 1947, and the creation of Pakistan, the battalion was allotted to the new Pakistan Army. The Sikh soldiers from the battalion were transferred to the Indian Army.

28TH Punjabis (4/15TH)

The 28TH Punjabis was raised in 1857 with the class composition of Sikhs, Punjabi Mussalmans, Pathans and Dogras, as the 20TH Regiment of Punjab Infantry. It was designated as the 28TH Punjabis in 1903.

In 1862, the regiment took part in operations in Assam. During 1860, the people in the Khasi and Jaintia Hills suddenly became troublesome, eventually breaking out in rebellion a year later. A strong force which included 20TH Regiment of Punjab Infantry was employed to suppress this rising. The principal scenes of action were in the area around Jowai, 32 miles east of Shillong, which was besieged by the rebels for nearly three weeks, and was only relieved with much difficulty, fighting, and a number of casualties. It was not till November 1863, after every glen and jungle had been searched out by the troops, and the last rebel leader had been captured, that the troubles in these hills was stamped out.

During the Second Afghan War of 1878-80, a British force of 6,000, which included 28TH Punjabis, under General Roberts met an Afghan Army of 18,000 men at Peiwar Kotal, Charasia and Kabul. The British skilfully routed the Afghan army, causing heavy casualties and capturing all their artillery. Peace was concluded in May 1879 and the Amir accepted a British mission based at Kabul.

On the North-West Frontier the regiment participated in the Black Mountain Expedition (1891), Mahsud Waziris (1901), and Zakha Khel (1908).

During the Mohmand expedition of 1908, Havildar Wadhawa Singh was awarded the I.D.S.M., for gallantry during the punitive action.

During the First World War, they were stationed in Ceylon on garrison duty and were called out to suppress the riots in 1915, which they did brutally. Many atrocities were committed by the Punjabis during Marital Law that prevailed in the country. Following the incidents of the riots, 28TH Punjabis was transferred to Mesopotamia, where they fought in the bloody battles on the Tigris Front, as the British made desperate efforts to relieve their besieged garrison at Kut-al-Amara.

15TH Punjab Regiment

28TH Punjabis (4/15TH)

In 1917, the regiment took part in the Third Battle of Sannaiyat, the Capture of Baghdad, and the actions at Istabulat and Tekrit. Jemadar Ran Singh, Lance-Naik Lal Singh and Sepoy Mansa Singh awarded the I.D.S.M., for their gallantry against the Turks in Mesopotamia.

In 1918, the 28TH Punjabis participated in the British campaign in Palestine, and fought in the Jordan Valley from 19TH February to 4TH May, the battles of Megiddo, Sharon and Nablus from 19TH to 25TH September, and the continuation of the Final Offensive beyond the Jordan from 26TH October to the Armistice in 31ST October 1918. Havildar Basant Singh, Jemadar Sundar Singh, and Sepoy Indar Singh were awarded the I.D.S.M., for their gallantry during the Palestine operations.

In 1921, Sepoy Ishar Singh was awarded the Victoria Cross for exceptional valour during the Waziristan Campaign near Haidari Kach. When the convoy protection troops were attacked, he was No. 1 of a Lewis Gun- Section. Early in the action he received a very severe gunshot wound in the chest, and fell beside his Lewis gun. Hand-to-hand fighting having commenced, the British officer, Indian officer, and all the Havildars of his company were either killed or wounded, and his Lewis gun was seized by the enemy. Calling up two other men he got up, charged the enemy, recovered the Lewis gun, and, although, bleeding profusely, again got the gun into action. When his Jemadar arrived he took the gun from Sepoy Ishar Singh, and ordered him to go back and have his wound dressed. Instead of doing this the Sepoy went to the medical officer, and was of great assistance in pointing out where the wounded were, and in carrying water to them. He made innumerable journeys to the River and back for this purpose. On one occasion, when the enemy fire was very heavy, he took the rifle of a wounded man and helped to keep down the fire. On another occasion he stood in front of the medical officer who was dressing, a wounded man, thus shielding him with his body. It was over three hours before he finally submitted to be evacuated, being then too weak from loss of blood to object. He later achieved the rank of Captain, and served in the Second World War In addition to the Victoria Cross, he was awarded the prestigious Order of British India, First Class, which carried with it the title of 'Sardar Bahadur'.

1921-22, a major reorganization was undertaken in the British Indian Army leading to the formation of large infantry groups of four to six Battalions. Among these was the 15TH Punjab Regiment, formed by grouping the 28TH, 26TH Punjabis with the 25TH, 27TH, and 29TH Punjabis. The Battalion's new designation was 4TH Battalion, 15TH Punjab Regiment.

During the Second World War, the Battalion fought in the Burma Campaign with great distinction. During 1941 and early 1942, the Japanese army had driven Allied troops (British and Indian) from Burma. During 1943, the Allies had tried a limited offensive into Arakan, the coastal province of Burma. The aim had been to secure Akyab Island at the end of the Mayu Peninsula.

15TH Punjab Regiment

28TH Punjabis (4/15TH)

The island possessed an important airfield, which featured prominently in Allied plans to recapture Burma. This offensive had failed disastrously.

The failure of successive British offensives in the Arakan, the steamy coastal region from which it was hoped it would be possible to gain access to central Burma, had reinforced the Japanese high command's low opinion of their opponent's abilities as jungle fighters. They were confident of victory, but were soon to be taught a terrible lesson.

A 130-miles (210km) road wound north from Imphal to the hill town of Kohima before running on to the railhead at Dimapur. It was Kohima's only contact with the outside world and would link the two remote settlements in the high hills of Assam in some of the most savage fighting of the war. Two divisions of the Japanese 15th Army crossed the Chindwin River and moved on Imphal. The third headed for Kohima. Both the Japanese and the British were operating under severe disadvantages. Time was not on Mutaguchi's side. Once battle was joined, his troops could rely on no more than a month's supplies. In May, the monsoon would arrive, making offensive operations all but impossible. In contrast, the commander of the British 14th Army, General William Slim, had been preparing to go over to the offensive and was not best placed to receive an attack in a sector where there were such poor communications and few facilities for the basing of large numbers of troops now committed to the front. Nevertheless, Slim had one invaluable advantage, under his superb leadership, Fourteenth Army had been transformed from the shattered force which had been driven out of Burma in the spring of 1942 into a highly motivated army, but it had yet to fight a full-scale battle against experienced Japanese troops who had been ordered by the super-aggressive Mutaguchi's to fight to the death. British were prepared for the Japanese thrust. Ample evidence of the build-up was provided by aerial reconnaissance. Nevertheless, Slim was surprised by its initial speed. By April 5TH the Japanese had cut the Imphal-Kohima road and isolated the settlements. Slim ordered his subordinate commanders not to withdraw without permission from higher authority.

It was imperative to deny the Japanese the mountain roads which led down into the Indian plain. Imphal and Kohima would have to be held at all costs, with last-minute reinforcements rushed in from Dimapur. Two battalions, supported by artillery, were positioned 2 miles (3km) west of Kohima itself on the highest hill in the ridge, later to become known as Garrison Hill.

Fighting began on the 30TH as General Sato's 31ST division pushed back the scattered units of the Assam Rifles and other regiments which were defending the approaches to Kohima. Commander at Kohima, Colonel Hugh Richards, had a force of approximately 1200 men to resist the all-out attack of 12,000 Japanese jungle veterans. He had to rely on the arrival of a breakthrough force from Dimapur, the British 2ND Division, without which his defences would be overwhelmed.

15TH Punjab Regiment

28TH Punjabis (4/15TH)

The Japanese arrived on April 5TH. In the teeth of desperate resistance they took the strongpoints on the hills and hummocks around Kohima. The pattern of the battle was now set. Men crouched in slit trenches sometimes only yards away from the enemy. One officer of the West Kents calculated that from the plop of a grenade being fired to its arrival was no more than 14 seconds. The intensity of Japanese artillery, mortar and sniper fire in suck a small space meant that movement between units was virtually impossible by day and extremely hazardous at night. Few of the men locked in this fight for survival had a clear idea of what was happening beyond the lip of their own trench.

Day and night the British and Indian troops were subjected to Japanese broadcast appeals to them to surrender. Sato's aim was to exhaust the defenders of Kohima. Japanese artillery was most active at dawn and sunset, shredding nerves as well as destroying targets. When darkness fell, the Allied troops stood to in the dark before the moon rose, straining to catch the rustle of Japanese infiltrators moving behind them. As one of Kohima's defenders observed, this stoked the fear that when he awoke the occupants of the next gun pit might be the enemy. On April 11TH Stopford sent 5TH British Infantry Brigade up the Dimapur-Kohima road. Two days later it had smashed its way through to the Jotsoma 'box' held by 161ST Brigade, by now, the situation at Kohima was desperate. A message was sent to the 5TH Brigade that unless help arrived within 48 hours Kohima would fall. On the 17TH the Japanese launched their fiercest attack on the slopes of Garrison Hill. Phosphorous bombardments were followed by howling infantry assaults with grenades and machine-guns. To the din was added the fire of the defenders' howitzers. By the night of the 18TH the men holding Garrison Hill were on their last legs. The Japanese swarmed everywhere but were unable to mount a co-ordinated battalion-strength attack which would have spelled the end at Kohima. The ground around Garrison Hill - just 350 yards (320m) square - was now all that was left of the perimeter which had held on April 5TH. The most savage fighting of the battle erupted in mid-May. The sliver of ground at stake was the British Deputy Commissioner's bungalow and its adjacent tennis court.

This had been seized on April 9TH by the Japanese, who had built a warren of bunkers and weapons pits on the surrounding terraced hillside. The task of winkling out the Japanese was given to the men of the 2ND Battalion Dorset shire regiment. It was a dirty business made more difficult by the terrain which denied the Dorsets any armoured support. A solution was found by the Royal Engineers who cut a path to a spur behind the bungalow. They then winched a Grant tank up and pushed it down the slope. It came to rest on the baseline of the tennis court, where its commander, Sergeant Waterhouse of the 149 Royal Tank Regiment poured a hail of fire into the Japanese bunkers at no more than 20 yards (18m) range. The Japanese fled on to the waiting rifles of the Dorsets. Only the chimney stack of the bungalow remained.

15TH Punjab Regiment

28TH Punjabis (4/15TH)

The rest of the landscape around was a shell-churned rubbish dump alive with rats. When he saw it, General Stopford compared it with the Somme in 1916: "One could tell how desperate the fighting had been". By now the Japanese had run out of time, supplies and ammunition. On May 31ST, Sato ordered his men to withdraw to Imphal. Exhausted and riddled with disease, they were harried all the way by the Allies. Imphal was relieved on June 22ND, after over 80 days of siege, and now it was the turn of Mutaguchi's to throw in the towel. Early in July, his 15TH Army pulled out, the survivors struggling down liquefied roads to cross the Chindwin on to the Burma plains. Only 20,000 of the 85,000 Japanese who had come to invade India were left standing.

In February 1944, Japanese troops infiltrated through the division's front and overran the divisional HQ. Units of the division took part in the subsequent Battle of the Admin Box, in which the Japanese failed to capture the positions.

On March 2ND 1945, the Japanese were holding a strong position astride the Kamye-Myingyan road. The attack on the first objective was successful and one platoon was ordered to attack a village to the right. This platoon's attack, with the aid of tanks, advanced very slowly under very heavy enemy fire. Naik Gian Singh was in command of the leading section. The enemy was well concealed along the cacti hedges but Naik Gian Singh soon observed enemy foxholes some 20 yards ahead. Ordering his light machine-gunner to cover him, he rushed the enemy foxholes alone, firing his Tommy gun. He was met by a hail of fire and wounded in the arm. In spite of this he continued his advance alone, hurling grenades. He killed several Japanese including four in one of the enemy main weapon pits. By this time a troop of British tanks moved in support and came under fire from a cleverly concealed enemy anti-tank gun. Naik Gian Singh quickly saw the threat to the tanks, and ignoring the danger to himself and in spite of his wounds, he again rushed forward, capturing the gun and killing the crew single-handed. His section followed him, and he then led them down a lane of cacti hedges, clearing all enemy positions, which were being firmly held. Some 20 enemy bodies were found in this area, the majority of which fell to Naik Gian Singh and his section. After this action, Naik Gian Singh was ordered to the Regimental First-Aid Post but, in spite of his wounds, requested permission to lead his section until the whole action had been completed. This was granted. There is no doubt that many casualties to Naik Gian Singh's platoon were prevented by his acts of supreme gallantry, they enabled the whole operation to be carried out successfully with severe losses to the enemy. Although wounded, the magnificent gallantry, devotion to duty and leadership of Gian Singh throughout this action could not have been surpassed. Gian Singh was awarded the Victoria Cross in 1945.

15TH Punjab Regiment

28TH Punjabis (4/15TH)

On the 18TH March 1945, Lieutenant Karamjeet Singh Judge was ordered to capture the Cotton Mill area on the outskirts of Myingyan. Up to the last moment Lieut. Karamjeet Singh Judge dominated the entire battlefield by his numerous and successive acts of superb gallantry. Although cover around the tanks was non-existent, Lieutenant Karamjeet Singh Judge remained with the tanks, regardless not only of heavy small-arms fire directed at him but also of extremely heavy shelling directed at the tanks. Lieut. Karamjeet Singh Judge succeeded in recalling the tanks and personally indicated the bunkers for the tanks to deal with, thus allowing the infantry to advance. In every case Lieutenant Karamjeet Singh Judge personally led the infantry charges against the bunkers and was invariably the first to arrive. In this way, this brilliant and courageous officer eliminated ten bunkers. On one occasion, as he was going into attack, two Japanese with fixed bayonets suddenly rushed at him from a small nullah at a distance of only ten yards. He killed both. About fifteen minutes before the battle finished, a last nest of three bunkers was located in a position that was difficult for the tanks to approach. An enemy light machine-gun was firing from one of them and holding the advance of the infantry. Undaunted and at great personal risk, Lieutenant Karamjeet Singh Judge directed one tank to within 20 yards of the bunkers, and then threw a smoke grenade as a marker. After some minutes firing from the tank, he asked the commander to cease firing whilst he went in with a few men to mop up. He then went forward and got within 10 yards of the bunker, when the machine-gun opened fire again, mortally wounding him in the chest. By this time, however, the remaining men of the section were able to storm this strong point and so complete the long and arduous task. During this battle, Lieutenant Karamjeet Singh Judge was an example of cool and calculated bravery. In three previous and similar actions, this young officer had already proved himself an outstanding leader of matchless courage. In his last action, in which he was killed, Lieutenant Karamjeet Singh Judge gave a superb demonstration of inspiring leadership and outstanding courage. He was awarded the posthumous Victoria Cross.

Performance of the 4/15TH Punjab Regiment in Burma in particular was outstanding. The battalion suffered 921 casualties and was awarded numerous gallantry awards including two Victoria Crosses to Lieutenant Karamjeet Singh Judge and Naik Gian Singh.

After the independence of the subcontinent in 1947, and the creation of Pakistan, the battalion was allotted to the new Pakistan Army. The Sikh soldiers from the battalion were transferred to the Indian Army.

15TH Punjab Regiment

29TH Punjabis (10/15TH)

The Regiment was raised in 1857, as the Jullundur Punjab Battalion, with the class composition of Sikhs, Punjabi Mussalmans and Jats. It was designated as the 29TH (Punjab) Regiment of Bengal Native Infantry in 1864. Subsequent to the reforms brought about in the Indian Army in 1903, the regiment's designation was changed to 29TH Punjabis.

The regiment took part in the Bhutan War of 1864-66. Britain sent a peace mission to Bhutan in early 1864, in the wake of a civil war there. Bhutan rejected the peace and friendship treaty it offered. Britain declared war in November 1864. Bhutan had no regular army, and what forces existed were composed of guards armed with matchlocks, bows and arrows, swords, knives, and catapults. The fort, known at the time as Dewanigiri, at Deothang was dismantled by the British during 1865. The British initially suffered a humiliating defeat at Deothang and when they recaptured Dewanigiri they destroyed much in an attempt to compensate. War lasted only five months and, despite some battlefield victories by Bhutanese forces, resulted in Bhutan's defeat, loss of part of its sovereign territory, and forced cession of formerly occupied territories.

The regiment took part in the Second Afghan War of 1878-80. The war ended when the British emerged victorious against the Afghan Army. The Afghans agreed to let the British attain all of their geopolitical objectives from the Treaty of Gandamak. Most of the British and Indian soldiers withdrew from Afghanistan. The Afghans were permitted to maintain internal sovereignty but they had to cede control of their nation's foreign relations to the British.

Subedar-Major Jagat Singh, Havildar Gurmukh Singh, Havildar Natha Singh, Lance-Naik Sher Singh and Sepoy Hira Singh were awarded the I.O.M., for their conspicuous gallantry during the Second Afghan War.

The Zaimukhts inhabit a triangular district bordering on the Kurram Valley to the south and Orakzai territory to the north in the North-West Frontier. No trouble arose with them until Afghan War of 1878, when they proceeded to harass the line of communication of the British force operating in Afghanistan. Transport difficulties prevented at first the despatch of an expedition against the Zaimukhts. However, early in December, 1879, the force that included the 29TH Punjab Native Infantry concentrated at Balish Khel, and, moving in south-easterly direction, invaded the hostile territory on the 8TH, after some preparatory reconnaissances of the route had been made. Having destroyed the villages on the way the force reached Chinarak on the 12TH. The detachment was left at Chinarak, next day on Zawo, the chief Zaimukht stronghold. A narrow ravine seven miles long leads from Chinarak to Zawo, flanked on either side by a difficult path across the hills. It was decided that the main body should advance by the ravine, with a flanking force on the right, or eastern route. Owing to the difficulties of the road the progress of the main body was very slow, and they halted for the night at Bagh.

15TH Punjab Regiment

29TH Punjabis (10/15TH)

The force on the right of the main line of advance met with some resistance from the enemy, who were found occupying a strong position along a ridge due east of Bagh, running at angles to the direction of the march. The attempt by four companies to carry the position by a frontal attack having failed, two companies of the 29TH Punjab Native Infantry, supported by two mountain guns, were directed to make a turning movement to the left and attack the enemy's right. At the same time the 85TH Regiment renewed their attack from two different directions. After a short hand-to-hand struggle, the Punjabis were in possession of the whole ridge, where they remained for the night. The advance was resumed early next morning, and the pass leading to Zawo gained after a short fight. The Punjabis, as on the day before, guarded the right of the main column, and was able to drive off some hostile reinforcements, that were seen moving on Zawo from the east, besides clearing the ground to his front, and destroying a group of villages in rear. As soon as the heights around Zawo had been crowned, a detachment was sent down from the pass to destroy the place, while the main body waited on the Kotal. The enemy rendered their submission six days later after the destruction of Zawo.

The Regiment took part in various expeditions on the North West Frontier, notably; Black Mountain Expedition, 1888, the First Miranzai Expedition, 1891, and, the Mahsud Blockade, 1901. Subsequent to the reforms brought about in the Indian Army in 1903, the regiment's designation was changed to 29TH Punjabis.

During the First World War, the regiment served with distinction in the German East Africa. In particular, by threatening the important British Uganda Railway, von Lettow hoped to force British troops to invade East Africa where he could fight a defensive action. In 1912, the German government had formed a defence strategy for East Africa; the military would withdraw from the coast into the hinterland and fight a guerrilla campaign.

On September 1ST, 1914, the 29TH Punjabis disembarked at Mombasa and were at once sent up the country by rail. Half of the 29TH Punjabis were left in the Voi Tsavo area and the remainder was sent to Nairobi, where Brigadier General Stewart had established his headquarters. On September 4TH, the British force received information that a German force was advancing on Tsavo. This German force had compelled a small British detachment on the upper Tsavo to withdraw, after an encounter near Mzima. The bulk of the 29TH Punjabis were concentrated at Tsavo, leaving a detachment at Voi. The two companies of the 29TH Punjabis with some troops of the King's African Rifles were sent up the Tsavo Valley on September 5TH. This force failed to make contact with the German force and presumed that the German force had slipped pass it in the bush.

15TH Punjab Regiment

29TH Punjabis (10/15TH)

Then they were ordered to turn and attack the German force in the flank and rear. Driving it into Major James's troops, who were in position astride the Tsavo River five miles west of Tsavo. However, the German force of 300 men with 2 Pompoms and 3 Maxim Guns, took rear guard unaware with heavy fire. After the encounter, the German force retired, receiving a severe mauling. In this encounter 2 soldiers were killed and 9 wounded of the 29TH Punjabis.

During the remainder of the month, skirmishes took place between the German forces and the Punjabis at Kissu, Campi Ya Marabu, Marajarni, Ingito Hill, and Mzima Camp. On October 7^{TH,} a German force about 300 strong entered the Gazi area and started firing on the British force there. In the counter-attack, one company of the 29TH Punjabis hit the German force's right flank while one company of the Jind Infantry (Sikh Princely States unit) attacked the left flank of the German force. This double enveloping movement with the frontal attack by the Indian units compelled the German forces to retreat.

Longido is an isolated hill situated to the north- west of Kilimanjaro Mountain. Reports were received that it was garrisoned by about 1,200 German soldiers. It was decided to launch an attack on Longido Hill from a place on the Manga River in British East Africa. The units detailed for the attack, included 29TH Punjabis, 27TH Mountain Battery and the Kapurthala Infantry (Sikh Princely States unit). The decisive attack column included 29TH Punjabis and a section of the 27TH Mountain Battery. On the morning of November 3RD, a small German column suddenly opened fire in the mist, on 29TH Punjabis. During the fire exchange, both sides suffered casualties.

The 29TH Punjabis continued its advance and captured a position to the west of the main German position. The Germans being reinforced advanced as darkness came on, their guns opening fire with fuses at zero. At this juncture, withdrawal was ordered with the Punjabis resisting the German attack. The retirement of 29TH Punjabis was carried out in orderly manner to the Manga Camp. This expedition was a total failure. It required a thorough knowledge of the topography of that area, which the British force, did not posses to gain victory. Until June 1915, no major battle was fought in East Africa, only minor skirmishes took place all along the border.

Eventually, Major General decided to undertake an offensive action, and the object he selected was Bukoba town, situated on the western shore of Lake Victoria. Before making any attempt on Bukoba, all precautions were taken to keep the plan of attack a secret. To capture Bukoba, the total fighting strength of the force which included 29TH Punjabis, was about 1,600 men. The whole force assembled at Kisumu and started for Bukoba by ship on June 20TH. On the following night it reached off the western shore north of Bukoba. The German observation post at the Busira Island noticed the arrival of the force and fired a rocket signal on June 22ND.

15TH Punjab Regiment

29TH Punjabis (10/15TH)

Before the disembarkation could take place it was found that the German force had a gun in the area, and therefore, the disembarkation was moved to the north of Bukoba (a few yards south of the main landing place). As the force began moving towards Bukoba, the German gun was knocked out of action by the 28TH Mountain Battery. The German force had to retire under the pressure of the fire of the 28TH Mountain Battery. The victory was complete, and the German flag was hauled down. All the troops were able to disembark and moved in different directions to occupy various places. On July 13TH, 1915, a force that included the 29TH Punjabis fought an action near Mbuyuni. Thinking that the Germans were in too great a strength, the force was ordered to withdraw.

Minor engagements continued till the beginning of 1916. In the meantime, the British protectorates of Uganda, Rhodesia and Nyasaland also joined in the attacks on the borders of German East Africa and the Government of Belgium Congo, too agreed to co-operate in the attacks from the west of the enemy. Towards the end of 1915, the British Government decided the South African troops to German East Africa. These units started moving to British East Africa from December 1915, onwards and by the end of March 1916, all the units, comprising about 18,700 men, which had been detailed for East Africa, had reached there.

In 1916, General J.C. Smuts was given the task of defeating Lettow-Vorbeck. Smuts attacked from several directions: the main attack was from the north out of British East Africa, while substantial forces from the Belgian Congo advanced from the west in two columns, over Lake Victoria into the Rift Valley. Another contingent advanced over Lake Nyasa from the south-east. All these forces failed to capture Lettow-Vorbeck and they all suffered from disease along the march. The Germans nearly always retreated from the larger British troop concentrations and by September 1916, the German Central Railway from the coast at Dar es Salaam to Ujiji was fully under British control.

Major-General J.L. van Deventer of South Africa took over command of the campaign. Van Deventer began an offensive in July 1917, which by early autumn had pushed the Germans 100 mi (160 km) to the south. On 23RD November, Lettow-Vorbeck crossed into Portuguese Mozambique to plunder supplies from Portuguese garrisons. The Germans marched through Mozambique in caravans of troops, carriers, wives and children for nine months but were unable to gain much strength. Lettow-Vorbeck divided the force into three groups on the march. One detachment of 1,000 men under Hauptmann Theodor Tafel, was forced to surrender, after running out of food and ammunition; Lettow and Tafel were unaware they were only one day's march apart. The Germans returned to German East Africa and crossed into Northern Rhodesia in August 1918. On 13TH November the German Army took Kasama, which had been evacuated by the British. Lettow-Vorbeck marched his army to Abercorn and formally surrendered on 23RD November 1918.

15TH Punjab Regiment

29TH Punjabis (10/15TH)

In spite of defective organisation and unprecedented difficulties, the Indian Army played a significant role in the East African Campaign. In the early phase of the campaign, the Indian Army could not do well as it was not properly led, but later, under able commanders, it proved invaluable to the Allies.

Subedar Udham Singh. Jemadar Pala Singh, Jemadar Bhagwan Singh and Sepoy Puran Singh, were awarded the I.D.S.M., for their gallantry during the East African Campaign.

From East Africa the 29TH Punjabis were ordered for service in Palestine. After a period of stalemate in Southern Palestine from April to October 1917, General Edmund Allenby captured Beersheba. Having weakened the Turkish defences which had stretched almost continually from Gaza to Beersheba, they were finally captured by 8TH November, after the Battle of Tel el Khuweilfe, the Battle of Hareira and Sheria and the Third Battle of Gaza, when the pursuit began. During the subsequent operations, about 50 miles of formerly Turkish territory, was captured as a result of the victories at the Battle of Mughar Ridge, fought between 10TH and 14TH November, and the Battle of Jerusalem fought between 17TH November and 30TH December. Serious losses on the Western Front in March 1918 during Erich Ludendorff's German Spring Offensive, forced the British Empire to send reinforcements. During this time, two unsuccessful attacks were made to capture Amman and to capture Es Salt in March and April 1918, before Allenby's force resumed the offensive during the manoeuvre warfare of the Battle of Megiddo. The successful infantry battles at Tulkarm and Tabsor created gaps in the Turkish front line, allowing the pursuing Desert Mounted Corps to encircle the infantry fighting in the Judean Hills and fight the Battle of Nazareth and Battle of Samakh, capturing Afulah, Beisan, Jenin and Tiberias. In the process the British destroyed three Turkish armies during the Battle of Sharon, the Battle of Nablus, and the Third Transjordan battle, capturing thousands of prisoners and large quantities of equipment. Damascus and Aleppo were captured during the subsequent pursuit, before the Turkish Empire agreed to the Armistice of Mudros on 30 October 1918, ending the Sinai and Palestine Campaign. The British Mandate of Palestine and the French Mandate for Syria and Lebanon were created to administer the captured territories.

1921-22, a major reorganization was undertaken in the British Indian Army leading to the formation of large infantry groups of four to six Battalions. Among these was the 15TH Punjab Regiment, formed by grouping the 28TH, 26TH Punjabis with the 25TH, 27TH, and 29TH Punjabis. The Battalion was redesignated as 10TH (Training) Battalion of the 15th Punjab Regiment, based at Sialkot. During the Second World War, 10/15TH Punjab was converted into the 15TH Punjab Regimental Centre.

After the independence of the subcontinent in 1947, and the creation of Pakistan, the battalion was allotted to the new Pakistan Army. The Sikh soldiers from the battalion were transferred to the Indian Army.

16TH Punjab Regiment

30TH Punjabis (1/16TH)

The 30TH Punjabis was raised in 1857, as the 22ND Regiment of Punjab Infantry. It was designated as the 30TH Punjabis in 1903.

The regiment was raised during the upheaval of the Indian Mutiny, by Captain Nicholls at Ludhiana on 10TH June 1857, as the 22ND Regiment of Punjab Infantry. The men were mostly drawn from other infantry and police Battalions in the Punjab and their class composition was Sikhs, Punjabi Mussalmans, and Dogras. For the next two years, the regiment remained engaged in suppressing the rebellion. The following anecdote is typical of its activities. On 6TH, November, 1859, the right wing of the regiment entered the thick jungle bordering the Kalanadi River, where a band of mutineers was reported to be hiding in difficult country scored with deep ravines. The regiment carried through a most successful night operations which received special recommendation in the subsequent report to the commander of the Saugor Field Force. The name of Subedar Kan Singh was brought to his notice for conspicuous gallantry, Kan Singh thus becoming the first man in regimental history to gain this distinction.

The regiment took an active part in the Bhutan War of 1865, which began on 28TH, November, 1865, and lasted some four months. The Bhutanese were not lacking in courage, but rather sinews of war. In describing an early engagement an account states: "In advancing to the foot of the ascent leading up to the fort the troops were exposed to volleys of stones and arrows, two men being killed and several wounded". The real enemy in fact was sickness. In the 22ND Regiment of Punjab Infantry, fifty-four men died and seventeen were invalided out from this cause.

By 1880 the Second Afghan War had been in progress about a year. Negotiations for peace had been disrupted by a treacherous attack on the British Embassy in Kabul, and Lord Roberts had marched on Kandahar and occupied it by 13TH, October, 1879. On arrival at the Frontier, the 22ND Regiment of Punjab Infantry joined the 2ND Khyber Division engaged at that time in establishing a direct line of communication between Pashawar and Kabul. They were soon to see action. On 14TH, January, 1880, some 5,000 Mohmands with twenty-five standards were observed form Dakha Fort encamped on a plateau overlooking Kabul River and about five miles to the East of the Fort. Another body of about 3,000 were descried on the Gara Heights three miles to the South East. It was decided to drive the tribesmen away from these positions. On the morning of 15TH, January, a force was drawn up on the plain immediately south-west of Dakha Fort facing the three thousand Mohmands on the Gara Heights. The main force had marched six hours earlier and was assumed already to be in position to cut off the enemy's retreat. The attack began with the guns opening fire on the advanced Sangars of the tribesmen at range of 1,000 yards, while the infantry made a feint as if to threaten the enemy's north flank nearest the River.

16TH Punjab Regiment

30TH Punjabis (1/16TH)

The main infantry assault began in three echelons; 300 rifles forming the line of skirmishers, with 200 in support and the remainder in reserve. The attack was carried through with great dash and the Heights gained with the loss of only one man killed and three wounded. The force had crossed the Gara Pass but unfortunately the main body had encountered unexpected difficulties in traversing the route selected for them, and failed to close the gap in time to cut off the enemy's retreat by raft and ferry across the Kabul River. The river was at this point un-fordable and further action was delayed for a day pending the construction of rafts. This enabled the enemy to escape without further loss, but although in this respect the combined movement as planned had failed, later it became known that the defeat of Mohmands on the Gara Heights had created panic in the tribe and the country was deserted for miles around.

The regiment took part in various minor operations until in 1881; it received orders to join a punitive column operating against the Mahsuds. The column comprised about 4,000 fighting men, and 4,000 followers. Little opposition was met with. By the middle of May the regiment left Razmak and returned to Bannu having reconnoitred the then little known areas of the Blanki Narai, the Shani Plain, and the Shaktu Algad.

In March, 1895, the regiment left Rawalpindi to join the Chitral Relief Force. The advance through Malakand began on 1ST, April. The operations came to an end by the end of the month. In 1897, the Afridis and Orakzais demanded the abandonment of the British posts on the Samana Ridge and the withdrawal of all forces from the Swat Valley. They followed up this demand by attacking and capturing forts Ali Masjid, Mandi and Landi Kotal. The Sikh garrison at Saraghari fell after a heroic resistance died to a man. A punitive force assembled under Lockhart at Kohat. It was organized into two infantry divisions, the 1ST and the 2ND. The 30TH marched from Pashawar arriving at Hangu on 20TH September to join the 1ST Infantry Brigade of the 1ST Division. The two divisions were to traverse and ravage the territory of the Afridis and the Orakzais.

The 22ND Regiment of Punjab Infantry marched from Pashawar arriving at Hangu on 20TH September to join the 1ST Infantry Brigade of the 1ST Division. On 20TH October the advance began with an attack by 2ND Division on the heights above Dargai. The Afridis stood their ground and fought. After severe action the heights were captured. On 21ST the regiment moved up to Chogra Kotal, just short of Dargai Heights. Two days later it took over the Dargai Heights, and remained there until 24TH November, on which date it rejoined the 1ST Brigade. Meantime the operations carried out by the 2ND Division had succeeded in establishing complete domination of the Central Tirah, and plans were being prepared to return to India. The 1ST Division was ordered to withdraw down the Mastura Valley over hitherto unexplored Sapri Pass and there to re-assemble with the 2ND Division at Bara, with the re-occupation of the Khyber in view.

16TH Punjab Regiment

30TH Punjabis (1/16TH)

The plan also required the destruction en- route, of certain villages in the Waram Valley, home of the Aka Khels. Six companies of the 22ND Regiment of Punjab Infantry were allotted to the column to which this subsidiary task was assigned, and on 9TH December this force left the main column, crossed the hills, and entered the valley. The Aka Khels were taken completely by surprise and, though they kept up a continuous fire and later in the day were re-enforced by a large party of Jakka Khels, towers and houses extending for three miles down the valley were successfully destroyed.

On 16TH, January, a Piquet of 2 N.C.O.s and 18 men of the 22ND Regiment of Punjab Infantry., moving out to take up a position, found it held by 40 to 50 Afridis, who opened up heavy fire on the forward section commanded by Lance-Havildar Kesar Singh. One man was killed and two wounded, while Kesar Singh himself was grazed by three bullets. In spite of the superior strengths of the opposition, the Piquet succeeded in putting the Afridis to flight and occupying the position. Lance-Havildar Kesar Singh was awarded the I.O.M. for his gallantry. This was the last action in which the regiment took part in this campaign.

Subsequent to the reforms brought about in the Indian in 1902, the regiment's designation was changed to 30TH Punjabis.

During 1902, the 30TH Punjabis were selected to go to China to join the China Expeditionary Force. It arrived off the coast of China in the Gulf of Pe-Chhi on 12TH July, and disembarked at Sinho. The role attached to 30TH Punjabis on arrival was primarily railway protection. The stay of the regimenting China came to an end in July, 1905, when it returned to India.

When the Great War broke out the regiment was serving on the North-West Frontier, and provided large drafts of officers and men for the units on active service on other theatres of war. On 1ST November, 1916, the regiment was ordered to German East Africa. By middle of 1916, two- thirds of the country was in allied hands, and Dar-es-Salaam had surrendered.

The German forces were, however, still a formidable challenge. Their commander, Colonel Paul Von Lettow-Vorbeck, saw that his role was to hold out as long as possible, and to involve the maximum number of British troops who would be prevented from being used against Germany in the main theatre of war. In this he achieved considerable success. The basis of his strategy was planned retreat. He fought delayed actions from carefully selected positions, but avoided set battles. He always survived to fight another day. His small force of German officers and African Askaris was adept in all the skills of bush and jungle warfare. It lived on the country and on captured supplies, and it developed a technique of disengaging and melting away into the bush, which seldom failed to leave the British forces baffled. On 31ST, December, the brigade commenced to advance towards Kisswani, and was involved in a sharp action, in which the Germans disengaged.

16TH Punjab Regiment

30TH Punjabis (1/16TH)

Before he could withdraw over the Rufiji River, a brisk action ensued, in which the 30TH Punjabis suffered the regiment's first casualties, and the enemy was again able to disengage and withdraw into the jungle. The regiment in the advance guard was in time to bring machine-gun fire on the retreating enemy, but not in time to prevent his crossing and destroying the only bridge. In order to give no respite, it was decided that a bridge-head should be established on the other side of the river, during the hour of darkness, and the task was allotted to 30TH Punjabis. As the regiment crossed the river, it ran into opposition, and was heavily engaged in a fire-fight, when the company commanders were instructed to fall back gradually. In this battle the 30TH single handed engaged a considerably superior force. Although suffering heavily in the process, it beat the Germans back and secured the bridgehead for the brigade. Spasmodic fighting continued at the bridgehead for several days, and then on the 16TH, January, the Germans withdrew from the trap long before the jaws could close.

Immediate awards for gallantry of I.D.S.M. were made to; Subedar Thakur Singh, Jemadar Hakam Singh, and Havildar Lal Singh.

In an action fought by the 30TH Punjabis at Tandamuti Hill on 3^{RD,} August, 1917, the Germans were astride the trolley line and constructed a strong-point covering a loop in it; to secure their right flank they had fortified Tandamuti Hill about mile and half to the east, while to protect their left, they had dug in on the heights known as the Kipaniya Ridge, about a mile west of the trolley tracks, The three positions were quite independent of each other, and dense bush covered the whole area. All the frontal attacks failed and the Germans finally decided to abandon the Tandamuti positions. Throughout September, the advance along the Lukuledi River continued slowly. Finally they started closing on the Germans around Mahiwa. The Germans fought series of bitter and bloody actions around Mahiwa. Although the Germans survived, fighting around Mahiwa marked the close of major operations in East African Campaign. On November, 7TH, as the British forces closed in, the Germans slipped across the border into Portuguese East Africa. The 30TH Punjabis embarked at Lindi and sailed for India, and reached Karachi on 10TH, January, 1918.

In 1921-22, a major reorganization was undertaken in the British Indian Army leading to the formation of large infantry groups of four to six regiments. Among these was the 16TH Punjab Regiment, formed by grouping the 30TH Punjabis with the 31ST, 33RD and 46TH Punjabis, and the 9TH Bhopal Infantry. The 30TH Punjabi's new designation was 1ST Battalion, 16TH Punjab Regiment.

The outbreak the Second World War had found the battalion serving on the North-West Frontier. It was taking part in minor operations against the tribes, while constantly despatching officers and men for service in other theatres of war. In February, 1940, the battalion moved to the Ahmedzai Salient. This is a well defined tract of tribal territory which buts the Kohat-Bannu road.

16ᵀᴴ Punjab Regiment

30ᵀᴴ Punjabis (1/16ᵀᴴ)

During the winter months of 1939-40 marauding tribesmen had been making frequent incursions into British territory. Operations began on 11ᵀᴴ, February, to deal with this nuisance. In this preliminary phase an unfortunate an unfortunate incident took place. 'A' Company holding a position in the centre of the brigade front was unfortunately left with both sides exposed. The tribesmen were quick to occupy positions overlooking and to open heavy fire. The commander and two other ranks killed and four wounded. A counter attack by the whole 1/16ᵀᴴ Punjab Regiment extricated the unfortunate company. For gallantry in this action Lance-Naik Gurbaksh Singh was awarded the I.D.S.M.

In early September, 1942, the 1/16ᵀᴴ Punjab Regiment received orders to proceed to the Eastern Frontier. Transfer of the 1ˢᵀ Battalion to the eastern front coincided with a general lull there as the Japanese were re-grouping their forces after their drive through Burma. Early in February, 1943, to join the 23ᴿᴰ Indian Division the Battalion proceeded from Chittagong by rail to Manipur Road, moved to Imphal, and then across the frontier into Burma at Tamu. Between the end of February and July, the battalion was mainly employed in routine patrolling in the teak forests of the Kabaw Valley. By 1ˢᵀ November, 1943, the battalion had moved to Tiddim area. From Tiddim the battalion marched down to the road to Milestone 52. On 12ᵀᴴ November, in bright moonlight a Japanese company attacked a platoon on point 653. The platoon under Jemadar Ishar Singh shot steadily and well, repelling repeated Japanese assaults. As soon as light started coming up, a company counter attacked and the Japanese withdrew. The body of a Japanese officer complete with sword was recovered from the front of the position. Jemadar Ishar Singh was awarded the I.D.S.M. for his fine leadership in this action. However, the battalion suffered heavy casualties during the action on Milestone 52. The Japanese made no effort to exploit their gains from Milestone 52. During the months from March to May, 1944, the battalion fought with great distinction in the actions at Kasom and Shongphel.

On 11ᵀᴴ, May, the battalion once more had to take to the hills. Japanese guns had been shelling the Palel air strip from the neighbourhood of Phalbung. The free use of airfields was vital for the supply of the troops beleaguered on the Imphal Plain. The battalion received orders to advance on Phalbung and capture or drive out the guns. The country around the Imphal Plain was mountainous in the extreme. The few tracks generally ran along the tops of ridges. Any movement by wheeled vehicles was impossible. The battalion set out and harboured the first night on a high hill near Mawchi some eight miles from Phalbung. On the 12ᵀᴴ, it continued to march towards Phalbung, but late in the morning the brigade commander, met the Battalion at Maibi Khunou. He said that a Patiala company had encountered some Japanese at Khudei Khunou, two miles down the track, and was in the process of clearing the village. As was usual in the Naga Hills, the track followed the crest line of a high ridge. The small Naga villages, presumably for reasons of defence, were mostly built on the ridge tops.

16TH Punjab Regiment

30TH Punjabis (1/16TH)

Colonel Newel noticed a spur which came up from the valley below and ran into Japanese position from the left. He ordered 'B' Company 1/16TH Punjab Regiment under Major Kehar Singh to take over the frontal position from Patiala Company. Kehar Singh was to engage the Japanese along the ridge and to 'jitter' the right flank without becoming seriously engaged. 'A' and 'C' Companies he ordered to descend some way into the valley below, cross onto the spur leading into the Japanese position and then by ascending the spur, assault the Japanese from the left flank. The guns he directed to put down slow accurate fire on the Japanese while the outflanking movement was in progress, 'C' Company moved off followed by' A' Company. The movement went through as planned. At this juncture, 'A' Company formed up in jungle assault formation with all automatic weapons in front. With a loud battle-cry the swept forward, shooting from the hip as they went. The firing reached a crescendo then the Japanese suddenly broke, and the dauntless company reached the summit. On 14TH May, the battalion went on to occupy Phalbung. During the actions from 16TH May to 7TH June, at the regiment was the part of the force which utterly destroyed the 15TH Japanese army. The Japanese capitulated on 15^{TH,} August, 1945, and the 1/16TH Punjab Regiment were ordered to Malaya for occupational duties. Then battalion was then moved to Java. On 3RD, October, the battalion landed at Tanjoeng Prior and moved to Batavia. Their task was to restore law and order, and hand the country back to the Dutch. The battalion was made responsible for the southern sector of Batavia. It took over responsibility for six Japanese internment camps still housing over 5,000 Dutch women and children, a civil hospital, a gas works, a power station, a telephone exchange and various dumps of arms, ammunition and military equipment. The situation in Batavia deteriorated steadily, Jemadar Sohan Singh was murdered while investigating a sniping incident and a full scale operation was mounted against the Indonesians. On 8TH February, 1946, the battalion left Batavia for Buitzenborg on occupational duties and ordered back to Batavia on 10TH June. The Battalion finally sailed for India on 18^{TH,} November, 1946. Their role in suppressing the movement for Indonesian independence had been distasteful one.

After the independence of the subcontinent in 1947, and the creation of Pakistan, the battalion was allotted to the new Pakistan Army. The Sikh soldiers from the battalion were transferred to the Indian Army.

31ST Punjabis (2/16TH)

The 31ST Punjabis was raised in 1857, as Van Cortland's Levy. The regiment was designated as the 31ST Punjabis in 1903. The regiment was raised during the upheaval of the Indian Mutiny, by General Van Cortland at Ferozepore on 22 May 1857, as 'Van Cortland's Levy' and afterwards 'Bloomfield's Sikhs'. On 7TH June 1857, the 'Bloomfield's Sikhs' marched to Hariana, which was in state of rebellion.

16TH Punjab Regiment

31ST Punjabis (2/16TH)

Within a fortnight of leaving Ferozepore, they fought an action at Udaiki and at the assault and capture of the fortified villages of Khairaki and Saharun, sustaining a loss of six killed and 33 wounded. Whilst in the Field recruiting parties were sent out to enlist Sikhs and Mussalmans in the Lahore, Ferozepore and Patiala. Transfers were made from the 1ST Punjab Infantry, and the 1ST Company, Punjab Sappers and Miners, which had been part of the Sikh Army, was bodily transferred to the Corps. The class composition of the regiment had already been laid down, as Sikhs, Punjabi Mussalmans, Dogras, Hill Rajputs and Gurkhas.

In August, 1857, two companies held Hissar and beat back an attack made by rebel force. In September, a detachment took part in the capture of the fortified village of Mangali and assisted at the assault and capture of Jamalpur. On 16TH, November, the regiment was engaged in the action at Karnoul.

With the sister regiment the 30TH; the regiment took an active part in the Bhutan War. The war, began on 28TH, November, 1865, and lasted some four months. The Bhutanese were not lacking in courage, but rather sinews of war. The real enemy in fact was sickness. In the 31ST regiment, seventy-nine men died of fever. Battle casualties were light. After a stint with the punitive expeditions on the North-West Frontier, the regiment proceeded to Malta. After an uneventful stay at Malta, with the Indian Expeditionary Force, the regiment sailed for Cyprus, and after about a month, returned to India.

Then alongside its sister regiment again, it was ordered to Afghanistan, to take part in the Second Afghan War. Negotiations for peace had been disrupted by a treacherous attack on the British Embassy in Kabul, and Lord Roberts had marched on Kandahar and occupied it by 13TH, October, 1879. On arrival at the Frontier the 30TH and 31ST both joined the 2ND Khyber Division engaged at that time in establishing a direct line of communication between Pashawar and Kabul. On 14TH, January, 1880, some 5,000 Mohmands with twenty-five standards were observed encamped on a plateau overlooking Kabul River and about five miles to the East of the Dakka Fort. The 31ST rapidly drove the enemy before them and cleared the plateau. On March, 26TH, a Detachment marching to join Headquarters at Gandamak halted the night at Fort Battye. Next day 1,200 Shinwaris and Khugianas delivered a determined attack on the Fort. The detachment of the regiment was encamped in a low walled enclosure outside the Fort itself. Lieutenant Angelo was killed in the first rush. However, the detachment under Subedar Sher Singh fought with utmost courage and the attackers eventually withdrew. Colonel Hannah in his account attributed holding of the Fort to the presence of the detachment.

For services in Afghanistan Subedar Sher Singh was admitted to the Order of British India.

16TH Punjab Regiment

31ST Punjabis (2/16TH)

On the 15TH September the regiment left for Rawalpindi to accompany the Chitral Reliefs, and went as far as Baradum beyond the Lowarai Pass, returning to Rawalpindi on the 9TH November. While the 31ST was at Rawalpindi, parties of Mounted Infantry were sent for service with Mounted Infantry Companies in Somaliland (November 1902) and Tibet (January 1904), and another party did duty with the Ekka Corps formed for service in Tibet.

Subsequent to the reforms brought about in the Indian Army in 1903, the regiment's designation was changed to 31ST Punjabis.

The beginning of the Great War, found the 31ST Punjabis serving on the North-West Frontier. Numerous drafts were sent to other regiments denuded of trained men. The regiment embarked for Mesopotamia on 9TH December, 1915. Disembarking at Basra on 15TH December, the regiment joined the 34TH Brigade and at once moved by steamer to Kurna and thence in sailing boats across the Hamar Lake to Hakika. Here the Regiment in conjunction with H.M. Gunboats, made small expeditions to punish raiding lake tribes and was employed in escorting river steamers and convoys of Lake Bellums between Nasiriyah and Kurna. In August, 1916, the regiment rejoined the 34TH Brigade at Khanisiyah, but was again detached in November, to Tel El Lahm to guard the railway then in the process of construction from Basra to Nasiriyah; the detachment guarding the railhead was encamped for some time at Ur of the Chaldees. In January, 1917, the 31ST Punjabis moved to Nasiriyah, the Headquarters of the newly formed 15TH Division. The regiment remained at Nasiriyah till the 4TH April when the 15TH Division having been transferred to the Tigres, and encamped at Maghil.

The 31ST Punjabis remained quietly between Samara and Tekrit till September, 1918, when having been specially selected for service with the Salonika Force, moved by rail and River to Basra, and embarked on 4TH October, 1918, and disembarked at Salonika on the 25TH. On the 7TH November the regiment moved by sea to Chanak in the Dardanelles and remained there till transferred to March, 1919, to Constantinople, Turkey, as part of Allied occupation forces. In May 1919, the 31ST Punjabis took over the Bosporus defences. Detachments were furnished in 1919 and 1920 at Gumuldjina, Osmanie, Buyuk Dere Fort, Yenikeui, Chiboukli, Killos, Pirgos and Beikos. In a raid at Yenikeui and Stenia, organised to search for hidden arms, a Sikh Sepoy was killed. In October, 1920, the 31ST Punjabis returned to India after 5 years overseas service.

In 1921–22, a major reorganization was undertaken in the British Indian Army, leading to the formation of large infantry groups of four to six Battalions. Among these was the 16TH Punjab Regiment, formed by grouping the 31ST Punjabis with the 30TH, 33RD and 46TH Punjabis, and the 9TH Bhopal Infantry. The Battalion's new designation was 2ND Battalion, 16TH Punjab Regiment.

16TH Punjab Regiment

31ST Punjabis (2/16TH)

During the Second World War, the battalion fought in the Malayan Campaign. The Battle of Malaya began when the 25TH Army invaded Malaya on 8TH December 1941. Japanese troops launched an amphibious assault on the northern coast of Malaya at Kota Bharu and started advancing down the eastern coast of Malaya This was made in conjunction with landings at Patani and Songkhla in Thailand, where they then proceeded south overland across the Thailand-Malayan border to attack the western portion of Malaya. The Japanese were initially resisted by III Corps of the Indian Army and several British Army battalions. The Japanese quickly isolated individual Indian units defending the coastline, before concentrating their forces to surround the defenders and forcing their surrender. The Japanese forces held a slight advantage in numbers on the ground in northern Malaya, and were significantly superior in close air support, armour, co-ordination, tactics and experience, with the Japanese units having fought in China. The Allies had no tanks, which had put them at a severe disadvantage. The Japanese also used bicycle infantry and light tanks, which allowed swift movement of their forces overland through terrain covered with thick tropical rainforest, albeit criss-crossed by native paths.

2/16TH Punjab Regiment which formed a part of the 11TH Indian Davison, had started to occupy Jitra positions on 8TH December, 1941. The Jitra positions were overrun and captured by the Japanese. The defeat of Allied troops at Jitra by Japanese forces, supported by tanks moving south from Thailand on 11TH December 1941 and the rapid advance of the Japanese inland from their Kota Bharu beachhead on the north-east coast of Malaya overwhelmed the northern defences. With virtually no remaining Allied planes, the Japanese also had mastery of the skies, leaving the Allied ground troops and civilian population exposed to air attack. On 23RD December, Major-General David Murray-Lyon of the Indian 11TH Infantry Division was removed from command to little effect. By the end of the first week in January, the entire northern region of Malaya had been lost to the Japanese. By this time the casualties had so reduced all battalions that the remnants of 2/16TH Punjab Regiment were also to fuse into a single unit. Throughout these operations the Japanese had relentlessly pursued the retreating Punjabis. 2ND and 3RD battalions of the 16TH Punjab Regiment just managed to cross over the Causeway into Singapore. They were taken prisoner by the Japanese following the British surrender on 15TH February 1942. A large number of recommendations for awards were sent in, but owing to the confused state of affairs, few were granted. The exception was the award to Major Pritam Singh who was awarded the Military Cross, for his gallant leadership during the Malayan Campaign.

On the release of the 1/16TH Punjab Regiment from captivity, it was re-raised in 1946. After the independence of the subcontinent in 1947, and the creation of Pakistan, the battalion was allotted to the new Pakistan Army. The Sikh soldiers from the battalion were transferred to the Indian Army.

16TH Punjab Regiment

33RD Punjabis (3/16TH)

The 33RD Punjabis was raised in 1857, as the Allahabad Levy. It was designated as the 33RD Punjabis in 1903. The regiment was raised during the upheaval of the Indian Mutiny, by Lieutenant EH Longmore at Allahabad on 23RD December 1857, as the Allahabad Levy. It was initially composed of low-caste Hindus, but in 1890, it was reconstituted with Punjabi Mussalmans. From this date, the regiment was continually being called out to quell riots round about Allahabad.

On February the 15TH, 1887, the regiment left India for service in Burma, where it remained until the 13TH, April, 1890. These three years saw the regiment continuously engaged in semi-bush warfare against half-civilised dacoits. The Regiment was split up into well-scattered detachments which were more or less continuously employed in chasing and punishing dacoits. Actual casualties due to action we very slight, but towards the end of the campaign sickness took heavy toll of the fighting strength.

On 10TH, November, 1894, the regiment received orders to proceed to Dera-Ismail-Khan. From this date it remained with the Waziristan Field Force until 21ST, March, 1895. From 1895 until June 1897, ordinary peace training was carried on. In June 1897, after hurried mobilisation the regiment marched to Mian Shah, where they remained with the Tochi Field Force until 1899. On the 24TH December, 1899, the was once more reorganised it was changed from a class Punjabi Muhammadan regiment to a class company regiment composed of Sikhs, Punjabi Mussalmans and Pathans. Subsequent to the reforms brought about in the Indian in 1903, the regiment's designation was changed to 33RD Punjabis.

During the First World War, the 33RD Punjabis served in Egypt and disembarked on Suez on November 19TH, 1914. The regiment proceeded to Ismailia where it remained improving general defences until December 5TH when it crossed the canal and encamped at Moascar Camp. From this date until the end of April defensive positions were reconnoitred, improved and manned. During April and May there was a certain amount of sniping which culminated on the 31ST May, by an enemy party about forty strong attacking a company Piquet. The attack was beaten off.

After this incident there was very little enemy activity, and on August the 25TH, the 33RD Punjabis received orders to proceed to France. The Regiment disembarked at Marseilles on the 3RD September, and then proceeded to billets at La Gorgue. On September 25TH, the 33RD Punjabis made their first real entrance into the furnace of European warfare. On September 25TH, 1915, the regiment took part in the Battle of Loos. In conjunction with the general advance ordered for this section, and when the preliminary bombardment had taken place, the 33RD left their trenches, and after a gallant struggle captured the German trenches immediately to their front.

16TH Punjab Regiment

33RD Punjabis (3/16TH)

Unfortunately the success was merely local, and the troops on the flanks bad not been able to accomplish such a long advance, consequently, in order to conform with the new line, the hard earned objective had to be vacated for position further in rear. Sepoy Lachman Singh was awarded the I.D.S.M. for his conspicuous gallantry against the Germans in France.

Leaving Marseilles on 6TH December, 1915, the regiment sailed for Port Said. By 13TH December, they were once again defending the Canal. From December 13TH until February 15TH, 1916, the regiment with its Headquarters at Ismailia was responsible for railway defence between Suez and Qantara.

On February 15TH, the regiment embarked for Aden, where they arrived on the 21ST February. They proceeded to Sheikh Othman, where they took up and outpost line of defence. On the 16TH March, an attack by the Aden Force was made on Imad. In this action a Company and the Machine-Guns were with the attacking column; the remainder of the regiment was in general reserve north of Helwar. With the exception of a patrol between Dardamas and Dar-ul-Mansur coming into contact with about 20 to 25 of the enemy on the 10TH April, 1916, and extricating them without loss under the fire of the cavalry patrol, nothing of importance occurred until October. During October the Turks began to show signs of activity and on the night 13TH-14TH shelled Sheikh Othman. On the 25TH a flying column encountered Turks and drove them out of a position near Hatum. The enemy casualties were estimated at 20 killed and wounded.

From Aden the Regiment proceeded to German East Africa. The German forces were, however, still a formidable challenge. Their commander, Colonel Paul Von Lettow-Vorbeck, saw that his role was to hold out as long as possible, and to involve the maximum number of British troops who would be prevented from being used against Germany in the main theatre of war. In this he achieved considerable success. The basis of his strategy was planned retreat. He fought delayed actions from carefully selected positions, but avoided set battles. He always survived to fight another day. His small force of German officers and African Askaris was adept in all the skills of bush and jungle warfare. It lived on the country and on captured supplies, and it developed a technique of disengaging and melting away into the bush, which seldom failed to leave the British forces baffled. The 33RD Punjabis disembarked at Kilwa on 8TH May. From Sangino Camp a detachment proceeded to Wungui and another detachment proceeded to Beumont's Post. On the 26TH one of patrols at Beumont's Post, encountered the enemy with a total loss to the regiment, two Sepoys killed and one wounded. Three days later a patrol was ambushed at the same place and every one was killed. Reconnoitring patrols established the fact that Kimamba Hill was occupied by the enemy, and on June 29TH, the commanding officer decided to clear the hill. This was carried out through with only one casualty to the Regiment. On July 19TH, the regiment was once again engaged in a heavy but successful battle at Kibunburu and Narungomba.

16TH Punjab Regiment

33RD Punjabis (3/16TH)

During these two more or less successful battles, Jemadar Bachint Singh and 12 men were killed. The regiment sailed for India on 9TH February, 1918. This date marked the final stage in the Great War as far as the 33RD Punjabis were concerned.

Subedar Amar Singh and Havildar Mehr Singh were awarded the I.D.S.M. for their conspicuous gallantry against the Germans East Africa.

On returning to India from East Africa, the regiment continuously mounted punitive expeditions against the various tribesmen on the North-West Frontier of India. On 12TH January, 1921 until May 1922, the Regiment joined the Corps of Occupations in Turkey.

In 1922, a major reorganization was undertaken in the British Indian Army, leading to the formation of large infantry groups of four to six Battalions. Among these was the 16TH Punjab Regiment, formed by grouping the 31ST Punjabis with the 30TH, 33RD and 46TH Punjabis, and the 9TH Bhopal Infantry. The Battalion's new designation was 3RD Battalion, 16TH Punjab Regiment.

In 1931, the Battalion was sent to Burma to take part in the operations subsequently known as 'The Burma Rebellion.' In some eighty miles from Rangoon, on Christmas Day, one of the tribal leaders known as 'The Golden Crow,' who is apparently the object of superstitious reverence, led about 500 tribesmen out of the jungle in a foray of killing, burning, and looting. There was a sharp encounter with the police, and a British forest engineer was murdered. The battalion was sent to reinforce the local police. On the completion of active operations in Burma the battalion returned to India.

During the Second World War, the battalion fought in the Malayan Campaign. The campaign began on 8TH December 1941 when Japanese forces landed in Singora and Patani in southern Thailand, and Kota Bharu in northern Malaya. Early in 1941, the 3/16TH Punjab Regiment, received orders to go overseas as part of the 15TH Indian Infantry Brigade. The battalion embarked at Bombay on March 7TH and on the morning of 17TH March, anchored off Penang and became part of 11TH Indian Division, with the task of defending the airfields at Alor Star and Sungei Patani. A special operation was planned therefore to block the Japanese advance. An improvised force known as 'Krohcol' (As Krohcol was not fully assembled 3/16TH Punjab Regiment began the advance alone), was to launch itself some 30 miles into the Thai territory and secure a position known as 'The Ledges'. Krohcol crossed the frontier into Thailand on the 8TH, and was immediately faced by road blocks and manned by some 300 Thai armed constabularies. It had been hoped that the Thai would not oppose the entry of British troops; their action in doing so delayed the advance of the column, by dusk that evening, was only about three miles beyond the border. After a night of sniping, the advance continued on the 9TH in the face of further opposition from the armed constabulary. All opposition however ceased suddenly, and Betong was occupied that evening.

16TH Punjab Regiment

33RD Punjabis (3/16TH)

The next morning (10TH) the column moved forward in trucks to a point six miles short of the Ledge position, from where it continued the advance on foot. Before it had covered the next mile, the advanced guard came under fire from enemy troops and an encounter battle developed. Heavy fighting ensued, but the enemy, who was in considerable strength and supported by light tanks, checked the advance. By nightfall on the 10TH, 3/16TH Punjab Regiment, with two companies cut off, was forced to take up a defensive position some twenty-five miles beyond the frontier, after destroying a road bridge to provide a tank obstacle. Meanwhile, 5/14TH Punjab (Less one company) and 10TH Mountain Battery had arrived at Kroh. During the afternoon of the 11TH, 3/16TH Punjab Regiment, repelled repeated strong attacks along the road, but casualties began to mount.

The Sikh mortar crew did splendid work despite casualties in the observation post which had been located by the Japanese. When the Havildar was wounded, Lance-Naik Tehl Singh ran from the mortar to the observation point to observe the strike and then back to adjust the aim. His enthusiasm was great tonic and his skill was enough to silence the enemy on more than one occasion. He then set up his mortar within a few yards of Battalion H.Q. which made things rather uncomfortable. Evidence received later indicated that the first few bombs from this new position fell right among the Japanese, breaking up the attack they were mounting.

Lieutenant Colonel Moorhead, who had correctly estimated the enemy strength as three battalions, realized that an early withdrawal was his only course of action. He explained the position to Murray-Lyon and was given permission to withdraw at his discretion. Accordingly he made preparations to pull back early next morning. At dawn on the 12TH the enemy renewed his attacks astride the road, and in addition attempted to by-pass the defences by working south along the right bank of the Patani River. Moorhead then ordered the withdrawal to begin. A further enemy attack supported by artillery upset his plan and it was only with great difficulty and further heavy casualties that he managed to disengage. During the afternoon 3/16TH Punjab Regiment, reduced to about half its original strength, passed through 5/14TH Punjab Regiment in position north-east of Betong and that evening reached the prepared defensive position on the Baling Road three miles west of Kroh. The threat to 11TH Division resulting from the Japanese advance along the Patani-Kroh road continued to grow.

Following up his successes of the 12TH, the enemy quickly made contact with 5/14TH Punjab Regiment during the night of the 12TH/13TH. To avoid becoming too heavily engaged this battalion withdrew about noon on the 13TH to Betong, from where, after destroying the road bridge, it moved to join 3/16TH Punjab Regiment in the defensive position west of Kroh. This withdrawal uncovered the road running south from the village of Kroh through Grik t link with the main west coast road at Kuala Sangsar. North of Grik, it was more than a narrow unmetalled track fit for use by light motor vehicles in dry weather.

16TH Punjab Regiment

33RD Punjabis (3/16TH)

Nevertheless, as the Japanese infantry could use it, it represented serious threat to the line of communication serving 111 Corps. On the 14TH 'Krohcol' was placed under the command of Brigadier Paris, and he was ordered to protect the right flank of 11TH Division's communications against any enemy advance along the Kroh-Baling road. At Baling, information was passed to Brigadier Paris of the various paths down which the Japanese might come from Kroh and which would bring them out below Baling. The 3/16TH Punjab Regiment had been fighting the Japanese 42ND Infantry Regiment supported by tanks virtually single handed. No praise is too great for this splendid feat of arms without which the fate of 11TH Division might well have been sealed in the first week of the campaign. On the morning of 16TH December, General Heath, decided to withdraw 11TH Division to the line of the Krian River. Krohcol was disbanded. The 3/16TH Punjab Regiment, supported by 10TH Mountain Battery, was ordered to cover the right flank by holding the river crossing at Salema.

At the Krian River crossing, the 3/16TH Punjab Regiment, contacted the Japanese on bicycles as they approached the bridge, they were scattered by well aimed Light Machine Gun bursts. Shortly after, an attempt was made to cross the ford; this too was driven off with the able assistance of the Mountain Battery. A long stand on the Krian River was not considered possible, and when on the 20TH the enemy reached Salema, 3/16TH Punjab Regiment was given permission to withdraw at discretion. On 27TH December, the 3/16TH Punjab Regiment arrived at Kampar, and were delighted to find itself in the 6/15TH Infantry Brigade and the 2/16TH Punjab Regiment serving alongside it. The Kampar position was one of the strongest in Malaya. The 28TH Brigade held a hill position around Kampar, and when the Japanese attacked on 31ST December, they beat them off with such a heavy loss they did not try again in this area. As the last elements of the 2/16TH Punjab Regiment were withdrawing the Japanese attacked and they had to put in a counter-attack to get clear. To cover the withdrawal of the 12TH Brigade, the 2ND and 3/16TH Punjab Regiment, took up a rear guard position to cover the road junction at Bidor. Early in January, because of their severe losses, amalgamation of 2ND and 3RD Battalions was carried out. Lt.-Col. Moorhead was appointed to command the combined Battalion. The 16TH Punjab withdrew to Singapore on 29TH January, and was taken prisoner by the Japanese following the British surrender on 15TH February 1942. . On the morning of 17TH February all the Indian ranks were separated from their British officers and sent off to a separate camp. A large number of recommendations for awards were sent in, but owing to the confused state of affairs, few were granted. The exception was the award of I.D.S.M to Lance-Naik Narinjan Singh.

On the release of the 2ND Battalion from captivity, it was re-raised in 1946. In 1947 at the creation of Pakistan, the battalion was allocated to Pakistan Army. The Sikh soldiers accompanied Major Harchand Singh to the Sikh regiment at Ambala on 14TH August, 1947.

16TH Punjab Regiment

9TH Bhopal Infantry (4/16TH)

The 9TH Bhopal Infantry was raised in 1859, as the Bhopal Levy. It was designated as the 9TH Bhopal Infantry in 1903. The regiment could trace its origins to 1818, when it was raised at Sehore, as a mixed force of infantry and cavalry by the State of Bhopal for service with the British. The contingent comprised at this time Sikhs, Muhammadans and Rajputs indiscriminately mingled in eight companies of infantry. The cavalry mainly came from the Punjab. The gunners were a mixture of Brahmins and Muhammadans recruited only from Oudh. It was known as the Bhopal Contingent and was employed to keep peace in the lawless regions of Central India.

During the Sepoy Mutiny, the contingent fought at Indore and Sehore. Thereafter the infantry were drafted into various bodies of police, which policed northward and eastward. Following the upheaval of the Indian Mutiny, the contingent was reorganized by Lieutenant Colonel James Travers, VC, as the Bhopal Levy in May 1859. In 1865, it was redesignated as the Bhopal Battalion.

In 1878, the battalion participated in the Second Afghan War, where it operated on the Line of Communication. In 1887 all the companies adopted one class system. Subsequent to the reforms brought about in the Indian Army in 1903, the Bhopal Battalion's designation was changed to 9TH Bhopal Infantry.

Opportunities for sport for the 9TH were not lacking. A good many of the men became expert in marking down tigers and running a beat. On one occasion in 1896, a tiger had been wounded, and turned back on the beaters under the command of Havildar Badhawa Singh, a staunch Sikh. The bearers took to the trees, covered by Badhawa Singh with an old Martini Henry carbine and six rounds of ammunition. The tiger's wounds prevented it moving very fast. Badhawa Singh coolly fired at it. The tiger turned towards the firer, but before it could get to him Badhawa Singh shot off his six rounds, and then hastily swarmed up the nearest tree, encouraged by the tiger striking at him from below. The officers following up the tiger then arrived and despatched the brute. On examining the body it was found that all six shots of Havildar Badhawa Singh had got home.

During the First World War, the 9TH Bhopal Infantry was dispatched to France in 1914. It reached Marseilles on September 26^{TH,} 1941. At Marseilles the regiment was re-armed with new rifles and ammunition. As they had arrived wearing tropical uniforms, warm clothing also had to be issued. The regiment suffered heavy losses at the Battle of Neuve Chapelle. The Officer Commanding 9TH Bhopal Infantry was given orders to move forward and assist Royal West Kent Regiment, and carry them forward into their trenches, which they were to occupy. The regiment moved forward from Rouge-Croix with its right on the main La Bassée Road.

16TH Punjab Regiment

9TH Bhopal Infantry (4/16TH)

In darkness and enclosed country, bogs and barbed wire fences, cohesion was lost, but eventually the whole battalion reached the Royal West Kent's trenches, which had never been vacated by them. Companies commenced entrenching at once, but it was found that the left of the West Kent's was in the air, hence fresh dispositions were made. The situation was critical. The enemy had practically enveloped the left of the West Kents and were actually firing into them from the rear.

The 9TH Bhopal Infantry, arriving on the right flank of the Germans, forced them to retire and so protected the Royal West Kents. As soon the positions were occupied the men entrenched, and the Patrols watched the front up to Neuve Chapelle. Frequent attacks were made by the enemy during the night, searchlights played on the left all night; several snipers remained behind the line causing a number of casualties. At about 11 a.m. a bombardment of the guns commenced and lasted fifteen minutes. Written orders were received for an attack to be made by troops facing Neuve Chapelle. The attack was not co-ordinated, units advancing independently. The original trenches from which the Wiltshires had been driven out the previous evening were reached. The enemy then started a severe bombardment on this thin line, and supported it with a strong counter-attack, which drove in the left and then gradually forced the rest of the line to give way. In the withdrawal, unsupported by fire, the regiment suffered many casualties, eventually the remnants of the regiment collected on the road south of Rouge-Croix.

Amongst the casualties, Subedar Partab Singh was killed. Subedar Major Bhur Singh and Havildar Amar Singh were awarded the I.D.S.M. for their gallantry in the battle of Neuve Chapelle.

On the night of November 4TH/5TH the regiment took over trenches from Royal Scots Fusiliers. These trenches were held till November 8TH. During this period no serious attack was made, but the regiment was subjected to severe bombardment which caused heavy casualties. The total number of casualties was one Indian officer (Subedar Major Bhur Singh) and 75 other ranks.

On November 22ND orders were received to relieve the Bareilly Brigade near Festubert that night. The relief was carried out in the dark. Nos. three and four companies occupied the fire trenches, Nos. one and two companies the support trenches. The 59TH Rifles, Frontier Force prolonged the line t the right, the 34TH Sikh Pioneers to the left. On the 23RD a heavy bombing attack began against the Sikh Pioneers. Both support companies of the 9TH were moved up to strengthen the Pioneers. As the Pioneer's front started to crumble the left flank of the 9TH became enveloped. Gradually the Germans surrounded the Nos. three and four companies, who were putting up a stout fight against heavily odds. The fighting became hand-to-hand; the men were handicapped by having no proper bombs to keep the enemy at a distance.

16TH Punjab Regiment

9TH Bhopal Infantry (4/16TH)

Gradually it became obvious that these two companies had been overrun. The 2ND / 8TH Gurkhas and 6TH Jats had been brought back, and they counter-attacked as soon as they arrived, but were unable to recover the lost ground. Meanwhile, several other units had been brought up and further counter-attacks launched without any real progress being made, until the arrival of the 1/39TH Garhwal Rifles and 2ND Leicesters. These two regiments organised a bombing counter-attack, one coming from the left and one from the right, and eventually gained the lost trenches.

The casualties in the Indian Corps in endeavouring to recover the ground had been very severe, for the fighting had been very largely hand-to-hand. The gallant way in which the 9TH Bhopal Infantry tried to stem the advance of the enemy down their trenches was shown by the number of bayonet wounds which the men received. Altogether the regiment lost over 200 men in this fight.

On 18TH December, the regiment rejoined the Ferozepore Brigade and took part in the battle of Givenchy. Describing the fighting round Givenchy, Sir James Wilcocks, the Commander of the Indian Corps in France says: - "Very little has hitherto been said about the work of the 57TH Rifles and one company of the 9TH Bhopal beyond mentioning the fact that they held their portions of the line throughout. The share taken by them deserves more detailed mention, as it was owing to their determination and tenacious grip of their trenches that communication with the French on their right was maintained, and that our line was kept intact in this section of the defence."

After two months of constant fighting the regiment badly required rest. Only handful of the original personnel remained, the reinforcements set haphazardly required time to settle down.

On April 22ND the Germans launched a heavy attack preceded by yellow cloud of gas. Caught completely by surprise, and lacking any protection against gas, the Algerian Division broke, leaving a gap of some four miles in the front. All the reserves of V Corps were used up in counter-attacks to prevent a further German penetration. The on the 24TH May, again under cover of gas, the Germans attacked the Canadians. Despite a desperate resistance with their flank uncovered by the French withdrawal, the Canadians were forced back fighting for every yard of ground. This was the situation which caused the urgent demand for the Lahore Division, and it was into this battle the Indian troops, quite unprotected against the new deadly weapon of gas, were to be hurled.

The attack at Neuve Chapelle opened on 9TH May. It was a complete failure. Sir James Wilcocks, in 'The Indian Corps in France' has given a vivid description of the scene:-

"The trenches, difficult to pass through, even when occupied only by the ordinary traffic, were now in a state which beggar's description. The German guns had been pounding high explosive and shrapnel into them all morning.

16ᵀᴴ Punjab Regiment

9ᵀᴴ Bhopal Infantry (4/16ᵀᴴ)

In many places the parapet had been blown in, blocking the way, while numbers of dead and wounded were lying at the bottom of the trenches. The direction boards had in many cases been destroyed, and men were wandering about, vainly attempting to find the nearest way to their units, or to the aid posts. The nearer one got to the front, the more of a shambles the trenches became- wounded men were creeping and crawling along amidst the mud debris of the parapet, many of them unable to extricate themselves, dying alone and unattended, whilst amidst this infernal scene the German shell continued bursting."

On May 6ᵀᴴ, the regiment was issued with gas masks for the first time. They consisted of flannel head-cover with eye-holes, the flannel being saturated with an anti-gas mixture. The regiment had landed in France with 807 all ranks. The battle casualties had amounted to 708. Nothing of note occurred until 5ᵀᴴ June, 1915, the regiment embarked at Marseilles for Egypt. After the trenches and thundering horrors of the Western Front, a tranquil sea voyage ended in the peaceful warmth of Suez. For six months the 9ᵀᴴ patrolled the banks and manned the defences of Suez Canal. The regiment re-organised and retrained.

On 5ᵀᴴ December, the regiment was ordered to Mesopotamia, and sailed for Basra, to join the 7ᵀᴴ Division of Tigres Corps. The regiment took part in The Battle of Wadi, on 13ᵀᴴ January 1916. It was an unsuccessful attempt to relieve beleaguered forces under Sir Charles Townshend then under siege by the Turkish Sixth Army at Kut-al-Amara. General Fenton Aylmer launched an attack against Turkish defensive positions on the banks of the Wadi River. The Wadi was a steep valley of a stream that ran from the north into the River Tigris, some 6 miles upstream towards Kut-al-Amara from Sheikh Sa'ad. The attack is generally considered as a failure, as although General Aylmer, managed to capture the Wadi, it cost him 1,600 men. The 9ᵀᴴ Bhopal Infantry who had sapped forward and held the jumping off line for 19ᵀᴴ Brigade had suffered the loss of three Indian officers and 60 other ranks in this action. The regiment could barely muster 200 rifles.

General Aylmer decided to direct his main effort to launch a frontal assault on the Hannah position. During the assault 7ᵀᴴ Division was in support of 13ᵀᴴ Division, the 9ᵀᴴ Bhopal Infantry leading the division. After a short bombardment the 13ᵀᴴ Division rushed the Turkish Fallahiyah position. 21ˢᵀ Brigade was now ordered to take over from the leading brigade of 13ᵀᴴ Division. The regiment relieved the 9ᵀᴴ Warwicks. Regimental patrols were at once sent out but found no sign of the enemy. Meanwhile, the other two brigades of 7ᵀᴴ Division concentrated behind 21ˢᵀ Brigade in order to carry out a dawn attack on Sannaiyat. In the face of heavy rifle and machine-gun fire from the front, and gunfire from both banks of the River, the attack petered out some 500 yards from the Turkish front-line.

16TH Punjab Regiment

9TH Bhopal Infantry (4/16TH)

The situation in Kut-al-Amara was rapidly becoming desperate, General Goring, who had taken over from General Aylmer, now planned a final attempt to relieve it by attacking Sannaiyat, which ended up in another failure.

In this battle the regiment took no part. The British failure led to Townshend's surrender, along with 10,000 of his men, in the largest single surrender of British troops up to that time. However, the regiment was part of the force in capture of Sannaiyat, on February 22^{ND,} 1917. The regiment fought its final battle in Mesopotamia, at Istabulat, in which it sustained considerable casualties. The allies had successfully pushed the Turkish army back and before the Turks were forced to ask for an armistice, the regiment returned to India on 20TH March 1918, with only 15 of the originals who had sailed for France in 1914.

In 1922, the regiment's new designation was 4TH Battalion (Bhopal) 16TH Punjab Regiment. During the Second World War, the battalion again fought with great distinction in the Italian East Africa, North Africa and Italy.

Originally colonised by the Italians in 1885, Eritrea was used as a staging ground for two Italian invasions of Ethiopia (or Abyssinia): the First and Second Italo-Abyssinian Wars. The second invasion was launched in 1935, four years before the outbreak of World War II in 1939. The Italians conquered Ethiopia in 1936 and incorporated it together with Italian Somaliland and Eritrea to form Italian East Africa, thus expanding the Italian Empire.

Following the Italian declaration of war on 10TH June 1940, Italian dictator Benito Mussolini ordered his troops to capture the British Somaliland and border towns in the Sudan and Kenya. In response, The British responded by building up a force of more than two divisions in Sudan and three in Kenya by early February 1941.

The 4/16TH Punjab Regiment had joined the Briggs Force, named after the commander of 7TH Brigade, in the Sudan-based forces. The 4/11TH Sikhs had been detached from the Briggs Force to Gazelle Force and were performing prodigies at the main Keren battle front. The aim of the Briggs Force was to create a diversion from the main thrust in the west by advancing on Massawa from the north, and the first task given to the battalion was to open a supply base at Mersa Taclai, a small anchorage on the Red Sea coast, just inside Eritrea. From here the country was as difficult as the battalion was to encounter anywhere. Roads were non-existent and the terrain, sand or boulder strewn gorges, made movement well-nigh impossible. The heat was intense and water scarce in the extreme. The advance continued through Elghena, where a rough track wound up into the hiss from the coast. Minor opposition was encountered here, and the Carrier Platoon took 40 prisoners on 22ND February. Eventually the battalion arrived at Mescelit Pass, the first of series of naturally strong defensive positions held the enemy. An attack was staged on March 1ST.

16TH Punjab Regiment

9TH Bhopal Infantry (4/16TH)

The 4/16TH Punjabi Regiment attacked the enemy's right flank. The battalion climbed the steep slopes and chased the enemy from the crests, and the position was taken. As the road beyond the pass was demolished with the enemy holding the hills in strength, it was decided to try another way round. The first serious opposition encountered was at Mount Engiahat, a formidable looking position surrounded by a range of high hills, all occupied by the enemy. It was now 13TH March and the renewed attack on Keren from the west and south by 4TH and 5TH Indian Divisions was due to start on the 15TH. The task of the 4/16TH Punjab Regiment supported by one battery 25TH Field Regiment, was the capture of Engiahat. Two companies feeling forward had a measure of success, but found them up against considerable opposition, and consolidated as far forward as possible. Between them and the enemy lay the only line of approach, a knife-edged feature which led up t the Italian main position some hundreds of feet above them.

It was extremely difficult to supply the forward companies. All ammunition, water and rations had to be manhandled up a long arduous climb in full view of the enemy. This was done by all available men in the battalion. The attack on Mount Engiahat went in on 27TH March. The main enemy force had evacuated the previous night leaving considerable amount of materials, particularly gun and rifle ammunition. Shortly after arriving on the objective it was heard that Keren had fallen. A few days after the fall of Keren, the brigade was directed on to Massawa. As the fall of the whole country was imminent it was important to save the installations of the main port from destruction. After being ferried over appalling country, the battalion arrived in front of the town which was heavily fortified and garrisoned by 10,000 of the enemy. The defences were formidable. They included two belts of wire extensively mined, and numerous static gun positions for a large range of artillery. After a long approach march through the night, the attack went in just before dawn on 8TH April. A hard fought action followed, which lasted 8 hours. An Italian frigate leaving the port added to the intense enemy fire, but the gunners of 25TH Field Regiment eliminated many enemy gun positions. Eventually the defences were overcome, the 4/16TH Punjab Regiment winning the race to the town by a short head, with Henry Pelly's carriers racing in along the shore. After a short stay at Massawa, the battalion was glad to leave its sweltering humidity and embark for the Western Desert on 23RD April, 1941. On 30TH April 1941, the 4/16TH Punjab Regiment concentrated in the familiar Baguush-Sidi Haneish area. The tactical situation facing the Western Desert Forces then presented a far more sombre picture than before the East African campaign. Rommel's Africa Corps had arrived on the scene and, stiffening the Italian Divisions in the theatre, bad pushed the British forces back to the Egyptian frontier, at the same time investing two divisions in Tobruk. General Wavell's immediate intention was to defeat the enemy armour in order to relieve Tobruk garrison.

16TH Punjab Regiment

9TH Bhopal Infantry (4/16TH)

On the 19TH November, the 4/16TH Punjab Regiment carriers were ordered to test the defence of Libyan Omar. They advanced in open formation from the north-west until a few hundred yards from the perimeter when a hail of fire of all calibres, came down on them. While withdrawing according to plan, one carrier was hit and stopped, but another went alongside to rescue the crew. The main attack on the Omars took place on 22ND November; the opening of the battle presented an impressive sight. A vast armada of tanks and Lorries sped over the flat plain. Ahead the horizon erupted in thunderous smoke, as the bombers and artillery laid into the enemy positions. The word came through that the battle for Omar Nuovo had been successful, and the 4/16TH Punjab Regiment were to pass through the gap made in the minefield from the north, and then head almost due west over the 4,000 yards which separated Nuovo from the larger Libyan position. The Royal Sussex were still mopping up when the battalion's troop carrying lorries entered the position, and the vehicles were sniped at by pockets of resistance while deploying to advance. Preceded by two squadrons of tanks and the Battalion's carriers, the vehicles swept in across the bumpy, dust ground, swaying and rattling. In front the shells of 25TH Field and 7TH Medium Regiments were churning up great fountains of dust and smoke. With only 800 yards to go, a cleverly concealed battery of 88 mm guns covering a minefield gap opened up with devastating effect. The first wave of tanks reeled out of line, broken and burning, and the second squadron, swinging away from this unbearable fire, blundered into a minefield where a dozen, disabled mines, were blown to pieces by these deadly guns. Only five tanks remained when the Punjabis reached the debussing line. Lieutenant Colonel Lavender at once launched three companies of the Battalion into the fray.

To quote from the Divisional History about this action by the Punjabis:-
"As at Omar Nuovo, the spirit of the infantry prevailed. Dashing through the gaps in the wire, the Punjabis fell with the bayonet on the first trenches and cleared them. A brilliant operation followed in which platoons and sections, methodically stalking enemy weapon pits and strong points, destroyed point after point. Moving always to the flank and skirting resistance, the Punjabis quartered the ground like terriers, ferreting out the defenders. The Sepoys packed their pockets with captured Italian grenades. As in East Africa, these small light missiles proved an excellent weapon. Hurling them high, the Punjabis, under cover of the bursts, raced in with the steel".

They performed valiant work by shooting into slit trenches with Brens from the flank and following up with No. 36 grenades. By nightfall, three more carriers had been lost. But without armour, it was impossible to penetrate the whole area that day, and a hard slogging match lasting a week was to begin. A depth of between 800 and 200 yards had been gained and 500 prisoners and several guns taken. The battalion had lost 147 killed or wounded of all ranks.

16TH Punjab Regiment

9TH Bhopal Infantry (4/16TH)

The next day another attack went in under the cover of a bombardment from the whole divisional artillery. Considerable progress was made and a further 1,000 prisoners taken. By nightfall the battalion was in possession of one third of the area, but the resistance had again stiffened in the northern and western sectors. The battalion sustained further 35 casualties in this attack. At dawn on the 27TH, after ten minutes artillery barrage, 4/16TH Punjab Regiment with a company of the 4/11TH Sikhs, put yet another attack; but after penetration of some 300 yards in which some men and guns were taken, they were pinned down by determined opposition at a cost of 44 Punjabi and 35 Sikh casualties.

On the 29TH it was decided to make an end of the Omar position. During the night the 3/1ST Punjab Regiment had infiltrated into the position from the north, with much gallantry but in some confusion. However, the order had been restored, and with their help and supported by 3 Matildas and the remaining 4/16TH Punjab Regiment's carriers, Lieutenant McKinley's company leapt into the assault. By nightfall, after hard fighting during which several carriers and one tank had been smashed, only 100 Germans stood at bay. These were the members of an M.G. Company, commanded by a brave, though brutal, German officer named Shoen, who had been largely responsible for the stiff resistance in the position. They slipped away during the night, but were eventually captured. Libyan Omar was at last clear but a cost of 215 of the battalion's strength in killed and wounded. In all 3,000 of the enemy had been wiped out.

On 8TH December, 7TH Brigade was directed on El Adem. Though Tobruk was now free, enemy resistance had hardened on the line Sidi Breghisc-Alam Hamza. On the 15TH, shortly after the brigade's gunners, 25TH Field Regiment, had fought their epic battle against German armour, the 4/16TH Punjab Regiment advanced to attack Point 201 on a three company front. Reinforcements to make good the recent heavy casualties had not arrived. Lt. Col. Lavender was able to put only about 180 rifles into action, though the task called for a full strength battalion. The attack began and the battalion pressed forward with the utmost determination to within 700 yards of the enemy positions when intense fire was opened on them. Without support, no further headway could be made, and sustained further 44 casualties. Then on the 17TH, thanks to a brilliant break through by the Poles in the north, the battalion managed to retreat 50 miles to Djebel Achdar and then proceeded to Derna.

By this time British supply lines were stretched like bow strings, and despite intensive bombing by the Desert Air Force, it was known that Rommel was getting considerable reinforcements and supplies over the short sea route to Tripoli. On 21ST January, 1942, the enemy forces, strong in all arms particularly in armour, flooded northwards from El Agheila, and 1ST Armoured Division were roughly handled. However, because of the overwhelming German force, the higher command authorised the British forces to evacuate Benghazi.

16TH Punjab Regiment

9TH Bhopal Infantry (4/16TH)

The battalion managed to retreat to a defensive position in the Egyptian border. The battalion now left the desert and went to Cyprus to rest and re-organise. August saw the 4/16TH Punjab Regiment back in Egypt preparing a defensive position at Damanhur in the Delta. Then the 4/16TH Punjab Regiment, took part in the victorious battle of El Alamein, being the first major offensive against the Axis since the start of the European war in 1939 in which the Western Allies had achieved a decisive victory. This victory turned the tide in the North African Campaign and ended the Axis threat to Egypt, the Suez Canal, and of gaining access to the Middle Eastern and Persian oil fields via North Africa. The 8TH Army pursued the Germans, as they retreated over the Tunisian frontier. The Germans were holding the Mareth line, heavily fortified defence, based on the Wadi Zig Zauo, a natural tank obstacle. The assault began on 20TH March. When the battle ended, the battalion had lost 50 killed and wounded. The battalion had taken 800 prisoners and considerable amount of enemy equipment. The Division had punched a hole through the position, and forcing the enemy to fall back on Tunis. At this time the welcome news arrived that the 4TH Indian Division, together with 7TH Armoured Division and 201ST Guards Brigade would reinforce the 1ST Army for the final drive on Tunis. General Montgomery had nominated his most experienced formations for the honour. It is difficult to conceive of a more poetically fitting situation in the history of war. The three formations which alone had begun the North African adventure in the far off days of Sidi Barrani were to be at the finish. The two armies met at Medjez-el-Bab. The 4/16TH Punjab Regiment waited their turn with 7TH Brigade in an assembly area which was literally under the muzzles of closely packed 25-pounders, and next morning after the success of 5TH Brigade, the noise of the barrage from this position was more unnerving than anything the enemy could produce. There was, therefore a sense of relief when the Battalion was unleashed, and the appointed objectives were taken. The end was obviously near when the drive began on 11TH May. The steady stream of prisoners grew to a flood, culminating in the surrender of General Von Arnim. Suddenly a determined enemy had turned into disciplined columns marching themselves into captivity. It was astonishing sight, 250,000 men had laid down their arms, and thus ending the Desert Saga.

Early in September the allies were ashore in Italy and a long struggle and even sterner mountains faced them. In view of this, the 4/16TH Punjab Regiment had move up, firstly to Palestine, and then to the Lebanon. Then in November the 4/16TH Punjab Regiment headed south through Sinai desert to Suez, there to take a ship. On 7TH December, 1944, its convoy anchored off Taranto, Italy.

It was decided that 7TH Indian Brigade should take over from 5TH New Zealand Brigade in the Orsogna sector, and by the 13TH January the battalion was in position between this town and the village of Ariela. Movement forward took place in drenching rain and at night, owing to the roads up the forward defence line being in full view of the enemy from Orsogna.

16TH Punjab Regiment

9TH Bhopal Infantry (4/16TH)

On 26TH January, it was decided to push forward one platoon from each of the forward companies. Unfortunately Lieutenant Sukhmandar Singh in attempting to establish contact with the platoon on their right got lost in the dark and was taken prisoner. The enemy shelling and mortaring became very fierce and his infantry attempted to infiltrate back into old positions, but the defensive fire proved too much for them. Towards mid-day however, it was decided to withdraw the two remaining platoons under the cover of smoke screen followed by artillery defensive fire. Only about one and half platoons came back and it was feared the rest had been taken prisoner. The defensive fire was brought down again, and this was followed by smoke screen through which the remaining men returned.

The battalion moved on to the Cassino front in February. Monte Cassino, a historic hilltop abbey founded in dominated the nearby town of Cassino and the entrances to the Liri and Rapido valleys. Lying in a protected historic zone, it had been left unoccupied by the Germans. They had, however, manned some positions set into the steep slopes below the abbey's walls. Repeated pinpoint artillery attacks on Allied assault troops caused their leaders to conclude the abbey was being used by the Germans as an observation post, at the least. Fears escalated along with casualties, and in spite of a lack of clear evidence, it was marked for destruction. On 15TH February American bombers dropped 1,400 tons of high explosives, creating widespread damage. The raid failed to achieve its objective, as German paratroopers occupied the rubble and established excellent defensive positions amid the ruins. Before the German defenders were finally driven from their positions, the battalion was replaced in the division, to give other regular units the chance for the final kill. Finally the Battalion returned to India on 29TH July 1945, nearly five years after leaving it.

During the Second World War the battalion had been awarded the following gallantry awards: - Havildar Sadhu Singh was awarded the I.O.M. Subedar Sardar Singh, the Military Cross and Jemadar Jaimal Singh, Sepoy Harbans Singh, Naik Jaswant Singh, Havildar Bhola Singh, Naik Hansa Singh, Naik Ludhar Singh, Naik Chanan Singh, Sepoy Narinjan Singh, Jemadar Ishar Singh, and Naik Piara Singh the I.D.S.M.

In 1947, at the creation of Pakistan, the battalion was allocated to the new Pakistan Army. The battalion had travelled a long way with its Sikh soldiers. The Sikhs went to India to join the Sikh Regiment, the unit allocated to India.

46TH Punjabis (10/16TH)

The 46TH Punjabis was raised in 1900, as the 46TH (Punjab) Regiment of Bengal Infantry. It was designated as the 46TH Punjabis in 1903 and became 10TH (Training) battalion of 16TH Punjab Regiment in 1922. In 1947, the 16TH Punjab Regiment was allocated to the Pakistan Army, and the Sikh soldiers routed to the India Army.

Probyn's Horse (5TH KEVO Lancers)

1ST Sikh Irregular Cavalry

1ST Sikh Irregular Cavalry was raised during the Sepoy Mutiny in 1857, by Captain Wales of the 18TH Irregular Cavalry. At the time of the raising the regiment contained large proportion of ex soldiers from the Khalsa Army. The Regiment was soon up to strength, and was sent out to the area between Lahore and Multan, to deal with some refractory tribes. The distance of 121 km., was covered by the 1ST Sikh Cavalry in a single day. The regiment was a motley collection, as the men reported with every type of horse, equipment, saddlery and weapon. The times were, however, critical for the British and this rough and ready but extremely serviceable unit was sent off to the United Provinces. The regiment took a prominent part in the capture of Lucknow. While following up a party of the enemy, Captain Wales was killed by a sniper and the command of the regiment went to Major Probyn, who had won the Victoria Cross in 1857. The regiment, thereafter, unofficially bore his name until it was officially recognised in 1904.

In 1859 the Chinese Government seized a Hong Kong ship which was carrying contraband opium. The British presented an ultimatum to the Government of Peking which required the Chinese to accept an envoy in the capital. When the ultimatum expired the allies invaded China. A joint Anglo-French expedition was decided upon and a cavalry brigade from India was to form a part of the joint force. Only volunteers could be sent overseas according to the conditions of service which obtained in the Company's army. 1ST Sikh Cavalry volunteered to a man for overseas service. The allied force, assembled in Hong Kong by July 1859. On 13TH August, the Taku Forts, which guarded the entrance to the Peiho River along which ran the route to Peking, were stormed. The Sikh Cavalry first saw action in China when the two Indian regiments counter-charged the Chinese cavalry which had charged the besieging artillery. The Chinese cavalry was pursued for miles. In the final battle for Peking the Sikh cavalry once again came into action. It routed the Chinese cavalry with such dash and determination that, thereafter, the Chinese cavalry never stood to meet the Sikh cavalry charge. The campaign came to close in November 1859, when the Chinese accepted the allied demands and the troops returned to India.

In the 1861 reorganisation the Sikh Cavalry became the 11TH Bengal Lancers. After the destruction of Sittana by the British in 1858, the Hindustani fanatics settled at Malka. After three years of tranquillity, they again began to disturb the peace of the surrounding district, aided and abetted by the clans bordering on British territory. Matters soon came to such a pass as it was determined that an effort should be made to exterminate for good and all the troublesome gang on both banks of the River Indus. The punitive expedition included the 11TH Bengal Cavalry. It took part in the hard fought action in the Ambela Pass, in which the power of the Hindustani fanatics was gone forever, but the toll taken of officers and men of the cavalry had been heavy.

Probyn's Horse (5TH KEVO Lancers)

1ST Sikh Irregular Cavalry

During the Second Afghan War, 1878-80, the regiment went with a column through the Khaiber Pass and saw action at Ali Masjid. Subsequently it sent an escort of 200 lances for the protection of the British party, which went to demarcate the Russo-Afghan boundary in accordance with the settlement of 1885.The regiment, saw much service on the North-West Frontier during the last decade of the 19TH century.

In 1891, they were employed in the Black Mountains. After the Black Mountain Expedition of 1888, the tribesmen agreed not to molest troops or officials moving along the crest of the main ridge which divided British from tribal territory. In March 1890, orders were issued for the construction of several roads leading up to the crest from the Agror Valley, and in October a force including the 11TH Bengal Lancers, was assembled at Aghi, with the orders to assert the rights of the Indian Government to move troops along the summit of the Black Mountain; but if the inhabitants were hostile, action was to be taken against them. After some hard fought battles the tribesmen submitted to the British terms, and the hostilities brought to an end.

In 1895 the 11TH Bengal Lancers formed a part Chitral Relief Force. The Chitral Relief Force was sent by the British authorities to relieve the fort at Chitral which was under siege after a local coup. After the death of the old ruler, power changed hands several times. An intervening British force of about 400 men was besieged in the fort until it was relieved by two expeditions, a small one from Gilgit and a large one from Pashawar.11TH Bengal Lancers formed part of the British force assembled at Pashawar under Major-General Sir Robert Low. On April 3RD they stormed the Malakand Pass which was defended by 12,000 local warriors. There were significant engagements 2 and 10 days later. Low was still crossing the Lowarai Pass on the day Kelly entered Chitral. Although Kelly got to Chitral first, it was the massive size of Low's force that forced the enemy to withdraw.

In 1897 the 11TH Bengal Lancers formed part of the Malakand Field Force. In 1897 occurred the most formidable outbreak the British arms have ever been called upon to suppress on the North-West Frontier India. The record of the operations of the Malakand Field Force, was one of struggles against climate the swollen Indus River, the heat, and the scarcity of water, were typical of the chief difficulties to be overcome by the troops when they clashed against the tribesmen. The rebellion was finally put down in October 1897.

Subsequent to the reforms brought about in the Indian Army in 1903, the regiment's designation was changed to the 11TH Prince of Wale's Own Lancers and finally in 1904 the name of their founder found a place in their new designation which became 11TH King Edward's Own Lancers (Probyn's Horse). During the First World War it served in the Middle East. In 1921, it combined with the 12TH Cavalry to become 5TH King Edward's Own Probyn's Horse and eventually in 1937 became, Probyn's Horse (5TH KEVO Lancers)

Probyn's Horse (5TH KEVO Lancers)

2ND Sikh Irregular Cavalry

2ND Sikh Irregular Cavalry was raised during the Sepoy Mutiny in 1857, by Captain Hockin of the 7TH Hariana Lancers. Delhi had been sacked by the time the regiment as raised, so it was sent to what is now Uttar Pradesh, to bring the country once again under British control.

The Sikh Irregular Cavalry, at that time, was composed of volunteers who had flocked to the colours with every imaginable horse, saddlery and weapon. Members could hardly form line but once shown the enemy, could ride hard and straight at him, whatever the odds. The regiment was employed in Avadh. At Keoti, in Rewa State, they captured a standard when they charged a formed body of 1,200 with only 61 Sowars of their own. After prolonged and bloody hand-to-hand encounter, the enemy was driven off the field with much loss.

The 1861 reorganisation, consequent to the Company's army coming directly under the Crown, changed the designation of the regiment to 12TH Bengal Cavalry. The regiment found its first opportunity to serve overseas in the Abyssinian Campaign of 1867. King Theodore had tried to get rid of foreigners from his country and the British decided to send an expedition from India. Due to the mountainous nature of the terrain, a major part of the cavalry with the expedition was used for the protection of the line of communication. The 12TH Bengal Cavalry was split into small isolated detachments manning posts along the single road from the coast to Magdala. These posts were subjected to frequent attacks by the Ethiopians yet the local population had to be dealt with sympathetically. The Commander-in-Chief, end of the campaign said in his report, "Seldom or never have the cavalry had such a variety of duties in maintaining communications for so many miles climbing over the mountains and through forest ranges, often benighted, where a false step would mean destruction, and in danger of treacherous attacks from the wild border tribes who are honoured among themselves for slaying with reason and without scruple."

On return from Ethiopia, the 12TH saw service in the Second Afghan War of 1878-80, when it joined Roberts in the Kurram, where it took part in the storming of Peiwar Kotal. Later, it joined the Kabul Field Force and took part in the battles at Shutargardan Pass, Charasiab and the fighting around Kabul. The reorganisation of 1903 did not materially affect the regimen as it only dropped the name of the Presidency from its designation to become the 12TH Cavalry. It did not see active service for many years but provided many drafts to other regiments. During the First World War the regiment saw service in Mesopotamia. The regiment arrived in Mesopotamia to take part in the capture of Baghdad and in the final advance to Mosul, which was taken on 3RD November 1918, but Turkey had already surrendered three days earlier.

In 1921, it combined with the 11TH King Edward's Own Lancers (Probyn's Horse to become 5TH King Edward's Own Probyn's Horse and eventually in 1937 became, Probyn's Horse (5TH King Edward V11's Own Lancers).

Probyn's Horse (5TH KEVO Lancers)

The Probyn's Horse was 'mechanised' in 1940 at Risalpur as part of 1ST Indian Armoured Brigade. It did not get any tanks until 1942 and was not fully armoured (with Shermans) until 1944. It then formed part of 255 Indian Tank Brigade and was concentrated in Kanglatongbi in Assam. The move forward from Kanglatongbi was carried out on the axis Palel, Tamu, Kalewa, Kan, Gangaw and Pauk. The regiment was put under the command of 7TH Indian Division in their task of advancing to and forming a bridgehead over the Irrawaddy. The assault across the Irrawaddy took place on the 14TH February 1945. Probyn's Horse was called upon to provide six officers and the Intercommunication Troop. This party controlled the crossing of the Division onto the South bank. 17TH Division commenced its crossing through the bridgehead on 17TH February. The Japanese had attacked the bridgehead from the air on 17TH February followed by ground attacks but it was too late to interfere seriously with the crossing. 255 Indian Tank Brigade started to cross with its tanks on 18TH February; all was now set for an armoured dash to Meiktilla, 136 km from the bridgehead.

The force earmarked to make dash from the bridgehead at Nyaungu to Meiktilla consisted of the 17TH Division with two motorised brigades, 48TH Indian Infantry Brigade and 63RD Indian Infantry Brigade. The Tank Brigade, with its two Indian regiments, Probyn's Horse and the Royal Deccan Horse had been placed under the command of 17TH Division. A force known as 'Tomcol' commanded by Major Tom Mudie the Deccan Horse, and consisted of the Scout Troops Probyn's Horse, the Royal Deccan Horse and motorised company 6TH Rajputs, had been formed with the object of passing through the bridgehead and establishing patrol bases. 'Tomcol' was the first to cross the Irrawaddy into 7TH Division's brigade-head on 18TH February followed by 48TH Brigade, and the Tank Brigade,

On 20TH February, 'Tomcol' followed by 48TH Brigade, established a firm base east of Pagan. Tomcol had met resistance at Sewa, and after an air strike, the enemy fled leaving behind a gun and ammunition dump. It was thought that he would return during the night, as Tomcol with infantry was unable to hold Sewa. Having arrived at Wetlu, Probyn's Horse was pushed straight forward to clear Sewa of the enemy. During the advance some small arms fire was encountered from what were subsequently found to have been enemy withdrawing down the Seiktein road. After clearing a group of villages, in which one Japanese officer was killed, the regiment moved to the south of Ngathayauk.

Early on the morning of the 22ND February, the regiment was ordered to clear up enemy resistance at Oyin on the Seiktein road. The infantry were dismounted from the tanks of the leading squadrons, and the advance was continued on both sides of the road. Snipers were soon spotted in the palm trees and bushes and several were killed. The village was found to be held, and the North and West edges were engaged initially. There were numerous fox holes and some bunkers in the village itself, in the hedgerows on the side of the road and in the hedges in a field to the West of the village.

Probyn's Horse (5TH KEVO Lancers)

The advance was carried out methodically by the leading squadron and company of infantry. The infantry was held up outside the village, so the tanks advanced slowly through the burning village. Japanese suddenly appeared and rushed forward and threw himself under the squadron commander's tank and detonated a box of explosives. The tank driver, Sowar Dayal Singh, was killed with the Japanese soldier and the tank's final drive was damaged. The Japanese infantry was found to be holding a line of hedgerows on a flank. A tank troop from the second squadron moved up to deal with them. Japanese rushed out of a hedge and climbed the second tank. The tank commander barely managed to close his cupola. The Japanese, while struggling to open the cupola, was shot by the third tank. Japanese rushed out about the same time and got under the third tank which managed to reverse just in time. The Japanese with his box of explosives was Singh, was shot through the head and another tank was attacked by tank hunting party when passing through some close country. The column reached Seiktein on 23RD February.

The next phase of the advance was the move to and capture of Taungtha, which was captured on the 24TH February. The next phase of the advance was the capture of Mahlaing and Thabutkon Airfield. On the 26TH February, 'A' Squadron Probyn's Horse supported 63RD Brigade in its attack on two villages on the western outskirts of the town. One troop led the assault on the smaller village. Two tanks covered the two flanks of the infantry and the third destroyed a large number of bunkers. The squadron provided close support for the capture of the larger village. The Royal Deccan Horse with supporting troops, had done a wide left hook over difficult country via Kwangtung and then captured Thabutkon Airfield, where a large consignment of Petrol was landed.

On the 27TH February one squadron of the Probyn's Horse was sent to the Thabutkon Airfield with the object of providing a protective screen for the landing of 99TH Indian Infantry Brigade who was scheduled to arrive by air. The squadron cleared the Thabutkon Airfield of all the enemy troops. 99TH Indian Infantry Brigade completed concentration in the Thabutkon area and was ordered to take over the defence of the Airfield.

On the 28th February, the force moved to a concentration area preparatory to the attack on Meiktilla. 'A' Squadron Probyn's Horse, in support of the 63RD Indian Infantry Brigade, was required t clear area Kyakpu in conjunction with 7 Baluch. The squadron deployed with three troops up in the forming-up place where the infantry got pinned down, while waiting for an air strike. The ground was covered by thick scrub and the village had strong stone buildings. The left troop became separated from its infantry and was attacked by tank hunting parties in the scrub, one tank was disabled but four Japanese were killed.

Probyn's Horse (5TH KEVO Lancers)

The troop, however, continued to advance through scrub systematically destroying bunkers. In the open ground beyond the scrub many more Japanese were killed. In the meantime the other two troops had also advanced ahead of the held-up infantry and reached the village. The Japanese had holed up in a strongly built red house. All tanks plastered the house with intense fire until 300 Japanese were killed. By the end of the day only a small part of the town jutting into the Lake was left in the hands of the remnants of the garrison. It was apparent that the enemy was determined to fight to the bitter end. This concludes the action with the 63RD Indian Infantry Brigade, and the squadron rejoined the regiment the following morning.

On 26TH February, all three brigades started moving on Meiktila. The Japanese became aware of the true size of the threat, and began preparing Meiktila for defence. The defenders numbered about 4,000. While they attempted to dig-in, the air-portable Indian 99TH Brigade was flown in to the captured airstrip at Thabutkon, and fuel was dropped by parachute for the armoured brigade. On 28TH February, 17TH Division attacked Meiktila from all sides, supported by massed artillery and air strikes. The 63RD Indian Brigade proceeded on foot to establish a roadblock southwest of the town to prevent Japanese reinforcements reaching the garrison, while the main body of the brigade attacked from the west. The 48TH Indian Brigade attacked from the north down the main road from Thabutkon. The 255TH Armoured Brigade left another roadblock to the northeast and made a wide sweep around the town to capture the airfields to the east and attack the town from the southeast. In spite of desperate resistance, the town fell in less than four days; the whole garrison of Meiktila had been killed to a ma.

The Japanese troops hastening to reinforce Meiktila were dismayed to find that they now had to recapture the town. The first attacks by the Japanese 18TH Division from the north and west failed, with heavy losses. From 12TH March onwards, they attacked the airfields east of the town, through which the defenders were supplied by aircraft. 9TH Indian Infantry Brigade was flown into the airfields from 15TH March to reinforce the defenders of Meiktila. Meiktila was now secure and the Japanese were gradually driven back. Tank-infantry columns sallied out of the perimeter and fought battles almost every day throughout the month of March.

A column composed of 'C' Squadron Probyn's Horse, one troop of 16TH Cavalry, two companies' infantry and an artillery battery was despatched to deal with the road-block. Tanks approached the block from the rear and were fired at by a 75 mm gun and a 37 mm gun, both of which were destroyed. A tank was lost to another 75 mm gun but the tank crew were recovered without any loss of life. The block at mile 342 and another one a couple of miles further, reported by the armoured cars, were both cleared. The column returned with four captured guns. On 6TH March, a column composed of Probyn's Horse, one squadron 16TH Cavalry, an infantry battalion and artillery support was sent out to sweep the area Yawadan-Hauze-Thedan and Wundwin.

Probyn's Horse (5TH KEVO Lancers)

A column consisting of two infantry battalions and one squadron Probyn's Horse advanced to mile 13 on the Mahling road, killing 70 Japanese and destroyed three guns. On 10TH March one squadron Probyn's Horse, two troops 16TH Cavalry, and one infantry battalion advanced to clear Mahling. After some hard fighting that day it was decided to carry out wide armour sweep the next day in order to establish the extent of the defences and estimate enemy strength. A large number of enemies were killed and a 75 mm gun destroyed. Several tanks were hit but no serious damage was caused.

On 14TH March two squadrons Probyn's Horse carried out a very successful sweep with a view to destroying Japanese guns which had taken up positions within range of the airfield. On the following day one squadron of the Regiment and 4/15TH Punjab carried out a sweep over the Meiktilla airfield, this enabled the resumption of the fly-in of 9TH Indian Brigade, which had been interrupted. Another operation was launched on 17TH March to prevent the Japanese firing on the airfield. 63RD Indian Infantry Brigade les a battalion and two squadrons Probyn's Horse commenced the task of clearing the area between the railway line on the west and Pindale on the east. It took three days hard fighting to complete the task. Two 105 mm guns, four anti-tank guns and two trucks were destroyed; 264 Japanese were killed.

Lieutenant Karamjeet Singh Judge of the 4TH Battalion, 15TH Punjab Regiment, British Indian Army was posthumously awarded the Victoria Cross (VC) for his deeds on 18TH March.

On 22ND March an attempt to clear few villages of the Japanese by two infantry companies supported by one squadron Probyn's Horse failed. During 23RD March, the Japanese launched a determined assault on the perimeter held by 48TH Brigade but did not succeed in getting over the perimeter wire, they left behind 120 dead. Next morning 63RD Brigade supported by two squadrons Probyn's Horse followed up the attacking force which was found entrenched in a village. In spite of an airstrike, artillery bombardment and two assaults by tanks and infantry, the village could not be cleared because of determined resistance by the enemy.

The Japanese infiltrated on to the airfield on 23RD March and destroyed two aircraft. 48 Brigade supported by both Probyn's Horse and Deccan Horse carried out sweeps from 25TH to 27TH March to clear the airfield. Their efforts succeeded only partially because the Japanese continued to hold a portion of the airfield. These partly successful Japanese efforts to hold on to a few surrounding localities marked the end of their efforts to recapture Meiktilla. The enemy realised that his best efforts had failed to make a serious dent in the defences and then he started to withdraw to the east and the south.

A sweep by two squadrons Probyn's Horse on 27TH March partially succeeded in clearing the Myindawgun Lake area. On 28TH March, 99TH Brigade attacked Japanese defences located in untankable terrain, while Probyn's Horse with infantry in support cleared the surrounding area. The brigade attack was only partially success but the tank sweep more fruitful.

Probyn's Horse (5TH KEVO Lancers)

The enemy, however, had had enough and withdrew during the night. The surroundings of Meiktilla were found free of the enemy the next day and Allied transport planes started to land again on 31ST March.

Now the story of the operations carried out by Probyn's Hose in Burma tells of the advance from Meiktilla southwards down the railway corridor from Meiktilla to Hlegu, 35 miles North of Rangoon. The total distance being over 300 miles, the whole advance being completed in 30 days.

The first phase of the advance was the capture of Pyawbwe by 17Th Division with under command 255 Indian Tank Brigade. 99TH Indian Infantry Brigade was to move out East from Meiktilla to Thazi, and thence South to capture Pt. 825, which lies about 3 miles North of Pyawbwe. 48TH Indian Infantry Brigade was to move South down the main road, take Yindaw and hold firm base there while 'Claudcol' and 63RD Indian Infantry Brigade was to turn east and attack Pyawbwe, from that direction. 'Claudcol' was to proceed to South to Ywadan, then North East to cut the main Rangoon road South Pyawbwe. 'Claudcol' under Brigadier Claude Pert, consisted of;- Tank Brigade HQ, Probyn's Horse, One Squadron Pavo Cavalry, Squadron 16TH Cavalry, 6TH Rajput, 4TH Grenadiers, 36TH Field Squadron Engineers and 59TH Battery RA.

On 5TH April 48TH Indian Infantry Brigade moved down the road brushing aside minor opposition until Yindaw was reached. It soon became apparent that the village was strongly held by about 1,000 Japanese, so it was decided that 'Claudcol' should take over the attack. On the 6TH April, Probyn's Horse under the command of 'Claudcol', moved from Ywathit to Kanbya by-passing Yindaw, which was subsequently evacuated some days later. Defences were found to be extensive and extremely well dug. The distance to Kanbya was short, but the Regiment experienced difficulty in getting into day dispersal area owing to a deep sandy nullah which soft vehicles were unable to negotiate until work had been done to it. It took considerable engineering effort but a diversion was prepared. The village was attacked on 8TH April by Probyn's Horse; No 3 Troop commanded by Risaldar Gurbachan Singh and No 2 Troop by Risaldar Ujagar Singh under the Squadron second-in-command Major Udham Singh, cut off the village from the flanks and the rear before the attack went in. The defenders suffered heavy casualties and the village was cleared.

In the evening the sappers were laying protective mines close to the column's harbour when a tank approached with headlights on. When the engineers tried to stop it, the tank quickly turned round and sped away; only then the engineers realized it was a Japanese tank.

On 9TH April 'Claudcol' smashed its way through Ywadan and several other villages. In the evening the column cut the Rangoon road south of Pyawbwe. Eleven Japanese Lorries came up from the south; three were hit and set on fire but the others managed to turn back and get away. A little later the few surviving tanks of the 14TH Japanese Tank Regiment approached, moving down the road from Pyawbwe. The leading tank noticed the burnt out Lorries, stopped for a while, and then moved closer.

Probyn's Horse (5 TH KEVO Lancers)

The leading tank was engaged by a Sherman of Probyn's Horse, which was harboured on one side of the road. As the leading Japanese tank was destroyed, the second tank turned towards the harbour and passed so close to the Shermans that their shots went over because of the low silhouette of the Japanese tank. The enemy again turned to get back to the road and was hit and destroyed. The third tank turned round and sped back in such a hurry that it went off the first bridge it came to and landed below on its turret.

On the 9TH April, 'B' Squadron Probyn's Horse, under the Squadron second-in-command Captain Udham Singh was ordered to carry out a Recce in force on the South West of Pyawbwe with a view to attack it on eh following day. No 1 Troop advanced from the start line with one platoon in the formation 'two up': Dafadar Tarlochan Singh's tank on the left, Jemadar Bhag Singh's tank on the right, and Dafadar Harnam Singh's in rear. When the troop had advanced nearly 300 yards, A Japanese ran away from the Canal. The infantry were immediately dismounted. When they were 100 yards short of the Canal, four inch mortars were fired at Dafadar Tarlochan Singh's tank. The troop halted and put down a troop shoot onto bunker position 200 yards to their front. During this time on 105 mm gun and one 75 mm gun were firing from the main road onto the rear of the troop. After the troop shoot No. 1 Troop advanced up to the Canal and Dafadar Tarlochan Singh's tank crossed the nullah covered by the other tanks. As it was crossing, 2 inch mortars again opened up. Jemadar Bhag Singh himself went forward and crossed without mishap. The troop destroyed all the bunkers and killed many Japanese who tried to run away. Later in the day the troop received orders to go forward without infantry. While doing so, Jemadar Bhag Singh destroyed an enemy battalion gun. Dafadar Tarlochan Singh's tank had its ammunition box, behind the driver, hit by a 4 inch mortar bomb. Although the armour was pierced no damage was done. Later the same tank was hit again by a hollow charge which penetrated but luckily hit the water containers first. One 75 mm shell hit the turret but failed to penetrate it, and yet another 37 mm shell shot away two track connectors. Orders were eventually given for the withdrawal of No. 1 Troop. Jemadar Bhag Singh was wounded by a 75 mm shell which hit his cupola as he was withdrawing.

No. 2 Troop with one platoon of infantry had been ordered to clear the village on the Thybin Canal and then find crossing on I.B. Canal and probe forward to the railway line. Reaching the Canal the troop was heavily shelled and it was silenced. The troop leader located and destroyed a battalion gun on the high ground near the railway line. Lieutenant Grover's tank stuck and while fixing the tow-rope Harcharan Singh was wounded, also Jemadar Sikander Singh was hit in the shoulder. The tank was pulled out and sent back with Jemadar Sikander Singh still commanding it. Harcharan Singh was carried back on Sowar Kishan Singh's shoulder for a distance of 300 yards then put onto Jemadar Sikander's tank. By this time it was getting late and orders were received for tanks and infantry to withdraw.

Probyn's Horse (5TH KEVO Lancers)

On the 10TH April, 'Claudcol' advanced North up the main Rangoon road towards Pyawbwe. The leading tanks 'C' Squadron Probyn's Horse destroyed three Japanese tanks which were covering the crossing over Chaung. The column advanced with two squadrons up, astride the main road and shot up several vehicles and dumps that it passed.

'B' Squadron was ordered to attack Pyawbwe with two companies of the Border Regiment. An artillery barrage was put onto the objective. During this time the infantry supported by two troops of tanks moved up the line of the I.B. Canal. The squadron second-in-command Captain Udham Singh had received orders to mover as soon as the barrage had started, and the squadron commander ordered to him to take up position north of the road and east of I.B. Canal in order that he might support the attack going on the south of the road.

All troops crossed the I.B. Canal safely, in spite of its having been mined. Progress was slow as the enemy was well dug in and possessed the odd L.M.G. which held up the infantry until they could be located. Meanwhile Captain Udham Singh's advance was progressing well and he was killing a number of Japanese. Jemadar Nazar Singh knocked out a 75 mm gun and Captain Udham Singh a 37 mm gun. Captain Udham Singh was ordered to come down from the north to cross the railway, and moved down the main road to join his HQ. This move was successfully carried out except that Risaldar Ujagar Singh's tank was blown up on a mine and had to be towed away under heavy shell fire.

Meanwhile to the immediate front of No. 3 Troop, across the road was an enemy position which was heavily engaged by tanks and infantry. It was not attacked as the squadron had reached its objective but the next day a considerable number of dead Japanese were found in the area.

With the tank Brigade steamrolling its way through the southern part of the town simultaneously, the whole town was cleared by evening. The tank Brigade harboured inside the town.

It was during this action on the 10TH April that Jemadar Gurbachan Singh was awarded the Military Cross. The citation of the award reads:-

"During the attack of Pyawbwe in Burma, on 10TH April 1945, Jemadar Gurbachan Singh was commanding a troop of tanks leading the attack. With superlative dash and vigour, and in order to give the maximum support to the attacking infantry, he led his troop unscathed through a heavily mined area onto the enemy position where he found himself almost on top of two enemy Light Machine Gun posts. Disdaining to reverse his tank, and leaning far out of his turret, he succeeded in throwing grenades into and destroying both positions. He then engaged and destroyed a 70 mm gun, a 37 mm gun, and a Light Machine Gun position, and forced a 75 mm gun to be pulled out of action that was later found abandoned. The alert, fearless, and dashing leadership of Jemadar Gurbachan Singh was commented on by all ranks taking part in the attack and was of great assistance in the capture of the position, which caused the enemy to withdraw that night. Jemadar Gurbachan Singh was strongly recommended for and awarded the Military Cross on 24TH May 1945"

Probyn's Horse (5TH KEVO Lancers)

After the capture of Pyawbwe, the 5TH Indian Division took over the lead from 17TH Indian Division. The Probyn's Horse having completed three days much needed maintainace, came under orders to move in the main body of 5TH Indian Division. On 29TH April the Probyn's Horse became the armour advance guard. A set-piece attack was mounted against the village of Payagyi with air and artillery support but the Japanese had already withdrawn, leaving behind much transport, equipment and stores.

With the fall of Payagyi the last motor able road east was denied to the Japanese. From that time onwards country tracks were his only escape. The same force continued the advance but halted south of Payagyi while the Probyn's Horse 'married up' with 7/10TH Baluch Regiment, and plan was made for the capture of the high ground of Pegu, as follows; Probyn's Horse less one squadron and 7/10TH Baluch less one company were to move South East from the road and attack the high ground North East of Pegu from the East. Meanwhile 63RD Indian Infantry Brigade with one squadron Probyn's Horse were to advance down the main road and join up with Probyn's and the Baluch on the objective.

The outflanking movement at first went smoothly and met with no opposition. The infantry reached the objective, and track was found by which tanks could get on with it in line ahead. During consolidation heavy fire opened up on the objective from short range. It was difficult to locate it owing to thick scrub. As it was getting late the force was called back to harbour. A.L.D. Gurdial Singh and Sowar Daman Singh of 'B' Squadron were wounded and three infantrymen killed. Meanwhile 'A' Squadron with 63RD Indian Infantry Brigade reached the northern approaches to Pegu.

It was learnt on 4TH May that Rangoon had been taken without opposition on 2ND May by a landing from the sea by the 26TH Indian Division. A newly formed Twelfth Army took over charge of operations in Burma. The main task of the Twelfth Army was the interception of the fleeing Japanese troops. The 255TH Tank Brigade which includes Probyn's Horse was moved to Rangoon as army reserve. They carried out extensive patrolling in their respective areas of responsibility to intercept the Japanese. The war in Burma ended with the Japanese surrender on 15TH August 1945.

Thus ends the story of the part played by Probyn's Horse in the reconquest of Burma. In five months the Regiment moved 400 miles when fighting its way through Meiktilla to Pegu in the vicinity of Rangoon. The Regiment remained in Burma until 1946, when it returned to India.

At the independence of the subcontinent in 1947, and the creation of Pakistan, the Probyn's Horse was allotted to the new Pakistan Army. Their Sikh Squadrons went to Scinde Horse, Indian Army.

6TH DCO Lancers (Watson's Horse)

4TH Sikh Irregular Cavalry

4TH Sikh Irregular Cavalry was raised in 1858, at the conclusion of the Sepoy Mutiny, at Lahore from Sikh volunteers. It straightaway went to garrison Delhi. The following year the regiment joined the Field Force sent out to intercept Tania Tope, who was reported to be making for Delhi. The regiment had gone out with minimum equipment as it was expected to return within a fortnight.

The main force went back to Delhi after ten days but the 4TH Sikh Cavalry was instructed to join the flying column of cavalry engaged in pursuing some troops that had taken part in the Sepoy Mutiny. The regiment joined the column 400 km. away by making six forced marches of 65 km. each. The column was in pursuit of Tantia Tope and followed him through Bikaner, Ajmer, and Guna to Shivpuri, where he was captured. The troopers of the 4TH Sikh Cavalry were all without shelter, while water and fodder for horses were extremely scarce in the country through which the column marched. Food was extremely costly if and when it could be procured. The regiment in spite of these unforeseen difficulties made no complaint.

Lieutenant Watson VC, who had been appointed to command the regiment, finally joined it in 1860. He could not do so earlier as he was employed on active service with the 1ST Punjab Cavalry. He commanded the regiment for eleven years and the regiment bore his name, unofficially, 1904, when it received official recognition.

The reorganisation of 1861 changed the designation of the regiment from 4TH Sikh Irregular Cavalry to the 13TH Bengal Lancers. In 1863, the regiment saw active service on the North West Frontier as a result of the tribal rising in Swat and was involved in the action in the Ambela Pass. The regiment next saw active service in the Second Afghan War of 1878-80. At the conclusion of which, the Afghans were permitted to maintain internal sovereignty but they had to cede control of their nation's foreign relations to the British.

During the Second Afghan War, the Afghans after their defeat at Ali Masjid fled to Bazaar Valley and started to harass convoys passing through the Khyber with the help of the Zakha Khel tribesmen. A punitive expedition, which included the 13TH Bengal Lancers, a designation adopted in 1864, was sent into the Valley, which did not succeed in eliminating raids on the line of communication of the army. Second expedition which again included the 13TH Bengal Lancers was sent in 1879. The expedition succeeded in finally making communications secure from raids in this area.

The 13TH Bengal Lancers first went overseas with the expedition to Egypt in 1882. During which the regiment repeatedly charged the enemy and routed them. The pursuit that followed was carried on Cairo, leading to the Arabi Pasha's surrender. Their performance so impressed the Duke of Connaught that he asked the Queen's permission become the Colonel of the 13TH Bengal Lancers. Queen Victoria confirmed the appointment and the Duke's name were added to the regimental title in 1884.

6TH DCO Lancers (Watson's Horse)

4TH Sikh Irregular Cavalry

The regiment again saw servicer on the North-West Frontier, when a major uprising by the tribesmen occurred in 1897. Two squadrons of the 13TH Bengal Lancers had the opportunity to launch a rare cavalry charge on a lashkar of tribesmen. The Mohmand tribe, inspired by the Mullah of Hadda, Najib-ud-Din, attacked the village of Shankargarh, some 18 miles north of Pashawar. Most of the villagers had taken refuge in Shabkadar Fort and the Mohmands, who numbered four to five thousand, made a planned assault on the fort. The fort stood on a mound and had 50 ft. high walls. It was held by a detachment of Border Police, who managed to repel the first attack. The 13TH Bengal Lancers went to the relief of the fort and the squadrons were ordered to charge the lashkar from a flank. The charge was made for two miles over very stony ground across the enemy's front. It was a complete success and the tribesmen were driven back to the hills. A Sikh signaller is said to have charged, with his long hair streaming behind him, with no other weapon except his signalling flag as he rode down several tribesmen. Dafadar Sewa Singh and Sowar Hira Singh were awarded the I.O.M., for their gallantry in the action at Shabkadar.

The regimental designation changed to 13TH Duke of Connaught's Lancers in 1903 and three years later sanction was given to the regiment to add Watson's name to become the He introduced new methods, which During the First World War the regiment was employed on the North-West Frontier until 1916, when they were ordered to Mesopotamia

Following the fall of Kut, the British ordered Major-General Stanley Maude to take command of the British army in Mesopotamia. He introduced new methods, and reinforcements, which included the 13TH Duke of Connaught's Lancers. Operations against Kut-al-Amara started on 16TH December. There were heavy rains which slowed down al movement, yet by the middle of January 1917, the right bank of the Tigres below Kut-al-Amara had been cleared of Turks. Within a month the right bank up to 20 km. west of Kut-al-Amara had been cleared, thus posing a serious threat to Turkish communications. Kut-al-Amara finally fell on 17TH September. The 13TH Lancers captured a standard, and had played a leading role in the capture of Kut-al-Amara.

Now commenced the pursuit to Baghdad in which the 13TH Bengal Lancers kept up a constant pressure on the withdrawing Turks. Baghdad was captured on 17TH March. After capturing Baghdad, British General Frederick Stanley Maude believed the British position was threatened by the Turkish forces of Khalil Pasha, who possessed 10,000 troops to the north of Baghdad, and Ali Ishan Bey's force who commanded 15,000 troops entering the region from Persia. In order to protect British gains in the region, in particular Baghdad, General Maude ordered the Samarra Offensive. The main British force advanced along both sides of the Tigris River. On 17 April, the British pushed the Turkish out of their trenches on the Adhaim River.

6TH DCO Lancers (Watson's Horse)

4TH Sikh Irregular Cavalry

This was a successful operation for the British as they suffered few casualties while capturing 1,200 Turkish soldiers.

On 19TH April the British built three strong posts a mile in advance, two on the east and one on the west bank of the Dujaila. The Turkish felt it was needed to contest this advance as if the Rail yard at Samarra was lost the Turkish would lose to ability to bring in reinforcements effectively to the region. The assault on the Turkish position at Istabulat started on 21ST April and on the 22ND the Turkish withdrew from their position.

Turkish Forces were forced to surrender the Samarra Rail Yard to British forces, ending their chance of retaking a dominant strategic position in the region. At the Battle of Istabulat, each side suffered approximately 2,000 killed. British casualties in the Samarra offensive as a whole were estimated at around 18,000 men; although a further 37,000 men were lost to sickness. The Turkish Empire lost about 15,000 men in the campaign, destroying the Turkish 6TH army.

Forming the final notable action presided over by regional British Commander-in-Chief Sir Frederick Stanley Maude the Capture of Tikrit was also one of the final significant engagements fought on the Mesopotamian Front. Maude despatched General Alexander Cobbe at the head of two divisions further up the River Tigris to tackle newly-established Turkish defensive positions some 13 km north of Samarra (itself taken during the year's earlier spring offensive). However before Cobbe could strike local Turkish commander Ismail Hakki Bey received news of the advance and made haste to withdraw his position to a position directly in front of the town of Tikrit. There, heavily protected Turkish trenches defended the town - built on cliffs over the River - in a ring on the west bank of the River Tigris. Cobbe nevertheless attacked Hakki's lines on 5TH November 1917, having been reinforced by a division of cavalry in the interim. Frontal attacks succeeded after three hours fighting in taking the Turkish front line, although heavy British cavalry losses were incurred during a charge on the Turkish second lines. Ultimately the Turks chose to withdraw, under skilful cover, further upstream to Fatah Gorge. Consequently Cobbe took possession of the town on 6 November but found it stripped of both men and supplies

The next objective along the Euphrates was the town of Khan al Baghdadi. Most battles in Mesopotamia had been tied to the Tigris and Euphrates Rivers. If an attack was successful, the loser would withdraw along the line of the River to prepared positions further back. Securing a proper victory was difficult. In an attempt to break with the usual pattern, the 15TH Indian Division were supplied with 300 Ford lorries, the 8TH Light Armoured Motor Battery (armoured cars), and the 11TH Cavalry Brigade. A mobile blocking force was assembled using divisional infantry in the Lorries, the armoured cars, the cavalry brigade, and one of the divisional artillery batteries equipped with double the usual number of horses. This mobile force was then sent on a wide flanking march around Khan Baghdadi, and dug in behind the Turkish positions.

6TH DCO Lancers (Watson's Horse)

4TH Sikh Irregular Cavalry

The remainder of the division then assaulted frontally in the normal fashion, and the Turkish retreated from the town. They then ran unexpectedly into the blocking force, and their discipline quickly crumbled. The entire force of about 5000 men was taken prisoner. The mobile force was then dispatched further up the Euphrates in the direction the Turkish had expected to retreat. 46 miles further upstream was the settlement of Ana. Here was the main Turkish supply base, which was now captured along with some high-ranking German officers attached to the Turkish Army. For most of the year 1918, the Mesopotamian theatre remained quiet. The British had to move troops to Palestine, and the Turks were enabled to receive reinforcements. Nobody wanted to fight in Mesopotamia anymore. Meanwhile the war was coming to an end and London was thinking about post-war arrangements. They saw a great interest in the seizure of Mosul and its oil resources. In addition to the oil, the area had to be cleared of the remaining Turkish influence, before the armistice was signed.

General Cobbe commanded a British force from Baghdad on October 23RD, 1918. Within two days it covered 120 kilometres, reaching Little Zap River, where it expected to meet and engage the Turkish Sixth Army operating under Ismail Hakki Bey.

Turkish forces retreated to Sharqat, a further 100 kilometres to the north, but nevertheless they came under attack by the British forces on October 29TH. Being aware of the armistice talks, Ismail Hakki Bey decided not to fight and not to attempt to break through. Within a day he surrendered although Turkish lines were not breached yet. Mosul was occupied by a British cavalry brigade on November 1ST, 1918, in violation of the terms of the armistice agreement. The war in Mesopotamia was over.

Dafadar Dalip Singh, Dafadar Ram Singh, Lance Dafadar Lashkar Singh, Lance Dafadar Arjan Singh, Risaldar Ram Singh and Sowars Mohan Singh, Ram Singh, Fauja Singh, Bhag Singh, Lakha Singh and Amar Singh, were awarded the I.D.S.M., for their conspicuous gallantry against the Turks in Mesopotamia.

Conditions in Mesopotamia defy description. Extremes of temperature arid desert and regular flooding; flies, mosquitoes and other vermin: all led to appalling levels of sickness and death through disease. Under these incredible conditions, units fell short of officers and men, and all too often the reinforcements were half-trained and ill-equipped. Medical arrangements were quite shocking, with wounded men spending up to two weeks on boats before reaching any kind of hospital. These factors, plus of course the unexpectedly determined Turkish resistance, contributed to high casualty rates. 11012 were killed 3975 died of wounds and 12678 died of sickness.

On returning to India from Mesopotamia the 13TH Lancers saw active service in Waziristan and the Third Afghanistan War of 1919.

In 1921, it combined with the 16TH Cavalry to become 6TH Duke of Connaught's Own Lacers (Watson's Horse).

6ᵀᴴ DCO Lancers (Watson's Horse)

16ᵀᴴ Bengal Lancers

The commissioner of Rohilkhand asked for volunteers from the area to fight for the British after the Revolt of 1857 and Captain Crossman raised the 'Rohilkhand Horse' which carried out the duties of subjugating Rohilkhand for the next two years. In 1862, the regiment was taken into Bengal Army as the 16ᵀᴴ Bengal Lancers. The regiment went to Duars in 1864 as part of the Bhutan Field Force. Duars is a region of north-eastern India, at the foot of Himalayas. It is divided by the Sankosh River into the Western and Eastern Duars. Both were ceded by Bhutan to the British at the end of the Bhutan War.

The regiment was disbanded in 1882, when three cavalry regiments were reduced in order to provide a fourth squadron to the other regiments. The Panjdeh incident fanned the British fears of a Russian invasion and an augmentation of three Indian cavalry regiments was sanctioned. The Bengal Army re-raised the 16ᵀᴴ and 17ᵀᴴ Bengal Cavalry while the Bombay Cavalry was raised in that Presidency. The re-raising of the 16ᵀᴴ Bengal Cavalry was carried out at Ambala in 1885.

Panjdeh Incident occurred at a place where the Russians had invaded far south in Asia, in the direction of British India. It was an area of northern Afghanistan, between the border with Turkmenistan and the Afghan city of Herat. Namely, the Russians occupied the Panjdeh oasis, suppressing the Afghans further south. Afghanistan became a buffer state between the Russian and British empires.

The regiment went on to serve on the North-West Frontier and participated in the Hazara expedition. The expedition ended with the Hasanzai and Akazai tribes requesting an armistice on October 19ᵀᴴ, 1888.

The 16ᵀᴴ which had become the 16ᵀᴴ Bengal Lancers, had an opportunity to go overseas with the expedition to China in 1900, put down what was referred to as the Boxer Rebellion. The Boxers, a xenophobic movement in China, carried out series of attacks on foreign missionaries, merchants and property. The Chinese government in June 1900 issued an edict, which amounted to support for the Boxers. The foreign legations in the Imperial capital Peking (Beijing) were besieged by the Boxers, and held out for three months despite having a small garrison. An international relief force was organised by seven nations. India sent a cavalry brigade which included the 16ᵀᴴ Bengal Lancers. On 30ᵀᴴ May the) the brigade disembarked from warships at Dagu and the 16ᵀᴴ Bengal Lancers, proceeded to attack the city of Tolieu, which soon fell. Various expeditions were then sent out to rescue missionaries. In the final assault on the Lichand-Kwang Pass, the 16ᵀᴴ Bengal Lancers dismounted to support the German infantry and were the first to reach the American Legation. The Americans presented the regiment with the 'Stars and Stripes' which had flown over the American Legation during the siege. The Chinese Government finally had to accede to all demands made by the foreigners and the Indian Cavalry Brigade was back in India by the end of 1901.

6TH DCO Lancers (Watson's Horse)

16TH Bengal Lancers

The reorganisation of 1903 changed the designation of the regiment to 16TH Cavalry. During the First World War the 16TH Bengal Lancers was sent to Mesopotamia in 1915, as part of the 6TH Cavalry Brigade. The 6TH Cavalry Brigade had frequent encounters with the enemy while on protective reconnaissance during March and early April.

On the morning of 11TH April, a patrol of cavalry reported a large body of Turkish cavalry and infantry close to Shawaibda, west of Shaiba. The patrol was unable to keep the enemy under observation as it was driven back by much a larger force of Turkish cavalry, which tried to occupy the watch tower and south Mound. The cavalry brigade turned out at the threat, and the enemy was driven back to Barjisiya wood. The brigade returned to camp at dusk.

The Turks now surrounded the British camp on all sides except the flooded side and it was decided to attack them on the 13TH. The 6TH Cavalry Brigade advanced from Kiln post to the north along the edge of the flooded area and contact was made with North Mound which was held by the Turkish infantry. A squadron charged an advanced post of the enemy and put the Turks to flight. The charge was pressed home until the squadron commander was killed and the squadron was recalled, but the Turks were unmistakably shaken. General Kennedy decided to withdraw the brigade and the position was cleared by the infantry later in the afternoon after suffering over hundred casualties. In this action the squadron lost 35 men and 70 horses.

The tide of battle fully turned on 14TH April when the Turks stated to withdraw from Barjisiya wood towards Nukhaila. An all out attack on the enemy was ordered by the British. The cavalry brigade was deployed on the right flank and ordered to threaten the Turkish line of retreat across the Nukhaila mud flats. The infantry launched a general assault and the cavalry supported them by dismounted fire from the right flank. The front line of trenches was captured and the bulk of the defenders killed. The enemy evacuated Barjisiya wood during the night and withdrew across the desert. The battle of Shaiba ended in victory for the British.

In order to advance to Amara, the right flank had to be secured. The 12TH Division was ordered to proceed to Ahwaz and carry out this task with the 6TH Cavalry Brigade and the 13TH and 30TH Infantry Brigades. The pipeline was also to be secured as the fuel supply had been interrupted. The British advanced on Amara from Qurna and Amara fell on 3RD June, and the cavalry squadron returned to Ahwaz. The encampment of the Arab tribe which had attacked a patrol was raided on the way back. Although most of the Arabs escaped, their ammunition and grain was captured and thus ended the expedition into Arabistan. The advance to Amara had been accomplished and oil began to flow once again to Abadan from 13TH June. The 6TH Cavalry Brigade, with the 23RD Cavalry (FF) which had arrived from India for patrolling duties along the Anglo-Persian Oil Company's pipe-line.

6ᵀᴴ DCO Lancers (Watson's Horse)

16ᵀᴴ Bengal Lancers

During December the Turks gradually closed in as the outposts were sniped at and some shells fell in the camp. It was decided to send the cavalry, additional transport and gun boats back to Ali Gharbi which was to be the covering position for the main British concentration at Kut-al-Amara. The beleaguered garrison at Kut-al-Amara surrendered to the Turks on 29ᵀᴴ April 1916. The efforts at relief had cost 40,000 casualties and failed to save the garrison of 8,000 out of which 6,000 were Indians. After the fall of Kut-al-Amara, major operations were carried out until the whole force was reorganised by General Maude who took command of the Mesopotamia Expeditionary Force at the end of August. Orders were now received for the relief of the three Indian Cavalry regiments in the 6ᵀᴴ Cavalry Brigade. The 16ᵀᴴ Cavalry was one of these regiments and proceeded to Loralai in Baluchistan in October 1916, much under strength.

The fall of Kut-al-Amara in April 1916, constituted a terrible blow to British prestige, and it appeared probable that a wave of fanaticism would sweep across Baluchistan to India. The assassination of King Habibullah of Afghanistan in February 1919, and the outbreak of the Third Afghan War in May of the same year, created a feeling of intense excitement, and it could not be expected that peace would remain unbroken. The breakdown of the militia system on the north-west frontier, arid the abandonment of Wana, the key position in neighbouring Waziri tribes were encouraged to launch a series of large scale raids in the administered areas. By November 1919, they had killed over 200 people and wounded a further 200. The first attempt to subdue them began in November 1919, when Major-General Sir Andrew Skeen launched a series of operations against the Tochi Wazirs. These operations were largely successful and terms were agreed. During 1920, 16ᵀᴴ Cavalry formed a part of the Derajat Column and committed to the fighting in Waziristan. The fighting continued for about twelve months and the British had to resort to using aircraft on a number of occasions to suppress the tribesmen. There were a number of successes, though, notably during the eight-day battle at Ahnai Tangi. When the Wana Wazirs rose up in November 1920, they appealed for help from the Mahsuds, but still recovering from their earlier defeat, no support was forthcoming and the Wazir opposition faded away. On 22ᴺᴰ December 1920, Wana was re-occupied. Minor raids by the Wazirs and forays by British forces continued into 1921, however, following the 1919–20 campaign, the British decided upon a change of strategy in Waziristan. It was determined that a permanent garrison of regular troops would be maintained in the region, to work in much more closely with the militia units that were being reconstituted following the troubles that occurred during the 1919 war with Afghanistan. As part of this policy, it was decided that a garrison would be maintained at Razmak.

In 1921, it combined with the 13ᵀᴴ Lancers to become 6ᵀᴴ Duke of Connaught's Own Lacers (Watson's Horse).

6TH DCO Lancers (Watson's Horse)

At the outbreak of the Second World War the 6TH Lancers proceeded to Iraq in April 1942. In September 1942, they were transferred to 6TH Indian Division in Persia to meet possible German threat through the Caucasus. The following year they returned to 8TH Indian Division for operations in Italy, as the reconnaissance regiment of the Division. It landed at Taranto on 24TH September 1943. It was reorganised on a special organisation current in Italy with five troops in each lancer squadron. Three of the troops were equipped with T16 Ben carriers at the scale of four per troop, one was a motor troop in tracked carriers and the fifth was a rifle troop divided into two self-contained half troops. The HQ Squadron had an intercommunication troop mounted in scout cars. Within two months of its arrival in Italy, one carrier troop in each squadron was issued with Humber mark IV armoured cars. In July 1944 a support group was added to the regiment's HQ Squadron. The support group had 8x self-propelled 75 mm guns mounted on half-tracks in a gun battery and 6x3 inch mortars in a mortar troop. The group provided immediate fire support to squadrons. The organisation changed again in October 1944 when each squadron had two Greyhound armoured car troops, one Humber armoured car troop, and one carrier troop had one rifle troop. Lieutenant Colonel Robinson was in command. The regiment had only a few junior Indian officers in it most were British officers. The class composition was Sikhs, Jats and Punjabi Mussalmans in its 'A', 'B', and 'C' squadrons respectively.

The 8TH Indian Division commenced its advance after putting a Bailey bridge over the Biferno. Divisional patrols reconnoitred forward on 22ND October. 'B' Squadron 6TH Lancers advanced on the left flank of the division. 1/12TH Frontier Force Regiment took over the feature occupied by 'A' Squadron. The 19TH Indian Brigade advanced with 'C' Squadron 6TH Lancers in the lead. Lancer patrols were also required to maintain contact with the British division on the right, across the Trigno River. The Indian planned a crossing with two brigades with the Lancers screening both flanks.

'C' Squadron 6TH Lancers and a squadron of the 5TH RTR were in support of 19TH Indian Brigade for crossing the Trigno. The task of the Lancers was to protect the vulnerable western flank of the bridgehead, there were some 6 pounder anti-tank guns towed by carriers in support. The operation, delayed by heavy rains, was launched on 2ND November. The left battalion had to be withdrawn due to heavy counterattacks but the other held on. Another attack the following night ground to a halt just short of objective. The enemy, however, withdrew and the Division occupied Palmoli on the next ridge on 5TH November. 6TH Lancer patrols entered Fresa on the northern flank but further progress was delayed by demolitions on roads where diversions soon turned into quagmire.

6TH Lancers deployed its squadrons on a 32 km front in order to obtain enemy information and identification. Base on information supplied by escaped British prisoners of war, a strong patrol from the Sikh squadron was despatched to confirm the presence of the enemy in a village 13 km away and 6 km inside German held territory and if possible capture a prisoner.

6TH DCO Lancers (Watson's Horse)

The patrol reached the village of Rossello undetected and advanced through it. Two Germans in their shirt sleeves came out of a building. One was shot dead and the other surrendered. The alerted Germans started to fire from all directions. The patrol withdrew with its prisoner without suffering any damage. Its withdrawal was covered by Gurdev Singh who earned a mention in despatches. The 8TH Division was now up against the main German defences of the 'winter line' across the Sangro River and faced the toughest task yet undertaken by it. The bed of the Sangro and the approaches to it were dominated by an escarpment and a ridge on the north bank into which were dug formidable German defences. They had fortified stone houses in villages and roads leading from the River to the defences were heavily mined. The 78TH British Division established a bridgehead across the swollen Sangro on 2ND November but continuous rain delayed forward exploitation by the 8TH Indian Division. Improved weather enabled tanks to reinforce the bridgehead. The 17TH Indian Brigade attacked Mozzagrogna on 27TH November and captured a part of the village after fierce fighting but had to withdraw because supporting tanks could not reach the objective. The second attack, the next night, was more successful. 6TH Lancers with two infantry companies and an anti-tank battery protected the left flank and maintained contact with the New Zealanders. 21ST Indian Brigade patrolled forward towards Lanciano with the Sikh squadron covering its left flank. By 30TH November V Corps was firmly established across the Sangro.

During the night 2-3 December dismounted patrols from the Sikh and Punjabi Mussalman squadrons entered the outskirts of Lanciano and confirmed that the enemy was making preparations to withdraw. German demolition parties preparing two bridges withdrew when disturbed by the patrols, enabling the bridges to be captured intact the next morning.

On 3RD December a squadron was operating on the left flank of the division. It advanced to Lanciano after cutting the road to Castel Frentano. As the leading armoured car rounded the last corner into town it came face to face with a German mark IV tank. The car fired two rounds, but the first shot from the tank set the armoured car on fire. The Lancers beat a hasty retreat. Patrols from the regiment and 3/15TH Punjab Regiment entered the town during the night and found it clear of the Germans. It was occupied the next day.

The Lancers fanned out of the town. 'A' Squadron advanced along one of the two roads going northeast to Saint Vito. It was held up 8 km short of the town by demolished bridges. 'C' Squadron advancing along the other road was stopped by another demolition east of Treglio. 'B' Squadron now moved along the track to Frisa, the objective of the Division. When it reached the demolished bridge half way to Frisa, it was fired at. It found a diversion and drove into Frisa where a German observation post was surprised and captured. Four machine guns located in a village 1500 m to the northeast engaged the squadron. The troop leader sent SDM Kirpal Singh and 7 Sowars to outflank the enemy. With his carriers he raced for the village.

6ᵀᴴ DCO Lancers (Watson's Horse)

The dismounted Lancers closed with the enemy with clever use of ground and after hand-to-hand fighting captured one machine gun and destroyed three. The regiment captured 25 prisoners of war in this operation.

General Montgomery decided further to strengthen his coastal thrust by advancing on a two-corps front. XIII Corps was brought in on the left of V Corps. The 8ᵀᴴ Indian Division swung towards Tollo to accommodate the 5ᵀᴴ British Division on its left. The Indian Division was to advance to Tollo via Villa Grande, while the Canadians were fighting in Ortona. The Canadians reached Ortona on 20ᵀᴴ December and captured the port from the 1ˢᵀ German Parachute Division after 8 days of bitter fighting.

On 17ᵀᴴ December, 6ᵀᴴ Lancers covered the advance of 19ᵀᴴ Brigade towards Villa Grande along two tracks. The advance was slow because of the close nature of the country which had extensive olive groves. German tanks fired from inside stone huts and infantry used them as strong points. The 3ᴿᴰ German Parachute Regiment, holding Villa Grande, had done a thorough job of preparing its defences. Houses were turned into strong points and dug-outs excavated under them to cover all approaches, which was also covered by anti-tank guns and mines were laid. The first attack by 19ᵀᴴ Brigade on 22ᴺᴰ January failed but the second on the following day, succeeded partially. The battle for Villa Grande raged for several days.

A subsidiary attack on Vezzani had better success. 'A' Squadron 6ᵀᴴ Lancers supported, by few tanks and a Punjabi company captured and secured the objective. The squadron was relieved by a battalion on 23ᴿᴰ December; the latter held a counterattack launched by the Germans. By 28ᵀᴴ December a major part of Villa Grande had been captured when the Germans vacated Ortona and Villa Grande. The Sikh Squadron held in readiness to exploit forward could not do so because of mines and demolitions. All three squadrons were employed dismounted to hold strong points on the eastern flank of the division. The Eighth Army's offensive came to a halt for the present. Winter blizzards precluded further operations until the spring.

By the middle of January 1944, the Adriatic front had become static. Eighth Army tried to prevent the Germans from moving troops away from the sector by frequent raids and offensive patrolling, but both sides found it expedient to thin out troops from the sector. Both sides reinforced the Tyrrhenian front where sanguinary battles were being fought after the Allies launched an offensive to break through the Gustav Line and capture Rome. The Adriatic sector remained active at a local level in spite of atrocious weather. During the winter of 1943-1944, all three Indian Divisions did tours of duty in the sector.

The 8ᵀᴴ Indian Division became responsible for a larger area covering the Orsogna and Casoli sectors. The 6ᵀᴴ Lancers moved to the left flank was up against the Maiella range. The Sikh squadron's rifle troop converted the village of Fallascoro into a strong point from where they sent out harassing patrols.

6TH DCO Lancers (Watson's Horse)

It was raided by 30 men of the 30TH German Reconnaissance Regiment on 3RD March but the Lancers stoutly defended their position. The battle lasted several hours before the enemy withdrew. The officer commanding the attacking party and three others were killed and four of the attackers were taken prisoner. Two men in the rifle troop were slightly wounded. The Lancers continued to send out patrols and laid ambushes throughout March, in spite of snow and bad weather. Their efforts yielded a steady dividend of prisoners and inflicted casualties on the enemy.

The 4TH Indian Division returned to the Adriatic sector after their gallant deeds in the Cassino area. It relieved the 8TH Indian Division, which went to the Larino area in the west close to the Cassino sector. There it took part in the assault on the Gustav Line and the advance up the Liri Valley. 6TH Lancers carried out a demonstration with its 'A' Squadron simulating a crossing and bridge-building opposite the Liri Appendix, 'C' Squadron being in support. The deception was most successful. German reaction to it was violent and very heavy fire, which would have done serious damage elsewhere, came down in the Lancers area without harm to anyone. By 14TH May the whole regiment was across with the Sikh Squadron bolding a firm base in the Liri Appendix. During the night 13-14 May, 78TH British Division passed through the 8TH Division's bridgehead in order to isolate Cassino. On the evening of the 14TH May, 3/15TH Punjab Regiment with 'A' Squadron 6TH Lancers and a tank squadron of the 12TH Canadian Armoured Regiment crossed into the bridgehead and advanced to cut the Pignataro-Cassino road. The ground was boggy and broken and the Germans offered stiff resistance. The tanks reached the objective but the infantry was held up. Although the attack did not succeed, it paved the way for the easy success of a second attack later during the day.

On the fourth day the Division enlarged the bridgehead further and broke through the Gustav Line while the Lancers protected the southern flank. 'C' Squadron met only slight opposition as it advanced towards the Liri River. A carrier had to be abandoned and the squadron took up position covering the Liri Valley. The 8TH Indian Division had accomplished it task of capturing the St. Angelo horse-shoe across the Gari River and was relieved on the morning on 17TH May. The Division had established the first, and for sometime the only, bridge over the Gari. This had turned a precarious crossing by the Eighth Army into a firm bridgehead which cracked the German defences. In five days of fierce fighting 400 German soldiers were killed and 600 captured.

On 17TH May the Eighth Army broke through the Gustav Line and finally succeeded in forcing the heroic defenders of Cassino and the monastery to abandon their defences. The Hitler Line took another week to overcome and then XIII Corps commenced its advance down the Liri Valley. During the advance the 8TH Indian Division was on the right and did its share of fighting in the crossing of the Melfa River. 'A' Squadron 6TH Lancers supported a battalion of 19TH Brigade in the capture of Roccasecca.

6TH DCO Lancers (Watson's Horse)

Passing the town on the west the squadron pushed north until halted by enemy fire. A column was sent up the Melfa gorge under the command of the squadron. It attacked the enemy's rear guard provided by German parachutists; the column killed 40 and took 14 prisoners. It came to halt when confronted with a 210-foot gap in the gorge.

The Corps once again met stiff resistance beyond Melfa. On 26TH May the Division outflanked the enemy advancing on Rocca d'Arce which it reached on 29TH May. For a month, thereafter, the Germans did not offer serious resistance to the Allied advance but merely relied on strong points to delay it through narrow valleys with steep hills and demolished bridges. The 8TH Division pursued the 1ST German Parachute Division to Altare and Viroli. It crossed the Liri on 30TH May and 19TH Brigade advanced on Monte S. Giovanni with 'B' Squadron 6TH Lancers sand a troop of New Zealand tanks protecting its flank. The squadron mopped up the Sona Road from Arce but 8 km north of it came up against a strong point held by the enemy supported by a Spitfire of the RAF, the rifle troop managed a limited advance. After heavy fighting the enemy withdrew during the night.

On 1ST June 'B' Squadron advanced to Viroli with a squadron of the 18TH New Zealand Regiment in support; 'C' Squadron was advancing on the right. The enemy had broken contact but when the column reached a high spur 14 km short of Viroli, the enemy column could be seen climbing Viroli hill. The Lancers took up the chase and a troop entered Viroli from the north along the main road. An anti-tank gun opened fire at point blank range and knocked out the rear armoured car. The other two were trapped and were hit a little later. The crew abandoned their vehicles, took cover beneath a culvert and called for artillery fire. A daylight attack by the infantry failed because every move was under enemy observation. The Brigade started to concentrate for and attack after dark. In the meantime, the enemy started to advance towards the dismounted lancers still holding their position outside Viroli. Two companies of infantry were rushed up to the aid of the lancers. The enemy was repulsed barely 50 m from squadron HQ. The squadron suffered seven casualties. The Germans withdrew from the Viroli after dark. The Division advanced across the country beyond Viroli because of congestion of Route Six. A Squadron 6TH Lancers acting as vanguard to 19TH Brigade had to be withdrawn because of extremely bad going which even the tanks found difficult to traverse.

From 9TH June the Tiber became the boundary between X and XIII Corps. X Corps advanced with the 6TH (British) Division and the 8TH Indian Division was kept in reserve for the advance to Terni. The 8TH Indian Division advanced with its three brigades up, with a squadron of the 6TH Lancers covering the advance on each axis. 'A' Squadron led the advance of 19TH Brigade along Route 79. It captured several German demolition parties and passed over several bridges prepared but not blown up. An ammunition dump was captured beyond Martana.

6ᵀᴴ DCO Lancers (Watson's Horse)

The squadron reached Berana on 16ᵀᴴ June; it was 9 km west of Foligno. 'B' Squadron advanced through the hills on the west of Foligno while the Corps reconnaissance regiment, 12ᵀᴴ Royal Lancers, were to go through the town. 'A' Squadron was the first to reach Foligno where it cut the enemy's escape route by securing the road junction northwest of the town. The driver of the leading car rammed and halted German staff car from which two officers were captured. 'C' Squadron also entered the town and drove the enemy towards the block held by 'A' Squadron. The Lancers killed 50 Germans, captured 135 prisoners including 8 officers, several vehicles, horses, a complete workshop, guns and other weapons.

'C' Squadron leading armoured car was hit by a self-propelled gun during its advance to Spello; the gun was destroyed by a patrol from 'A' Squadron. Another patrol came up a troop-carrying vehicle which was engaged and set on fire. A staff car was intercepted and two officers in it surrendered; one of them was shot when he drew a pistol and wounded an NCO. The patrol withdrew with its prisoners because a large enemy convoy appeared on the scene.

On 17ᵀᴴ June 'C' Squadron led the advance of 19ᵀᴴ Brigade to Bastia and 'A' Squadron covered the left flank. The former met only slight opposition until the outskirts of the town where and anti-tank gun knocked out two of the squadron's armoured cars and destroyed a jeep. A rifle troop, which dismounted to deal with the gun, was also pinned down and its troop leader Lieutenant Iqbal Singh killed. C Squadron made contact with the enemy on the line of the Chiascio River where one of its armoured cars was destroyed. Four tracked carriers were lost shortly afterwards resulting in the death of a VCO and two men wounded. 'B' Squadron took up the advance beyond Bastia but was held up by strong opposition 5 km past the town.

The 8ᵀᴴ Indian Division launched a series of attacks supported by armour till the end of the month. The 6ᵀᴴ Lancers was deployed on the left flank of the Division and maintained contact with the 6ᵀᴴ Armoured Division. The 10ᵀᴴ Indian Division relieved the 8ᵀᴴ Indian Division at this stage. Skinners Horse took over from the 6ᵀᴴ Lancers which withdrew to the Foligno area for rest and reorganisation.

The 8ᵀᴴ Indian Division rejoined XIII Corps and was allotted the task of advancing on the Arno on the Corp's left flank, and took over the its allotted sector on 22ᴺᴰ July. 'B' Squadron 6ᵀᴴ Lancers was deployed on the left flank of 19ᵀᴴ Brigade. Apart from protecting the flank it maintained contact with 11 Corps on its left. Advance was slow because of extensive mines and demolitions. On one day 180 'Schu-mines' were lifted from a two km stretch of the road. By 27ᵀᴴ July an advance of only 24 km could be made. On 28ᵀᴴ July 'C' Squadron was deployed on the right flank of the Division, the regiment was stretched over a 4,000-m frontage with two squadrons committed. On the evening of 1ˢᵀ August the Germans attacked a post held by 'A' Squadron with tanks and company of infantry and were repulsed.

6TH DCO Lancers (Watson's Horse)

The 8TH Indian Division had captured Castigliani on 1ST August and established a bridgehead across the Pesa, 16 km west of Florence. By 4TH August the southern outskirts of Florence was reached. The Corps reorganised on 7TH August and the 8TH Indian Division took over the sector to the south of Florence. The 6TH Lancers took over a sector in the foothills overlooking the Arno Valley. The Germans withdrew to their main defences behind the Magnone Canal so that a part of Florence south fell into Allied hands by 15TH August. The Indian Division was withdrawn for rest the following day.

The 8TH Indian Division established a bridgehead across the Arno on 25TH August and work commenced on the construction of bridges. The infantry commenced intensive patrolling across the River. The 6TH Lancers deployed on the right flank, commenced advance through the valley along the west bank of the Siave River. Advance was slow because of demolitions on the road which had been cut into the hillside with a vertical 50 foot drop into the River. In a stretch of 1000 metres there were 14 craters. The Division pursued the enemy vigorously but came up against strong German defence based on the line of the hills, the last line of defence ahead of the Gothic Line.

6TH Lancers were under the command of 19TH Brigade for an attack on Calvana. The attack did not succeed but the Germans, having completed their arrangements, withdrew to the Gothic Line on 8TH September. The Division followed up through extensive demolitions. On 12TH September the 6TH Lancers were deployed with its 'A' Squadron on the right flank of 21ST Brigade. The Seima River was crossed but no further progress was possible. On that day the 8TH Indian Division closed up with the bastion of the Gothic Line.

The Fifth U.S. Army's attack on the Gothic Line commenced on 13TH September and by the 18TH, 11 U.S. Corps had captured and 11 km stretch of it. The 8TH Indian Division was allotted the most mountainous terrain in the middle of its attack. The Germans held well-sited concrete defences and pillboxes hidden in well wooded mountains with plenty of cover. The 8TH Indian Division stormed and captured three bastions held by determined German infantry. The 6TH Lancers remained in reserve in the Molezzano area, while the Division attacked through the most difficult and wild terrain. By 18TH September the 8TH Indian Division had smashed its way through the mountainous portion the Gothic Line against an enemy who had every advantage of terrain. The 6TH Lancers were temporarily placed under the command of the 26TH Armoured Brigade from the middle of October to early November 1944 to operate in a dismounted role along with other British armoured regiments. The regiment was required to hold the high ground north of Benedotte with two squadrons up at a time. It not only held the allotted area also managed an advance of 11 km in two weeks in the Apennines under atrocious weather conditions. This was achieved by constant patrolling and raids on the enemy. Two regimental patrols were ambushed and suffered casualties.

6ᵀᴴ DCO Lancers (Watson's Horse)

On 26th December 19th Indian Brigade hastily occupied a defensive position north of Serchio and 21st Brigade moved up the next day to protect its flank and provide depth. The Germans approached the forward Indian positions on the evening of 27th December but did not make any effort to advance further. 'B' Squadron 6th Lancers, having arrived with the regiment on the evening of 28th December, advanced the next morning along the east bank of the River to make contact. The squadron had to deal with extensive mines and demolitions carried out by the U.S. troops before their withdrawal. By late afternoon the squadron occupied Baraga ridge. Two infantry battalions of the 19th Indian Brigade following the Lancers could not make much progress because of the difficult terrain. The squadron held the ridge during the night which passed off peacefully except for minor patrol clashes. On 30th December, 21st Brigade occupied the Baraga ridge and the Lancers armoured cars probed forward west of the River towards Molezzano. A couple of miles beyond Nebbiana they were engaged by intensive small arms and artillery fire. Two armoured cars of the squadron advanced along the other bank of the Serchio after the sappers completed a bridge at mid-day. Their advance was also held up by accurate enemy shelling. The situation was well under control.

Fifth Army sent an urgent call for a prisoner to obtain identification of the enemy. 'B' Squadron sent out a fighting patrol of a rifle troop to the village of Molezzano. It bypassed a strong point by making good use of ground and attacked an outpost in the village. The patrol captured and brought back three Italian Fascist prisoners at the cost of two of the patrol's men slightly wounded. Jemadar Jagir Singh was awarded a Military Cross for leading the patrol. By New Year's Day the Indian Division regained all ground that had been lost during the sudden German attack, and the enemy had gone back on the defensive. The 8th Indian Division was relieved by the Americans on 8th January 1945, and it moved to the foothills overlooking the Arno River and the city of Pisa for a spell of well-earned rest. In February the 8th Indian Division returned to the Eighth Army on the Adriatic coast.

The 8th Indian Division arrived on the Senio Line in early February and on the 25th assumed responsibility for a sector immediately to the right of the 43rd Lorried Brigade. The Division had relieved the 1st Canadian Division and taken under command the 2nd Armoured Brigade, already in sector. Here the Germans held both flood banks with elaborate defences constructed underground. Frequent clashes took place between the two sides which enabled the units to gain valuable information about the German defences which proved invaluable when the time came for the final offensive. The 8th Indian Division held this sector until the spring offensive which commenced on 9th April 1945.

The 6th Lancers was placed under the command of the 2nd Armoured Brigade and assumed responsibility for a sector from the 27th Lancers on 24th February. All three squadrons, reinforced by men from HQ Squadron, were in the line simultaneously.

6TH DCO Lancers (Watson's Horse)

The 8TH Indian Division had been pulled out of the line on 12TH April after it had broken through the German defences on the Senio and Santerno rivers. The first unit to be called up again was the 6TH Lancers, which was put under the command of V Corps on 17TH April. 'C' Squadron was allotted the task of providing left flank protection to the Corps along the Idice River. V Corps burst through the Argents gap on 20TH April as the Corps front broadened, the 8TH Indian Division was inducted on 21ST April with the task of advancing to Ferrara and the Po River along Route 16. The Division advanced astride the Prmaro River, with a brigade on each side. The Germans committed their 26TH Panzer Division in this area, to stem the Corps' advance. This German formation was considered one of the best in Italy and one of the few not seriously depleted in men and material.

'A' Squadron 6TH Lancers led the advance of 19TH Brigade along Route 16 against light opposition but through extensive demolitions. The squadron fought a minor action about 8 km from Ferrara against a German platoon supported by tanks. The squadron captured 15 prisoners and reached the railway line, 2 km south of the town by the evening of 22ND April but was held up by demolitions and strong opposition. Here the infantry relieved the squadron which had fought its last action in Italy.

'B' Squadron 6TH Lancers led the advance of 21ST Brigade along the west bank on a parallel road. One troop overcame strong opposition and negotiated demolitions to advance 16 km in one hour. It reached Ferrara airport and took many prisoners. Other troop of the Sikh squadron was on the southern outskirts of the town by the afternoon. Here many tanks were encountered which knocked out the leading armoured car and inflicted four casualties. On 23RD the squadron again led the advance of the brigade and reached the southern bank of the Po River and took 12 prisoners during the advance. The advance carried on and the Division commenced preparations to advance with the 6TH Lancers and 19TH Brigade. The 6TH Lancers started a race for Venice and covered 80 km in two hours, meeting no organised resistance but thousands of Germans intent on surrender. The regiment was halted by a direct order from the XIII Corps Commander, General Clarke., who insisted that the road must be cleared for his Corps of Americans, to have the privilege of entering Venice first! The 6TH Lancers withdrew to the Padna area. The war in Italy was over for the lancers. They returned to India in June 1945.

In August 1947, at the independence and the partition of the Indian subcontinent in the sovereign states of India and Pakistan and the division of the army the 6TH Duke of Connaught's Own Lancers (Watson's Horse) was allotted to the new Pakistan Army. Their Sikh Squadron went to the 8TH King George V's Own Light Cavalry, Indian Army.

Guides Cavalry (10TH QVO Frontier Force)

Corps of Guides was raised on 14TH December 1846 at Pashawar. It was raised from the veterans of the Sikh army at the conclusion of the First Sikh War. Sikhs, Pathans, Punjabi Mussalmans, and Dogras formed the bulk of their manpower. Initially composed of a troop of cavalry and two companies of infantry mounted on camels, the Guides were organized as a highly mobile force. Their mission was to maintain order on the Punjab Frontier. From this time on this history will chronicle separately their services.

The first occasion on which the newly raised Guides were employed was in July 1847, in collecting the revenue from the border clans. One night in July, two Dafadars and eighteen Sowars, marched from Kalu Khan in Yusafzai to surprise a village of Mugh Darah in the Panjar Hills. The village was surprised and the men disarmed and three hundred head of cattle brought away. In September, a village called Babuzai, refused to pay its share of revenue and necessitated the employment of a considerable body of troops. The Cavalry portion of the Guides, one Jemadar, one Kot Dafadar, seven Dafadars, and twenty two Sowars, advanced from Katlang and attacked the village from the front. The village was burnt and the Guides Cavalry pursued the leader, Prasand Khan, and his mounted men for four miles, cutting off their retreat to the Bazdarah Valley and obliging them to see refuge in the village of Mian Khan, which was too strong to be attacked by cavalry unsupported.

The general unrest in the Punjab led to trouble at Multan, where Diwan Mulraj ruled the province under a treaty with the Sikhs. Mulraj now raised the standard of revolt and called upon all to join him in expelling the British from the Punjab. In the month of June the Cavalry of the Guides joined the force before Multan, and when the little army first took up its position on the right of a nullah at Suruj Kund, the Cavalry charged and silenced twelve wall-pieces mounted round the Bibi Pakdaman Mosque; but with the heavy odds against them they were unable to carry of the guns. Eventually Multan fell on 22ND January 1849. During the Multan troubles, there was Sikh uprising in the Punjab, which resulted in the Second Anglo-Sikh War. In February the Guides Cavalry fought in the final battle at Gujerat, pursuing the Sikhs to Rawalpindi where they surrendered. With the annexation of the Punjab, to the British Empire, some 80,000 square miles were added to British India, whose western boundary now marched with the mountain ranges, from Sind to Hindu Kush. Policing the North-West Frontier, now as it had become, were in the British hands.

The Guides had proved so useful and heroic that their strength was increased to three troops of cavalry.

The Guides Cavalry and Infantry participated in sixteen punitive expeditions between 1849 and 1857. Baizais (1849), Kohat Afridis (1850), Mohmands (1851), Ranzais (1852), Uthman Khel (1852), Waziris (1852), Black Mountain Tribes (1852), Jowakis (1853), Hindustani Fanatics(1853), Shiranis (1853), Kohat Afridis (1853), Mohmands (1854), Afridis (1854), Orakzais (1855), Miranzai(1855), Kurram(1856).

Guides Cavalry (10TH QVO Frontier Force)

On 26TH June 1849, 67 Sabres of Guide Cavalry rode during the night from Pashawar to Yar Husain in Yusafzai, attacked and destroyed the village of Bagh in the Panjar Hills next morning and returned to Yar Husain by noon, thus accomplishing a distance of fifty-six miles and burning the village in thirty-six hours.

On 6TH March 1852, thirty Sabres of the Guides Cavalry was at Gujargarhi, some five miles north-west of Mardan, awaiting the arrival of a survey party to which they was to provide escort, when they were attacked at night by 180 horsemen from Swat, headed by one Mukaran Khan, formerly of the Pashawar Police. These when challenged by the sentry, replied "Sahib," on which the Risaldar ran out, expecting to meet the survey officer; but seeing that the party was carrying matchlocks, he instantly realized they were enemies, and called out to his men " to look to themselves for the enemy was upon them." Mukaran Khan's men now galloped into camp, discharging their matchlocks into the standing tents, not one of which had fewer than eight or ten bullet-holes through it. Fortunately all the Guides had rushed out of the tents, sword in hand, on the alarm being given, and breaking up into small parties, they defended the camp on foot, finally driving out the enemy. In this affair one Sowar was killed and two were wounded.

Early in 1852, one Ajun Khan took up his quarters in Uthman Khel villages, and began raiding the British border. Finally in April, collecting some two hundred men, he attacked Charsadda, the headquarters of the district, plundered the treasury, and murdered certain government officials. With a week Sir Colin Campbell was moving against him from Pashawar, with a force of 1,593 of all ranks, while 250 men of the Guides Infantry and a Squadron of the Cavalry joined the column at the Kabul River. Sometime after Campbell's men had settled in for the siege, Ajun Khan decided to take the fight to the besiegers and advanced on the British stealthily. The force was caught unawares, but an outlying picket of 20 men of the Guides Cavalry was the nearest group to the enemy. A young subaltern of the Guides, Lieutenant G N Hardinge, saw the situation and rode out to the picket and led them in a desperate charge against the Pathans to give the rest of the Force time to get into formation. This charge was such a shock to the enemy that it was entirely successful, and Hardinge, though wounded managed to return with most of his men and a captured standard. On 11TH May the force under General Campbell, covered by the skirmishers of the Guides Infantry, moved on the village of Nawe Dhand, which was carried and burnt, and on the 12TH the column advanced seven miles to Gandera, attacking and destroying Prang Ghar, the stronghold of the Uthman Khel, who were in some force and offered considerable opposition. The Guides again covered the advance, and one of them wounded and Ajun Khan's headman, who was found to be in possession of the weapons of a thanedar who had recently been murdered in Hashtnagar. In this three day's fighting the Guides had one Sepoy killed and Jemadars Ousan Singh, Pir Baksh and eight other ranks wounded.

Guides Cavalry (10TH QVO Frontier Force)

It was very evident that Ajun Khan's men had been permitted to pass through, if they had not actually been harboured in, Ranzais territory; and it was decided to proceed against this tribe, who had also refused to pay the fines levied upon them for other acts of misconduct. On 15TH May a force, numbering considerably over 3,000 including the Guides, was assembled at Shergarh, just outside Swat border, under the command of Sir Colin Campbell. From reports received it was clear that numbers of tribesmen were flocking from all parts to defend Shahkot, the principal village of Ranzais and that many Ghazis had come over the passes to encourage the faithful and urge over the waverers. On the 18TH May the force moved on Shahkot, situated between a very deep and narrow nullah on the east and some hills on the west, where the enemy was holding a position about a mile and a half long. The Infantry of the column, led by the Guides, cleared the ravine and the village and occupied the high ground beyond, while the Guides Cavalry charged the enemy and cut down many of them, pursuing the rest as far as Dargai, there miles away at foot on the Malakand Pass. Of the forty casualties sustained by the force, half were men of the Guides, who lost eight men killed and twelve wounded. The Ranzais now made overtures for peace, accepted the terms offered them, and settled down to rebuild their villages and till their lands; while all through the hot weather of 1852 the Guides were employed in guarding and patrolling the Frontier and in providing parties for the workmen engaged in erecting a fort at Abazai.

In 1853 during the punitive operations against the Kohat Afridis, when the force entered the Valley there were not more than two hundred men to resist; but before they returned, the number had increased to some three thousand, tens and twenties pouring in all morning from all the villages and hamlets within many miles, the intelligence of the attack being conveyed to them by the firing. In the fighting the Guides lost Sowars killed, while nine were wounded, their casualties actually amounting to half those of the whole force. In this action Subedar Kor Singh and Sowar Dal Singh distinguished themselves by their gallantry were awarded the I.O.M.

During the Sepoy Mutiny, the regiment was ordered to go to Delhi on 13TH May 1857 to help suppress the mutineers. They set off from their base at Hoti Mardan at 6pm. On the way they were required to take punitive action against a rebel village called Karnal. They were also held up at Attock and Rawalpindi, these delays amounting to more than 5 days. But this hardly slowed them down because they arrived at Delhi on the morning of 9TH June, having covered a distance of 580 miles in 26 days. They started to pitch camp but 3 hours after their arrival they were in the thick of the fighting.

The enemy, having ascended the hill, were close to the right Piquet, when the Guides Infantry arriving on the scene were instantly thrown into skirmishing order and, with a shout, dashed to the front. The rebels fell back in confusion and the Guides followed hard on their heels, friend and foe pouring together on the main road.

Guides Cavalry (10TH QVO Frontier Force)

The Guides Cavalry were watching the opportunity to assist their Infantry comrades, and were now moved forward to attack, but had not advanced fifty yards when they came upon a body of some 150 of the enemy cavalry drawn up on a cross road; these Guides at once charged and the enemy broke and fled. Dafadar Dal Singh was awarded the I.O.M. Kot-Dafadar Tarlok Singh particularly distinguished himself in this action, while Sowar Jiwan Singh was promoted Dafadar during this action. During the course of the siege the enemy delivered no fewer than 26 separate attacks upon this part of the line, and these occurred almost daily. The Guides spent 4 months at Delhi, the cavalry constantly employed around the city. The latter were especially important in their support of the 9TH Lancers against the batteries at Kishenganj. The 9TH were so depleted that the Guides cavalry were ordered to take their place. They performed so well that the commander of the 9TH commented that "they stand like the Lancers." To appreciate this praise it has to be understood that at that time native units were not expected to be as committed and disciplined as their European counterparts. The following officers and men were awarded the I.O.M. during the campaign of 1857:- Jemadar Dal Singh, Risaldar Prem Singh, Dafadars Avtar Singh, Ishar Singh, Nihal Singh, and Kala Singh. Twenty-two men of the Cavalry were specially promoted for their gallantry in the field.

When Delhi fell the Guides went home to the frontier, to take part in further punitive operations until the Second Afghan War:- Waziris (1859), Mahsuds (1860), Ambela (1863), Black Mountain tribes (1868), Jowakis (1876), Afridis (1877).

In 1860, Mahsud Waziris who, to the number of some 3,000, had made an attack on the town of Tank, standing in a plain about five miles from the foot of the hills on the Dera Ismail Khan border. Such aggression called for severe punishment, while there was a long score outstanding against the Mahsuds which demanded early and prompt settlement. A large force was assembled on 16TH April at Tank, which included 108 Sabres of the Guides Cavalry. The force entered the hills on 17TH April, and arrived unopposed at Palosin Kach. The Guides Cavalry marched with the main column to Haidar Kach and Barwand, punishing troublesome sections before returning to Palosin. The main camp had been pitched on the left bank of the Tank stream. On the 23RD April, some 3,000 Waziris, overpowered the Piquets, and dashed on the Guides. The Guides though surprised in their tents made a respectable resistance, falling back inch by inch on the guns. Here the Guides contrived to get together some men, who with fixed swords and bayonets advanced on the enemy bearing down on them and clearing the camp. In spite of the surprise, the Waziris had all been evicted from the camp within fifteen minutes of their first appearance, leaving ninety-two of their dead within the camp and forty more in the ravine close by. The force advanced and attacked the enemy positions one after another, each point being at once occupied by skirmishers and the whole range of the hills was cleared of the enemy. The force then marched on and reached Bannu on 20TH May, when the force was broken up.

Guides Cavalry (10TH QVO Frontier Force)

In the year 1858, the Guides had taken part against the Hindustani fanatics and the Khuda Khel had been that then Hindustanis had been ejected from their settlement at Sittana and had settled at Malka, on the northern slopes of the Mahaban Mountain; but in 1861 they had come down to a place called Seri, close their former haunts, and began abducting Hindu traders from across the Hazara border. Repressive measures were undertaken against those tribes who had allowed the raiders passage through their territories, and for a brief period matters improved; but in the spring of 1863 murder and outrage began again, and with the connivance of the Gaduns and Utmanzai, the Hindustanis in the summer suddenly reoccupied Sittana, began preaching of a Jihad, and made many attacks on the posts and villages on the British border. A blockade of the Utmanzai and Gaduns was now imposed, and on 28TH July 1863 a detachment of the Corps of Guides with too troops of Cavalry, marched from Mardan to protect the border village of Topi, thirty-miles distant, from a threatened attack by the Gaduns of Mahaban and the Hindustani fanatics of Sittana. By a forced march Topi was reached on 29TH.

The prompt arrival of the Guides saved Topi from immediate attack, but the Hindustanis and Gaduns continuing to show a hostile demeanour, the Guides were ordered to remain at Topi and form part of the force blockading the offending tribe. On the night of 3RD September the usual night patrol was out, composed of a Dafadar and three Sowars, and came across the advance guard of a party of 250-300 Hindustanis, who had come down from Sittana under their leader, one Mullah Abdulla, with the intention of surprising the Guide's camp at Topi. Coming upon this party in the dark, the patrol promptly charged, shouting "Fall in, fall in !" when the enemy, thinking that the surprise had failed and that they had the whole detachment in the front, at once turned about and fled, their leader showing the way. The Guides had no casualties, but they killed one of the enemies and mortally wounded and brought in another, besides some arms which some of the Hindustanis had thrown away in their flight.

These blockade measures proved insufficient, and the Hasanzais, instigated by the Maulvi of Sittana, made an unprovoked attack upon and destroyed several villages in Amb territory and as it seemed now clear that most of the tribes had thrown in their lot with the Hindustanis against the British, and expedition for their punishment was determined upon. This was to be on a large scale, and contained two troops of Guides Cavalry. Near the village of Ambela the road was found to be held by the enemy in force, and a gallant charge by the Guides Cavalry cleared the road to the village, which was destroyed. Three times in the course of this month the Guides Cavalry were engaged with the enemy. During this expedition the Bunerwals sided with the British, by destroying the stronghold of their own allies. Finally it was decided to require these tribes to perform similar service to that demanded of the Bunerwals i.e. the destruction of the Hindustani fort and the settlement called Mandi near Sittana. This was done and the force was broken up, the Guides Cavalry returning to Mardan on 11TH January.

Guides Cavalry (10TH QVO Frontier Force)

In January 1866 the Guides Cavalry was again called out on service, this time against the Sam Baizais, who for the past fifteen years had been guilty of numerous raids into the British territory and who had flocked to assist the Bunerwals during the Ambela campaign. Their punishment was long overdue, and accordingly on 15th January 1866, a force of some 4,000 men with twelve guns was assembled at Nowshera, moving out next day to Mardan, where it was joined by 275 Sabres and 450 Bayonets of the Guides. It was found that the mere approach of a punitive force had itself been sufficient to cause some of the villages to come to terms, but the troops marched on, destroying the villages of Sanghao, Mian Khan and Barmol, and the inhabitants of these were required to rebuild upon other less inaccessible sites. The object of the expedition having been carried out, the force marched back and was broken up.

Lord Lytton, the newly arrived Viceroy to India, notified Sher Ali, the Afghan ruler that he was sending a "mission" to Kabul. The Amir refused Lytton permission to enter his kingdom. Initially, the Viceroy did not take action against the kingdom until 1878, when Russia's General Stolyetov was admitted to Kabul, while Lytton's envoy, Sir Neville Chamberlain, was refused entry at the border by Afghan troops. The Viceroy affronted by the insult, decided to crush his neighbour and launched the Second Afghan War on November 21st, 1878, with a British invasion over the high passes. General Roberts gained a victory at the Peiwar Kotal and General Sam Browne took Ali Masjid and advanced on Kabul and General Donald Stewart occupied Kandahar. The Guides Cavalry formed part of the cavalry brigade of Sam Browne's force and the Guides Infantry were in his 2nd Infantry Brigade. Sher Ali fled hi capital and country, dying in exile early in 1879. The British army occupied Kabul, as it had in the first war, and a treaty signed at Gandamak on May 26th, 1879, was concluded with the former Amir's son, Yaqub Khan. The following Sikh officers and men of the Guides Cavalry were awarded a collective I.O.M., for their conspicuous gallantry in a cavalry charge against a large body of fanatical Khugiani Ghazis near Fatehbad on 2nd April 1879; Dafadar Jiwan Singh, Ressaidar Nand Singh, and Sowars Diwan Singh, Kadoo Singh, Prem Singh and Yakub Singh.

Accordingly, Sir Louis Cavignari was appointed a Her Majesty's Envoy at the court of Kabul. The Guides had only just arrived at Mardan on their return from the Afghan frontier when they were instructed to detail and escort for the Kabul Mission, and to join Sir Cavignari at once at Thal. The composition of the escort was: - Cavalry, 25 Sowars and 52 Sepoys. This party marched for Kohat on the night of 26th June under Lieutenant Hamilton. The Mission left Ali Khel in the Upper Valley on 18th July and on crossing the frontier was received by Sirdar Khushdil Khan, late Governor of Turkestan, who had been deputed by the Amir to conduct it to Kabul. Next day the march to Kabul was begun and the capital was reached on the 24th July, 1879. Here the Mission was met with every sign of friendship and respect, and was lodged in a spacious building in the Bala Hissar, 250 yards from the Amir's palace. This satisfactory state of affairs was not destined to last.

Guides Cavalry (10TH QVO Frontier Force)

Some two or three after the arrival of the Mission, six regiments of Afghan infantry arrived form Herat and encamped for three days at Debori, about two miles out of Kabul. On morning of the fourth day they marched through the principal streets of the city, headed by their officers and with the bands playing. During the march they abused the envoy by name. They also abused the Kazalbashis, loyal to the Amir, and taunted them with not being men, adding that they, the Heratis, show them how to act and put an end to Cavignari.

On 3RD September without any warning, Afghan soldiers attacked the Residency. British officers and Indian troops of the Guides faced countless Afghan soldiers and civilians. Soon all the British officers were dead. The Guides fought desperately, even charging out of the Residency to bayonet the crews of Artillery brought against them, The Afghans set the Residency of fire and the buildings started to collapse. All day the Afghans called upon the Guides to surrender, promising them their lives. The Guides rejected the offer and after 12 hours of fighting the few remaining men commanded by a Sikh Jemadar, Jiwand Singh, fixed bayonets and charged out to their deaths. Thirty six of the Guides Cavalry and Infantry sacrificed their lives, and by their deeds they conferred undying honours on the Sikh nation. Over 600 Afghans dead bore witness to the heroic sacrifice of this small force. Following are the names of the fallen, given for Cavalry, so all may remember the richness of their inheritance:-

Jemadar Jiwand Singh, Dafadar Hira Singh, Sowars Amar Singh, Wazirs Singh, Rattan Singh, Mul Singh, Jiwan Singh, Harnam Singh, Thakur Singh and Dewa Singh.

The sacrifice of these gallant men is commemorated in the impressive Guides Memorial at Mardan with the following words: "The annals of no army and no regiment can show a brighter record of devoted bravery that has been achieved by this small band of Guides. By their deeds they have conferred undying honour not only on the regiment to which they belonged but on the whole British Army."

The massacre at Kabul led to the resumption of hostilities and in December 1879, the Guides were dispatched to join the Kabul Field Force under General Sir Frederick Roberts at Sherpur Cantonment near Kabul.

Roberts felt that it was essential that the British troops make some kind of blow against the Afghans before the snows made campaigning impossible. He advanced his forces out of the Kurram valley towards Kabul, issuing a proclamation to the people of Kabul that he was returning there in order to punish the murderers of the British mission and that anyone found in possession of a weapon would be considered just such a perpetrator. Just south of Kabul his forces encountered a large force of thirteen Afghan regiments and twenty guns overlooking a village known as Charasiab. The battle at Charasiab was a critical one. The courage and resource of the troops won the battle against great odds. Roberts advanced into Kabul and almost immediately begun to punish local Afghans with a series of public hangings.

On October 28TH the Amir Yakub Khan he publicly announced that he was going to abdicate, and on the 1ST December he departed for India for good.

Guides Cavalry (10TH QVO Frontier Force)

During November and the first week in December of the Guides Cavalry, fifty-four Sabres were at Jagdalak Kotal and 103 Sabres at Pezwan Kotal. The precariousness of Roberts' position was made evident on December 11TH as his forces were split to comb the countryside surrounding Kabul looking for hostile forces. One of these forces, under Massy, found just such a force. Unfortunately, it was far bigger than anyone had suspected; some 10,000 Afghans in a continuous, unbroken line of two miles length. Roberts sent some forces to help Massy extricate himself from his very dangerous position. A propitious rear attack by the force headed by General Macpherson allowed General Massy to fully disengage and head for the relative safety of the camp at Sherpur. The Guides Cavalry were ordered out of Sherpur to cut off the retreat of a body of the enemy, who were moving along the Siah Sang heights towards Kohistan. They were successful in intercepting them, and cut up a good number of the enemy, who fought obstinately and caused some loss on the cavalry, with three Sowars killed and Kot-Dafadar Bhup Singh, one trumpeter and six Sowars wounded. The British forces would spend the next couple of days in enforced captivity at their base at Sherpur. Reconnaissance forces sent by the British were coming under increasing pressure as the sheer number of Afghans made any movement outside the encampment all but impossible. On the 14TH, Roberts was forced to send out a force to try and disperse Afghans amassing less than a mile and half away from the base. At first it seemed successful, but as more Afghans appeared, they were forced to withdraw to the safety of the compound once again. Having lost the initiative and the ability to dictate circumstances, they would have to just wait for the Afghans to attack at their own leisure.

Roberts did not have a great number of forces available to him in Kabul, so a number of relief columns had been organised and were heading towards Kabul from the Khyber Valley. However, the emboldened confidence of the Afghans had made the whole country far more difficult and dangerous to traverse. The relief column led by Gough came under repeated attacks and pressures from surrounding tribes. As the relief column approached Sherpur on the 23rd of December they suddenly began to hear gunfire from the direction of Roberts' camp. The Battle of Sherpur had begun that very same day; the relief column had no way of knowing if they were marching to relieve the base, or to meeting their own deaths at the hands of a victorious Afghan army. Fortunately for them, the first forces they came across were a troop of Lancers pursuing the Afghans from the battlefield. It was clear that they would now be spending a cold, but relatively safe winter in Kabul. Winter brought a temporary end to the campaigning of all forces in Afghanistan. But, the British were still no closer to achieving any kind of lasting diplomatic solution. It was clear that as soon as the snows lifted, the Afghans would be back to their traditional warlike ways and carry out yet more attacks on the British and their supply columns.

Meanwhile in April, Stewart had begun to move a large force from Kandahar to Kabul in some sort of attempt at consolidating commands and forces.

Guides Cavalry (10TH QVO Frontier Force)

Just outside of Ghazni the column was confronted by a well positioned force of some 9,000 Afghans in the hills immediately to his front. Reinforced by a force, which included the Guides Cavalry, he attacked the enemy, who were seen flying from the villages and orchards. Stewart then advanced into Kabul to find that the political and diplomatic landscape had changed in Afghanistan. It was becoming clear that Abdul Rahman was the only candidate who was powerful enough to wield power and yet still remain palatable to the British and their war aims. There was still more negotiating to do, but essentially he was the only serious candidate that the British could support and he duly became Amir on July 10TH. It looked as if the British could withdraw with their pride reasonably intact once again. During the Second Afghan War, the Guides Cavalry were foremost. They led the Khyber column right up to Jagdalak, and when called on rode straight into Kabul. They were at the capture of Takht-i-Shah on 13TH December 1879, and of the Asmai Hill on the 14TH, and held the most exposed part of the Sherpur cantonment. Everywhere their conduct was magnificent. During the campaign they had 2 British officers, 2 Indian officers, 7 non-commissioned officers and 35 Sowars killed and 4 Indian officers, 9 non-commissioned officers, and 32 Sowars wounded.

The Corps was more or less continuously engaged in frontier actions. Bunerwals (1886), Hasanzais (1888), Black Mountain Tribes (1890), Darband (1891), Isazai (1892).

In 1895, a coup d'état in Chitral cost the life of the ruling chief. The victors attempted to destroy the troops in Chitral, who were besieged in the Chitral fort. To rescue them, a couple of hundred miles of continuous frontier hills or as much by almost non-existent precipitous roads from Gilgit, was a very great problem. While Gilgit was cut off by vast snowbound passes, an attempt from Nowshera-Mardan was possible and the Guides, Cavalry and Infantry, joined the relief force now assembling. At the Malakand Pass, on April 3RD, 1895, the invading troops overwhelmed some 12,000 Chitralis, who lost more than 500 men before giving up control of the pass.

After the successful actions of the Malakand Pass, during which the I.O.M., for conspicuous gallantry was awarded to Dafadar Tota Singh and Lance-Dafadar Sobha Singh of the Guides Cavalry, they carried out various operations against the tribals including the punitive actions during the Pathan Revolt of 1897-98. The conflagration began in Waziristan and then spread along the whole length of the frontier from Gomal up to the hills near Mardan. It took months to quell the Pathan Revolt. On 1ST August, Dafadar Sham Singh and Sowar Gurdit Singh were awarded the I.O.M., for their gallantry. Again on 2ND August, as the Guides Cavalry near the Chakdara bridge, which was still intact, the garrison of the fort made a sortie and drove the enemy from the right bank of the River, so preventing them on the advancing Guides Cavalry. The cavalrymen took up the pursuit and drove the enemy to the neighbouring hills and into the village of Chakdara. When the relief column arrived to invest Chakdara, most of the enemy had completely disappeared.

Guides Cavalry (10TH QVO Frontier Force)

At the outbreak of World War I, the Guides Cavalry remained in India for service on the North-West Frontier. In April trouble arose on the frontier and the Guides were called, as so often in the past, to hold back the more aggressive of the tribesmen of the Border. The trouble was due to fanatical Mullahs who preached against the British in Mohmand country, and on 13TH April 1915, a report was received that Mohmands were collecting with a view to raiding Shabkadar. Accordingly, on the 15TH Khyber Movable Column marched from Pashawar to Shabkadar. Guides with 100 sabres and 100 rifles, marched to Abazai to reinforce the garrison of the fort, which consisted a detachment of Guides. On the 18TH the Khyber Movable Column fought an action against Mohmand tribesmen in the vicinity of Hafiz Kor in which the detachment of Guides at Abazai, without waiting for orders, joined and rendered valuable assistance by operating against the enemy's flank. Meanwhile at Mardan the remainder of the Corps had been mobilised and hastily marched to the Mohmand frontier. On their advance the Mohmand tribesmen were reported to be dispersing, and the Guides after spending a few days in Shabkadar marched back to Mardan.

The Frontier did no remain quiet for long, and within a month of the Guides returning to Mardan signs of trouble became apparent in Swat where the tribes were engaged in inter-tribal quarrels. Matters came to a head in June when the advance of a tribal Lashkar on Adinzai threatened the safety of Chakdara fort and also of Chitral road. Accordingly Malakand Movable Column with the Guides Cavalry was concentrated at Chakdara. The rapid concentration of the troops had an excellent effect and prevented any outbreak the time. The Guides carried out various operations against various tribes until 1917.

For month after month of this year the Cavalry of the Guides pursued the even tenor of their way at Mardan, and many must have begun to wonder whether the greatest of all wars would come to an end without the Guides Cavalry having an opportunity to take part in it. Meanwhile, as the time went by the calls made by other corps for officers and men was repeated and insistent. In January 1917 draft of one Indian officer, Jemadar Ganda Singh, and fifty-five rank and files as reinforcement for the 10TH Lancers, were sailed for Mesopotamia. On 22ND September orders were received for the Guides Cavalry to proceed on active service to Mesopotamia and to embark at Karachi on 2ND October.

On 8TH October the transport carrying the Guides Cavalry sailed from Karachi. The following are the names of Sikh officers who left India for Mesopotamia with the Regiment: Risaldar Dayal Singh, Ressaidar Jiwand Singh, Ressaidar Bhagwan Singh, Jemadar Beant Singh, Jemadar Wasawa Singh and Jemadar Arjan Singh.

The Guides Cavalry arrived in Mesopotamia at a time when the campaign had taken a very favourable turn. Early in the spring of 1917 Kut-al-Amara had been captured and Bagdad had fallen, and before the summer heat, the British troops, advancing north of Bagdad, had captured Samara and had driven the remnants of the Turkish forces into the fastness of the Jebel Hamrin. In November 1917, they joined the 11TH Indian Cavalry Brigade and fought in the Battles of Sharqat.

Guides Cavalry (10TH QVO Frontier Force)

Activity on the Mesopotamian Front had been muted in the months leading up to the action fought at Sharqat. However Lloyd George's government in London ordered Marshall to remove as much remaining Turkish influence from the region as possible in the weeks immediately prior to the anticipated Turkish armistice, as had earlier been achieved in Palestine. Thus Sir Alexander Cobbe was commanded to lead a combined Anglo-Indian force from Baghdad on 23RD October 1918. Its progress was remarkably swift: within two days it had covered 120km, reaching Little Zab River, where it expected to meet and engage the Turkish Sixth Army operating under Ismail Hakki Bey. However Hakki determined to retreat his army once it became clear that Cobbe's force was endangering his army's rear. Retreating therefore to Sharqat a further 100 km to the north, he nevertheless came under attack by Cobbe on 29TH October 1918. Within a day Hakki surrendered to Cobbe. However with the Turkish Empire in disarray an armistice was both desirable and imminent, and was consequently agreed within a matter of days. During this last battle in Mesopotamia 18,000 Turk soldiers were taken prisoner by the British, whose losses ran to a little under 2,000 men.

Immediately the news of the Turkish Surrender on the Tigris was received General Maud determined to exploit the victory to the full by pushing on to Mosul, the headquarters of the 6TH Turkish Army. Mosul itself was peacefully occupied by an Indian cavalry division two weeks after the Sharqat encounter, falling to the British on 14TH November 1918.

After the armistice, the Guides Cavalry proceeded to Kasvin in Persia to join what was known as Norper Force to counter any threat to British interests from the Russian Bolsheviks and Persian socialists. On July the Guides detachment at Menjil while on patrol encountered about a hundred dismounted men of the enemy and engaged them for about six hours. Two days later a patrol, with four machine guns, also became engaged with an enemy body and was reinforced and extricated in a most spirited manner by a Jemadar and nine men. The squadron of the Guides left camp soon after midnight on 14TH August by a track through the hills, with the idea the enemy at dawn at Yuz Bashi Chai, about fifteen miles down the road. The country to be passed over was found, however, to be more difficult than had been expected, and at dawn of the 15TH squadron was still some distance from the enemy. But the Bolshevik troops, estimated at about 150 cavalry, 200 infantry and four guns, had also selected this day to advance, and being surprised while entangled in the hills, they fell back as soon fore was opened on them, losing forty men and three Lewis guns. On 27TH October news of somewhat disturbing character reached Kasvin to the effect that the Persian Cossacks had fallen back and disintegrated; that the Bolshevik troops had occupied Resht, and that the advance position in that direction was exposed to intermittent shelling. The Guides were directed to march at once in order to intercept a body of some 200 Cossacks with two machine and two mountain guns, said to be moving round the north of the town and making for Teheran, The party was to be turned back by force if necessary.

Guides Cavalry (10TH QVO Frontier Force)

The squadron started in twenty-five minutes and came upon the Cossacks in a village about five miles distant and *persuaded* them to return quietly.

The Cossacks, never very satisfactory allies, had been completely demoralized by a Band of Russian adventurers who were supposed to command them; almost the first act of General Sir Ironside, who arrived about this time from Constantinople to take command of 'Norper Force', had been to eject all Russians neck and crop from the country.

They returned to India in 1921. The end of the war also spelt the end of the Corps of Guides as a unit. In the post-war reorganization of the Indian Army in 1921, the corps was broken up and the cavalry and infantry became separate units. The Cavalry became 'Guides Cavalry (10TH Queen Victoria's Own Frontier Force)'.

In May 1930, the trouble began with the Red Shirt movement, by name of Khudei Khitmatgar (Persian: "Servants of God"), in support of the Indian National Congress, an action started by Abdul Ghaffar Khan of the North-West Frontier Province of India. Abdul Ghaffar Khan was a Pakhtun and was called the Frontier Gandhi. It was a semi-rebellious body with vast following in semi-military guise, and was involved in series of troubles which had become very dangerous and beyond the power of the civil authorities to control. Military assistance was now called for, and on 30TH April 1930, the Guides Cavalry was ordered to the plague spot of Charsadda, to help evacuate political prisoners. This was carried out satisfactorily and the Battalion was back in Mardan the next day. This, however, was but a commencement of perpetual sallies from Mardan to various troubled areas to arrest offenders or disperse gatherings and was to continue for seven years of trouble and war.

A few weeks after the Red Shirt troubles, some five thousand Afridi tribesmen has assembled on the western sided of the Afridi plain between 31ST May and 3RD June, and some two thousand had reached the outskirts of Pashawar. The authorities were alarmed that a large force had succeeded in getting into close touch with the rebels of the city. In a few days, bombed and attacked by troops, the Afridis had retired back to the hills for the moment. The news of this invasion had spread to the neighbouring country and everywhere raids were prevalent. On 1ST August the Afridis Jirgas decided to launch another attack on Pashawar. Within a week 5,000 men succeeded in evading a military force watching the border. Another lashkar joined them and at least 2,000 Afridis were in the gardens around Pashawar engaged in attacking the military posts. In the meantime the Afridis were attacking the trains on the railway line, which had to be protected, and various troops began to arrive. An extended campaign was inaugurated to clear up the invasion and generally advance on the Khajuri plain, and by the end of September the situation was well in hand. Among the troops hurried up were the Nowshera Brigade and the Cavalry Brigade, which included the Guides Cavalry. The Guides Cavalry constantly clashed with the Afridis, however, the position ended in a stalemate, and it was decided to withdraw the Cavalry Brigade from an operation for which they were not suited. The Regiment on 12TH June was ordered to return to Mardan.

Guides Cavalry (10TH QVO Frontier Force)

On 13TH June the regiment it received orders to go to Swabi, to deal with disturbances. The Afridi inroads had lowered all the respect for law and order, and the country needed quieting. It arrived at Swabi and left to round up the villages of Marghuz, Miani, Kotah, Yar Hussain and Tordher. The trouble was now over, and the Cavalry returned to Mardan.

The Afridi incursions into Pashawar Valley were not over. The loot acquired was to produce a larger inroad, which meant no rest for the Guides Cavalry. They had arrived in Mardan on the 28TH and on the 29TH were ordered to march to Pashawar to rejoin their Cavalry Brigade. During this long and trying period the movement of the Cavalry Brigade undoubtedly kept the countryside clear of the enemy. The end of it was that in a long, trying days the Guides Cavalry had been able to get on terms with the intruders and do more than exchange a few shots with them.

The Guides Cavalry was kept busy during the following punitive expeditions on the frontier until 1940; Mohmands (1933-35), Waziristan (1936-39).

On 26TH September 1940, the Guides Cavalry was mechanized as a Light Reconnaissance Regiment equipped with wheeled armoured carriers and 15 cwt trucks.

On 4TH April the political coup took place in Iraq, the Regent escaping to Egypt and one Rashid Ali declaring himself Regent. In 1941 a Squadron of the Guides Cavalry, was dispatched to Iraq, in accordance with the treaty with Iraq, especially to watch the large British oilfields. The Squadron arrived at Basra on 2ND July and Baghdad on the 14TH. The rebel party, whose principal rebel leaders having fled to Persia, asked for and armistice on 31ST May, which was accepted, and the royal Regent had returned, and the Squadron was employed in rapid movement about the country.

In early August the Squadron was sent down to Basra to join the 8TH Indian Division for the invasion of Persia. The invading force seized Abadan Island, ten miles below Khorramshahr, secured the oil works, Khorramshahr itself, while the Navy seized the port of Bandar Shaper, on the Khor Musa, an inlet a few miles east of the Shatt.

The share of the Guides Squadron was straightforward and important as it led the advance. When the Navy opened fire, and as the Squadron advanced on the wireless station, they were met by the gleaming light of Admiral Bey Endor's car as he tried to get away. Meeting the Guide's advanced armoured cars, he left his car, entered the wireless station, and there he met his death. The Squadron crossed the defence ditch fairly easily, getting behind and capturing the wireless station. They then moved north towards Pul-i-Nao, crossed over, and joined the infantry regiment in their clearing operations, and then returning to the wireless station. From here they marched up-River to Marid. On the 26TH, after covering the advance of the 18TH Brigade to Marid, they were ordered to cross the Karun and at early dawn on the 27TH to reconnoitre up the west bank towards Dorquain, an oil pumping station, where the Anglo-Iranian Company's families were rescued.

Guides Cavalry (10TH QVO Frontier Force)

On the 28TH came the news of the Persian surrender, and the Squadron parked that night at Kot Abdullah, north of Ahwaz and on the 30TH it returned to Dorquain. In September, the Squadron and the 2ND Gurkhas were sent to Shahgan some twenty miles east of Dorquain to bring in 1,000 Persian troops who had fled from Abadan and suffered terribly from thirst and heat. The road had been strewn with corpses. They surrendered eagerly but would not face the road again and were brought to Ahwaz in Lorries, and that was the finish.

From Persia the battalion was ordered to Egypt via Syria. Starting on the 29TH and marching 460 miles, they were ordered to Damascus, showing the flag, supporting the Free French. Eleven days were spent in Damascus itself where, the first armoured units to be seen, the Guides received much attention. On 14TH April they marched north to Homs and then back to Der-ez-Zor on the Euphrates. It was the station of the Free French, who received them enthusiastically. From there they marched on 4TH May to continue their reconnaissances of armoured vehicle routes and the flag-showing, via Bab and Djerablous to Aleppo. By 21ST May they were back in Damascus, having received on the 20TH the long-awaited orders for North Africa.

Just as Rommel was attacking and stretching out south to Bir Hacheim that the Guides Cavalry marched in from Syria. On 24TH May 1942, before the final smash up in "The Cauldron", they were pushed out into the Wadi Natrum, coming under the orders of the 10TH Indian Motor Brigade. They were now well on the road to the front. The fighting in the "Witch's Cauldron" south of Acroma, was now at its height and more debris and rear services of the Eighth Army were coming through, the seriousness of the situation being apparent to all. By 18TH June the British line was hastily formed on the Italian frontier, or had withdrawn north to Tobruk. The Guides Cavalry were now ordered to turn westward, a fresh and unshaken armoured unit, for reconnaissance purpose only. But of all things, what was essential was the combating of Axis penetration and reconnaissances. The situations, however, was growing worse and worse, and on the very day the force had hurriedly occupied Tobruk and had not had time to organize their defence, were smothered. The only possible course was to withdraw farther rather than attempt to hold the line, and on the 23RD the Regiment was ordered to pull out and get back as fast as it could to the vicinity of Fuka.

By now General Auchinleck had taken over the actual command from General Ritchie, and had been compelled by the state of to the troops and armour to give up any idea of holding a line at Matruh, which line indeed Rommel was endeavouring to encircle. The troops retiring was fighting fiercely, counter-attacking or breaking out.

In marching to Fuka on the 23RD the Regiment itself was heavily bombed and machine-gunned, Sowar Bij Singh mortally wounded. On the 26TH and 27TH the Regiment was practically covering the rear of the Eighth Army on the edge of an escarpment facing west, while the Axis troops were pushing on down the coast, a movement which had caused the Brigade some anxiety.

Guides Cavalry (10TH QVO Frontier Force)

On the 27TH there was "the father and mother" of a tank battle on their front between the Huns and the 22ND Armoured Brigade, and the Regiment was also being engaged with patrols. When this fight was over, it was ordered back some ten miles, while the enemy had got as far as Baggush on the coast. During this movement a Squadron covered the rear, and three vehicles had to be destroyed to save them from the enemy. Next day orders came from the Brigade to move fifteen miles south and 100 miles east, taking with them a mixed force of gunners who had become detached from the 50TH Division. Halting the night in the desert, they arrived at the Ruweisat Ridge, having been bombed and machine-gunned without loss. Here were many staff officers arranging to get the troops into position on the El Alamein position, from which the Rommel was soon to be beaten back, and orders from the 30TH Corps now directed them to cover the front and work in with the 18TH Indian Infantry Brigade.

October had almost run out and the great hour had arrived. On the 23RD the artillery opened the ever-memorable Fourth Battle of Alamein that was to put Egypt out of Axis thoughts forever. For the Guides Cavalry the only excitement was the capture of two escaped German prisoners. On the 5TH came orders to join the Eighth Army, now pushing after Rommel's defeated troops, and be at Amirya by the 10TH. Rommel had returned from his leave a few days before Montgomery opened, in time to see a heavily protected convoy making for port devastated from the air. At Mena on the 8TH the actual orders to march to the Eighth Army came, and on the 10TH came the route to be followed from Mareopolis, via El Amein and Sidi Abd-el-Rahman, and on the 11TH they had marched accordingly. As Colonel Walton went to contact the rear of the Eighth Army a despatch rider arrived with the orders for the unit to return to Amirya. It was on loan from PIA Force to help the Eighth Army when its armoured force was broken. The German approach to the Caucasus was ominous, the hour of PAI Force might soon come back, and back to PAI Force it must go.

. Form 11TH November to the 20TH it remained at Mareopolis, its actual orders to march to Baghdad coming on the 17TH, and on the 21ST it marched for Ismailia and the Canal. By the 29TH it joined the 5TH Indian Division at Quetta camp and the next day marched to Latafiya, where the whole January 1943, was spent. Not long after their return to PAI Force the Cavalry was ordered back to India, with great hopes of going to Burma. This was not to be, and they were sent back to the Frontier on detachment at various places in Waziristan.

Risaldar-Major Rattan Singh was rewarded with the Membership of the Order of the British Empire. Two pensioned Sardars, who had rejoined, received recognitions. Risaldar Ganda Singh, O.B.I., I.D.S.M., being made an Honorary Lieutenant, and Risaldar Makhan Singh, received the O.B.I.

At the independence of the subcontinent in 1947, and the creation of Pakistan, the Guides Cavalry was allotted to the new Pakistan Army. Sikhs were posted to the Poona Horse, Indian Army.

Pavo Cavalry (11ᵀᴴ Frontier Force)

1ˢᵀ Punjab Irregular Cavalry

The 1ˢᵀ Punjab Irregular Cavalry was raised by Henry Daly at Lahore n the spring of 1849. Volunteers were available in large numbers from the disbanded regiments of the Khalsa Army of the Sikh Kingdom. The regiment was raised as a part of the force for the protection of the Frontier from Hazara to Sind. When the annexation of the Punjab brought the frontier of British India up to the north-western hills, the Indian Government decided to continue the payments to the Kohat Pass Afridis, which had been customary in the past in return for the protection of the road through the Pass.

On February 2ᴺᴰ 1850, however, a serious attack was made on a party working on the road near Kohat within British territory. The regiment formed part of the force for reinforcing the garrison of Kohat, and exacted punishment from the authors of the raid. In March 1852, operations became necessary, against Ranzais, a Swat clan living between British territory and the Swat River, in consequence of various raids which were made across the border and the asylum afforded to outlaws. The regiment after a sharp fight captured and destroyed the village of Shahkot. Soon after the annexation of the Punjab the Afghans set up a claim to the Kurram and Miranzai Valleys, and even sent troops to occupy the places. The inhabitants at once protested to the Indian Government, and offered to pay annual tribute in return for inclusion of their country in British territory. The offer was accepted, and the Afghans were forced to withdraw. Shortly afterwards the presence was reported in the neighbourhood of the Miranzai Valley of bands of Waziri raiders. The regiment caused the dispersion of these bands, and chastised the tribes for such disturbances.

The regiment helped in disarming a part of the garrison of Multan at the outbreak of the Sepoy Mutiny in 1857. One squadron was sent to Delhi and after the sack of the city, went to Agra, where they captured five standards and three guns. They were part of the force which relieved Lucknow and took part in the pacification of Rohilkhand. The rest of the regiment was employed in the Punjab and went on to take part in the pacification of Avadh until 1859, when detachments were employed in aid of the Civil Power. Then the regiment went back to their duties on the North-West Frontier,

The 1861 reorganisation changed the designation of the regiment to the 1ˢᵀ Punjab Cavalry. The Tochi Valley is inhabited by a tribe called the Dawaris. The first occasion on which the Indian Government came in contact with the Dawaris was in 1851, when they took part in an attack on one of the border posts, but were driven off with heavy loss. After this little trouble arose until 1870, when the Dawaris lent their assistance to the Waziris in acts of hostility towards the Indian Government. As a punishment for their complicity in these outrages the Dawaris were ordered to pay a fine, but half of the tribe not only refused to comply with this demand, but sent an insulting letter to the British Authorities, in addition to treating the envoys despatched to them with great indignity.

Pavo Cavalry (11TH Frontier Force)

1ST Punjab Irregular Cavalry

The 1ST Punjab Cavalry formed part of the troops to chastise the refractory section of the Dawari tribe. The force carried out brilliant and decisive little series of operations against the Dawaris. In the final action the cavalry was speedily down upon them, and sabred large of their number, when the rest, seeing that all was lost, throwing down their arms as they ran, surrendered as prisoners.

The 1ST Punjab Cavalry took part in capturing Kandahar, during the Second Afghan War and distinguished itself in the action at Ahmed Khel in April 1880. After the withdrawal from Afghanistan the regiment was back their duties on the North-West Frontier. Dafadar Chait Singh, Lance-Dafadar Gujar Singh and Sowars Buta Singh and Jowahir Singh, were awarded the I.O.M., for their conspicuous gallantry during the Second Afghan War.

In 1893 the British persuaded the Amir to agree to a commission comprising officers from Afghanistan and British India to establish the border between Afghanistan and the independent tribal areas. A strong military escort was allocated to the Border Commission at Wana. This force, denominated the 'Waziristan Delimitation Escort', and included the 1ST Punjab Cavalry. In order to join the Border Commission at Wana the force marched from Dera Ismail Khan to Khajuri Kach arriving on 18TH October 1894.

On 3RD November 1894 in the pitch dark the camp at Wana was attacked by around 2,000 tribesmen in one of the most dramatic episodes on the North West Frontier. 3 rifle shots rang out. These shots were immediately followed by wild yells and frenzied drum beating as tribesmen poured out of the nullas concealing their approach to the camp perimeter. Many of the Piquets and support posts raced back to the perimeter as instructed and the wave of tribesmen struck the camp just 3 minutes after the first warning shots.

Many encountered the charging tribesmen as they came out of their tents, fighting in the dark, bayonet against sword and shield. Several horses of 1ST Punjab Cavalry were injured or killed by the tribesmen. With full daylight, the General, ordered out the squadron of 1ST Punjab Cavalry. Led by Major O'Malley 61 troopers of the squadron headed north towards the Inzar Kotal in pursuit of the tribesmen. The pursuit followed the tribesmen to the Inzari Pass, leading into Mahsud country. The cavalry were able to catch and kill some 50 tribesmen over a distance of around 11 miles. The pursuit was abandoned once it was clear that the Mahsud lashkar had dispersed leaving no worthwhile force to pursue. Some form of retribution against the Mahsuds was considered essential. The Mahsud Maliks were offered terms which involved the supply of hostages, the expulsion of the Mullah Pawindah from Waziristan until the boundary marking was complete and the return of the loot taken in the attack on 3RD November 1894. The period for compliance was given and extended to 12TH December 1894. The punitive operation was carried out on Christmas Day 25TH December 1894 with little opposition and a trawl of cattle seized and villages burnt.

Pavo Cavalry (11TH Frontier Force)

1ST Punjab Irregular Cavalry

On 19TH January 1895, all the British terms were complied with. A permanent post was established at Wana. Dafadar Thakur Singh, Sowar Man Singh and Sowar Khanda Singh were awarded the I.O.M., for their gallantry during the operations at Wana.

The large scale insurrection by the tribesmen in 1897 found the 1ST Punjab Cavalry as part of the Tochi Valley Field Force in Waziristan. The rebellion started with an attack by the Madda Khel section of the Waziris in June 1897. The 1ST Punjab Cavalry supplied detachments along the line of communication. The task of the detachments became more ardours as the threat of an attack was ever present, with minor actions fought by the squadrons. The rebellion was finally put down in October 1897.

During the First World War, the regiment continued to be employed on internal security duties. Finally before the final advance against Kut-al-Amara started in December 21ST Cavalry had arrived in Mesopotamia and played a leading role at the recapture of Kut-al-Amara. Baghdad was captured on the 17TH March. In the course of the long pursuit 800 prisoners were captured. One wing of the 32ND Lancers, together with 21ST Cavalry, during the course of the pursuit, charged a Turkish column and captured about 1,000 prisoners. The advance continued to the towns of Haditha and Ava, which was soon captured with over 5,000 prisoners. Preparations were now made for the final defeat of the Turks in Mesopotamia. It was decided to advance on Mosul from Samarra. Mosul was taken on 3RD November 1918 but Turkey had already surrendered three days earlier. The Indian cavalry was a major component of the force in Mesopotamia. The 21ST Cavalry played a leading role in the final defeat of the Turks, before being ordered to take part in the Anglo-Afghan war of 1919.

The Third Anglo-Afghan War was one of Britain's briefest, lasting just over 3 months during the summer of 1919, from May 6th to August 8th. The conflict began as the result of Afghan incursions into British-occupied territory across the border with India.

Over 10,000 British-Indian troops were mobilized. British tactics included what was colloquially referred to as "butcher and bolt" operations, in which villages would be destroyed, their inhabitants killed, and troops would immediately return to their base, making no attempt to occupy any territory. Kabul and the Afghan fort at Dakka were successfully bombed using the relatively-new technology of biplanes,

The war was ended by the Treaty of Rawalpindi, with both sides claiming a measure of victory – the Afghans successfully asserting their right to conduct their own foreign affairs (one of the first acts of which was to recognize the new Bolshevik government in Russia), and the British re-establishing the ante bellum border and discontinuing their subsidy to the Amir.

On the 6TH June 1921, the amalgamation of 21ST Calvary and 23RD Cavalry took place, to be known as: - Pavo Cavalry (11TH Frontier Force).

Pavo Cavalry (11TH Frontier Force)

3RD Punjab Irregular Cavalry

3RD Punjab Irregular Cavalry was raised at Pashawar of the Bengal Cavalry during the spring of 1849 as a Frontier Force Regiment, from the disbanded regiments of the Khalsa Army of the Sikh Kingdom. The regiment moved to Amritsar in February 1850, was utilised in suppressing a revolt by the 66TH Bengal Native Infantry in Govindgarh Fort. The regiment lost nearly 300 horsed due to Surra in 1852. This was such a serious loss that the Government had to sanction a loan t the regimental Horse Fund to enable the regiment to be remounted. The regiment continued on duty along the Frontier during the Sepoy Mutiny against the British in 1857, when a body of 50 Sabres took part in operations against the Bozdars, a Baluchi tribe. The regiment had its share of fighting in keeping the tribesmen in check as they had decided to take advantage of the disturbances in India.

In 1860 the regiment took part in the Mahsud blockade. In 1860 the Mahsud country was overrun, in punishment for a long series of outrages, culminating in an attempt to plunder and burn the border town of Tank. The tribe, however, did not submit, and after the withdrawal of the troops was put under blockade. Different sections of the tribe, and from 1877 onwards the whole of it, remained under embargo, on account of repeated violations of British territory, almost without intermission, until the next expedition was undertaken.

During the Second Afghan War, the 3RD Punjab Cavalry was at Kabul with Roberts and advanced to Kandahar, with the relieving force, taking their share in Robert's victory at the Battle of Kandahar on 1ST September 1880. The regiment was back on the Frontier at Kohat when the Mahsud campaign started and did a remarkable march of 120 km to Bannu n 28 hours. They were engaged in operations in the Kurram Valley during the tribal uprising in 1897-98 and took part in the action at Samana Ridge. However, they were employed in small detachments which brought much hard work but little glory!

The reorganisation of 1903 brought a radical change in the designation of the regiment as their number was changed to 23RD and the territorial title was dropped.

The 23RD Cavalry had been deployed on internal duties in Lahore during 1914. This was a time of unrest in the Punjab with the early stirrings of an independent movement particularly among the Sikhs who had started Ghaddar or Revolt movement. The Sikh squadron of this regiment refused to carry out repressive measures among their own kith and kin. Several men were tried by court martial and sentenced to death.

During the First World War the regiment sent off officers and men as drafts to regiments actively engaged in operations in France and the Middle East. However in May 1915, 23RD Cavalry was sent to the Persian Gulf, and assumed responsibility for patrolling the oil pipeline. The regiment was in Ahwaz with detachments along the pipe line from May 1915 to October 1917 when they were relieved by the 5TH Cavalry.

Pavo Cavalry (11TH Frontier Force)

3RD Punjab Irregular Cavalry

On its relief from patrolling the oil fields in 1917, the regiment was ordered to Mesopotamia, to confront and pursue the Turkish Army to its final defeat and destruction. The regiment was then attached to the 15TH Division for the forthcoming operations to clear the Euphrates of Turks below Hit. The Division moved to Sahilya with great secrecy in order to attack Khan Baghdadi, the main Turkish base in the region. One column of all arms was to advance on Khan Baghdadi supported by a similar column and third column was to be in reserve. The columns advanced during the night of 25TH March 1918, and the infantry attacked the next morning. Two squadrons of cavalry escorted the guns to a position which enfiladed the Turkish trenches. The advance continued to the towns of Haditha and Ava, which were soon captured with over 5,000 prisoners. Western Mesopotamia was now clear of Turks. Preparations were now made for the final defeat of the Turks in Mesopotamia. It was decided to advance on Mosul from Samara. The Indian cavalry had its share of honour in the advance to Kirkuk in which the 23RD Cavalry and 32ND Lancers took part. The 23RD chased a Turkish battalion, sabred 100, and captured 350 of the Turks. In the final advance to Mosul most of the Indian cavalry regiments fought at Sharqat including the 23RD Cavalry. Mosul was taken on 3RD November 1918, but Turkey had already surrendered three days earlier.

The Indian cavalry was a major component of the force in Mesopotamia. The 23RD Cavalry played a leading role in the final defeat of the Turks, before being ordered to take part in the Anglo-Afghan war of 1919. The war was ended by the Treaty of Rawalpindi, with both sides claiming a measure of victory.

On the 6TH June 1921, the amalgamation of 21ST Calvary and 23RD Cavalry took place, to be known as:-

Prince Albert Victor's Own Cavalry (11TH Frontier Force)

Pavo Cavalry as a part of the 3RD Indian Motor Brigade had landed in Egypt in February 1941. Its motor regiments carried out some training after vehicle deficiencies were mad good. The men were issued with battle dress trousers and leather-jerkins. In early March the Brigade moved to Mersa Matruh for acclimatisation and training in desert warfare. At the end of the month the formation was moved to El Adem, outside Tobruk. From there troop-strength reconnaissance parties were sent out to Derna, Trigh-el-Abid, Tengender and Msus to enable regiments to become familiar with their likely area of operations and gain confidence in their ability to navigate in the desert.

The 3RD Indian Motor Brigade had moved to Tmimi, where the brigade commander and party joined it early on 4TH April. After a brief halt the brigade left for Mekili, and commenced straight away on its defences. The brigade occupied perimeter about 4,000 m in circumstances, with the northern flank resting on the ridge and the southern flank on the scrub.

Pavo Cavalry (11TH Frontier Force)

Later the enemy fire shifted to brigaded HQ area. An enemy vehicle towing a gun appeared and started shelling the brigade defences. The Sikh squadron of the Pavo Cavalry sent a patrol which chased away the gun. Then an Italian lorried infantry launched an assault from the east on the Pavo defences but it was easily repulsed; 37 prisoners were taken. The Pavo Cavalry went on to capture a German patrol in three scout cars.

Then the Germans sent their first ultimatum, asking the brigade to surrender, through a staff officer who came up to the Pavo perimeter under a white flag. The ultimatum was rejected and the German officer sent back. On 7TH April the Germans sent another ultimatum, emphasising the fact that the brigade was completely surrounded and had no option but to surrender. The ultimatum was again rejected. In the afternoon Italian lorried infantry launched a mounted assault on the south-western face of the perimeter. The leading Italian lorry was hit and destroyed; its occupants dismounted with their hands up. The last demand for surrender, signed personally by General Rommel, offering 'honours of war' was also rejected. A German Fiesler Stork spotter plane had appeared overhead and started to put down artillery fire as soon as the envoy got back with the rejection. The shelling lasted an hour and half, the Pavo Cavalry suffered three casualties. Eventually the brigade was ordered to withdraw to El Adem.

The gallant stand at El Mekili by the 3RD Indian Motor Brigade, equipped with totally inadequate means of defence against tanks or rather with no such means of defence, against practically the whole might of Africa Korps, must rank one of the most gallant actions of World War 11. Apart from the display of sheer bravery, the results achieved make it one of the crucial actions of the War.

After early reverses, the British drove the Axis armies back into Libya, relieved the garrison in Tobruk, and forced Rommel to pull back on January 6TH 1942, to El Agheila (on the border of the Libyan provinces of Cyrenaica and Tripolitania). Throughout its stay in the Western Desert the Pavo Cavalry had suffered heavily, with very large casualties. It was sent to the Suez Canal and then to Syria and Iran until the end of 1942. In January 1943, the regiment returned to India.

In March 1944, it was back in action against the Japanese in Burma, where it greatly distinguished itself against the Japanese. It took part in the relief of Meiktilla and went on to fight at Monywa, Mandalay, Myinmu Bridgehead, Capture of Meiktilla, the Irrawaddy and finally Rangoon. With the capture of Rangoon, Burma was effectively liberated.

In December it was sent to Dutch East Indies. The Indonesians had declared their independence from Dutch rule and resisted its imposition. The resulting chaotic situation required full military operations in order to restore semblance of order. After the pacification operations the Pavo Cavalry returned to India in May 1946.

In 1947, at the independence and partition of the Indian subcontinent the Pavo Cavalry was allotted to the new Pakistan Army. Its Sikh squadron was transferred to the 3RD Cavalry, Indian Army.

19TH King George V's Own Lancers

18TH Bengal Cavalry

The 18TH Bengal Cavalry was raised in 1858 at Gwalior for service in Central India, consequent to 1857 Sepoy Revolt. A unit known as Tiwana Horse had also been raised for service with the British by the Tiwanas, a Rajput Muslim class in the district of Jhelum. This unit was joined with the 2ND Maratha Horse and taken into Bengal Cavalry in 1861 as the 18TH Bengal Cavalry. The regiment saw service in the Second Afghan War (1878-80) on line of communication duties, escorting convoys through the territory of the Wazirs and the Mahsuds, who missed no opportunity for a raid. Their duties, in small detachments, were exacting and strenuous for both horse and man.

The next spell of fighting in which the 18TH Bengal Lancers, as was the new designation of the regiment, took part was in the Kurram Valley expedition and with the Tirah expedition during the general uprising by the North-West Frontier tribes in 1897-98. The regiment was the Divisional Cavalry regiment to the Tirah expedition and such had the major responsibility for providing reconnaissance and mobile protection to the column.

They became Lancers in 1885. This designation was not to last for long. The Prince of Wales, during his visit to India in 1906 became Colonel-in-Chief of the regiment. Consequently their title was changed to the 18TH (Prince of Wale's Own) Tiwana Lancers. Their regimental was once again changed to 18TH King George's Own Lancers.

When World War One started, the 18TH Lancers had a detachment escorting a boundary commission in North Persia. The British officer was ordered to return to India alone, the escort of 20 men under a Viceroy's Commissioned officer marched back to India covering 2,600 km of often hostile territory with only one man and one horse dead. The Indian officer was personally decorated by the King with the Order of British India.

Eventually the regiment arrived in France in December 1914 in the Meerut Cavalry Brigade of the 2ND Indian Cavalry Division. A total of fourteen regiments of the Indian cavalry went to France in 1914. There were two regiments each in the three cavalry brigades in each of the two cavalry divisions and one regiment in each of the two infantry divisions as divisional reconnaissance regiments.

In those early weeks of the war the Indian Force took part in the First Battle of Ypres from October to November 1914. In the early spring of 1915 the Indian Force provided the lead division in the Allied offensive in French Flanders against the German Army at the Battle of Neuve Chapelle (10TH-13TH March 1915). They continued to fight in French Flanders in 1915 in the Battle of Aubers Ridge (9TH May), the Battle of Festubert (15TH-27TH May) and the Battle of Loos (25TH September – 8TH October 1915).

During the winter months of November and December 1915 arrangements were made to remove the two Indian infantry divisions of 1ST Indian Corps from the Western Front.

19TH King George V's Own Lancers

18TH Bengal Cavalry

The two divisions of 1st Indian Corps were sent to the Mesopotamian theatre of war. The two Indian cavalry divisions remaining in France were renamed from March 1916 as the 4TH and 5TH Cavalry Divisions. They were in the order of battle for the British offensive on the Somme battlefield from 1ST July 1916. Indian cavalry units were involved as mounted troops and dismounted infantry troops in battles on the Western Front from that time until their removal to Egypt in March 1918. Battle actions in France included the Battle of Bazentin (14th-17th July 1916, the Battle of Flers-Courcelette (15th-22nd September 1916), the advance to the Hindenburg Line in the spring of 1917 and the 1917 Battle of Cambrai (20th November - 8th December 1917).

Cambrai was the last battle for the Indian Cavalry in France. This brought to close the three and a half years eventful active service by the Indian Cavalry in France.

The Sowars were put into the front line the moment they arrived, often issued with rifles they had no experience of handling before, facing, for the first time, artillery and, later, gas. Field Marshal Sir Douglas Haig sent the following farewell message:

"As the Indian Cavalry regiments are now leaving France, I wish to record my very great appreciation of the valour, determination and devotion to duty shown by all ranks in the field. Indian officers, non-commissioned officers and men have been absent for more than three years in a foreign country, thousands of kilometres from their homes and families, in a climate to which they are totally unaccustomed, and have their gallant deeds added even greater lustre to the already glorious names of their respective regiments."

After leading the British forces in a successful campaign in Palestine and capturing Jerusalem in December 1917, the regional commander General Edmund Allenby lost many of his infantry troops to the Western Front when the Germans launched their massive spring offensive in 1918. Meanwhile, after a change of command—Erich von Falkenhayn was replaced by Otto Liman von Sanders—the German and Turkish forces in the region dug in, resisting several British attacks and even regaining some ground by the summer. After new units arrived from France, which included the 18TH Lancers, Allenby's forces were up to full strength, and the general prepared to launch a new offensive in September. Beginning with a midnight bombardment on September 19TH, the British troops in Palestine went on the attack, executing a classic feint manoeuvre: after directing one attack up the Jordan Valley as a diversion, Allenby switched the force of his offensive to the west and up the coast, As Allenby reported, the attack met with smashing success: "On the north our cavalry, traversing the Field of Armageddon, had occupied Nazareth, Afulah, and Beisan, and were collecting the disorganized masses of enemy troops and transport as they arrived from the south. All avenues of escape open to the enemy, except the fords across the Jordan between Beisan and Jisr-ed-Dameer were thus closed."

19TH King George V's Own Lancers

18TH Bengal Cavalry

Megiddo fell with little resistance the same day, and the aerial bombing of roads, railways and troop formations in the area over the following week disrupted all Turkish and German operations. From September 20TH to September 21ST alone, Allenby's troops took some 7,000 Turkish prisoners. As the demoralized Turks retreated northward and eastward, they were attacked by more Allied aircraft. General von Sanders was forced to flee Nazareth as well, still wearing his pyjamas.

The British attack at Megiddo set off a string of victories that led straight through the rest of the month, including the fall of both Beirut and Damascus to British control. The 18TH Lancers reached Aleppo on 31ST October, when Turkey sued for peace, signing an armistice with the Allies on October 30TH, 1918. November 1920 found the 18TH Lancers back in India. The 18TH Bengal Lancers amalgamated with 19TH Bengal Lancers in New Delhi on 23RD August 1921 to form, 19TH King George V's Own Lancers.

19TH Bengal Lancers

The 19TH Bengal Cavalry was raised in early 1860 by Lieutenant Fane as Fane's Horse at Cawnpore. This raising took place at a time when a number of cavalry regiments were being disbanded, among them being the 3RD Hodson's Horse. The raising was specifically for service overseas, as there were some reservations about the wisdom of sending a Bengal Cavalry regiment with personnel recruited prior to the making of world-wide service liability, a condition at recruitment. Most of the men from the 3RD Hodson's Horse joined Fane's Horse, which was recruiting Sikhs and Pathans.

Fane's Horse was part of the cavalry brigade, provided by India, despatched to China to enforce the right of Britain with other European powers to keep envoys at the Chinese capital. The seizure of a British ship smuggling Opium by the Chinese authorities was made an excuse for declaring war in 1859. The other units in the cavalry brigade were the 1ST Sikh Irregular Cavalry and a regiment of British Cavalry. The force assembled at Hong Kong. An earlier attempt by a naval party to take the Taku Forts, which covered the entrance to the Peiho River leading to Peking, had failed. These were now successfully stormed after the Indian cavalry had routed the Chinese cavalry, which tried to charge the besieging artillery. The Chinese cavalry was pursued for several miles. In the final battle for Peking, the Indian Cavalry Brigade with Fane's Horse in the van completely vanquished the Chinese cavalry that thereafter, it never stood up to the Punjabis.

In the reorganisation of 1861, the Fane's Horse was taken into the Bengal Army as the 19TH Bengal Cavalry to be subsequently designated 19TH Bengal Lancers (Fane's Horse).

The regiment saw service during the Second Afghan War 1878-80. The Second Afghan War was fought, as had been the first, to eliminate the Russian influence in Afghanistan.

19TH King George V's Own Lancers

19TH Bengal Lancers

In 1878 two British forces advanced towards Kabul through the Khyber Pass and the Kurram Valley respectively and the Afghans, having been defeated, and agreed to receive a British Envoy. Next year the Afghans attacked the British Residency in Kabul and the Envoy and his escort of seventy Guides were killed, after resisting to the last round. The British advanced again and this time occupied Kabul. There they were virtually besieged, but eventually drove off their opponents.

In 1880 trouble arose at Kandahar, previously occupied with little opposition, following the British force at Maiwand. Roberts, who was commanding at Kabul, was due to evacuate the country and` he did so by marching part of his army to Kandahar and defeating the Afghans in that area before returning to India. During the war the regiment took leading part in the defeat of the Afghans at Ahmed Khel. The following Sikh officers and men of the 19TH Bengal Lancers were awarded the I.O.M. for conspicuous gallantry in action during the Second Afghan War:

Dafadar Naurang Singh, Dafadar Hardit Singh, Kot Dafadar Hukam Singh, Ressaidar Jowahir Singh, Lance Dafadar Kehar Singh, Lance Dafadar Sardar Singh, and Sowars Gulab Singh, Khushal Singh, Ram Singh and Avtar Singh.

The regiment was again on the North-West Frontier for the Zakka Khel and the Mohmand operations of 1908. In the spring of 1908, British and Indian forces waged two campaigns on the North West Frontier. The first, briefer campaign was launched against the Zakka Khel, south of the Khyber Pass, and the other, more serious affair, was directed against the Hill Mohmands, north of Pashawar. Both were long established enemies of the British and on numerous occasions in the past had been the target of punitive expeditions.

On the outbreak of World War One, the 19TH Lancers were in Sialkot Cavalry Brigade and sailed with them for France in November 1914. With its sister regiment the 18TH Lancers, the regiment served with the Indian Corps in France until the Corps's withdrawal in 1915. Then with the cavalry brigade Battle until the battle of Cambrai in December 1917, it then once again with its sister regiment proceeded to Palestine. Dafadar Mehar Singh and Jemadar Bishan were awarded the I.O.M. for conspicuous gallantry in action on the Western Front.

After its exploits in Palestine, similar to that of the 18TH Lancers, the 19TH Lancers were back in India early in 1921.

The 19TH Bengal Lancers amalgamated with 18TH Bengal Lancers in New Delhi on 23RD August 1921 to form, 19TH King George V's Own Lancers.

After mechanisation in 1940, the regiment moved to Sialkot in 1941, to join the 1ST Indian Armoured Division as its reconnaissance regiment. It moved with the Division to Karachi and was equipped with Humber armoured cars in 1942. The 31ST Armoured Division HQ moved to Iraq without its regiments in June 1942. The regiment moved to Madras in 1943 on coast watching duties against an expected Japanese landing. In 1944 the regiment was equipped with Sherman tanks and joined the 50TH Indian Tank Brigade at Neera, near Poona.

19TH King George V's Own Lancers

The Brigade was allotted to the XV Indian Corps in Arakan and moved there during November 1944. The terrain in Arakan was not suitable for large-scale employment armour. It could only be used in a supporting role and in small detachments because of jungle-clad hills, steep valleys and numerous unfordable chaungs which restricted tank movement and their scope for manoeuvre. Tanks had, however, proved their worth particularly for bunker busting and with skill and determination tanks could be taken where required. Regiments of Indian Armour had at last been equipped with tanks with a suitable gun and were available in sufficient numbers.

19TH Lancers allotted one squadron to 25TH Division for employment in the coastal sector, one squadron to 82ND Division for employment with the 2ND West African Brigade and one squadron to Corps reserve, to be employment with 25TH Division, when required.

The 74TH Indian Brigade commenced advance along the Mayu coast on 12TH December and by 29TH reported it clear; there had been little opposition. On 14TH December the 1ST West African Brigade entered Buthidaung which had been abandoned by the Japanese, but offered some resistance on a hill south of the town. Their bunkers were promptly destroyed by tanks of 'B' and 'C' Squadrons 19TH Lancers.

The planned assault landing to capture Akyab was advanced to 3RD January 1945. A day before the schedule landing, it was discovered that the Japanese had evacuated Akyab. The 25TH Indian Division landed the next day and was supported by one troop 19TH Lancers. Plans were now finalised for carrying out assault landings on Myebon peninsula by the 25TH Division and 3RD Commando Brigade. Myebon peninsula, 56 km from Akyab down the coast, commanded the Kyatsin River in the Dinbon Chaung, both waterways were in extensive use by the Japanese to support their troops in the Kaladan Valley. Only a limited number of troops could be employed because of the shortage of landing craft.

The landing on Myebon was to be carried out by the Commando Brigade followed a day later by the 74TH Indian Brigade. The shortage of landing craft also forced a choice between taking either tanks or artillery guns for fire support the choice made was to land only tanks in the initial stage and proved a wise one. The commandos landed on 12TH January 1945, following an air strike and a naval bombardment. The Japanese held well-constructed bunkers covered by an anti-tank ditch. Initial resistance was light but stiffened later. The falling tide created difficulties for the following infantry waves. By the time HMIS Narbada approached to land a half squadron of the 19TH Lancers, there was 400 m of deep mud in front of the landing site. The first tank landed in 4 feet of water over deep mud. The tank moved a little then bellied. Water entered through the hull gunner's hatch. HMIS Narbada steamed up the Myebon River and attempted to land tanks again under the cover of its guns. The second tank managed to get ashore but heavy enemy fire prevented further landings. The engineers had, in the meantime, reconnoitred another beach where the remaining six tanks managed to get ashore before nightfall.

19TH King George V's Own Lancers

On 13TH January the commandos attacked a strongly held hill feature, west of Myebon village. Fire support was provided by the half squadron and fire was controlled by a forward tank officer. A method of attacking a heavily wooded hillside had been standardised. An air strike with napalm removed most of the vegetation, prior to the assault. Supporting tanks engaged the defences thus revealed with high explosive shells as the infantry crossed the start line. Targets not spotted by tanks were indicated by a FTO who carried a 38 radio set and accompanied the leading company commander. When the infantry was about 50 m short of the objective, tanks switched to shooting with solid armour-piercing shot. With the infantry only about 5 meters away, the tank fire lifted to engage the crest of the hill with co-axial machine-gun fire. Bunkers were engaged with solid armour-piercing shot in order to splinter the supporting timber. High explosive with delayed fuse was fired into slits and if there was some doubt that all slits were not exposed, then a white phosphorus smoke shell was fired through the exposed slit, smoke emanated from all slits of the bunker. In this particular attack indirect fire was also brought down in order to clear a part of the jungle and improve observation. Guns were landed the next day and tanks relinquished the role of providing indirect fire support.

The commandos attacked Point 200, another strongly held defensive position; intimate fire support was provided by tanks from the base of the hill but when the Commandos got close to the crest of the hill, they were held up by intense machine-gun fire from well sited bunkers. No further advance could be made until the bunkers were destroyed. Tank fire from the base of the hill was ineffective against the bunkers which were defiladed behind a false crest. One tank managed to climb the steep hill and knocked out several bunkers at a range of about 40 m. In an effort to get into position to engage the last bunker, the tank toppled over backwards and tumbled down the hillside. Point 200 was, however, captured. An attack on 17TH January gained barely a foothold on the hill. The enemy was finally cleared by a tank troop, supported by an infantry platoon, outflanking the position and destroying several bunkers dug into brick foundation of the Pagoda.

The only escape route for guns and vehicles, let open to the Japanese withdrawing against the West African Division was road Myhaung- Tamandu. It was decided to put a block on this road at Kangaw, in spite of air photographs showing extensive digging and prepared defences in the area. 3RD Commando Brigade sailed up the Dainbond Chaung on 22ND January and landed 2.5 km from the village. A beach-head was secured without much difficulty.

The next day, 51ST Indian Brigade commenced landing in the afternoon. One troop 'A' Squadron 19TH Lancers landed with the leading battalion. The Brigade completed concentration on 27TH January and the following day attacked the village and hills covering the road. The Japanese, having realized the gravity of the situation, mustered all available troops and launched eight counterattacks during the first night. It was decided not to attack the other features equally strongly held, because had already been effectively cut with the ground gained.

19ᵀᴴ King George V's Own Lancers

The Japanese were holding the Kangaw Gap with regiment less a battalion supported by a field regiment and an engineer company. This force decided to capture a feature located between the beach and Kangaw village and thus effectively cut off the Indian Brigade. At first light, the Japanese launched their heaviest and most desperate counter-attack of the whole campaign. The enemy secured a foothold on the feature and their assault engineers broke into the harbour of the tank troop.

Tank crews were alert and manning their tanks. Nevertheless, the Japanese set fire to one tank; the crew perished inside. The track of another tank was blown, but the third tank fought back and with the help of the motor platoon 2ᴺᴰ Grenadiers, the enemy engineer party was decimated. Indian and British troops, after desperate hand-to-hand fighting, which went on for three days, finally threw out the enemy from their defences. Over 700 Japanese dead bodies had been counted lying around their defences.

On 11ᵀᴴ February one company 8ᵀᴴ Hyderabad supported by the tank troop of the 19ᵀᴴ Lancers, attacked a feature still in Japanese hands. Tanks promptly silenced enemy guns and the feature was captured. A column consisting of tanks and an infantry company had been kept ready to pursue the remnants of the enemy but its start was delayed by the spring tide which flooded the Kangaw area. The column could not leave until 20ᵀᴴ February but by then the Japanese had abandoned their vehicles, thrown their guns into Chaungs and escaped over minor hill tracks. The 22 day battle had been one of the hardest fought in Burma. The enemy lost over 2,000 men and had to abandon all his vehicles, guns and equipment.

Final phase of operations in Arakan required the capture of two passes through the Arakan, which linked it with the Irrawaddy Valley. 25ᵀᴴ Indian Division was given its last task of capturing Ruwya and A Squadron was with the division to support in these tasks. One troop gave excellent support to 53ᴿᴰ Brigade to Ruwya and thereafter supported 74ᵀᴴ Indian Brigade in its advance to Tamandu.

The 19ᵀᴴ Lancers fought their last action of the war on 1ˢᵀ April 1945 in support of the West African Division which was short of artillery support. The 19ᵀᴴ Lancers made a significant contribution to success in the Second Arakan Campaign, by close support it provided to the infantry, and took part in almost every major engagement in the Arakan.

The regiment was withdrawn from the Arakan on 8ᵀᴴ April to Ramree Island from where the amphibious operation was launched for the capture of Rangoon. The regiment landed at south of Rangoon on 2ᴺᴰ May 1945. It returned to India in June and then moved to Pashawar.

In August 1947, at the independence and the partition of the Indian subcontinent in the sovereign states of India and Pakistan and the division of the army the 19ᵀᴴ King George V's Own Lancers was allotted to the new Pakistan Army. Their Sikh Squadron went to the Skinners Horse, Indian Army.

Burma

Burma, located on the edge of British India, was a thorn in the side of the British East India Company. King of Ava, increasingly became expansionist, and aggressive towards the British-held territories. In 1766, the Burmese had seized Tenasserim from Siam. 1784 saw the incorporation of Arakan into the kingdom of Ava and 1813 saw the conquering of Manipur, which lay near the Surma Valley. This expansion and advance towards the Indian border made an Anglo-Burmese War inevitable. The final straw came in September 1823, when the Burmese seized the Shalpuri Island near Chittagong, which was owned by the East India Company. The declaration of war came on 24TH February 1824. It was a hard fought battle. Artillery had to be manhandled through the jungle, soldiers were falling thick and fast due to disease and each town was heavily defended. However, the Burmese army were slowly pushed back up the Irrawaddy Valley. By February 1826, the Anglo-Indian army had advanced three hundred miles to the town of Yandaboo. The advance on the capital began on 9TH February 1826 and was reached just two weeks later. The King of Ava sued for peace and signed a treaty by which he agreed to pay the expenses of the war and forego a considerable part of his territory. Thus closed the first Burmese war, resulting in the loss to the Burman monarch of all the territories, which his ancestors had taken, from the Siamese, and of Arakan, which had been conquered by his father and his exclusion from all interest in Assam, Cachar, and Manipur, where his predecessors had been paramount. By 1886, Britain had incorporated it into the British India. Indians, particularly Sikhs formed the backbone of the various forces Britain raised in Burma. Burma's oldest local military formation was the Burma Military Police (BMP). It was a colonial gendarmerie, with a very limited police role, and the main armed pillar of British rule. Each battalion of the BMP had a mounted infantry detachment of Sikhs, whose duties included standing watch over the frontiers and the regions that had not been brought under formal British control. Burma was administered as a province of British India until 1937, when it became a separate, self-governing colony, independent of the Indian administration. On separation from India the BMP was divided into two forces. Six battalions made up the new Burma Frontier Force tasked with border protection. Three less armed battalions remained the rump of Burma Military Police. During the World War Two, the Japanese succeeded in expelling the British from most of Burma. Lightly armed units suited to irregular jungle and hill fighting was ordered to hold fixed positions against massive artillery and air attacks. Disintegration became rampant in Burma Army formations and other units as they trudged through the hills and jungles to India, and the Sikhs back to the Indian Army.

The British counter-attacked using primarily troops of the Indian Army, and by July 1945, they had defeated the Japanese and retaken the country. Burma became independent from the United Kingdom on 4TH January 1948

Burma Military Police

Upper Burma was formally annexed on 1ST of January 1886, and the work of restoring the country to order and introducing settled government commenced. This was a more serious task than the overthrow of the Burmese government and occupied years. This was in part due to the character of the country, which was one vast military obstacle, and in part to the disorganization, which had been steadily growing during the six years of King Thibaw's reign. It was recognized that troops alone could not suffice for the work of pacification, that difficulties in Burma could only be overcome by the creation of an efficient Military Police. In 1886, the Government of India sanctioned the raising of the Military Police to facilitate the withdrawal of the main part of the regular forces in Burma. The military police battalions were organized like regular army regiments and their duties were entirely military. The Military Police at the end of 1888 included 3,937 Sikhs. The force was the first line of defence against intermittent revolts and unrest. The organization of the Military Police and the establishment of Military Police posts, in place of posts held by troops, contributed greatly towards the progress of pacification. As soon as the pacification of any district was sufficiently advanced, the military posts were withdrawn and Military Police posts established. Between these protective Military Police posts, the Civil Police, consisting of the locally recruited Burmese, held intermediate posts. To enable long marches and prompt pursuits to be made, each battalion had a mounted detachment, often of Sikhs, whose duties included standing watch over the frontiers and the regions that had not been brought under formal British control. During 1887-88, great progress was made in the pacification of Upper Burma. The Burma Military Police units also patrolled the remote jungles and frontiers, clashing with head-hunters, and border raiders. The result was, however, not affected without much toil and hardship. The story is a record of endless marches by day and night, through dense jungle where the path could hardly be traced, along paths so thick in mud that the soles of men's boots were torn off as they marched, over sandy tracts devoid of water, over hills where there were no paths at all. Rarely was there the chance of an engagement to cheer the troops; stockades were found empty, villages deserted, camps evacuated. Yet everywhere there was the probability of sudden ambush from every clump of trees or line of rocks, or at any turn of the road by arrow-firing tribesmen, were just one of the occupational hazards.

During the First World War, the Burma Military Police Battalions were milked dry for volunteers to serve in various regiments of the Indian Army in Egypt, Persia, and Mesopotamia. During the Second World War, at the bludgeoning Japanese attacks, one battalion was transferred to the Burma Frontier Force, the remnants trudged through the hills and jungles to India, where they joined the newly raised battalions of the Burma Regiment. The Burma Military Police were not reformed at the re-occupation of Burma by the British in 1945.

Burma Military Police

South Persia was in the British sphere under the terms of the Anglo-Russian Convention of 1907. British officials were increasingly concerned about the security of the trade routes from the Persian Gulf to the hinterland because of the value of the trade to the Indian government and the strategic importance of maintaining Britain's ascendancy over the Persian Gulf. In the years leading up to World War One, the government had lost control over the provinces, with banditry, armed robbery, and attacks on foreign residents had increased. A British-controlled force had become more pressing, given the interest in the nascent Anglo-Persian Oil Company. The British proposed to mend matters by undertaking punitive operations against the offenders, in the first place against those in the vicinity of the main trade routes. This work had to be carried out mainly by the Indian troops, and mainly by the Burma Mounted Rifles.

The Burma Mounted Rifles was raised in May 1916 from the Burma Police Battalions. It had 'class squadron' structure of two Sikh squadrons and a Punjabi Muslim Squadron. It served in South Persia as part of Sykes's Mission from April 1917 to May 1919, and eventually reverted back to the ranks of Burma Police Battalions. Following are the highlights of the actions fought by the Burma Mounted Rifles in South Persia and the gallantry awards made to the Sikh soldiers and officers.

In June 1917, the Burma Mounted Rifles were sent to Dehbid for keeping order in that district, where raids were continually being made on caravans travelling between Isfahan and Shiraz .On 1ST June, a Squadron of the Burma Mounted Infantry on their way to Dehbid came into collision with a band of robbers belonging to a Khamseh tribe and pursued them for some miles, inflicting casualties without loss to them. On the 18TH and 19TH June part of the Burma Mounted Infantry detachment at Dehbid were engaged in that vicinity with a Robber Band that had looted a donkey caravan. The action was most effective, nine of the robbers being killed or wounded and eighteen captured, while part of the lost property was recovered. This affair had an excellent effect in the neighbourhood.

The Kurshuli tribe were camped in a village some 30 miles of Dehbid. They had been responsible for much of the raiding and it was decided t punish them. On the 4TH July a force, consisting, a squadron BMR left Dehbid for this purpose. Troops under Jemadar Partab Singh pursued the tribesmen into the hills then returned re-join the party that had taken up position in readiness to attack fort Kafta. The column under Jemadar Partab Singh had been under arms for over fifteen hours and had covered distances varying from thirty-three to forty-six miles. It was by this time very tired and hungry, but they responded with spirit to the order to assault the fort.

Burma Military Police

The fort, of thick mud walls, was situated on the top of a low isolated hill. Round the base of the hill were the walls of a deserted village. On every side of the position stretched, for more than a mile, sun-baked mud flats utterly devoid of cover and on which the spurt of every bullet could be noted. It was extraordinary how weary men forgot entirely their fatigue as soon the attack started. The men showed great dash in the attack. The possession of the fort ensured an enormously strong position and overlooked from nowhere. Sir Percy Sykes in his History of Persia writes: 'This feat of arms produced a much greater effect, inasmuch as the distance marched, the small size of the column and strong position of the Kurshulis, who were expecting an attack and had received help from neighbouring tribes.' For his gallantry in this action, and in the engagements of Meshed i Murghab and Khuramin on 1ST and 19TH June 1917. Jemadar Partab Singh was recommend for the award of IOM, but the award was reduced that of IDSM. In the same action Dafadar Chanan Singh was recommended for the award of IOM, but the award was reduced that of IDSM.

Sir Percy Sykes urged the necessity for punishing the robber tribes who had been guilty of a long series of depredations on the Kerman – Yezd, Shiraz – Isfahan, and Shiraz – Saidabad roads. A small column with one Squadron of the Burma Mounted Infantry, marched off from Qawwamabad on 20TH September. Having destroyed several forts and having captured or destroyed a considerable amount of forage, the column halted at Abadeh Kaleh on 25TH to destroy several more forts. Starting on its march again on the same day, the column found its way blocked by a body of some five or six hundred Lashanis, who were holding a position round the village of Khwaja Jamali. Two Troops of the Burma Mounted Infantry were sent to attack and turn the enemy's left flank, which they did, compelling the tribesmen to flee northwards. Jemadar Partab Singh was awarded the IOM for bold and intrepid leadership in the action of Khwaja Jamali while Jemadar Hazara Singh was 'Mentioned in despatches 'for intrepid and good leadership in the same action.

On 25TH January, the Burma Mounted Infantry encountered about 200 raiders in the vicinity of Gumun and attacked and killed 25 and wounded about 80, destroyed two of their camps, and recovered a considerable number of plundered animals. They completely routed the raiders, burning their remaining camp and recovering many more animals they had plundered.

For their gallantry in action at Gumun the following Sikhs ware awarded the gallantry medals. Sowar Uttam Singh was recommended for the award of Victoria Cross, but the award was reduced to that of IOM. Risaldar Gulzar Singh was recommend for the award of IOM, but the award was reduced that of IDSM. Jemadar Partab Singh was recommend for the award of IOM, but the award was reduced that of IDSM bar. Lance Dafadar Wariam Singh was recommended for the award of IOM, but the award was reduced to that of IDSM. Sowar Saudagar Singh and Signaller Man Singh were awarded the IDSM.

Burma Mounted Rifles

The operations against the Chah Haqis and the Labu Muhammadis included two Squadrons of the Burma Mounted Rifles. They drove the tribesmen into the high hills to the West and pursued them for some distance, which coming after sixteen hour's fighting and having covered about fifty miles was a fine effort.

Colonel Grant, receiving information that a well-known robber chief, Mullah Qurban, with a strong following, was near Ziarat, decided to take action against him. One Squadron of the Burma Mounted Rifles, reinforced by another half Squadron, gradually drove the enemy, who fought hard, first off the hill immediately behind Ziarat and then up the rocky slopes as far as the snow-line. During the day Colonel Grant received information that many of the Chehar Rahis, abandoning their forts had betaken themselves to the main tribal stronghold on the Kuh-I-Khan, which was about twelve miles West of Ziarat. Here, in a position which they deemed impregnable, they were said to be prepared to fight. The attack on the Kuh-I-Khan stronghold started with the Infantry capturing the enemy's main position. With the fire from Lewis guns of the Burma Mounted Riles very few of the enemy escaped.

It is estimated that 3,000 Qashqais had invested Khan-I-Zinian, a military post held by the South Persia Rifles. On 24TH May three Squadrons of the Burma Mounted Rifles marched out to attack the tribesmen besieging the garrison. They engaged the enemy in some very stiff actions. It was calculated that the enemy strength in action had been about 4,500 Qashqais and 300 Khamseh men. They had been well armed with two machine guns, rifles and plenty of ammunition; and they had fought bravely and estimated to have sustained between 600 and 700 casualties.

Learning that there were about thirteen hundred tribesmen at Ahmadabad, another three or four hundred at Chenar and between two and three thousand Qashqais at Deh Shaikh, Colonel Orton decided to take the offensive and during the fighting that ensued the Qashqais displayed great bravery and in places got within two hundred yards of the Burma Mounted Rifles, but the increasing volume of fire they encountered was too much for them and they had fallen back, having sustained heavy losses. Colonel Orton had achieved his objective most successfully, it being estimated that of about 3,200 tribesmen engaged, 200 had been killed and 300 wounded; the total British losses being 5 killed and 24 wounded. Next day Sir Percy Sykes telegraphed India expressing his high appreciation of the discipline, gallantry and soldierly spirits of the Burma Mounted Rifles.

A force, commanded by Colonel Orton, left Shiraz on 20TH October with a column composed of three Squadrons of the Burma Mounted Rifles, two sections of 36TH Mountain Battery and 124TH Baluchis to take action against the Qashqais at Firuzabad. On 24TH October, it was evident that the enemy intended to stand and fight and about 2.50pm they were seen in occupation of a ridge Westward of Ibrahim Bad village.

Burma Mounted Rifles

Meanwhile Colonel Dyer, with two Squadrons of the Burma Mounted Rifles, their advance supported by the fire of the mountain guns, had secured a minor ridge some 1,200 yards North of the enemy's main position. The Baluchis were sent forward to secure the left flank about Ibrahimabad and to attack this position. The remaining Burma Squadron and a Baluchi Company were retained as a reserve. Two of the Baluchi Companies gained a knoll about 1,000 yards Northwest of the enemy's position without difficulty; the third Company, securing the left flank about Ibrahimabad. These movements had brought the enemy's main position under accurate gun fire and a cross fire from the Lewis guns and rifles of the Burma Mounted Rifles, with a result when an attack was launched it attained complete success within twenty minutes. So far, the Indian casualties had been only seven, all among the Baluchis, but the enemy, had lost about eighty killed and wounded.

In the meantime a Squadron of the Burma Mounted Rifles had inflicted severe loss on the Qashqais. The Squadron had reached Deh-I-Barm unobserved and taken up a concealed position in front and in the village, while sending some scouts towards the enemy's camp. These scouts afterwards came galloping back to the village pursed by some five to six hundred Qashqais horsemen. The Burma Mounted Rifles then opened fire with their Lewis guns and rifles with devastating effect before the Qashqais could wheel off and get out of range. Nevertheless, and in the face of this heavy fire, the tribesmen made two or three gallant attempts to gallop in again, so as to recover their wounded men and rifles. But as they only sustained further casualties without succeeding they finally abstained, and at dusk the Burma Mounted Rifles withdrew to Gilak without molestation. After dark the Qashqais returned and carried off their wounded, subsequently estimated at 100, leaving 103 dead where they had fallen. The following Sikh soldiers were awarded gallantry medals for their conspicuous gallantry against the tribesmen. Risaldar Gulzar Singh was awarded the I.O.M. for conspicuous gallantry on the 25TH May 1918. Jemadar Kishan Singh was awarded the IOM for conspicuous gallantry on the 23RD October 1918. While Lance Dafadar Hukam Singh, Dafadar Ralla Singh, Dafadar Mohar Singh and Sowar Uttam Singh were awarded the IDSM for their conspicuous gallantry in South Persia. Dafadar Gulab Singh and Lance Dafadar Ganda Singh were recommend for the award of IDSM but downgraded to 'Mention in Despatches' for period 1ST April 1917 to 31ST May 1918

The Burma Mounted Rifles evacuated South Persia in May 1919, leaving behind them a reputation for discipline and gallantry.

Some Sowars of Burma Mounted Rifles reverted back to the ranks of Burma Military Police, whilst some took their discharge from the army and went back to the Punjab. Very little has appeared in print about this short lived unit, although its presence in South Persia is noted in numerous times in the official history 'Operations in Persia'.

85TH Burma Rifles

85TH Burma Rifles was raised in Mandalay in 1917 with predominately Indian volunteers from the Burma Military Police. It was trained in India before being shipped to Mesopotamia. Its four companies were set up on class or racial lines from various races, like Indian Army regiments, and included platoons of Sikh soldiers. The regiment numbered almost 1, 500 officers and men by the end of the war.

Sheikh Mahmud led the first Kurdish revolt in British controlled Southern Kurdistan (Iraqi Kurdistan) in May 1919. After seizing control of the region, Sheikh raised a military force from his Kurdish tribal followers and proclaimed himself 'Ruler of all of Kurdistan'. Tribal fighters from both Iran and Iraq quickly allied themselves with Sheikh Mahmud as he became more successful in opposing British rule. As the British became aware of the sheikh's growing political and military power, they were forced to respond militarily. Two British brigades that included the 85TH Burma Rifles were deployed to defeat Sheikh Mahmud's fighters at Darbandi Bazyan near Sulaimaniyah in June 1919.

The Sikh military police veterans of 85TH Burma Rifles were in continuous actions against nationalist Kurds while in Mesopotamia. They returned to Burma in 1920 to amalgamate with the 70TH into a single regiment, the 70TH Burma Rifles. The regiment became the 20TH Burma Rifles as part of the 1922 reorganisation of the Indian Army. After the British formally separated Burma from India in 1937 the 20TH Burma Rifles was allocated to Burma and renamed the Burma Rifles.

Burma Rifles

The regiment served through the Japanese invasion of Burma during the Burma Campaign. All the Burmese battalions disintegrated during the Japanese invasion and were disbanded. The wholly Indian 8TH battalion of Sikhs and Punjabi Mussalmans was reduced to around 250 men by early April 1942, mainly due to battle casualties. The 8TH fought well in the early battles and was regarded as the best of the Burma Rifles battalions. The battalion underwent re-fitting and formed a composite battalion of 1ST battalion, The Burma Regiment, with the 7TH battalion, which had reached India in May. The regiment was reorganised as a conventional infantry battalion of four companies. In January 1946 the battalion was transferred to Syriam and in May 1947 formed part of a force involved in operations against dacoits. On 4TH January 1948 Burma became independent and the Burma Regiment was absorbed into the new Burma Army, which unlike its Indian and Pakistani counterparts did not retain the regimental structure and traditions of the former Indian Army.

The Burma Regiment

The Burma regiment was formed in India in September 1942 from the Indian soldiers who had survived the retreat from Burma. Of the six battalions raised to form the Burma regiment three regiments were composed entirely of Sikhs and Punjabi Mussalmans in equal numbers and the other three of Gurkhas.

In the reconquest of Burma, the 1ST Battalion fought at Kohima with the 33RD and 9TH Indian Infantry Brigades. The Battle of Kohima was the turning point of the Japanese U Go offensive into India in 1944 in the Second World War. The battle was fought in three stages from 4 April to 22 June 1944 around the town of Kohima in north-east India. It is often referred to as the 'Stalingrad of the East'. From 3RD to 16TH April, the Japanese attempted to capture Kohima ridge, a feature which dominated the road by which the besieged British and Indian troops of IV Corps at Imphal were supplied. By mid-April, the small British force at Kohima was relieved. From 18TH April to 13TH May, British and Indian reinforcements counter-attacked to drive the Japanese from the positions they had captured. The Japanese abandoned the ridge at this point but continued to block the Kohima–Imphal road. From 16TH May to 22ND June, the British and Indian troops pursued the retreating Japanese and reopened the road. The battle ended on 22 June when British and Indian troops from Kohima and Imphal met at Milestone 109, ending the siege of Imphal. In 2013, the British National Army Museum voted the Battle of Imphal and Kohima 'Britain's Greatest Battle'

At the end of the war the battalion went first to Singapore and then went on to serve at Palembang, Sumatra, landing in October 1945 and leaving a year later.

The Governor of Burma awarded the Burma Gallantry Medal to officers, NCOs and men of the Burma forces for acts of conspicuous gallantry in the performance of their duties. Following Sikh soldiers of the Burma Regiment were awarded the Burma Gallantry Medal for their gallantry against the Japanese in Burma.

Havildar Nikka Singh, Jemadar Ghur Singh, Jemadar Jaman Singh, Jemadar Trilok Singh, Naik Partab Singh, Lance-Naik Indar Singh, Lance-Naik Karnail Singh, and Sepoys Kehar Singh, Nand Singh, Arjan Singh, Sardar Singh, Phuman Singh, Tara Singh, and Sardara Singh.

The Regiment was transferred to the new Burma Army in 1948 and the Sikh officers and men were absorbed in the Sikh regiments of the Indian Army.

Burma Frontier Force

The Burma Frontier Force was formed following the separation of Burma from India from units of the Burma Military Police. With the Japanese invasion the Allied retreat from Burma began and by April 1942 the units of the BFF had disintegrated, firstly through desertion and casualties and later as a result of the decision to allow men to return to their homes if they so wished. The majority of the Sikhs and Gurkhas continued the retreat into India where it was later decided to form them into The Burma Regiment.

Shanghai Municipal Police

The relations between China and Britain detrioted so much that the British declared war on China in November 1839. The Chinese were technologically no match for the British, and the military was poorly trained for such a showdown. In August 1842, the Treaty of Nanjing officially ended the brutal war. The treaty, among other things, handed Hong Kong over to the British, opened new ports including Shanghai, and granted Britain to be the 'most favoured nation'.

Shanghai International Settlement was created in 1854 to serve the British, French and American foreign concessions in Shanghai, China. In 1863, the British and American concessions formally united to become the Shanghai International Settlement. As more foreign powers entered into treaty relations with China, their nationals also became part of the administration of the settlement. Shanghai International Settlement always remained a predominantly British affair. The Shanghai International Settlement always remained Chinese sovereign territory. The Shanghai Municipal Police brought order to the bustling activity of the International Settlement. Dating back to 1854, the Shanghai Municipal Police had grown from a small complement of Britons recruited from the Hong Kong police into a large ethnically diverse force. The Sikh Branch recruited in 1884 from officers who had retired or left from Sikh military detachments in China, reached about 800 men. They were very effective in keeping the generally lawless elements of the population, under effective control and in the prevention of rioting and mob violence within the International Settlement. In 1927 the cause for alarm stemmed from the threat that the Chinese Nationalists would seize Shanghai and endanger the foreign residents there. The Mounted section of the Sikh Police was mobilized to patrol the limits of the International Settlement. Shanghai was once again threatened in early 1932 after hostilities broke out between the Chinese and the Japanese. The fighting became so intense that the Sikh Mounted Contingent and the American 4TH Marines manned the barricades of the International Settlement. The 1937 situation developed into a series of potentially explosive crises as both sides resorted to aerial bombing with considerable carelessness and accompanying indiscriminate antiaircraft and artillery fire. Again Sikh reinforcements were rushed in to support the 4th Marines. The 4th Marines was withdrawn early in 1938 when a shift of the scene of Sino-Japanese hostilities left Shanghai relatively safe.

The Shanghai Municipal Police was disbanded in 1943, when the settlement was retro ceded to Chinese control. In the decades that followed the founding of the People's Republic of China, the country's Sikh population virtually slowly disappeared.

'Sikh is the figure above all others who today represents the treaty port period in Shanghai's popular memory. They formed a surrogate military reserve for the Shanghai Municipal Council. Tall and imposing, Sikh added a touch of imperial authenticity to the squatter settlement'. (Bickers)

Auxiliary Military Police Battalion

One of the most novel and interesting organizations in China under the supervision of the Provost Marshal was the Auxiliary Military Police Battalion. The Battalion was formed in Shanghai on 1ST November 1945. The organization at that time was composed principally of Sikhs under the supervision of British citizens who were former members of the International Settlement Police Force The Battalion was used to supplement American troops who were engaged in protecting United States property. The outfit was clothed in U.S. Army uniforms, using a Geneva insigne on the left sleeve and the name of the AMP on the shoulder. The system of the rank is the same as the Army and the insigne is worn on the right sleeve. Auxiliary Military Police Battalion deactivated in 1949.

Hong Kong Police

For several decades Hong Kong was a 'rough-and-tumble' port with a 'wild west' attitude to law and order. Consequently many members of the Police force were equally rough individuals. After his appointment as Superintendent of Police in 1862, William Quinn, who had served in the Bombay police force, decided to recruit police officers direct from India. However, he was not impressed with the work of the police officers recruited from Bombay, and began recruiting Sikhs from the Punjab instead. The Sikhs, with their generally strong physique and presence, were effective in the opinion of the British, in intimidating the Chinese Secret Societies and deterring the activities of the other 'Eastern criminal classes'. They built up a healthy respect among the population, with their strong-armed policing and military capabilities. Their performance proved more satisfactory and the Force continued recruiting them over the years. In deference to their customs and religious beliefs, the Hong Kong Police Force allowed them to retain their turbans and exempted them from wearing police caps. With more Sikh police officers recruited into the Force, many high-ranking British police officers were sent to India from time to time to learn their language. This arrangement continued until just before the Second World War. Just prior to the British capitulation to the Japanese during the Second World War, commissioner Penne-father-Evans issued instructions to members of the Force to assist the Japanese invaders in maintaining law and order in the event of a Japanese occupation of Hong Kong. The Force was urged to serve under the Japanese so as to protect local residents from harsh and unfair treatment by the Japanese and their Chinese collaborators. To this end, some members of the Force had no choice but to work for the enemy. After the Japanese surrender, doubts about the willingness of Hong Kong people to accept Indian officers who had worked, and often abused their authority, under the Japanese administration forced authorities to wind down the Sikh contingent. However, some individual Sikh police officers with impeccable service records were retained until the early 1960s.

Hong Kong & Singapore, Royal Garrison Artillery

The Hong Kong and Singapore Royal Garrison Artillery was one of the largest colonial units of the British Empire. It garrisoned the two colonies that gave the regiment its name and operated outposts dotted across the Indian Ocean for more than a century. A Royal Artillery company was based in Hong Kong for the first time in 1842. To spare the British gunners enervating labour of moving guns and ammunition, native auxiliaries were recruited from India in 1847. Two double companies of Lascars were formed in an 1891 reorganisation, each composed of a company of Sikhs and a company of Punjabi Mussalmans in equal numbers. It was recognised that these units were no longer just Gun Lascars. They were capable of operating batteries themselves and not just as assistants to European Gunners. Imperial policing became the regiment's regular duties. During the Boxer Rebellion, armed with Maxim and Mountain guns, helped to defend the besieged international settlement at Tientsin and then took part in the subsequent march on Peking. The mountain gunners blasted their support when the Russian and French troops stormed the Chinese capital. In 1903 the British sent an expeditionary force into Tibet. A short but confused war ensued in which the Mountain Gunners held a 'world record' for setting up an assault at 17,200 feet in the Himalayan Mountains.

With the outbreak of the First World War in 1914 the Hong Kong and Singapore Battalion, Royal Garrison Artillery, was employed on coastal defence duties at Hong Kong, Singapore and Mauritius. In 1915 No. 1 Battery composed of big brawny Sikhs, two hundred and forty strong, was formed into a 6-gun Mountain Battery and equipped with 10-pounder guns, embarked for Egypt. After a tour of duty in the Suez Canal defences, the Battery took part in the western desert campaign. In early 1916, the Battery was stationed at Abassia, where it was re-equipped with camel instead of mule transport and then attached to the Imperial Camel Corps. It then saw service in Palestine where it took part in the battles of Maghdada and Rafah. In January 1917, it was again re-equipped, this time exchanging its 10-pounder mountain guns for 2.75-inch guns. The Battery then took part in the three battles of Gaza, the action at Nebi Samil, the capture of Jerusalem and the attacks on Amman. With the limited range of its guns, the Battery had to fight from a position well forward in both attack and defence. Its personnel were highly regarded for their bravery in action and professionalism. The Distinguished Conduct Medal is the second highest award for gallantry in action, after the Victoria Cross. Only Seven DCM medals were ever awarded to the Indian soldiers of whom, the following four were awarded to the Sikh gunners for their conspicuous gallantry in the Desert and Palestine Campaign. Havildar Fateh Singh (26TH April 1917) Havildar Kishen Singh (3RD September 1918) Havildar Chajja Singh (1ST May 1918) and Havildar Rur Singh (21ST October 1918)

Hong Kong & Singapore, Royal Garrison Artillery

In the early 1930's HKSRGA comprised a mountain battery and three heavy batteries in Hong Kong and a single heavy battery in Singapore. Three new heavy batteries were formed in 1938, with one each allotted to Hong Kong, Singapore and Penang in Malaya. The formation of the Anti Aircraft Battery, for the first time, started in September 1938 when the Sikhs from 2ND Mountain Battery were attached to 7TH Anti Aircraft Battery. The Record of Service of the Battery records this period in these words, "This marks the beginning of the period when the Sikhs proved that they could deal with any peacetime crises and that no form of equipment could daunt them. On 8TH December 1938, they formed two anti aircraft sections. It is heartening to see their adaptability. HKSRGA gun crews fought in the first battles on the mainland when the Japanese attacked Hong Kong on 8TH December 1941. The gunners were soon overwhelmed by the much more numerous and experienced Japanese artillery. Gun crews fired over open sights at attacking Japanese infantry in often-vain attempts to save their guns. Just seven men survived when a section was overrun on Tytam Hill. HKSRGA survivors who had lost their guns were formed into infantry units. The men were untrained in the infantry tactics and most of them were killed or captured by the Japanese. Sections of the regiment cut off and surrounded in different parts of the island fought to the end. HKSRGA sustained heavy losses in the battle for Hong Kong and virtually all of the survivors taken prisoner.

HKSRGA unit were among the first troops to engage the Japanese forces that attacked the string of British airfields defending northern Malaya. The gunners at Khota Bharu and Alo Star valiantly struggled to protect the airstrips against repeated air strikes by Japanese bombers and fighters. With most British aircraft lost or out of action, the RAF began to abandon the airfields. Repeatedly the RAF and the infantry guarding the airfields retreated without warning, leaving the gunners virtually alone to defend the airfields. Nonetheless, the gunners fought hopeless rearguard actions, and inflicted rising toll on the attacking Japanese as they retreated to Singapore. During the long withdrawal, the gunners shot down 51 planes and claimed another 30 probable kills. They accounted for most of the 72 planes reported shot down by the British forces during the campaign. Fourteen of the regiment's guns bad been destroyed or lost and dozens of its men killed, wounded or posted as missing by the time Malaya were abandoned. All the surviving HKSRGA guns were deployed to face the coming invasion of Singapore Island. There was no sign of the British infantry that had been positioned nearby, so the gunners destroyed their guns and fought as infantry suffering heavy losses. The survivors were either butchered or taken prisoners by the Japanese. At end of the war, and the rush to end British rule, of the Indian subcontinent, raised question about the HKSRGA future. India and Pakistan were unlikely to countenance the recruiting of their citizens to uphold British imperialism in Asia. And with that, a proud regiment passed into history.

Malay States Guides

Britain made a fairly slow colonial advance into Malaya, now named Malaysia. By 1826 the Crown Colony of The Straits Settlements–Penang, Malacca and Singapore – had been established. But lawlessness on the peninsula along with piracy off its coast began to threaten the stability of the Straits Settlements, and in 1874 the Pangkor Engagement was signed. This treaty between Britain and Sultan Abdullah of Perak, whose territory was seriously disturbed by warfare between opposing gangs of Chinese tin miners, opened the gateway to British administration of the peninsula by British Residents. Perak was a state that stretched about 160 kilometres down the coast in between Penang and Malacca, and ran inland for around 80 kilometres. The local Malay administrators imported experienced Chinese miners into Perak to exploit this mineral wealth, but the Chinese brought their own fierce inter-clan rivalries with them and large-scale disturbances and fighting broke out which the Malays were unable to contain. In 1873 a larger-than-life British colonial adventurer named Captain Speedy resigned his post as Penang Superintendent of Police in order to take up a new job as Chief of Police in the Larut area, where he worked under the local Malay Sultan's administrator known as the Mentri. Speedy went to Lahore in India and returned with just over a 110 Sikhs, ex-soldiers of the Indian Army. This force was called the Perak Armed Police but became known as the Perak Sikhs and the unit was stationed at Bukit Gantang and Taiping. The Mentri financed the arming of these policemen, including the purchase of two Krupp's field guns, and the force was deployed around Perak to enforce the ruler's authority. As a result of the Pangkor Engagement the first British Resident in Perak, James W.W. Birch, was appointed on 4TH November 1874. Malay chiefs and officials feared that Birch would threaten traditional customs such as debt-slavery, and 1 it was decided to kill Birch with the hope that the British would then go away. The only men that Birch could call upon to help him in his duties were the dispersed, ill-trained and only partially disciplined Perak Sikhs. On 2ND November 1875 James Birch and his orderly Sepoy Ishar Singh were murdered at Pasir Salak. Ishar Singh was probably the first Sikh to die on duty in Malaya.

The commander of the Sikh escort, Lieutenant Thomas Francis Abbott, had in fact been shooting game on the opposite bank of the River when the attack occurred. On hearing of the attack Abbott retreated down the River to the Residency fort at Banda Bahru which he defended with around 50 Sikh Sepoys.

A British Resident had been murdered and in retribution the power of the Empire had to be seen to be applied with a vengeance. The Perak War had begun.

The Sikh Sepoys fought alongside British forces in the Perak War. The major actions in the Perak War were concluded by the end of 1875 and the war was declared and was over in March 1876, recalcitrant Sultans and Chiefs having accepted defeat. Three insurgent leaders were hanged and three others were banished from Malaya.

Malay States Guides

The Sikhs of the Perak Armed Police were now trained effectively and reinforcements were recruited from the Punjab. Captain Speedy resigned his commission in 1877 and left Malaya. In 1879, Lieutenant R. S. F. Walker took over the command of the Perak Armed Police. In 1883, Walker was sent to India to engage about 250 Sepoys for the Perak Armed Police. He went to the Punjab to recruit Sepoys from the well known Sikh Regiments; 14TH Sikhs, 15TH Sikhs, and 45TH Sikhs. Many of those selected had seen active service on the North West Frontier of India. In 1884, Walker (now promoted to Lieutenant Colonel) changed the name of the Perak Armed Police to '1ST Battalion Perak Sikhs'. At this time, the strength of this police force was 650 men. Some of these policemen were sent to Parit Buntar and Telok Anson. A section of this force was mounted on horses as cavalry troopers. In the 1880s, in the State of Selangor, Captain H.C. Syers had a force of about 530 Military Police known as the Selangor Sikhs. Similarly, W.W. Douglas had 75 Sikh Police in Sungei Ujong in 1881. During the insurgency operation between 1889 and 1894, 11 Sikhs had been killed fighting the rebels. Troops from various forces helped to suppress a rebellion in Pahang in 1891. Malay chiefs rebelled after the British persuaded the Sultan to strip one of them of his title. The ensuing guerrilla war was one of the few serious attempts to resist encroaching British rule. On 18TH May 1892, Mat Kilau and Dato Bahaman were compelled to flee to Kelantan and Terengganu. In June 1892, they crossed the border from Terengganu into Pahang and attacked the stockade at Kuala Tambling, which was manned by 11 Sikh police officers. During the attack, five Sikh police officers were killed and the rest managed to escape. During their flight, Ram Singh and Kishen Singh fought heroically against some of the rebels. Kishen Singh died fighting while Ram Singh suffered more than thirty wounds and yet managed to reach Pulau Tawar and raise the alarm. Ram Singh was awarded the Imperial Service Medal for his bravery and courage. The Sikhs retook the fort and later overran the rebels' stronghold at Jeram Ampai, forcing Mat Kilau and Dato Bahaman to flee north. During the attack on Jeram Ampai, four Sikhs were killed and four wounded. The British had deployed 200 Sikh police officers from Singapore, Perak, and Selangor for the anti-insurgency operations in Pahang and for the pursuit of the rebels into Terengganu and Kelantan. Private Ishar Singh was killed and Privates Kharak Singh and Teja Singh were wounded during the attack on the rebels' fort in Pahang. By late 1895, the insurgency in Pahang was practically over. In 1896, Walker decided to set up a military force, which could carry out their military duties without being called to do police work as well. This led to the formation of the Malay States Guides and Walker, now promoted to Colonel, became its first commandant. Sikhs from the Police forces of Perak, Selangor, Negeri Sembilan, Pahang and even Singapore volunteered to join the Malay States Guides. Its total strength was 900 personnel comprising six companies of Infantry and two companies of Artillery.

Malay States Guides

And after some uncertainty as to whether, as 'colonial' troops, they might be entitled to British awards including the Distinguished Conduct Medal and the Military Medal; it was resolved in July 1916 that Indian awards would be more suitable, in the form of the Order of British India, the I.O.M., and the Indian Distinguished Service Medal. The rationale was influenced by the fact that during WW1 the Malay States Guides was integrated, albeit *pro tem*, with Indian formations within the orbit of Simla and the Government of India.

The infantry establishment of the Guides called for three double companies: one of Manjha Sikhs, another of Malwa Sikhs, and a third of Punjabi Muhammadans and Pathans. A depot company trained recruits and specialists. The artillery establishment, a mountain battery, was equipped with four 10-pounder mountain guns carried on mules purchased in North China, although there were insufficient numbers of mules for all four guns. Of the two sections in the battery one was composed of Sikhs and the other of Punjabi Muhammadans and Pathans. An important non-military duty of the unit was to supply the Fire Brigade for Taiping town with equipment provided by the Perak Government. Despite using 1902-pattern rifles the unit marksmanship results were satisfactory. The establishment of thirty qualified signallers with requisite equipment was complete. A further thirty-five men possessed signalling certificates. All Indian ranks had received an increased pay award on 1ST January 1913. The Malay States Guides was, in theory, ready to go to war.

At the same time, the police forces of the states, consisting of Malays and the remaining Sikhs, were placed under a Federal Commission of Police, with Deputy Commissioners or Superintendents in the states. The dual organisation of police, which had resulted in units not fully effective either as police or soldiers, thus came to an end.

Colonel R.S. Walker, C.M.G., retired in 1910. Colonel Murray was appointed Commandant of the Malay States Guides. Colonel O.H.B. Lees was seconded from the Indian Army as the Commandant of the Malay States Guides in 1913.

The Malay States Guides mobilised for war on 6TH August 1914, and were posted Singapore, and satisfactorily performed routine security duties. But the regiment had been selected for service in East Africa. When preparations for the move to East Africa began the Indian officers and rank and file refused to embark, stating that their contracts did not specify service outside Malaya. This action shocked the British military establishment and also exposed the lack of knowledge of the British regimental officers about the concerns and intentions of their own soldiers. Initially disbandment of the regiment was proposed but wiser councils ordered a return of the infantry to Taiping where, after reflection on both sides, new contracts including provision for overseas service were offered and accepted by all ranks. The mountain battery was retained for duties in Singapore.

Malay States Guides

On 15TH February 1915 a mutiny broke out in Singapore involving half of the 5th Light Infantry, an Indian Army regiment. Around a dozen of the Malay States Guides gunners joined the mutineers. However, the remainder of the battery remained loyal and distanced itself from the mutiny, which was by now becoming bloody and brutal. After the suppression of the Mutiny, an enquiry had cleared the Sikh gunners of any association with the mutiny; the loyal gunners were re-armed and returned to duty. Later in 1915 an insurrection broke out in the Malay state of Kelantan and 'A' company of the Malay States Guides infantry was sent there. The single-company was increased in size to around 200 men by attachments from other companies. The Guides moved up the coast by boat to make a beach landing, successfully defending their camp from an insurgent night attack; next day an enemy group, poorly armed with old muskets, was caught in the open and the Guides were able to kill and wound several insurgents. Hard jungle patrolling then became the norm for a few months until the last of the insurgents had surrendered or been killed. The Guides suffered only one casualty when a soldier drowned in the Kelantan River. It was then decided to send the regiment to join the Aden Field Force.

After being inspected by the General Officer Commanding Troops, Straits Settlements, the Malay States Guides embarked on the transport ship *Arankola* and sailed for Aden on 26TH September 1915. A port call was made at Colombo, Ceylon, where the regiment went on a route march. Three machine guns and two tripods were issued at Colombo by the Army Ordnance Department. Aden was reached on 9TH October, and was immediately allocated a sector of the Sheikh Othman defence line, relieving the 56TH Punjabi Rifles (Frontier Force), who departed for Egypt. The companies were employed on manning static defence Piquets by day and night, learning desert entrenching and wiring skills under Captain C.F. Stoehr of the 3RD Sappers and Miners, practising field firing under Major Borton, and taking part in minor tactical manoeuvring against Turkish intrusions near Sheikh Othman. There were regular arrests of local and Somali women suspected of spying, and night patrols attempted to apprehend enemy agents signalling from the minarets of mosques and other high places in Sheikh Othman. The effects of the exposure to the dry, hot and harsh climatic conditions in Aden gave rise to dysentery-types of sickness throughout the unit until the soldiers' bodies, diets, and drinking habits had adjusted to their unaccustomed environment.

The mountain battery wished to train for mobile operations but more mules and drivers were needed if four guns were to be deployed in a Mobile Column. Army HQ in India stated that no more resources were available and so the battery reduced its mobile element to one section of two guns. Even so, compared to Indian Army establishments there was still a deficiency of thirteen drivers, nine mules, three syces and four ponies. The other two guns were positioned in the Sheikh Othman defence line.

Malay States Guides

Those men that marched outside the British defence line found the terrain to be rolling country consisting mainly of sand dunes, with patches of dense camel-thorn and scrub and every now and then a solitary tree or group of ruined buildings. A skilful Turkish commander, Said Pasha, operated from Lahej with 2,300 Turkish soldiers, 650 local Arabs and Somalis, and nineteen artillery pieces. Said Pasha maintained Piquets on wells and vital ground features and he could reinforce threatened locations quickly. In early January 1916 reports came into Aden Headquarters suggesting that Said Pasha was extending his influence over former friendly tribes to the east of Aden. A decision was taken to counter this by mounting a demonstration against the Turks Piqueting the important Hatum Ridge. A manoeuvre was planned that was intended to entice the enemy into an inopportune counter-attack across open ground where he could be punished by the British artillery. The Malay States Guides would be the decoy that attracted the Turkish counter-attack.

All the nominated units were ordered to leave behind specific numbers of men in order to maintain the Sheikh Othman garrison at a respectable strength. Medical support was provided by two Indian Sections and one British Section of the Combined Field Ambulance stationed at Sheikh Othman. Each unit was to set up its Regimental Aid Post 100 metres behind the firing line, commanded by the unit Medical Officer. Casualties for evacuation then had to be carried to the Dressing Station in the rear from where they would be evacuated by Desert Carts with canvas covers to Sheikh Othman; there casualties were to be taken over by No.10 Stationary Hospital and moved by motor ambulance to the base hospital in Aden.

The Malay States Guides was the advance guard, marching out at 02.15 hrs, 12TH January 1916, and reaching the Hatum area, about ten kilometres distant, at dawn. The regiment then acted as a protective screen for the main body that entrenched a position behind the screen. Elements of the column marched to Fiyush to reconnoitre that area but maintained close contact with the troops at Hatum.

Colonel Lees deployed his No's I and II double-companies forward. No. 5 Coy Sappers and Miners supported the Malay States Guides throughout the day. The artillery battery commanders went forward to reconnoitre. Around 07.00 hrs the Turks noticed the British movements and commenced shelling the area where Nos. I and II double-companies met. The shell-fire searched the area with shrapnel; the Turkish range and fuse settings were accurate and the guns appeared to be concealed behind Subah. Luckily for the Guides and the Sappers & Miners the Turkish artillery observers could not see exact targets and so the enemy guns continued to search with fire rather than engage specific groups of men with concentrations of fire. The enemy shelling intensified around 08.30 hrs and the Turks then moved forward to attack, coming to within 550 metres of the Guides' positions.

Malay States Guides

The Guides had been sheltering from enemy observation behind a low ridge but now they had to come onto the crest of the ridge to engage the enemy with rifles and machine guns. The Turkish artillery observers could now see them and accurate fire came down causing casualties. As more Turkish troops appeared to his front Colonel Lees started to withdraw at around 09.30 hrs; the Guides withdrew 400 metres and took up new fire positions. During this withdrawal the British guns concentrated fire on the presumed enemy artillery locations, neutralising their activities whilst the Guides scrambled back with their casualties.

Half an hour later Colonel Lees noticed that the number of enemy infantry to his front had diminished and so he advanced again, but this time about 700 metres forward, driving enemy skirmishers before him. The Guides were again exchanging rifle fire with the enemy, and attracting accurate Turkish artillery fire that caused further casualties. As an enemy attack was now predicted, the British artillery batteries came into action. The 15-pndr camel battery stayed in the rear, using three positions from which it gave very effective fire support to the Guides. Much sand was blowing in the air, reducing visibility, and the guns of the 4TH Hampshire Battery and Guides guns came into action to a flank but forward of the Guides infantry. These two units attracted heavy enemy rifle fire and Captain William Leslie, the Guides Battery commander, was shot off his horse by a bullet to the head that killed him instantly, at which point Jemadar Sawan Singh took command. The Hampshires' and Guides' guns were then re-deployed to come into action further to the rear.

Around noon the situation had become very unpleasant for the Guides and Colonel Lees commenced a tactical withdrawal starting with his right flank that was now being enfiladed by the enemy. The Turks then built up strength in front of the Guides left double-company and the company commander was ordered to make a fighting withdrawal. Colonel Lees concentrated his men on the screening positions that they had first occupied at dawn, and halted the Turkish advance.

The 10-pndr Camel Battery was used in direct support of the Guides now and its fire effectively deterred a Turkish attack. After ninety minutes of fighting from the screening position, the Guides left flank was being turned again and Colonel Lees withdrew his three double-companies and the Sappers & Miners into the main position at 14.30 hrs, where the Guides role was taken over by the 126TH Baluchis, the Guides going into reserve.

Meanwhile the cavalry had been tasked to get behind the Turkish left flank and disrupt enemy activities; however the enemy artillery fire directed against it was so effective that the mission could not be achieved, and the cavalry was shelled out of each area that it occupied. At 15.00 hrs the Turks attacked the 126th Baluchis but a double-company of the 109TH Infantry moved up in support and the attack failed.

Malay States Guides

Thirty minutes later Brigadier Walton decided that his Moveable Column had achieved all that it reasonably could do, and he called-in the Fiyush elements and ordered a return to Sheikh Othman. This decision was no doubt influenced by the aggressive and courageous actions of the enemy infantry and horsemen, the accuracy of the Turkish guns and the proximity of nightfall which would have been of more benefit to the enemy that to the Moveable Column. Overnight the column would have had to stay in an entrenched square formation, taking casualties from both artillery shrapnel and the small-arms fire of Turkish raiding parties.

The Mobile Column withdrew in good order; another enemy attack was repulsed at 16.30 hrs but after that the Turks were disinclined to follow-up the British withdrawal. The Malay States Guides covered the withdrawal supported by the Sappers and Miners and the company of $1/4^{TH}$ Buffs, and at 22.15 hrs that night the Rear Guard arrived back at Sheikh Othman.

The Malay States Guides infantry had fired 16,574 rifle and machine gun rounds in action and the section of guns had fired 191 rounds of shrapnel; the regiment had been blooded on the battlefield and had come through the action very creditably, as Brigadier General Price told the unit when he later congratulated them. Throughout a difficult day's fighting in the desert the Guides' internal administrative systems worked well; orders were issued and executed, casualties were evacuated, signals were sent and received, ammunition and water was moved forward when needed, and all of this was performed whilst under effective enemy fire. Said Pasha had been shown that a British column could swiftly come out from Sheikh Othman to operate and cause the Turks attrition when they attacked. The local tribes had been shown that whilst the British could not defeat Said Pasha, neither could he defeat the British. However it has to be said that Said Pasha would not have been disappointed at the result of the engagement. He had seen-off a British column and the poor visibility had prevented the British artillery, which fired a total of 1,138 rounds, from inflicting too many casualties on his attacking infantry and horsemen.

But a price had been paid by the Guides. William Leslie was the sole casualty suffered by the Guides artillery, but the Guides infantry had lost three men and an attached mule driver killed and two more men who died of wounds. Two Indian officers and six men were seriously wounded and one British officer and thirteen men were less seriously wounded.

Awards for the Hatum action granted to the Malay States Guides;

Military Cross

Captain Thomas Blanford

I.O.M.

Havildar Kehar Singh and Naik Sawan Singh

Malay States Guides

The Malay States Guides remained in Aden until 1919 and the operations in which they were involved were very similar to the Hatum action. Moveable and Flying Columns went out into the desert to confront the Turks, British posts were defended against Turkish raiders and Turkish posts were raided by the Guides. The following citations give an idea of the tactics employed:

"On the night of the 15TH-16TH February 1918 this Indian officer commanded a platoon in an enterprise against an enemy Piquet. He personally volunteered to go forward and exactly locate the Piquet and by doing so materially assisted the success of the operation. Subsequently in the attacks, he led his platoon with great gallantry and determination." Jemadar Gurdit Singh was awarded the I.O.M. while Jemadar Bogh Singh, Infantry; Naik Santa Singh, Infantry; Sepoy Lal Singh, Infantry; Havildar Bagga Singh, Infantry; Sepoy Surain Singh, Infantry ;Havildar Wir Singh, Artillery ; Gunner Abdul Rahim, Artillery; and Gunner Roshan Din, Artillery, were awarded the I.D.S.M.

On the Heliopolis (Aden) Memorial in Egypt are inscribed the names of thirty-five men of the Malay States Guides who died in Aden, while another name is inscribed on the Heliopolis (Port Tewfik) Memorial. Names can also be seen on Great War memorials in Malaysia.

By the end of the Great War the strength of the regiment were around 500 men, a big reduction from the established strength of over 900 that had been in service when war was declared. Fighting and harsh climatic conditions had led to many casualty and medical evacuations from Aden; the three years of war in that theatre had taken a heavy toll. Most men wished to return to the Punjab and the pleasures of family life. After consultations and discussions, and ever-mindful of how he had been let down early in the war by the refusal to serve overseas, Colonel Lees recommended the disbandment of the regiment. The Rulers of the Federated Malay States were advised to accept this decision. The Indian officers and men were given three options: to serve in the Federated Malay States Police or the Indian Army, with previous military service counted for both options, or to become redundant on generous terms. It appears that 200 men opted for the Federated Malay States Police and just one man opted for the Indian Army; the remainder accepted redundancy and returned to the Punjab.

Thus the brief but interesting life of the Malay States Guides ended in 1919. The regiment was what it was – a colourful addition to the entourage of its owners, the Sultans of the Federated Malay States. Malay States Guides went to serve for over three years in one of the most physically demanding and under-resourced operational theatres of the Great War – and the regiment served and fought well.

North Borneo Defence Force

North Borneo is located on the northeastern end of the island of Borneo. It was part of Brunei and Sulu Sultanates until 1878. In 1878, Alfred Dent formed a British syndicate and persuaded the Sultan of Sulu to cede parts of North Borneo to the syndicate. Later British North Borneo Company was formed which took over the concession granted to the syndicate. British North Borneo Company applied for and received a charter from Queen Victoria in 1881. British Protectorate was declared over the northern part of Borneo in 1888, which included Sarawak, Brunei and the state of North Borneo. The Crown took over external affairs, while the Chartered Company remained in control of internal administration of their territory until 1942. The Japanese Army occupied North Borneo from January 1942 to August 1945, and after the war the territory was under the British Military Administration from September 1945 until July 1946, when it became a crown colony. It is now the state of Sabah, East Malaysia

One of the earliest problems for the owners of North Borneo had been to maintain peace amongst the various tribes and security for the company officers. The Chartered Company officials soon found that owning 30,000 square miles of territory was only one aspect of the story. Keeping it and deriving beneficial income was another. One of the first tasks was to establish law and order. In order to do this, they had to have a police force. Since the local natives considered the British as transgressors in their land, hostility towards the authority of the British North Borneo Chartered Company was natural. The first contingent of police was, therefore, made up of Sikhs. They were eagerly sought for recruitment because of their proven loyalty and bravery. The original force after its formation in 1881 was composed of Sikhs who were brought into the country by Captain Harrington. Captain A.M. de Fontaine, who succeeded Harrington in 1883, commanded a mixed force of Sikhs, Dyaks, and Malays, numbering 300 in all, the Sikhs being used for military duties.

In May 1884 when 'amok' (from the Malay meaning "mad with uncontrollable rage") at Kawang occurred, Jemadar Asa Singh, Sergeant Major Narain Singh and Private Gendah Singh were the first fatal casualties among the Sikh police. Among the enlistments during this year was Natha Singh who retired with the rank of Jemadar in 1911. He took part in the Omadal expedition in 1884 and the Padas expeditions in 1885, 1887 – 1889 and was severely wounded in the Ranau expedition in 1898. He was one of the first recipients of the North Borneo Silver Cross for Valour which was awarded to him for bravery shown during the Padas Damit Expedition in 1888 during which operations another Sikh officer, Jemadar Maha Bir Singh, was killed. Other recipients of this medal from among the Indian ranks are Sergeant. Major Juar Singh who won his decoration for his plucky conduct at Seganan in Darvel Bay in 1891; Regiment Sergeant Major Shere Singh who received the Cross for long service and good conduct in 1895 and who died in 1899 at Sandakan after 19 years service in the Force.

North Borneo Defence Force

North Borneo Armed Constabulary was constantly in action against bandits and rebels. These involved the pursuit of bandits and rebels, largely via Rivers meandering through mangrove swamps and the across jungle clad hills, in tropical rainstorms (with rainfall up to 200 inches a year, mostly in the afternoons) with ambushes and much sweat and toil by Sikh and Malay police, Dyak guides and local Dusan and Kadazan porters.

In June 1892, Mat Kilau and Dato Bahaman, the rebel leaders, crossed the border from Terengganu into Pahang and attacked the stockade at Kuala Tambling, which was manned by 11 Sikh police officers. During the attack, five Sikh police officers were killed and the rest managed to escape. During their flight, Ram Singh and Kishen Singh fought heroically against some of the rebels. Kishen Singh died fighting while Ram Singh suffered more than thirty wounds and yet managed to reach Pulau Tawar and raise the alarm. Ram Singh was awarded the Imperial Service Medal for his bravery and courage. The Sikhs retook the fort and later overran the rebels' stronghold at Jeram Ampai, forcing Mat Kilau and Dato Bahaman to flee north. During the attack on Jeram Ampai, four Sikhs were killed and four wounded.

Antanum or Antanom was a famous and influential Murut warrior from North Borneo who according to local oral history claimed to have supernatural powers. Because of this he was able to receive support from the chiefs and villagers from around the villages of Keningau, Tenom, Pensiangan and Rundum and led the Rundum uprising against the British North Borneo Company but was killed during fighting with the Sikh police in Sungei Selangit near Pensiangan in 1915.

As part of the Second World War Japanese forces landed in Labuan on January 1, 1942, and continued to invade the rest of North Borneo. The North Borneo Armed Constabulary with only 650 men hardly provided any resistance to slow down the Japanese invasion. From 1942 to 1945, Japanese forces occupied North Borneo, along with most of the island.

In June 1945 the Australian 9th Division landed in Brunei and liberated much of North Borneo before the end of the war. North Borneo was placed under British Military Administration until restoration of civil government on July 15, 1946

In 1950 the North Borneo Armed Constabulary and Sarawak Constabulary were merged to form the Royal Malaysian Police

The Sarawak Rangers

Sarawak is one of two Malaysian states on the island of Borneo. It is the largest state in Malaysia and is situated on the north-west of the island. In 1839, Sarawak, then a dependency of the Brunei sultanate, was in rebellion against the central power. Looking for commercial ventures with his well-armed schooner, a young British adventurer by the name of James Brooke arrived on the scene. He soon found himself involved in the local disputes. The young Brooke assisted the Sultan's representative to bring peace to the area. For his services, the Sultan made him the Rajah of Sarawak in 1841. James Brooke tried to expand his territory; strived to pacify the many warring tribes and to stamp out the practices of head hunting and piracy. In 1857, the Chinese uprising started in the gold mining town of Bau, which is about 20 miles from the town of Kuching. Sir James Brooke fled to Singapore, where he took refuge with the Governor of the Straits Settlements. He subsequently recruited Sikh officers for the Sarawak Police Force in Singapore. The first batch of Sikhs arrived in Kuching, led by Dewa Singh Akhara. These Sikhs played an important role in bringing peace, law, and order to the area. The Sikhs recruited later joined the Sarawak Police forces stationed at Miri and Bua. The Government also employed them as prison wardens. The Sarawak Rangers were a Para-military force founded in 1862 and were highly skilled in jungle warfare and general police duties, being equipped with various western rifles, cannons and native weaponry. Most of the Sarawak Rangers were Malays and Dyaks from the jungle. One or two British officers ran the force with the help of Sikh NCOs. Sikhs were recruited as ordinary soldiers in 1902, and by 1907, there were 66 Sikhs in the Sarawak Rangers. They were based in a number of forts constructed at strategic locations in towns and at River mouths. Aside from protecting Sarawak's borders, they were used to fight any rebels and were engaged in a number of campaigns during their history. Suppressing intermittent rebellions and riots were the Rangers main tasks.

The Sarawak Rangers were disbanded for a few years in the 1930s, only to be reformed and mobilised for the Second World War in which they attempted to defend Sarawak from Japanese invasion in 1942 at the start of the Pacific War. After the abdication of Charles Vyner Brooke in 1946, the Sarawak Rangers became a colonial unit under direct British control and saw action in both the Malayan Emergency and the Borneo Confrontation. In 1963, after the formation of Malaysia, the Sarawak Rangers became part of the Royal Ranger Regiment.

Lieutenant Colonel Harbajan Singh commanded the Royal Ranger Regiment from 1ST May 1987 – 31ST December.

Central African Rifles

David Livingstone was a Scottish pioneer medical missionary with the London Missionary Society and explorer in Central Africa. During his explorations, he reported on the extent and evils of the slave trade in Central Africa and died near Lake Bangweulu in 1873. Then the Free Church Mission of Scotland founded the Livingstonia Mission at Cape Maclear on the lake. Trade followed, when in 1879, the African Lakes Company was formed. In 1883 a British Consul was appointed and in the following year the African Lakes Company built a trading station at Karonga, at north-west of the lake, which was placed under the charge of Mr. Montieth Fotheringham, the Company's agent. The Arab slavers had divided up the land between themselves, and the arrival of the British at Karonga was a threat to the slaver's livelihood and the three Arab slavers, Mlozi, Kapakopa, and Msalema therefore built themselves stockades about seven miles from Karonga to consolidate their hold on the northern end of the slave route. Mlozi was half-bred Arab; Kapakopa, and Msalema, his two colleagues were ordinary Swahilis, indistinguishable from the natives. In 1887 Mlozi massacred a number of Wakonde tribesmen and as a result the Karonga station had to be abandoned. Montieth Fotheringham described how the half-caste Arabs had fallen on the tribe at Kambwe Lagoon, giving no quarter. Village after village was burnt and the, fugitives hunted out of the hills, and driven into lagoon amongst the reeds which were set on fire. There was no escape and as the flames spread the fugitives either had to leap into the lake to be eaten by crocodiles or shot down by the Arabs waiting for theme on the bank. In 1888 Montieth Fotheringham returned to Karonga with a force of five hundred tribal levies. He eventually defeated them in a battle. However, there was so much plunder that Fotherigham's levies just disappeared back to their villages with whatever they could carry. Captain Lugard was on leave in the area and volunteered his services to command a relief expedition; He enlisted a force of about 220 tribesmen. He was determined to attack the slaver's stockades which were formidable affairs. Lugard's force was really insufficient to tackle the slaver's strongholds with their ditches and walls 14 feet high, and in a night attack of Kopakopa's stockade Lugard was shot and wounded in both arms and chest while he was climbing over the wall leading the assault. The attack was repulsed and Lugard was lucky to survive.

In January 1889, Armstrong 7-pdr screw guns arrive as a gift from the Nyasa Anti-Slavery and Defence committee. It had a muzzle velocity of 1440 ft/sec and a range of 4,000 yards, but was not particularly effective against the stockades. Msalema's and Kopakopa's stockades were bombarded but no reduced. In October, H.H. Johnston, the British Consul, made a treaty with the slavers allowing them to retain their stockades. The arrangement however, was more of a truce than a peace.

In May 1891, when British Protectorate over Nyasaland was proclaimed, Harry Johnston was appointed Her Majesty's Commissioner for British Central Africa.

Central African Rifles

Harry Johnston made arrangements for the establishment of an armed force with a nucleus of Indian troops loaned by India. Captain C.M. MacGuire raised a force of seventy volunteers from the Indian Army, from the 23RD Sikh Pioneers, 32ND Sikh Pioneers and the Hyderabad Lancers (the Lancers were eventually replaced by the Sikhs) This Sikh contingent was to form the first armed force of the new Protectorate and designated as the Central African Regiment. Until the slaver's final defeat, a number of expeditions were mounted against them.

The first expedition was mounted against the Yao slaver Chimkumbu in July 1891. He had settled amongst the peaceful Nyanja people of Mlanje, whom he had been gradually subjugating. The occasion of the expedition was an attack on two British coffee-planters. Accordingly, Captain MacGuire was dispatched with a force of fifty Sikhs to bring Chimkumbu to reason. As the Sikhs advanced, they were repeatedly attacked by the Yaos, but went on to defeat Chimkumbu's force and capture his town. As Chimkumbu fled, his brother was taken prisoner and a large number of slaves found in the town were released.

A more serious situation arose in September south of Lake Nyassa, where Mponda, who controlled upper course of the Shire, was attempting to interfere with the free passage of River steamers. Johnston and MacGuire, with seventy-eight Sikh Sepoys, with a 7-pounder gun, decided to take action against Mponda. One of the reasons for Johnston's desire to deal with Mponda was that a local chief, Chikusi, had appealed to him for protection against the slave raider. As a gesture of defiance, Mponda had beheaded fourteen of Chikusi's people and had stuck their heads on posts round his stockade, which was already decorated with the skulls of a hundred other victims. On reaching the neighbourhood of Mponda's, MacGuire thought it advisable to fortify his camp. On the opposite bank of the Shire Lake to Mponda's stronghold, Captain MacGuire built a fort and named it Fort Johnston. The work had to be done secretly and at night, as Mponda was highly suspicious. It became first of a succession of forts established throughout the Protectorate in the next few years. From this base, MacGuire, moved off to attack Mponda's stronghold. Meanwhile when a slave caravan bound for Kilwa arrived, a Yao chief Chindamba, arranged to sell all his slaves to the Kilwe traders. MacGuire immediately attacked Chindamba, drove his people into the hills, and destroyed his town. Mponda welcomed the opportunity and had no difficulty in capturing Chindamba's people in the outlying villages to be sold as slaves. Johnston issued an ultimatum to Mponda that unless the slaves were freed he would attack the town. At Mponda's refusal to comply Captain MacGuire and the Sikhs drove the Yaos out of town and destroyed the stockades. On October 22ND Mponda handed over Chindamba's people and large number of other slaves who were to be sold to the Kilwa traders. Three days later, he came over to Fort Johnson and signed a treaty abolishing the slave trade in his territory.

Central African Rifles

Harry Johnston next turned his attention to the slave raiders near Lake Nyasa and Lake Shirwa. Here again the Yao chiefs were the culprits, encouraged by the Arab and Swahili ivory merchants, wanting slave porters. The principle villain in this region was Makanjira. On October 28TH 1981, Harry Johnston, Captain MacGuire and the Sikhs embarked on the steamer, *Domira*, to sail up the Shire and attack Makanjira's town. Makanjira's men opened fire on the steamer as soon as it approached the shore and MacGuire replied with incendiary shells from the 7-pounder, which set the town alight in four places. Johnston and thirty-four Sikhs boarded the barge, which had been towed behind the steamer, and landed on the west side of the town, while MacGuire bombarded the eastern side. When it became too dark to serve the gun, MacGuire landed ashore in the Domira's boat with six Sikhs and made straight for the guns in the hands of the slavers. He captured the guns and before withdrawing, set fire to a slaver's new dhow that was almost ready for launching. Next morning MacGuire renewed his attack on the town, defeated the Yaos in a pitched battle in which several Sikhs were severely wounded, and saw to it that the town was completely burnt to the ground and destroyed another two dhows. Four Sikh soldiers earned the I.O.M. for their conspicuous gallantry in this action

The expedition against Chief Makanjira had hardly returned to Zomba when news came of depredations by Kawinga, a powerful Yao Chief. He was a notorious slave trader and lived on the northwest shore of Lake Shirwa, and commanded an important route to the coast. In 1889, he was reputed to have sent as many as a thousand slaves to the markets of Kilwa and Quinlimane. When MacGuire tried to storm Kawinga's stronghold he was wounded in the chest and his attack was repulsed, but Kawinga was forced to sue for peace. Kawinga was duly repentant and paid a fine of five tusks. Sixty-nine Sikh soldiers had taken part in this expedition. They had suffered several casualties and four of them were awarded the I.O.M. for their conspicuous gallantry.

Captain MacGuire returned to complete the building of Fort Johnson, which was to be permanently garrisoned. Makanjira possessed a fleet of slaving dhows and information came that two of them were hidden in a small cove. The chance was too good to miss and MacGuire embarked with a small force in the *Domira*. MacGuire set off in the Domira with a few Sikhs. Landing with a small force of 28 Sikhs, on 15TH December, he was about to demolish the dhows when Makanjira, with 2,000 followers, attacked him and forced his party back to the beach. There he found his boat had been wrecked by a storm which had arisen, and the *Domira* herself in endeavouring to come as close as possible inshore, had stuck on a sandbank, not far off the beach. After three Sikhs had been killed, MacGuire told the others to wade out to the *Domira* whilst he and a few men as rearguard kept off the Yaos with the bayonet. As MacGuire withdrew and was pulling himself aboard the *Domira,* he was shot dead.

Central African Rifles

The Sikhs struggled on board with the loss of three killed and defended the stranded steamer against all comers for three days. Makanjira then enticed the doctor and chief engineer on shore with a promise of surrendering MacGuire's body, and treacherously murdered them. Once again the stranded *Domira* was besieged, this time for five days and owing to the efforts of the second engineer and the Sikhs, who behaved splendidly throughout, the *Domira* escaped, firing her gun into Makanjira's hordes as she drew away. Nine Sikhs were killed during this operation. Three Sikh soldiers were awarded the I.O.M. for their conspicuous gallantry during the operation.

Soon after MacGuire's death, Zarafi attacked Fort Johnson. The commissioner, Harry Johnston, hurried north to its relief with some British volunteers and the remaining Sikhs. Siege was raised and some of Zarafi's villages were raided and burnt in revenge. For the time being, however, his subjugation could not be attempted. The Sikhs, who had actually wept over MacGuire's death, were at this time reduced to 63 effectives, of whom ten were suffering from wounds. Mr. J.G. King, who had been left in charge at Fort Johnson, with the help of one hundred Angoni and an inadequate force of thirty-five Sikhs and thirty Zanzibaris, set off to attack Zarafi. At the foot of the slavers' fortress, King was seriously wounded, losing six of the Sikh soldiers killed and losing a 7-pounder gun in the bush. Johnson was obliged to remain on the defensive until the arrival in June 1892 of Captain C. E. Johnson, the new commander with a draft of 60 Sikhs. During 1893, the armed forces of the Protectorate were reorganized and strengthened. The original contingent of Sikh soldiers, who had given valiant service, returned to their homeland at the end of their three–year engagement. Captain Johnson asked in future only Jat Sikhs should be sent and it was decided to increase the number. Soon a draft of 100 Sikhs arrived under command of Lieutenant C. A. Edwards and a second draft of the same strength of Sikhs under Lieutenant W. H. Manning arrived from India. The military force now numbered 3 British officers, 200 Sikhs, and 150 native regulars. Though the Sikhs were still the mainstay of the force, the need to train local troops was at last realized, for the Government of India were growing disturbed at the frequent requests for Sikh soldiers to serve in Africa, as it was anxious to preserve the recruitment of Sikhs for its own use.

The Yaos on the Upper Shire, inspired and led by Chief Liwondi, were another thorn in the Commissioner's flesh. In the campaign against him, the plucky little *Domira* again found herself in an unenviable position when she went aground in the Shire opposite one of Liwonde's towns and the crew was trapped in the fire between defenders and attackers. The arrival of reinforcements for the Administration's forces relieved the position and Liwonde's capital town was captured and burnt down. The Chief Liwondi himself escaped and gave occasional trouble for the next few years.

Central African Rifles

Lieutenant Edwards led a punitive expedition and after a brief campaign subdued Yao chief Nyassera. Soon afterwards, trouble arose with the Mlanje chief Mkanda. By that time, the second draft of 100 Sikhs had arrived. An expedition was organized and after several days hard fighting among the crags and precipices, Mkanda's strongholds were captured as he fled into exile.

The main trouble spot during 1893 was Kota-Kota, on the western shore of Lake Nyasa, ruled by an independent potentate called the Jumbe. Puffed up by his victory over Captain Maguire, the troublesome Makanjira attacked Chief Jumbe, who was friendly to the British. By the middle of 1893, Makanjira had captured most of the territory until Jumbe was penned in Kota-Kota itself. Johnston decided that the time had come to settle accounts with Makanjira. The first step was to deal with a rebel called Chiwauru, who had overthrown Jumbe and established his stronghold at Kisamba. Johnson and Edwards marched with 113 Sikhs and some Makua tribesmen and attacked Kasamba's fortified village, which was surrounded by an eight-foot high wall. Covering fire from a 7-pounder gun had little effect and eventually Johnson ordered the assault. The Sikhs charged gallantly for the eight-foot high wall. The first to scale the wall was shot dead, but his comrades soon reached the top and had the mass of natives below at their mercy. Chiwauru was killed, the town taken and hundreds of captured slaves released. The expedition then crossed the Lake and meted out similar treatment to Makanjira's town and a number of smaller towns and villages, including the village where Maguire, Boyce, and MacEwan had met their deaths. Fort Maguire was erected on the Lakeshore and garrisoned by Sikhs. Early in 1894, Makanjira attacked the fort but was defeated with heavy loss. His power at last was broken and he sought refuge in Portuguese territory. Havildar Bulaku Singh was awarded the I.O.M. for conspicuous gallantry in this action.

In November 1894, Johnston obtained permission to negotiate in India an agreement for two more drafts of Sikhs to serve in Central Africa for a period of three years. He expressed the highest admiration for the services rendered by the previous drafts. Johnson was allowed to select up to twenty from any of the Sikh or Punjabi units: no less than 500 of the 900 men in one regiment alone offered them as volunteers and Johnson considered that he had obtained 'the very cream of the Sikh regiments.'

Early in 1895, trouble again arose with the Yao chiefs, Kawinga, Zarafi, and Matapwiri, as they decided that the time had come to drive the British out of the Shire Highlands. Kawinga began operations with a raid near the Scottish Mission. A force of six Sikhs and a few Atonga sent against him fortunately took the precaution of constructing a strong *boma* (an enclosure) around their post, for within a few days Kawinga attacked it with 2,000 warriors. The handful of men held on grimly and when reinforcements of Atonga arrived, sallied out with the last few rounds of ammunition, and routed the enemy with a spirited charge.

Central African Rifles

Meanwhile Captain Manning, with a force of 55 Sikhs and about 200 Africans, attacked Kawinga's stronghold and captured it after two days siege. Matapwiri was tackled next. In September, a mixed force set out from Forts Lister and Anderson and approaching Matapwiri's village at night, achieved complete surprise and easy victory. In the following month, with a punitive force of five officers, 65 Sikhs and about 230 native troops, Lieutenant Edwards took Zarafi's upland villages by storm. Zarafi fled to the Portuguese territory.

Mlozi and his confederates were again threatening Karonga and raiding the countryside for slaves. An attempt at negotiation failed completely. A force of 6 officers, 100 Sikhs, and 300 native troops was therefore assembled at Fort Johnston and taken by steamer to Karonga. On 1ST December, Lieutenant Smith posted detachments round Mlozi's stockade. Next morning a force of Sikhs and sailors from the gunboats bombarded Msalema's stockade, the nearest to Karonga and captured it with little difficulty. Kopakopa's stockade was similarly captured and then the forces started bombarding Mlozi's stockade. A shell was dropped on Mlozi's hut and he was wounded. Rumour spread among his followers that he had been killed. Desperate and angered by this news, the defenders made a furious sortie, which was met by the Sikhs, who fought their way over the walls of the stockade. About 200 of the enemy were killed for the loss of one Sikh, three others killed, and six wounded. Mlozi was tried and hanged the next day, and the Arab stockades were then systematically destroyed.

'A parley was held with Mlozi the chief under a flag of truce, and he was offered his life if he would surrender; but he refused, choosing to fight to a finish. The earthworks were at last blown down by artillery and Sikhs let go. They stopped at nothing in their mad rush to victory. All the stockades fell in rapid succession. Mlozi was captured, tried, and executed for the brutal massacre of those grand Wakonde in the lagoon.' (Swann)

Immediately after Mlozi's defeat, Lieutenant Edwards began further expeditions against disaffected chiefs. His first move was to send Lieutenant Alston with 149 Makua and 40 Sikhs to join A. J. Swann, the political officer at Kota-Kota, in an expedition against the Chewa chief Mwazi, an ally of the Arabs. Swann had brought 2,400 auxiliaries, who were kept in reserve while Aston attacked with the regular troops. At the sight of Mwasi's warriors brandishing their spears behind the stockades the Makua hung back, so the Sikhs stormed the stronghold. Mwazi escaped, but Saidi Mwazungu, the ringleader in the treacherous Makanjira murders of 1891, was captured, tried, and hanged.

In January 1896, Edwards sent an expedition against the paramount Angoni chief Tambala. Tambala's village was perched on the flat of a hill with three precipitous sides and a fourth covered with large boulders. The village was bombarded by artillery from another hilltop and the stronghold captured. The operation met only with partial success, for although Tambala's stronghold was captured, the chief escaped and joined the Chewa raider Odete.

Central African Rifles

To break the Tamabala – Odete alliance, Manning left Kota-Kota on 6th October and five days later, was climbing the mountain slopes by a little-used track, with a force of 24 Sikhs and about 80 Africans. One by one, the raiders' villages were surprised and rushed and finally the main stronghold on the mountain peak was stormed, where Odete and other chiefs submitted.

Captain Stewart led the expedition against Chikusi, which included 58 Sikhs. Marching by way of Liwondi, through country thoroughly devastated by the raiders, he reached Chikusi on 21st October. Manning's force arrived next day, and on 23rd the village was taken. Chikusi was captured, tried, found guilty and shot. In December 1898, the existing troops of the Central African Rifles were designated 1st Battalion, and an authority was issued for a 2nd Battalion to be raised for Foreign Service.

Northern Rhodesia

Across the Northern Rhodesian border, the Angoni tribe were living around the area of Fort Jameson, where a trading company tried to expropriate a large tract of Angoni land by a fraudulent concession. Consequently, the Angoni threatened the Company. The Company frantically appealed for help. British Central Africa Protectorate had undertaken to provide military support for Northern Rhodesia when that was requested. A military force was despatched across the border to reach Fort Jameson. As Captain H. E. J. Brake with six rifle companies of Africans, 118 Sikhs, Maxim Guns, and two 7-pounder field guns moved his force to occupy commanding ground nearby, the Angoni were observed concentrating a force of around 10,000 warriors in the villages. Brake's use of Maxim guns, 7-pounders, rifle volley-fire, and finally a silent advance with the bayonet destroyed the Angoni will to fight. Then a new body of at least 500 warriors in full wardress approached, a Maxim burst, and a bayonet charge that was not faced up to caused the rapid dispersal of the survivors of this 500. During the next few days, Brake's men patrolled the area, skirmishing with and completely dispersing the Angoni fighters. The old Chief Mpeseni could no longer control his son Singu and the younger warriors. On 30th January Lieutenant J. S. Brogden captured Singu. After a trial by Drumhead Martial, (a swift military trial held in the field), Singu was summarily shot in front of a collection of chiefs on 5th February. On 9th February, Chief Mpeseni surrendered and was exiled for a year to Fort Manning. With his banishment, resistance to the British halted.

1st Battalion Central African Rifles continued its task of pacification even beyond its borders. On the eastern frontier, two chiefs named Nkwamba and Mataka kept raiding both sides of the border, which culminated in killing two European traders. The punitive force led by Captain Pearce left Zomba with 9 officers, 119 Sikhs, and 269 Askaris and after very little resistance destroyed Nkwamba's village in the Namweras Hills. However, Mataka proved more troublesome and escaped to the Portuguese territory.

Central African Rifles

Ashanti

The Ashanti were a powerful and highly organized group of tribes living in the north of the Gold Coast Colony (now Ghana). The consciousness that the Ashanti were a great people was aroused by their wise man Anoky, who affirmed that the spirit and the strength of the nation were enshrined in the Golden Stool. All chiefs were 'enstooled', not crowned, for in Ashanti it was the symbol of royal authority. The British had conducted operations against the Ashanti in 1873-74 and in 1895-96. After the last occasion, King Prempeh was deported and a treaty was drawn up with the remaining chiefs. In March 1900, the British Governor visited Kumasi, held a meeting with the chiefs, and asked why, as representative of the paramount power, the Golden Stool had not been brought from its hiding place for his use. This demand was a serious blunder and precipitated a rebellion among Kumasi, Ofinsu, Ejisu and Adansi sections of the tribe. To put down the rebellion, troops were ordered to the Gold Coast, which included 1ST Battalion, Central African Rifles with four British officers, seventy-three Sikhs, 276 African Askaris and a machine gun detachment. They left Zomba for the Gold Coast, under the command of Major Cobbe, with half of 2ND Battalion to follow from Berbera. Cobbe and his men were in action in August and suffered heavy casualties in thick bush. 'All ranks, especially those fine soldiers the Sikhs, behaved admirably' wrote Colonel Wilcocks, the commandant of the West African Frontier Force in his despatch, 'and if it were not for this impossible bush we should soon wipe out most of the Ashanti'. Lieutenant Colonel Brake and four companies of 2ND Battalion arrived on 13TH August and were in action a week later. At the battle of Obassa on 30TH September, the Ashanti held firm and continued to fire volley after volley at close range, so the assault could not be pressed. It was plain that the undertaking was beyond the capacity of the advance guard and its supporting troops. Colonel Wilcocks himself came forward. As a former officer of the Indian Army, he placed great reliance on the Sikhs and telling them that he would watch the charge, he ordered them to attack the centre of the stockade in the teeth of the Ashanti fire. As the bugles sounded, the Sikhs dashed down the slope, followed by the rest of the line. This charge decided the issue of 'a somewhat doubtful day.' The Ashanti still fought on but gave way before the Sikhs, as they came under devastating enfilading fire that rapidly spread panic and completed the rout. Obassa was a hard fought victory over a most courageous enemy.

The Sikhs fought several actions in conjunction with the West African Frontier Force. When the campaign ended, they earned high praise from Colonel Wilcocks for their discipline, drill, and shooting. They returned to Nyasaland via the Mediterranean, having gone around the cape, so they circumnavigated Africa.

Naik Hira Singh, a volunteer attached to the Central African Rifles, was awarded the I.O.M. for conspicuous gallantry in action. He was foremost in the attack as the Ashanti fled to the bush.

Central African Rifles

Gambia

Gambia is a country in Western Africa. It is the smallest country on mainland Africa. Gambia shares historical roots with many other West African nations in the slave trade, which was the reason to the establishment of a colony on the Gambia River, first by the Portuguese and later by the British. The West African coastline had been an important source of slaves for European and American traders, but during the 19TH Century, the trading emphasis moved towards obtaining African agricultural and mineral commodities in exchange for European manufactured goods. This led to European expeditions methodically exploring the hinterland of the West African coast. Both France and Britain were interested in the territory now known as The Gambia, and eventually an amicable agreement was reached by which Britain controlled a strip of land on each side of the navigable course of the River Gambia, whilst France controlled the land surrounding the strip. Britain established a capital at Bathurst (now named Banjul) on the coast, built Fort Bullen at Barra Point on the north side of the River mouth and Fort James 19 miles further upstream on James Island. They suppressed slavery and administered Gambia from a headquarters in Sierra Leone. The agreement with the French had settled the boundaries of Gambia in 1889, but this meant little to the native slave raiding chiefs, who were accustomed to operate indiscriminately on both sides of the frontier. One of these chiefs, Fodi Kabba, had been driven out of the colony in 1892 and had settled at Medina, beyond the frontier in French territory, whence he raided impartially in all directions. On 14TH June 1900, two travelling commissioners were murdered with their police escort of six constables, as many chiefs refused to recognize British authority. In 1901, a military expedition was authorized against the rebellious chiefs, which was afterwards prolonged to settle matters with the slavers. As Gambia possessed an armed police force of only 100 men, it was decided to employ four companies of 2ND Battalion, Central African Rifles and four companies of West India Regiment from Sierra Leone. The command of this Field Force was given to Lieutenant Colonel Brake of 2ND Battalion, Central African Rifles, who travelled to Bathurst on the *SS Dwarka*. At Bathurst, with the rest of the Field Force, including four companies of West India Regiment, they sailed up the River and eventually landed at Tendaba. Their objective was the stockade town of Dumbutu, which they reached after a three-hour advance through long grass. Two companies of 2ND Battalion, Central African Rifles, under Major Plunket, moved round to the left flank to get between the village and the French border. Surprise was complete and when the defenders finally surrendered, more than forty were dead and over 200 men and women were captured. Losses on the British side were one carrier killed and four men wounded. There were some sweeping–up operations, including tax collection and capture of over 200 rifles. Brake and his men went to the Gold Coast next, to put down mutiny in the West India Regiment. On January 1902, the regiments of Central African Rifles were amalgamated in to the King's African Rifles.

Uganda Rifles

In 1890 Captain Lugard, arrived with a few soldiers impose Imperial British East Africa Company's rule on the Kabaka (King) of Buganda. Lugard made a treaty with the Kabaka and went on to annexe Ankole and Toro. After a civil war, between the various religious groups, the Foreign Office, in view of the complaints made by the French Missions, appointed Colonel J.R.MacDonald to carry an enquiry into Lugard's activities. The government of India had seconded two British officers and Jemadar Bhagwan Singh with 30 men of 14TH and 15TH Sikh Regiments as an escort for Macdonald's party.

After Britain declared a provisional protectorate over Uganda in 1893, the colonial authorities formed a military unit of 600 regulars and 300 reservists, most of whom were Sudanese. In 1895 the colonial authorities organized these soldiers into rifle companies, which became known as the Uganda Rifles. Despite the good reputation they achieved, many Sudanese became disillusioned with the rigors of military service in a foreign country under British command. Their grievances included loneliness, low pay, poor food, bad officers, and frequent reassignments, often to remote areas. When the colonial government failed to resolve these problems, the Uganda Rifles mutinied in 1897. The mutineers made for the fort at Lubwa, hoping to raise the garrison and join forces with the disaffected Muslim elements in Buganda. The whole force, numbering about 600 Sudanese and 200 Buganda Muslims, was admitted to the fort.

Meanwhile Colonel Macdonald had occupied a hill dominating the fort with 10 Europeans, 17 Sikhs, and half-trained Swahilis. On the following day, the mutineers attacked MacDonald's force for five hours, but were defeated and driven back into the fort. This was a remarkable feat by the Sikhs, who with their Maxim guns had performed prodigies of valour, and the half- trained Swahilis and by the fact, the mutineers were led by experienced native officers.

Writing about the Sikhs, Macdonald stated. 'This detachment fully maintained the great reputation of the Sikhs, and fought with such gallantry that they secured the admiration of all'. Ten Sikh soldiers were awarded the I.O.M. for conspicuous gallantry during these operations. In October, the Foreign Office was warned that the local forces were unable to cope with the situation, and advised to order to Uganda the 300 Sikhs of the East African Indian Contingent, then at Mombasa and to arrange for a battalion from India to replace them. In November, the Sikh Contingent began to move inland. 150 Sepoys, under Lieutenant Scott, were going forward from the railhead on 23RD and another 70 Sepoys following soon afterwards. On February 23RD Captain Harrison led an attack on the rebel stockade of Kabagambi, when, 500 yards from the fort, the mutineers came out to meet them. Severe fighting took place and the mutineers were driven back into their fort. After some desperate fighting at close quarters for two hours, the Sikhs captured the fort. After one of the stiffest fights of the campaign since the first attack on Lubwa Hill of October 19TH, Sikhs had gained a most brilliant victory over the mutineers.

Uganda Rifles

Realizing that after the mutiny the armed forces would have to be completely reorganized, Ternan suggested that 400 Indian troops should be enlisted, as the backbone of the forces. The Foreign Office, therefore, lost no time in asking the Viceroy of India whether 400 men, Sikhs or Punjabis preferred, could be recruited for Uganda on the same terms as those supplied for British Central Africa. In March, 1898, Captain J. T. Evatt was appointed to raise the first Indian Contingent, 400 strong, for service in the Uganda Protectorate. Throughout June and July, operations continued in Bunyoro against those chiefs who supported the rebellion. In July, the mutineers who had built another stockade near Mruli, showed fresh signs of aggression. To prevent their escape across the Nile a force assembled in secret on the further bank. Under the cover of darkness, they surprised and overcame an enemy Piquet on a hill overlooking the mutineer's fort. At daylight on 4TH August, the stockade was bombarded and stormed, 40 mutineers being killed and two men of the Uganda Rifles slightly wounded. This ended the main operations against the mutineers; Macdonald reported that they had fought five major and seven minor engagements, and 35 skirmishes. Altogether, some 2,000 troops had been employed and 3,000 Buganda auxiliaries equipped with firearms. Supported by a hastily raised body of several thousand carriers, these troops made many arduous marches throughout an area exceeding 40,000 square miles. Seven Europeans and 280 Indians and Africans were killed and five Europeans and 555 Indians and Africans were wounded during the mutiny operations. In his final despatch, Major Macdonald stated, 'The detachment of Sikhs, men selected from 14TH and 15TH Sikhs, fought with such determined and conspicuous gallantry as to add to the already high reputation of these regiments.'

The arduous nature of the campaigning in Uganda can be visualized from the following description written by one of the officers who took part. "Passing through one of these swamps is a most tiring experience. Now clutching hold of the papyrus at the side, now stepping from one bit of floating vegetation to another, one tries in vain to save oneself from sinking deeper than necessary, until at last a treacherous root gives way, and down one goes into a quagmire of evil-smelling mud and water, only to recommence the whole process again. Except where the papyrus and weeds have been beaten down in forming a passage across them, there is no water to be seen and from a distance one of these sluggish River swamps appears like a beautiful green lawn of varying shades. This appearance is in reality caused by the great heads of the papyrus with their innumerable little delicate spikes, supported four or five feet above the level of the marsh by the long thin stems growing out of the tangled mass of vegetation, the troops made many arduous marches throughout an area exceeding 40,000 square miles. At midnight on 31ST December 1901 'Uganda Rifles', had ceased to exist; the formation of the King's African Rifles (KAR) began a moment later.

Kings African Rifles

On 1ˢᵀ January 1902, the Kings African Rifles came into being, with the original forces of the protectorates incorporated as follows: -

1ˢᵀ (Central Africa) Battalion,	(Formerly 1 C.A.R.)
2ᴺᴰ (Central Africa) Battalion,	(Formerly 2 C.A.R.)
3ᴿᴰ (East Africa) Battalion,	(Formerly 2 E.A.R.)
4ᵀᴴ (Uganda) Battalion	(Formerly Uganda Rifles)
5ᵀᴴ (Uganda) Battalion	(Formerly Uganda Rifles)
6ᵀᴴ (Somaliland) Battalion	(Formed in 1904)

We will only record the military history of the units in which the Sikh soldier was present at that moment.

British Somaliland

1884, Britain declared a protectorate over northern Somaliland. The emergence in 1900 of Muhammad Abdille Hassan (the "Mad Mullah") and his band of dervishes represented a serious challenge to colonial rule in British Somaliland.

The Mullah's repeated raids into British territory induced the Government, at the end of 1900, to sanction the raising of a local force for the defence of the Protectorate. At this time, the Mullah's force was reported to consist of some 1,200 horsemen and 6,000 foot, with about 300 rifles between them. A defence force under Lieutenant Colonel Swayne was raised, consisting of a Camel Corps of 100 men, Mounted Infantry of 400 and two corps of 500 Infantry each. With this force and with the co-operation of the Ethiopians in the east, the Mullah was driven into the Dolbahanta country. The enemy's strength at this time was estimated at about 5,000 men. In April 1901, Colonel Swayne moved to Burao, which was made an advance base; from there he advanced to Samala, where he built a *Zariba`* (an enclosure of bushes or stakes protecting a campsite) which he garrisoned with a force of 470 men. The main body then pushed on towards the Mullah's position, which side stepped the advance and delivered three determined attacks on the *Zariba* at Samala. The Mullah's forces were beaten off with the loss of 600 killed and wounded. As they retreated, they were intercepted at Odergoeh by the main column and their retreat became a rout as they fled over the border to Mudug.

In December 1901, the Mullah once again entered the Protectorate, where his force was daily increasing. Caravans of rifles, smuggled into the country through Mijertein ports, were reported to be reaching him at Mudug. Colonel Swayne, with a force of 1,200 infantry and 70 mounted troops, reinforced by 300 men from 2ᴺᴰ Battalion, Kings African Rifles, and the secondment of Sikh signallers from 5ᵀᴴ Battalion, Kings African Rifles, and the Sikh Contingent of Central African Rifles, he moved to Burao. On 26ᵀᴴ May, he marched south from Burao with the largest force he could muster. The authorities in Central Africa were asked by the Foreign Office to dispatch an officer and 60 Sikhs, with a maxim gun to garrison Berbera and other posts on the line of communication.

Kings African Rifles

British Somaliland

In October, Colonel Swayne commenced his advance on Mudug, and while advancing through the thick dense bush at Erigo, the Mullah's Dervishes attacked his force. They were attacked from all sides by riflemen and spearmen and some of the Somali Levies panicked, but the Sikhs and companies of Kings African Rifles stood firm. When the enemy had been driven off, most of the scattered camels and their loads were recovered, but the Dervishes carried off a maxim gun, which had been dropped by its bearers during the action. To drive the Mullah out of the Mudug area reinforcements from British Central Africa, East Africa, Aden, and India were ordered to embark for Somaliland. By the end of 1902, British forces totalled 2,674 ranks. As soon as a flying column could be ready, Bohotle, which was surrounded by hostile Piquets, was relieved and garrisoned Central African contingent of Sikhs. The column was further strengthened by two guns of a battery of 7-pounders loaned from Aden. 21 Sikhs of the Indian Contingent, who proved themselves excellent gunners, served them, and the unit was known as Kings African Rifles Camel Battery.

On 17TH April, Lieutenant Colonel Cobbe was commanding a Flying Column ahead of the main body moving against the Mullah. He had orders to secure the water supply at Wardair. Having established a *Zariba*, (a camp fortified with a thorn hedge) near Gumburu, he sent forward 'A' Company 2ND Battalion Kings African Rifles, 48 men of 2ND Sikh Regiment and two maxim guns under Lieutenant Colonel Plunkett to secure the return of a small scouting party. Colonel Plunkett, in his eagerness to engage the enemy, was drawn on to a distance of four miles from the *Zariba* where he was attacked by the whole of the Mullah's force, numbering perhaps some 14,000 men. The British column of 224 of all ranks had apparently formed three sides of a square in single rank on the march out, with the Sikhs in the front face. Afterwards a half company was thrown across the rear face. The troops were attacked by about 4,000 horsemen and 10,000 warriors, apparently commanded by the Mullah in person. With the fanatical contempt for death that they always showed in his presence, the dervishes swept from all sides upon the square, first horsemen, then riflemen on foot, and finally hordes of spearmen who broke into the square with the weight of their headlong rush, heedless of the devastating fire of maxims and rifles. All were successfully repelled until the ammunition ran out. The Sikhs had taken with them 100 rounds per rifle in their pouches. There was no reserve ammunition. Moreover, the Sikhs used solid bullets not suited to stop a charging savage. When the ammunition started to run out the order was given to breakout with the bayonet and charge back to the *Zariba*. Plunket was killed and the little force was borne down and overwhelmed. No European or Sikh survived the fight.

Kings African Rifles

British Somaliland

On 22ND April, a column of 213 all ranks, which included 85 Sikhs of the Central African rifles, under the command of Major Gough, advanced and established a base at Danot. From Danot Major Gough decided to push on to Daratoleh, which was held by a strong force of the enemy. The column had not marched far before the mounted infantry fought an action against the Mullah's scouts and reported a large enemy force in front. Gough at once dismounted his men and formed a square with the Camels in the centre. The ground was dead flat; with thorn bush 15-20 feet high. A short period of extreme tension followed and then the attack broke in a sudden uproar of rifle fire from the long grass and thorn bush, at a range of 20-50 yards. The attack continued for three hours, while the square remained steady and the Maxim guns were moved by the Sikhs from point to point to counter each threat as it developed. As the ammunition was running short, Gough decided to retire. Just then, the Dervishes were apparently reinforced as their assault, which had gradually slackened, was suddenly renewed. Throughout the afternoon the retirement continued, the Dervishes continually harassed the flanks and the rear. They were driven off by repeated bayonet charges. During the retreat Captain Bruce fell shot through the body. Major Walker, Sergeant Nderamani, and a Corporal of 2ND Battalion K.A.R., Lance-Naik Maieya Singh of the Central African Rifles and Sowar Umar Ismail of 6TH Battalion K.A.R remained behind to fight off the Dervishes pressing around them. For the parts they had played in this action, Rolland and Walker and later Gough were awarded the Victoria Cross, the men of the K.A.R., the African D.C.M. and Lance-Naik Maieya Singh the I.O.M. British casualties were six officers and 38 other ranks killed or wounded, whilst the Dervishes lost about 150 killed or wounded.

After these reverses, British prestige was at stake and forces were increased to more than 8,000 troops, were employed, in the hope that the Mullah's power would be permanently shattered. The enemy's force was concentrated at Jidballi, where the Mullah received a most crushing defeat. Edgerton described the disciplined fire of the Sikhs and K.A.R. as 'terrific'. The Mullah's casualties in the actual fight at Jidballi was very large, and the morale of his Dervishes as a fighting body had been destroyed, and their numbers, estimated at 6,000 to 8,000 before Jidballi, could not have exceeded 800 on the conclusion of the campaign.

In March 1905, the Illig or Pestalozza Agreement was concluded between the Italian Government and the Mullah, whereby peace was declared between the Dervishes on the one hand and the British and Italian Governments on the other. The Mullah was assigned a port and certain territories in Italian Somaliland, beyond which he and his Dervishes undertook not to encroach. The Mullah also agreed to become an Italian protected subject. This agreement was, however, nullified soon after it was concluded, as the Mullah left Italian territory, and by 1907 had re-established himself on the British side, raiding and looting everywhere.

Kings African Rifles

British Somaliland

The Mullah had built a series of forts on the plateau of the Burao range. The Burao range rises a sheer 1,100 feet out of the plain and is intersected with deep ravines covered everywhere with boulders and thick scrub. The forts are remarkably well sited and very strong. The walls are 9 to 12 feet thick at the base, 16 to 20 feet high, and 24 feet wide, provided with well made machicouli galleries, but badly constructed loopholes, and each fort is capable of holding between 50 and 70 men. The sides of the cliffs are honeycombed with caves, some of which are capable of containing 100 men and animals. The attack was well executed; 60 to 70 dervishes fled out of the fort and down the hill, suffering some casualties. A fort in the Valley near the wells and 800 feet below my position was shelled, whereupon the enemy evacuated the forts and caves in the valley and fled eastwards. The troops were not in sufficient strength to leave a post at Shimber Berris, and, as anticipated, the Dervishes returned in about a fortnight. The General Commanding Officer Aden placed an officer with thirteen men, of 23RD Sikh Pioneers at our disposal. So I was enabled to concentrate a force, partly mounted and partly dismounted, of 15 officers, 570 rank and file, (Sikhs and Somalis), six machine guns and two guns in the neighbourhood of Shimber Berris on 2ND February. On 3RD February, I advanced in two columns against the forts of the Burao. Although the Dervishes had commenced construction of new forts, the hilltop was unoccupied and the Sikh Pioneers blew up the forts. The following morning, 4TH February, the column was transferred from south to north of the Burao by a pass seven miles west of Shimber Berris and was concentrated on the plain close to that place by noon. The enemy were holding two forts overlooking and flanking a deep Nullah and a fort at the far end of the Nullah, also in occupation of the numerous caves in the hillsides.

The two flanking forts were captured after two hours fighting, but the enemy developed a heavy fire from the caves, and from the middle and the vicinity of the fort. The guns were brought forward and with machine guns engaged the middle fort and the caves at close range. The enemy's fire slackened, and the Dervishes were observed to be evacuating the fort and retiring southwards up the ravine. The Sikh Pioneers to place a charge of guncotton against the door, under a hot fire from the occupants inside. The fort and its defenders were blown up, hand grenades were thrown into caves, known still to be occupied, and the two flanking forts were blown up. The next morning all the caves were found to be evacuated. Leaving a tribal post at Shimber Berris, the column returned to Burao on 7TH and 9TH February.'

Mullah died at the age of 56 in November 1920 and thus ended the life of a man who for twenty years had fought great odds and managed to elude all the forces the British and Ethiopians could deploy against him.

Eventually the various Battalions of the Kings African Rifles became the nucleolus of the Armies of their respective countries.

Free Indian Legion

Indische Freiwillegen - Legion Regiment 950

The troops of the Free India Legion were derived from Indian prisoners of war captured during the battles for Tobruk. They were flown to Berlin in May 1941. Initially they were set up in Annaburg, and then transferred to Frankenberg Camp, from where they were sent to Konigsberg for training and induction. It was at Konigsberg that uniforms were issued, in German Fieldgrau with the badge of the leaping tiger of Azad Hind.

The legion was transferred to Zeeland in Netherlands in April 1943 as part of the Atlantic Wall duties, and to France in September 1943, attached to 344 Infanterie Division, and later the 159 Infanterie Division of the Wehrmacht.

The 1ST Battalion was reassigned to Zandvoort in May 1943 where they stayed until relieved by Georgian troops in August. In September the battalion was deployed on the Atlantic coast of Bordeaux on the Bay of Biscay. The 2ND Battalion moved to the island of Texel in May 1943 and stayed there until relieved in September of that year. From here it was deployed to Les Salles D'Ollonne in France. The 3RD battalion remained at Oldebrook as corps reserve till the end of September 1943.

Indische Freiwillegen Legion Der Waffen SS

The legion was stationed in the Lacanau region of Bordeaux at the time of the Normandy landings and remained there for four months after D-Day. On the 8TH August its control was transferred to the Waffen SS. On 15TH August 1944, the unit pulled out of Lacanau to make its way back to Germany. On the journey from Poiter to Chatrou it suffered casualties while engaging French regular troops in the town of Dun. The unit also engaged against Allied Armour at Nuis St.Georges while retreating across the Loir to Dijon, and was regularly harassed by the French Resistance. The unit moved from Remisemont, through Alsace, to Oberhohofen near the town of Heuberg in Germany in the winter of 1944, where it stayed till March 1945.

The 2ND Battalion, 9TH Company, of the Legion also saw action in Italy. Having been deployed in the spring of 1944, it faced the British 5TH Corps and the Polish 2ND Corps before it was withdrawn from the front to be used in anti partisan operations. It surrendered to the allied forces in April 1945, still in Italy.

With the defeat of the Third Reich imminent in May 1945, the Indian Legion sought sanctuary in neutral Switzerland. The remainder of the unit undertook a desperate march along the shores of Lake Constance, attempting to enter Switzerland via the Alpine Passes. This was, however, unsuccessful and the Legion was captured by the US and French forces and delivered to British and Indian forces in Europe.

They would be later shipped back to India where a number of the troops would stand trial for treason.

Azad Hind Fauj

Azad Hind Fauj
The Azad Hind Fauj or 'The Indian National Army' (I.N.A.) was an armed force formed during World War Two with the aim to overthrow the British rule in colonial India. Initially it was composed of Indian prisoners of war captured by the Japanese in Malaya and Singapore. Significant portions were also recruited from Indian civilians in Japanese controlled Malaya and Burma.

The hostilities had started with the German invasion of Poland on 1ST September 1939. The United Kingdom declared war against Germany. India, then ruled by the British, automatically joined in the war under the governor general's proclamation of 3RD September 1939. While the smaller Indian political parties such as the Muslim League, Hindu Maha Sabha and the Shiromani Akali Dal were prepared to support government's war effort, Indian National Congress refused to cooperate.

A resolution passed by its Working Committee on 15TH September 1939, and subsequently endorsed by the All India Congress Committee and the plenary session of the Congress, declared: "India's sympathy is entirely on the side of democracy and freedom, but India cannot associate herself with a war said to be for democratic freedom when that very freedom is denied to her..." The resolution demanded that the British government pronounce in unequivocal terms their war aims and "in particular how those aims are going to apply to India and to be given effect to in the present." Congress led ministries in eight of the provinces resigned and the party planned a programme of individual Satyagraha or protest. In fact a group of left wingers in the Congress had already formed a separate party, the Forward Block, under the leadership of Subhas Chandra Bose. This group wanted to take advantage of the situation and to intensify their struggle for independence.

Subhas Chandra Bose was arrested on 2ND July 1940. He went on an indefinite hunger strike on 29TH November and was released on 5TH December, but was kept under police surveillance in his ancestral house in Calcutta. Giving the police the slip, Bose reached Berlin on 28TH March 1941 after a hazardous journey through north India, Kabul and Moscow.

Subhas Chandra's call to Indian prisoners of war was well received and 1,200 men, mostly Sikhs, were recruited during the first six months for a training camp set up at Frankenberg. This camp was the precursor of the Azad Hind Fauj. It was initially named Lashkar-i-Hind or Indian Legion and its strength in the West rose in due course to 4,500. The name of the political organization corresponding to the Indian Independence League in the East was the Free India Centre.

Japan's entry into the War on 8TH December 1941 and her rapid conquest of Malaya and Singapore, with Thailand's capitulation into neutrality, radically changed the situation so far as India was concerned. Certain Indian nationalist sections such as the Socialist Party and Forward Bloc entertained hopes of liberating the country with the Japanese help.

Azad Hind Fauj

Azad Hind Fauj
Indians, mainly Sikhs, living in Malaya, Singapore and other countries of the region had set up two secret anti British groups, led by Giani Pritam Singh and Swami Satyananda Puri, respectively. Major Fujiwara, a Japanese officer, head of the field intelligence section, had even before the declaration of war by Japan, contacted Giani Pritam Singh and reached an agreement of collaboration with him at Bangkok on 4TH December 1941. Following the Japanese advance in North Malaya, Fujiwara and Pritam Singh reached Alorstar on 14TH December 1941 for discussions.

On 17TH February 1942, one of Japanese the prisoners, Captain Mohan Singh of the 14TH Punjab Regiment, was appointed the leader of the movement. Kuala Lumpur fell on 11TH January 1942 with 3,500 Indian prisoners of war and Singapore on 15TH February 1942, with 85,000 troops of whom 45,000 were Indians. Mohan Singh asked for volunteers who would form the Azad Hind Fauj to fight for freeing India from the British yoke.

A large number, again mostly Sikhs, came forward. Mohan Singh established his headquarters at Neeson in Singapore with Lt Col. Niranjan Singh Gill as Chief of Staff, Lt. Col. J.K. Bhonsle as Adjutant and Quarter master General and Lt. Col. A.C. Chatterjee as Director of Medical Services. The Azad Hind Fauj, however, was formally established on 1ST September 1942 by which date 40,000 prisoners of war had signed a pledge to join it.

Meanwhile another organization, Indian Independence League, had materialized under the leadership of Rash Behari Bose, veteran Indian revolutionary, who had escaped to Japan in June 1915 and become a Japanese citizen. He arranged two conferences of Indians in the East to discuss political issues. During the Tokyo Conference, on 30TH March 1942, besides establishing the Indian Independence League, resolved to form an Indian National Army. The Bangkok Conference, on 23RD June 1942, formally inaugurated the Indian Independence League adopting the Congress tricolour as its flag. One of the 35 resolutions passed by it invited Subhas Chandra Bose to East Asia.

Through another resolution Captain Mohan Singh was appointed commander in chief of the Indian National Army. The Indian Independence League established a Council of Action, with Rash Behari Bose as president and Mohan Singh as one of the four members with charge of the military department. News of the Quit India movement launched by the Congress Party in India in August 1942 afforded further encouragement, and the Azad Hind Fauj was formally inaugurated on 1ST September 1942.

Difficulties, however, arose soon after. Mohan Singh (now General) was disillusioned regarding the intentions of the Japanese, who wanted to use the Indian National Army only as a pawn and a propaganda tool. He was also dissatisfied with the functioning of the Council of Action and the Indian Independence League, who failed to secure Japanese recognition and official proclamation regarding the existence of the Fauj.

Azad Hind Fauj

Azad Hind Fauj
The other members of the Council of Action, on the other hand, were unhappy with Mohan Singh for his arbitrariness in military matters. The crisis came on 8TH December 1942 when the Japanese arrested Colonel Niranjan Singh Gill branding him to be a British agent, without informing General Mohan Singh, whose protest was ignored and who was not even allowed to see Colonel Gill. On the same day the three civilian members of the Council of Action resigned. On 29TH December 1942, General Mohan Singh was subsequently arrested by the Japanese and exiled to Palau Ubin, an island off of Singapore. Thousands of INA soldiers returned to the status of POWs again.

The Indian National Army was disarmed. Efforts to revive it were made by Rash Behari Bose who appointed a committee of administration to manage its affairs. Subhas Chandra Bose, popularly called Netaji (lit. respected leader), left Europe on 8TH February 1943 and arrived at Tokyo on 13TH June 1943. After discussing matters with the Japanese Prime Minister, General Tojo, he came to Singapore on 2ND July 1943. Two days later Rash Behari Bose handed over the leadership of the Indian Independence League to him. On 5TH July 1943 Netaji revived the Azad Hind Fauj, giving it the battle cry "Chalo Delhi" ("March to Delhi") and the salutation "Jai Hind" ("Victory to India").

On 23 October 1943 he proclaimed the setting up of the Provisional Government of Azad Hind, which was recognized within a few days by nine countries, including Japan, Italy and Germany. On 6TH November 1943, the Japanese premier announced the handing over of the Andaman and Nicobar Islands to the Provisional Government. Netaji organized the Fauj into three brigades for taking part in Japan`s offensive campaign on India`s eastern borders. After initial hesitation of the Japanese field commander, Field Marshal Terauchi, to associate Indians with actual fighting, it was agreed to employ one brigade, as a trial, attaching smaller Indian detachments to different units of the Japanese army as irregulars.

Accordingly, a new brigade of three battalions was raised by selecting the best soldiers out of the other three. Commanded by General Shah Nawaz Khan, its 1ST Battalion operated on the Arakan front and had its first notable success in May 1944 when it captured the British post of Mowdok in the Indian territory, about 80 km to the east of Cox Bazaar, and holding it till September 1944 in the face of repeated counterattacks by British forces. The other two battalions also gave a good account of themselves in Falam and Haka area. Meanwhile, Subhas Chandra Bose had brought forward his headquarters to Rangoon.

An Officers Training School for INA officers, led by Habib ur Rahman, and the Azad School for the civilian volunteers were set up to provide training to the recruits. A youth wing of the INA, composed of 45 Young Indians personally chosen by Bose and affectionately known as the Tokyo Boys, were also sent to Japan's Imperial Military Academy to train as fighter pilots.

Azad Hind Fauj

Azad Hind Fauj
Also, possibly the first time in Asia, and even the only time outside the USSR, a women's regiment, the Rani of Jhansi regiment was raised as a combat force. The plans decided between Bose and Kawabe envisaged the INA was to be assigned an independent sector of its own in the U Go offensive and no INA unit was to operate less than battalion strength. For operational purposes, the Subhas Brigade was assigned under the command of the Japanese general Headquarters in Burma. Advance parties of the Bahadur Group also went forward with the advanced Japanese units early during the offensive. As Japan opened its offensive towards India, the INA's first division, consisting of four Guerrilla regiments, was divided between the diversionary Ha Go offensive in Arakan 1944, with one battalion reaching as far as Mowdok in Chittagong. A Bahadur group unit, led by Shaukat Malik, took the border enclave of Moirang in early April. The main body of the first division was however committed to the U Go Offensive directed towards Manipur, initially successfully protecting the Japanese flanks against Chin and Kachin guerrillas as the Mutaguchi's three divisions crossed the Chindwin River and the Naga Hills, and later directed towards the main offensive through Tamu in the direction of Imphal and Kohima. However, by the time Khan's forces left Tamu, the offensive had been held, and the troops were redirected to Kohima. By the time Khan's forces reached Ukhrul in the vicinity of Kohima, Japanese forces had begun their withdrawal from Kohima. The first division suffered the same fate as did Mutaguchi's Army when the siege of Imphal was broken. With little or no supplies and supply lines deluged by the Monsoon, harassed by Allied air-dominance and local Burmese irregulars, the INA began withdrawing with the 15TH Army. The INA suffered terrible fate as wounded, starved and diseased men succumbed during the hasty withdrawal into Burma. The INA lost a substantial amount of men and materiel in the retreat, and a number of units were disbanded or used to feed the newly formed units of the second division.

As the allied Burma campaign began the following year, however, the INA remained committed to the defence of Burma, and was a part of the Japanese defensive deployments. The second division, tasked with the defence of Irrawaddy and the adjoining areas around Nyaungu was instrumental in opposing Messervy's 7TH Indian Division when it attempted to cross the river at Pagan and Nyaungu during Irrawaddy operations. Later, during the Battles of Meiktilla and Mandalay, the 2ND division was instrumental in denying the British 17TH Division the area around Mount Popa that would have exposed the Flank of Kimura's forces attempting to retake Meiktilla and Nyaungu. Ultimately however, the division was obliterated. As the Japanese situation became precarious, Azad Hind withdrew from Rangoon with Ba Maw's government and the Japanese forces for Singapore along with the remnants of the first division and the Rani of Jhansi Regiment. Nearly 6000 troops amongst the surviving units of the Army remained in Rangoon and surrendered as Rangoon fell.

Azad Hind Fauj

Azad Hind Fauj
Rangoon was occupied by the British early in May 1945. On 16TH May, Shah Nawaz, Gurbaksh Singh Dhillon and many other officers and men of the Azad Hind Fauj surrendered at Pegu in Lower Burma where after the Azad Hind Fauj ceased to exist. The War ended with Japan's surrender on 14TH August 1945. Subhas Chandra Bose died in an air crash on 18TH August 1945. Officers and men of the Indian National Army were brought back to India and were interrogated and divided into three categories: white or loyal in their allegiance to the British throughout; grey or those whose loyalty was doubtful; and black or those who admitted that they had joined the Azad Hind Fauj.

The white were reinstated with benefits of seniority and arrears of pay; the greys were kept under observation, and were later graded into either white or black. The black were summarily dismissed and their arrears of pay and allowances were confiscated. Mohan Singh and Niranjan Singh Gill were set free. Shah Nawaz Khan, Gurbaksh Singh Dhillon and Prem K. Sehgal were, as a test case, put on trial in open court in the Red Fort at Delhi.

They were charged with treason and with waging war against the King. This aroused within India wide sympathy for them. The INA trials that attracted more attention in India than the war time activities of the unit. The decision to hold the trial in public became a rallying point for the independence movement so much so that the release of INA prisoners and suspension of the trials came to be the dominant political campaign in precedence over the campaign for Freedom. Newspaper reports around November 1945 reported executions of INA troops, which deteriorated already volatile situations. Opposition to the trial of the officers for treason became a major public and political campaign, and the very opening of the first trial saw violence and series of riots in a scale later described as sensational. It also saw a campaign that defied communal barriers. The trial began on 5TH November 1945. Eminent lawyers and public men such as Tej Bahadur Sapru, Bhulabhai Desai and Jawaharlal Nehru defended the accused in court. There were riots in their favour in several places between 21ST and 24TH November. The court on 31ST December 1945 sentenced all the three to transportation for life. The government, however, yielded to the outburst of popular sympathy and the British commander in chief, Sir Claude Auchinleck, quashed the sentence on review.

On 3RD January 1946, Prem Kumar Sehgal, Gurbaksh Singh Dhillon and Shah Nawaz Khan, quietly emerged from imprisonment in Old Delhi's Red Fort. They were leading officers of the Indian National Army and had been in the vanguard of Subhas Chandra Bose's renegade force. Now they were free men and, within days, found themselves national heroes. People interpreted their release as a decisive victory against the British Raj. The trials had been a disaster for the British rulers and had gripped the imagination of the Indian people.

Azad Hind Fauj

Azad Hind Fauj

As the word spread of the men's release they were swept along the cramped streets of Old Delhi in a growing tide of supporters, cheered and hoisted on shoulders, and everybody clamoured to shake their hands. Indian National Congress politicians rushed to the scene to be among the first to congratulate them. Over the coming days, the men paraded around Delhi, Lahore and across the country. Everywhere they went admires mobbed them, thrust forward autograph books and strong heavy garlands of flowers around their necks.

The Red Fort, the sandstone fortress built by the Mughal emperors in the heart of New Delhi, was a spectacularly ill-chosen as the location for the trial. The fort, which had been used as a barracks by the Indian Army ever since the Sepoy Mutiny of 1857, was the symbolic seat of South Asian power. So, too, the British decision to try the three officers together, a Sikh, a Hindu and a Muslim. This just added piquancy to the symbolism of the event. The Congress Party used the trials as a way to try to build pan-religious solidarity and some of the finest legal minds in the country had represented the men as their defence barristers.

The vehement outpourings of anger that greeted the INA trials, and widespread rejoicing at the release of the prosecuted men, were the hardened form of nationalism. Everywhere there was a new belief in the power of violence to release India from colonial control, and an upsurge of post-war euphoria which gripped civilians and soldiers alike. Policemen, Magistrates and Military Generals became reluctant to intervene in a cause which had captured the imagination of people of all regional and religious backgrounds. Military commanders of the Indian Army had feared mutiny if the INA men received the death sentence. As it was, over 20,000 members of the Royal Indian Navy would mutiny during the coming weeks in any case.

The upsurge of political zeal was inextricably linked with ongoing demobilisation. As over 2 million soldiers were demobilised from the Indian with everything that had gone before and the Imperial rule had lost its final shreds of legitimacy. Army in the aftermath of the war, and began to return to their villages, they started to ask how they would be rewarded for their sacrifice during the war. This was the moment the British rule in India became untenable. It marked a decisive break

Prem Kumar Sehgal, once Military secretary to Subhas Bose, explained that although the war itself hung in balance and nobody was sure if the Japanese would win, initiating a popular revolution with grass-root support within India would ensure that even if Japan lost the war ultimately, Britain would not be in a position to re-assert its colonial authority, which was ultimately the aim of the Azad Hind Fauj.

The Independence of India arrived in 1947.
Rarely have the vanquished helped win so much.

Indian Long Range Squadron

The ILRS formed in January 1942, at Damascus in Syria, under the umbrella of the Indian Armoured Corps. It was modeled on the Long Range Desert Group, and composed almost entirely of Indian volunteers from the 2nd Royal Lancers (Gardner's Horse), PAVO Cavalry (11TH Frontier Force) and 18TH King Edward VII's Own Cavalry. All three regiments were then serving together in the 3rd Indian Motor Brigade. It was designed for operating behind enemy lines in Syria, Iraq and Persia in case of a Nazi attack through the Balkans into the Middle East.

In May 1942, two ILRS patrols were attached to the LRDG in the desert for operational experience. In October 1942, the whole ILRS came under command LRDG, operating behind enemy lines from Siwa, Kufra and Hon on similar tasks to those allotted to the LRDG. It was attached to General Leclerc during the march north through the Fezzan to Tripoli. Following the Battle of the Mareth Line in 1943, the Squadron was released from the LRDG by FM Montgomery and sent to India as it was unlikely to find further scope for its activities in the country the Eighth Army was then entering (North Tunisia).

After a period spent at Ferozepore in India, the ILRS was deployed to Zahidan, Baluchistan and Persia where it saw the war out patrolling the volatile Persian/Afghan/Russian border to discourage any Soviet infiltration into this oil-rich border region

The ILRS was disbanded in 1947 when India was partitioned. The Jats, Rajputs and Sikhs of 'J', 'R' and 'S' Patrols went to the 2nd Royal Lancers, 3rd Cavalry and 18th K.E.O. Cavalry, allotted to India. The Muslims of 'M' Patrol were absorbed into the PAVO Cavalry (Frontier Force), allotted to Pakistan.

Sikh officer of Indian Long Range Squadron

Appendix

Indian Order of Merit

The East India Company first introduced this medal in 1837 and it was proposed for "conspicuous gallantry in the field". The Indian Order of Merit was the highest gallantry award available to Indian soldiers between 1837 and 1911, when the eligibility for the Victoria Cross was extended to Indian officers and men. The Indian Order of Merit ranks high among the oldest and most venerable of decorations for bravery, pre-dating the Victoria Cross by nineteen years and the United State's 'Medal of Honour' by twenty-four years. The order was removed when India became independent in 1947.

Victoria Cross

The Victoria Cross (VC) is the highest recognition for valour "in the face of the enemy" that can be awarded to members of the British and some Commonwealth armed forces (British Empire personnel prior to the Commonwealth). In 1911 King George V extended this to include officers and men of the Indian Army. Previously the equivalent award for which these soldiers were eligible was the Indian Order of Merit.

Indian Distinguished Service Medal

Instituted in 1907, the Indian Distinguished Service Medal was awarded for distinguished services in the field for Indian commissioned and non-commissioned officers and men of the Indian regular forces. The order was removed when India became independent in 1947.

Military Cross

The Military Cross is awarded to commissioned officers of the substantive rank of Captain or below or Warrant Officers for distinguished and meritorious services in battle. "…gallantry during active operations against the enemy."

Distinguished Service Order

The Distinguished Service Order is a military decoration awarded for distinguished leadership during active operations against the enemy.

Order of the British Empire

The Most Excellent Order of the British Empire is a British order of chivalry established on 4TH June 1917 by King George V for those who have played a distinguished role in any field in their region or country. Appointments are made on the advice of the governments of the United Kingdom and some Commonwealth realms.

Military Medal

Awarded to non-commissioned officers and men of the army for individual or associated acts of bravery brought to notice by recommendation of a commander-in-chief in the field

Bibliography

Ahmad R.N. (2006) *Unfaded Glory*, The 8TH Punjab Regiment, The Naval &Military Press, Uckfield.

Anderson R.H., 45TH Rattray's Sikhs, 1 (Reprint) The Naval &Military Press, Uckfield.

Anon, *History of the Guides,* Part 1 (Reprint) The Naval &Military Press, Uckfield.

Anon. (1938) *History of the Guides 1846 – 1922*. Gale and Polden: Aldershot.

Betham Geoffrey, (1956) *The Golden Galley,* The Story of the Second Punjab Regiment, Oxford University Press

Bird wood, F. T. (1950) *The Sikh Regiment in the Second World War.* Jarrod & Sons: Norwich

Condon W.E.H., *The Frontier Force Rifles*, (Reprint) The Naval &Military Press, Uckfield.

Corrigan Gordon, (1999) Sepoys in the Trenches, Spellmount Ltd. Kent

Dhesi N.S. (2010) *Sikh Soldier, Battle Honours*, The Naval &Military Press, Uckfield.

Dhesi N.S. (2010) *Sikh Soldier, Gallantry Awards*, 1 (Reprint) The Naval &Military Press, Uckfield.

Dhesi N.S. (2012) *Sikh Soldier, Warriors & Generals*, The Naval &Military Press, Uckfield.

Dhesi N.S. (2013) *Sikh Soldier, Policing the Empire*, The Naval &Military Press,

Dhesi N.S. (2014) *Sikh Soldier, At War,* The Naval &Military Press, Uckfield.

Doulton (1951) *Fighting Cock,* 23RD Indian Division, Gale and Polden, Aldershot.

Duckers, Peter. (1999) *Reward of Valour, I.O.M.* Jade Publishing Ltd.: Lancashire

Fanshawe H.D., (1917) *The 18TH Indian Division,* in Mesopotamia, 1 (Reprint) The Naval &Military Press, Uckfield.

G. S. Sandhu, (1981) *The Indian Cavalry*, Vision Books, New Delhi, India

G. S. Sandhu, (1987) *The Indian Armour*, Vision Books, New Delhi, India

General Staff, Army Headquarters, India. (1921) *Operations in Waziristan, 1919-1920*. Superintendent Government Printing: Calcutta.

Government of India. (1942) *The Tiger Strikes*. Government of India: Calcutta.

Government of India. (1944).*The Tiger Kills*. HMSO: London.

Government of India. (1946) *The Tiger Triumphs*. HMSO: London.

Grant, Sir James Hope. (1875) *Incidents in the China War of 1860*. Blackwood and Sons: London.

Bibliography

Heath, I. (1999) *The North East Frontier*. Osprey Publishing Ltd.: Oxford.

History of the Sarawak Rangers (1981) Malaysian Armed Forces College

Hudson H. *History of the 19TH KGO Lancers*, The Naval &Military Press, Uckfield.

India Army Intelligence Branch, (2006) *Frontier and Overseas Expeditions from India,* (Vol.V1). The Naval and Military Press Ltd.: Uckfield.

John Gaylor, (1992) *Sons of John Company*, Spellmount Ltd. Kent. UK.

Kirby Woodburn, *History of the Second World War,* 5 Volumes, The Naval &Military Press, Uckfield.

Lawford J.P., (1967) Solah Punjab, The History of the 16TH Punjab Regiment, Gale and Polden, Aldershot, UK.

M.I. Qureshi, (1958) *The First Punjabis*, Gale and Polden, Aldershot, UK.

Macmunn, Sir George, *History of the Guides*, Part 11, (Reprint) The Naval &Military Press, Uckfield.

Macmunn, Sir George, (1936) *The History of the Sikh Pioneers*. Sampson Low, Marston and Co. Ltd.: London.

McLYnn Frank, (2010), *The Burma Campaign*, The Bodley Head, London

Moyse-Bartlett, H. (2002) *The King's African Rifles* 1 (Reprint) The Naval &Military Press, Uckfield.

Nevill, H. L. (2005) *Campaigns on the North–West Frontier*. The Naval &Military Press, Uckfield.

Norie E.W.M., (1903), *Military Operations in China.* 1 (Reprint) The Naval &Military Press, Uckfield.

Page, Malcolm. (1998) *K.A.R. A history of The Kings African Rifle*. Leo Cooper: South Yorkshire.

Raj Kumar, (2004) *Military System of the Sikhs*, Commonwealth Publishers, New Delhi.

Renfrew Barry, (2009) *Forgotten Regiments*, Terrier Press, UK

Rutter, Owen. (1922) *British North Borneo*. Constable and Co Ltd.: London.

Shorey, Anil. (2005) *A Legendary Force: 1st Patiala*. Manas Publications: New Delhi.

Singh, Inder. (1965) *History of Malay States Guides*. Cathay Printers Ltd.: Penang.

Stevens G.R. *Fourth Indian Division*, (Reprint) The Naval &Military Press, Uckfield.

Tugwell W.B.P. *History of the Bombay Pioneers,* (Reprint) The Naval &Military Press, UK

Index

1st Patiala Infantry 17
23RD Sikh Pioneers 37
32ND Sikh Pioneers 44
51ST Sikhs 157
52ND Sikhs 166
53RD Sikhs 169
54TH Sikhs 177
55TH Coke's Rifles 199
56TH Punjabi Rifles 203
57TH Punjab Rifles 211
62ND Punjabis 73
66TH Punjabis 79
69TH Punjabis 104
72ND Punjabis 108
74TH Punjabis 115
76TH Punjabis 90
82ND Punjabis 95
87TH Punjabis 116
89TH Punjabis 103
90TH Punjabis 135
91ST Punjabis 142
92ND Punjabis 145
93RD Burma Infantry 149
Abyssinia 37
Ad Teclesan 173
Aden 40
Adriatic front 163
Afghan 169
Afghanistan 283
Afridi 339
Agordat 91
Ahluwalias 9
Ahmad Khel 166
Ahmad Shah 157
Akyab Island 252
Aleppo 115
Alexandria 42
Amir Amanullah 20
Arabs 41
Arakan 77
Ashanti 386

Attariwala Sardars 12
Ayub Khan 39
Aziziya Canal 137
Bala Hissar 187
Barentu 171
Basra 193
Batavia 285
Battle of Hanna 68
Beersheba 129
Bhangis 9
Bhutan 231
Birjand 61
Boxer Rebellion 237
Bozdar 199
Brigadier B S Sidhu 20
British Central Africa 385
Burma 180
Chakdara 18
Chattar Singh Attariwala 12
Chhamb, 23
Chillianwala 13
China 56
Chitral Fort 47
Cis Satluj 8
Cis Satluj Sikhs 16
Subedar Gurbux Singh 246
Colonel Ishar Singh 19
Colonel Nand Singh 24
Ctesiphon 70
Cyprus 173
Dal Khalsa 16
Damascus 91
Dardanelles 129
Datta Khel 153
Delhi 185
Derna 76
Dewanigiri 44
Dologorodoc 91
Donbaik 155
Dujaila 206
Durbar 11

Index

Durrani 9
Dutch 22
Dutch East Indies 78
Duzdab 61
East Africa 109
Egypt 244
El Arish 19
Eritrea 295
Euphrates 314
Fallujah 137
Faridkot Sappers and Miners 34
Gallipoli 104
Gaza 238
General B. S. Sidhu 22
General G. S. Harika 20
German 16
Ghilzais 39
Gorchurra 9
Gothic Line 31
Great Bitter Lake 66
Greece 98
Guides Infantry 162
Gujarat 13
Gurkhas 196
Gustav Line 263
Gyantse 40
Habbaniya 137
Haifa 194
Hajipur 12
Hazara 12
Hindu Kush 46
Hindustani Fanatics 157
Hong Kong 238
Imphal 246
Indonesia 22
Ipoh 133
Iraq 64
Ismailia 66
Italy 93
Japanese 96
Jassa Singh Ahluwalia 32
Java 86

Jhangar 23
Keren 91
Khalsa 343
Khyber Pass 352
King Theodore 303
Kirkuk 116
Kissoue 92
Kohima 242
Kota Bharu 285
Krasnovokdsk 61
Kurdistan 362
Kut-al-Amara 60
Lahore 9
Lebanon 61
Lhasa 40
Libya 90
Lieutenant Bhag Singh 112
Lieutenant Colonel Bishan Singh 34
Lieutenant Colonel Ishar Singh 19,
Lieutenant Jasmer Singh 19
Lieutenant Kalwant Singh 82
Lt Col. Niranjan Singh Gill 396
Lieutenant Sher Singh 197
Loos 219
Mad Mullah 390
Maharaja Ranjit Singh 32
Maharajah Ala Singh 24
Maharajah Dalip Singh 11
Mahsuds 39
Maizar 160
Maj. Gen. Natha Singh 28
Major Amar Singh 163
Major Amrik Singh 184
Major Bhag Singh 113
Major Budh Singh 19
Major Himmat Singh Sandhu 164
Major Inder Singh 31
Major Narain Singh, 376
Major Sarbjit Singh Kalha 83
Malakand 189
Malaya 395
Malerkotla 24

Index

Manipur 84
Manzai 43
Marseilles 57
Massawa 172
Maungdaw 180
Mayu Peninsula 82
Mazhbi Pioneers 36
Megiddo 351
Meshed 359
Mesopotamia 16
Metemma 170
Miranzai 190
Mosul 228
Moulmein 85
Muar 134
Mughal 400
Mulraj 12
Multan 9
Nabha Akal Infantry 30
Naushera 23
Nawab Muzafar Khan 32
Neuve Chapelle 58
New Guinea 118
Operation Gulmarg 23
Orakzai 190
Palestine 193
Panchas 11
Panzer units 93
Pathans 157
Patiala 281
Peiwar Kotal 333
Peking 37
Persia 61
Phulkians 8
Port Said 60
Punjab 72
Punjab Regiments 72
Qantara 104
Ramadi 137
Ramgharias 9
Ramree 97
Rangoon 97

Razmak 153
River Gari 164
River Santerno 165
Rommel 174
Ronconfreddo 94
Russian Turkestan 200
Ruweisat Ridge 102
Salonika 128
Samara 193
Sannaiyat 207
Sardar Charat Singh 34
Sardar Didar Singh 30
Sardar Fateh Singh 32
Sardar Kahan Singh 12
Shabkadar 18
Shaiba 69
Shaikh Othman 206
Sheikh Saad 58
Sher Ali 239
Shimber Berries 41
Sidi Barani 90
Sikh Confederacies 9
Sikh Gorchurra 9
Sikh Kingdom 158
Sikh Princely States Forces 16
Sikkim 45
Singhpuria 9
Sirhind 224
Sittana 301
Somaliland 390
Somaliland Contingent 41
Sudan 190
Suez 19
Suez Canal 19
Sukkarchakkias 10
Sungei Patani 133
Surabaya 114
Syria 140
Taimur Shah 9
Taiping 368
Taranto 140
Tartars 42

Jemadar Nand Singh VC
(11TH Sikh Regiment)

Major Parkash Singh; VC
(8TH Punjab Regiment)

Forgotten Regiments

The history of the Sikh Soldier's battles and campaigns pertain to the bloodstained Mughal period, the tyrannical Afghan period, the feat of arms and the glorious period of the Sikh Empire. The greatest legacy of the Sikh Soldier is the conquest of Hazara and Peshawar and the barring and bolting of the North-West Frontier of India. The Frontier was the main gateway and the first home of all successive waves of invaders from time immemorial that poured into India. It was fated to be a 'perpetual field of battle'. "Maharajah Ranjit Singh had wrested from the Afghans their fairest provinces, not only those east of Indus where Kabul rulers could claim no racial affinity, but Pashawar itself and Bannu, fertile gardens inhabited by proud people of Afghan and Pathan stock." If it were not for this achievement, the entire trans-Indus territories, would have been lost to India forever, and would have remained part of Afghanistan.

At the fall of the Sikh Empire, and the destruction of the Khalsa armies, and with a tradition of soldiering behind him, The Sikh Soldier went soldiering to the far corners of the British Empire. He found employment overseas in two related kinds of imperial enterprise: the initial conquest of new territories, extending the territories of the British Empire, and subsequent suppression of rebellions. The reputation of the Sikh soldier as the premier colonial soldier was so great that from the outset the colonial administrators insisted that Sikhs, and Sikhs alone, must be supplied to them for the paramilitary policing needs of the colonial forces. They were extensively used as the 'Motor Muscle' of imperial authority. Subsequently they trained the native soldiers to meet the requirements of their respective countries.

In the organized regiments of the Indian Army, the Sikh Soldier fought in the majority of the Battles of the British Empire and went on to fight in the trenches of France and Flanders to the sands of the African Sahara, from the deserts of the Middle East to the steaming jungles of Burma.

In August 1947, at the independence and the partition of the Indian subcontinent into the sovereign states of India and Pakistan and the division of the army in 1947, the Punjab and the Frontier Force regiments were allocated to the new Pakistan Army. Whole regiments were escorted across the border and lost to the Sikh Soldier, although the parting was always tearful and emotional.

The Sikh Soldier had left his footprints of glory and sacrifice in the history of these Forgotten Regiments, which are lost to him forever.

Narindar Singh Dhesi is the author of five books on Sikh Soldier i.e. Sikh Soldier: Battle Honours (ISBN 97884574891), Sikh Soldier: Gallantry Awards (ISBN 97818457), Sikh Soldier: Policing the Empire (ISBN 9781781519851), Sikh Soldier: Warriors and Generals (ISBN 978783310234), and Sikh Soldier: At War (ISBN 8781783311262).

They are available from the Naval and Military Press.

www.ingramcontent.com/pod-product-compliance
Lightning Source LLC
Chambersburg PA
CBHW080633230426
43663CB00016B/2849